Behind the Disappearances

Behind the Disappearances

Argentina's Dirty War Against Human Rights and the United Nations

Iain Guest

University of Pennsylvania Press
Philadelphia

Library of Congress Cataloging-in-Publication Data

Guest, Iain.
    Behind the disappearances : Argentina's dirty war against human
rights and the United Nations / Iain Guest.
        p.   cm. — (Pennsylvania studies in human rights)
    Includes bibliographical references.
    ISBN 0-8122-8204-3. — ISBN 0-8122-1313-0 (pbk.)
    1. Human rights—Argentina.   2. United Nations—Argentina.
3. Political persecution—Argentina.   4. Disappeared persons—
Argentina.   5. United States—Foreign relations—Argentina.
6. Argentina—Foreign relations—United States. I. Title.
II. Series.
JC599.A7G84   1990
323.4'9'0982—dc20   90-35689
                                               CIP
                                              Rev.

*To all families everywhere who never give up,
particularly my own*

Contents

Appendices

Acknowledgments

This book has been a long haul, and I cannot hope to thank everyone who has helped me in its preparation. But the following deserve special mention.

I am particularly grateful to the European Human Rights Foundation, and the Joseph Rowntree Social Service Trust, both of which helped with grants. Malcolm Harper and Lord Chitnis were instrumental in ensuring the Rowntree grant.

I owe a special debt to Theo van Boven, who gave me access to his files and took me through the story of his dismissal at a time of great personal stress. In spite of everything we laughed a lot, and I'm gratified that events in Argentina have vindicated him so completely.

Patricia Derian and Jerome Shestack were patient with me. Jeane Kirkpatrick, Michael Novak, Elliott Abrams, Richard Schifter, and Mark Colville also gave generously of their time before I knew whether I was even writing a book—while no doubt aware that I was not sympathetic to their views.

The following helped with the material on Argentina. Emilio and Isabel Mignone recalled the immensely traumatic circumstances of Mónica's disappearance. The prosecution staff at the 1985 trial of the former military commanders put up with my presence at a time when our two countries were still in a state of suspended hostility. Tom Farer recalled his participation in the important OAS mission to Argentina in 1979. Gregorio Dupont, Juan Gasparini, Juan Mendez, Patrick Rice and Julio Cesar Strassera helped to fill in gaps. Anna Rasmussen and Robert Cox reviewed the text and made valuable comments.

Roberta Cohen, Holly Burkhalter, Michael Posner, and Maggie Nicholson from the Lawyers Committee for Human Rights gave me valuable advice on U.S. human rights policy. Philip Alston and Peter Davies encouraged me to persevere, while Margo Picken, Nigel Rodley, Toine van Dongen, and Niall MacDermot all reviewed the material about the United Nations and made helpful suggestions. Many friends in the U.N. provided information, documents and comments, while requesting anonymity.

I have talked to many human rights campaigners on the front line, starting with Emilio Mignone and the Mothers from Argentina, and the relatives of Chile's disappeared. Roberto Cuéllar, José Estéban González, Julia Esquivel, and Alejandro Artucio helped with El Salvador, Nicaragua, Guatemala, and Uruguay respectively.

Raymond Bonner kindly gave me access to his treasure-trove of cables and documents on El Salvador. Margaret Roman from the Information and Privacy Staff, which administers the Freedom of Information Act, responded to my queries with unfailing courtesy. Stephen Feingold, my lawyer, tenaciously appealed several FOIA cases. Gloria Loomis cheerfully guided me through the publishing labyrinth.

Among those who reviewed the entire text, Jack Donnelly, Howard Tolley, David Weissbrodt, and Laurie Wiseberg all gave me invaluable advice. Alison Anderson, from the University of Pennsylvania Press, and Mindy Brown, the copy editor, asked all the right questions and did a superb job beating the final text into shape. Special thanks to Bert Lockwood and Arthur Evans, two friends whose unerring editorial judgment and hard work ensured publication.

Tom Bliss, my father-in-law, read early chapters and brought common sense to the project, while my mother has reminded me throughout how mothers care. But the final word—for once—must go to Patricia my wife, without whom this book would not have been written.

Introduction

One of my goals in writing this book has been to show that the United Nations can be interesting, important, and useful to the United States.

This may strike many Americans as wildly ambitious. During the 1980s, it has been an article of faith at the highest levels of government that the U.N. is "politicized," its human rights machinery "selective," its officials underworked and overpaid.

Whether or not this is true of 1990 lies beyond the scope of this study, but it was certainly not the case in 1980. I have tried to show that the U.N. was never more effective in promoting human rights than on the eve of Mr. Reagan's accession, and that this was largely due to its vigorous—if belated—response to the disappearances in Latin America.

The book shows how, after seizing power in 1976, Argentina's military rulers set out to cripple the U.N.'s human rights machinery in an effort to muzzle international protest, and how—with support and encouragement from the Carter Administration—the U.N. fought back. This fight rejuvenated the U.N.'s ponderous human rights machinery. But the gains were wiped out after 1981, when the Reagan Administration threw its support behind the Argentinian military regime as part of a profound shift in U.S. policy.

The 1981 American assault was aimed at the entire U.N. system, and ten years later the U.N. has still not recovered. It is still demoralized, still short of funds, and certainly not up to the growing number of challenges in the areas of health, environment, trade, drug abuse, refugees, and peacekeeping that are being dumped into its lap. As far as human rights are concerned, the most serious development in my view has been the de facto merging of the two entirely separate roles—political mediator and human rights advocate. To be a successful human rights advocate, the U.N. must confront governments. This it no longer does, and it is certainly not in the interests of the United States. A U.N. human rights program that courageously addressed abuses in China, for example, would take some of the pressure off the Bush Administration.

Readers may question my choice of the disappearances as a vehicle for such a thesis, when so much has already been written about this dismal episode. One thinks of Jacobo Timerman's *Prisoner Without a Name, Cell Without a Number,* and *Nunca Más (Never Again),* the 1984 report by CONADEP, the Argentine national commission on disappearances. These are without doubt two of the best human rights books ever written.

There are several reasons for the choice. One is that the disappearances had such a profound impact, not just on the U.N., but on U.S. human rights policy as well. Argentina came to symbolize Carter's confrontational approach to human rights, as well as the change that occurred under President Reagan.

Another reason is that the diplomatic fall-out from the disappearances has been almost completely ignored by authors. This is hardly surprising, because a U.N. conference hardly compares for excitement with a march by the Mothers in the Plaza de Mayo. But I hope to show that Geneva was an important theater in the dirty war, both to the Argentinian Junta and to the relatives of its victims.

The third reason for this book is personal. Between 1977 and 1985 I reported on human rights issues while working from Geneva for the *London Guardian* and *International Herald Tribune.* In 1982 I learned that Gabriel Martínez, Argentina's ambassador, had used my newspaper articles to accuse Theo van Boven, head of the U.N.'s human rights secretariat, of passing me information and of violating the U.N.'s rules of confidentiality. The accusation was a lie—van Boven and I were hardly acquainted—but it was just one of many devices used by Martínez to obstruct a U.N. investigation into the disappearances. He was a formidable operator.

I began to dig deeper when van Boven was dismissed from his post in 1982. My inquiry was rounded off in 1985, as it was for many of the actors in this story, when I attended the trial of the nine former military commanders in Buenos Aires. There I obtained access to many of the cables and memoranda written by Gabriel Martínez from Geneva, and found that he had sent some of my articles back to Buenos Aires, carefully annotated. Martínez had always refused interviews with me, so this was like finding family photos in the possession of a total stranger—slightly eerie.

The material that I collected in Argentina and Geneva forms the basis for this book. I hope it gives a flavor of what it is like for a government to be on the receiving end of a major international human rights campaign. This is something that rarely features in human rights literature.

The final reason for choosing the disappearances is that the trauma did not end for Argentina with the transition from dictatorship to democracy in 1983. This is the case throughout much of Latin America. Indeed, during the 1980s the travails of transition have replaced torture and the disappearances as the Latin American human rights story, even if they have received far less attention from the human rights community.

How can a nation heal such self-inflicted wounds as the disappearances? This is not a new problem. It faced Germany after the Second World War, it faces Chile today, and it will no doubt face other nations in the future. But few nations in history have found it so wrenching as Argentina. Alfonsín's dilemma in 1983 was the following. How far could he go in punishing the killers? If he went too far, he provoked another coup; but if he tried to sweep the disappearances under the carpet, he left a huge pool of grieving relatives whose bitterness would serve as a permanent reminder of the horror.

Alfonsín gets surprisingly little credit for a bold attempt to satisfy both sides, probably because he ended up by satisfying neither. Many feel he went too far in punishing the military, and that this provoked the debilitating series of military mutinies that unsettled his entire term of office. Argentina's military is still convinced that its dirty war was justified and is making ominous noises about intervening again if the economy collapses. This was obviously not Alfonsín's intention. On the other hand, the relatives of the disappeared feel he did not go nearly far enough.

Although my own sympathies are with the relatives, it is not my intention in this book to take sides in this debate, vital though it is. What I do feel is that the United Nations took the wrong side by siding with Argentina's military in 1983 on the argument that this would ease the country's transition. This was a political decision that should not have been made by a human rights advocate. Pressured by the Reagan Administration, and scared of their own shadow, U.N. human rights officials in 1983 ignored the fact that they had a different mandate from that of an elected president like Alfonsín. The U.N.'s task is narrow: to promote universal human rights standards and take the side of victims. By abandoning this mandate in 1983 and 1984, the U.N. lost credibility with its natural constituency and deprived Argentina's democrats of a point of reference that could have helped in the war of nerves with the military.

Because this story ends in 1985, it inevitably leaves loose ends untied. I can only hint at Argentina's political problems since the 1985 trial. Readers may find my treatment of the U.N.'s human rights work after 1985 equally cursory. I do not, however, want to leave the impression that the U.N.'s human rights machinery collapsed completely after 1985. The U.N. Working Group on Disappearances celebrated its tenth anniversary in March 1990, and it has certainly improved since 1983. Finally, human rights experts may find my account of U.S. human rights policy incomplete.

But then this book examines no more than a slice of history. Furthermore, I have tried to tell a story, not write a treatise.

Geneva, March 1990

Prologue: Buenos Aires, September 11 1985. Generals in the Dock

Outside the courthouse it doesn't feel like the trial of the century. A thin curtain of rain is falling on the handful of curious bystanders standing behind the wooden barriers and the blue-uniformed police look bored as they amble around, trying to keep warm and dry. By now the novelty has worn off. The trial of the nine former military chiefs who ruled Argentina between 1976 and 1982 has been grinding on for almost five months, producing an avalanche of numbing statistics and horrifying detail. By now there are no more tears left to cry. Perhaps that was President Raúl Alfonsín's intention. If so, holding this trial is a shrewd move.[1]

Inside the gray and echoing building, the trial is taking place in an elegant wood-paneled room that resembles the dining room in an Oxford college. The six judges, members of Argentina's federal appeals court, are seated on a raised dais in front of a large stained-glass window. To the right of the judges, slightly lower, sits Julio César Strassera, who is leading the prosecution. Strassera has the sort of solid, down-to-earth qualities one associates with a Julius Caesar, and he sports the drooping moustache made fashionable by President Alfonsín. This gives him a slightly mournful expression. Given the context, it seems appropriate.

The word "disappearance" does not feature in Argentina's penal code, but "homicide," "illegal deprivation of liberty," "torture," "falsification of documents," "kidnapping of minors," and even "slavery" do. They form the basis of Strassera's charge against the nine defendants.[2]

Strassera has chosen 709 individual victims to illustrate the pattern of murder. Many have become household names in democratic Argentina and a handful have survived to give a damning account of their ordeal in detention centers: Miriam Lewin de García carried a cyanide tablet but was unable to swallow it fast enough to thwart her kidnappers; Adriana de Laborde gave birth to a child in a police truck and was made to clean up her own placenta; together with two other women, Ana María Martí delivered a report to the French National Assembly in late 1979 which remains one of the most memorable and authentic documents to emerge from the dirty war; Jacobo Timerman, the newspaper publisher, galvanized the human rights debate in the United States during the first months of Ronald Reagan's presidency by his dramatic account of torture and anti-Semitism.

Yet almost all of the 709 victims chosen by Strassera are certainly dead, and many are presumed to have died in the navy mechanics school in the middle of Buenos Aires. They include Mónica Mignone, whose abduction turned her father Emilio into one of Argentina's foremost human rights activists; Dagmar Hagelin, a young Swedish girl whose disappearance caused an international uproar; Léonie Duquet and Alice Domon, two French nuns; and Azucena Villaflor de Vicenti, the first, inspiring, leader of the Mothers of the Plaza de Mayo.

Here, too, is the name of Zelmar Michelini, an Uruguayan senator whose murder in Buenos Aires in 1976 attracted international attention to the danger facing Argentina's refugees; Oscar Smith, a trade union leader whose disappearance sparked a flicker of independence from Argentina's muzzled Supreme Court; Rodolfo Walsh, an investigative journalist, murdered for criticizing the economic policies of the Junta; Elena Holmberg, an Argentinian diplomat who contributed to the Junta's disinformation campaign and ended up strangled and dumped on a mud flat.

Gradually, over these four months, the ghosts have started to slip into this court. Some have come vividly alive again as witnesses have recalled seeing them in the detention centers. Now they seem to fill the benches, as if silently waiting to pass their own verdict on Argentina's "dirty war." What did they think of in those final terrifying moments, as they went to their deaths? The testimony has been so detailed that it is impossible not to speculate.

*   *   *

Throughout the four months that Strassera presented his case, the nine defendants did not personally attend their trial. For the last week they have been present in the courtroom to hear his final summary. Their presence has revived public interest in the case. Each time they arrive, relatives of the disappeared press against the barriers to catch a glimpse of the old enemy, holding the banners and signs they had carried on countless marches through the nearby Plaza de Mayo. The signs read "aparición con vida, castigo a los culpables," which translates as "appearance alive, punishment to the guilty." This is the message that has held the relatives together for nine years. Now at least the second demand is being partially met.

Spectators point and whisper as the nine file into the courtroom through a door on the left, looking straight ahead, with the occasional "abrazo" for a defense lawyer. Retired Lieutenant General Jorge Videla, head of the first Junta, enters first and sits down, brushing against the lens of a television camera. Then the six judges appear and everyone rises, including the nine defendants. There is something hugely significant in this act of simple obedience to civilian judges by the former dictators.

How strange the change from major to minor! Here are the men who dispensed life and death to their fellow citizens through seven long years, oversaw the extermination of as many as ten thousand Argentinians, presided over the disintegration of Argentina's economy, and threw the country into a disastrous foreign war. Methodically and carefully, they took it on themselves to dismantle one of Latin America's oldest constitutions.

Such ordinary men. Videla and Leopoldo Galtieri have refused to wear uniforms in protest. Videla, who presided over the worst years, never looked the part in a uniform; now he looks more like a bank clerk than ever. He has spent much of his time in jail praying furiously, and is suffering from anemia. Galtieri looks physically smaller, stripped of the regalia he loved so much.

What order will they sit in, and will they talk to each other, these men who feuded and squabbled incessantly? Necks crane in the audience, hungry for the tiniest detail. Retired Admiral Emilio Massera, who directed the horrors at the navy mechanics school, is puffy-faced and wearing glasses, clearly happy to be back in uniform after several months in jail on a charge of having disposed of his mistress's husband. He seems unaware of the specks of dandruff on the dark blue collar that are visible to the audience behind.

Retired Brigadier Omar Graffigna, Air Force Commander in the second Junta, is stooping and white haired. He was always the most diffident of the military leaders and now he looks what he is, an old man who has retired. Yet his men are still unashamed of their role in the dirty war. One story currently going the rounds tells of how they threw one pregnant woman out of a plane. She was trembling violently. "So much for the

Montoneros' vaunted bravery," goes the punchline. It still gets chuckles in the mess.

Nothing about the trial has been left to chance, not even the allocation of tickets. Each of the nine defendants is entitled to four tickets a day, as is each of the eight human rights groups. That leaves human rights with 32 tickets and dictatorship with 36, almost equal, but not quite. Such facts are deeply symbolic, and serve as a reminder that the trial is part of a complex political package.

President Alfonsín has made a studied attempt at neutrality. The same day that he ordered the trial of the nine, on December 13 1983, he also signed a decree calling for the trial of seven leaders of the guerrilla movement. He is trying to satisfy the human rights movement without humiliating the armed forces. It's a delicate balancing act.

Relatives of the disappeared were furious at the implication that the misdeeds of a handful of guerrillas could be equated with state terror. At the same time, many relatives have derived intense personal satisfaction at seeing the nine in the dock and in testifying against them. The trial has rounded off a cathartic year of nonstop testimony during which many relatives have recounted their ordeal several times over, most recently to the Argentine National Commission on the Disappeared (CONADEP), established by Alfonsín. The mere act of speaking out has acquired special significance among human rights groups throughout Latin America. They call it the "denuncia" and the English translation, "denunciation," cannot begin to convey the full psychological importance. Now the "denuncia" is bearing fruit.

It seems an eternity since prosecutor Strassera opened his case on April 22 with the words: "I am not alone. I am accompanied by the 9,000 disappeared." Finally, at 5:20 on the afternoon of September 18, he ends on a stirring emotional note: "I want to use a phrase which doesn't belong to me, because it belongs to all the Argentinian people. Gentlemen of the court, Never again!"

There is a burst of applause from the gallery, one of the few signs of emotion from an audience that has concentrated fiercely on every detail during the whole four months. Dr. Carlos Arslanian, the presiding judge for this session of the trial, calls for order. Strassera and his assistant embrace. Videla turns to the audience with a long and threatening look. Roberto Viola, who succeeded Videla as President, mutters "sons of bitches" under his breath. Suddenly, the crowd is breaking up, and the nine defendants begin filing out.[3] The defense will start their replies next week, and the trial itself will last several more weeks. But this is the emotional climax. The ultimate denuncia.

*   *   *

Prosecutor Strassera has mounted an enormous effort in his case against the nine. Between April 22 and August 14 he called a total of 833 separate witnesses, including 12 foreigners, 64 military officials and 13 priests. In a large office behind the courtroom a team of 30 clerks and lawyers have worked round the clock for weeks collecting documents from embassies, police stations, judges, and military offices. They have amassed 400,000 pages of evidence and taken 1.3 million photocopies. The documents that arrived from Argentina's embassy in Geneva alone weigh 700 kilos.[4]

Much more is on trial than nine bedraggled former dictators. On trial is Argentina's judiciary. With the exception of a few courageous lawyers like Emilio Mignone, the judiciary surrendered during military rule and in so doing gave respectability to the policy of disappearances. Even prosecutor Strassera made compromises.[5]

These six judges have a daunting task. Will they give the nine former dictators a fair hearing? If they do, it could conceivably lead to acquittals, which would be a body blow to the relatives. If they don't, it will turn the trial into a vindictive political gesture by Alfonsín's government that will further discredit the judiciary. The judges have to satisfy a deep yearning for revenge, while at the same time fulfilling the dispassionate requirements of justice. This is a tall order.

On trial too, of course, is military rule itself. Between 1930 and 1983 Argentina's military passed its own verdict on democracy and seized power no fewer than five times. The nations of Latin America have been so notoriously prone to military government that it became fashionable among North American political scientists in the early 1980s to suggest that Latin America was somehow incapable of true democracy, and that abuses like torture were routine and even justifiable. Here is Argentina's answer to that thesis. Here is the most coup-prone country in Latin America breaking the cycle of military rule and insisting that democracy, not "authoritarian" military rule, is its natural form of government. Perhaps the pendulum will swing back in Argentina and the military will again seize power. But right now, in September 1985, that seems unlikely.

The rest of the continent is watching carefully. Several other military regimes followed the Junta's example and used disappearances to stamp out

opponents while escaping accountability. Disappearances became standard operating procedure for what have been called "authoritarian" military regimes.

Most of Latin America's dictators have since surrendered power to democracy. Senior officials in the Reagan Administration see this as one of
the crowning achievements of Mr. Reagan's presidency. They argue that
only democracy is capable of guaranteeing human rights. But to Latin
Americans, it seems much less straightforward. Uruguay, El Salvador,
and Guatemala have also made the transition from military rule during
Reagan's presidency, but all remain tormented societies because the military have refused to permit any inquiry into their misdeeds. If democracy
means peace, then Reagan's boast is clearly unjustified. Even Nicaragua's
Sandinistas are paying the price for ignoring the disappearances that occurred immediately after their 1979 victory.

Argentina's democratic government has gone further than any other
nation to punish the military, because here in Argentina the demoralized
military has less bargaining power since its failure on the Falkland Islands.
But has it gone far enough? Argentinian human rights groups say no, but
by the end of the trial they are subdued and out of step. The film *The
Official Story* about a couple who adopted the child of a disappeared
couple captures the national mood. Beautifully filmed and beautifully
acted, it nonetheless hints at the past instead of confronting it directly.
Most Argentinians feel that if Argentina's democracy is to survive, it will
have to make similar compromises. But the relatives disagree. Sad and
introspective, they have withdrawn into a private world and lost the
sparkle that was so appealing during their darkest hour. Old friends find
messages unanswered, appointments ignored.

Is President Alfonsín right? Is compromise the proper response to a
crime so deliberate and gross, as the disappearances? The question nags at
everybody, yet few have an answer. Alberto Amato has covered the trial
for a newspaper and he fears for the future: "One has to ask oneself how
it is possible to live in this country with people who murdered, people
who tortured and still walk among us; with fathers who will grow old
without their sons, and sons who will have to grow up without fathers.
Four months of testimony have left me totally devastated."[6]

He is not the only one to ask whether Alfonsín's gamble had paid off.
Nine aging men are in the dock, but thousands disappeared. Has Alfonsín
made too many compromises?

I

After the Coup

1. Mónica Disappears

The doorbell rang harshly, echoing from one side of the stairwell to the other, forcing its way into the innermost recesses of the darkened apartment. The effect was terrifying. Emilio Mignone awoke with a start, his heart racing.

As he groped for a dressing gown Mignone glanced at a clock. It was five in the morning. What in God's name was going on? How had anyone managed to get into the apartment building? Visitors to Number 2949 on the Avenida Santa Fe have to announce themselves down in the street before they are admitted through the heavy wrought-iron gate. Had the system failed?

"Who is it?" Mignone peered through the peephole.

"Open up, it's the army," came the reply. Mignone could just make out a group of men. He asked if they carried any identification. In reply, one of them waved a machine gun.

Outside, the big city was still asleep. In the poorer parts of Buenos Aires it was a fitful, troubled sleep. Six weeks earlier, on March 24 1976, the Argentinian armed forces had seized power from President Isabel Perón. Emilio Mignone, a lifelong member of the Peronist movement, was dismayed, but many Argentinians were frankly relieved after a year of escalating violence and up on the Avenida Santa Fe, one of the great arterial roads that slice through Buenos Aires, most people slept more easily. Underneath, subway trains have elegant wooden carriages and polished mirrors, while above ground visitors think they're in Milan instead of South America. The architecture is baroque and the shops sell fashionable jeans, Italian ice cream, and freshly made pasta. The effect is overwhelmingly middle class, and light years away from the sullen "villas miserias" (shanty towns) that encircle Buenos Aires. The family of the Minister of Planning, General Díaz Bessone, and a retired admiral lived on the same block as the Mignones, and both houses were under constant police surveillance. If any district in Buenos Aires could be considered secure in the spring of 1976, this was surely it.

When Mignone opened the door, five men pushed past and started to fan out through the apartment. They were wearing what appeared to be military trousers and boots with civilian shirts, and they carried grenades and automatic weapons. Mignone began to gather his wits and note details. It was his lawyer's training. The group leader appeared to be about thirty-four years old. He had a large nose, brown eyes, and brown hair. A younger man with fairer hair guarded the telephone. He looked nervous, and he jumped to the curt orders of the group leader like a junior officer. A third man acted more like a policeman and carried what appeared to Mignone to be a standard police sidearm.

Mignone thought at first that they had come for him. It would have made sense because he was rector of a progressive university, as well as being a well-known lawyer with long ties to the Peronist movement. On the morning of the coup, soldiers had come to the university, menaced students, and hammered on the doors. Soon afterward, the university was closed and Mignone went briefly into hiding. But this morning, at least, he was not the target. This morning they had come for his daughter Mónica.

Mónica, the second of Mignone's five children, was an educational psychologist at a local hospital and a teaching assistant at her father's university. She had been working late and had let herself in with her own key the night before. She was suffering from flu and had planned to sleep late this morning. Her elder sister Isabel was on a trip abroad.

At twenty-four Mónica Mignone was past the age at which young women leave home in Europe or North America. There were, however, compensations. The Mignones' apartment was spacious and she was exceptionally close to her family. They in turn were proud of her. She was hard-working and serious. As were they all. The Mignones were a cultivated, self-confident family without any of the arrogance that foreigners find so distasteful in the inhabitants of Buenos Aires, "los porteños" (people of the port). They had a large circle of acquaintances, but they also valued their privacy. Once the door to the apartment was closed, it held the family more tightly together. Like so many Argentinians, they sought consolation against an unfriendly world in the privacy of the family. Any intrusion was thus doubly intolerable.

While one of the strangers herded the rest of the family into the kitchen, the leader of the group and one other forced their way past Emilio Mignone into Mónica's room. By now Mónica was awake, and very frightened. She had managed to slip her address book to her sister Mercedes, who took it to the bathroom. The intruders started to ask Mónica questions. What was in this bag? They opened it up, and took out texts that she had prepared for work. They then turned up some political books. There was nothing remarkable in this. The Mignones were avid readers and the apartment was always strewn with books of every political persuasion. Suddenly, however, it all seemed terribly ominous. Even reading seemed incriminating. Mónica was told to dress.

Emilio Mignone was now recovering from the initial shock. How could he regain control, play for time? "Are you from the intelligence service?" he asked. "Yes" replied the group leader, "we're from the First Patricios." That made sense. The First Patricios was one of the regiments of the First Army Corps based at Palermo, a nearby neighborhood that was famous for its picturesque Italian restaurants. "Don't worry," continued the stranger, "the armed forces don't arrest people for their ideas. We want to take your daughter and talk to her about a friend. She'll be back in a few hours."

Mónica was dressed by now. The leader of the group told her to bring money for the return taxi fare, which was reassuring. Her parents hugged her. Suddenly, as quickly as they arrived, the strangers were leaving. Emilio had one last glimpse of his frightened daughter as she squeezed into the narrow elevator between the burly men and their machine guns. The operation had lasted exactly forty minutes. It had been carried out like clockwork, almost as if it was part of a military exercise. Emilio pushed the thought from his mind. Five armed men against an unarmed, frightened, twenty-four-year-old young woman? Impossible! Yet throughout the whole operation there had not been any intervention from the police officers guarding the nearby house of General Díaz Bessone! Why?

Then the panic came. As he ran downstairs Mignone forced himself to recall each minute detail, particularly the faces. Large nose, brown hair. If he ever saw those faces again. He heard the sudden acceleration of cars outside. Now he realized why the intruders had not needed to announce themselves at the gate. The heavy, reassuring lock had been forced in.

He rushed outside. The air had been let out of all four tires on his car. Any pursuit was impossible. His daughter Mónica had disappeared. Why had he opened the door?[1]

The Predictable Coup

On Sunday March 21 1976, everyone knew that a coup was coming when members of congress began to remove refrigerators and filing cabinets from their offices. On Tuesday it was reported that units of the armed forces had moved into position and that all leave passes had been canceled. That same night, President Isabel Martínez de Perón held a lengthy cabinet meeting. Weary ministers emerged expecting to talk about national elections, which were planned for December. Instead, they were asked by journalists when they expected to be thrown out of office.[2]

By morning, the journalists had their answer. The coup began on a brisk, stern note with the proclamation of a "Process of National Reorganization." A short communiqué on the national radio announced that the three service chiefs had formed a junta that would make all decisions jointly. The army Commander, Lieutenant General Jorge Videla, had been chosen President and would act, as it appeared, like the chairman of a board. Ten hours after the coup, Videla was sworn in at the army headquarters by the country's chief notary. Inevitably, the ceremony was described as "austere." Journalists, like everyone else, had a stock of clichés ready. And why not? After all, they had seen it all before. This was the sixth time that the army had seized power since 1930. Thirty of the last forty-six years had been spent under military rule.[3]

So turbulent were these years that it was easy to forget Argentina's tradition of democratic government. Argentina was the first country in Latin America to throw off Spanish rule (in 1810). In 1853, after forty-three difficult years of consolidation, it adopted a liberal constitution that laid a heavy emphasis on protecting individuals against abuse by authority. The document allowed for some individual rights to be suspended in times of extreme emergency, but its authors also were aware that this exception could be abused and they carefully defined its nature and duration. The President was given the power to arrest and detain people during the emergency, but not to punish them. This form of administrative detention was known as PEN ("poder ejecutivo nacional"). Habeas corpus was available, and the detainees themselves were given a choice between exile and jail. This was known as the "right of option."[4]

For almost eighty years, as Argentina struggled with growing pains, this structure worked. Outsiders had an impression of a restless but fundamentally stable democracy. Then, in 1930, the military deposed President Hipólito Yrigoyen and began a trend: the military seized power in 1943, 1955, 1962, 1966, and 1976, and with each successive coup extended its involvement in civilian life. By 1976 Argentina's armed forces were running steel mills, petrochemical plants, electronics factories, newspapers, and radio stations. They were even manufacturing underwear. One army enterprise,

"Fabricaciones Militares," was the largest single employer in the country.

Yet, in spite of this tradition of military involvement in civilian life, Argentina's armed forces were physically and psychologically isolated from civilians. Young recruits were taken in at the age of sixteen and required to live on, or next to, the base until they reached the rank of Lieutenant Colonel, some twenty years later. They were bound by a medieval code of honor, and by a military code of justice that was totally separate from the civilian code and called for total obedience to the orders of superior officers.[5] All this further widened the gulf between military and civilian life.

The succession of coups exposed one of the original assumptions behind the 1853 constitution, that any suspension of normal government could be controlled and kept within democratic limits. The military found it increasingly easy to argue that the country was sufficiently threatened to require military rule until order, and democracy, could be restored. The only possible legal challenge, from the Supreme Court, was easily circumvented. In 1930, the Court set an unfortunate precedent by recognizing the military regime that had deposed Yrigoyen. Thereafter, the military stifled any legal objections in advance by purging the court. Without an independent judiciary, the constitution's safeguards against individual abuse were hopelessly fragile.[6]

It was, of course, possible to argue that the military had no legal right to purge the Court, but by the time of the 1976 coup this seemed like sophistry. The constitution had been abused so often that it hardly seemed relevant. Did it really matter whether Isabel Perón was overthrown unconstitutionally when forty-four people died in the week of constitutional rule before the coup? By 1976 government by the military was the rule rather than the exception. Was it not perhaps time to accept the fact that Argentina was ill-suited to Western-style democracy?

Following the 1976 coup, many Argentinians concluded sadly that democracy had failed to create a sense of national identity out of the country's many ethnic components. Emilio Mignone, whose grandparents had come from Genova, Italy and the French Basque country, describes Argentina at the turn of the century as a mixture of "British money, French culture, and Italian people who spoke bad Spanish." It was as much a melting pot as the United States, but somehow the mixture had failed to gel. Argentinians were left with a profound sense of insecurity and even self-loathing. One description, of a "man on the defensive," seemed appropriate.[7]

Political scientists found it fascinating. Jeane Jordan (later Kirkpatrick) was a student when she first became interested in political systems that were, as she would write, "neither democratic nor totalitarian." She was teaching at Washington's Trinity College when she began research on a book about Juan Perón, the dominant political figure of postwar Argentina.[8] Perón's presidential style was highly autocratic, and Peronism, the movement he created, was a heady mixture of nationalism and working-class populism that relied on bruising mass marches as much as reasoned debate. Perón's political legacy was thus part democratic and part authoritarian, but Jeane Kirkpatrick's book, when it was published in 1971, stressed the authoritarianism. (Even the title was suggestive: *Leader and Vanguard in Mass Society*.) Perón succeeded, wrote Kirkpatrick, because Argentinians had little confidence in democracy. In spite of the inspiring 1853 constitution there was, she wrote, a "legitimacy gap" in the Argentinian system: "No procedure was recognized as the legitimate route to power." Instead, one found constant instability, constant violence, constant conflict, and constant competition.[9] Perón was simply more competitive and ruthless than his competitors.

To his Argentinian supporters like Emilio Mignone, the fact that Perón submitted to elections and won in fair votes in 1946 and 1951 gave him political legitimacy. But this is blurred over in Kirkpatrick's book. Perón himself and Peronism were too autocratic to warrant the label of "democratic." When the Army and Church joined forces to oust Perón in 1955, it was as if they, not Perón, were the servants of democracy. "The overthrow of Perón," she wrote, "signified an end to the rule of a popular tyrant."[10]

No one who reads Jeane Kirkpatrick's book could be surprised that the soldiers were back in power in 1976. Against such a background as Argentina's, military rule was the norm rather than the exception. Many American conservatives would take this a stage further and argue that it was unrealistic to expect "authoritarian" regimes to live up to the standards of behavior expected of Western democracies. In 1974 Ernest Lefever would describe the widespread torture that followed the 1973 coup in Chile as in the "Iberian tradition."[11]

One obvious drawback to this theory was the fact that Latin American constitutions, like Argentina's, invariably outlawed torture. Was this not as clear-cut and binding as anything in the American constitution? No, came the answer. Such rights and freedoms should not be interpreted at face value but instead seen in Latin America's "authoritarian" or "Iberian" context. In 1978, Howard Wiarda would describe them as "ideals, aspirations and future goals for society. They are not presumed to correspond to actual operating reality, nor is any regime expected to live up to them completely. . . . What in the United States is considered a fundamental right often occupies a third or fourth order priority in Latin America."[12]

This analysis suggested three things. First, that "authoritarian" military regimes of Latin America should be exempted from the universal standards of behavior demanded by international instruments such as the 1948 Universal Declaration of Human Rights; second, that the torture they invariably generated was inevitable and even justifiable; and third, that military rule was as legitimate as democracy, perhaps even more so, if it could keep order. As we shall see, this theory would prove profoundly influential in the early years of the Reagan Presidency.

The Roots of Authoritarianism

Why was Argentina, and Latin America, so ill at ease with democracy? The question may seem inappropriate in 1990, but it was impossible to avoid after Videla, Massera, and Orlando Ramón Agosti assumed power in 1976.[13]

There tended to be two very different answers. One blamed the United States. It was accepted wisdom among left-wing intellectuals in North and South America that the United States had pursued two broad goals since the Second World War: the first to create a favorable economic climate for U.S. multinational corporations, the second to expunge all traces of Communism from its southern neighbors.[14] To do this, went the argument, the United States had indoctrinated a whole generation of Latin American military commanders in the so-called doctrine of "national security," which interpreted any movement for social reform as "Communist subversion."[15] "National security," as its name suggested, placed the security of the state before the security of the individual. It was no coincidence that Latin America's first right-wing death squads made their appearance in the wake of the 1964 military coup in Brazil, the first to invoke the doctrine.[16]

Advocates of the second, very different explanation agreed with Jeane Kirkpatrick and Howard Wiarda that authoritarianism was embedded in Latin American society. As late as 1986, Lawrence Harrison would write: "You don't have to live in Latin America very long to appreciate how badly most human beings are treated in comparison with the Western democracies, and how much nonsense cultural relativism is. I speak now not just of economic opportunity but also of justice, social responsibility and political participation, rare commodities in most Latin American countries."[17]

Which of these two theories applied to Argentina in 1976? Emilio Mignone was better placed than many to answer the question. Mignone was a lifelong follower of Perón and a devoted member of Argentina's highly conservative Catholic Church. Both were uniquely Argentinian. Both exhibited a strong streak of authoritarianism. Both discouraged dissent. (Argentina's Church leaders had a long tradition of accommodation to military rule, and were fervent supporters of Videla's Junta.) Both, moreover, were often at odds with each other.[18]

Why was Mignone attracted to Perón? Why was he not repelled by the mass marches? The Mussolini-style fascism? Perón's autocratic style? The main reason was that Perón had given Argentina's working classes a voice in the political system. As in the United States, Argentina's unions had grown out of city sweatshops at the turn of the century, their numbers swollen by a huge wave of European immigrants, including Emilio Mignone's grandparents. When Perón took office in 1947 only 600,000 Argentinians were unionized. By 1955 the figure stood at six million.[19] Living standards had soared and rural peasants brought into the political system, shattering the power of the oligarchy once and for all. To Emilio Mignone this was an achievement that far outweighed the darker, authoritarian side of Peronist rule.

Mignone was well aware of the excesses of Peronism and of his Church's collaboration.[20] At the same time he also believed, like many Peronists, that the doctrine of national security had been imposed on Argentina from outside, further weakening democracy. Argentina's first national security regime seized power in 1966 under the leadership of General Juan Carlos Onganía, a fanatical right-wing Catholic. Following the 1966 coup, Argentina's soldiers, already isolated from civilian life, were taught that the "subversion" of their fellow countrymen posed more of a threat to Argentina's security than external foes. (It was no coincidence that the army was so much larger than the air force or navy, nor that the army divisions were based in the centers of major cities instead of in isolated rural areas, as is the case in the United States.) Here was one important reason why the armed forces turned against civilians with such extraordinary cruelty after the 1976 coup, and why many former military officials still feel proud of their "dirty war" against subversion.[21]

By 1976, these strands, external and home-grown, had come together in

Argentina to produce a profound gulf between civilians and the military; deep-rooted hostility between Peronism and the armed forces; and a society that was profoundly suffocating, profoundly discouraging to individual spirit.

But if any one factor had to be singled out as responsible for the "authoritarianism" that seemed so close to the surface, it was the military's obsession with keeping Juan Perón out of Argentinian politics. After his overthrow and expulsion in 1955, Perón's followers were forced by law to vote, but forbidden to vote for Perón. Here, clearly, was one reason for the "legitimacy gap" noted by Jeane Kirkpatrick. As she herself wrote, "behind most of the electoral manipulation since 1955 has been the problem of how to contrive elections that could not be won by the followers of Juan Perón."[22] Remarkably, the majority of Perón's followers remained loyal to the constitution. Wrote Kirkpatrick: "They voted; they did not engage in massive illegality."[23]

Inevitably, though, some—younger and more radical—turned to violence.

The Subversives

They called themselves "Montoneros," after guerrillas who had specialized in fighting the Spanish from horseback, and they announced their presence on May 29 1970 with the kidnapping and murder of General Pedro Aramburu, a former President. It was the first of a long series of provocative actions that held the country in thrall and helped to win the Montoneros a reputation for ferocity throughout the Continent. Throughout 1971 and 1972, they stepped up their attacks. Banks were robbed, police stations attacked, factory managers assassinated, and bodies dumped in the streets dynamited or "carbonizado" (burned beyond recognition). It was a frantic, fearful period.[24]

For a brief period in 1973 it seemed that the Montoneros might win. The military conceded that Perón could no longer be barred from political life. Perón returned at the end of 1972, and chose a stalking horse, Héctor Cámpora, to stand for the presidency and open the way to his own re-election. With his election, Cámpora declared an amnesty which effectively legitimized the Montoneros and the ERP (Revolutionary Army of the People), the other main guerrilla group.

Young Argentinians talk wistfully of the period as a golden age for left-wing politics. Montoneros served in Cámpora's short-lived administration and even held provincial governorships. Several Montonero leaders visited Perón in Europe and presented him with a list of three hundred names the Montoneros wanted to see in government. Perón enjoyed such massive personal support that it was assumed he would be able to reconcile the two extremes (revolutionary left and fascist right) that had both invoked his name. The Montoneros seemed ready to put aside their campaign of violence and embrace democracy.

It was not to be. After his return, Perón spurned the chance to create a broad-based political coalition by rejecting Ricardo Balbín, a popular politician, as his Vice-President, in favor of his third wife Isabel, a former dancer. It was a grotesquely inappropriate choice. Perón also turned fiercely against the Montoneros, ridiculing what he termed their "infantile" revolutionary ideas. Well before his landslide victory in the elections on September 9 1973 it was clear that Perón himself was endorsing the right wing of his movement.

On September 6 1973, the ERP broke the uneasy truce with an attack on the headquarters of the army health service in Buenos Aires. The ERP lost several fighters in the attack and switched to Tucumán, where it announced the creation of a "liberated zone." It also established links with like-minded guerrillas from Uruguay and Chile.[25] On September 25, after several of their own supporters had been murdered, the Montoneros assassinated José Rucci, the Secretary General of the Labor Federation and a close friend of Perón. On November 21, apparently in retaliation, a right-wing Peronist death squad known as the Triple A ("Alianza Anti-Comunista Argentina") made its appearance by bombing the car of Hipólito Solari Yrigoyen, a deputy of the Radical party and nephew of the former President.

Perón himself died on July 1 1974, and the Presidency passed to his widow, Isabel, whereupon all pretense of a truce vanished. Firmenich held a press conference to announce that the Montoneros were resuming the armed struggle and going underground. On September 19 1974, they kidnapped two businessmen, Juan and Jorge Born, and extracted the colossal sum of sixty million dollars in ransom money. On February 26 1975, the Montoneros kidnapped and killed John Patrick Egan, the American consul in Córdoba.

Looking back on this chaotic period, Juan Gasparini, himself a leading Montonero who was to survive the dirty war, concludes that both Perón and the Montoneros willfully threw away the chance of reconciliation.[26]

Martin Andersen, a journalist, has gone further and suggested that the Montoneros' uncompromising approach was instigated by the Argentinian intelligence services, which recruited Firmenich with the aim of provoking the 1976 coup and justifying the slaughter of Montoneros in the dirty war. What is certain is that, in spite of a spate of spectacular bombings and killings in 1975 and 1976, the Montoneros committed military and political suicide faster and more spectacularly than virtually any other Latin American guerrilla group. They lost eighty percent of their fighters and much of their leadership in 1976. They lost most of the remainder in 1979 when Firmenich, who had slipped out of the country and danger, sent several of his colleagues back for an abortive "counteroffensive."[27]

How much support did the guerrillas enjoy? In retrospect it is impossible to draw the line between active combatants and sympathizers. Emilio Mignone's own estimate is that at the peak of their popularity the Montoneros were able to muster at most five hundred combatants and the ERP less than two hundred, compared to the 135,000 men in the armed forces. But this is not to underestimate the widespread support enjoyed by the ERP and Montoneros, or the panic they produced in 1974 and 1975.[28]

Isabel Perón concluded that the powers at her disposal were inadequate to cope with the twin menace, and on November 6 1974 she declared a state of siege. On February 25 1975, under the powers granted by the state of siege, Isabel Perón passed decrees ordering the armed forces to put down an ERP uprising in Tucumán. On October 6 1975, following a major attack by the Montoneros against an army base in the province of Formosa, she extended the decrees to the rest of the country.[29]

The October 6 decrees asked the armed forces to "aniquilar la subversión" (annihilate subversion) but did not give them a free hand. Two councils were established to lead the campaign and both were headed by civilians. The aim was to keep the armed forces on as tight a rein as possible without curbing their ability to crush the guerrillas.[30] Isabel Perón's government also passed a range of complementary laws designed to combat terrorism and made excessive use of the executive power granted under the state of siege. (By the time of the coup on March 24 1976, the number of PEN detainees stood at at least 5,182.) Many of these measures were bitterly criticized by human rights groups as unconstitutional. But the means, and the will, clearly existed to fight terrorism without resorting to mass murder.[31]

By the end of 1975 the Montoneros and the ERP had suffered decisive defeats. "Operation Independence" in Tucumán had broken the ERP. The

Montoneros were more resilient, although several ambitious operations ended in bloody failure and they were badly hurt when Roberto Quieto, their leading military strategist, was arrested on December 28 1975 while sunning on a beach with his family. Quieto was accused of turning informant and condemned to death by his ertswhile Montonero colleagues. It was an empty gesture. He disappeared and was presumably killed by the army.[32]

By the beginning of 1976, left-wing terrorism was sullen, brutal, and terrifying, but it had ceased to pose a mortal danger to the state. One secret intelligence report prepared for the foreign ministry and clearly not intended for publication showed that "subversive actions" fell dramatically from an all-time high of 520 in September 1974 to 200 in January 1976.[33] There was no justification for an army coup to wipe out left-wing "subversion."

Cleansing the Disease

Right-wing terrorism, however, was on the increase. People were abducted and killed by the Triple A death squads and the bodies dumped in exposed places. During 1973 there were 19 such murders. In the first three months of 1976 alone the figure rose to 549.[34] On August 8, Mariano Grondona, a well-known journalist, had a narrow escape when he and his wife were seized outside their tennis club, and blindfolded before being driven off to a secret destination to be harangued about the evils of subversion in front of a portrait of Adolf Hitler.[35]

Lawyers who took up the cases of left-wing activists were singled out by the Triple A. In March 1975 Heleno Fragoso, Vice-President of the Brazilian Bar Association, visited Argentina on behalf of the Geneva-based International Commission of Jurists and found that thirty-two defense lawyers were in jail without having been charged. Fragoso brought back copies of two sinister anonymous pamphlets that were being distributed in Buenos Aires. One, signed by "Comando Puma," contained death threats against eight lawyers. Within two months of the 1976 coup, four had disappeared and the rest had fled abroad. Fragoso's findings thoroughly alarmed the International Commission of Jurists, and gave the organization an interest in Argentina that was to plunge it into direct conflict with the military junta after 1976.[36]

Right-wing terror, however, was of no concern to the armed forces.

Following the coup, Vice Admiral César Guzetti, the Foreign Minister, explained what he understood by "subversion": "My concept deals with organizations of the left. There is no such thing as subversion of the right. The social body of the country is contaminated by a sickness that is eating away at its guts and generates antibodies. These antibodies should not be seen in the same light as the disease itself." Coming from a senior minister this was a strange and sinister comment. Instead of sowing terror, the Triple A was apparently seen as a cleansing influence.[37]

By now, the armed forces had also begun their own clandestine campaign against subversion. In February 1975 General Acdel Edgardo Vilas, one of the commanders of Operation Independence in Tucumán, set up his headquarters in a former school in the town of Famailla. As the military operation progressed, suspects were rounded up, brought into the school, detained in eight former classrooms, and given electric shock treatment. The technology was relatively primitive, and the electric current was produced by turning the handle of an old field telephone. Yet something devilish had been set in motion. Famailla was the first of hundreds of clandestine detention centers that would be set up by the armed forces, and it was operating over a year before the coup.[38]

Declaration of War

By early 1976, Argentina was poised once again to join the other Latin American nations under military rule. The 1976 coup was very much a continuation of the trend of militarization that had begun in 1930. Videla, Massera, and Agosti were personally committed to the doctrine of national security and eager to play a leading role in the hemispheric crusade against "subversion."[39]

But there the similarity stopped. Using the pretext of left-wing terrorism, Argentina's armed forces were preparing to take an unprecedented gamble. They were planning to launch an undeclared war against their own people, the likes of which had never before been seen in Latin America.

In September 1975 a group of senior army generals met to plan their campaign. They included Jorge Videla, the Commander, Roberto Viola, the Chief of Staff, and the heads of the army divisions. They agreed that if left-wing terror were to be stamped out, the overall population would have to be thoroughly terrorized in order to deny the guerrillas a popular base. But it would have to be clandestine. The generals were determined not to make the same mistakes that Pinochet had made in Chile. They would not round up thousands of people in the football stadium and haul them away to be tortured in front of television cameras. They would not shoot foreign television reporters or set fire to books and invite foreign journalists to watch the fun.

Nor would they commit the error of Argentina's previous military rulers, who had seized power with the limited aim of restoring order and returning power to civilians. This time, they would hold power indefinitely. Never again would Argentinians be beguiled by the subversive nationalism of Peronism.

According to Rodolfo Peregrino Fernández, a well-placed official in the Interior Ministry, it was left to General Cesareo Cardozo, director of the War College, to sum up the September 1975 meeting.[40] The document was ready early the following year, and it proposed a secret war against subversion. The day of the coup, it was sent out to all senior officers in the three services in the form of an "orden de batalla" (battle order).[41] The dirty war was about to begin. A month later, Mónica Mignone disappeared.

2. The War Begins

Argentina's first sight of its new leader was reassuring. Lieutenant General Jorge Videla was not bull-necked and pugnacious like Augusto Pinochet of Chile. While Pinochet glowered and frowned, Videla seemed mild, simpático. If his was the face of military rule in Argentina, it did not seem unpleasant.[1]

It was accepted wisdom that Videla was desperately reluctant to assume the highest office. One report described him as "tormented by the prospect of a new military government."[2] In December 1975 he had refused to cooperate with air force officers who seized two bases and called for Mrs. Perón's ouster. His stock rose enormously in March 1976 when a bomb exploded in a parking lot just before he arrived. After his investiture, Videla remained accessible. Robert Cox, editor of the English-language *Buenos Aires Herald,* would later recall a meeting between a small group of journalists and Videla soon after the coup: "I did not know President Videla personally, but I came away with the image of a friend, not only my friend, but a friend of the Argentinian people. The meeting was extremely warm. I remember when we left commenting that Videla appeared to be a marvelous fellow."[3]

There was a powerful dose of wishful thinking about these first impressions. People wished Videla well. They wanted him to succeed. The one quality they could not invest him with was magnetism. Videla seemed most at home kneeling at a church pew, where he was frequently photographed. Thin and angular, he looked like an efficient office manager rather than a three-star general. Of all the Latin American dictators, Videla was the least charismatic. He looked to be what he was, a compromise President who could present a reasonable, even humane, face to the outside world. A "blando," not a "duro."[4]

The air force representative in the Junta, Brigadier General Orlando Ramón Agosti, had the most overtly anti-Peronist past.[5] Fifty-two-year-old Admiral Eduardo Emilio Massera, the navy commander, was the oldest and also the most flamboyant member of the three. "Handsome, dark haired, athletic, and sociable" gushed a profile in the *New York Times* on March 25 1977. Massera had been placed in charge of security for Juan Perón's triumphal return from exile and Perón was sufficiently impressed to promote Massera to the top navy post over several more senior admirals. (The appointment was agreed on August 23 1974 by the Peronist-dominated Congress.)[6] The connection with Perón evidently fueled Massera's personal ambitions. It opened the door to membership of the ultra-secret right-wing Italian brotherhood known as the P 2, whose grandmaster, Licio Gelli, had long been a close friend of Perón. Massera's P 2 connection was to become useful after he resigned from the Junta in September 1978.[7]

By March 1976 Massera had over forty decorations from foreign governments and, more important, total control over the Argentinian navy. A generation of senior officers were indebted to him, and he responded like a godfather, dispensing patronage and calling in dues. It was clear that he had a fertile mind and lively intelligence. What was not known at the time of the coup was the extent of his personal ambition, nor his ruthlessness.

One of the first tasks facing Argentina's new military rulers was to divide out the spoils and apportion government ministries. Two ministries went to each of the three services. Another two (Education and Finance) went to civilians. The army received Interior and Labor, which were considered crucial for the fight against "subversion." The air force received Defense and Justice, while the navy took over the Foreign Ministry and Social Welfare. This would have suited Massera well. The prestigious Foreign Ministry would afford him unparalleled opportunities for personal aggrandizement.

Under Massera, the navy hijacked the Foreign Ministry. Within twenty-four hours of seizing power, the Junta announced that all diplomats would be checked out and anyone found to be "ideologically unreliable" dismissed. Three days later, thirty ambassadors were retired. Within two months, they had been followed by another fifty career officers from Argentina's 800-strong diplomatic corps. Meanwhile, unqualified navy officers occupied key positions. Admiral César Guzetti was appointed Foreign Minister, with Captain Gualter Allara as his deputy. When foreign correspondents filed their stories on the March 24 coup their copy was checked by navy officers, who had taken over the ministry press office. During the months that followed, navy personnel would come and go between the

Foreign Ministry and the navy's chief concentration camp, and several would take part in kidnapping and torture.[8]

These developments spelled ruin for a diplomatic corps that had retained a reputation for excellence and independence throughout the forty turbulent years following the 1930 military coup. Competition for places was fierce. Only one in every ten applicants could expect to enter the "Instituto del Servicio Exterior de la Nación," the training school for young diplomats that looked out over the cranes and derricks of the port. The course itself was grueling but rewarding. Ahead stretched a pampered life and foreign postings among Argentina's seventy-nine embassies around the world. Most important, it offered a chance to serve a branch of government that had remained relatively unscathed by the successive military coups and untainted by ideology.

This now changed abruptly. Anyone who challenged Massera found himself in deep trouble. Gregorio Dupont was a second secretary in the Foreign Ministry at the time of the coup. In October he was astonished to learn that Massera proposed to send an ambassador to attend the independence ceremony of Transkei, one of the controversial South African homelands. Aware of the damage this would do to Argentina's reputation within the Nonaligned Movement, Dupont drafted an alarmed memorandum. He was immediately called in by Deputy Foreign Minister Allara and warned that he had challenged a personal decision by Admiral Massera.[9]

Allara listened as Dupont warned of the diplomatic damage that would result, but it was no use. Dupont had crossed Massera. Shortly afterward Dupont found himself at a dinner party where the conversation turned to Massera's chances of ever becoming President. Dupont voiced skepticism. He did not know at the time that one of the dinner guests was Massera's mistress. Dupont began to receive threats against his life. Within a month he found himself drummed out of the diplomatic service. He could not know that worse was to come and that his brush with Massera would lead to personal tragedy.[10]

The Assault on Law

Argentina's judiciary was allowed to survive because the Junta required a veneer of legality for its acts and decrees and its assault on "subversión."

But any spark of independence was quickly snuffed out. At the time of the coup, the country was still under the state of siege declared by Isabel Perón on November 6 1974. The day of the coup, the Junta extended the state of siege, and arguing that this provided a legal justification embarked on rule by a series of executive directives, many of them unconstitutional.[11] The Supreme Court was purged, the Prosecutor General and federal judges replaced, and all new judges were required to swear an oath of loyalty to the acts and objectives of the Process of National Reorganization. Habeas corpus and the right of option were both emasculated. The Junta suspended the right of option on the day that it seized power. Shortly afterward, notices began to appear in courthouses saying that no habeas corpus writs could be accepted without a lawyer's signature. This had never before been required.[12]

The next move against the independence of the legal system was scandalously and cruelly illegal. Under Argentina's constitution, everyone is entitled to a defense lawyer. The Junta's response to this was simple and brutal. Between 1976 and 1983 no fewer than 109 lawyers disappeared, 24 were murdered, and more than 100 detained without being tried and charged.[13]

This intimidating attack completely undermined habeas corpus. When Ragnar Hagelin tried to submit a writ on behalf of his daughter Dagmar, he approached almost a hundred lawyers before he found one willing to take up the case.[14] Even when lawyers could be found who were courageous enough to file the writ, judges were either too intimidated or too sympathetic to the Junta to take action. They never demanded the right to investigate a center in person or call key witnesses. Between 1976 and 1979, judges received at least 5,487 submissions for habeas corpus in Buenos Aires alone. Not one resulted in a serious investigation. During the dirty war, only two detainees, including the newspaperman Jacobo Timerman, were released as a result of a habeas corpus writ.[15]

Judges had another important function that might have checked the murder if it had been taken seriously. When someone dies from foul play in Argentina, judges pass the case on to a prosecutor and order an investigation. During the dirty war they turned a blind eye to the evidence. Miguel Angel Sosa was kidnapped on May 25 1976. The autopsy report concluded that he had been tortured and shot in the head at close range. This case should have been vigorously pursued by the investigating judge. Instead he wrote out a letter to Miguel's family saying that their son had been found dead and then "forgot" to send it. The oversight would launch

Emilio Mignone on a grim search for clandestine graves that would, eventually, expose the complicity of his profession.[16]

Early in 1976, Rubén Bossio and his co-workers at a morgue at the city of Córdoba began receiving corpses that were torn, lacerated, and peppered with bullet holes. They noticed that the doctors rarely performed autopsies on these bodies, but limited themselves to signing the death certificate that had come from police doctors or the Third Army Division, based in the city. For three years Bossio and his co-workers kept their suspicions to themselves. But by June 30 1980 so many mutilated corpses had piled up in the small hospital waiting for burial that the conditions of work had become unbearable. They wrote a despairing letter to President Videla: "Mr. President. It is impossible to describe what we have to live with. Some of the bodies have been more than than thirty days without being refrigerated. There is a cloud of flies over the bodies, which are covered by a layer of ten and a half centimeters of worms and eggs which we take away in buckets."[17]

Did all of this mean that the legal safeguards in Argentina's constitution, and the rights to due legal process, were not to be taken at face value—as some American scholars would assert? Clearly not. Indeed, in a sense, the disappearances were a testament to the legal tradition in Argentina. The armed forces knew their murderous campaign was illegal. This is why it had to be conducted in secret, away from prying eyes.[18]

The Wizard Crushes the Unions

Never before, throughout Latin America's flirtation with the doctrine of national security, had "subversion" been so broadly defined. Evening classes were banned, oceanography and folklore eliminated from university curricula. Even *The Little Prince* disappeared from libraries and bookstores. The charge was all-embracing. Most important, it allowed for an all-out assault on Argentina's powerful trade unions.

"Subversion in the work place." The phrase featured obsessively in secret army directives, but what it really meant was organized labor exerting the rights to strike and bargain collectively, rights that would be taken for granted in most Western countries. There were two reasons why the Junta had to crush Argentina's powerful unions. One was to destroy the political base for Peronism, the other to open up Argentina's economy and reverse the years of economic nationalism. Perón had thrown up trade barriers against imports in an attempt to build up Argentina's own industry, and the Junta was determined to put an end to such protectionism. Down came the barriers, up went the peso, and in came the loans. It was the pure free-market policy embraced by Pinochet in neighboring Chile, but it could only succeed if labor was cowed.

The man who directed it, Finance Minister Alfredo Martínez de Hoz, was a scion of the landowning oligarchy who had already held the post briefly in a previous government and had won a reputation as a strike-breaker while president of ACINDAR, Argentina's largest steel concern.[19] Some of the Junta's earliest, and harshest, edicts were directed against unions. Strikes, collective bargaining, closed shops, even meetings, were banned. The umbrella General Confederation of Labor had its authorization suspended, and some fifty labor leaders were banned from political activity. Military officers were put in charge of powerful unions. Factories were raided and workers hauled away to detention or death.[20]

For a privileged few, however, it was the time of "plata dulce" (sweet money). Wrote one journalist:

> Affluent families still remember this period as the time of "give me six," because the goal of shopping sprees in Europe or the United States was to purchase six of everything. "We'd go into a shoe store in New York and buy six pairs for everybody," a businesswoman remembered. "One time our youngest daughter wasn't there and we weren't positive of her shoe size. So we got two pairs at size four and a half, two pairs at size five, and two pairs at size five and a half."[21]

Middle-class Argentinians were reassured and worried less about the mysterious disappearances. International bankers vied with each other to lend money to Argentina at low rates of interest. American businessmen were charmed and labelled Martínez de Hoz the "Wizard of Hoz." Politicians rushed to issue him with invitations. One of his admirers was former Governor Ronald Reagan, who met the Wizard during a trip to the United States and wrote a glowing newspaper article in October 1980:

> Martínez de Hoz is the architect of what may turn out to be one of the most remarkable economic recoveries in modern history. . . . The armed forces stepped in, as Martínez de Hoz explained, to bring continuity and to keep the country afloat. In this civil war atmosphere "no quarter was asked and no quarter was given," he said. "It is a sad reality that there will be a certain number of people that the government will never be able to account for."[22]

In spite of the compliment, Martínez de Hoz's economic strategy was anything but an exercise in what would come to be termed Reaganomics. Instead of curbing public spending, he budgeted huge amounts on highways and housing. He also pampered the military. (Here perhaps there were similarities.) 1.8 billion dollars, equivalent to half the country's total exports, was earmarked for defense in 1977. Military wages were increased by 120 percent in February.[23]

Martínez de Hoz borrowed over a billion dollars in under a year, helped by that vague and mystical quality known as "international creditworthiness." No single institution or individual bestowed the mantle on Argentina, but the International Monetary Fund approved of the Wizard's free market polices and the private banks were flushed with petrodollars that had to be loaned. Slowly but surely, the familiar cycle set in. Each dollar borrowed had to be repaid, but earnings from Argentinian beef and grain failed to match the cost of essential imports and repayments on debts. Local industries caved in under foreign competition. Unemployment and inflation started to rise. Incomes fell. The chill was soon felt in the "villas miserias" and working-class neighborhoods. The once-powerful unions were unable to help: even their welfare programs had been taken over by the military government.

In March 1977, Rodolfo Walsh, one of Argentina's foremost investigative journalists (as well as a top Montonero leader) wrote a bitter denunciation of the Junta's economic policies:

> There are parts of Greater Buenos Aires where infant mortality has reached 30%—a figure which puts us on a par with Benin, or the Guineas. There are huge urban areas with little or no electric light, without water because the big industries have pumped the underground reservoirs dry. Networks of streets have been reduced to a continuous pothole because you pave the roads only in the military suburbs. The business associates of Martínez de Hoz have polluted all the beaches of one of the most beautiful rivers in the world by pouring effluents directly into the estuary.

It was the sort of eloquence that had won Walsh a distinguished reputation. But by now no paper would touch it, so on March 24 1977 Walsh published his tract as an open letter. It ended on a prescient note. "These are the thoughts I wish to share with the members of the Junta on this first anniversary of your disreputable government, without hope of being listened to, in the certainty of persecution."

Walsh asked his family to send a copy of his letter to Patricia Derian, the U.S. Assistant Secretary of State for Human Rights, who was present in Argentina on a visit. (The letter reached the U.S. embassy on April 11, after Derian had returned to Washington.) The following day Walsh disappeared. His letter had been a suicidal act by a desperate man, crushed between the fanaticism of the army and his own Montonero comrades. Some say he was killed with a gun in his hand, others that he died under torture at the navy mechanics school (ESMA). If the latter, then he might have suffered the fate of being tortured by Lieutenant Enrique Yon, an operative at the ESMA who was married to a niece of Martínez de Hoz. Walsh's body was seen at the ESMA by Martín Gras, a detainee who survived.[24]

The disappearances and Martínez de Hoz's free market economic policy remained locked in a deadly embrace for four long years. It was a brutal, all-out attack on the principle of free labor association—a fact that soon became clear to the Geneva-based International Labor Organization and the U.S. embassy in Buenos Aires.[25] Of 8,960 disappearances reported to the 1984 CONADEP commission, no fewer than 30.2 percent were workers.[26]

Chopping up the Parsley

The dirty war developed its own slang. Young people like Mónica Mignone who had no direct connection with the guerrillas were called "perejil," which meant literally "parsley" but came to mean "small fry." This did not stop them from being "chupado" (sucked in). The language was chilling, but apt.

The war spun out of control. Intelligence officials at the ESMA and other centers acted on the slightest piece of information, no matter how flimsy. If someone's face appeared on a wanted poster they pulled in his tailor, his barber, anyone remotely connected to the wanted man. Someone has been shot trying to run a police checkpoint? Take down all the names in the address book found on the body and pull them in; then round up any former classmates who might have shown any inclination toward left-wing politics.

Bizarre mistakes were made. One victim was abducted because he belonged to the Argentinian Federation of Psychiatry, which happened to share the same initials (FAP) as one of the three left-wing revolutionary movements (Armed Peronist Forces). One curious fourteen-year-old boy wandered into the ESMA by accident. When they discovered his father was a Communist he was atrociously tortured to death.[27]

The same pattern that emerged in the kidnapping of Mónica Mignone and her friends appeared in several other cases. During the "night of the pencils" of September 16 1976, ten schoolchildren were kidnapped because they had signed a joint petition asking for student-rate bus tickets. The children paid dearly for their subversion. They were starved, beaten, chained, and tortured with the omnipresent cattle prod. Only three lived to tell the tale.[28]

The oldest recorded victim of the dirty war was seventy-seven-year-old María Hourcadie de Francese.[29] One of the youngest was Claudia Victoria Poblete, who was just eight months old when she was seized by police on November 28 1978 with her mother, Gertrudis Hlaczik. Claudia's father, José Poblete, was arrested the same day. Gertrudis and José were both invalids, and both were seen by other detainees at the Olimpo detention center, where they were apparently singled out for special treatment because of their disabilities. The guards mocked José and called him "Shorty" because he had no feet. One detainee recalled seeing him dragging himself along the floor as he tried to reach a toilet. Later his wheelchair was spotted in a pile of garbage, a sure indication that he had been killed, or "transferred." The same fate presumably awaited his invalid wife, who was seen being beaten and pulled around by her hair, naked, shortly after her abduction. What became of their daughter Claudia is not known.[30]

For one Western diplomat who lived through it all, the horror was the innocence of most of the victims. Looking back, he recalled with great sadness the way they walked to their deaths like Jews to the gas chamber.

> They simply didn't know the ground rules. They were the sort of people who would have been willing, even eager, to help police with their questioning. They had nothing to hide. Sure, they were members of the Young Peronists; sure, they had known future Montoneros at school, played football with them, gone to movies with them. They simply did not realize that the association, however distant, was a sentence of death.[31]

"Desaparecido." Originally coined in Guatemala in the 1960s, the word became synonymous with Argentina. To this day, no one knows how many disappeared. The Permanent Assembly of Human Rights, the first Argentinian human rights group to take up the issue, compiled 5,900 documented cases. CONADEP, the commission that was established by

Argentina's democratic government in 1984 would register a total of 8,960. This, too, was almost certainly an underestimate.[32]

There was no precedent for such an assault by a government against its own people. Historically, the nearest equivalent to the disappearances were the Night and Fog decrees used by the Nazis to remove several hundred members of the Resistance and sow terror in Nazi-occupied Europe. Hundreds disappeared in Guatemala and Brazil in the 1960s. Some seven hundred disappeared following the 1973 coup in Chile, and as noted above at least three hundred were abducted and murdered by the Triple A in Argentina itself before the 1976 coup.[33]

What made the dirty war different from these miserable episodes was the scale and method. Never before had the the resources of a state been geared to systematic torture and murder. The Junta turned disappearances into a government policy and in so doing gave new meaning to the concept of state terror. It was as deliberate, methodical, and calculated as collecting tax, and as such very much out of character with the haphazard brutality of previous military regimes. Here was one more reason why the disappearances could not be described as a product of Latin American authoritarianism, or in the "Iberian tradition."

By 1981 the urge to pin labels on human rights abuses would be overwhelming. What of the disappearances? One shrewd analysis was prepared in late 1980 by Claus Ruser, a senior diplomat at the U.S. embassy in Buenos Aires. Looking back over the previous four years, Ruser offered the following definition of what he aptly termed "the tactic of disappearances":

> Disappearance is a euphemism for the unacknowledged detention of any individual by security forces. Based on everything we know we believe that detainees are usually tortured as part of interrogation and eventually executed without any semblance of due process.[34]

Three key elements are noted here. First, there is the total involvement of the government. While it is often hard to identify the authors of human rights abuses, there could be no such doubts about the disappearances. Second, there is the physical violence, the routine use of torture.[35] Third, there is the indifference to law, noted earlier. Or was it rather fear of the law? From the moment that their first victim disappeared, Argentina's military rulers were trapped in a vicious circle of their own making. Spurred on by the fear of eventually being called to account, they tried to spread responsibility as widely as possible throughout the armed forces. "Under the current system," wrote Ruser, "the military are responsible as an institution but the individual is free from accountability." This meant that victims of torture had to be killed to ensure that they never gave evidence.

Absent from Ruser's shrewd but bloodless analysis was the psychological impact on Argentinians that came from knowing that their government, defender of law, had cast law aside. This added a new dimension to the terror, as was surely intended. The disappeared knew that they were totally at the mercy of the torturers. They could be skinned alive and no one would ever know. For the relatives it was almost as bad. They lived on the edge for month after month, fearful one moment and hopeful the next, paralyzed by the memory of loss and the feeling of guilt. For them the wound would never heal. It was like ripping a wing from a butterfly.

By the middle of 1977, Argentinians were able to answer some of the questions they had begun to ask immediately after the coup. The basic justification for the coup, the threat from terrorism, clearly no longer applied.[36] By now, "subversion" had come to mean democratic rights and a social conscience.

Of all the labels applied to the Junta, fascism seemed the most appropriate. How else was one to describe the experience of guardsman Carlos Beltrán, after he was told to accompany a group of guards and four prisoners from the army camp of La Perla? One of the four prisoners was a pregnant woman. They were driven out to a rocky area beyond the camp, where the youngest prisoner was given a shovel and told to dig a ditch. Beltrán would recall what followed before the CONADEP commission:

> I was standing with the oldest of the four prisoners. I could see that he was praying very slowly, and crying. No one spoke. A profound silence reigned. The captain made the man who was digging stand at the . . . edge of the ditch. When I indicated that I would not do it, "Gino," the four sub-officers, and the First Lieutenant began to fire on the detainees . . . The three men remained motionless after the shots, but the woman was able to stagger to her feet and walk a few paces. The "Captain" drew his pistol and shot her in the head.[37]

3. Torture at the ESMA

After Mónica Mignone's abduction, her mother Angélica Mignone had a sudden second sense that Mónica might not have been the only target, and she immediately took a cab to the home of Mónica's best friend, a young woman named María Marta Vasquez. She arrived too late: Vasquez had already been taken away. The kidnappers had said that Mónica was to be questioned at the Palermo army barracks. Angélica and Emilio waited several hours and then drove to the barracks. Here they found, to their consternation, that camp officials denied any knowledge of their daughter. They then went to their local police station to submit a report and asked about the police guard outside the nearby homes of retired General Díaz Bessone and Admiral Rojas. Had they not seen anything? No, they were told, because the police guard had been withdrawn that night. It was beginning to dawn on the Mignones that their daughter had been picked up in an operation by the armed forces. They were dumbfounded. It was still early days. The word "desaparecido" was not yet in vogue.[1]

Emilio Mignone embarked on a feverish search, exploiting any contacts he had among the military. Doors opened into elegant offices with thick carpets to reveal dignified men in immaculate uniforms. But the answer was the same: no news of Mónica. Mignone had only one important clue to work on. Five of Mónica's friends, including María Marta Vasquez, had disappeared the same night. Later in the morning a sixth, Mónica Quinteiro, had been picked up outside her office. Each operation had been meticulously carried out, except that one group had stolen 12,000 pesos, a television, a record player, a radio, and a blender.

The seven friends were fairly typical of young middle-class Argentinians in 1976. They were impatient with the bourgeois society that had rewarded their parents, frustrated by years of stifling military rule, and devoted to the memory of Juan Perón. But if they saw violence as the way to achieve change, they kept it well hidden. Mónica Quinteiro was, perhaps, the one exception. She was a left-wing professor and Montonero sympathizer. For some years she had worked as a catechist in the Bajo Flores, one of the huge slums that surround Buenos Aires, with two progressive priests, Orlando Yorio and Francisco Jalics. The two priests were viewed as such mavericks by their superiors that they were even forbidden to celebrate mass in the slum.

By the time of the coup, Mónica Mignone was also spending several hours a week in the slum. One week before they were kidnapped, Mónica Mignone and María Marta Vasquez had visited Yorio for a personal discussion. Nine days after Mónica was kidnapped a band of heavily armed men surrounded the house where the two priests lived, ransacked the place, and took the two men away. A raid of this size in a crowded slum was bound to attract attention, and when the local inhabitants inquired the intruders said they were from the navy. A few days later, when another priest visited the navy mechanics school in the capital he found himself giving communion to a detainee that he knew well. It was his fellow priest Yorio.

For Emilio Mignone, the snippets of information were all beginning to fit into a wider pattern. He stepped up his efforts and gained a meeting with Oscar Montes, the Chief of Naval Operations, who had overall responsibility for navy counterintelligence in the capital.

"I don't see why you've come," said Montes truculently. "I can't give you any information. The navy is not responsible."

"You're not telling the truth," replied Mignone.

Montes lost his temper. "Why are you calling me a liar?"

Because," replied Mignone, "our daughters were close to the two priests Yorio and Jalics who were arrested on May 23 by men from the navy."

"Yes," replied Montes, "that's right. Those two Third World priests were detained because one of them in particular is very dangerous."

Mignone pounced on the comment. "That's very interesting. I think we're making progress." Montes realized he had said too much, and the interview finished abruptly, but Mignone's suspicions had been confirmed.[2]

Three months passed. Then, on October 23, Mignone heard that the two priests had been released. He hurried over to the home of Yorio's mother, where the priest was recovering. Yorio had a strange tale to tell. After being taken from the slum, he and Jalics had been driven blindfolded to an unknown destination and interrogated for several days before being moved again. Five months later, without warning, they were released. Yorio remembered the interrogation well. His captors had asked about his meeting in the slum with Mónica Mignone and her friend María Marta Vasquez, details which only the two young women could have known. At one stage they asked about "Mónica," but Yorio was uncertain whether they were referring to Mónica Mignone or her friend Mónica Quinteiro. On another occasion, he was aware of being in a crowded room. He heard someone whisper his name in a weak voice. He was sure it was Mónica Quinteiro.

During his detention, one of his interrogators made a revealing comment to the priest Yorio: "We know you're not violent. You're not guerrillas. But you've gone to live with the poor. Living with the poor unites them. Uniting the poor is subversion." Emilio Mignone realized at last why his daughter had disappeared. He also understood the rationale behind the dirty war.

The Navy Prepares for the Dirty War

Mónica Mignone's parents now suspected that she was, or had been, held at the navy mechanics school in the capital. They also knew she was considered to be a "subversive" because of her work in the slum. As the number of disappearances soared, they were beginning to realize how dangerous that could be. Yet the navy officially denied any knowledge or involvement. What had happened? Was she well? Was she being fed? Did she have clean clothes? Angélica and Emilio Mignone must have spent hours asking themselves those questions that parents never stop asking of their children. Anything to avoid facing the unthinkable. And the more they learned of the navy mechanics school, the more Emilio wished he had never opened the door to the intruders.

The school lay in the middle of Buenos Aires, on the Avenida Libertador San Martín. On weekends, a stream of traffic took Argentinians north to the affluent suburbs. Directly opposite, a Gillette factory turned out razor blades. Next to it was a cafe where factory workers could retire to drink "maté," the thick green tea to which Argentinians are addicted. Nearby rose the walls of the city's main football stadium.

Surrounded by bustling city life, the school itself was spread out over several spacious acres. It could take approximately five thousand officers and cadets and offered a wide range of technical courses. Great care went into maintaining the whitewashed buildings, with their red-tiled roofs and green shutters. Over the entrance visitors could read the words "Escuela Superior de Mecánica de la Armada" (the school became familiar to Argentinians as "the ESMA"). The door was flanked by two navy cadets with peaked hats and gleaming ornamental swords. "Look at us with respect and be grateful," they seemed to say to the civilians who teemed past outside, "because our job is to protect you." At the time of the coup in 1976, most Argentinians wanted desperately to believe it.

They did not know that the school had already been transformed into the navy's nerve center in the war against subversion. The first recorded case of a clandestine kidnapping by a navy squad occurred in February 1976, a month before the coup.[3] Following the coup, the strategy of secret arrest and detention received the imprimatur of the junta, and the transformation of the ESMA was completed. Over the next three years, it would claim the lives of almost 5,000 Argentinians.

After the outline of the dirty war was agreed in September 1975, the country was divided into a series of security zones which were apportioned between the services under the overall command of the army. The First Army Corps, under General Carlos Guillermo Suárez Mason, took overall control of Greater Buenos Aires, within which the city center went to the navy, operating out of the ESMA, and the Western suburbs went to the air force.[4]

Army Colonel Roberto Roualdes was appointed overall coordinator and each service was required to report daily to the First Army Corps on the status of each prisoner. Once a suspected subversive had been identified and a kidnapping operation planned, the local police were contacted. They were told the time and location of the planned kidnapping, asked to declare it a "free zone," and ordered to stay clear. This explained why the local police made no move to interrupt the patrol which had seized Mónica Mignone. Initially, the system worked remarkably well considering the rivalry among the three services and their chiefs. But Massera was greedy. He wanted the top Montoneros, and he extended the navy's operations into the suburbs. By the end of 1977 the division of responsibility between the services had broken down and Suárez Mason, an obsessive administrator, was forced to draw up a secret plan to install some order.[5]

The services set up several counter-insurgency task forces ("grupos de tarea"). Each service was then left to organize itself internally. The navy's areas of responsibility were divided into eleven sectors, each with its own operational "work groups." Massera created an elite group, based at the ESMA and known simply as the GT 3/32, to cover the all-important capital.[6]

Within the ESMA, the officers' quarters, a roomy building set apart from the main complex, was overhauled and turned into an elaborate concentration camp. The basement was transformed into an interrogation center, hospital, and photo laboratory, which were connected to the ground floor by a well-guarded stairway. On the ground floor the results of interrogation were analyzed and the next operation planned. Officers lived on the second and third floors. The third floor was also converted into a series of small cubicles, known as the "capucha" (hood), where prisoners were kept. On the same floor was a "pañol" (storeroom) where the "botín de guerra" (war booty) from raids was kept. In 1977 a third area, known as the "pecera" (fishbowl) because of its glass partitions, was created where prisoners could work. When the third floor got too crowded, cells were also extended to the loft, known as the "capuchita" (little hood).

Massera chose the GT 3/32 members with care. Jorge Radice, an accountant by training, helped keep an account of the war booty. Luis d'Imperio was an essential addition because he commanded the contingent of navy planes at the small city airport which were used to take prisoners up and drop them over the river Plate. The GT 3/32 grew quickly in number and prestige, and within months of the coup it was independent from the navy's intelligence service as well as the third task force (of which it was technically a part). Rubén Chamorro, the ESMA director, was promoted from a captain to the rank of rear admiral with orders to report directly to Admiral Massera himself. Captain Jorge Acosta, chief of the intelligence unit, assumed control of the GT 3/32 after a vicious power struggle among the officers.

The GT 3/32 members gave themselves childish pseudonyms while taking pride in divulging their real names. Detainees at the ESMA knew that the "Son of Sam" was really the son of General Carlos Suárez Mason, head of the First Army Corps, and that the good-looking "Angel" was an admiral's son, Lieutenant Alfredo Astiz. Captain Enrique "Cobra" Yon was married to the niece of Finance Minister Alfredo Martínez de Hoz. Their connections were impeccable. They were Argentina's brightest and best, and they turned their talent to torture.[7]

Thanks to the evidence of a handful of detainees who survived, they would become household names in Argentina, and their escapades would be followed as eagerly as a soap opera. Behind the whitewashed walls,

"Dolphin" Chamorro and his underlings squabbled, tortured, murdered, and loved. Most of it was sheer horror, of a kind that no scriptwriter could have invented. The rest was melodrama. Prisoners learned not to stare at Coca, Chamorro's black mistress. They also gave a wide berth to Miriam Vantman, a Montonero who was kidnapped, tortured, and then taken to bed by "Gabriel" Jorge Carlos Radice, one of the most ferocious members of the GT 3/32. Adolfo "Gerónimo" Dunda served as the group's chief of operations at a time when his own sister-in-law María Hilda Pérez de Dunda was detained in the ESMA. She gave birth to a baby on May 10, 1977.[8]

Admiral Emilio Massera urged them on. He addressed the inaugural meeting of the GT 3/32 and urged it to respond to the enemy "with the maximum violence." Massera himself reportedly participated in some of the group's earliest operations under the pseudonyms of "black" and "zero," even torturing suspects to emphasize his support. On one occasion, he visited the hooded, shackled prisoners and wished them a happy Christmas. On November 2 1976, he gave an address at the school that was a masterpiece of cynicism. "Slowly," he said, referring to the left-wing terrorism, "a machine of horror spread its evil over the innocent. We will not allow death to prowl unchecked in Argentina." Upstairs, in a tiny cell, lay sixteen-year-old Cecilia Inés Cacabellos with a hood over her head and her hands chained behind her back.[9]

Ana María Meets Caroline

Ana María Martí, one of the few detainees to be released from the ESMA, bore many similarities to Mónica Mignone. She was a committed Peronist and a social worker, and her ordeal began under equally terrifying circumstances. On March 28, 1977, in the evening, she approached the ticket office at a small railway station in the suburbs of Buenos Aires. The ticket clerk looked at her. She sensed he was trying to tell her something. Moments later, a hand clamped tightly around her neck and several men pushed her down a small flight of stairs toward three waiting cars. One was a Ford Falcon without license plates. Her kidnappers shouted "Keep away, this is a drug arrest!" while they bundled her down behind the back seat.[10] From her cramped position Ana María Martí found herself facing a young man with light brown hair. By now, Lieutenant "Angel" Astiz was one of the stars of the GT 3/32. When he leaned over and started to frisk her for weapons, she pushed him away. He muttered angrily at her. "Okay, be brave. We'll see how brave you are when you've met Caroline." Ana María had no idea what he meant.

By now Astiz would have radioed back to the ESMA base, which was known as "Selenio" (moon), and reported another successful operation. The car pulled in through the back gate. Ana María Martí was hooded and bundled out. She felt herself being pulled down the stairway to the basement. Unknown hands snatched at her. Commands were barked. Doors slammed and opened. Suddenly the hood was pulled off. Several men were standing before her wearing uniforms. "Where would you least like to be?" snapped one. By now, the stories of torture and death had begun to filter out from the ESMA. Where would Ana María Martí least like to be? She had no doubts at all. "ESMA," she answered. Her captors grinned. They seemed pleased. "That's just where you are," said one of them. This, Ana María later learned, was Antonio Pernía. Pernía was known by two "noms de guerre" "Thunder" and "Rat." He used to shoot tranquilizing darts into prisoners to work out precisely how long it could take to subdue a prisoner during a kidnapping. It was all very scientific. They could not afford to lose precious time.

It was time for Ana María to meet "Caroline." Caroline was the name given to a thick broom handle with two long wires that ran through and out at the end, like the antennae of a large insect. Caroline had been invented and christened by an electrician at the ESMA who was known to the detainees by his nickname "the electric cat."

Torture had been practiced in Argentina since the 1930 coup, in spite of being expressly outlawed in Argentina's constitution and penal and military justice codes. Dr. Leopoldo Lugones, police chief under the first military regime, took advantage of Argentina's predilection for beef and used the electric cattle prod or "picana" to extract information from detainees. The "picana" became the favorite instrument of torturers throughout Latin America, and Eduardo Pedace, an Argentinian pathologist, became the world authority at identifying the unseen burns it caused.[11]

Nothing, however, remotely resembled the scale on which torture was practiced in Argentina after the 1976 coup. At the ESMA, it took place in three basement rooms next to the photo laboratory and infirmary. Sometimes there was a doctor on hand to gauge the amount of suffering the prisoners could take and revive them before they died. Nine doctors were seen in the hospital by detainees. One, who had been given the macabre name of "Mengele," was present as Ana María Martí was stripped and tied to the steel bed frame. She watched, dazed, as Caroline was attached to a box on a table. The insect's antennae were throbbing and dancing with the current, its jaws open. They closed on the steel frame. Then came the agony, unspeakable agony, as the insect moved hungrily over her body, probing, spitting and spluttering while Antonio Pernía's grin hovered above.

It was unhurried and methodical. If the victim was a woman they went for the breasts, vagina, anus. If a man, they favored genitals, tongue, neck. The aim was to cause disorientation as much as pain. Sometimes victims twitched so uncontrollably that they shattered their own arms and legs. Patrick Rice, an Irish priest who had also worked in slums and was detained for several days, recalls watching his flesh sizzle. What he most remembers is the smell. It was like bacon.[12]

After electric shock torture, prisoners were warned not to drink. Carlos Muñoz, another ESMA detainee, recalls one friend who was so thirsty after hours of Caroline that he drank from a toilet bowl and died of a heart attack thiry minutes later.[13] All the EMSA detainees were tortured, irrespective of their age, sex, or background. It made no difference why they had been abducted or whether they belonged to a guerrilla group. They all went through the same, terrifying ritual. And all around, outside, the city of Buenos Aires teemed with people going about their business.[14]

In the Hood

After torture, the ESMA detainees were moved up into the "capucha" (hood) on the third floor, where they were chained down in tiny cells separated from other cells on either side by a low wooden partition. Above them, a naked light bulb hung from the sloping roof. This the prisoners were only dimly aware of because they were kept hooded. Sometimes they managed to lift the hood and snatch a few words with a neighbor.

The guards were known as "verdes" (greens) from the color of their uniforms. They were young cadets who came mainly from poor families. Some of them were even more savage than their superiors, but others were gawky and embarrassed, and so recently acquainted with mother love that they were openly distressed for the wretched women who groped their way to a filthy shower or communal toilet. This had not been in the manuals. Jorge Carlos Torres, one of the greens, would testify at the 1985 trial that some guards suffered from mental disorder because of the experience.[15]

Ana María Martí remembers the way night merged into day. Real sleep was impossible with the light above her, and she was constantly jolted awake by loud music. They played slushy, romantic songs by Julio Iglesias to make the prisoners weep. It was hard to stay awake or sleep. Martí tried to think of her two children and mentally reorganized the furniture in her house until she dozed off. "I never thought I would die. But then I remember waking up to the sensation of fear. I had forgotten where I was. I felt the heat rise, the panic. I felt like vomiting."

Many of the prisoners could not take it. Sixty-year-old Lola de Lévenson, in a cubicle next to Ana María Martí, went crazy and began taunting the guards. "Don't imagine I'm going to stay here," she screeched, "I'm going to fly away like a bird." They watched, laughed, and tied a heavy iron ball and chain to her foot, which the exhausted old woman was forced to pull around. It was like a scene from the Inquisition.

Eventually, de Lévenson was "transferred", which in the language of Argentina's dirty war meant killed. It took time for this to emerge. In February 1977 an army deserter known as Tincho, who had joined the Montoneros and been captured, was taken down to the infirmary, given an injection, and taken by truck to the Aeroparque. Groggy, he was pushed up the steps of a plane. Then they asked him his name and number. They had made a mistake. He returned to the ESMA and recounted his story, whereupon the prisoners began to understand what they faced. Anyone marked for execution was given decent food and cleaned up. (It would be harder to explain if corpses turned up showing signs of obvious maltreatment.) Not surprisingly, there was always great tension the day the trucks arrived and the numbers were called. It usually happened on Wednesday. According to Norma Susana Burgos, another survivor, Tincho was subsequently killed.[16]

Sometimes they were thrown out of planes fully conscious, sometimes drugged with sodium pentathol. Sometimes, mercifully, they were killed first with an injection of curare and the belly was slit open so that the body would sink. "Fish food," they were called. The decomposed corpses floated over the river Plate and were washed up on Uruguayan beaches with hands and arms severed or jaws smashed to make identification impossible.[17] Corporal Jorge Carlos Torres, one of the young guards, would later recall hearing that bodies were being burned and buried in a nearby sports field behind the school. When he went to the field he found a blue plastic bag containing a fetus.[18]

Inside the ESMA, captivity was punctuated by moments of raw terror. On one occasion Ana María Martí was told to collect some clothes from the "pañol" (storeroom) on the third floor. The door opened on piles of musty clothing, taken from the disappeared persons, and the booty from their houses. Here, in 1978, Ana María Martí gazed on the scene that had greeted the Allied troops who liberated Belsen and Dachau in 1945. The storeroom was tended by an old man who was known as Pedro the Witch and smelled of death. As she was pushing through the hideous heap she came upon two shirts that had belonged to her two children. Further on she recognized an old refrigerator from her own house. It still carried the flower decorations she had put on it to cover the cracks. Her house evidently belonged to the navy Commander in Chief Admiral Massera. But what of her children, aged six and nine? What had become of them?[19]

Behind its whitewashed walls and green shutters the ESMA produced life as well as death. As the numbers of prisoners grew and as the GT 3/32 extended its operations, so did the ESMA's services, including the business of child rearing. Up in the "capucha" were three rooms reserved for pregnant women. Their babies were delivered in the infirmary down in the basement, next to the torture rooms. Ana María Martí saw many pregnant women lying on mattresses, waiting to be taken down to the basement. Increasingly, they came from outside the ESMA. In a rare example of cooperation, other task groups used to avail themselves of the school's efficient services.

What should have been the supreme experience of a young woman's life turned into a sinister, fearful ordeal. As soon as María del Carmen Moyano began to feel contractions, she was taken down to the infirmary, where Dr. Jorge Magnasco, a fat gynecologist, and Dr. "Tommy" Martínez, a forty-year-old dermatologist, were waiting to deliver her child. María beseeched the doctors to allow her closest friend at the ESMA, Sara Solarz de Osatinsky, to be present.[20] They agreed, no doubt anxious to quiet the frantic woman. But when Sara was brought down to the infirmary a new problem arose. María couldn't bear the sound of the clanking chains around her friend's wrists and ankles, and she grew hysterical. Just about then her daughter was born. María was immediately taken away, presumably to her death.

Ana María Martí and Sara Osatinsky learned that a list had been com-

piled of navy wives who had no children and were anxious to adopt. Rubén Chamorro used to give guided tours for senior navy officials around
the rooms where the pregnant women were waiting to deliver their children. They must have known that the women would be slaughtered after
giving birth. So, probably, did the prisoners, although the ESMA officials
tried to prevent panic by inviting them to write a letter to their families
after they had given birth. The letters were never delivered. Ana María
Martí recorded the names of fifteen mothers who gave birth while she was
at the ESMA. They included María Pérez de Dunda, the sister-in-law of
one of the GT 3/32 officers, Adolfo "Gerónimo" Dunda. Dunda expressed
surprise to learn that his own niece had been born in the infernal basement
of the ESMA. None of his brother's family had the slightest knowledge of
the whereabouts of the baby.[21]

Alfredo Astiz, Angel on the Prowl

Some of the ESMA torturers, like Antonio Pernía, were sadists. Others,
like Lieutenant Alfredo Astiz, were in it for the cause. In time, Astiz would
acquire almost mythical status as an internationally-known torturer and
come to personify the cruelty and cowardice of the dirty war. But what of
the person behind the myth?[22]

His father had been an admiral, and the family owned property at an
exclusive seaside neighborhood near the naval base of Mar del Plata. He
had been raised in privilege, but instead of turning against the establishment, like so many young Argentinians, Astiz embraced it and joined the
navy. Once at the ESMA, he chose a brizarre string of noms de guerre
including "Angel," "the Blond," and "Crow."

To Ana María Martí, Astiz was the personification of terror. Late at
night, she would be startled out of sleep to find him leaning against her
stall, nonchalantly describing his latest exploit. Other prisoners give a
more nuanced portrait. Juan Gasparini, another ESMA survivor, presents
Astiz as a peculiar combination, part fanatic and part a muddled young
man very much out of place among thugs like "Tiger" Acosta who compared torture to making love.

Gasparini was a year younger than Astiz. They had been born in the
same city, attended the same school, and worked out at the same sports
center. Their paths then went different ways. While Astiz joined the navy,

Gasparini joined the Montoneros.[23] Gasparini was waiting one day outside an interrogation room in the ESMA when his former acquaintance walked past. The surprise was mutual. "What are you doing here?" asked Astiz, apparently for once at a loss of words. "What are you doing?" responded Gasparini, equally taken aback. Astiz told him that he was a lieutenant in the navy and one of the GT 3/32 operatives. The encounter may well have saved Gasparini's life, and this fact has tempered his otherwise savage recollections of the ESMA, and of Astiz. Astiz, he has concluded, was not the monster that headlines would subsequently make him out to be.

At times, Astiz appeared disgusted by the cruelty and the blood; at other times he gloried in it. He drew consolation from talk. Other members of the GT 3/32 group, says Gasparini, had inferiority complexes and talked in clichés about "flagrant subversion." Astiz, in contrast, liked to debate with the prisoners and considered himself an expert in international affairs. He told Gasparini that he had sent a telegram of congratulation to Margaret Thatcher when she became prime minister of Britain. Gasparini never heard him utter the word "terrorism."

In spite of his good looks, Astiz was desperate for company and approval. He fell in love with a former Montonero, Silvia Labayru, who had been sucked into the ESMA and had turned to collaboration, but lost her to his best friend in the GT 3/32, Alberto González Menotti. Gasparini evidently offered a shoulder to cry on. Late one Saturday evening, Astiz came to Gasparini's cell, ordered the guard to unlock his shackles, and took his former school acquaintance out on a drinking spree. "The melancholy flowed in torrents from him," recalls Gasparini. Astiz poured scorn on Acosta and the others, and expressed sympathy and understanding for the Montoneros who were dying in the ESMA. "You're not killers, you just think differently."[24]

Clearly affected by the intimacy of the occasion, Astiz promised Gasparini that he had nothing to worry about as long as he was at the ESMA. He was true to his word, although Gasparini suffered greatly at the hands of Astiz's friend González Menotti, who kept him constantly shackled and refused to treat his leg wounds.[25]

Today, Juan Gasparini lives in Geneva, nursing his physical scars and his memories of the ESMA. He harbors no illusions about his benefactor. Astiz was one of the most ruthless and effective ESMA operatives, more sinister than the psychopaths because he knew he was living out a lie. "He was not a torturer in the classic sense," Gasparini would write. "His business was abduction. He provided the human material for the ESMA, and he did it knowingly. He was not taking orders."[26]

Astiz Captures Dagmar Hagelin

Throughout 1976 the machinery of torture and death at the ESMA ran smoothly. Then, on January 26 1977, Astiz committed a blunder that ensured his own international notoriety and did more than any other incident to alert the world to the horror of the disappearances.

It began when the ESMA interrogators obtained under torture the address of María Antonia Berger, one of the most wanted Montonero guerillas. A squad then "chopped up" Norma Susana Burgos, an acquaintance of Berger, in the sector of El Palomár. Seven members of the squad, including Astiz, then settled down in the bushes around the Burgos house to wait for María Antonia Berger.[27]

At 8:30 the following morning, a friend of Norma Burgos arrived at the house. Dagmar Hagelin was a young woman with joint Swedish/Argentinian nationality who looked and acted older than her seventeen years. She planned to inquire whether Norma would be interested in going on holiday with the Hagelin family. She approached the house and knocked on the door. Norma's father opened it. He later told Dagmar's father that one of the navy squad had whispered "There's the blonde!" as soon as he caught sight of Dagmar, presumably mistaking her for María Berger.

Just at that moment, there was a shout: "Stay where you are!" Norma's father saw the look on Dagmar's face turn to fear. She turned and ran. Alfredo Astiz and a policeman set off in pursuit. Dagmar was a good runner and started to pull ahead. By now people had started to spill out onto the pavement. Astiz shouted out again but the girl kept running. With a swift movement, Astiz pulled his pistol from the holster, took aim with both hands, and fired a single shot. It caught Dagmar in the head and she fell to the ground.

Astiz and the policeman then "split." The policeman noticed a Chevrolet taxi outside a house, ran to it, and demanded the keys from the driver, Oscar Eles. "It's not working very well," pleaded Eles. "It doesn't matter. This is police business," replied the policeman. He snatched the keys, drove to the corner where Dagmar was lying, and tried unsuccessfully to open the trunk while Eles watched. The car returned and he was

told to get in. They drove back to the spot. Eles helped to pick up the wounded girl and put her into the trunk. She appeared to be still conscious, but bleeding from the head. As they closed the trunk on her, she raised her arms in protest. Astiz and the policeman jumped in and drove off.

This much was later recounted by Norma Burgos's father to Ragnar Hagelin. It was left to Norma and Ana María Martí, who both survived the ESMA, to fill in the grim details.[28] Norma Burgos had herself been taken back to the ESMA. The day after Dagmar Hagelin's abduction, January 27, Burgos was taken down to the infirmary in the basement, hooded and shackled. The hood was lifted slightly and she saw two navy officers whom she later came to recognize as Francis William Whamond and Alfredo Astiz. Between the two men lay Dagmar Hagelin, chained to a bed. She was apparently conscious, but still bleeding from a wound above her left eyebrow. Burgos assumed that the two officers wanted to gauge her reaction to seeing Hagelin. It was complete astonishment. Astiz then told Dagmar that he had fired the shot and observed that he and she looked "Nordic" because of their blond hair.

Three days later, Burgos was again taken by Whamond to the infirmary to see Hagelin, who was wearing a bandage on her wound but looked much weaker. One hand was chained to the bed. "There, you can see that the lady is alive; and you're going to live too," Whamond told Burgos in an apparent attempt to calm her. She saw Hagelin fleetingly again, a week later. Shortly afterward she passed the room. Dagmar was gone but her sandals were still there. She also saw Dagmar's shirt in the storeroom, a sure sign that the young woman had been killed. (Norma retrieved the shirt and later gave it to Dagmar's father.)

Several survivors from the ESMA would recall having seen Dagmar Hagelin alive in the camp. Gasparini remembers how the rumors started to circulate, as they always did when foreigners had been kidnapped. He was waiting outside the torture rooms when the Swedish girl was dragged past him down the corridor by two guards. She had a large bandage that covered her head and she couldn't walk. Another detainee told Norma Burgos that he had overheard two officers discussing the case: apparently, Dagmar Hagelin's injury had made her incontinent and caused paralysis in her feet. It was generally assumed that the wounded young woman was killed in the ESMA by Jorge "Tiger" Acosta, director of the GT 3/32.

Astiz expressed regret when he told Ana María Martí about this grim episode on a later occasion. He confessed that it had been an error which had, he implied, caused recriminations within the Junta. But there was no time for remorse. Astiz the Angel had embarked on something even more exciting than kidnapping. He had managed to infiltrate a group of persistent women who were pestering the junta for information about their disappeared children.

4. The Relatives Resist

As the details about the ESMA began to emerge and as he narrowed his search for his missing daughter, Emilio Mignone became the Junta's foremost critic.

He did not, at first sight, seem threatening. There was no Latin charm, no crinkling smile, no bear hug. He had few of the social graces and he looked with some suspicion at strangers. When he talked he gobbled the words and slurped his sentences, like someone drinking soup too fast. No one could have been more different from the arrogant, self-confident military men who dispensed life and death to their fellow countrymen. Mignone seemed vulnerable, disorganized and friendless. As a result, many in the military thought they could ignore him. This turned out to be a serious miscalculation.

Mignone had an amazing capacity for work. He could wake up refreshed at three o'clock in the morning and write fifty pages on the origins of democracy in Argentina. Michael Posner, Executive Director of the New York-based Lawyers Committee for Human Rights, visited the Mignones and remembers the carefully controlled clutter. Others recall a desk covered with pictures of his children, including Mónica. They helped him to remember the events of May 24.

Over the years, Mignone made mental notes of hundreds of other disappearances. Posner accompanied Mignone on one of the many trips he made to Washington to testify before the U.S. Congress. He came in, recalls Posner, "with those great big sad Italian eyes" looking diffident and shy. Then he started talking, and people started listening. Quietly but precisely Mignone began to marshal the facts and sort them out, moving on from the immense trauma of his daughter's kidnapping to the wider agony of his country. He was, thinks Posner, the most impressive witness he ever saw on Capitol Hill.

Mónica Mignone's sister Isabel remembers the way her father's obsession took root. Initially, he was optimistic. Then he began to get rebuffed. His inquiries met with blank stares and telephone calls went unanswered. Before her eyes, Isabel saw her father grow withdrawn, sad, and guilt-ridden. He became uncompromising and belligerent, as if challenging them to kidnap him too. He was invited to a reception at the U.S. embassy in Buenos Aires. Tex Harris, an embassy official, sat Mignone at a table with another guest, Admiral Fracassi, and asked them to find some common ground. Mignone later confessed that he found the idea rather strange, but he obliged and quickly made his views clear.

"You wouldn't understand because you're a civilian," replied Fracassi. "This is the Third World War. If we shot people in public, the Pope wouldn't be too happy."

"But you shoot unarmed people who have never held a gun in their lives," said Mignone, warming to the argument.

"Because they're ideologues. They are the most dangerous, they have to be disposed of first."

"If that's your view, Admiral, you are undoubtedly a murderer," said Mignone bluntly.

"From your point of view, I probably am," replied Fracassi.

"No," said Mignone. "From any objective point of view, you are." [1]

That was a remarkable conversation to hear at a cocktail party, but people gathered round. Mignone was earning a reputation as someone who was ready to stand up to the Junta and challenge the logic of the dirty war. He was becoming a formidable opponent.

If Mignone's quest was dangerous, it was also extraordinarily macabre. The corpses had started to turn up within weeks of the coup, dug up from secret graves or washed up on the shore. Thirty more were found at Fátima, in Pilar, in August. It was fairly clear what was happening to the disappeared ones, yet Mignone and his wife steeled themselves, and went along to watch. The bodies were all in the final stages of decomposition, and were impossible to identify. Soon afterward another seventeen bodies were washed up on the Atlantic coast. The Mignones went over and talked to local police and doctors. Again, no news of Mónica. They continued to scour the graveyards and morgues.

For the relatives of the disappeared, this would prove to be the grimmest, most nerve-racking part of the quest. Part of them wanted to solve the mystery once and for all, yet another part dreaded learning the answer at the lip of a newly opened grave. Would the next grinning skull, with the dank kerchief around the eyes and the neatly drilled bullet hole, turn out to be the missing son or daughter? Perhaps it was just as well that so few bodies could be identified. This was not the way for Emilio and Angélica Mignone to remember Mónica.

Initially, there was very little that lawyers like Emilio Mignone could do. But they did what little they could, and on April 18 1977, a year after his daughter's disappearance, Mignone and a group of lawyers entered a habeas corpus petition with the Supreme Court on behalf of 1,221 petitioners representing 1,541 desaparecidos, including Mónica. The case became known as "Pérez de Smith et al.," and it turned out to be a milestone. The case went to the Supreme Court three times. After the third submission, on December 21 1978, the Court explained that it did not have the jurisdiction to hear the case, because the authorities had flatly declared they had no knowledge of the disappeared.

The Court found itself unable to pass a judgment, but observed that the refusal of the security forces and other authorities to cooperate had created a major obstacle to the proper functioning of the habeas corpus procedure. It observed: "This court considers it its unavoidable duty to bring this situation to the attention of the executive, and to urge it to employ the measures within its power to create the conditions to enable the judiciary to rule on the cases brought before the courts."[2] This was the nearest thing to a rebuke from the muzzled judiciary, and General Videla himself publicly acknowledged the significance of this decision. It suggested that the embers of judicial independence still flickered.[3]

The Permanent Assembly

When a son or daughter disappeared in Argentina, distraught parents did what the Mignones did and went to the local police station. In the early days, it was a chaotic free-for-all as they blundered from station to station. They would try to work out which barracks or police station their child had been taken to and set out at dawn with clean clothes and some food to wait for the release. Sometimes they would be let in, more often they waited outside. The more aggressive ones obstructed traffic and shouted "Murderers!" at the doors. None of it did any good. They heard what Emilio and Angélica Mignone had heard: no lists, no news. It was time to return home to a cold house, carrying the clothes and uneaten food.

After so many years of military rule there was no civil rights body, no ombudsman, to turn to. The closest equivalent was the Argentinian League for Human Rights, which had been formed in the 1930s to defend persecuted Communists. But the League remained closely associated with the small Argentinian Communist party, which supported Videla, and took no risks after the 1976 coup.

On December 18 1975, a broad coalition of prominent Argentinians had formed the Permanent Assembly on Human Rights in response to the killings by the Triple A. Its members included Raúl Alfonsín, a deputy in the Radical Party, and Emilio Mignone. After the coup, the Permanent Assembly opened an office, coined the term "desaparecido," and began methodically collecting files on individual cases. Its reputation spread inside and outside the country, and it began to attract volunteers from among the relatives, but its approach remained essentially passive. It mounted no investigations and organized no protests. Even the term "desaparecido" was neutral: it gave no hint of what was known, that the disappearances were a methodical campaign by the security forces.

Three months after the coup, a new organization arose out of the League. Seventeen-year-old Gustavo Cabezas took one of the small buses, or "colectivos," that run between the suburbs of Buenos Aires and the center of town. The bus arrived just as a large military operation was in progress, and everyone was ordered to lie down. One girl tried to run and was shot dead in front of the horrified passengers. Gustavo was hauled into a truck and driven off.

His mother Thelma then embarked on the same fruitless search that had taken Emilio and Angélica Mignone to police stations and the First Army Corps. Her search took her to the League for Human Rights. There she found other relatives in the same predicament, and they decided to form a group which they named "The Commission of Relatives of Detainees and Persons Disappeared for Political Motives." Thelma Jara de Cabezas, a fifty-two-year-old housewife, was its first secretary.[4]

So many people were disappearing by early 1977 that the inquiries were beginning to disrupt the routine business of government. A new office was opened in the Interior Ministry, where relatives could report a disappearance. Each case was then allotted a number. The theory was that whenever information was received it would be passed on to the relatives. None of the inquiries produced any results.

The Crazy Mothers

On Saturday April 30 1977, the relatives' patience finally snapped. Most of the fourteen middle-aged women had been looking for their children for months, but as the days had given way to weeks and then months it seemed as though their ordeal was only just beginning. Each time they had been received with indifference or insolence by Interior Ministry officials.[5]

Azucena Villaflor de Vicenti broke the impasse. She was a stocky former switchboard operator who radiated energy and impatience. "We're wasting our time. Why don't we go to the government house and talk to Videla directly?" María Antokoletz, whose son had disappeared, remembers the moment clearly. The other women murmured among themselves, looked puzzled and then interested. What did they have to lose? They made their way out of the building and headed off toward the Plaza de Mayo. They arrived at the square at 11:00 A.M.[6]

The Plaza is to Buenos Aires what Times Square is to New York City or Trafalgar Square to London. On one side is the squat, whitewashed colonial building where Argentinian revolutionaries formed the first local government in 1810. Opposite, low-slung and red-bricked, is the "casa rosada," the President's residence and the seat of government. As the women entered the square, their enthusiasm began to give way to apprehension. Protests were strictly illegal. So were gatherings, and a "gathering" was defined as anything involving more than two people. Suddenly the idea seemed fraught with danger.

The women began to mill around, talking. They hadn't known each other personally before, but they suddenly realized they had much in common and they found that it helped just to talk. Suddenly, the tension that had been bottled up for so long began to come out. One of history's most remarkable human rights movements had been born.

The fourteen women struck a note of open defiance that would become one of their trademarks. They knew that the mere act of meeting, let alone seeking an audience with Videla, was an act of open defiance. That was fine. They wanted to be noticed. The square was almost empty that Saturday, and Azucena suggested returning when more people would be present in the square. The women were very clear about one thing: they wanted to shake Argentinians out of their apathy. Maybe that would force someone into telling them where their children had been taken.

Azucena de Vicenti suggested the following Friday. They could all meet about 3:00 P.M. after they had finished the household chores. (Like most mothers they were nothing if not practical.) Another of the women, Dora Peñales, then raised an objection. Friday was an unlucky day. Thursday would be better. So Thursday it would be. What time? Why not 3:30 in the afternoon, just after the banks closed? That should ensure plenty of onlookers, which could be helpful if there was trouble with the police. They were aware of the risks. Just before the first meeting, they telephoned several foreign journalists, including the local Agence France Presse correspondent Jean-Pierre Bousquet.[7]

The following Thursday this small group of fourteen middle-aged housewives began to confront the all-powerful military Junta. They met at one of the large benches in the square and plotted their next move. At first, people did not know what to make of them as they sat on the park bench and swapped stories of the latest frustation at the Interior Ministry, or the rising price of groceries. It was immensely therapeutic.

Azucena de Vicenti was in favor of a joint letter to Videla asking for an audience. She was revealing herself as a natural leader. They had unwittingly created a unique women's movement. It was quite unlike anything in the West, where women campaigned under the banner of "liberation" to claim equal political rights, equal wages, or the right to have an abortion. The Argentinian women who went each Thursday to the Plaza de Mayo did not want abortion legalized—most were Catholics, and housewives. They did not favor equal wages for women—most had never worked. When, by 1980, their fame had spread sufficiently for them to send a delegation to a United Nations Conference on Women, they found themselves profoundly uncomfortable with some of the demands being made by radical Western delegates.

If they were out of place abroad, the Mothers were unique in Argentina. Although Eva and Isabel Perón had stamped their mark on Argentinian politics and Argentinian women were far better educated than their counterparts elsewhere in Latin America, Argentina was still a country of "machismo," a country where the woman's place was in the home bringing up children.[8] The disappearances shattered this tradition because they were a direct challenge to women. Homes were broken into, families destroyed, personal belongings stolen, children kidnapped. This was an invasion of the women's domain. There were also practical reasons why a disappearance would have to be investigated by the mother instead of the father of the family: the father had to work, and additionally any sort of protest could sign his own death warrant.

As the weeks went by, membership grew. Rene Epelbaum, who had lost two sons and a daughter, heard of the Mothers from a friend. Another early adherent was Angélica Mignone, Mónica's mother. Around the middle of 1977 Hebe de Bonafini, a stocky aggressive woman, also began to attend the weekly Thursday vigil. There were no formal membership, no fees, and no organization although Azucena was unofficially recognized as the leader. Personal initiatives were welcome, but all that was required for membership was attendance. For some time they even had no name. The one they eventually adopted, "Mothers of the Plaza de Mayo," was, like the movement, innocent and straightforward.

So was their distinctive emblem. They attended a religious ceremony in Luján, and they wanted to stay together in the large crowd. Someone suggested wearing white diapers around their heads. It was appropriate, given that they were all mothers, but could anything have been more out of keeping in stern, authoritarian Argentina? A baby's diaper against the cattle prod, a group of middle-aged women against the generals. The character of Argentina's human rights movement was being molded. The white head scarves proved instantly recognizable, and other groups agreed not to adopt the same emblem.

The Mothers continued to picket the Interior Ministry, police stations, churches, barracks, and morgues. At each place they told other anguished mothers about the weekly Thursday meetings. There had been no reply to their letter to Videla. This simply increased their determination, until eventually Interior Minister General Albano Harguindeguy agreed to meet with a delegation. Harguindeguy had played an important role in putting down the ERP in 1975. He had been appointed chief of the federal police by Isabel Perón for a short time in 1976, in the hope that the army could be further co-opted into the fight against terrorism. With the coup, he was promoted to the Interior Ministry, which he would direct until March 29 1981. He was intimately tied up in the policy of disappearances, and he knew exactly what was going on. His task was to blunt any criticism.[9]

Azucena de Vicenti went to the meeting with two other Mothers. They found Harguindeguy in a truculent mood. "Your daughters were prostitutes, your sons were guerrillas who have left the country or been killed by other guerrillas," he said. De Vicenti replied that the Mothers would not leave the Plaza de Mayo until their sons and daughters were restored to them. Harguindeguy told them to sort that out with the police. And the police, he warned, would be less cooperative from now on.

Harguindeguy was right, but once again the Mothers reacted in a way that would mark their movement. They were seventy in number by now, and they took up most of the bench space at the Thursday vigils. The police forced them to move on, so they started walking around the square. The walk became as familiar as the white scarves. The next few weeks saw many clashes with the police, some of them violent. On one occasion they were chased out of the square into the busy traffic. When the women tried to seek shelter in the cathedral opposite, they found the doors closed against them.

Still, the Mothers began to win small victories. Harguindeguy's deputy, Ruiz Palacios, gave up the fight to bar them from the Plaza, and on August 15 he introduced a system of allocating ten tickets at a time to relatives seeking information in order to ease the congestion in the Ministry. But there was still no information. On October 15, three hundred Mothers gathered outside the defunct Congress building, while a deputation went inside carrying a petition with 24,000 signatures. All three hundred women were rounded up and questioned. Most locals steered clear of the weekly vigils, but foreign journalists started to appear in the square, much to the anger of the Junta. The Mothers were described as "locas" (crazy), but this only served to whet curiosity.

The Grandmothers

In October 1977 a separate but related group emerged from the Mothers movement. On November 24 1976 armed troops had surrounded a house in La Plata. Inside were a desperate woman and her three-month-old daughter. The mother took her baby and tried to escape, but was spotted and shot dead. Her husband had gone underground. Seven months later, on August 1 1977, he was also killed as he tried to enter a friend's house. His mother, María de Mariani, was not allowed to bury her son or daughter-in-law.[10]

It was the sort of brutality that had turned the Mothers into determined campaigners, but the death of her son and daughter-in-law disqualified María de Mariani from membership in the Mothers, whose children had disappeared, not died. But what had happened to the three-month-old infant, Clara Anahi de Mariani? María de Mariani went to the headquarters of the Fifth Police Precinct in La Plata, where she managed to gain an interview with a senior police official. He told her that the infant was still alive, but that he would deny ever having told her.

Fortified and encouraged, the sixty-one-year-old de Mariani started out on a search to track down her granddaughter. In the process, she met other women in the same predicament. Either their daughters had been pregnant at the time they were kidnapped, in which case they had given birth inside a detention center, or the infant had been kidnapped together with the parents. In November 1977, the grandmothers decided to form their own distinct organization, "Grandmothers of the Plaza de Mayo." They had much in common with the Mothers, but there was one crucial difference. All the evidence suggested that their grandchildren had survived, to be adopted by military families. This clearly was not the case with the adults who had disappeared. It suggested that the Grandmothers' task of location would be easier than the one facing the Mothers.

The Mothers and Grandmothers would be accused of being "politically motivated." This charge was richly ironic, coming from an illegal regime that was murdering its political opponents by the hundreds. The Mothers were not "political" in the normal sense of the term. There was no opportunity for political statement of any kind, political parties had all been banned, and the Mothers certainly had no platform beyond demanding the release of their children. Yet, to some extent the charge was true because in Argentina, in 1977, "political" meant the same as "subversive." It was used to describe any statement or activity that challenged the authorities.

The challenge from the Mothers was indeed bold and forthright. Many families paid money to the security forces, and others lived in hope that, if they kept quiet or worked discreetly through the Church, their children would eventually be released. The Mothers were the first to realize that this hope was empty.

Supping with the Devil

Nine days before the first historic gathering of Mothers in the Plaza de Mayo, Bishop Miguel Esteban Hesayne had his own disturbing encounter with Interior Minister Harguindeguy. Hesayne was self-effacing and universally admired in his large diocese of Viedma, bordering the Río Negro. As a result, he received an unusually large number of appeals from desperate parishioners who had lost relatives. He was already deeply troubled when he arrived for the meeting with Harguindeguy. He left with a feeling close to despair, something he had not previously felt in his fifteen years as a priest.

Hesayne's concern stemmed from Harguindeguy's open confession that torture was being routinely used by the security forces. Harguindeguy had been characteristically blunt. "Suppose you've caught a kid who planted a bomb in a house where two hundred people live. You've got ten minutes to find out where he put the bomb. Would you use torture?" Hesayne was appalled. As soon as he returned, he collected his thoughts and rushed off a letter to Harguindeguy. "I left our interview," he wrote, "anguished, pained, and weighed down with a great fear for the future of our country. The Minister of the Interior, who is responsible for keeping order, admitted that torture is used. Torture is immoral. It is violence and violence is anti-human and antichristian."[11]

This unsettling experience turned Hesayne into a critic of the Junta, but he was very much an exception. Two bishops and twenty priests, nuns, and seminarians disappeared or were killed in the dirty war, yet the Church hierarchy barely raised a voice in protest. Military chaplains were fervent supporters of the Junta, with Christian von Wernich, the chaplain to the Buenos Aires provincial police force, acquiring a particularly unsavory reputation. Even Monsignor Pio Laghi, the Pope's nuncio, was not immune from the charge of collaboration.[12]

Shortly after her son Jorge disappeared, on February 8 1977, Hebe de Bonafini met the Bishop of La Plata, Antonio Plaza, in the cathedral. It was well before the formation of the Mothers. Plaza took her aside and said he wanted her to meet someone who had news of her son. He took her into a small office in the cathedral, where he introduced her to a retired policeman named Sosi. It soon became clear that the bishop and his friend were more concerned with gaining than imparting information. Sosi started to ask questions about her son, who had been a guerrilla. What had Jorge done? Who were his friends? Where did they live? Where did they work? At the fourth question, Hebe de Bonafini suddenly realized that she was being interrogated. She said something very unchristian to the two men, and ran out of the cathedral. Later in the year, in December 1977, Hebe de Bonafini lost a second son.[13]

The passivity of the Church in the face of the disappearances played an important part in shaping the direction of the human rights groups. Hebe de Bonafini never forgot or forgave. She was one of the earliest and most uncompromising adherents of the Mothers, and her deep distrust of the Church soon became group policy. Many other Mothers shared her sense of betrayal when their letters to local priests and bishops went unanswered. On several occasions, when they sought refuge from baton-wielding police in the cathedral in the Plaza de Mayo, the doors were shut in their faces.

Two human rights groups that had strong religious connections were the Ecumenical Movement for Human Rights and the Service for Justice and Peace. Created in 1966, Justice and Peace had moved from Uruguay to Buenos Aires following the imposition of military rule in Uruguay. Its director, Adolfo Pérez Esquivel, was a sculptor and professor of architecture. There was nothing remotely charismatic or even outspoken about Pérez Esquivel. He was a Woody Allen look-alike who rarely raised his voice and never lost his temper. He had begun teaching sculpture in 1956 and his works were dotted about the capital. In 1972 he helped to organize a nationwide protest against political violence. After taking over Justice and Peace, Pérez Esquivel became a frequent visitor to the slums of Buenos Aires. His message was simple and to the point: peace is not possible without social justice.

Pérez Esquivel was not particularly well known outside Argentina, and within the country he seemed anything but threatening, with his lack of personal ambition and general air of untidiness. But the Junta knew better, and on April 4 1977 he was arrested when he went to get his passport renewed. Pérez Esquivel was kept incommunicado for thirty-two days and spent another fifteen months in detention at a center in La Plata before being released. But at least he was alive. Others were not so lucky.[14]

Kidnapping at the Holy Cross

Even the sober English-language *Buenos Aires Herald* played up the story. "15 People Grabbed!" shouted the headline on the morning of December 8 1977.

From the start it was clear that this had been a coordinated operation. The previous evening, a group of forty Mothers and relatives had gathered at the Holy Cross Church for a mass on behalf of the disappeared persons. The meeting had been held under the auspices of the Ecumenical Movement for Human Rights. All the participants were Argentinian except Alice Domon, a forty-year-old French nun who spent a lot of time in the slums and even more time encouraging the Mothers. She lived in the same house as Sister Léonie Duquet, another French nun. Their presence was a tangible reminder to the Junta that the Mothers' efforts had not gone unnoticed abroad.[15]

After the mass, the relatives and Sister Alice gathered on the steps of the church. They had spent two weeks collecting 140,000 pesos ($250) for an advertisement in *La Nación,* one of the larger local newspapers. The advertisement contained the names of two hundred fifty disappeared persons, under the challenging query: "Are our missing alive or dead?" It had been Azucena de Vicenti's idea. Many of the Mothers had scrimped and saved to raise the money. It was the first time they had carried their denuncia into the local newspapers.

They had brought some of the money to the mass. Suddenly, six cars drew up. Five Renaults and one Ford Falcon, all without license plates. Armed men in civilian clothes jumped out, produced police credentials, and started bundling women into the cars. Two of them seized the money that had been collected for the advertisement. María del Rosario Cerruti, one of the fourteen founding Mothers, had a remarkable escape. She was pushed roughly against a wall and told to go home. "This is a drug bust," they said. Then the cars were pulling away, tires screeching. It was over in a matter of minutes. Among the missing were Sister Alice and Esther Cariaga, a Paraguayan under the protection of the U.N. High Commissioner for Refugees (UNHCR).

Azucena Villaflor de Vicenti, the recognized leader of the Mothers, had not been present at the mass. She was picked up on Saturday morning while shopping near her home. Onlookers would recount how she had thrown herself on the ground and begged her kidnappers not to take her because of her daughter. They had kicked her into the car. It was not easy because she was fat, and the car drove off with her feet sticking out of the window.[16]

When Azucena de Vicenti's relatives went through the familiar routine and tried to register the kidnapping with local police, they were told they would have to wait for twenty-four hours. The same day Sister Léonie Duquet, the second French nun, was also kidnapped. It was December 10, International Human Rights Day. Argentina's military rulers could not have sent a clearer message to their critics abroad.

The following day, it was learned that a new name had been added to the list of victims. Gustavo Niño was a good-looking young man who had started attending meetings of the Mothers two weeks before the operation. He had presented an identity card (7696527) and said his brother had disappeared. He wanted to help, to do something. Perhaps fund-raising? The Mothers liked him. He was young, rather dashing, and blond for an Argentinian. He also had a sense of humor and that was an asset. They took him to their hearts. It now appeared that Gustavo Niño had also been seized in the sweep.

Ana María Martí soon learned Niño's real identity when Lieutenant Alfredo Astiz, alias the Angel, stopped off at her tiny cell on the third floor of the ESMA. Astiz had played a key role in the operation. Posing as Gustavo Niño he had infiltrated the Mothers with Sylvia Labayru and had identified the leaders outside the church. Afterward, long afterward, it all made sense to María Cerruti. She remembered seeing young "Niño" pointing out key Mothers to the gang. Astiz himself boasted loud and long about this exploit when he prowled the corridors of the ESMA.

On December 15 an army communiqué announced that the Montoneros had contacted the Agence France Presse office claiming reponsibility for the kidnapping, and had sent a photo of the two nuns with a note from Sister Alice that described themselves as "prisoners of dissident groups." There was no mention of the other victims. It had been a crude fake.[17]

Observers at the U.S. embassy were highly sceptical of the faked claim, but totally in the dark about what had really happened. According to one cable the security forces were involved, and the finger seemed to point to the navy. But publicly Admiral Massera was trying to shift the blame: only the army, he suggested, would have been capable of such a "muddled, ill-judged caper."[18]

He knew, of course, that the kidnapped Mothers were now deep inside the ESMA. Ana María Martí would later recall how she heard a strong, clear voice ring out on Christmas day, saying "Today is the day of our Lord." A guard whispered that it was a "sister." Later she met Sister Alice in a shower. Her face was bruised. They only had time for a hurried conversation, and each asked the other her name. (This was standard procedure among detainees in case either survived.) The guard told Sister Alice not to drink water, which was a sign that she had just been given electric shock treatment.

The two French nuns were never heard of again, although ghoulish stories emerged about their torture and death. One report said that the corpses were washed up on the Uruguayan side of the river Plate, without hands. According to another, the two women were buried in a large common grave at El Vesubio, a notorious army center. Inside the ESMA itself, Juan Gasparini pieced together the rumors and concluded that Jorge "Tiger" Acosta had made the decision to have the nuns killed, afraid that Massera would order their freedom. To have yielded to pressure from French diplomacy and the army would have been a major sign of weakness in Acosta's never-ending war: if anyone walked out of the ESMA alive, it was because the Tiger so decided. Acosta entrusted the assassination to Antonio "the Rat" Pernía. Gasparini thinks the two nuns and the rest of the group were taken by launch one night out into the river Paraná and killed.

Later, Gasparini had the temerity to tell Pernía that he had made a grave mistake. "It was the only way to stop them screwing around with human rights," replied the Rat.[19]

Like the death of Dagmar Hagelin, the disappearance of the nuns would return repeatedly to haunt the Junta, as well as cripple Massera's personal political ambitions.[20] It had been a singularly brutal operation, even by the standards of Argentina, but the Junta had underestimated the courage and resilience of the Mothers. The morning after the mass kidnapping, the advertisement appeared in *La Nación*. The kidnappers had only stolen a fraction of the amount collected. The following Thursday the women were out at the Plaza de Mayo wearing their distinctive white scarves. The Junta had failed to break its critics.

For thousands of grieving Argentinians like the Mignones, December 25 1977 brought a sorrowful Christmas. An editorial in the *Buenos Aires Herald* summed up the national spirit after eighteen months of "National Reorganization": "Argentina is an impoverished, unhappy, country hag-ridden by mysteriously intractable problems and tormented by devils that will not let themselves be exorcised." There was only one redeeming feature, the resilience and courage of the relatives. Argentinians did not know it at the time, but they would have good reason to be grateful to Emilio Mignone, Adolfo Pérez Esquivel, and the crazy Mothers. They showed the outside world that there was decency as well as death in Argentina. This could be immensely important if the dictators ever stepped down. Democracy would need the reassurance that someone had resisted.

5. The Truth Comes Out

They were the first to alert the outside world to the turmoil in Argentina, and they were easy to spot as they prowled around the tiny alleyways and impossibly narrow streets that arch off Corrientes, the thick bustling artery of downtown Buenos Aires. No matter what the weather they were always hunched up against an imaginary wind. They wore badly fitting clothes. Occasionally, they would stop at a kiosk to enquire furtively about a periodical, before ducking into a cheap hotel to pass the rest of the day behind drawn curtains.

They were refugees. Human flotsam, they had retreated before the tide of military rule as it spread slowly south through the continent. Juan Perón had issued an open invitation to Latin American refugees when he returned to Argentina in 1973, but the impression of security was illusory. Argentina had ratified a 1951 convention on refugees and agreed to accept refugees, but it had entered a debilitating reservation: it would only accept refugees from Europe. This meant that Nazi war criminals could ask for asylum, but anyone fleeing from Chile, Brazil, and Bolivia would be liable to expulsion at a moment's notice.[1]

As a result, thousands of Latin Americans who sought refuge in Argentina were left without any formal legal protection. They were in mortal danger. Even as Perón issued the invitation, his Minister of Social Services José López Rega was building the right-wing Triple A movement. The Triple A would prey upon the refugees, most of whom had fled because of their left-wing political views. Guy Prim, who worked in Buenos Aires for the U.N. High Commissioner for Refugees (UNHCR) recalls his horror when a refugee staggered into his office with the letters AAA burned into his flesh. The noose was tightening, and after the March 24 coup in Argentina it snapped shut. The Junta issued a decree stating that any foreigners whose presence "affected national security" would be liable to expulsion from Argentina. A church hostel for refugees was raided, the director detained, and the refugees beaten up and issued with expulsion orders. It was a taste of things to come.[2]

It was particularly terrifying for the Uruguayans. Zelmar Michelini, a well-known member of the Uruguayan Senate before its dissolution, was working as a newspaper editor in Buenos Aires and living with two of his sons at a small hotel. His wife and seven other children had remained in Uruguay. Another prominent Uruguayan exile was forty-three-year-old Héctor Gutiérrez Ruiz, speaker of the defunct Uruguayan Chamber of Representatives. He had lived in Buenos Aires with his wife and five children since 1973. Like Michelini he had been a vigorous proponent of Uruguayan democracy, and like Michelini he remained an obvious threat to the generals who had snuffed it out.[3]

On the morning of May 18 1976, Gutiérrez Ruiz and Michelini were abducted from the center of Buenos Aires in another operation that was to have major international repercussions. On May 21 the government issued a press release expressing "deep concern" and promising an "exhaustive investigation." This was ominous. The families of Gutiérrez Ruiz and Michelini waited throughout that day and the next. No one came to conduct an investigation. Mrs. Gutiérrez Ruiz went to the post office and sent three telegrams, one appealing to Mrs. Videla, the wife of the President. When she returned to the house she was told that her husband was dead. The bodies of the two men and a young Uruguayan couple had been found in the trunk of an abandoned red Torino coupe the previous evening. Michelini and Gutiérrez Ruiz were still handcuffed. They had been shot several times.[4]

Following the murders, UNHCR officials in Buenos Aires found themselves submerged by appeals from panic-stricken refugees. Guy Prim stretched the rules and hid several terrified refugees in his own house. The effect of the murders on Prim's superiors at UNHCR headquarters in Geneva was equally decisive. Even if they had wanted to ignore the crisis, which they did not, they were obligated to demand protection for refugees. On June 26 the agency issued a worldwide appeal to governments to help resettle the refugees in Argentina.

On July 13, twenty-three more Uruguayans were kidnapped in Buenos Aires.[5] If this operation showed complicity between the security forces of the two governments, it also alerted international opinion to the fact that foreigners were not exempt from the terror. Because Argentina was a young country of second- and third-generation immigrants, thousands of its citizens had dual nationality. Almost six hundred foreigners were to disappear in the dirty war. Between 1976 and 1983 fifty governments, including China, Saudi Arabia, and the Soviet Union, would make diplomatic inquiries about 2,928 desaparecidos.[6] Only a small percentage were their own nationals and virtually all of the inquiries took the form of discreet submissions—what would come to be termed "quiet diplomacy." But many governments protested because the Junta had broken the most basic rule in diplomacy: it had killed foreigners.

The case that provoked the most fury was the disappearance of Dagmar Hagelin, the young Swedish woman who had been shot and wounded by Astiz. Within two weeks of Hagelin's abduction, the Swedish cabinet met and sent an outraged telegram to Argentinian Foreign Minister Guzetti protesting that in no civilized country in the world would an animal, let alone a human being, be thrust wounded into the trunk of a car. Shortly after the protest, her father Ragnar went to visit Guzetti with the Swedish ambassador, Bertil Kollberg. Guzetti showed his irritation and started to gesticulate. "Listen to me, the girl is Argentinian. She was born here. She's no more Swedish than I'm Italian. Look at me. Guzetti. G-U-Z-E-T-T-I." Ambassador Kollberg took no notice. For him the law was the law, and as far as the law was concerned Dagmar was Swedish.[7]

To the outside world, Dagmar Hagelin came to personify the horror of the dirty war and the innocence of its victims. Her ghost returned again and again to haunt the Junta. "Swedish-Argentine relations, far from normal or friendly, have sharply deteriorated—as a result of the disappearance," observed the U.S. embassy in Stockholm in a March 1977 cable. When, in July 1980, an official in the Argentinian Foreign Ministry was asked to review the record, he wrote that Hagelin's disappearance had caused a complete rupture in relations between Buenos Aires and Stockholm. Overall, he concluded, the disappearance of foreigners had caused untold problems for the Foreign Ministry and had "seriously disturbed" the country's bilateral relations.[8]

This would not have happened if Ragnar Hagelin had chosen "quiet diplomacy." Eventually, he would write a moving book about his fruitless search for Dagmar. "She was," he wrote in the preface, "a girl of 17 years, full of life and illusions. A girl who had just left the age of dolls; who believed in life, in love, in the magic of everyday things. She was a girl (or should I say is?) whose only crime was to be a youngster at a time when youngsters were killed in the streets or kidnapped in universities, in factories, or bars." Ragnar Hagelin was a sad man when he wrote these words, but he had performed a major service for his daughter and for thousands of other desaparecidos and their relatives, by insisting that their ordeal could not be ignored by the international community.[9]

Rodolfo Matarollo

The man who did more than anyone else to break the story of the disappearances to a disbelieving European public was a highly articulate Argentinian lawyer named Rodolfo Matarollo who had left Argentina before the coup and settled in Paris. There he found a large and highly political community of 25,000 Latin Americans, many of them refugees who were lucky to be alive.

Like so many before him, Matarollo drank in the heady atmosphere of Paris. During the day, he worked in the French government's refugee office. In the evening he spent long hours in smoky cafes or at political meetings, anguishing about the fate that had befallen his country and plotting revenge. In his spare time he was active in two organizations that were outspokenly critical of the Junta. These were the Argentine Human Rights Commission (CADHU) and the Argentine Information and Solidarity Center (CAIS). CADHU was formed in Argentina in 1975. It moved abroad the following year when two of its founding members disappeared, and it was to prove to be a thorn in the side of the Junta throughout 1976 and 1977.[10]

In Paris, Matarollo also acted as a lawyer for Julio Cortázar, a renowned Argentinian poet and fierce critic of military rule. Matarollo was popular and visible among left-wing circles in Paris and he formed a friendship with several prominent French radicals. It was well known that before fleeing Argentina Matarollo had been a lawyer who had specialized in defending political prisoners. It was also known that he had been the editor of a left-wing magazine, *Nuevo Hombre* (New Man), which was associated with the ERP, one of the two main guerrilla groups. Less well known was the fact that he had also been a leading member of the ERP political wing.

Matarollo's background, and his activities outside Argentina, will play an important part in our story. What are the facts? His career as an ERP activist was outlined in several Foreign Ministry memoranda in the author's possession and reprinted abroad in several accounts sympathetic to the Junta.[11] According to these reports, four extreme left-wing Latin American organizations met in the Argentinian city of Mendoza in February 1974 to coordinate their activities: the Left Wing Revolutionary Movement (MIR) from Chile, the Tupamaros from Uruguay, the National Liberation Army from Bolivia, and the ERP from Argentina. The result was the formation of an umbrella organization named the "Junta de Coordinación Revolucionaria" (JCR). The JCR set up its headquarters in Buenos Aires, with Matarollo playing a key role. But in spite of some halfhearted contacts with Cuba, the group never remotely began to fulfill its military objectives, and after the ERP was broken as a fighting force Matarollo left for Paris. There, according to the Junta, he continued his subversive campaign and played a crucial role in poisoning international public opinion against the Junta.[12]

CADHU and CAIS were soon feeding information about the disappearances to solidarity groups throughout Europe and North America. Branches of CADHU were set up in Mexico, Rome, and Geneva. In September 1976, CADHU scored a major political coup when two of its leading members, Gustavo Roca and Lucio Garzón Maceda, were invited to give testimony before the U.S. House Subcommittee on Human Rights and International Organizations.[13] CADHU was quick to capitalize. In December 1976 Horacio Lofredo, an engineer with joint U.S.-Argentine citizenship, and Olga Talamante, a young American who had herself been imprisoned in Argentina, established a CADHU branch office near Washington's Dupont Circle. Talamante and Lofredo were well placed to take advantage of the dramatic shift in U.S. human rights policy that followed Jimmy Carter's election as President, and operating on a shoestring budget they led the fight to cut off U.S. military aid to the Junta.[14]

The network caught fire in Europe. One Argentinian Foreign Ministry memo noted no fewer than eight separate anti-Junta groups in Paris alone.[15] Under Matarollo's guidance, CADHU pounced on anything likely to embarrass the Junta and sent a steady stream of reports to anyone and any group remotely sympathetic. It is not surprising that Rodolfo Matarollo emerges as a sinister, subversive figure in articles and books sympathetic to the Junta. More surprising, perhaps, is the fact that there was no record of any terrorist activities in his brief biographical file at the Argentinian Foreign Ministry. The file gives his occupation as a defense lawyer and contains nothing to suggest that Matarollo was ever anything other than a political activist.[16]

The crucial point about Matarollo was this: did his sympathy for the left-wing guerrilla movement in Argentina discredit him as a witness against the Junta? If another human rights group took him at face value, was it "politically motivated?" The regime in Argentina certainly thought so. To judge from Foreign Ministry documents, the Junta could never understand why Rodolfo Matarollo was allowed to live in France and travel freely throughout Europe, nor why CADHU's reports were accepted by Europeans and Americans who had little sympathy for the ERP's brand of left-wing revolution.

It was not hard to see why Matarollo was taken seriously. The most compelling reason was that he would have been killed if he had stayed in Argentina. When Heleno Fragoso visited Argentina in March 1975 for the International Commission of Jurists, he found that twenty-six lawyers had received death threats. They included Matarollo and his partner, Roberto Sinigaglia. Matarollo left later that year; Sinigaglia remained. On May 13 1976 he was arrested, beaten up, and dragged away in central Buenos Aires just as he was entering a law firm office. He never reappeared.[17] People asked themslves which was a greater threat to democracy in Argentina, the systematic murder of lawyers who defended political detainees or the ERP's revolutionary rhetoric and halfhearted military escapades? The question was rarely posed that way, but when it was, Rodolfo Matarollo provided an answer. With his spectacles and plump cheeks, he looked anthing but "subversive."

Matarollo was also helped by the fact that CADHU's information was generally superior to the material put out by the Junta. The Junta described people like Matarollo in lurid terms and complained incessantly of an "international Marxist conspiracy" to undermine the prestige of Argentina. This was not credible outside Argentina, given that the Junta's main foreign support was coming from the Marxist Soviet Union. One document at the Foreign Ministry contained a list of what it described as "Montonero political contacts in France." The list was headed by the name of François Mitterrand. This was far too crude to strike a chord in Western Europe, least of all in a sophisticated city like Paris. By 1978, moreover, French public opinion was reeling from the disappearance of the two French nuns.

CADHU's reports also had a lurid quality to them. They talked of secret concentration camps like the ESMA, of skin being peeled off prisoners, and electric saws being taken to hands, feet, and fingers. But they also gave dates, times, and names. They reprinted Emilio Mignone's letters and Rodolfo Walsh's despairing open letter that had led to Walsh's own disappearance. CADHU was not only the best, it was the only source of information on Argentina during the first terrible year of killing. It was hardly surprising that people turned to it for information and ignored the "political motivation" of its members.

The Junta Turns to Madison Avenue

As they began to lose the international information war, Argentina's military rulers turned to Madison Avenue to counter the threat. Burson Marsteller was one of the largest public relations companies in New York City, and following the coup it received a large fee to help the Junta clean up its image in Europe and North America. The firm responded as it would have done to a similar plea from an ailing car company, with a lengthy project proposal. Its recommendation? Not to end the killing, but to launch a major propaganda effort in eight key countries—the U.S., Britain, Japan, Canada, Colombia, Mexico, Holland, and Belgium. It identified fifty-three influential foreign journalists and suggested that they be courted and invited to Argentina, which it described as "a mysterious country of large clean beaches, rugged and imposing mountains, an almost endless unfolding of flora and fauna both familiar and unique, enthusiasm, beauty, technology," and, most important, "commercial opportunities."[18]

The Junta agreed. By May 1978, according to one report, between thirty and forty of the fifty-three journalists had visited Argentina, newspapers were reflecting what a BM vice-president described as "greater balance," and a series of large paid advertisements had appeared in notable newspapers making extravagant claims that even the Junta stopped short of.[19]

On October 8 1978, the Junta won some breathing space when the CADHU office in Washington was forced to close. Midway through 1977, during the frantic debate over U.S. aid to Argentina, someone had informed the U.S. Justice Department that CADHU was not registered as a foreign lobbyist. The Department filed a suit. Under the settlement, the highly effective CADHU team of Olga Talamante and Horacio Lofredo were forced to write a humiliating apology to those they had contacted.[20]

This eased the pressure on the Junta in Washington, and under the prodding of Burson Marsteller its propaganda grew more sophisticated. In the first week of 1979 a seminar was held at Georgetown University in Washington. Its goal, in the words of one Argentinian author, was to explain that "military rule was the best thing that could have happened to Argentina." Among the speakers were ten members of the Argentinian government, a once and future Argentinian Foreign Minister (Nicanor Costa Méndez), and a group of American luminaries that included Jeane Kirkpatrick, Walter Rostow, and William Rogers. The seminar was financed with the help of a twenty-five-thousand dollar subsidy from a right-wing businessman, Piñero Pacheco, who had close ties to the Junta.[21]

Burson Marsteller may have helped to polish the Junta's image in the United States, but in the long run it did a major disservice to Argentina by allowing the Junta to think that the problem was merely one of presentation, and that it could be solved by impugning the motivation of critics like Matarollo. Videla and his colleagues clung to the illusion, and Argentinians went to their deaths. Inevitably, embassies became adjuncts of the propaganda machine and the dirty war acquired an international dimension.

The Dirty War Spreads to Paris

The first and most formidable obstacle facing the Junta in implementing the Burson Marsteller strategy was itself. Behind the official portrait—stern, patriotic, efficient—Videla, Massera, and Agosti feuded, squabbled, and fought. It was perhaps inevitable that their first major attempt to improve Argentina's image in Europe should end in a grotesque failure, causing immense damage to the prestige of Argentina's diplomatic corps.[22]

In May 1977, Argentina's ambassador to Paris, Tomas de Anchorena, hosted a meeting of Argentinian ambassadors in Western Europe and proposed the creation of an office at his embassy to counteract the adverse publicity coming from exiles like Matarollo. The other ambassadors were enthusiastic and the idea was referred back to Deputy Foreign Minister Gualter Allara. It met with quick approval and on June 30 1977, under decree 1871, a new office known as the "pilot center" was established at the embassy in Paris. De Anchorena received one hundred thousand dollars from a special presidential contingency fund to cover expenses. He appointed one of his diplomats, forty-seven-year-old Elena Holmberg, to serve as the center's press attaché.[23]

Holmberg was a career diplomat who also happened to be the niece of a former President and a personal friend of General Videla, as well as an ardent supporter of his Process of National Reorganization.[24] Under de Anchorena's supervision, Holmberg began a discreet program of disinformation at the embassy in Paris, stressing the positive aspects of life under the Junta and cultivating contacts among the local press. Any useful information was relayed back to the press office at the Foreign Ministry, run by the navy.

The trouble began in September 1977 when two ESMA operatives, Federico Gonzales and Jorge "Puma" Perren, arrived unexpectedly at the embassy in Paris to start working at the pilot center. Their instructions were apparently to conduct a more aggressive campaign of disinformation than Holmberg, and to infiltrate the exile groups, particularly CAIS and CADHU.[25]

In January 1978 two more ESMA officers (one of them Enrique Yon) arrived at the embassy in Paris, followed soon afterward by Antonio "the Rat" Pernía, the torturer who shot darts at his victims, and Lieutenant Alfredo "Angel" Astiz. After the spectacular kidnapping of the thirteen Mothers at the Church of the Holy Cross in December 1977, Astiz was an acknowledged expert at infiltration, and using the pseudonym of Alberto Escudero he began to attend CAIS meetings in Paris. Unluckily for him, he was spotted by some exiles who recognized him from Mothers meetings in Argentina. His cover blown, Astiz only just escaped with Enrique Yon from France into West Germany.[26]

By the summer of 1978, the pilot center in Paris had become an extension of the ESMA GT 3/32 group and Elena Holmberg had been elbowed aside. She complained incessantly to her ambassador, de Anchorena, who protested to Videla and earned a reprimand from Foreign Minister Admiral Oscar Montes. Montes was clearly not going to cross his superior, Massera. It was intolerable for everyone involved, and in October 1978 Holmberg was recalled to Buenos Aires to work in the press office at the Ministry. The pilot center had long ceased to bear any resemblance to the operation proposed by de Anchorena. Indeed, it was fast becoming a springboard for Admiral Emilio Massera's own grandiose ambitions.

To understand Massera's intentions fully, we must take a step back into the twilight world of the dirty war. Massera wished to succeed Videla as President, something that the army had no intention of allowing. By March 1977 Massera's relations with his two colleagues in the Junta had cooled to the point of open hostility. With the dirty war against subversives won and many of the top Montoneros safe within the walls of the ESMA, Massera began to make plans to break with the Junta and launch a new political party, named Social Democracy. He evidently hoped to emulate Juan Perón, who had made a successful transition from military to civilian life. Perón's widow, former President Isabel Perón, had been transferred to house arrest at a navy base where, it was rumored, Massera urged her to run as his vice-presidential candidate and even courted her. Massera opened sumptuous offices in a building owned by Licio Gelli's Banco Ambrosiano. He had the use of a navy-owned radio station and newspaper. Booty from the dirty war provided him with funds. Now all he needed was manpower. Incredibly, he turned to the former Montoneros who were lying manacled at the ESMA and to their desperate relatives outside.

This fact helps to explain one of the great mysteries about the dirty war, the fact that approximately one hundred detainees survived the horror of the ESMA, some to identify their tormentors. Massera was more personally committed to the strategy of torture and disappearance than the other two members of the Junta, but at the same time he was also more fascinated by the nature of the "subversion" he had pledged to eliminate. He admired the Montoneros' ruthlessness and intelligence. Why toss away such a valuable resource?

Jorge "Tiger" Acosta agreed wholeheartedly. The success of the GT 3/32 group in rounding up the Montonero leadership had given the navy, and Acosta himself, huge prestige within the armed forces and an edge over the rival army. Acosta apparently viewed himself as Massera's future Interior Minister, but both realized that if they were to be credible to Peronists as civilian politicians they would have to call a halt to the slaughter of the Peronist Montoneros. Acosta thus dispensed mercy to Ana María Martí, Juan Gasparini, and the lucky handful of survivors, just as he had dispensed death to thousands of other ESMA detainees.

The interrogation of some prisoners had already begun to yield interesting results. At least one Argentinian author, Horacio Verbitsky, credits these prisoners with helping to toughen the navy's position on Argentina's territorial conflicts with Britain, Chile, and Brazil, and reinforcing the idea that the Malvinas/Falkland Islands should and could be taken by force from Britain. Verbitsky says the idea caused such excitement among Massera's officers that the GT 3/32 temporarily suspended kidnapping and sent out patrols to distribute leaflets advocating seizure of the Falklands and the Beagle Channel. This prompted a bitter reproach from Massera's colleagues in the Junta. According to Verbitsky, some prisoners found the idea of working with Massera appealing. They compared it to the 1974 alliance between Portuguese officers and revolutionaries in Mozambique and Angola which had put an end to the Portuguese dictatorship.[27] On a less exotic note, prisoners at the ESMA were put to work cleaning, preparing documents for foreign escapades, analyzing newsapers, and forging Chilean money in preparation for a possible war with Chile over the Beagle Channel.

These actions produced new stress within the walls of the ESMA as a few "lucky" prisoners found themselves forced to choose between death and collaboration. Some, known as "ministaff," needed no prodding and willingly committed themselves to the cause, and even the beds, of their tormentors. Others, like Gasparini and Ana María Martí, known as "staff," chose to live while at the same time vowing revenge.[28]

Gradually, prisoners found themselves working less on navy intelligence and more on Massera's personal projects. Miriam Lewin de García, a young student who had tried and failed to swallow cyanide before being abducted, was forced to work for Massera from the ESMA even after Massera retired from the navy in September 1978.[29]

Massera's search for political recruits among his victims extended beyond the ESMA camp to their relatives. Emilio Mignone's third meeting with Massera occurred early in June 1979 after Mignone received a call from Massera's office saying that he had news of Mónica. Mignone hurried over. After he was thoroughly frisked by Massera's bodyguards, Massera made it clear to him that he had no news about Mónica, but he did tell Mignone that the two French nuns were dead, killed by the army. "Videla is a son of a bitch," he said portentously. "Then there's at least one thing we can agree about," said Mignone. To Mignone's astonishment, Massera then began to sound him out about joining his new political party. He was trying to recruit a man whose own daughter had probably been tortured and killed by navy officers. There seemed to be no limit to Massera's cynicism.[30]

Death from the Pilot Center

At the same time that he was trying to recruit the ESMA detainees, Massera was fighting a vicious war against his colleagues in the Junta. The most distinguished victim, Héctor Hidalgo Sola, was none other than Argentina's ambassador to Venezuela. Apparently with Videla's approval, Hidalgo Sola had spoken openly of the need for a return to democracy, and was even rumored to be Videla's choice to head an interim government. Hidalgo Sola was abducted on July 18 1977 during a visit to Buenos Aires. Several other notable journalists and lawyers who were involved in the scheme were abducted or had their houses bombed by the GT 3/32 as part of Massera's campaign to "reestablish democracy."[31]

To be credible as a political figure, Massera had to improve his image abroad. The murder of the two nuns had made this very difficult, and he set about trying to undo the damage. Massera put out feelers to French President Valéry Giscard d'Estaing, and on November 8 1978 he arrived in Paris. Lieutenant "Cobra" Enrique Yon, now at the pilot center, made the hotel reservations. The meeting was brief and, from Giscard d'Estaing's perspective, cool. In the presence of an interpreter, Massera handed Giscard d'Estaing a list of thirty-two names of French nationals. Twelve names were preceded with an asterisk, indicating that they were dead. They included the names of the two French nuns, Léonie Duquet and Alice Domon. Both women, according to Massera, had been detained and killed by the First Army Corps. It was another lie. Giscard d'Estaing was suitably skeptical, although he did not release Massera's list until 1985.[32]

Massera had more success at Georgetown University's Center for Strategic and International Studies, which invited him to speak and gave him a platform to express his disagreement with Videla and the economic policies of Martínez de Hoz. Massera told the audience that no more than four hundred people had disappeared and that he had told Videla to release the names. Later, in the elevator, he warned a correspondent for the *Buenos Aires Herald* that he did not want this to appear in the paper.[33]

Massera's machinations combined with the failure of the Junta's propaganda war in Europe to produce one of the most bizarre incidents of the dirty war. Massera by now was playing for very high stakes indeed, using the pilot center in Paris to try to strike a deal with leaders of the Montoneros. According to one newspaper report in *Le Monde,* Massera met with Mario Firmenich, the head of the Montoneros, in an effort to arrange a truce. The rumor caused stupefaction in Argentina.[34]

One person who evidently knew about Massera's activities in Paris was Elena Holmberg, the former press officer at the pilot center. Following her return to Buenos Aires in September 1978, she met several times with Gregorio Dupont, her former colleague at the Foreign Ministry who had himself been dismissed for crossing Massera. Late one December afternoon the two went for a drink at a bar. The city was buzzing with rumors about Massera's reported meeting with Firmenich. Dupont was curious. "Do you think it's true?" he asked. Elena Holmberg then blurted it out: not only was it true that Massera had met with Montoneros, but he had given them a huge sum of money—a million dollars, maybe more. Dupont was staggered. "For God's sake, Elena, keep this to yourself!" he said. "Don't tell anyone, because it could get you killed."[35]

Dupont was right. On December 20 1978 Elena Holmberg arranged to have dinner with some visiting French journalists. She never arrived. Three weeks later, on January 11 1979, her body was found floating in the river Luján. She had been strangled—another victim of the same vicious "Process of National Reorganization" that she herself had supported. Gregorio Dupont concluded that his friend's fate was sealed when she spoke about Massera to her colleagues at the Foreign Ministry press office, who included several navy officials seconded from the ESMA.[36] Later, Dupont realized that if he had let Holmberg continue with her story he might have learned the full tantalizing account of Massera's intrigues. He could not suspect, at the time, that the brief encounter had also left him a marked man.[37]

So Argentina's flirtation with propaganda culminated in a grotesque and tragic failure that forced the disappearances once more into the news and revealed the sinister nature of Argentina's military regime. This was hardly the consequence intended by Burson Marsteller. In July 1980, one official in the Foreign Ministry, asked to review Argentina's propaganda effort between 1976 and 1980, would pour scorn on the Burson Marsteller contract and the amateurish bungling at the pilot center in Paris.[38]

To this day, no one has come out with a convincing firsthand account of why Massera met with Firmenich and whether his aim was to buy off the Montoneros or to co-opt them into his new political party. It hardly mattered to relatives like Emilio Mignone. What mattered was that Massera was prepared to reach an accommodation with the die-hard guerrillas, after thousands of innocents like Mónica Mignone had been kidnapped and slaughtered on a trumped-up charge of "subversion." To the end the relatives reserved a special loathing for Massera.

6. Amnesty's Fraught Visit

In the spring of 1977, an Argentinian bishop, Argimiro Moure, received nine remarkably similar letters from West Germany asking him to intercede on behalf of Rubén Becerra, a professor who was detained in a prison in his diocese. The bishop was not fooled. He knew that he had been targeted by the human rights organization Amnesty International. The bishop was an ardent supporter of the Junta and on August 9 he sent an irritated reply to one of his correspondents, Rudolf Rengstorf, a Catholic priest in the West German town of Menlen. Moure pointed out that Becerra was a "union agitator." "Amnesty," he went on "is mounting a cowardly, unjust, and unworthy campaign against Argentina from the safety of Germany." [1]

Anyone who supported the Junta's campaign of mass murder would have sympathized with the bishop. Amnesty International had become an international mouthpiece for the disappeared and their relatives; it picked up their reports, stamped them with Amnesty's own mark of approval, and fed them to governments, the media and even the United Nations. This posed an infinitely greater threat to the Junta's image than Argentinian exiles like Rodolfo Matarollo, who had a clear political bias. Amnesty claimed no ties to any government or ideology, and it insisted that such rights as freedom from torture had no political hue. They were "universal" and "inalienable."

Argentinian government documents written during the dirty war referred to Amnesty in terms of acute frustration and very little consistency. At one moment Amnesty was "Marxist," at another a brilliant tool of Western democracy. But the essential point was that, to governments that it criticized, Amnesty was the ultimate political machine. In addition, Amnesty dealt only with governments, but seemed blind to the greater evil of terrorism. Terrorists, to Amnesty, were common criminals. One could almost hear the teeth gnashing in Buenos Aires. How naive could they be, these human rights campaigners?

Worst of all, Amnesty was accountable to no one. It scampered out regularly to issue a provocative report, exploiting its privileged access to outlets like the BBC World Service, and then retreated to the security of plush offices in London or Paris. By what right did this self-appointed watchdog presume to challenge the established rules of diplomacy and criticize the internal affairs of sovereign states like Argentina? This, at least, was the accepted wisdom in Buenos Aires in mid-1977, when Bishop Moure answered his West German correspondents; yet it had all looked very different a year earlier, when the Junta had invited Amnesty to visit Argentina and view the situation for itself.

Amnesty International was young to enjoy such a high international profile. It had been created in 1961 when an English lawyer, Peter Benenson, read about two young Portuguese students jailed for raising a toast to freedom. Benenson wrote an article calling for the creation of an organization to work for people in detention. From that modest source sprang a mighty torrent of indignation. By 1976 Amnesty had 97,000 members in 74 countries.[2]

Its concern was with "prisoners of conscience," a broader concept than "political prisoners" because it covered those detained for their religion, race, color, or language, as well as for political views. Its strength lay not just in this clarity of purpose but in the way it had harnessed the guilt of the educated middle class. Amnesty brought the "picana" and political prisoners into the living room alongside potted plants and Beaujolais nouveau, and local branches responded with that perseverance which is the hallmark of middle-class volunteers. It was always hard to know how many prisoners owed their release to Amnesty pressure. (The estimate in 1976 was 1,200.) But spirits never flagged.[3]

Amnesty's two basic tools were the letter and the newspaper article. Once a local group adopted a particular prisoner it would direct a series of letters to a far-off minister or bishop in the detainee's country and back them up with embarrassing articles in the foreign press. In 1974, Amnesty created an "urgent action" program for rapid intervention when lives were threatened. One hundred and forty-nine cases were taken up in 1976.

National sections required accurate information, and this was provided by a large team of researchers at the international secretariat in Central London. Here, disheveled enthusiasm gave a misleading impression of disorganization. The secretariat protected the precious Amnesty formula carefully, issued precise instructions to branches, and allowed very little room for local initiative. Information, too, was tightly controlled. There were very few leaks from Amnesty researchers and journalists ignored an embargo at their peril.

All this gave a curious flavor to the Amnesty movement. One moment it seemed as packaged as a Burson Marsteller project proposal, the next it seemed to be operating on pure inspiration. When members of the American section opened their Amnesty newsletter they read about the "prisoner of the month," a new "harassment" campaign, and the latest on the "adoption campaign," all written in a jaunty style and offered like special bargains at a supermarket. New prisoners of conscience were unveiled with a flourish. In the same newsletter members might be asked to write "courteously worded letters" to the thuggish Admiral Massera complaining about the fact that Mónica Mignone and Dagmar Hagelin were being skewered by electric cattle prods.[4]

There was one driving principle behind Amnesty that helped to account for this peculiar mixture. Amnesty was the first nongovernmental human rights organization to realize that it would be accused of "political motivation" once it singled out governments for criticism. As a result, Amnesty made elaborate efforts to meet this charge and remain above the political fray. It was careful to invoke the Universal Declaration of Human Rights or a government's own laws. No one qualified as an Amnesty "prisoner of conscience" if he or she had advocated violence, no matter how just the cause. No national section could adopt prisoners from the same country, and no researchers could investigate their own governments. When in doubt, the policy was to err on the side of caution. When war broke out between Britain and Argentina in 1982, British and American sections suspended their letter-writing campaigns on behalf of Argentinian prisoners.

It was, in fact, Amnesty's lack of "political motivation" that provoked one of the major internal eruptions during the 1970s. Cosmas Desmond, a priest who had himself been detained in South Africa and had been adopted as an Amnesty prisoner of conscience, was elected head of the British national section. Desmond resigned after a stormy few months, complaining that Amnesty had disqualified itself from adopting Nelson Mandela, the jailed symbol of black opposition to apartheid, on the grounds that he refused to forswear violence. This fundamental complaint, which Desmond later expressed in an eloquent book, was that Amnesty was not sufficiently political.[5]

Others have put this differently and charged that Amnesty ignores the root causes of repression and concentrates on the symptoms. What sense did it make for the Swiss section to campaign for a handful of prisoners in Argentina like Becerra, while Swiss banks were underwriting Alfredo Martínez de Hoz's economic strategy and so financing the disappearances? One could say that Amnesty may have salved the middle-class conscience, but that it also sucked off a lot of middle-class energy that could have been more usefully channeled.

This is not, it must be stressed, a conventional view. Amnesty has done more to challenge and expose the cruelty of governments than any other organization, and if human rights is now an accepted part of foreign policy, then Amnesty can claim much of the credit. The point is that supporters and critics alike agree about this: Amnesty is as near to being apolitical as it is possible to be. Perhaps there was a special concentration, almost venom, in Amnesty's comments and campaigns on Latin America, but if so it was due to the volume of information available and to Amnesty's own mandate. In the stilted vocabulary of human rights, Amnesty dealt with violations of the "right to life" and other acts of violence by governments, particularly torture. Latin American dictatorships were the classic violators of these rights. It was thus entirely logical that the full fury of Amnesty's middle-class membership should be turned against the dictatorships in Chile, Argentina, and Uruguay.[6]

By October 1976 Amnesty's record was being carefully weighed in Buenos Aires. It was an awkward time for the Junta. In the United States, Jimmy Carter's campaign for the Presidency was stressing human rights and striking a chord. On October 18 Garzón Maceda and Roca, from CADHU, testified before Congress. Public opinion in Europe and North America was skeptical and hostile. The Junta decided to admit an Amnesty team of inquiry.

This was a clear gamble. Amnesty had sent a mission to Chile soon after the 1973 coup, and had issued a report that was devastating to Pinochet. But the Junta in Argentina had carefully weighed the pros and cons. It was probably noted in Buenos Aires that Amnesty sections were still only writing letters on behalf of a few hundred people detained under the continuing state of siege, and it was far from clear how the strict adoption procedure would apply to the thousands of desparecidos. Amnesty had excluded itself from adopting ERP or Montonero guerrillas because they advocated violence. In short, Amnesty's narrow, apolitical focus may have seemed to preclude the possibility of a damaging attack.

There were other potential benefits. One 1977 Foreign Ministry memo, written with the wisdom of hindsight, would explain:

It was obviously not going to be possible to obtain a fundamental change in Amnesty's outlook. That would have been utopian, considering the ideological basis for its actions. As a result, we sought the following limited results in authorizing the visit: First, convey an impression of firmness and conviction. Second, get a better understanding of the individuals in question, of the way they worked and their contacts, with whom we should then concern ourselves.[7]

In other words, working from the principle that it helped to know the enemy, this trip could be very useful indeed. The Junta would get a clear idea of how this important organization functioned. It would also have a chance to identify Amnesty's contacts in Argentina.

Creating a Climate of Skepticism

The Amnesty team was made up by Lord Avebury, a British peer, and Robert Drinan, the first Jesuit priest to have been elected to the U.S. House of Representatives. The third member, Patricia Feeney, occupied the Argentina desk at Amnesty's headquarters in London. Feeney, who was English, served as the team's translator.[8]

The visit opened on a cautious note on Saturday November 6. The group moved into the Presidente Hotel, which was expensive, but centrally placed for interviews. How were local journalists supposed to interpret the arrival of a "human rights mission"? This was not a time to take chances—forty journalists had already disappeared, so they concentrated on the personalities of "el team."[9]

Avebury the English peer and Drinan the Jesuit congressman were certainly an odd mixture. Avebury had won a sensational parliamentary election victory for the minority Liberal party in Britain before being elevated to the House of Lords, and he came across as shy, scruffy, and eccentric. His fellow countrymen were amused some years later when Avebury announced that he had bequeathed his body to a dog's home, for consumption by the inmates. (The offer was politely declined.) On a more serious note, Avebury was coordinator of the British parliamentary human rights group, a task he performed tirelessly. Drinan was also a character, with his "dog collar" and beetling white eyebrows. It was instantly clear that he was not shy. The *Buenos Aires Herald* called him "fiery but good-humored." It was one of the few kind descriptions of the week.

The mood remained polite, if wary, through Monday when the team met with Deputy Foreign Minister Gualter Allara to discuss the rest of the schedule.[10] Allara made an important concession. He agreed to allow the team to visit Villa Devoto, one of the prisons in Buenos Aires, to talk freely to prisoners. Avebury went to the prison the following morning, accompanied by a British diplomat. The newspapers were full of the latest terrorist outrage, which had taken the life of a retired mayor named Adolfo Wals. Avebury spent most of the day talking to eight prisoners. When he emerged at five in the evening, some journalists were waiting outside. There was some small talk but no interviews—this was a policy decision—and Avebury drove back to the hotel.

That, at least, was how Avebury saw it until he read a report put out later in the evening by the government press agency Telam. The report gave a mischievously inaccurate account of the jail visit. "After they left, an unknown man thrust himself forward and introduced the sister of a captain who had recently been assassinated 'by those delinquents you care about.' Lord Avebury did not comment. His clothes were rumpled and stained, particularly the lapels. He appeared distressed. 'Who finances Amnesty?' asked another journalist. 'I don't know,' replied Lord Avebury, through an interpreter." The Telam account was a complete fabrication.

Alerted by the Telam report, journalists gathered at the Presidente Hotel in the middle of the night and the mood turned ugly. They spotted Drinan in the hotel and crowded around him. Drinan turned on them and accused them of being police. One of the journalists tried to take Drinan's photo. Furiously, Drinan demanded the roll of film. Another journalist pursued him up a corridor. Trapped, Drinan turned. According to one account, he was about to throw a file at the man, "endangering his humanity," when Patricia Feeney, who had been watching the fracas with growing alarm, tried to calm things down. Drinan would have none of it. He asked her to record the names of the journalists in a notebook, suspecting correctly that few were genuine journalists.

Meanwhile Avebury had appeared and the questions turned to his visit to the prison. Avebury, according to another insinuating Telam report, was wearing red socks and a red tie. "I'm not interested in who's been killed by subversives," he said. He was asked whether subversives also kidnapped people. "I don't know," he replied. "I haven't asked them." What about Cuba? "I don't care who they've killed in Cuba." Another fabrication.

The papers were full of it the following morning. Avebury was astonished. The three drafted a reply to the Telam report, pointing out ten serious inaccuracies. The vilest charge of all, as Avebury later said, was the report about the incident after his visit to the Villa Devoto. The woman had been introduced to him inside the prison by the prison governor and Avebury had expressed regret and sympathy at her bereavement.

The following morning the Amnesty team was due back at the Foreign Ministry for a second and final meeting. According to the circular cable, it lasted three hours. The two sides parted company on a cordial note, but it could hardly be business as usual in light of the newspaper reports. It was now clear that the Junta, while maintaining the façade of cooperation, was trying to discredit Amnesty in order to prime the public for a critical report. Slur followed slur. Avebury ceased to be the diffident English lord and turned into a freak with food on his clothes, Marxist-colored ties, and even dubious sexual preferences. (One weekly magazine referred at length to the recent resignation of Jeremy Thorpe, the leader of Avebury's Liberal party. Thorpe had been involved in a sordid homosexual affair, and the magazine pointed out that Avebury was not only a close personal friend of Thorpe's but the godfather of his son.)

Drinan, too, had lost all his charm for the reporters. He was now "choleric and irascible." About the brush in the hotel lobby, one paper wrote:

> We can confirm it was the product of a fevered mind. During the altercation, a strange group of people approached. One introduced himself as "the creator of political science for true world peace," said he was a candidate for the Nobel Peace Prize, and asked protection for his companion, who was presumably threatened by mysterious secret delinquents. With a furtive expression, Drinan listened to both of them in spite of the fact that they did not speak English and he did not speak Spanish.

According to Patricia Feeney, this whole account was complete fantasy.

Another brush with the press came the following night. All three members of the team again refused to talk with the Argentinian journalists, but Drinan was seen giving a lengthy interview to an American news crew. This caused further resentment. Lacking hard news but under pressure to uncover something, one journalist discovered that the hotel bill came to 29 million pesos and that Patricia Feeney had paid it all in local currency.

On Friday evening, there occurred what was in many ways the most unnerving incident of them all. It took the form of a demonstration outside the hotel by a group of young people called the "National Patriotic Movement." They were heard chanting: "How can the church allow this priest Drinan to defend extremists and assassins? Why don't you leave our country, slaves to Communism! Argentines: you must know that Amnesty International is our enemy! It is cynical and impertinent."

Demonstrations were illegal in Argentina, yet the group entered the hotel while police watched, and distributed a printed communiqué with a strong undertone of fascism:

> These foreigners who offend our national dignity should know that we are fighting against Marxism: so that we can continue to believe in God; so that the family can continue to be the center of Argentinian life; so that fathers can continue to be the main educators of their children; so that our flag can continue to carry its traditional colors, a sun with blue and white.

The End of the Dialogue

It had been a thoroughly unnerving week for the Amnesty team. Inevitably, their side of the story had gone unreported. Drinan may have antagonized the local press, but it was only to be expected of a man who had an obsession with personal freedom. (He had once demanded to see his FBI file; after being refused he had taken the issue to court and won the case. Drinan was surprised to find that the file ran to 82 pages.) They returned tired to the hotel early in the trip to find a large contingent of security men waiting to "escort" them. They had not been told of this arrangement. Not only were their "escorts" probably engaged in the disappearances they had come to investigate, but they clearly intended to make a record of the team's contacts. The security officials remained with them throughout the week, and several witnesses from the Argentinian League for Human Rights were photographed. Drinan's suspicion was understandable and entirely justified. In spite of everything, a steady stream of Argentinians met with the Amnesty group and told their stories.

The worst moment came when Feeney and Drinan flew to Córdoba. Feeney met with a young student to hand over a letter from a mutual friend in London. When they returned to Buenos Aires, they learned that the young woman had disappeared. They spent a panic-stricken few days before they learned she was safe. In between, they tried to meet with witnesses. Drinan was particularly impressed by Emilio Mignone. He took up the case of Mónica Mignone and pestered the Argentinians during the trip until one of them confided nothing more that could be done. This confirmed what Mignone already suspected, that she was already dead.

Drinan met with Jacobo Timerman, the editor of *La Opinión*. Timerman had welcomed the coup, but he listened carefully to Drinan and contributed the most balanced account of the Amnesty visit in the local Spanish-speaking press. It was, in contast to the feverish accounts of his competitors, a long and cerebral analysis of the various dilemmas facing Amnesty as it grew beyond its original mandate. It also presented a nuanced account of a meeting with Drinan, who asked him about anti-Semitism. The Amnesty visit evidently gave Timerman food for thought.

The most sympathetic account, by far, was run in the *Buenos Aires Herald*. Robert Cox, the editor (who would himself leave Argentina after his son was threatened), demolished the Telam account of Avebury's visit to Villa Devoto and reminded his readers that Amnesty's mandate did not permit it to examine violations by terrorists. But even Cox was forced to admit that the Amnesty visit had generated enormous hostility. He ran the following letter from Norman Antelme at the top of the editorial page:

> Amnesty International please get the hell out of our country—you stink. Get yourselves a one-way Aeroflot ticket to Moscow, Cuba, Angola, Uganda, or some of the soap-box African "states" where you can really see some action—and then just stay there.

On November 15 1976, the visit came to an end on a final note of mutual incomprehension. The team had promised earlier that there would be a final press conference. When the journalists arrived at the hotel they were handed a written statement. There were more bitter complaints until Avebury agreed to sit down quietly and discuss the broad outline of the report they would be drafting.

It had been a tense visit, and it had raised many profound questions about the work of human rights groups. If the Junta was in the dock of international public opinion and Amnesty was the prosecutor, much would depend on the facts. The Foreign Ministry would charge Amnesty with accepting questionable allegations, but this ignored the fact that the policy of disappearances was designed to ensure that hard information was not available. Amnesty could not have done more to verify the unverifiable. Then there was the charge of "selectivity." Outside Villa Devoto, Avebury had been asked whether Amnesty was "selective" in picking on Argentina and ignoring other abusers like Cuba and the Soviet Union. Avebury had pointed out that Amnesty's annual report dwelled at length on the Soviet Union and that he personally had friends in jail in Russia.

He might have added that it had little bearing on what was happening in Argentina. They had ignored him.

Equally important was the issue of terrorism. *La Prensa* put it like this: "Whose rights are they defending? Only those in prison? Apparently, the rest of society has none. Amnesty remains indifferent to the brutal killings of innocent people. It cannot hope to inspire confidence and sympathy in our country." It would have been useless to reply, and explain Amnesty's mandate. They would not have listened. By 1976 Argentine society had been programmed to believe that any response to terrorism was justified, no matter how ruthless.

The report of the Amnesty visit was published on March 23 1977, one day before the first anniversary of the coup. The date was no coincidence, as one Argentinian Foreign Ministry memorandum noted. What was a useful journalistic "peg" to the Amnesty information office, was, to the Junta, further proof of Amnesty's desire to "cause embarrassment" and of its "political motivation."[11] Far more important, of course, were the report's contents. It was a sober, factual account of a year of mass murder (replete with names, dates, places) set out beside the Junta's lofty goal of "national reorganization." The Amnesty report was the first of a long series on the disappearances, and it set a remarkably high standard. True to form the writing was poker-faced and legalistic, conveying no hint of the torrid circumstances under which the information had been collected.

The Junta acted aggrieved and accused Amnesty of bad faith. But it had known far better than to think it would be rewarded for merely allowing the team to visit. It had been a calculated gamble, and it had been clear from the first day what the outcome would be.[12] Once it was clear that the gamble had failed, the Junta devoted all its energy into throwing the Amnesty team off balance, priming public opinion for a critical report, and storing up ammunition for the long fight that lay ahead. Wrote one angry Foreign Ministry official: "We have finished with trying to get Amnesty to understand our situation. The dialogue is now finished. We must seek other ways." In short, there would be no more concessions to nongovernmental critics, only implacable hostility. Critics would automatically be accused of infiltration by left-wing subversives and of launching a "political" campaign against Argentina, irrespective of the facts.[13]

The Amnesty visit to Argentina would turn out to be one of the most significant human rights missions ever undertaken by a nongovernmental organization. It had a profound effect on the individuals involved. It helped confirm Jacobo Timerman's growing doubts and turn him from a sympathizer of military rule into a critic. Robert Drinan found a new cause, and emerged as one of the most forceful advocates of suspending U.S. aid to Argentina in Congress. Eric Avebury also remained alert. On his return to Britain he began a long fight to win entry into Britain for refugees from Argentina. Patricia Feeney's knowledge of Argentina and the disppearances was immeasurably enhanced by the trip. It was a superb education, and it meant that future Amnesty reports and statements on Argentina would have added credibility and authenticity. Whenever relatives of disappeared persons passed through Europe they would head for the Amnesty offices, further enriching the organization's information.

As for the disappearances, the international community now had two different versions, one from the Junta, the other from Amnesty. Nine months after the Amnesty report on Argentina was released, the verdict was rendered: Amnesty won the 1977 Nobel Peace Prize. International human rights groups were indeed beginning to flex their muscles. It was just a matter of time before they took the case of the relatives to the world stage, at the United Nations.

II

Inside the United Nations

7. A Dangerous Place

The Palace of Nations is set in a spacious park overlooking Geneva's Lake Leman. During the summer, when the wind tugs at the small sailboats below, the view is invigorating. But throughout much of February and March, when the annual session of the U.N. Human Rights Commission takes place, the city is enveloped in thick, soupy fog. Underneath, the air becomes dense and almost suffocating. U.N. officials and diplomats pine for the pure white skiing slopes that lie above, and lethargy fills the Palace. Nothing could be further from the terror that enveloped Buenos Aires in 1976.

The Palace was built for the League of Nations, and between 1929 and 1936 it inched up, brick by marble brick, while the League itself veered giddily between promise and disaster. Fractionally larger than the Palace of Versailles, it still seems a fairy-tale building. But its beauty is cold, and it can be eerie walking these corridors on a foggy day, pursued by the echo of one's own footsteps. On such days, the Palace of Nations seems more like a mausoleum than a forum for debating contemporary evils like torture and disappearances.

Ironic mementos of the League are sprinkled throughout the Palace. In one room are marble floors from fascist Italy, in another wood panels from racist South Africa. The most magnificent decorations are in the chamber that used to house the League's Council. This is a series of superb if somber, monochrome paintings by a Spanish artist, José María Sert. Given to the League in 1936 by the Spanish Republican government, they depict man's conquest of disease, war, and slavery. The paintings were meant to be the crowning glory of the League's new Geneva headquarters. Instead, they turned into an ironic comment on its failure. By the time the paintings were finished, civil war was raging in Spain. José María Sert deserted the government which had commissioned his paintings and joined Franco.[1]

The League's Assembly met for the first time in its new headquarters in 1937. On the eve of yet another European war the Assembly voted to suspend the League, an act of heartbreaking irony which not only stamped the League itself as a failure but inspired Parkinson's law that an organization starts to disintegrate as soon as it builds its own headquarters. The lights went out in the beautiful new Palace to save electricity. Throughout the Second World War, the League's pulse continued to flicker until, on April 18 1946, the League Assembly resumed its 1939 session after one of the longest suspensions in history. By then the United Nations had been created in San Francisco and the Palace was converted into the U.N.'s European headquarters.

The U.N. Human Rights Commission meets each year in Conference Room 17 in a new wing of the Palace. If the rooms in the older League building are steeped in history, Room 17 is neutral, anonymous and bland. Is this a room for people? It's hard to say. There is no chewing gum on the microphones or initials carved in the wood paneling. Within minutes of the end of a meeting, invisible hands have sharpened the black pencils, straightened the little blocks of notepaper, and swept up doodles in preparation for the next conference.

The U.N. Human Rights Commission comprised thirty-two governments in 1976 and, like Room 17 where it met, it seemed disturbingly detached from the real world. Delegates used a diplomatic code. They never lost their temper. They described each other as "honorable" instead of the scoundrels many of them were. Rather than "taking up an issue," they confessed to being "seized" by it. They talked of U.N. agencies as "organs." Here was a foreign language. To normal people, the idea of an "organ being seized" sounds agonizing. Here in the U.N. it meant action.

The dress, like the language, was neutral and anonymous. The U.N.'s most precious asset is the cultural diversity of its member nations, but little of that appeared at the Commission. This was the home of the business suit and nylon shirt. When a delegate from India entered in a sari, or a Saami native from Norway wore traditional costume, the dull canvas came brilliantly alive with color. So overwhelming was the pressure to conform that when the real world did intrude one's first reaction was usually embarrassment. When, in 1980, a group of Argentinian Mothers entered the public gallery and silently donned their symbolic white scarves, the effect was shocking. Scarves, like emotions, were out of place here. The Mothers were gratified because they had come to shock, but they found it hard to understand. They were also puzzled by the fact that peacocks still roamed in the grounds outside the Palace, at the bequest of its donor. Baby carriages, however, were strictly forbidden. The Palace, it seemed, was not for people.

The Search for the Single Standard

To understand the challenge that this peculiar institution posed to the Argentinian Junta in 1976, we need to take a step back and retrace the evolution of international human rights law. Drawn up in 1945 in the aftermath of the Holocaust, the Charter of the United Nations stated unequivocally that violations of human rights were a matter of legitimate concern to the international community. It was ambiguous on how far the U.N. and its members could go in protesting against such violations without "interfering" in a state's internal affairs. Even so, it was clear that sovereignty of the state was no longer the undisputed foundation of international diplomacy.[2]

The Charter made no attempt to define human rights. This omission was partly rectified on December 10 1948, when the U.N. General Assembly adopted the Universal Declaration of Human Rights, which set out a list of articles.[3] Seventeen of them enshrined individual political rights and freedoms, such as the right to free expression and freedom from torture. Another six contained economic, cultural, and social rights to food, education, and even leisure. The Declaration was drafted and adopted in two years, which was double-quick time for the U.N., and one should not underestimate the achievement. The challenge to governments here was clear and undeniable, and it was to provide groups like Amnesty with an indispensable tool in the years ahead.[4]

At the same time, it exposed a formidable inbuilt contradiction. The United Nations is a body of governments, but by adopting the Universal Declaration the U.N. threw down the gauntlet to governments and sided with their victims. It was clear from the outset that for this formula to stand any chance of success three factors would be essential. First, the U.N.'s human rights machinery, particularly its secretariat, would have to work independently of governments. Second, human rights bodies like the Commission would have to rise above their (governmental) composition. Third, governments themselves would have to exhibit statesmanship and tolerance and accept U.N. criticism of their own behavior in the wider interests. This was wildly utopian given the international climate in 1948.

Indeed, the Universal Declaration raised expectations of its parent, the United Nations, that could never be realized.

The Universal Declaration did even less for linguistic clarity. Its legalistic terminology ensured that the vocabulary of human rights is opaque and often misleading. When the U.S. State Department referred to "unlawful or arbitrary deprivation of life" instead of "killing" in its 1984 annual review of human rights, it received the annual Newspeak prize from the National Council of American Teachers.[5] The teachers had a point. Under President Ferdinand Marcos of the Philippines, security forces did not "kill," they "salvaged." A U.N. resolution which describes murder as "deprivation of the right to life" is equally distorting because it creates a comforting buffer between the act and the description. If delegates at U.N. meetings talked of "inserting a cattle prod into young women" instead of "torture," they might remind themselves of their real business.

Leaving aside this linguistic fog, are the rights in the Universal Declaration really "universal?" This was the key question in 1948; it remains the key question today; and it was certainly the key question in 1976 when much of Latin America was under military rule and there was, as we have seen, a growing body of opinion in the United States that such "authoritarian" regimes could not be expected to live up to the same standards of behavior as Western democracies. Clearly, the more "universal" the rights in the Declaration, the more realistic it was to expect Argentina's military rulers to respect them, and the more plausible it was for Amnesty and others to complain when they didn't.

The fact that eight of the U.N.'s fifty-six member states abstained on the final vote on December 10 1948 suggests the answer was no: the Declaration was not universal. The severest disappointment was registered by the Soviet Union, which argued that the Declaration was a product of Western democracy. The Soviet Union was, at the time, openly violating much of the Declaration, but it was also concerned that the U.N. would turn into a tribunal and sit in judgment on member states. Saudi Arabia abstained because the Declaration allowed people to change their religion, which it claimed was forbidden by the Koran. South Africa raised the fear that the Declaration would in time become binding and acquire the force of customary international law.[6]

The voice of the Third World was not yet being heard in the U.N. in 1948, but some Third World scholars have subsequently argued that the Declaration's heavy stress on individualism is at odds with many of the collective values of tribal society, particularly in Africa.[7] Latin America participated at the San Francisco conference, and the American Declaration of the Rights and Duties of Man—adopted six months before the Universal Declaration—is virtually identical. But most Latin American constitutions, like Argentina's, were drawn up as a reaction against Spanish imperialism and expressed the same commitment to individual freedom as the U.S. Bill of Rights. What can be said, with confidence, is that the Universal Declaration owed much to Western documents and the Western concept of human rights. It drew on Western legal instruments and reflected the distrust of government authority that underpins Western democracy.

Thirty years of "standard-setting" then followed as the United Nations attempted to build on the Universal Declaration. By 1976, the corpus of international human rights law had expanded into a formidable thirty-nine conventions and non-binding declarations, and the urge to set standards had spread far beyond the U.N., to specialized agencies like the International Labor Organization and UNESCO, and regional organizations like the Council of Europe and the Organization of American States.[8]

How successful was this elaborate creation? Anyone unschooled in the art of compromise would probably answer, not very. As newly independent nations joined the U.N. it become progressively harder to draft conventions that would be universally acceptable and still precise enough to be useful. As a result, the U.N. was forever striving to enshrine new rights, while at the same time being forced to make crippling concessions to governments in order to achieve their agreement. These concessions were apparent both in the texts, which contained major omissions and ambiguous definitions, and also in their application: many of the laws were not legally binding, while those that were imposed no obligation on governments that had not ratified them.[9]

Some rights, like property, were squeezed out. Others, like freedom of religion, were weakened. Still others fell through the net completely: in 1976, there were still no conventions expressly protecting migrants and children. Although a number of instruments outlawed torture, they were either not legally binding or else not yet subject to any enforcement procedure.[10] The U.N. had failed to build on the Nuremberg trials and to expand the concept of an "international crime"—a failure that would, as we shall see, affect the campaign against torture and even disappearances.[11] To cap it all, the whole shaky edifice was constantly being disturbed by East-West hostility. After helping to draft the Universal Declaration and mold international human rights law in its own image, the United States turned its back on international human rights treaties in the 1950s. The Soviet Union spotted its opportunity and ratified almost all the conventions, even though its system and practice at the time were fundamentally at odds with many of their provisions. This was a sure recipe for mischief.[12]

What remained in 1976 was a vast array of international laws with varying levels of acceptance and hence "universality." At the core, enjoying general acceptance, was something that lawyers like to call the "right to life." Given the ambiguity in this term, and its association with the abortion controversy, perhaps U.S. Secretary of State Cyrus Vance described it better in a 1977 address as "the right to be free from governmental violation of the integrity of the person."[13] Here, in many ways, was the fundamental right—common to all societies, endorsed in all constitutions, and given preeminence in international law. Here was the very right that was being abused by Latin America's "authoritarian" military regimes, particularly in Argentina.

Civil liberties of the kind abused by "totalitarian" regimes like the Soviet Union did not enjoy the same degree of acceptance, either in practice or in international law. Whereas people could, under international law, be prevented from meeting or leaving their country during an emergency, they could not be deprived of their right to be free from governmental violence.[14] There was sound common sense to this. As a U.S. federal judge wrote in 1980: "While Americans feel strongly about freedom of speech and the press . . . such rights are not yet universal and we would be arrogant and self-righteous to apply them to all societies. The right to be free from torture, however, is . . . a right that exists regardless of the economic or social organization of a society."[15]

Other standards that were more or less universally accepted were the right to seek asylum and the right not to be subjected to the evils of racism, apartheid, genocide, and slavery. All were subject to individual conventions, even if most contained unsatisfactory omissions and ambiguities of the kind mentioned above. At the next level were to be found the rights to food, education, shelter, and health care—usually described as cultural, economic and social rights. These had been featured in the Universal Declaration and had been turned into a separate, legally binding instrument, much to the disgust of American conservatives, who viewed economic rights as socialist and who saw them as goals for government action instead of legal rights that can be claimed by individuals.[16]

Yet it was President Franklin Roosevelt who had placed economic rights on the U.N. agenda with his famous "four freedoms" speech to Congress in January 1941. One of the freedoms was "freedom from want," and in a subsequent war-time address on January 11 1944, Roosevelt described the rights to work, food, and even a "decent home" as "self-evident economic truths." Likewise, the Carter Administration had no trouble accepting the concept of "economic rights."[17]

At the next level came collective rights like "self-determination," which were accepted in principle but not particularly well defined. Then came the concept of the "right to development," which was endorsed by the U.N. General Assembly in 1977 in the face of fierce opposition from Western states that felt it devalued the concept of a right and diverted attention from individual political rights. Finally, at the outer edge, came controversial practices like female circumcision and particularly unpleasant forms of punishment like the stoning of prostitutes (allowed by the "Sha'aria," or Islamic code of justice) and even the death penalty (opposed by Amnesty International as a violation of the right to life). With each succeeding stage, the degree of agreement (and hence of universality) diminished, and the U.N.'s involvement became harder to justify.[18]

How did this affect the disappearances? In one respect, like torture, they fell through the net. Just as there was no convention outlawing torture in 1976, there was no instrument that specifically dealt with disappearances. On the other hand, a huge range of international laws referred indirectly to the crime, just as they did to torture.[19] This pinpointed the real problem over universality. Most of these actual rights—certainly the crucial rights to life—were universally accepted, even if there were wide differences of interpretation. What were not universally accepted were the legal instruments. The United States certainly did little to help by refusing to ratify the conventions, particularly the International Covenant on Civil and Political Rights. This made it easier for the really violent regimes like Argentina's Junta to follow suit.

Foxes in Charge of the Chickens

Apart from their lack of universality, the other obvious drawback to international human rights laws in 1976 was their implementation. While governments like Argentina publicly paid lip service to the right to life, they were busy snuffing it out behind the whitewashed walls of the ESMA.

This fact exposed a crippling weakness in the U.N. A law is worth less without a judge, jury, and court, and the United Nations had none of these. It dropped the idea of establishing an international criminal court at the insistence of the American Bar Association and the Eastern Europeans.[20] The International Court of Justice was only allowed to arbitrate if the disputing parties specifically accepted its competency to do so. The generally accepted method for implementing conventions required governments to do no more than submit regular reports. This system was just being consolidated in 1976. On September 20, forty of the governments that had ratified the International Covenant on Civil and Political Rights met and elected a committee of eighteen independent members to review the government reports, but it was quite unclear how forceful they would be in exposing government lies or whether they would be able to escape the clogging paperwork.[21] Perhaps most serious, by 1976 there was still no way for individuals to lodge complaints with the U.N. against their governments, such as existed in the European system.[22]

Almost by process of elimination, this left the U.N. Human Rights Commission as the principal outlet for victims of human rights abuses and their families. The Commission was judge, jury, and police force rolled into one. It was here that the battle over disappearances would be fought.[23]

The year 1976 found the U.N.'s human rights machinery at a turning point. For thirty years scholars, governments, lawyers, and human rights activists had struggled to clarify the ambiguity about "interference" in the U.N. Charter. Could the U.N. criticize governments that were violating human rights without "interfering" in their internal affairs? Of course, said groups like Amnesty International. Of course not, replied governments like Argentina. Given that governments comprised the U.N., they usually carried the day. Even individual communications were considered too controversial.[24]

Gradually, as for any law, the ambiguity over "interference" was resolved on a case by case basis. South Africa was placed in the dock as early as 1947. Given that hostility to racism was built into the U.N., this was inevitable and understandable even though in time the U.N.'s treatment of South Africa would strike many Americans as "selective."[25] In December 1967, the U.N. General Assembly set up a special committee of three governments to monitor Israeli practices in the occupied Arab territories.

This too would anger Americans, but again it was less than surprising. Israel's policies in the territories clearly threatened international peace and also raised legitimate human rights concerns. From the perspective of human rights, the problem was not why this investigation into Israeli practices had been set up, but how to investigate more countries.[26]

By a coincidence, on June 6 1967—the day that the Six Day War broke out in the Middle East—the U.N. further clarified the ambiguity over "interference" with a resolution (#1235) allowing the Commission to review not just apartheid in South Africa, but situations which appeared to reveal a "consistent pattern of gross violations similar to apartheid." In 1970 another resolution (#1503) took this a stage further. It allowed for the individual petitions that were arriving at the U.N to be sifted for "gross violations" and a blacklist of violating governments to be drawn up. Slowly, but surely the taboo against "interference" was crumbling.[27]

Following the coup d'état in Chile on September 11 1973, it appeared to collapse completely. The U.N. had not, until now, concerned itself with military takeovers, however brutal, because that would have placed half the U.N.'s membership in the dock. Furthermore, army coups posed no obvious threat to international peace. Pinochet's strike in September 1973 changed this. The coup that killed Salvador Allende produced much misery inside Chile, but a fortuitous convergence of interests outside. Allende had brought Chile into the Nonaligned Movement, and the Nonaligned used the U.N. Human Rights Commission to retaliate against Pinochet. The Soviet Union, which had been steadfastly against any strengthening of the U.N.'s human rights machinery, abruptly changed its mind after Communist trade unionists were detained and tortured. Western Europe was disgusted and angered at the excesses. Amnesty International and the International Commission of Jurists sent missions to Chile and wrote devastating reports.[28]

Each searing image added to the sense of outrage, and by the time the U.N. Human Rights Commission met six months later, in March 1974, disgust had transcended ideology. Salvador Allende's widow Hortensia addressed the Commission. A year later Theo van Boven, a member of the Dutch delegation, started to circulate the idea of a working group on Chile similar to those established on Southern Africa and Israel. The Chileans eventually agreed on condition that no East Europeans were represented. The Soviets raised no objections.[29]

The Chilean coup had a dramatic impact on the U.N., but it was not enough to prize the Commission out of its basic mold. The Commission remained a product of the U.N.—inherently biased in favor of governments and unwilling to challenge governments that violated international human rights law. No attempt was even made to bar violators from membership, with the result that in 1976 Iran and Uruguay both sat on the Commission. Later in the year the U.N.'s Economic and Social Council (ECOSOC) elected Idi Amin's Uganda to the Commission. Argentina was not a member, but there was little doubt that a body of this nature would be instinctively sympathetic to the Junta, and hostile to its critics.[30]

Nor, in 1976, could the relatives hope for much from the U.N. secretariat. Kurt Waldheim looked on human rights as a political embarrassment and was happy to delegate any responsibility in the area. In Geneva, a small core of forty-seven international civil servants serviced U.N. meetings under the direction of Marc Schreiber from Belgium. Schreiber was shrewd but unwilling to use his position to challenge governments. Following the coup in Chile, the U.N. Sub-Commission on Prevention of Discrimination and Protection of Minorities decided to place detention and torture on its regular agenda and invited human rights groups like Amnesty to submit information on torture. Schreiber was so terrified that the government names would leak out that they were put into sealed envelopes and handed personally to the subcommissioners.[31]

Drowning in Red Tape

All of this increased the importance of nongovernmental organizations. Outside the United Nations, groups like Amnesty International and the International Commission of Jurists were making headlines with tough, hard-hitting reports. But inside the U.N., they were drowning in red tape.

They were known as "NGOs," and by 1976 three hundred and seventy-seven were participating in the U.N.'s economic and social work, including human rights. They were a strange breed. To the Junta they appeared threatening and powerful, but in Geneva they seemed vulnerable. Some had extravagant titles that suggested global ambitions, like "Women's International League for Peace and Freedom," but operated out of small cluttered offices. Others, like the World Council of Churches and the International Committee of the Red Cross, had budgets of several million dollars and large headquarters.

Some were young, brash, and confident; others seemed to be of another era, with little to show for past efforts but a brass plaque and an impressive letterhead. Some, like the World Peace Council, were Communist-affiliated. Others, like Amnesty and the International Commission of Jurists, were Western in their approach to human rights (stressing individual freedom), although they also valued their independence. The ICJ, which will play an important part in our story, was established after a conference in Berlin in 1952 with the aim of exposing abuses in Eastern Europe. It expanded its scope to the rule of law as a whole, but remained committed to the Western principle of an independent judiciary. What all these NGOs had in common was a consuming interest in the United Nations. Their representatives whiled away many long hours at meetings, waiting to buttonhole diplomats and putting up with rebuffs from arrogant diplomats.

The U.N. offered them the chance to speak at meetings and have their documents distributed, but they had to pay a heavy bureaucratic price for the privilege. Every effort was made to keep them on the tightest possible rein and ensure they did not lead the U.N. to "interfere" in the internal affairs of governments. In order to qualify for accreditation (known as "consultative status"), an NGO had to prove it was financially independent and that it would refrain from "systematically engaging in unsubstantiated or politically motivated acts" against governments.[32]

No one could really quarrel with the demand for financial independence, although it nearly caused the International Commission of Jurists to be struck off the list in 1970 after it was revealed that the ICJ had indirectly received CIA money.[33] Altogether less reasonable was the prohibition against "politically motivated" attacks. Here was the old red herring. When the Junta leveled this charge against Amnesty International following Amnesty's momentous visit in 1976, it was dismissed with derision. Inside the United Nations, however, the charge was written into the rules. Here was a powerful weapon for the Junta.

Throughout the 1970s, the game swung back and forth. The rules appeared to relax in 1974, when Hortensia Allende was allowed to criticize Chile publicly in the U.N. Human Rights Commission. The following year they tightened again. In an effort to avoid mentioning a government by name, one hapless speaker referred to a "small, landlocked country somewhere in Latin America." He was challenged by the chairman to name the country (Paraguay) and immediately was ruled out of order. This was worthy of Alice in Wonderland: merely mentioning a government by name constituted U.N. "interference." Much more important, it signaled a major attempt by governments, headed by Iran and the Soviet Union, to regain the initiative and muzzle their NGO critics.[34]

The Junta's Assessment

There is where it stood on March 24 1976, when the Junta seized power in Argentina. What could the U.N. and the other international organizations offer the relatives in their struggle? At first sight, very little. Fundamental rights and prohibitions, such as the right not to be tortured, were not universally accepted. It was quite unclear how far the U.N. could go without "interfering." The U.N.'s implementation procedures were hopelessly weak. NGOs were drowning in a sea of red tape.

Back in Buenos Aires, however, it did not seem so simple. Over the years, Argentina's successive military regimes had endeavored to keep their international legal obligations to a minimum. Some, however, could not be avoided. Argentina was a member of the United Nations and the Organization of American States, and so was bound by the human rights provisions in both charters.[35] The government of Juan Perón had also voted for the Universal Declaration on December 10 1948, and by 1976 the Universal Declaration had acquired considerable moral and legal force. Argentina had joined the Convention of Vienna, which among other things protected diplomats and foreigners. It had ratified the two important ILO conventions; one allowing for the right to form free trade unions (#87) and the other to bargain collectively (#98). Argentina was also a party to the Geneva Conventions.[36] Above all, as we have seen, Argentina's own laws accepted the primacy of the right to life, which was one reason why the disappearances had to be clandestine.

Weighing these factors up, the Junta realized that it had to be careful. In one frank memo, written in 1977, an official at the Foreign Ministry issued a warning:

> Our situation presents certain aspects which are without doubt difficult to defend if they are analyzed from the point of view of international law. These are: The delay incurred before foreign consuls can visit detainees of foreign nationality. (This contravenes article 34 of the Convention of Vienna.) The fact that those detained under Executive Power (PEN) are denied the right to legal advice and defense. The complete lack of information on persons detained under PEN. The fact that PEN detainees are not processed for long periods of time. The fact that there are no charges against detainees. The kidnapping and disappearance of people.[37]

However weak the U.N.'s implementation procedures, Argentina's diplomats were aware that the U.N. and OAS had assumed the right to take
action against a "consistent pattern of gross violations of human rights"
by governments; and nothing, they knew, was more "systematic," more of
a "pattern," and more "gross," than the disappearances. In addition, the
U.N. had taken action against a military dictatorhip (Chile), ignoring the
Charter's prohibition against "interference" in a member's internal affairs.
NGOs like Amnesty International and the International Commission of
Jurists were clearly spoiling for a fight. ·

Even the U.N.'s Human Rights Commission was an object of dark
menace—"the anteroom to the tribunal of international public opinion,"
as one 1977 memo described it. All in all, it was hardly surprising that the
official in the Foreign Ministry issued his blunt warning: "Even if the
international organizations cannot themselves impose concrete or binding
sanctions . . . they can exert a moral pressure which can have an indirect
effect on bilateral relations with other countries."[38]

The pressure was already building. Within six months of the coup, the
International Labor Organization had published a list of detained and
disappeared trade unionists and had rebuked the Junta. UNESCO was
shortly to follow suit.[39] The evidence was growing, moreover, that such
pressure could have tangible results. The U.N. had already sponsored oil
and arms embargoes of South Africa.[40] The U.S. Congress was showing
signs of following the example: it had already passed a series of laws cutting U.S. military aid to governments which practiced human rights
abuses. The most important law (502B) even used wording identical to
that of the United Nations: "a consistent pattern of gross violations."[41]

One other point needs to be made. Critics often point to the slowness
with which the U.N. takes up violations, even violations on the scale perpetrated by the Khmer Rouge in Cambodia between 1975 and 1979, and
Idi Amin's terrifying regime in Uganda. (Pol Pot, Idi Amin, the Shah of
Iran, Anastasio Somoza, and Macías Nguema all fell from power just as,
or even before, the U.N. took action.) It is true that years can pass before
the machinery can be cranked up, true that the U.N. cannot intervene
rapidly like the Red Cross to save lives, true that the whole U.N. system is
impossibly ponderous. But what critics often ignore is the fact that once
the machine starts it cannot be turned off at a stroke. The governments of
Kampuchea, Equatorial Guinea, and Uganda even remained under review
for crimes committed by the ousted regimes. How much harder it would
be for a regime like the Junta if and when the U.N. ever took action on

the disappearances in Argentina! Even if the killing stopped, the pressure would not necessarily cease.[42]

No, this was not a time for the Junta to relax. There was real danger lurking behind those echoing marble corridors in Geneva. It would require a special kind of response from a special kind of diplomat.

8. The Godfather

Apart from a certain swagger, there would have been nothing to distinguish Gabriel Martínez when he arrived at the U.N.'s Palace of Nations to present his credentials on the morning of May 29 1974, certainly nothing to suggest the ruthlessness that would later become his hallmark. Onlookers would have noticed a stocky, balding man with a confident chin and a broad smile. The impression was one of alertness and intelligence. It was appealing, if also slightly unnerving. Most people found the white marble and bare corridors of the Palace soporific. Gabriel Martínez appeared to find them a tonic.[1]

Europeans usually distrusted Martínez when they met him for the first time. Emilio Mignone—poor Mignone with the sad, haunted look—took time to warm to strangers, and this made strangers warm to him. Martínez, in contrast, tried to overwhelm with charm. He would spot people from a distance and bear down, wreathed in smiles. The victim would find himself trapped in an "abrazo" (the traditional Latin American greeting), one hand plucking at a sleeve, another pinching an elbow, a third pummeling a hand, a fourth draped around a shoulder. Where were all the hands coming from? You never knew.

Western diplomats, who were to become Argentina's fiercest critics, were at a particular disadvantage. Being Anglo-Saxons they shrank from physical contact, but being diplomats they were trained not to show it. Martínez gleefully exploited their discomfort. The "abrazo" was his first weapon, his way of throwing people off guard—of showing that he, Gabriel Martínez, had absolutely nothing to apologize for. He loved to see his victims squirm.

His appointment as ambassador to Geneva by President Juan Perón in 1974 had been entirely logical. His curriculum vitae suggests a precocious intelligence and a flair for finance: divisional chief at the age of eighteen; economic councilor in the Argentinian embassy in Chile at twenty-five; diplomatic postings in Bonn and Brussels; chief of the department of foreign trade at thirty-six; another diplomatic posting in Chile, just in time to observe Salvador Allende's election; back to Buenos Aires as Under Secretary for Foreign Trade.[2]

By now, there would have been little that Martínez did not know about trade, and this was a vital qualification for Argentina's ambassador in Geneva. Geneva was headquarters for the General Agreement on Tariffs and Trade (GATT), the focus for efforts to liberalize world trade, and Argentina's economy was heavily dependent on exports of wheat, meat, and leather. Also in Geneva, and of keen interest to Argentina's powerful labor unions, was the International Labor Organization (ILO). By 1974 the United Nations Conference on Trade and Development (UNCTAD) in Geneva was already trying to achieve across-the-board debt relief and a boost in commodity earnings for developing countries.[3]

His knowledge of the U.N. would have been one reason why Martínez kept his job after the 1976 coup instead of joining the thirty ambassadors unceremoniously dismissed by the Junta. The free-market economic policy of Martínez de Hoz depended squarely on Argentina's being able to sell raw materials and borrow money. This made UNCTAD and GATT crucial. The ILO would require special attention as the Junta set out to crush labor unions; so would the Geneva-based office of the U.N. High Commissioner for Refugees. Then there would be the task of confronting the U.N.'s human rights machinery.

Most important, from the Junta's perspective Martínez was ideologically sound in spite of a close association with Peronism. He had been a protege of José Ber Gelbard, Perón's powerful Minister of Finance, and reportedly served as an economic adviser to José López Rega, Isabel Perón's Minister for Social Welfare and architect of the right-wing death squads. In January 1974, Martínez reportedly accompanied López Rega to Libya on a mission to negotiate a trade deal. The trip was a disaster. The Argentinians agreed to provide meat to Libya in exchange for oil, but according to subsequent reports Argentina paid far more than the market price for the oil and López Rega pocketed the difference. In May 1975 Jacobo Timerman of *La Opinión* asked one of his journalists to investigate the Libyan-Peronist connection, suspecting the germ of a nuclear power deal. A few days later the man's corpse was found with the fingernails pulled out.[4] López Rega himself left Argentina in 1975 at the insistence of the armed forces. He was subsequently traced to the Swiss town of Lausanne, thirty minutes away from Martínez's office in the Argentinian mission in Geneva.

Argentina's Diplomats Under Pressure

The years 1976 and 1977 were traumatic for Argentinian diplomats in Europe and in North America. They found themselves summoned, not invited, for frosty interviews about torture at the ESMA, and about prisoners being chopped up by electric saws and dropped from airplanes. They had no answers. All they could do was bluff it out and return red-faced and humiliated to the bosom of their embassy.

One 1977 internal Foreign Ministry memorandum conveys some of the confusion.

> It began with tactful diplomatic inquiries. Then it rapidly grew in scope and intensity into an an aggressive, open campaign against our country and its government. Our diplomats—principally those in the U.S. and West Europe—found themselves bearing the brunt. They were totally unprepared. They could not compete with those who were behind this campaign to isolate Argentina.[5]

Did Argentina's diplomats know what was happening back home during the dirty war? Gabriel Martínez, when called to the witness stand at the 1985 trial of his former military chiefs, would plead ignorance. His role, he would maintain, had been that of a messenger, transmitting complaints from the United Nations back to Buenos Aires. After all, was not diplomacy neutral? Here was the time-honored excuse of the diplomat, pleading due obedience to higher orders and ignorance about his political masters' acts and intentions.

The facts about Argentina between 1976 and 1983 are unusually difficult to unravel because the Foreign Ministry had been taken over by the navy, which was itself playing a key role in the disappearances. Following the coup, a new department was created under Deputy Foreign Minister Gualter Allara to centralize all the information on disappearances, to prepare coherent responses to inquiries, and to meet with foreign diplomats. Several career foreign service officials looked on the office as a source of disinformation and refused to serve in it.[6] In principle, the new department was meant to work closely with the Ministry of the Interior, which was responsible for internal security. But nothing was that simple under the Junta's Process of National Reorganization. As a result, cases like that of the young Swedish woman Dagmar Hagelin, of critical concern to Argentina's image abroad, went through layer upon layer of bureaucracy until the facts vanished altogether.

Dagmar Hagelin, it will be recalled, had been kidnapped by Alfredo Astiz and the navy GT 3/32 squad and taken to the ESMA. The Swedish protest would have been directed by Argentina's embassy in Stockholm to Allara's new department at the Foreign Ministry in Buenos Aires. From there it would have been forwarded to the Interior Ministry, even though Allara's navy colleagues in the GT 3/32 had kidnapped the girl. (Some of the GT 3/32 operatives were by now serving in the ministry press office). Interior Ministry officials then drew up a file (#217/734) on the Hagelin case and initiated inquiries of other security branches, including the navy. The file notes that the navy's intelligence service furnished a reply on September 8 1980. The reply was "negativo" (no information) because the girl had long ago been killed—by the rival navy GT 3/32. Back the reply would have gone to the Foreign Ministry, for transmission to the Swedish government.[7]

It was a façade, but it had advantages. Rather like dirty money, each successive stage took off a little more grime, pushed the truth further into the background, and made the plea of ignorance more plausible. In addition, it also slowed down the process. But did this mean that Foreign Ministry officials were "unaware" of the facts? Junior civil servants probably were. The author of one 1977 memo complained about "the excessive delay—no doubt justified—in obtaining information which will enable us to respond to the charges, particularly those which involve foreign nationals."

"Of course," he continued, "we fully understand the security considerations. I'm simply trying to identify a problem which exists and which has repeatedly made governments more resentful and impatient."

But the author could not plead ignorance about the role his ministry was playing in the disappearances: "Our ambassadors have been instructed to develop a persistent, aggressive approach in order to clarify the aims and methods of terrorism . . . They are to reply to any and all criticism firmly . . . present a positive image of our country."

On this important point the memo is brutally frank. It shows clearly how Argentina's once-proud diplomatic corps was to be used by the Junta to blunt criticism in the United Nations and to give the Junta time to finish the killings at home: "The aim is to delay criticisms of supposed violations of human rights in order to gain time and permit the necessary freedom of maneuver so as to bring the struggle against subversion to a happy conclusion."[8] As a result, when ambassadors asked for information about cases like the disappearance of Dagmar, these junior officials were

able to cable back: "Nothing known." But they could not plead ignorance. Even less could senior ambassadors like Gabriel Martínez, who were
playing a critical role in extending and defending the dirty war outside Argentina. Many of Martínez's cables were sent "exclusive" to his
Foreign Minister. This was the most confidential form of diplomatic
communication.

In short, Argentina's ambassadors had been told to defend a policy they
knew to be indefensible, and in violation of international law. They had
been told to lie.

Diplomat of Many Talents

Whatever talent this called for, it came popping and fizzing out of Argentina's ambassador to the United Nations in Geneva. In one respect Gabriel
Martínez was not so exposed as his colleagues in the capitals: while the
ambassador in Paris or London might be made to feel the host government's disgust at what was happening in Argentina, any disapproval expressed at the U.N. would be much more muted. But in other respects the
Geneva post was more demanding, because of the range of issues covered.
It called for immense nerve and stamina. Martínez had both in abundance.

A trade specialist, he had not, until 1976, had to deal with human rights.
But it soon became clear, after the coup, that it would consume much of
his time. He began to work himself into the subject.

This was no easy task. By 1976, as we have seen, the U.N.'s human rights
machinery had grown into an unwieldy mass of overlapping committees
and agencies that spewed out resolutions. But Martínez approached the
task as he did everything else—thoroughly and carefully. He realized that
before the rules could be broken, they had to be understood. He never
made the mistake of underestimating the task ahead. No corner of the
U.N. bureaucracy was too remote to be ignored, no delegate too insignifi-
cant to be courted, no scrap of information too trivial to be recorded and
cabled back to Buenos Aires.[9]

By mid-1976 Martínez was formidably well equipped to play his part in
the strategy outlined in the Foreign Ministry memo. He was capable of
speaking with authority on a remarkable range of subjects. Diplomats
from other nations took note and began to turn to Martínez for advice.
He was happy to oblige, never sure when it might become useful in Argentina's diplomatic counter-offensive. Back home in Buenos Aires, he

began to acquire the reputation of a workaholic. Colleagues in far-flung embassies began to wonder whether this Martínez dominating the cable traffic was the same affable trade expert they had known.

In many respects, he was the complete diplomat—fluent in several languages, nerveless, indifferent to the dislike he aroused. Throughout countless statements he was rarely known to falter in midstream or drop a pencil. His statements often ran to an hour or longer and were frequently delivered off the cuff. He could be vicious one moment, purring with compliments the next. But other diplomats understood this sort of thing. They were all playing the same game and they never knew when they would be roasted, particularly when it came to human rights.

Yet, in spite of his diplomatic abilities, no one did more to strain and abuse the frail conventions of diplomacy. Martínez was far more than a diplomat. Like Alfredo Martínez de Hoz, he was a full-blooded apologist for the Junta. He absorbed the philosophy and used the same fascist language about "antibodies" and "antisocial elements." In Argentina people were either useful or dangerous, friend or foe, patriot or subversive.

The same applied to the United Nations. Like Daniel Moynihan, Martínez saw the U.N. as a "dangerous place." Here, as in the ESMA, opponents were to be neutralized and, if necessary, eliminated. There are four recorded cases of the dirty war spreading to Geneva, and Gabriel Martínez was almost certainly involved in some, if not all. The cruelest involved Antonio Jakasa Vitaic, a member of the Argentinian employers' federation. Vitaic was a delegate to the ILO's governing body, and one of the ten members of the ILO committee that monitored violations of the right to form free trade unions. In November 1976 the committee took up the case of Argentina, with Gabriel Martínez almost certainly present. Six months later, on May 6 1977, Vitaic disappeared in Argentina, never to reappear. In 1981 Martínez was seen in the Palace with an army intelligence officer known as "Cortez" who had interrogated prisoners inside the ESMA. "Cortez," it appeared, had now joined Martínez's delegation in Geneva as an adviser.[10]

This gave a cruel, biting edge to U.N. debates on the disappearances. It was almost as if the door had slipped open, letting in a whiff of Argentina's dirty war. You shivered, but you also listened. Relatives of the disappeared certainly saw the sinister side of Gabriel Martínez as soon as they started to come to Geneva. Occasionally they would approach him in a corridor. He would listen coldly and then stalk off without a word of sympathy. It was disturbing to find someone who identified so completely with Videla's regime in neutral Geneva and a reason, in those early days, to doubt the U.N.'s commitment to human rights.

During his years in Geneva, Gabriel Martínez imposed his personality on the U.N. unlike any other ambassador. He became a full-blooded apologist for Argentina and indeed for the whole tortured Continent: godfather to other beleaguered ambassadors, and a high priest of the doctrine of state security.

Martínez Suffers a Reverse

Gabriel Martínez had two broad aims. The first was to prevent any public debate that could lead to criticism of the Junta by name. Second, he had to ensure that Argentina stayed off the U.N.'s confidential blacklist of "gross violators." He threw himself into the fray and emerged bloodied.

In August 1976, less than three months after the Uruguayan refugees Héctor Gutiérrez Ruiz and Zelmar Michelini were murdered in Buenos Aires, the annual session of the Sub-Commission began in Geneva. It was the first major U.N. human rights meeting after the coup in Argentina and two thousand refugees appeared to be in imminent danger. Could not the Sub-Commission do something? Several subcommissioners thought so, and began to work out the draft of a resolution. Argentina had no member on the Sub-Commission and Martínez was attending the meetings as an observer, but he kept abreast of the discussions and on August 28 cabled back confidently to Buenos Aires that the Western authors of the resolution were showing "great flexibility." They had also assured him that their purpose was not to criticize Argentina, but to "help it resolve a problem."[11]

This was far from clear from the resolution, which was less about refugees than about the disappearances. It mentioned Argentina by name, and it cleverly saw to it that four separate U.N. bodies—and the U.N. Secretary General—took note. Martínez woke up to the danger. He tore into the resolution and its sponsors, but to no avail. The resolution was accepted. Argentina had been criticized by name. It was down in black and white in U.N. press releases, summary records, and diplomatic cables back to capitals. Even worse, it was on the desk of the U.N. Secretary General, and on the agenda of the Commission next year. It was a major reverse for Martínez.[12]

There was worse to come. Every October, the program and the budget of the UNHCR are reviewed at an annual meeting. The High Commissioner in 1976 was Prince Sadruddin Aga Khan. Sadruddin was immensely wealthy, but he also had as much heart as money. He was an early supporter of Greenpeace before it became fashionable, and a strong opponent of nuclear power. He cared about refugees and was ambitious for his agency.

The Prince had been brooding for weeks about the alarming cables that been coming in from his officials in Buenos Aires and he began his traditional opening remarks with the following words:

> Mr. Chairman, distinguished delegates. Once again we meet in the calm and peaceful atmosphere of Geneva to discuss human problems which stand out in sharp contrast to the quiet environment. Let me illustrate through concrete examples: on 18 May in a Latin American country two refugees who were both well-known personalities in their country of origin were abducted from their residence very early in the morning by a non-identified armed group. Three days later their corpses were discovered along with those of two other refugees in an abandoned car. [13]

The ghosts of Michelini and Ruiz were returning from the grave to haunt the Junta. Martínez snapped back an angry reply accusing the refugees of being linked to "subversion and terrorism." It was a sneering, impertinent way to answer a prince, but more important were the sinister implications for the remaining refugees in Argentina.

This is an instance of Martínez initiating policy. The cable he had received from Buenos Aires on October 5 said simply that the two men had been killed by "terrorists." [14] Why then Martínez's suggestion that they too were "subversives"? Simple. He was carrying out orders to neutralize the United Nations. The truth was irrelevant.

Early in 1977, taking his cue from Martínez, a memo-drafter at the Foreign Ministry in Buenos Aires would accuse the UNHCR of "politicization" and lament the "left wing infiltration" into its Geneva headquarters. [15] Set up to protect refugees, the agency was seen as "subversive" in Buenos Aires merely because it was trying to do its job.

9. The Junta Counterattacks

Gabriel Martínez could afford no more reverses. He now adjusted his sights and turned on the nongovernmental organizations. It would develop into a memorable confrontation, but like a stone tossed into a still pond, it started with small ripples when the owlish Rodolfo Matarollo arrived in Geneva in August 1976, accompanied by Lidia Massafero, a leading Montonero in exile who was also high on the Junta's wanted list.

Rodolfo Matarollo, as readers will recall, was the ERP sympathizer who had helped turn the independent Argentine Human Rights Commission (CADHU) into a formidable arm of propaganda against the Junta and a highly effective monitoring group. Matarollo made a very good impression in Geneva. He was personable, persistent, and well-informed; among those he talked to was Alejandro Artucio, a former defense lawyer from Uruguay who—like Matarollo—had courageously represented captured left-wing guerrillas until he too was sucked into the maw of Uruguay's torture centers and political imprisonment. Artucio was now working with the International Commission of Jurists in Geneva and he told the Secretary General of the ICJ, Niall MacDermot, about Matarollo's presence.[1] MacDermot asked Matarollo if he would like to talk on behalf of the ICJ before the U.N. Sub-Commission. Matarollo jumped at the offer. MacDermot was a towering figure who had rescued the ICJ from its damaging association with the CIA and restored it to the forefront of the international human rights movement. This would be a huge boost.

Niall MacDermot had taken over the discredited ICJ in 1970 at a moment of deep personal crisis. His had been, up to this point, a brilliant career: barrister, member of Parliament, Secretary to the Treasury, and Housing Minister in Britain's Labour Government. MacDermot had been widely expected to go even higher and friends were astonished when he suddenly resigned his parliamentary seat in September 1968. Shortly afterward he chose exile at the ICJ in Geneva. Two years earlier MacDermot had divorced his first wife and married a Russian translator at the United

Nations in Geneva. Friends assumed that it was time to wipe the slate clean and start afresh, but they were wrong. Between 1966 and 1968 Ludmila MacDermot was repeatedly harried by the British secret service on the vague suspicion that she was a Soviet spy. Even though he was a minister, MacDermot was unable to call off the interrogators, and he resigned in disgust.[2]

His first task was to rescue the ICJ from financial ruin. (He found, on arrival, that the ICJ's annual income had shrunk to just $9,000.) Within two years he had succeeded, drawing heavily on his political contacts.[3] It was now time to restore the ICJ's credibility and this MacDermot achieved by a combination of astute strategy and force of personality. He encouraged challenging seminars on controversial issues like human rights in single-party states and the "right to development"—two concepts that were anathema to the ICJ's more conservative members and arguably at odds with its fundamentally Western view of an independent, apolitical judiciary. This—together with MacDermot's consistently harsh criticism of South Africa and Israel—endeared him to influential governments like Tanzania, and helped the ICJ win back credibility in the Third World.[4]

In many ways MacDermot was an anachronism, a throwback to an earlier era. Long after leaving Britain, he continued to look and act like a British cabinet minister with his mane of white hair, craggy features, and rich aristocratic delivery. He loved his British-made Rover car, the BBC World Service, and the London *Times*. His pinstriped suit stood out among the long hair and jeans worn by many other human rights lobbyists. He discouraged intimacy and he could be cuttingly rude to people who thought they were his friends. But this only added to the impression of incorruptibility. As a former minister he owed no one any favors. No one talked down to MacDermot, and no one ignored him. Diplomats deferred to him and dreaded his rebukes. It was immensely reassuring to other human rights lobbyists in Geneva, who suffered from a permanent inferiority complex when dealing with diplomats like Gabriel Martínez.

When Artucio recommended that he speak to Rodolfo Matarollo, MacDermot did not hestitate. He helped Matarollo work on the statement to ensure that it represented ICJ policy, but Matarollo delivered it in his personal capacity as an exiled Argentinian lawyer. It was the first time that an ICJ statement was delivered by someone other than a staff member.

Matarollo's statement was the nearest thing to a firsthand account from Argentina, and for several days the ICJ basked in the approval of other NGOs. Gabriel Martínez was appalled. He protested angrily that Matar-

ollo belonged to a terrorist organization and that the ICJ had violated the
U.N. rules banning "politically motivated" statements by NGOs. He was
of course partly right: Matarollo was a left-wing political activist with
known connections to a guerrilla organization. Asking him to speak for
the ICJ had, to say the least, been a calculated risk by MacDermot.

MacDermot rationalized it easily. The ICJ's concerns were law and lawyers, and in Latin America of 1976 both were endangered species. In 1975
Rodolfo Matarollo had met Heleno Fragoso when Fragoso visited Buenos
Aires on behalf of the ICJ and just escaped with his life.[5] Someone had to
speak up for the legion of murdered lawyers and Matarollo was the right
man at the right time. There was, after all, no proof that he had been
involved in terrorism (as even the Junta privately conceded). MacDermot
would later compare Matarollo to a member of Sinn Fein (the Irish Republican movement) who was not an IRA gunman. It could be said that
this distinction was naive. Yet the British government had accepted it
when MacDermot was a British minister, even when Ulster was on the
brink of civil war. Sinn Fein was not outlawed.

Was MacDermot trying to force the issue and challenge the arcane rules
governing the accreditation of NGOs to the U.N.? He denies it, but it
would have been in character. Certainly, he never imagined for a moment
that Martínez would pounce the way he did.

Shot Across the Bows

MacDermot was happy with Matarollo's statement, but uneasy about the
virulence of Gabriel Martínez's response. He had every reason to be. Toward the end of 1976, a young woman presented herself at the office in the
U.N. headquarters in New York which services the NGOs. The young
woman said she was completing a degree at Columbia University and
asked whether she could consult the files. The NGO office is one of the
sleepiest corners of the U.N. Its staff was impressed by the young woman's
brisk manner and flattered that anyone could be interested. Ana Carmen
de Richter, from the Argentinian mission to the U.N. in New York, then
began to do some homework on the ICJ and the other organizations that
had had the temerity to criticize her government.[6]

She discovered that under the rules NGOs are supposed to submit
regular four-yearly reports to show what they have done to "further the
aims of the United Nations." The rule had been allowed to lapse long ago.

The Argentinians spotted their chance. They proposed that the U.N. committee should review accreditation at a special meeting in New York, early in 1978.

It was a stealthy attempt to turn the clock back and get the NGOs to be denied access to the U.N., but senior U.N. officials in Waldheim's coterie raised no objections. The proposal was accepted by ECOSOC on May 23 and communicated to the groups by Diego Cordovez, an ambitious Ecuadoran who was working his way up the ladder of the U.N. secretariat. On August 31 Cordovez asked governments if they had any information they wanted to furnish. Argentina replied promptly with a long letter accusing four NGOs, including the International Commission of Jurists, of making a "politically motivated" attack. There was a particular irony to this charge which Martínez might have appreciated. One of the most critical NGO statements had been written by a South African intelligence officer, Craig Williamson, who had secretly infiltrated the Geneva human rights groups.[7]

Feigning indifference, MacDermot kept up the pressure on Argentina throughout 1976 and into 1977 with a steady stream of letters. November 18 1976: Roberto Bergalli, a magistrate, has been detained without charge. Why? June 22 1977: Jehovah's Witnesses are banned for refusing to salute the Argentinian flag. Could the distinguished ambassador send over copies of the relevant law? Such pinpricks must have reinforced Martínez's determination, and as the time for the review in New York approached, Niall MacDermot suddenly realized there could be trouble. It was, after all, only eight years since the Soviets had tried to bar the ICJ from the U.N. in the wake of the CIA scandal, and the tone of Diego Cordovez's letter suggested that the U.N. hierarchy sympathized with the Argentinians.[8]

MacDermot submitted a detailed rebuttal of Martínez's letter and prepared to attend the New York meeting if his presence was required. Martin Ennals, Secretary General of Amnesty International, did actually make the trip. He arrived in the middle of the fiercest blizzards in the history of New York. Others, less fortunate, were delayed by the snow. They included most of the Argentinian contingent. Even the weather was against the Junta.

Encouraged by the absence of a high-level Argentinian team, the four beleaguered organizations all replied robustly. One of their representatives then dropped a minor bombshell by disclosing that Rodolfo Matarollo had in the past worked for the provincial government of Buenos Aires. This came as a total surprise to the junior Argentinian official who was

monitoring the debate, and clearly cast doubt on Matarollo's guerrilla connections because terrorists do not feature on the government payroll.
Someone had slipped up. It was so embarrassing that someone back in
Buenos Aires tried—unsuccessfully—to erase the official's complaint from
the cable.[9]

The meeting closed on an inconclusive note. Later, no one was quite
sure whether it had been a warning shot against the NGOs by Argentina
or whether the NGOs had indeed been saved by New York's fickle
weather. Martínez portrayed it as a success. A year later, in a March 26
1979 cable to the new Foreign Minister Carlos Washington Pastor, he
would boast that he had "moderated" the behavior of the NGOs.[10]

It had certainly shown Martínez's skill in turning the U.N. rule book
against Argentina's critics. In the summer of 1976 he had been isolated,
vilified, and shunned. Within eighteen months he had turned an obscure
U.N. committee from the epitome of U.N. indolence into a band of vigi-
lantes, ready to pounce at the first sign of "political motivation." Henceforth, new NGOs would have to run a formidable gauntlet before they
were admitted. Overnight, the committee had been "politicized."[11]

It had been a close shave. Niall MacDermot decided henceforth that he
would only ask ICJ officials or members of affiliates to speak on its behalf.
He now knew that Martínez was a formidable adversary. He had also seen
the way that U.N. bureacracy could be manipulated. What neither he nor
Martínez knew was that their feud was only just beginning.

Argentina off the 1503 Blacklist

Martínez's other main target during these months of 1976 and 1977 was the
U.N. Sub-Commission on Prevention of Discrimination and Protection
of Minorities. This body, which meets every summer for four weeks, has
several important functions. One is to draw up the confidential 1503 blacklist of gross violators. The other is to offer NGOs the chance to contribute to a freewheeling public debate. Both posed an obvious threat to
Argentina.[12]

The twenty-six subcommissioners, who like to be known as "experts,"
are supposed to be independent, but at any given time no more than a
third can be counted on to take their independence seriously. Another
third are invariably government officials, and the remaining third uncom-
mitted. It was this last third that Martínez had to influence. They would

determine whether the disappearances were openly debated and Argentina's name placed on the confidential 1503 blacklist, or whether the U.N. maintained its long tradition of sycophancy to governments. For the second year running, Rodolfo Matarollo played into Martínez's hands.

Matarollo was everywhere that summer, buttonholing delegates and lobbying journalists. One of the subcommissioners he talked to was Beverly Carter, the tall black American Ambassador to Liberia. As an ambassador, Carter was technically not independent. But he was also nobody's catspaw; he had fallen out with Secretary of State Henry Kissinger over a hostage incident in Zaire.[13] Martínez also spotted the Italian subcommissioner, Antonio Cassese, huddling with Matarollo during a coffee break. On August 23, during a discussion on torture, Cassese referred to "reliable sources," including Matarollo's group CADHU, that suggested fifteen thousand people had disappeared in Argentina.

Martínez replied the same morning by accusing Cassese of sympathizing with terrorism because of his meeting with Matarollo. This was a monstrous charge and Ben Whitaker, the British subcommissioner, told Martínez to apologize or withdraw. "Countries which practised terrorism," said Whitaker, "should not use the same tactics in the United Nations."[14] Oblivious to the indignation he had aroused, Martínez left the room without apologizing to Cassese. Following a recess, the Sub-Commission met to review what had happened in private, and the details of Martínez's covert operation emerged.

José Caicedo Perdomo from Colombia, one of the more independent subcommissioners, announced that Argentina had threatened to cancel trade agreements with Colombia if he took a firm line on disappearances. Bali Ram Bhagat, from India, disclosed that he had been approached by the Argentinian ambassador in New Delhi before leaving. Beverly Carter, the American, let it be known that the Argentinian Foreign Ministry had protested his meeting with Matarollo during a visit to Argentina by U.S. Assistant Secretary of State Terence Todman. (This was ironic, because Carter had in fact been refusing Matarollo's request for a longer interview.) The Sub-Commission came out of its huddle and issued a short statement reminding the world that it was an independent body and rejecting "insinuations to the contrary or any intimidation against its members." It was an unprecedented diplomatic rebuke.

There was a mood of satisfaction during the following week—a sense that Martínez had been humbled and the Sub-Commission's independence vindicated. What they did not know was that Martínez had no sooner left the room than he fired off a cable to Kurt Waldheim, the U.N. Secretary General, protesting Whitaker's remarks and asking for "light to be shed on the legal validity" of his exclusion from the debate. This was the way Martínez would operate again and again; and it would have had more effect on the U.N. mandarins who surrounded Waldheim than newspaper headlines.[15]

Martínez certainly thought he had won this round. Two years later, in a March 26 1979 cable to Foreign Minister Washington Pastor, he would point out that "although they later made a declaration on the impartiality and independence of the experts . . . the Sub-Commission did not return again to the case of Argentina in public."[16] This was absolutely true. There was no further debate, and no resolution. To this extent, it was a step backward from the previous year, when the Sub-Commission had at least expressed concern on behalf of the refugees.

It was now time to ensure that the Sub-Commission did not impale Argentina on the confidential blacklist, established in 1970 under ECOSOC Resolution 1503. This formidably complex procedure is known familiarly as "1503" to human rights buffs, who treat it like a tired old acquaintance. But do they love it or loathe it? That is impossible to say. Life without 1503 would be drab and lifeless, mainly because no other procedure so richly sums up their frustration with the U.N.

1503 plays a critical part in our story. Here is how it works. Individual communications that arrive at the U.N. are reviewed in a general way by a small group of U.N. officials in Geneva under the watchful eye of Jakob Möller (a former magistrate in Iceland before he joined the U.N.) to see whether they appear to reveal a "consistent pattern of gross violations" by a government. Möller's staff present their findings to five members of the Sub-Commission who meet for two weeks before the full session in August. These five prepare a preliminary blacklist of governments, which is rubber-stamped or modified by the full Sub-Commission. This blacklist then passes to the Commission six months later, where a similar procedure is followed. The Commission endeavors to strike up a dialogue with offending governments, on the assumption that they will cooperate because the procedure is confidential. If improvements are not forthcoming, the case is thrown open to the public.

This at least was the principle in 1976. The practice was very different. After five years in operation, it was abundantly clear that as well as being breathtakingly complex, 1503 was exerting little if any pressure on governments. It was hardly surprising, because 1503 had been created with two unrelated goals. The first was to reprimand governments, but in private. The second was to make use of the thousands of individual communications that were arriving at the U.N. 1503 was not, in any sense, a petitions procedure that permitted Emilio Mignone to appeal to the U.N. on behalf of his disappeared daughter. Individual victims like Mónica Mignone were only important insofar as they helped show a "pattern."

From start to finish the 1503 procedure was riddled with built-in obstacles. The Soviet Union was opposed to the procedure (which it considered too inquisitorial), yet was given the power of veto over all communications concerning the right to leave.[17] It was anything but confidential: details were always being leaked, to the fury of all concerned, and on one occasion a confidential debate was even mistakenly broadcast to the U.N. press room. Another mistaken assumption was that confidentiality encouraged dialogue. In 1976 the U.N. secretariat sent 54,510 communications to 33 governments for comment. Only 128 replies were received.[18] This was hardly surprising: no government will accept that it is guilty of a "pattern of gross violations," irrespective of whether the case is heard in private or public. What would it take for the Commission to throw up its hands in exasperation and throw a case public? In 1976, no one knew the answer because it had never happened. Even Idi Amin's Uganda had escaped censure.[19]

Yet however fragile 1503 might have been, however remote the prospect that it might embarrass Argentina, Gabriel Martínez could take no chances. It was absolutely imperative that his country's name be kept off the blacklist. Frail as it seemed to outsiders, the 1503 blacklist of "gross violators" was the first step on the way to public condemnation by the U.N. Commission—the "antechamber of international public opinion," as the 1977 memo-drafter had termed it.[20]

By the summer of 1977, hundreds of individual communications on Argentina had arrived at the U.N. Three were chosen as representative.[21] These three communications contained more than enough data to indicate a "consistent pattern of gross and reliably attested violations," but they never made it past the first all-important hurdle of five subcommissioners. The Soviet, Pakistani, and Nicaraguan delegates all cast their vote in favor of the Junta. Beverly Carter and Jonas Foli, the Ghanaian, disagreed. But Argentina had been let off the hook.

This vote was a crushing disappointment for the dwindling number of people who put faith in the confidential 1503 procedure.[22] That the Nicaraguan dictator Somoza should side with the Argentinian Junta was hardly surprising. More significant perhaps, was the Russian vote. On August 19 1977 the two countries signed a massive trade agreement.[23]

In spite of the alarms and bad publicity, it had been a remarkably successful session for Martínez. Argentina had been kept off the confidential blacklist, and there had been no resolution in public. The nongovernmental organizations were subdued. Martínez had gained valuable time for his military masters.

Martínez Keeps His Nerve

Throughout the last crucial months of 1977, and into the following year, Gabriel Martínez kept his nerve. He knew that this was not the time to relax. His expulsion from the Sub-Commission had shown the problems of being a mere observer. It was, he realized, essential to try and get an Argentinian member elected. Even better if he could eliminate Argentina's more obvious enemies from the Sub-Commission.

Over the next six months, the Argentinian Foreign Ministry deployed its formidable muscle to this end. It paid dividends at the Commission in March 1978 when several of the subcommissioners who had caused irritation to Argentina were voted off the group. The independent José Perdomo from Colombia and Bali Ram Bhagat from India were not even renominated by their governments. Antonio Cassese from Italy was nominated, but heavily defeated. He too, had paid the price of independence. Marc Shreiber had been as outspoken on the Sub-Commission as he had been timid directing the U.N. Human Rights secretariat: he, too, was voted off. Ben Whitaker of Britain, a former member of parliament and one of the most outspoken subcommissioners, was narrowly reelected. The real winner, incredibly, was Argentina, whose candidate, Mario Amadeo, won election with a handsome twenty-six votes.

Amadeo was an old diplomatic war horse and lawyer who had served as foreign minister in the military regime that threw Perón out in 1955 and now served the Junta with equal loyalty while managing to appear compassionate. Early in 1979 Amadeo would participate at the controversial Georgetown seminar. He would also draft a controversial September 1979 law that declared dead any "desaparecido" not found within ninety days.[24]

Following the 1978 elections, the supposedly independent Sub-Commission now contained eight serving diplomats (five of them ambassadors), four ministers, and two former ministers. It was less independent than ever.

The 1978 session drew near. Martínez and Amadeo made a powerful team, with Martínez giving the orders and Amadeo doing public relations. The same three communications were up for consideration as in the previous year. This time, however, the five-man working group decided by three votes against two to put Argentina's name on the blacklist. Sergei Smirnov from the Soviet Union and Shariffuddin Pirzada from Pakistan again voted in favor of Argentina. Beverly Carter from the United States voted against, together with the subcommissioners from Nigeria and Colombia.

The case then went to the full Sub-Commission, where Mario Amadeo put on a convincing performance in the closed session. He looked a bit like a bloodhound with drooping eyes. Yes, he admitted, Argentina's prison system left a lot to be desired. But, he went on, "disappearances for political reasons had stopped." If disappearances were occurring in the cities it was "the same sort of thing that happens in New York." Amadeo then came to the crux of his argument: because of the large number of individual cases contained in the three communications, the government had not had sufficient time to review them. It needed another year.[25]

Ahmed Khalifa, the Egyptian, said that he had been enormously impressed by Mr. Amadeo's "emotional" statement and urged that Mr. Amadeo should be given another year. Carter of the United States and Whitaker of Britain both disagreed, but other influential Nonaligned delegates rallied to the emotional Amadeo. They were headed by Walima Warzarzi from Morocco (whose duties were vaguely defined as a Moroccan "roving ambassador"). Incredibly, Argentina was off the blacklist for yet another year by a vote of fourteen to six. This was a triumph for Gabriel Martínez, but not for human rights. Thousands of Argentinians had now died, but the United Nations was even unwilling to censure the Junta in private.

Martínez was not quite through. Isabelle Vichniac, the local Geneva correspondent of the French newspaper *Le Monde*, wrote a piece exposing the Soviet vote in favor of the right-wing Argentinian Junta.[26] She was right to dwell on it. This cynical alliance between a right-wing Junta that was murdering left-wing "subversives" and the left-wing Soviet Union was one more reason to open up the confidential procedure to the public scrutiny it so richly deserved.

Instead, the Sub-Commission turned furiously on Vichniac and demanded an investigation into the source of her information. This was intimidating both for Vichniac, an elderly woman, and the French sub-commissioner, Nicole Questiaux, who was the obvious suspect. It was also an unconscionable assault on freedom of information because the blacklist was a legitimate target for any self-respecting journalist. Isabelle Vichniac would have been within her rights had she turned her back on the whole charade—or followed up with another article. Instead she agreed to sign a pledge that she had not received the information from the U.N. secretariat.

This happened at Martínez's insistence. He had cleverly turned an embarrassing leak to his advantage by diverting the challenge against two of his foes—the U.N. secretariat and the French subcommissioner Nicole Questiaux. By now the storm had broken in France over the disappearance of the two French nuns. Questiaux might be less eager to intervene against Argentina in the U.N. if it could be implied that she had broken the U.N.'s cherished rule of confidentiality.

Gabriel Martínez had good reason to congratulate himself. As he cabled back to Foreign Minister Washington Pastor, he had managed to avoid the "institutionalization of the case of Argentina" before the United Nations. It had been a brilliant, ruthless campaign. He had fulfilled the requirement of the 1977 memo, and gained time for the killers.[27]

Back home, the "parsley" had all been "chopped up." Mónica Mignone, Dagmar Hagelin, Daniel Antokoletz, and the legion of other "desaparecidos" were all dead. Gabriel Martínez was undoubtedly an accessory.

10. Martínez Against the U.N. Middleman

By the middle of 1977, Gabriel Martínez had identified another enemy in the United Nations. On May 1 Theo van Boven, a Dutchman, had taken over as director of the U.N.'s Human Rights Division, or secretariat, in Geneva. Van Boven promised a new, more active style than his predecessor Marc Shreiber and his appointment posed a clear and unequivocal threat to Martínez. Before the year had ended the two men were locked in a bitter personal feud that was to have a decisive impact on the evolution of the U.N. secretariat.[1]

When someone joins the United Nations staff, he or she has to take a short but simple oath of loyaly to the U.N. and sever all political ties to his or her own or any other government. The concept of a committed, independent civil service able to withstand government pressure was, as we have seen, central to the vision of the United Nations. By 1977, however, the dream was far from being realized. The Soviet Union still refused to let its nationals in the United Nations work independently and Americans applying for U.N. jobs had to undergo an FBI security check before joining. Alarmed at Dag Hammarskjöld's activism, the superpowers had decided that future U.N. secretaries general would be elected on the basis of compliance rather than ability. As a result, the lackluster Kurt Waldheim was embarking on a second term. The independence of U.N. staff was only one of the obstacles to building the U.N. secretariat. It was endlessly difficult to establish fair salaries and balance out geographical quotas against efficiency.[2]

At the same time it was clearer than ever in 1977 that an independent secretariat offered the best—perhaps the only—chance of the U.N. rising above the inbuilt contradiction of its governmental composition. The secretariat had initiated many of the most exciting programs to emerge from the U.N. system in the 1970s: primary health care, which called on governments to prevent killer diseases caused by foul water and malnutrition; a "basic needs" development strategy to bypass the affluent and concentrate on the needy; the call for a "New International Economic Order."[3] These and other programs, richly promising in many ways, posed a direct challenge to governments, nowhere more so than in human rights. The U.N. could not possibly fulfill its potential in this controversial area if U.N. officials were not prepared to stand up to governments.

As a result, few corners of the U.N. were more exposed or exciting than the Human Rights Division. The Division acted like a prism, catching and magnifying the larger issue of the independence of U.N. officials. The director of the Division has wide discretion over the bureaucratic terrain where Gabriel Martínez had chosen to wage his guerrilla warfare. The Division advises on resolutions, prepares background documents, and services meetings and investigations; it is often left to the director to decide if names slip in or out of preparatory documents, or if groups like Amnesty International are allowed to attend meetings. If van Boven took his job at all seriously, it was inevitable that he would clash with Martínez.

In terms of personality, the two men could not have been more different. While Martínez strutted, van Boven ambled. While Martínez oozed ego, van Boven had none—at least none that was visible. Largely as a result of his confrontation with Martínez, van Boven would become a celebrity in Holland. But he was surprised when a friend wanted to rush out a book of his speeches and completely unaware of his market value. He was transparently, even painfully, honest—a quality he shared with Emilio Mignone but not with Gabriel Martínez. Martínez had turned lying into an art, but van Boven went to the other extreme and made it appear like original sin. This put him at something of a disadvantage in an organization run by Kurt Waldheim.

He had the air of an absentminded professor, and was often scruffy. He wore strange corduroy shoes, rumpled jackets, and yellow ties. Women wanted to mother him and tidy him up. He looked younger than he was, with his thick, wavy head of hair and his English was good, although names sometimes got mangled. Answering a question or giving a briefing, he would lower his head and clasp his hands, as if in prayer. Friends often described him as "religious," and he had written a thesis on religious liberty. But he was a man more of conviction than of religion, like so many Dutch. He could be intensely stubborn and very naive. Those, too, tend to be Dutch traits.

Van Boven was born in 1934 at Voorburg, an affluent suburb of the Hague, and earned law degrees in Holland and the United States before entering the diplomatic service at the age of twenty-six. Thereafter, his career in the Foreign Ministry ran strangely parallel to that of Gabriel Martínez in Argentina, until the two collided in Geneva. Unlike Martínez, however, van Boven believed in international law and he did not consider the U.N. dangerous. He had started attending U.N. seminars in 1964 and served on the Dutch delegation to the U.N. Human Rights Commission for several years. It was here that he helped to launch the U.N working group on Chile in 1975. In 1974 he was elected to serve on the Sub-Commission.

This was an impressive curriculum vitae when, in 1976, Secretary General Kurt Waldheim began looking for a new director for the Human Rights Division. The Dutch were underrepresented in the higher echelons of the U.N. and van Boven was impatient for change. Van Boven's two predecessors had lasted in the job for twenty and ten years respectively, but if this pointed to a five-year term for himself he did not let it show. He moved his family into a large, rambling house opposite the International School in Geneva, where the children of diplomats were consuming large quantities of marijuana in protest against Swiss conformity.

Initially, van Boven was helped by Kurt Waldheim's indifference. The trio of Americans who worked under Waldheim on human rights at the U.N. headquarters (William Buffum, Jay Long, and Donald Fitzpatrick) also left van Boven to his own devices. But while this gave van Boven a relatively free hand, it also meant that he could expect little support in the event of a crisis. Waldheim refused to upgrade the Human Rights Division, which left it marooned in the upper echelons of the U.N. bureaucracy with plenty of responsibility but little clout. Van Boven's own grade was also just below the level where he could call in political support.[4]

Van Boven gave early hints of impatience with the U.N. in interviews, but he was also very much a U.N. man, and much given to using jargon like "standards," "machinery," and "organs."[5] He gave terrible press briefings and never betrayed the secrets of the 1503 confidential procedure. Journalists would emerge disappointed because he refused to be drawn into criticism of the Soviet Union or the United States. He was a loyal servant of the U.N.

At the same time, van Boven made it clear that he was anything but "neutral." On a narrow reading of the U.N. Charter, the main duty of U.N. officials is indeed to remain neutral and avoid "interfering" in the sovereignty of governments. According to a more progressive interpretation, they have a duty to promote the goals of the Charter and this calls for taking initiatives, confronting governments, abandoning neutrality. In

May 1961, Dag Hammarskjöld delivered a famous statement in favor of an activist secretariat in a speech at Oxford. If neutrality meant resisting influence, he said, then this was in line with the U.N. Charter. If it meant not taking a position, then it was not: "The international civil servant cannot be accused of lack of neutrality simply for taking a stand on a controversial issue when this is his duty and cannot be avoided."[6]

Van Boven made it clear that he was keen to take initiatives. On February 6 1978, in his opening statement to the Human Rights Commission, he would observe:

> If one tries to work for the cause of human rights, as we do on a daily basis . . . it is impossible to remain indifferent when confronted with the many appeals which are directed to the United Nations. Peoples . . . are vesting their hopes in the United Nations which has proclaimed ideals of freedom, justice and peace and which has reaffirmed faith in fundamental human rights in the dignity and worth of the human person. Large masses, many of them young children and young people, see no meaningful future because they lack the most basic needs of existence. Large groups of people live in desperate situations because of their race, their sex, their religion, their ethnic origin or their convictions.[7]

Behind these words lay an important message. Van Boven would not be afraid to take a stand. It was just a matter of time before this would bring him into conflict with governments like Argentina, and invite the charge that he was making a "politically motivated" attack as well as "interfering" in their internal affairs.

The War of Nerves

It needs to be stressed that this charge was even less plausible when directed at the director of the Human Rights Division than at NGOs. The Charter, for all its ambiguities, was relatively explicit about what it saw as the main obstacle to an efficient and competent secretariat:

> In their performance of their duties the Secretary General and the staff shall not seek or receive instructions from any government or from any other authority external to the organization. Each member of the United Nations undertakes to respect the exclusively international character of the responsibilities of the Secretary General and the staff and not to seek to influence them in the discharge of their responsibilities.[8]

It is quite clear from this statement what the founders of the United Nations were concerned about. They had few illusions that members of the secretariat would take their duties so zealously as to interfere in the "internal affairs" of governments. But they did realize that an international civil service would be bombarded with political pressures from governments, and that it would require considerable courage to resist. That is why, when someone joins the United Nations, he or she pledges not to "interfere," but rather to remain independent from governments. The corresponding obligation on governments is to respect this independence. This is quite different from the rule requiring nongovernmental organizations not to make "politically motivated" attacks on governments.

The first pressure on van Boven came from the Soviet Union. Strictly speaking, the Soviet Union should have been denied any posts in the U.N., because it had refused to accept the principle of an independent secretariat. (All Soviet officials in the U.N. are seconded from the Soviet government.) The Soviets were particularly keen to gain access to the unit in the Human Rights Division that handled confidential communications. Here they could learn the identity of Eastern European dissidents. In spite of American charges to the contrary, they did not succeed. Van Boven adamantly refused to appoint a Soviet to the unit that handled communications. This won him no compliments from his superiors or Western states, but it did ensure the unending hostility of the Soviets.[9]

Russian displeasure was, however, child's play compared to what van Boven was putting up with from Gabriel Martínez. Martínez moved quickly to throw van Boven off balance. Within days of van Boven's moving into his office Martínez sent him a note demanding to know why a statement by Rodolfo Matarollo had been printed in summary records. It is standard U.N. practice for public debates to be recorded unless a special decision is taken to the contrary, but Martínez's note suggested that van Boven had deliberately slipped Matarollo's statement in. Trivial, yes, but also unsettling.

Van Boven decided early on that he would operate an open-door policy, and be available to anyone—even Rodolfo Matarollo. Matarollo telephoned and arranged a meeting. Van Boven then found he had another appointment and asked his secretary to cancel the meeting. His secretary innocently telephoned the Argentinian mission by mistake to arrange another appointment. Given that Matarollo was on the Junta's list of most-wanted "subversives" this was quite a mistake, rather like ringing Ronald Reagan and rearranging tea with Angela Davis. Van Boven thought it was amusing and shrugged it off, but Martínez put on a show of fury. The operative word is "show" because Martínez no doubt realized this could be valuable ammunition against the Dutchman. He visited Luigi Cotta-favi, an indolent Italian count who headed the U.N. office in Geneva, and followed up with a cable to William Buffum, van Boven's superior in New York.[10]

Martínez began to wage a bureacratic war of nerves—a war of unset-tling memos and brusque phone calls. On August 22 1977 he appeared in van Boven's office to complain that the Sub-Commission had broken for lunch before he had time to respond to charges. His concern was that his reply would appear in a different summary record from the substance of the debate (on disappearances) that morning. He was also angry that one of his statements had taken a long time to circulate. This complaint, too, was forwarded to van Boven's chief, William Buffum.[11] Van Boven's rec-ollection of the incident is that Martínez "launched a tirade" and stalked out of the office. In the corridor a Spanish-speaking colleague of van Boven overheard Martínez say angrily: "He's kicked me in the balls." Van Boven has a strong sense of propriety and the remark shocked him. But Martínez was, at this moment, in no mood for pleasantries. Two days later he would confront Antonio Cassese and Ben Whitaker in the Sub-Commission and be asked to withdraw.

As the pressure on van Boven grew, neither Cottafavi nor Buffum com-plained, and their silence can only have encouraged Martínez. The Argen-tinian was beginning to achieve his objective. It was characteristic of Martínez to assume at the start that his opponent was weaker than he was. It was not always true, but such was his confidence that he usually man-aged to make it so. It might start with a trivial issue—a hurried comment to a journalist or an unfortunate error in documents. In themselves these were minor and routine. But once the ambassador of Argentina had com-plained, they became significant—popping up out of nowhere, knocking people off balance, consuming time, and demanding precise explanations.

Martínez employed these tactics against van Boven from the very start. They were calculated not just to intimidate but also to goad him into an unwise response. He also made a habit of going over van Boven's head to his superiors in New York, and making sure a copy went not just to Wil-liam Buffum, but to Secretary General Kurt Waldheim as well. This made the charges doubly, triply unsettling for van Boven, particularly as neither Waldheim nor Buffum made any effort to slap the Argentinians down. Jay Long, Buffum's assistant, was asked about this later in an interview. He shrugged it off: "The Argentinians were always up to something. It happened all the time. We didn't take it seriously."[12] That was a fatal mistake. It encouraged Martínez to twist the knife.

There is no particular reason to think that Martínez took his campaign on van Boven personally in these early days. He was too seasoned a diplomat to let emotions get in the way. Van Boven, on the other hand, did take the threats personally, as he was intended to. He began to find Martínez's speeches—and his comments about the need to "cleanse" Argentinian society—distasteful and even fascist. He began to sympathize with people like Matarollo, who were on the receiving end of the invective.

This began to blur his political judgment. On June 27 1978 van Boven received a letter from León de Cárdenas, a Uruguayan official at the U.N. asking for help in locating his twenty-three-year-old nephew Fernando who had been arrested in Buenos Aires. Van Boven sent the letter over to Martínez, together with a personal appeal. The letter began: "As you are aware the Division of Human Rights has been receiving over the last few years a large number of communications asking for assistance and seeking information concerning arrested and disappeared persons in Argentina."

Two weeks later Martínez wrote back a dark and glowering reply pointing out that no U.N. body had as yet passed judgment on these "politically motivated" communications. (This was of course true, thanks to the Soviet votes at the U.N. Sub-Commision.) "I take it badly," wrote Martínez, "that a U.N. official allows himself to prejudge these U.N. organs. Is the Director of the Division accustomed to doing personal favors, to bypass U.N. procedures?"[13]

"That," recalled van Boven later of the note, "was a nasty one." But his own note had been unwise. He had allowed himself to be goaded into a reply by Martínez and he should not have been surprised by the reaction.

A month later, at the summer session of the U.N.'s Economic and Social Council, Gabriel Martínez accused van Boven of "total impudence" in the way his office had encouraged "terrorists." It was another accusation that should have prompted a concerned and angry response from van Boven's superiors. Instead, there was a deafening silence. A deep enmity now existed between Theo van Boven and Gabriel Martínez. It was such an open secret that Pierre Sanon, van Boven's deputy, who was on friendly terms with Martínez, offered to bring the two men together at a lunch. Van Boven curtly refused.[14]

As 1977 gave way to 1978 without any visible U.N. pressure on the Junta, van Boven began to feel that the U.N. was betraying the relatives of those who had disappeared in Argentina. He loathed the Argentinian and the loathing was reciprocated. In a cable back to the Argentinian Foreign Ministry in 1979, Martínez described van Boven as "consistently hostile" to Argentina.[15]

It is clear that van Boven had lost some of the detachment required of an international civil servant. But his clash with Martínez must be put into perspective. Neither he nor Martínez were able to remain neutral on what was happening in Argentina. But there can be no doubt about which man better served human rights and the aims of the U.N.

Van Boven Visits Chile

In July 1978, Theo van Boven took part in a U.N. human rights investigation in Chile. It had been almost five years since Pinochet had seized power. Many outraged reports had been published, but Pinochet had dug in tenaciously. Drawing on the advice of the "Chicago School" of American economists, he had anticipated Martínez de Hoz, opened up Chile's economy, and been rewarded with an economic boom that kept Chile's powerful middle class content. By 1978 disappearances had stopped. Torture was still occurring, but was no longer spectacular as it had been at the time of the 1973 coup. The dictatorship was dour and stifling, but no longer glamorous. That role was now reserved for Argentina.

There was some argument, then, for seeing the U.N. visit to Chile in 1978 as a striking example of the U.N.'s tardiness, even irrelevance. This was not the case. The visit would turn out to be almost as significant for the U.N., and Theo van Boven, as the visit to Argentina had proved for Amnesty International in 1976.

As a Dutch delegate to the U.N. Human Rights Commission, van Boven had played an important role in establishing the special U.N. group on Chile in 1975. He had then watched with dismay as Chile had given and then withdrawn permission for the group to visit. For the last two years the U.N. had done little more than issue shrill denunciations. Pinochet had matched insult with insult. But behind the outraged façade, moderates in the Chilean government were urging Pinochet to admit the U.N. group. The word was passed to van Boven during the U.N. Human Rights Commission in March 1978 and negotiations then began between van Boven and a Chilean delegation in New York.

There was much at stake for van Boven. After one year as Director of the Human Rights Division, he was keen to push the U.N. into a more activist investigating role. At the same time, he was aware of the need not to set a precedent which would compromise future U.N. investigations. The U.N. would not pay any price for the privilege of visiting Santiago. The Chileans agreed that the U.N. team would have virtually unlimited access in Chile. The only concession made by the U.N. was to offer the Chileans the chance to comment on any report before it was published. The team set out for Santiago on July 12.[16]

On arrival they found that the Chileans had arranged for a fleet of limousines and a program of cocktail parties so onerous that the group would have little time for work. They refused the limos, took U.N. cars from the airport, and canceled all social engagements except those considered absolutely necessary. They could not turn down a visit to President Augusto Pinochet. It took place on the top floor of the Diego Portales building that Allende had built for the 1972 meeting of the U.N. Conference on Trade and Development. Ushered in by armed guards, they found Pinochet dressed in civilian clothes and seated behind an empty desk. He lectured them about the evils of Marxism. Abdoulaye Dieye, a Senegalese judge who was the African member on the U.N. group, took issue with the dictator. Pinochet's brow darkened at being lectured by an African, but Dieye remained unperturbed. Van Boven recalls that Felix Ermacora, the Western representative, seemed distinctly uncomfortable. Ermacora, an Austrian, was a right-wing politician himself.[17] At the end of the meeting, van Boven had the distinct impression that Ermacora clicked his heels, Prussian-style.

The investigation began. They went to poorhouses and the prison in Valparaiso. They talked with three former democratically elected presidents of Chile. They even visited the Villa Grimaldi, one of the places where officials from DINA, the secret police, had tortured their prisoners. It had since been turned into an officers' club. It was an unlikely group that turned up at the Villa Grimaldi. The U.N. team was accompanied by General Odelier Meña, head of the intelligence service (CNI) which had replaced DINA. They also took along two Chileans, Rodrigo Muñoz Muñoz and Héctor Zamorano, who had been tortured in the Villa Grimaldi. Together they tramped through the elegant building. The officials denied that any torture had taken place there. Preposterous notion, said General Meña. The two former prisoners knew better and they had one concrete lead to follow. Photographs had been taken of them during their detention at the villa and published in newspapers. One of the photos showed what appeared to be tiles at eye level on the wall behind. Muñoz Muñoz thought that the tiles had been colored blue.[18]

They had been hooded during their ordeal, but they still remembered a lot. Just about here, said Zamorano pointing, there would have been a stairway; and there it was. And here, said Muñoz Muñoz, was the court-yard and the bench where his jailers had made him sit, manacled and blind-folded, and forced him to eat excrement. Wasn't there an iron gate somewhere over there to the right? Everyone looked. There was a gate. Here was where they had been stripped, plunged into water, had electric shocks applied to their genitals. Over there was the tree where they had been tied, blindfolded, before a mock firing squad.

The Chileans had made elaborate, but not quite successful, attempts to eradicate all traces of the villa's former functions. The group visited one room. What did they see but blue tiles at eye level. General Odelier Meña reddened. But he still managed to stay silent. Muñoz Muñoz talked of the men who actually tortured him. Once the hood had slipped, and he had caught a glimpse of a thin man with a moustache and black curly hair. He described it as a "Turkish" face. The group came out of the main building. Muñoz Muñoz suddenly froze and pointed. "Standing over there by that car. That thin man." The group went over. The man looked blank and said he was a chauffeur.

Muñoz Muñoz's claims might not have stood up in a court of law, but the group had no trouble believing him. The marks on his body from repeated beatings and electric shocks were certainly convincing.[19]

"Hats Off to Those Fascist Bastards"

Approximately eight hundred people disappeared in Chile during and af-ter the 1973 coup, and the U.N. group proposed an international panel of inquiry.[20] The proposal was quickly rejected by the Chileans on the grounds that it would be "selective." "Why not a panel on missing Cam-bodians or Vietnamese?" they asked.

In spite of this, the group managed to arrange a dramatic meeting with relatives of disappeared persons. This was not on the official itinerary; the group members and U.N. staff left their base at the Economic Commis-sion for Latin America by a side entrance. The rendezvous turned out to be in a movie theater. Halfway there, two members (Dieye and Kamara) got cold feet. They said that they had nothing to offer the relatives and that the meeting could turn into a shambles. Felix Ermacora, however, opted to continue with McCarthy and van Boven. Ermacora usually struck van Boven as inflexible and pedantic, but on this occasion his inflexibility seemed admirable.

The meeting was dignified yet emotional. Over four hundred relatives were present, almost all women, and they were carrying photos of their sons and daughters. They broke into applause when the group entered the cinema, and eight of the women then came forward and told their story. "We know you can't offer us anything," they began, hesitantly. "Don't worry. It's enough that you're here." They referred repeatedly to a torturer named Osvaldo Romo. Eventually, the U.N. visitors got up to leave. Van Boven lingered and the women started singing a hymn. They came up and hugged him, weeping and begging him not to abandon them.

Van Boven found it profoundly moving. Suddenly, those dry, interminable speeches and reports had been translated into shattered families. On the way back to the hotel he tried to get his feelings under control. What could be done? He toyed with the idea of refusing to leave the country until the Chileans started coming up with some answers. He dismissed the idea; it was clearly not practical. But he did resolve that the regime should be made to answer for the disappearances, and that it should not be rewarded with a clean bill of health simply for having allowed in a U.N. team of inquiry. Shortly afterward one of the U.N. secretaries pointed out in a matter-of-fact way that many more people were disappearing in Argentina than had ever disappeared in Chile. Van Boven was thunderstruck.

Even Felix Ermacora, who had seemed uncomfortable at the tears in the theater, found himself absorbed by the intellectual challenge. He took up the issue with the Chilean government, and found that the Ministry of the Interior had a thick file on each case. This appealed to the lawyer in him. It was tidy and methodical. When the three members of the group divided up the information in preparation for drafting the report, Ermacora asked for disappearances.[21]

The Chileans tried to the end to influence the U.N. group. Van Boven found himself put in the first-class section on the flight back to New York. He did not want any favors and asked for a second-class seat. Sorry, came the smooth reply, but there were no second-class seats left. Each member was also given a full-size portrait of Pinochet. In general, though, the Chilean government lived up to its side of the bargain. There were no retaliations or reprisals; the visit was fully covered and advertised in the press. The visit was even extended three days beyond the original schedule. The mood of the U.N. team was summed up by one of its members: "Hats off to those fascist bastards."

But if the Chileans had expected a reward, they did not get it. The U.N. group produced a massive report of two hundred and thirty-one pages with eighty separate annexes which covered everything from the Chilean constitution to the visit to the Villa Grimaldi. Stuck in the middle was a bizarre centerfold showing Muñoz Muñoz's wounds. The report also took in health, unemployment, the government budget, child welfare, and even labor legislation (in an effort to underline the pitiless nature of Pinochet's right-wing economic policies). This was stretching human rights to the limit. Most governments would have viewed it as "interference" in their internal affairs, but it was also one of the most useful, and imaginative, reports ever produced by the U.N.

The Chileans were torn between pride at having been the first country to admit a U.N. human rights inquiry and bitter fury at the tone and scope of the report: "The working group has overstepped its mandate. . . . it has also stretched the definition of human rights to incredible limits."[22] They had cooperated, but instead of being rewarded and encouraged, they were getting punished.

Worse was to come. The group was abolished by the Human Rights Commission in February 1979 only to be replaced by a thicket of three new probes, no less thorny: a new fund for Chilean torture victims, a separate report on Chile's disappearances, and an annual report on general human rights abuses to be presented at the Human Rights Commission and General Assembly. It was the U.N. Human Rights Commission which took these decisions, but the Chileans blamed van Boven. The Americans never forgave or forgot. Gabriel Martínez, the Argentinian ambassador, also took note. His cables repeatedly pointed to the way the case of Chile had been "institutionalized."[23]

This raised a crucial issue. Should a government be rewarded simply for allowing a human rights team into the country? Some of van Boven's U.N. colleagues, including William Buffum and Jay Long, certainly thought so. But van Boven believed, as Amnesty had believed in Argentina, that his first obligation was to the victims not the villains. He had seen the United Nations in a different context on this trip. People had come up to him in health clinics and whispered messages: "Don't let us down—you're all we've got." More dispassionately, lawyers who worked with the Chilean Church had also urged keeping up the pressure. Anything else, they said, would be seen as condoning the past killing and torture.

"Be very careful of the notion of improvement," they added. "One murder may appear to be an improvement over two, but it is still murder. Besides, nothing has really changed underneath. Barring an accident Pinochet is in power until 1990. What happens if things take a sudden and drastic change for the worse? If the economy collapses and people start rioting? If the regime suddenly turns its fury on us—the human rights groups? What would the U.N. do? Apologize? Crank up another investigation?"

No, they insisted, the U.N. had a duty to keep up the pressure. Anything less would be a betrayal. Van Boven agreed. He never saw his role, or that of the U.N., as helping to inch Chile towards democracy. The role, he thought, was human rights, not political mediation. Nor was this the time or the place for neutrality. The U.N. simply had to take a firm stand on behalf of the victims of Pinochet's miserable regime. There could be no compromising.[24]

This visit to Chile accelerated a change in van Boven that had already been set in motion by the attacks of Gabriel Martínez. He was becoming, in U.N. terms, an "activist," shedding his neutrality, taking sides. It was at this point, too, that his fascination with Latin America began. He was an unlikely convert. He didn't speak Spanish and he had never visited the continent, as student or holiday-maker. He was initiated into its mysteries by desperate, obsessed people whose relatives had been tortured and killed. It was intense, passionate, intoxicating. He was ready to take on the Junta over the disappearances in Argentina.

11. The Junta's Bluff

On December 20 1978, the U.N. General Assembly finally passed a resolution expressing deep concern over the "disappearance of persons as a result of excesses on the part of law enforcement and security authorities." This was the fruit of three years of debate by the United Nations system, and still it did not refer to Argentina by name. Yet Gabriel Martínez realized that it represented a threat, as he pointed out in a cable. The noose was beginning to close. The International Labor Organization had publicly condemned the wholescale assault by the Junta against Argentinian labor unions earlier in 1978. UNESCO was preparing to take up the disappearances at its next session in May 1979.[1]

The next hurdle facing Martínez personally would be the session of the United Nations Human Rights Commission, due to start in Geneva on February 1 1979. Martínez was now a master of U.N. procedure, but he also knew that this was no time to relax. Critics were crowding in on every side. Martínez was immediately made aware of the unfriendly atmosphere in Geneva as the Commission began its work. He complained in a March 26 cable back to Buenos Aires that the relatives of disappeared persons in Argentina had sent a letter to each delegation on the Commission. In addition, he wrote, Mothers had appeared in the U.N. Palace wearing their distinctive white scarves. Outside the building, their supporters staged a brief demonstration. Then there was the "hostile attitude" of the U.N. secretariat and its director, Theo van Boven. Martínez probably knew that it was during this session of the Commission that van Boven first met personally with the Argentinian Mothers. Van Boven found it almost as moving as his meeting with the Chilean relatives in the Santiago cinema the previous summer.

Martínez was joined on Argentina's delegation by Enrique Ros, Argentina's ambassador to the United Nations in New York. The two made an effective team, but they were at a technical disadvantage because Argentina was still not a member of the Commission. This meant they would have to marshal their defense from the sidelines.

Soon after the opening of the session, seven Western delegations proposed a resolution that went considerably further than the General Assembly resolution and called on the U.N. Secretary General to collect and analyze information on disappearances. The resolution mentioned Argentina by name. It was coming close to proposing the kind of working group set up on Chile, which would undoubtedly would have meant the "institutionalization" of the charges against Argentina.

During his four years as ambassador, Gabriel Martínez had built up a formidable number of personal contacts as well as foes and he now began to call in some favors, starting with the Yugoslavians. Martínez later said in a cable that he immediately got "total agreement" that the "unfair Western resolution" had to be blocked.[2] He then sat down and drafted an innocuous-looking amendment to the Western resolution which was accepted by five Nonaligned delegations. Martínez then canvassed the six Socialist government delegations on the Commission and found them happy to offer support. This must have been reassuring.

The tables had been turned. The Western group was now on the defensive. Under the U.N. rules, amendments to resolutions must be put to a vote before the actual resolution and the Argentinians appeared to have a majority for their counterproposal. Negotiations between Argentina and the West to find a compromise text began in a small room behind the Commission. The meetings went on late into the night in a mood of mutual suspicion. Martínez and Ros could be seen stalking in and out, with Martínez clearly relishing the attention. The tension began to seep out into the corridors where the Mothers were waiting anxiously. Martínez and Ros were cocky. They insisted that they could win in a vote. The Nonaligned, after all, accounted for sixteen of the thirty-two seats on the Commission.

In private, however, the Argentinians were much less confident. They realized that although Nonaligned countries shared broad foreign policy goals there was no single issue that united the group, least of all human rights in Argentina. Besides which, the Junta viewed the Nonaligned Movement with considerable ambivalence. It despised the least developed nations, and often broke ranks with them. A comprehensive analysis produced by the Argentinian Foreign Ministry in 1980 would recall that the Junta had increased its commercial ties with hated South Africa and adopted an "ambiguous" position on liberation movements and Palestinian rights. This was a snub to the Nonaligned.[3]

Still the Western negotiators declined to call Martínez's bluff. As a result, they lost yet another round. Accounts vary about how the negotiations broke down. In one of his round-up cables, Martínez states that the negotiators agreed upon a compromise text, which was promptly rejected by the United States, causing great consternation.[4] One participant in the talks remembers it differently. He remembers the Argentinian team repeatedly asking for more time and dragging out the negotiations until the eleventh hour. Yvon Beaulne, the Canadian, then impatiently demanded a reply. Martínez and Ros stood up from the table without a word and walked out. By now it was too late to salvage a resolution, and the issue was postponed for another year, until the 1980 Commission meeting.

Martínez had gained more valuable time and he was elated. "Once more our delegation was able to avoid the condemnation and institutionalization of 'the case of Argentina' in the United Nations," he boasted in a cable to his foreign minister.[5] He was right. But Martínez also knew that the humiliated Western delegations would not forgive him when the Commission next met in a year's time. One cable from the U.S. ambassador in Geneva, William Vanden Heuvel, concluded bitterly that Western tactics had failed precisely because they had been aimed at "appeasing" Argentina.[6] It was time for Martínez to pull another rabbit out of the hat. He turned for help to a most improbable ally.

Confidential U-Turn

For three years Gabriel Martínez had threatened, bullied, and destroyed careers to keep Argentina's name off the U.N. 1503 blacklist. Now he did an extraordinary 180-degree turn and advised the Junta to cooperate. This was the way he put it, in a March 26 cable:

> For obvious reasons I believe it is useful to ensure the confidential passage of the communications and not—this time—to interrupt the denunciations on disappearances. This will have the following result at the 1980 session of the Commission: First, the debate on Argentina will be closed. Second, it will preclude any other action to reopen the issue in a public debate. We should facilitate the passage of some communications in the Sub-Commission.[7]

This was breathtakingly cynical and breathtakingly clever. It was cynical because Martínez had for three years employed a vicious campaign of innuendo and denigration to keep Argentina off the blacklist. It was clever because he realized that, since Argentina could no longer hide behind confidentiality, the only option was to use it. Martínez's own analysis evidently suggested that the risks were slight. During 1979, according to his files, the U.N. human rights secretariat inquired about 13,124 individual cases from sixty-one governments. It received back information on precisely 235.[8] Suddenly Gabriel Martínez turned into an ardent advocate of "quiet diplomacy."

The attitude of the five members of the Sub-Commission who were supposed to review communications at the first all-important stage must have seemed equally reassuring. The Latin American and African subcommissioners failed to attend, while the three that remained included two of Argentina's allies: Pirzada of Pakistan and Smirnov of the Soviet Union.[9] The group agreed to send on the names of seven governments to the full Sub-Commission: Argentina, Chile, Tunisia, Uruguay, Central African Empire, Indonesia, and Paraguay. In the case of Argentina, they even decided to add a further three communications to the three pending from the previous year. One had been prepared by a group of exiled Argentinian lawyers, including Rodolfo Matarollo.

This decision did not deserve to pass unnoticed. It was the first time in four years that a Soviet had voted to criticize Argentina in the U.N. over human rights. Smirnov and Pirzada had faithfully voted on behalf of the Argentinian Junta for three consecutive years. It would have taken only one of them to have cried off and the group would have lacked the necessary quorum of three. The only possible explanation is that both Pirzada and Smirnov had been co-opted into Martínez's scheme. Both, moreover, reversed this early vote and abstained during the final vote of the full Sub-Commission. The last thing they wanted was to appear enthusiastic.[10]

Argentina's abrupt change of strategy was bound to prove acutely uncomfortable for Mario Amadeo, the Argentinian subcommissioner who had pleaded for one year's grace the previous year and promised to personally investigate the disappearances. He must have known at the time that this was a promise he could not keep and that he was just another pawn to be sacrificed by the Junta. In a court of law, Amadeo would have been accused of contempt, but this United Nations body of "independent experts" did not even protest. It was with a touch of regret that they voted by 18 to 1 to send the name of Argentina on to the full Commission meeting the following February. The sole opposing vote was cast by the independent Mario Amadeo.

The subcommissioners had no way of knowing that they had fallen neatly into a trap set by the man who had harried and bullied them for four long years. How Martínez must have chuckled! In a September 6 cable following the vote, he even complained, tongue in cheek, that Amadeo's task had been made harder by the "tardy and partial replies" from Buenos Aires to the three communications that had remained pending since the previous year.[11] It had all been planned. He would now be able to argue that because the name of Argentina was on the U.N. confidential blacklist no individual cases could be discussed in any public debate. He was like a general retreating in good order, turning every hillock to his advantage and laying nasty surprises for the enemy.

Following this supposedly "confidential" decision, an article in the Argentinian newspaper *Clarin,* dated September 22 1979, gave full details of the confidential voting pattern. This could not have been done without their authorization of the Junta, but it was one final cynical gesture. Just a year earlier the Argentinians had menaced the correspondent for *Le Monde* for making similar disclosures.

Javier Pérez de Cuéllar, the Quiet Diplomat

Shortly after this meeting, Gabriel Martínez received convincing proof that that the U.N.'s confidential 1503 procedure could indeed provide Argentina with a refuge, when a U.N. emissary returned from a secret mission to Uruguay. The emissary's name was Javier Pérez de Cuéllar. He had gone to Uruguay to investigate a prison that was almost as notorious as Argentina's ESMA.

Liberty jail owed its name to an anonymous handful of bars and whitewashed houses that lay fifty-three miles to the west of Montevideo, on the main road. Inhabitants of the small, dusty pueblo tried to ignore the prison that sat, glowering, on the brow of the hill. They shut their doors when the military convoys thundered through the village and the helicopters flew in low over the fields before settling inside the prison perimeter. Unlike the ESMA, which was surrounded by bustle and traffic, photos of Liberty jail, taken with a telephoto lens, tended to exaggerate its size and isolation. They showed a massive, squat building, surrounded by barbed wire fences and outbuildings that rose above the fields. It looked half like a concentration camp, half like a nuclear power plant. Certainly, it needed to be big because Uruguay had very few large prisons and even fewer top security jails. The Uruguayan armed forces were ill-prepared for the logistics of guarding, let alone brainwashing, thousands of political prisoners.

Uruguay had suffered a cataclysmic descent into repression and terrorism during the second half of the 1960s when world meat prices plummeted, threatening Uruguay's cradle-to-grave welfare services. At the same time, agitation began among the poor sugarcane cutters and lead to the emergence of the Tupamaros. Named after Tupac Amaru, an Indian king who had fought the Spaniards, the Tupamaros grew into one of the most celebrated, ruthless guerrilla movements in Latin America.

A state of siege was declared in 1968. In September 1971 the army invited itself to take control of the war against the Tupamaros. On April 14 1972 the screw tightened further with the declaration of an internal state of war. By the end of 1972 all the Tupamaro leaders were in jail and the threat was extinguished, but the soldiers liked the taste of power. In 1973 they tired of the charade. The deputies were physically ejected from the ornate Congress building. Sentries moved in, urinated in corners, and set up braziers on the ornate wooden floors. Democracy had been snuffed out in the Switzerland of Latin America.[12]

Thousands of Uruguayans were detained and tortured, and hundreds disappeared for long, terrifying periods. Among them were Alejandro Artucio, the lawyer who would work with the ICJ in Geneva, and professor José Luís Massera, a world-renowned mathematician and first secretary of Uruguay's Communist party. Another well-known detainee was Miguel Angel Estrella, one of Latin America's best-known pianists.[13]

On August 15 1976, after nearly a year in jail without being charged, Professor Massera was finally accused of belonging to a "subversive association"—he wasn't present at the hearing—and sentenced by a military judge to twenty years in prison. It was, as his family and friends pointed out, tantamount to a death sentence for a sick, sixty-five-year-old man. It also made legal history. Massera's case was the first to be examined by the Human Rights Committee, comprising eighteen international lawyers—the only U.N. procedure which allows for individuals to lodge complaints against their governments. On April 18 1978, the committee found that Massera's detention violated nine key provisions in the International Covenant on Civil and Political Rights. Several months later the decision was made public. This was a major step toward toughening human rights law and rectifying some of the flaws noted earlier.[14]

Throughout the mid-1970s, the U.N. Human Rights Commission—an entirely separate body—was wrestling with the decision of whether to indict Uruguay for a "consistent pattern of gross violations" in public or private. The name of Uruguay entered the confidential 1503 blacklist in 1976. This left the U.N. Human Rights Commission with four options: drop the case altogether (politically impossible); "keep it under review" (as it had been doing without results for three years); send an emissary to Uruguay; or throw the case open. That no action had been taken between 1976 and 1979 was due to Carlos Giumbruno, Uruguay's delegate on the Commission. Giumbruno was a marvelous ham actor. He trembled, sweated, and sobbed. He also made sure that his delegation included at least two young women wearing tight skirts. What delegates did not know, as he talked with a quavering voice about the "ravages of subversion," was that his own nephew was behind bars in Liberty jail.

Faced by Giumbruno's histrionics, the Commission could not accuse Uruguay of refusing to cooperate, so instead of throwing the case open the Commission chose the third option of "direct contacts" and turned to U.N. Secretary General Kurt Waldheim to appoint an emissary. On August 24 1979 the president of Uruguay, Aparicio Méndez, wrote back saying that the government was prepared to cooperate. On December 10 1979, International Human Rights Day, Waldheim's Peruvian-born under secretary general for political affairs, Javier Pérez de Cuéllar, left New York for Montevideo.[15]

Pérez de Cuéllar was a man of vast experience and very little obvious personality. He had been one of Peru's most experienced ambassadors before joining the U.N., having served in Paris, London, Brasília, La Paz, and Moscow. His diplomatic career culminated, as it does for many Third World leaders, at his country's mission to the U.N. in New York. During this period, 1971 to 1975, he served as a spokesman for developing countries on economic matters. As such he would have been well known to the trade expert Gabriel Martínez in Geneva and Argentina's Minister of Finance Martínez de Hoz.

In October 1975 Waldheim invited Pérez de Cuéllar into his inner circle to handle the impossible job of bringing peace to the divided island of Cyprus. The assignment lasted until December 1977, and it was there that Pérez de Cuéllar made his mark as a patient, tactful mediator. In February 1979 Waldheim asked him to take the important post of under secretary general for political affairs. Within a year Pérez de Cuéllar had been handed another impossible job—trying to negotiate a withdrawal of Soviet troops from Afghanistan.

The key words throughout this impressive career were "tact" and "discretion." Pérez de Cuéllar was neutral—the quintessential "quiet diplomat." He was not a fanatical supporter of military rule, like Gabriel Martínez, but he certainly shared Martínez's ability to swim with the prevailing current. When a military coup toppled the elected government of Belaunde Terry in Peru in 1968, Pérez de Cuéllar officiated at the inauguration of the new military president.[16] Pérez de Cuéllar's responsibilities in Waldheim's entourage included Latin American affairs. This, combined with his nationality, made him an ideal choice for the sensitive human rights mission to Uruguay.

Theo van Boven visited New York in December 1979, hoping to give Pérez de Cuéllar some information on the prisoners in Liberty jail. It was hard to pin Pérez de Cuéllar down, because he was so busy. When they finally talked, Pérez evaded the issue of Uruguay and recalled a recent visit to North Korea which, he said, was very beautiful. Van Boven tried to remind Pérez de Cuéllar that the Human Rights Commission wanted some first-hand information about individual detainees, particularly Professor Massera and Miguel Estrella. Pérez de Cuéllar, however, saw his role rather differently. In his report he listed his priorities as showing respect for the sovereignty of the state, dealing only with the authorities (as opposed, presumably, to their critics), adopting a "cautious and flexible" approach, and working in strict confidentiality. Luckily, his report was leaked almost as soon as it was written.[17]

The Whitewash

About the same time, in early 1980, another report on Liberty jail was also leaked. For several years, the International Committee of the Red Cross had offered to visit detainees in Uruguay and had been rebuffed. In 1979, the regime finally relented. Jean-François Labarthe, a member of the Red Cross team, was a seasoned troubleshooter, but even he was not prepared for what he found in Liberty. He noted every aspect of daily life: the shaven heads; the rules that were suddenly and unpredictably changed; the petty restrictions against speaking, singing, even whistling; the simulated escapes (staged, said Labarthe, with guards dressed up as prisoners); the arbitrary punishment; the deliberate attempt to rob the prisoners of their identities. Labarthe estimated that ten percent of the prisoners in Liberty were mentally ill, and noted that "tens of thousands" of tranquilizers were handed out every month. The camp authorities put mentally ill prisoners in with the healthy, to break them both. The ill prisoner would then be interrogated about his cell mate. Wrote Labarthe: "When this mentally ill prisoner is returned to his cell, racked with guilt, he may attempt suicide."[18]

The effect of Liberty jail rubbed off on the hardened Labarthe and he found the interviews with the prisoners a considerable ordeal. "They no longer express any needs. They manage by trying to mask their pain and their unwillingness to show a deteriorated personality to a sympathetic interviewer. They tell the delegates of an anguished and impoverished life—of a silent isolation from persons, of psychological disturbances."

Officials at Red Cross headquarters in Geneva were appalled when Labarthe's report was leaked, but at least it showed that Red Cross officials understood horror when they were faced with it.[19] Javier Pérez de Cuéllar apparently did not. He prepared a majestically misleading report for the U.N. Human Rights Commission, based on the premise that the Uruguayan military had been right to introduce a state of siege, suspend the constitution, and pack legislators like Luís Massera off to Liberty jail. "No one," he concluded, "is being detained on account of his ideas."

Pérez de Cuéllar saved his best for the treatment of prisoners. He stated that he paid a "lengthy" visit to Liberty and also to Punta de Rieles, where the women were held. Prison conditions are "extremely reasonable." The guards are armed only with wooden truncheons for "purposes of self defense." Visits to prisoners are normal and regular. Correspondence (including parcels and foodstuffs) is allowed.

Something very odd is going on here. Is this the same Liberty jail witnessed by Labarthe of the Red Cross? The Liberty jail of "anguished and impoverished lives . . . silent isolation . . . psychological disturbance?" Clearly not. The decisions of the U.N. Human Rights Commission, a recent report of the Inter-American Commission on Human Rights, reports by Amnesty, the International Commission of Jurists, and the International League for Human Rights—all were studiously ignored. Javier Pérez de Cuéllar, the future Secretary General of the United Nations, had allowed himself to be hoodwinked by the Uruguayan torturers.

Pérez de Cuéllar might have learned a little more of what went on behind Liberty's grim walls if he had followed the instructions of the U.N. Human Rights Commission and spent some time with prisoners. He made the following breezy comment: "As for the physical condition of the detainees Mr. Pérez de Cuéllar found that they all appeared healthy. Among the many prisoners whom he was able to meet were Messrs. Altessor, Estrella, Massera and Turcanski."

Pérez de Cuéllar's report was due to be reviewed at the U.N. Human Rights Commission meeting in February 1980. Miguel Estrella, the pianist, had been released from Liberty jail and was living in Paris. Alejandro Artucio was by now in Geneva working with the International Commission of Jurists. When he got wind of Pérez de Cuéllar's report he telephoned Estrella, who then came to Geneva, where the Commission was meeting. After being introduced to Theo van Boven, who had personally campaigned for his release, Estrella sat down and wrote out a short note denying that he had ever been visited by Pérez de Cuéllar. Later, in a fuller statement, he did recall seeing someone in civilian clothes who had put his head around the cell door and wished him good day. Estrella had taken this man, presumably Pérez de Cuéllar, for an arms salesman.[20]

This was a serious charge to make of such a senior U.N. official, but van Boven insisted that it be passed to the president of the Commission, Waleed Sadi from Jordan, and circulated as an official U.N. document. Sadi showed the note to Mohamed al-Jabiri, the head of the Iraqi delegation and chairman of the group of five delegates reviewing the 1503 blacklist. Al-Jabiri read it out in public, much to the indignation of the Uruguayan delegate Carlos Giumbruno. The Human Rights Commission was now faced with a dilemma. Should Uruguay be "kept under review?" Should it be dropped from the 1503 blacklist? Should contacts be maintained? At first sight the case should have been dropped. Otherwise what point was there in sending an investigator and ignoring his conclusions? Such a move, however, would have been greeted with outrage by human rights groups. The whole thing had become acutely embarrassing.

Estrella's short note helped to tip the balance against Uruguay. Mohamed al-Jabiri recommended that it be entered in the U.N. records, that Uruguay be kept under review, and that Secretary General Waldheim persevere with direct contacts. One observer recalls that Carlos Giumbruno was almost in tears.

Javier Pérez de Cuéllar did not come to Geneva personally, and the task of informing him about the Commission's irritation fell to Theo van Boven. Van Boven is convinced that it sowed the seeds of future confrontation between them.[21] Equally important were the implications for the U.N.'s human rights machinery. This trip by Pérez de Cuéllar was the first example of a U.N. emissary assuming a political role. This was bad enough. That Pérez de Cuéllar sided with one of Latin America's most brutal regimes against its victims was almost incredible. In this, Pérez de Cuéllar was out of step with the general climate in 1979. But it might not always be that way.

As for the U.N.'s confidential 1503 procedure, it had played into the hands of the dictators. Gabriel Martínez had good reason to feel confident.[22]

Van Boven's Phone is Tapped

The end of 1979 found Martínez plotting his next move. He pulled it all together in one key cable, sent on September 13. His most startling comments concerned Theo van Boven. All pretense of balance has gone. Theo van Boven, said Martínez, must be destroyed:

> Van Boven is a declared enemy of our country. We must keep up active criticism in order to weaken his authority and prestige with other members. We can take advantage of the personality of Mr. van Boven, and the internal tensions in his Division that have resulted from irregularities in the Division and denunciations against officials, including the deputy director of the Division, Pierre Sanon. These irregularities are at present being aired at the level of the Secretary General of the United Nations, and have been reported in the press.[23]

This was a venomous cable, even more so because the "irregularities" that Martínez was referring to were indeed irregular. Pierre Sanon had been in Upper Volta's mission in New York when, in 1976, he was proposed for the prestigious job of Deputy Director of the Division, traditionally held by an African. He was rejected by the U.N. board on appointments as unqualified for the job, but made it through the second time round, helped by some energetic lobbying on his behalf by Jay Long, William Buffum's assistant. Sanon and Long were friends. Sanon also knew Martínez and had offered to mediate between the Argentinian and van Boven.[24]

Initially, van Boven took to Sanon and began to delegate responsibilty to him, ignoring the fact that he was unpopular with other staff members. By 1979, van Boven was preparing a conference in Africa to start the process of framing an African charter on human rights. The prime mover behind this was Kéba M'baye, a distinguished Senegalese jurist. Sanon and

M'baye had different views about the way the conference should be run and in May 1980 van Boven held a long telephone conversation with M'baye in Dakar about the seminar. Two days later Sanon was talking to van Boven's personal assistant, Bertie Ramcharam. To Ramcharam's surprise Sanon theatrically closed all the windows and the door to his office, before bringing out a small tape recorder and playing a perfect recording of the conversation between van Boven and M'baye. The recording began with van Boven's opening words, suggesting that his device was permanently attached, not switched on just for the conversation.

Ramcharam later said that he hesitated before telling van Boven. Van Boven took the news calmly at first, but two days later, after a long talk with his wife, his mood had changed. He was determined that Sanon had to go. William Buffum arrived in Geneva a few days later. When van Boven told him what had happened, Buffum agreed that it was intolerable and that Sanon should be suspended. Sanon was away on leave at the time and he was astonished and upset to learn the news on his return. Van Boven sent him off to New York to cover a meeting, to get him out of the way.

Sanon then started lobbying, and the next thing van Boven knew Buffum was on the phone saying that the Americans were trying to get Sanon a senior job in the office of the U.N. High Commissioner for Refugees. Would van Boven kindly not say anything to jeopardize the appointment? Van Boven was astounded. Buffum had changed tack completely and was now proposing that Sanon be promoted—after the fellow had been caught bugging his superior's telephone! Van Boven insisted that Sanon had to go. He even threatened to resign if the man got another job in the United Nations system. At this delicate juncture, the affair became public, with newspaper reports hinting broadly that Sanon might be a CIA agent.

Eventually, the U.N. established a team of inquiry. Sanon stopped working but stayed on in Geneva on his salary for several more weeks. It was an uncomfortable time for both him and van Boven. Before Sanon left Geneva at the end of 1979 he had one last emotional telephone conversation with the author, who broke the story. Almost sobbing, he said that his children had been abused at school and that his own career was at an end. It was a miserable end to a miserable affair, and to this day only Sanon knows the truth.[25]

Van Boven did not know that the incident almost cost him, and not Sanon, his job. William Buffum's deputy in New York, Jay Long, was a close friend of Sanon. Long conducted his own inquiry into the affair and accepted Sanon's explanation. He then spent considerable time weighing whether or not to recommend van Boven's dismissal. Van Boven, concerned at the long silence, talked to some American friends. The word got back to Assistant Secretary of State for Human Rights Patricia Derian, who asked Donald McHenry, U.S. ambassador to the United Nations, to make it abundantly clear to Buffum that van Boven had full American support. Derian did not know van Boven personally, and van Boven himself never knew how much he owed to the Americans nor how completely he was deserted by his superiors.

The Sanon episode would be a footnote in the main story were it not for the fact that Jay Long and van Boven never fully trusted each other again. Van Boven thought Long had intrigued against him, and Long evidently thought van Boven had acted like a clumsy Dutch peasant. It created a yawning, and potentially disastrous, split within the U.N. secretariat and played into the hands of van Boven's deadly enemy, Gabriel Martínez. The September 13 1979 cable shows that Martínez knew the scandal that could be exploited in his campaign. He knew that Under Secretary General William Buffum's confidence in his Dutch deputy had been shaken.

Of all the many cables sent by Gabriel Martínez, this is one of the most sinister. Nothing and no one would be allowed to stand in the way of Argentina's counterattack—least of all the fragile independence of the U.N. secretariat.

III

The Carter Years

12. Derian into the Lion's Den

Patricia Derian likes to show visitors a photograph taken during her official visit to Argentina in 1977 as U.S. Assistant Secretary of State for Human Rights. It shows her wedged between two generals, one of them President Jorge Videla, on a sofa. The military men are clearly as uncomfortable at her presence as she is at theirs. There are grimaces all around instead of smiles. Here is someone profoundly ill at ease with authority.[1]

By the time this remarkable picture was taken, the disappearances in Argentina were beginning to shape Jimmy Carter's human rights policy, much as they were doing to the United Nations in Geneva. They were also beginning to affect Patricia Derian personally, just as they were affecting Theo van Boven. We know how it happened to van Boven, but how did it happen to Derian? How did a former nurse from Mississippi find herself on a couch beside—of all people—Lieutenant General Jorge Videla?

For Derian herself, it began with the years of political and emotional upheaval that accompanied and followed the war in Vietnam.[2] By the early 1970s, she will say, there was a growing conviction in the United States that morality had to find its way back into American foreign policy. This intensified following the disclosure of CIA involvement in the 1973 coup which killed Salvador Allende in Chile and ushered an era of ugly military rule into one of Latin America's most democractic nations.

Congress then seized the initiative from an executive that was badly weakened by Watergate, and forced through a series of laws banning the delivery of U.S. aid to repressive regimes. The assault began in 1973, when Congress added an amendment to the 1961 Foreign Assistance Act expressing its sense that U.S. military aid should be denied to any government that held political prisoners. In June 1974 the administration announced that it was ignoring the suggestion because it was impossible to define "political prisoner."[3] Later in the year, Congressman Donald Fraser proposed another amendment (502B) to the Foreign Assistance Act calling on the president to deny security aid to governments that engaged in a "consistent pattern of gross violations of internationally recognized human rights." This was to set the tone for a range of legislative restrictions which were to spread to U.S. economic aid, international development banks, and even the private sector.[4]

Fraser was chairman of the House Subcommittee on International Organizations and Movements and a leading champion in Congress of human rights. The previous year, 1973, he had chaired a long and well-publicized series of hearings whose first witness had been Niall Mac-Dermot, the craggy, patrician Secretary General of the International Commission of Jurists. MacDermot had just returned from Chile, and he was still shaken by a remarkable conversation with Pinochet's Minister of Justice that he was able to share with Fraser's subcommittee. "Why are so many prisoners denied access to lawyers?" he had asked. "Why should they need lawyers?" came the Chilean's reply. "They haven't been charged with any crime."[5]

By 1975 502B was still only a "sense of Congress" amendment, which meant it was not binding on the executive. But the sense was clear enough and it evidently did not please Secretary of State Henry Kissinger. Kissinger was happy to use American muscle to maintain U.S. hegemony over its self-proclaimed sphere of interest, even if it meant overthrowing democratically chosen rulers like Allende in Chile. Yet he had warned at his nomination hearings in 1973 against the United States interfering in the domestic affairs of other countries.[6] He consulted U.S. embassies about the human rights records of countries that were receiving U.S. aid, and then refused to release the findings. A State Department message to Congress argued that there was no "adequate objective way" of deciding which nations were the worst violators—a tacit admission that valued U.S. allies like the Philippines, South Korea, and Indonesia had lamentable records.[7]

The war of nerves continued. Congress insisted on restricting economic aid to Chile, and the administration made it up with credit to buy food aid.[8] In 1976, frustrated by Kissinger's stonewalling, Congress turned 502B from a suggestion into a mandatory requirement. This was vetoed by President Ford on May 7 1976. Congress and the administration then reached a compromise, which was signed into law by Ford on June 30 1976.

Both sides won something from the compromise. Congress won agreement that human rights was a "principal goal" of U.S. foreign policy. It was also agreed that the State Department would issue human rights reports on all governments receiving U.S. security aid. By now a solid institutional base had also been created. Fraser's 1973 hearings had recommended the creation of a new human rights bureau and the appointment of a human rights legal advisor, both within the State Department. Charles Runyon, a former Yale University law professor, was appointed to the legal post. Fraser then asked for the appointment of a human rights policymaker and James Wilson, a career foreign service officer, was duly moved to the office of Deputy Secretary of State Robert Ingersoll as Coordinator for Humanitarian Affairs.[9]

On the other hand, 502B contained a significant loophole. U.S. security aid could continue to gross violators "in extraordinary circumstances," or when it was in U.S. "national interests." The administration would have to justify any such exceptions, but the loophole would clearly be very useful to a Secretary of State like Kissinger, whose heart was clearly not in 502B.

The underlying disagreement between Congress and the executive over human rights was not just about which branch controlled foreign policy. It was about substance. To Kissinger, a foreign policy that penalized U.S. allies made no sense. Jeane Kirkpatrick would make the same point in a withering 1979 critique of Carter's human rights policy.[10]

Fraser's response was that if "security aid" meant training torturers then aid was being misused and no one's security was being enhanced. True, there was a strong reformist undercurrent to this. Fraser was quite prepared to use the leverage provided by American aid to promote democracy in non-Communist countries. He might also have pointed to the fact that the United Nations had been trying for ten years to assess human rights "objectively," albeit with varying degrees of success.[11] Equally important, the U.N. Charter gave governments the right—even the duty—to protest violations outside their own frontiers. Even the language of 502B was taken from the U.N.'s 1503 procedure.[12]

Yet Fraser's subcommittee was very different from the U.N. Human Rights Commission. In 1976, Leonard Garment, U.S. delegate to the Commission, bemoaned his recent experience in Geneva, which he described as "a nice forgotten place with a sleepy press corps and no spectator interest."[13] Donald Fraser's subcommittee, in contrast, hogged headlines and galvanized American lawmakers. It was also far more a tribunal than the U.N. Commission. In the dock—more often than not—were U.S. allies.

These governments were rarely given the right to respond, but their critics were welcomed, and unlike Senate hearings there was no ban on foreigners giving testimony. Rarely, if ever, were credentials challenged. When Fraser held a hearing on Argentina on September 29 1976 the witnesses included Gustavo Roca and Lucio Garzón Maceda, two exiled lawyers who, with Rodolfo Matarollo, were busy in CADHU. About the same time, Matarollo's testimony before the U.N. in Geneva was provoking a furious counterattack from Gabriel Martínez, but Maceda was listened to in respectful silence. Jacobo Timerman, the Argentinian newspaper editor, was so irritated that he wrote to Fraser complaining of Maceda's "obvious partiality" and asked for the chance to present a more balanced picture.[14] Fraser wrote back loftily, turning him down. He could afford to. Henry Kissinger and others may have fumed at Fraser, but if so they did it privately. The U.N. may have been "politicized," but U.S. congressional subcommittees were democracy in action.

By the time Gerald Ford put his signature to 502B, on June 30 1976, he and Kissinger were still on the defensive and Congress was far from satisfied. It was noted (and resented) that James Wilson, the new State Department Coordinator for Humanitarian Affairs, was a career diplomat whose expertise lay in Micronesia. Presidential candidate Jimmy Carter was beginning to exploit human rights in his campaign. Kissinger and Ford tried to hedge their bets. Aware of the strength of feeling against Pinochet, the administration vetoed a loan to Chile in the Inter-American Development Bank, and Kissinger even instructed the U.S. embassy in Buenos Aires to inquire on behalf of Argentinians whose disappearances had provoked a protest in the United States.[15]

At the same time, Kissinger also took the time to meet with Argentina's Foreign Minister, Admiral César Guzetti, at the Hotel Carrera in Santiago on July 10, and reportedly gave his blessing to the Junta's dirty war against subversion.[16] To the end, Kissinger remained deeply skeptical about loud diplomacy. On December 29 1976, just before the Carter Administration took office, the State Department released human rights reports on six countries (including Argentina) to the House Committee on International Relations. They were so weak that one newspaper observed: "The reports make us think that folks at State would have described Jack the Ripper as 'a person accused of certain misdeeds and limited mayhem although these allegations are not fully substantiated'."[17]

Fraser's hearing on Argentina in September 1976 had concentrated minds on the disappearances. Amnesty International had just sent a mission to Argentina and one of its members—Congressman Robert Drinan—had returned with fire in his belly. Americans were beginning to feel something devilish was loose in Argentina, and that whatever it was it was more significant even than America's security interests. On January 17 1977 twelve human rights groups, including Amnesty, sent a letter to newly elected President Carter insisting that he take firm action to stop the disappearances.

At this point, the Junta began unwittingly to mold U.S. human rights policy. Law 502B and the other laws were on the statute books, but they were awaiting a case and a judgment. There were a Bureau of Humanitarian Affairs and a Coordinator at the State Department, but they too were waiting to acquire an identity. Shortly after Carter's election, Congress upgraded the post of Coordinator to Assistant Secretary of State for Human Rights. The rest would be up to President Carter's nominee for the new post, and the most blatant abuse that he or she would face was clearly the disappearances in Argentina.

Fighting Clientitis

Patricia Derian had no experience in international human rights, and even less in diplomacy. By profession she was a nurse. In 1959 she moved back to her native Mississippi, where she joined a campaign to provide better public education and plunged into the civil rights movement. From there she moved into local Democratic party politics, where her instincts placed her firmly on the liberal wing of the party. Along the way she met her husband-to-be, Hodding Carter. When Jimmy Carter threw his hat into the ring, Derian was asked if she would support the former governor of Georgia in his battle for the presidency.

After Carter won the election, Patt Derian was offered two posts in the new administration. One was head of protocol, the other Coordinator (soon to be Assistant Secretary of State) for Human Rights at the State Department. She didn't take long to make up her mind. "I couldn't tap dance, so I chose human rights."[18] It was not quite that simple. Both by temperament and by experience, Derian was remarkably well-qualified to give substance to Carter's rhetoric. Human rights meant challenge and exposure, and Derian was comfortable in this role. She found it easier to identify with the cluttered offices of nongovernmental groups than the State Department, where she kept empty cartons in her office to remind people that she did not need to make compromises in order to protect a foreign service career. She even acted like an advocate, turning her job into one long challenge—to Argentina, to dictatorship, to language, even to her own colleagues at the State Department.

Her colleagues, in turn, were determined not to surrender bureaucratic turf to the newcomer. This behavior was predictable. Regional bureaus in the State Department are powerful fiefdoms, each one headed by an assistant secretary of state. Their relationship with the governments in their region is usually one of warmth and understanding, often described as "clientitis" or "clientism." Now this cosy relationship was about to be threatened. Instead of sending back good news, American embassies would be expected to report back on torture, disappearances, and murder.

Patt Derian was determined to make sure that the information was acted upon, and she decided that she would, in her own words, "beat the bureaucracy, force them to deal with me personally." She saw the job as that of a kind of human rights ombudsman: if they were chopping off hands in Pakistan or children were disappearing in Argentina, then it was her job to protest. Let others weigh the political and military consequences. She recalls one early meeting with Deputy Secretary of State Warren Christopher. Christopher asked whether she expected to win all her battles. "No," she replied, "But I'll expect to win my share." The choice of words was important. The emphasis was, from the start, on "winning," and "losing." Old timers at the State Department were quick to catch the whiff of approaching battle and scramble to keep their own powder dry.

Patt Derian plunged into an exhausting year of bureaucratic infighting to win what is termed in State Department parlance as "standing." "Standing" is a mysterious quality, hard to define but easy to measure, and as in the United Nations the first requirement is access to paper. Endlessly circulating, yet hidden beneath the waterline, cables and memos keep the ship of state afloat. Initially Derian was treated like a Victorian child, allowed to read but not contribute. She worked frantically to assert her presence. She might receive a tip in the cafeteria that a memo had been routed past her office to Warren Christopher, or return to find an anonymous note on her desk. Sometimes she was able to contact Christopher directly and get an important memo recalled. Sometimes it was too late.

It was incredibly wearing. She would spend long evenings poring over memos, trying to get acquainted with the system. Gradually she made her presence felt, helped by the aura of power that came from her past association with Jimmy Carter. She exploited the notion that she had a direct line to the White House. It was one of her most powerful weapons in those early days of bureaucratic infighting.

She threw her office solidly behind the United Nations over the definition of human rights, reaffirming the primacy of the issue of government violence and endorsing the concept of economic rights.[19]. At the same time, she turned quickly and savagely against the subtle, coded language of human rights. If people were dying at the ESMA, their "right to life" was not "violated." They were not "subversives" who were "salvaged." They were people who screamed their lives away lashed to an iron frame, with the image of Antonio "the Rat" Pernía slavering over them. This was how Derian talked at her press conferences. Slowly and deliberately, so that no one missed the point. She liked to see mouths fall open and pens scribble furiously. Of all her challenges to convention, her challenge to language was one of the most shocking.

Into the Lion's Den

Patt Derian was no sooner installed in her new office than she found herself pitted against the powerful regional bureau known as the American Republics Area (ARA), headed by Assistant Secretary of State Terence Todman. Todman and his staff, particularly John Bushnell, the senior Deputy Assistant Secretary, suffered from a chronic case of clientitis towards Argentina, and early in 1977 Todman suggested to Derian that she visit the country and talk to the Junta. She had no doubt it was a ploy and that Todman hoped she would be more sympathetic to Videla if she viewed the Junta's security problems at first hand. She thought hard about the suggestion, and realized that it was too soon to be traveling. But at the same time she also knew a trip would increase her "standing." So she decided to go.

If it was indeed a ploy by the ARA, it backfired spectacularly. Derian made three visits to Argentina in 1977 and they were to have much the same effect on her as the U.N. mission to Chile would have on Theo van Boven the following year. They would turn her into an outspoken and informed human rights advocate and send hostility to Videla's regime coursing through the State Department.

On her way to Argentina, Derian reviewed confrontations with Ku Klux Klansmen, angry sheriffs, and various other protagonists from her civil rights days, searching to recall details that could help with the forth-coming confrontation. She knew this would be no ordinary visit and that Carter's human rights policy would mean rewriting the rules of diplo-macy. Rather like Amnesty International, her very presence was a chal-lenge, her title proof that she came in the spirit of a prosecutor rather than ally. The fact that she was a woman would have made this doubly galling to the chauvinistic Massera and Videla. But the distrust was recipro-cal. Derian was appalled and disgusted by the reports coming out of Argentina.

The local papers gave her the benefit of the doubt when she arrived, much as they had done with the Amnesty team the previous year. "The Yankee envoy is optimistic!" ran one headline, before she met Videla on August 9. Two days later, just before leaving, she told reporters that the meeting had been "very cordial." When pressed about details, she said "I need a little time to think it all over."[20]

Behind the platitudes, a deep dislike had formed on both sides. Derian remembered the throbbing vein on Videla's forehead, his damp hand-shake. Videla, she recalls, was almost shivering throughout. It wasn't sur-prising that he looked uncomfortable seated next to Derian on the couch. This was a major personal and diplomatic confrontation between two al-lied governments.

Outwardly the Junta held Derian personally responsible for the tension with the United States and encouraged an abusive campaign against her, no doubt hoping to divert attention from the grave implications of the rift with the United States. She not only allowed Videla to cry "interfer-ence"—her personality virtually demanded it. In an otherwise sympathetic profile written in 1980, James Neilson, editor of the *Buenos Aires Herald,* would put Derian firmly in the category of "reformist-minded, outspoken, unputdownable American women . . . preaching, often nagging, some-times cajoling they have continued to ram their principles down the throats of Americans and others."[21]

Nagging, cajoling, meddling . . . these were useful words to the Junta. They played on the current of anti-Americanism—part jealousy and part fear—that lies beneath the surface of every Latin American country. The United States presumed to act as the hemispheric policeman, expunger of Communism, banker, arbiter of tastes and God knows what else—without consulting anyone. Why couldn't it leave well enough alone? What gave the United States the right to meddle—to interfere?

Interference. Here it was again, the crucial charge. Gabriel Martínez was using it against the International Commission of Jurists and Theo van Boven in Geneva. The Argentinian Junta used it against Patricia Derian. In one exceptionally influential 1979 article, Jeane Kirkpatrick would make much the same point, arguing that Carter and Derian were trying to impose democracy on societies that were simply incapable of living up to democratic standards of behavior.[22]

Yet in one respect, Derian's presence in Argentina was anything but "interference." During the early part of Carter's presidency, U.S. policy toward Latin America underwent a major change. Carter and his advisers were determined to usher in a new era. There would be no more invasions and no more covert CIA operations. Latin America's security value to the U.S. would no longer be exaggerated: henceforth, it would be viewed as just another region of the world with major economic and political problems that required U.S. understanding and money. This philosophy lay behind two major foreign policy goals of the new administration: starting a dialogue with Cuba and negotiating the Panama Canal treaties.[23]

Leaving aside the impact of this new policy on U.S. security—another major concern for Jeane Kirkpatrick—it has to be said that if the presence of Patt Derian on Videla's couch indicated U.S. "interference," it was certainly less lethal and threatening than the arrival of marines or a CIA operation. Derian was trying to save lives, not take them. But what ultimately rescued her human rights crusade from the charge of "interference" was the United Nations. The more successful the U.N. was in universalizing freedom from torture and government violence, the less plausible it was to charge Derian with "interference" when she sat on Videla's couch and protested about murder in the ESMA.

Jimmy Carter knew this. He knew that the United Nations—so fragile, so easily manipulated by diplomats like Martínez—complemented his human rights policy. From the outset he associated himself with the two key U.N. goals: drafting credible international standards and implementing them. Every nation had a right and a duty to protest when they saw these standards abused. This was not "interference." As Carter himself told the U.N. General Assembly on March 17 1977, in his first major foreign policy speech: "No member of the United Nations can claim that mistreatment of its citizens is solely its own business . . . no member can avoid its responsibilities to review and to speak when torture or unwarranted deprivation occurs in any part of the world."

Yet for this position to be credible, the United States itself had to submit to U.N. scrutiny. Shortly after his speech, Carter ended the long U.S. boycott of international human rights law and signed the two U.N. covenants, the International Convention on the Elimination of All Forms of Racial Discrimination, and the American Convention on Human Rights. Patt Derian led the political struggle (ultimately unsuccessful) to secure ratification of the treaties by the Senate.[24]

By the middle of 1977 it was also clear that the United Nations could draw the poison from bilateral confrontation. This was vital, because Carter's human rights policy virtually demanded such confrontation. The Argentinian Junta realized this clearly. One 1977 Foreign Ministry memo predicted accurately that the U.S. position in the U.N. and OAS would toughen noticeably as domestic resentment grew against Carter's human rights policy.[25]

The U.N.'s campaign to universalize human rights also made it easier to dismiss another of Jeane Kirkpatrick's charges—that Carter's human rights policy was an attempt to impose democracy. The charge itself was clearly correct, as the Argentinians themselves realized. One 1977 memo put it as follows:

> The [Carter] administration believes that its political and social model is decidedly superior to those of its ideological competitors, and it has decided to make use of this in the strategic confrontation. As a result, it is clear that the American position on human rights is neither accidental, nor totally emotional, nor idealistic. It will continue to feature in the administration's foreign policy.[26]

Publicly, though, the Junta could not protest, because it accepted the "right to life," claimed to be upholding "Western values," and had promised (ultimately) to restore democracy.

Interestingly, Derian's personality does not feature in these Foreign Ministry memoranda. The Argentinians knew that her challenging style was a symptom rather than a cause of the profound change that had taken place in American foreign policy. Indeed, one memo offered a rather sober account of Derian's views that contrasted sharply with the frenetic public campaign against her: "While our rationale was accepted, [she] pointed out that a wide gap exists between the theory and the actual treatment of these people . . . [and] argued that if the government made use of procedures outside the law, then terrorism will have achieved its objective."[27]

Meeting Pontius Pilate at the ESMA

For Derian herself, times, dates, and places have now merged with the passing of time, but she still remembers vividly the images of a country at war with itself. There was a crazy trip through downtown Buenos Aires. Derian was by now chafing at the extraordinary security precautions. Everywhere she went she was accompanied by four cars. The Americans were right behind her, under the watchful eye of the grizzled security chief at the American embassy. Behind them followed a convoy of three cars—one car from each of the three services. Exasperated, Derian told her driver to stop and got out. The cars behind screeched to a halt. The security man piled out and ran up to her. "What the hell are you doing? Get back inside."

She refused. "I'm a free agent. I want those cars sent away." She pointed to the three cars behind, filled with goons, the windows rolled down and their guns sticking out because there was no room for the hardware in the Falcons.

"Get inside," said the security man through gritted teeth. "This is not Disneyland."

"No," she insisted.

"Listen." The security man made a huge effort to remain patient. "Let me try and explain. I am watching you. They are watching each other. One is from the navy. Another is from the air force. The third is from the army. They want to be around in case any of the others snatches you. I've got the whole thing very carefuly worked out. Please don't blow it." Derian got back into her car, chastened. Later she heard that her hotel room had been searched.

She made a deliberate effort to raise morale among the relatives of the disappeared persons. She met with Emilio Mignone, the Mothers, and the Permanent Assembly on Human Rights. She had one meeting with the relatives in the large underground garage of the embassy to avoid Argentinian surveillance. She told them they deserved the Nobel Peace Prize. One onlooker remembers "a lot of bawling." She formed a deep attachment to the Mothers and would help form a support group for them in the United States when she left office in 1981. During her first visit she also met with Jacobo Timerman and his two sons. His paper *La Opinión* was the only local paper to grant her an audience. Timerman told her he thought he was a marked man. He was right.

She remembers the meetings vividly. These were people she could identify with. One very old woman related the way her neighbors' daughter
had disappeared. The body later turned up. It was dumped in her parents'
yard, naked but showing no outward signs of torture. Later the director
of the funeral home called to inform her parents that the girl's vagina had
been sewn up. Inside he had found a rat.

During the August visit, she talked to the Interior Minister Albano
Harguindeguy. It was about the same time that he talked to the Mothers
and he was much more frank with Derian. He was apprehensive about the
possibility of some kind of Nuremburg trial, and she advised him to call a
halt to the whole thing and send the soldiers back to the barracks. Jacobo
Timerman had disappeared and resurfaced between Derian's first and second visits, but he still remained in jail. She complained to Harguindeguy
that Timerman had probably been tortured and urged him to receive the
publisher. He replied that he would bring him out and let her talk to him.
No, she insisted, Timerman was his responsibility: he should do the talking. His voice got shriller. Eventually, he did agree to see Timerman, but
not before he had asked who the hell this woman was—Timerman's
cousin? The frustrated query made its way out into the press and was taken
by some as fact. It was the only time any of the military men lost his
temper to her face. Timerman remained deeply grateful for her intervention.

Derian's most vivid memory was of meeting Admiral Emilio Massera
at the ESMA. Accompanied by a senior official from the U.S. embassy,
she drove in through the gates just before eleven on the morning of August 10 1977. Maybe she paused to look at the guards in their trim uniforms
and the elegant paintwork. For some time now, terrifying stories had been
trickling out about this building.[28]

Massera and Derian both knew what was happening at the ESMA—
this was at the very height of the killing—but for several minutes they
both kept up the diplomatic pretense. She began by stating that violations
of human rights in Argentina had placed obstacles in the way of normal
relations between the two countries. Massera looked grave and nodded, as
befitting a member of the ruling Junta. She found herself wondering what
he was thinking—perhaps how she would have looked strung out on an
iron frame down in the basement?

It would not have been that surprising. He was, after all, a man who
had overseen torture. Derian persisted. She asked about the reports of
torture. Massera said the navy had never tortured anyone, that it was the
army. Derian began to show her impatience. She said there had been tes-

timony of torture taking place in the very building where they spoke. In fact, she continued, she had even seen a rough diagram, showing that prisoners were detained in the floor below. "It's possible that they're torturing people down there even now, while we're talking."

She was right. Just one floor down, in the "capuchita" (little hood) prisoners were hooded and manacled. Among them were daughters and sons of the women she had met at the American embassy, including Mónica Mignone (if she had survived this long). Billy Lee Hunt, an American, had disappeared on April 18—perhaps he too was being held at the ESMA. Ana María Martí was down there. So, probably, was Alfredo Astiz, angel on the prowl. It was an eerie feeling, knowing that hundreds of men, women and children had passed through this building like animals through an abattoir. There but for fortune . . .

Massera paused, grinned, and rubbed his hands together as if washing them. She noticed that he had sparkling teeth. "Ah," he said, "you know that story about Pontius Pilate." So ended one of the strangest encounters ever to take place between the United States and an ally.

13. The Allis Chalmers Controversy

It was not long before American opinion began to look for concrete results from Patt Derian's whirlwind activity. How many lives were being saved? How much torture prevented? How many prisoners were being released? It was frustratingly difficult to give precise answers. Occasionally people like Jacobo Timerman would emerge, loudly proclaiming their gratitude. But such cases apart, it was depressingly easy to argue that very little had been achieved when set against the antagonism provoked. What use was the pressure if Massera continued to lie?

If the cynics had had access to some of the memoranda prepared by Argentina's Foreign Ministry, they might have been less scathing. There is an embattled mood about these documents. They show that the new American policy on human rights was a body blow to the confidence of the Junta and they warn of worse to come: of American votes in international institutions, of cutbacks in arms and spare parts. They seem at a loss for a reply, yet desperate to avoid a complete break with the United States.[1]

Only over the question of security do they grow shrill and accusatory. What rankled, clearly, was not Derian's criticism but the fact that Argentina was not considered sufficiently important to U.S. security interests to qualify for exemption under the 502B legislation. On February 24 1977, Secretary of State Cyrus Vance told a Senate subcommittee that military aid to Argentina would be reduced from $48.4 million to $15 million. Ethiopia and Uruguay would suffer similar reductions. South Korea, said Vance, would remain unaffected because of its strategic importance to the United States. The Argentinians were humiliated. Together with three other governments, they announced they would accept no U.S. military aid for 1978.[2]

There followed a torrent of private and public protests. The decision was "arbitrary," says one document. It was "immoral and unilateral," says another. It was a unilateral violation of the agreement signed between the United States and Argentina on May 10 1964, says another. This memo goes on to suggest that Argentina was deliberately chosen by some Democrats as a test case for President Carter's human rights policy with the knowledge that the risks to American security were minimal. It also complains that the United States seemed to care about its own security, but not about Argentina's. The frustration and bitterness are palpable.[3]

In fact, Derian's staff cared a lot about the security of Argentina—or rather Argentinians. A good case could be made for the argument that providing any kind of aid to Argentina's navy would merely strengthen the navy GT 3/32 squad and send more Argentinians to their deaths. If, furthermore, U.S. aid did anything at all to encourage the quixotic Admiral Massera to contemplate an invasion of the Falkland Islands and threaten America's ally Britain, then it was doing little for U.S. security either.

Such considerations should have made it any easier for Derian to block security aid for Argentina, but they did not. The compromise agreed upon between Congress and the Ford Administration over 502B in 1976 had allowed for security aid to be maintained under "exceptional circumstances" or when U.S. "national interests" were involved. As the Carter Administration broadened its definition of U.S. security, it became more reluctant to describe any ally as a "gross violator." Being a superpower meant—almost by definition—that any event affected U.S. security and this was much exploited by regional bureaus, anxious to play up their clients' importance. The bureaus also took it for granted that American arms enhanced, rather than threatened, the security of the recipient.

ARA officials argued long and hard on behalf of Argentina. Were the United States and Argentina not engaged in joint navy patrols in the South Atlantic? Was not a key foreign policy goal to prevent the proliferation of nuclear power? Well, Argentina had nuclear power. Then there were the Panama Canal treaties. As they ran into domestic opposition in the United States, Carter was forced to turn the treaties into a hemispheric issue, and even Videla and Pinochet were invited to Washington for the signing. All of this enhanced the ARA argument that Argentina was an important ally.

Derian and her staff fought unceasingly against such claims. No quarter was asked and none was given. In April 1977, as the memos were beginning to rain down, Cyrus Vance established a committee, the Inter-Agency Group on Human Rights and Foreign Assistance, under the chairmanship of Deputy Secretary of State Warren Christopher, to review each proposed loan.[4] The human rights legislation now extended to economic aid and multilateral banks, and such was the volume of work that a subgroup was set up. It began meeting every six weeks or so to confront some familiar

issues. How did one define "gross violators?" How could a country's security importance be measured? What, indeed, was "security assistance,"
and did spare parts qualify? The sound of battle echoed around Washington. It gave an impression of an administration at odds with itself and
contributed to Carter's subsequent reputation as a flip-flop president.[5]

Although the discussion touched on virtually every type of aid, the key
issue was U.S. military assistance and arms sales. Since the signing of the
joint U.S.-Argentina military treaty of 1964, Argentinian armed forces had
grown increasingly dependent on the United States. More than three
thousand Argentinian servicemen had already been trained in the United
States and in the Panama Canal zone, and in the process deep personal
friendships had formed. Even after the reduction in military assistance
announced by Vance in March 1977, the U.S. Defense Department still
asked for seven hundred thousand dollars to train two hundred seventeen
Argentinian military personnel. (Fourteen were to be trained in "intelligence techniques" which could clearly have been useful in the dirty war.)
In addition, Argentina still had over $54.4 million of American credit in
the pipeline waiting to be spent.[6]

Overall, the United States sold Argentina $120 million worth of spare
parts in 1977 and 1978. Trade, in fact, boomed. This sat awkwardly with
the administration's public posture and irritated liberals in Congress. On
May 23 1977, Congressman Gerry Studds introduced an amendment in the
House of Representatives to cut off all military aid to Argentina. It narrowly failed by 200 votes to 187. A year later, in June 1978, Senators Edward Kennedy and Frank Church proposed a total cutoff in all military
sales and aid. Hubert Humphrey engineered a compromise (section 620B
of the Foreign Assistance Act) under which the cutoff would take effect as
of September 30 1978, giving the Junta several months grace.

"Cut 'Em Off at the Cheese"

The bureacratic tensions in Washington were reflected and magnified in
American embassies throughout the world. Suddenly, American diplomats were being asked to act as inquisitors instead of friends, and to inquire about morgues instead of military maneuvers. The pressure was
most intense on officials in the political section. Until now their work had
involved analyzing the various political currents in the host country. Now
they acquired the added responsibility of contributing to the annual State

Department human rights reports called for under 502B. This upset the traditional hierarchy. Carter's policy had turned relatively junior positions into some of the most exposed and sensitive in the embassy—something that could only be highly disconcerting for an ambassador.

Tex Harris's career in the U.S. foreign service had been relatively un-eventful until he arrived as a first secretary in the political section at the newly built U.S. embassy in Buenos Aires in 1977. He found an air of studied indifference toward the disappearances. There was only one en-trance into the embassy compound, and it resembled a round piece of cheddar cheese with a slice cut out of it. This was as far as the distraught relatives got before they were turned away. The official policy was "cut 'em off at the cheese." There was no reason to act otherwise. The conventional wisdom in the intelligence and military sections was that the disappear-ances were the work of "extremists" of the right and left who were uncon-nected with the security forces. As result, the embassy's records amounted to just two yellow sheets that carried at most twenty names.

Tex Harris has a large physique and plenty of energy, and he quickly set about trying to persuade his ambassador, Raul Castro, to change policy. Shortly after arriving, Harris appeared on the fringes of one of the Thursday vigils by the Mothers at the Plaza de Mayo. María Antokoletz recalls it well. It was raining. After the vigil broke up, Harris approached, and they took a subway train to the Plaza Italia near the embassy. It devel-oped into a close relationship. Harris would provide the Mothers with translations of American articles about Argentina and let them know of visiting American dignitaries.

The relatives were finally permitted into the embassy by Castro, and the trickle became a torrent as word got around. Harris acquired a Swiss as-sistant named Blanca Vollenweider—the last survivor from a USAID mis-sion in Argentina. Vollenweider would take names and addresses in one room, while Harris would conduct interviews in the next. Gradually they built up a record of the reports using small five-by-eight cards. It was before the days of the personal computer, but Vollenweider and Harris had remarkable memories and they worked late into the night battling Argentina's confusing system of double surnames. The relatives began to queue up outside the embassy, ignoring the large white van that was filled with Argentinian security officials and sophisticated electronic devices.[7]

Harris was interviewing thirty, then forty families a week. If any of the kidnappings had the remotest connection with the United States, or had provoked a query from Congress, he would bring it up at one of his regular meetings with officials from the Foreign Ministry working group on human rights. On October 31 1977, he handed over a list of sixteen names. One of the queries had come from Rosalynn Carter, the President's wife.[8]

There were many such cases—Jews, in particular, were being singled out—and the speed of the inquiries clearly astonished the Argentinians. One exasperated Foreign Ministry memo written in 1980 complained: "The U.S. embassy was constantly making official and informal efforts with our government to stress U.S. interest in human rights." The process began to develop a momentum of its own, with the initiative increasingly coming from Congress. David Stockman was one of many congressmen who contacted the embassy on behalf of two "desaparecidos."[9]

Castro brought the full weight of the embassy's own contacts to bear when two Americans, Jon Pirmín Azorena and Billy Lee Hunt, disappeared (in separate incidents) in 1977. When U.S. military attachés inquired of their contacts in the Argentinian military, they were told to look no more. It was never formally confirmed that the armed forces were responsible, but the inference was unmistakable. The cases caused particular indignation among Derian's staff and in the embassy.[10]

To many of the foreigners who worked in Buenos Aires during the dirty war, Tex Harris was a larger than life figure. He met regularly with other Western diplomats at a local restaurant called the Basque, where they would drink beer and review the latest kidnappings. He appeared before congressional hearings, which was unusual for a relatively junior foreign service officer, and prompted a stream of admiring articles in the press. On the question of disappearances he was, to judge from the comments about him, anything but neutral. Like Derian, he openly identified with the relatives, stretching his brief to the limit.

Harris is still serving in the State Department and unable to talk about this turbulent period. But it is clear that an extraordinary tension developed between Harris on the one hand and Ambassador Raul Castro and Deputy Chief of Mission Max Chaplin on the other, that mirrored the division in Washington between Derian's office and the ARA bureau. Max Chaplin was a foreign service officer with long experience in Latin America who made no secret of his contempt for Derian's human rights crusade. Raul Castro was a Mexican-American who had been governor of New Mexico and ambassador to El Salvador and Bolivia before being posted to Buenos Aires. For many people he was an equivocal figure. On the one hand he was a shining example of American success. He used to recall the discrimination suffered by his parents in their fight to make good, even using the derogatory term "wetback" to describe his own family. (He liked to tell the story of how he had been leaning against the fence of his ranch in New Mexico, surveying his cattle, when a police officer drew up and demanded his ID. Castro did not have it on him, so the officer promptly arrested his own governor.)

The Argentinians were furious at Castro's appointment, which they regarded as an insult, and sneered at him behind his back. Openly, however, they fawned over him. Castro responded with warmth and understanding for Videla and his cronies, and he evidently dreaded having to deliver rebukes from Washington. After one bruising session with the army chief of staff Roberto Viola in June 1978 he cabled back: "I have a strong feeling President Videla will also go through some agonizing moments. They sincerely feel they are the defenders of a free world by defeating terrorism and that the USG [U.S. Government] is not giving them enough time to move in politically dangerous areas." Like the ARA bureau in Washington, Ambassador Castro clearly had a bad bout of clientitis.[11]

The potential for division in the embassy existed from the moment that Harris began to compile records. When challenged, the military and intelligence sections clung to the same arguments being advanced by the ARA in Washington: even if the violence was indeed the work of security forces, the United States simply could not afford to alienate people who looked likely to be in power indefinitely. Harris, echoing Patt Derian, would present the human rights case. Castro's own instincts were to agree with his military attachés, and he was disconcerted by Harris's role as a troubleshooter. On the other hand, Derian's star was rising in Washington. It was a recipe for trouble.

In Washington itself, Harris's reports were having a critical effect on the Christopher group. Aware of this, his colleagues in the embassy would try and delay the transmission of the reports and attempt to balance his invariably gloomy picture with some redeeming features. Derian protested angrily that Harris was being muzzled and the Christopher group denied vital information, and it was agreed that when Harris uncovered particularly sensitive information he would avail himself of the diplomatic back channel and draft what is termed an "official informal letter." Copies would be posted to ARA and Derian's human rights bureau, with a third copy going to Ambassador Castro. William Hallman, the political counselor and Harris's superior at the embassy, is quite clear that Harris saw Derian, not Castro, as his spiritual chief. Ambassador Castro was furious. He had surrendered control over his embassy.

A hint of the disarray emerged during the November 1977 visit by U.S. Secretary of State Cyrus Vance to Buenos Aires. According to press reports, Vance presented Videla (and Massera) with a list of 7,500 names of disappeared persons and a list of disappeared Argentinian artists. This was a diplomatic rebuff of the highest order, but Castro did much to undermine the impact at a subsequent press conference when he insisted the list had been prepared by human rights groups in the United States and merely passed over by Vance as a courtesy to the Junta. The Argentinian Foreign Ministry gleefully circulated a cable around embassies in an effort to repair the damage and present this as an example of the confusion that existed in the U.S. embassy.[12]

Relations between Harris and Castro took a sharp turn for the worse after a Dallas firm (E Systems) won a contract to supply a computerized ID system for police cars in Buenos Aires. The Dallas firm applied for credit from the U.S. Export-Import (EXIM) Bank, which supports American exporters doing business in high-risk countries.[13] The commercial and intelligence sections at the embassy both supported the sale, but Harris opposed it on grounds that it would facilitate the kidnapping. The two sides refused to back down and in the end both drafted position papers. Castro was out of the office, and on return he hurriedly signed off on the cable. His colleagues at the ARA were furious: ambassadors were meant to accept decisions, not dabble in democracy. Castro received a reprimand. He drafted a second cable explaining that he had been out of the office and recommending in favor of the EXIM credit.

Meanwhile Derian's staff drew on Harris's report and argued that the proposed ID system would help the kidnapping squads like the navy GT 3/32. The credit was refused and it fell to Ambassador Castro to break the news to the Argentinians. The atmosphere in the embassy deteriorated sharply.

Allis Chalmers Tests the Water

The bureacratic tension in Washington and Buenos Aires came to a dramatic climax in July 1978. Argentina and Paraguay were cooperating on a joint hydroelectricity project to dam the river Paraná at Yacyreta, and the U.S. firm Allis Chalmers had put in a bid to build a plant for an Argentinian shipyard, Astilleros Argentinos, to supply twenty-seven turbines for the dam. On April 3 1978, Allis Chalmers had asked the EXIM bank for a "letter of interest" that would signify EXIM's willingness to support the firm if it went ahead with the project.

It was immediately clear that more than money was involved in the request. On June 23, during a meeting in Washington, Argentina's Deputy Foreign Minister Gualter Allara told David Newsom, U.S. Under Secretary of State for Political Affairs, that Argentina could easily find financing for the project elsewhere.[14] Yet Argentina encouraged Allis Chalmers to approach the EXIM bank. Why? Because it had become a crucial test case for Patt Derian and the Junta in their escalating war of nerves. The economic policy of Martínez de Hoz depended on loans at low rates of interest, and these in turn were only coming in because Argentina was considered "creditworthy." EXIM's continuing approval was thus essential, as is clear from cables to and from the U.S. embassy in Buenos Aires.[15] Patt Derian is convinced that the Junta had an additional aim: it wanted to break the back of her campaign.

Feathers flew when the contract was discussed in the Christopher group at the State Department. Eventually, the argument was settled after one of the strangest episodes in the annals of American diplomacy. What follows is a reconstruction from several sources.

In Buenos Aires, Tex Harris made enquiries about Astilleros Argentinos, the Argentinian company, from Peter Jones, a colleague in the commercial section of the embassy. Jones was absent from his office, so Harris asked a secretary for any relevant files. These showed that Astilleros Argentinos was owned by the same Argentinian navy that was running the ESMA concentration camp. Shocked by the discovery, Harris wrote a letter which he dutifully sent to Derian, ARA, and his ambassador.

Either Castro or Chaplin—it is not clear who—ordered the letter stopped because it contained "policy" instructions. According to one onlooker, William Hallman then cornered Harris just as he was to give his explosive letter to the registrar for posting to Washington. The two men argued for half an hour. Eventually, Hallman looked at his watch and remarked that Harris had missed the post. He was wrong. After Hallman left, Harris persuaded the registry clerk to reopen the mail, and the letter was winging its way to Washington, where it helped to swing the Christopher group against the Junta. On July 20 the State Department announced that it could not recommend that EXIM issue a letter of interest to Allis Chalmers. Rarely, in the history of diplomacy, had so much hung on one letter.[16]

The backlash came quickly, in Buenos Aires and the United States. Ambassador Castro received an irate delegation of American businessmen at the embassy, who warned him that Argentina would take its business elsewhere.[17] In the U.S., Allis Chalmers mounted a major lobby in an effort to get the decision reversed, with help from William Coleman, a highly respected black civil rights lawyer and member of the NAACP. David Scott, the chairman of Allis Chalmers, let it be known that the Yacyreta contract could be worth eighteen million man-hours to American workers—an argument that was particularly influential in states where the firm had plants. Other U.S. firms rallied round. On August 8 1978 James Cormack, president of the Sherer Corporation, wrote to Senator Robert Griffin of Michigan warning that his firm's plans to produce pharmaceutical drugs in Argentina could be jeopardized. Wrote Cormack: "Our views towards Argentina are positive, both economically and in terms of the political stability achieved by the current government."

Patt Derian began to feel the pressure. Even Andy Young, the U.S. Permanent Representative at the U.N. in New York and an outspoken champion of human rights, entered the fray and sent a warning to Zbigniew Brzezinski, Carter's National Security Adviser, that Derian was "denying jobs to U.S. workers."[18] Eventually, on September 26 1978, the EXIM decision was reversed and a letter of interest was issued to Allis Chalmers.

This strange episode marked the high-water mark of Patt Derian's crusade in the State Department. Between July and September 1978 the mood in Congress shifted from sympathy with the human rights policy to concern over its economic cost. A survey was commissioned from commercial sections in all embassies on the potential effect of the human rights policy on American jobs. The replies were predictably exaggerated. Were it not for Derian's antics, they implied, U.S. exports would be booming. The survey was not taken too seriously—in State parlance it was treated as "GIGO" ("garbage in garbage out")—but Congress decided that EXIM loans would henceforth be excluded from the scope of the human rights legislation.[19] Human rights was on the retreat, and once again Argentina was responsible.

Maneuvers at the OAS

As soon as she realized the tide was turning, Patt Derian urged that Argentina be held to some conditions. Secretary of State Cyrus Vance agreed and David Newsom, Under Secretary of State for Political Affairs, was dispatched to Buenos Aires with a package of proposals. If Argentina were to invite the Inter-American Commission on Human Rights to visit Argentina and restore the "right of option" which allowed detainees to choose between jail or exile, the U.S. would soften its line. Newsom repeated the proposal when he met Argentina's Deputy Foreign Minister, Gualter Allara, in Washington on June 23 1978.[20]

The Inter-American Commission on Human Rights (IACHR) is the human rights investigating arm of the Organization of American States. It comprises a secretariat and seven individual members, all of whom serve in an independent capacity, and like the OAS system as a whole it had been invigorated by Carter's 1977 decision to sign the American Convention on Human Rights.[21] This was a clear sign that the United States would extend its human rights campaign into the OAS, and it opened up another front in the Junta's diplomatic war. The IACHR was viewed as particularly threatening in Buenos Aires, where any activism in the cause of human rights was suspect. "Some government officials have claimed that the [IACHR] members share a leftist political bias coupled with zealous determination to castigate military governments," wrote Ambassador Castro in one cable.[22]

In June 1977, at the OAS annual assembly on the Caribbean island of Grenada, Secretary of State Cyrus Vance met with Argentina's Foreign Minister Oscar Montes for what one Argentinian Foreign Ministry memo described cautiously as a "broad exchange of views." According to the memo, Vance listened sympathetically to Argentina's concerns, and the two men agreed to maintain "bilateral discussions about human rights and terrorism." This was clutching at straws. Vance was courteous, but he gave Montes little cause for encouragement. Indeed, as the memo makes clear, the U.S. played a decisive role in defeating an Argentinian resolution to have the danger of terrorism recognized. The defeat left a bitter taste.[23]

During the assembly Foreign Minister Montes also met with Andres Aguilar, a Venezuelan jurist who was president of IACHR. Montes said the Junta was keen to cooperate. The reaction was skeptical. Reports of disappearances in Argentina were now flooding in to the OAS headquarters in Washington, but not one case had been satisfactorily resolved. Argentinian diplomats in Washington were skillful and charming but—like Gabriel Martínez in Geneva—they were following instructions and playing for time. In February 1978 the IACHR made a formal request to Buenos Aires for a visit. The request was turned down.

It was now time for the 1978 OAS assembly in Washington. Carter delivered a speech which was seen as remarkably bellicose in Argentina, but its impact was partly offset by some behind-the-scenes maneuvering by OAS Secretary General Alejandro Orfila, who was Argentinian and known to be sympathetic to the Junta. Orfila hosted a meeting between Andres Aguilar, the IACHR president, and Foreign Minister Montes at his house in Washington, after which Montes invited the IACHR to pay a special visit to Argentina to "verify the juridical/legal conditions" there.[24]

The IACHR did not, traditionally, accept such restrictions on its visits, and back in Buenos Aires the U.S. embassy was informed that Montes's invitation would mean a very restricted visit indeed—little more, in fact, than a series of discussions with judges. "It is not envisioned that the Commission would take testimony from individuals, nor would it visit jails or meet with human rights groups," cabled Castro.[25] IACHR reviewed the Argentinian invitation and decided it was unacceptable. The mood at the State Department toughened, and the decision was made to turn down EXIM funding.[26]

Montes returned to Buenos Aires from Washington under a cloud, and a bitter argument erupted within the Argentinian military over whether to issue an unconditional invitation to the IACHR.[27]

By August the issue had split the "duros" (hawks) from the "blandos" (doves).[28] Eventually, the doves won the day. At 9:30 A.M. on August 31, Castro received an enigmatic phone call from Viola saying that his personal emissary, Lieutenant Ramírez, was coming over for a talk. Viola said he could not discuss the matter over the phone. Ramírez arrived and said it had been learned that Vice President Mondale was heading the U.S. delegation to the swearing-in ceremony of Pope John Paul I in Rome. Videla was due to leave for Rome the following day. It was the perfect opportunity for a meeting. Sensing a breakthrough, Castro cabled to Washington, pleading for Mondale to accept: "A negative answer would be a bombshell in our relations, and another affront to their dignity and sovereignty," he wrote.[29]

Washington agreed. By now the Allis Chalmers affair had generated a huge controversy, and the State Department was desperate to close a deal with Argentina. A message from Mondale was sent to Videla through Argentina's representative at the Vatican, whereupon more bureaucratic infighting erupted in Washington.[30] Mondale's office asked for a copy of the draft 1979 report on human rights in Argentina, which was in the final stages of completion by Derian's office. The draft was returned to Derian with eighty-one suggested changes, each one of which had the effect of softening criticism of the Argentinian regime. Derian took the draft to

Vance and said that she would resign if the changes were made. She stayed put, together with the original version.

Mondale requested total secrecy from the Argentinians, but the upcoming meeting was immediately leaked by the Italian press. Unlike Mondale, Italian public opinion was less than delighted at the prospect of hosting a visit by Videla. (Several Italians had disappeared in Argentina.) On September 4 Mondale and Videla worked out a deal and a timetable. The United States would give the green light to EXIM funding before September 15, the deadline for bids for the Yacyreta project. The Junta would issue an invitation to the IACHR before October 23, the IACHR deadline. Thereafter, the United States would send Assistant Secretary of State Viron Vaky to Argentina as proof that relations were healing.[31]

Who blinked first? To judge from the exchange of cables, it was the Americans. The Carter Administration was desperate to put an end to the Allis Chalmers controversy. But at the same time, it could not be seen to be making a deal. As a result, the United States tacitly agreed to reverse the EXIM decision without extracting any firm concessions. The Argentinians were not even asked to restore the all-important "right of option." Ambassador Castro, who acted as the intermediary, was happy to oblige. He was desperate to believe the best of the Argentinians, particularly the avuncular General Roberto Viola. Castro's cables back to Washington portrayed the whole exchange as immensely reassuring.[32]

The second EXIM decision, in favor of Allis Chalmers, was announced and the press correctly linked it to the Mondale-Videla meeting. The Junta then delayed issuing its invitation to the IACHR until October 16 1978. According to Castro it demanded only one condition: there must be no visit to any army bases. Said one Argentinian contact: "Videla himself would be booted out of the military camps if he wished to enter for purposes of snooping around." Castro predicted that the IACHR would visit in the second quarter of 1979.[33]

Derian had been frozen out of the actual negotiations, and the gloom deepened in her office as the Argentinians procrastinated. This caused acute concern in human rights circles, both in Buenos Aires and in Washington. One evening, Augusto Conte MacDonell arrived at Emilio Mignone's apartment in a state of high excitement. He had heard that prisoners were being killed in centers like the ESMA which the IACHR would probably want to visit. The same rumor had reached independent human rights groups in Washington and it provoked an agonized debate about whether or not to endorse the IACHR mission.[34]

The Dam Breaks

The doubts persisted as the IACHR visit approached, and pressure on the seven human rights groups in Buenos Aires increased. On April 30 1979 Thelma Jara de Cabezas, the secretary of the group of relatives of detainees and disappeared, herself disappeared, provoking an international outcry. One month before the team arrived, in August 1979, the police raided the offices of three human rights groups on the orders of a notoriously right-wing judge and seized three thousand signed testimonies that were being prepared for the IACHR. The Minister of the Interior, Albano Harguin-deguy, was unrepentant, even proud, when he talked to journalists. It was not a good omen.[35]

The charge that prisoners were killed in advance of the IACHR inquiry was never substantiated, but it is certain that the delay allowed the Junta to clean up some of the more disreputable centers. By 1979, the population of detainees at the ESMA had been reduced to one hundred. In the summer, sixty were taken by police launch to an island in the river estuary north of Buenos Aires. Those that remained were given uniforms of the prison staff. One of those taken to the island was Thelma Jara de Cabezas.[36]

Meanwhile, efforts were made to change incriminating features at the ESMA school. When Mario César Villani was brought back to the school on November 18, following the IACHR visit, he noticed that the stairway to the basement and torture rooms, which had become a familiar calvary to the detainees, had been replaced by an elevator. The IACHR would visit the ESMA, along with several other notorious centers, but find no evidence of detainees. It would, however note the evidence of reconstruction.[37]

The IACHR finally arrived in Buenos Aires on September 6 1979—almost a year after the meeting between Mondale and Videla in Rome. The chances of probing into the disappearances had been harmed by the long delay, yet the door was finally being thrown open on Argentina's dirty war. The effect was as dramatic as a blindfold suddenly taken off a prisoner at the ESMA. Newspapers carried banner headlines when the team arrived. One paper showed IACHR president Andres Aguilar wearing a Sherlock Holmes hat and puffing at a pipe. "What is he looking for?" asked the headline. Everyone knew the answer. The line of people waiting to see the IACHR team wound like a live animal for block after block, past the Plaza de Mayo where the Mothers held their regular Thursday processions. In the plaza, the weeping relatives mingled with exuberant Argentinians who were celebrating the victory of the national junior soccer team. It was, remembers Tom Farer, the American member of the IACHR, a remarkable sight.

The IACHR team separated to conduct interviews. Tom Farer went to two prisons, at La Plata and Mendoza, where he was, in his own words, "engulfed in human suffering." At La Plata, he decided the safest place to conduct interviews was in the chapel. The weather was freezing, so he wore a raincoat, sweater, and gloves as he sat at a pew taking testimony from three o'clock in the afternoon until one-thirty the following morning. Farer was appalled by the conditions in the prisons he visited—young people cramped into tiny cells, forbidden exercise or newspapers, harshly beaten. This treatment, he told his hosts crisply, was "cruelty, punto." For the first time, Farer became aware of the sheer scope of the disappearances. The IACHR received a remarkable 5,580 allegations. No fewer than 4,983 concerned cases that were new to the IACHR.[38]

Farer also visited the cemetery in La Plata, where he was told that burials were being performed at night. He looked at some of the corpses, observed the bullet holes, and noticed that army physicians had prepared the death certificates. These, he assumed, were the bodies of desaparecidos. The IACHR report would be the first independent confirmation of something that relatives like Emilio Mignone had long suspected: the disappeared persons were being buried in secret graves.[39]

The Junta cannot have expected a sympathetic report, but it was clearly not prepared for the massive 374-page indictment that was handed in to the Argentinian embassy in Washington on December 14. The report was devastating in its frankness and detail. It also firmly rejected the argument that the IACHR should have investigated violations by terrorists.[40] The first draft had been written by Edgardo Paz Barnica, from Honduras, and Edmundo Vargas Careno, the IACHR executive secretary, but the final version was the product of an exhaustive review by the whole team and a vindication of their independence.

Emilio Mignone was in the United States when the report was released. He hurriedly collected 500 copies and smuggled them into Argentina. Here was an important psychological boost. At last the relatives had something tangible to show for their international campaign. This was appreciated by the Junta, which refused to release the OAS report.[41]

Argentina's military rulers realized at once that the report was one of the most serious diplomatic reverses they had faced since taking power. On

January 3 1980, Foreign Minister Carlos Washington Pastor drafted a confidential memorandum for President Videla on the new crisis, lamenting
the "hardness of its [IACHR] conclusions, the obvious politicization, the
lack of balance and the attempt to generate worldwide publicity, as well as
its determination to ascribe responsibility to the armed forces. The international political repercussions could be considerable."[42]

Worse still, this promised to be merely the beginning. The Junta would
have to submit a convincing reply no later than February 29 1980. If it
failed to reply, the chances were that the next OAS General Assembly (in
November) would pass a resolution criticizing Argentina by name. This,
according to another worried document, was exactly what Patt Derian and
others wanted as Jimmy Carter entered his reelection campaign: "Human
rights has been the political theme of the Carter Administration par excellence. Some people in Washington feel that it would be a crowning success
if the majority of governments in the Latin American region pronounced
themselves in favor of the report's recommendations."[43]

Two major hurdles thus faced the Junta in 1980—the U.N. Human
Rights Commission meeting in February, and the OAS General Assembly
in November. Foreign Minister Washington Pastor was to spend much of
the year fighting off this twin challenge, and on December 18 1979 he summoned several key ambassadors, including Gabriel Martínez, to Buenos
Aires for a council of war. A single task force was set up to prepare the
two replies for the OAS and U.N. Gabriel Martínez and Enrique Ros,
Argentina's ambassador to the U.N. in New York were designated to prepare the U.N. reply, which would then serve as the basis for a reply to the
OAS. Martínez asked one junior diplomat at the Argentinian mission in
Geneva, Roberto Saracho, to cooperate. Saracho refused, and was instantly demoted by an angry Martínez.[44]

These arrangements were outlined in a top-secret memorandum from
Foreign Minister Washington Pastor to President Videla, dated January 3.
Like some of Gabriel Martínez's more memorable cables, this document is
a striking mixture of humiliation, frustration, and resolution. It also gives
some important insights into the ways the U.N. and the OAS were viewed
in Buenos Aires. The OAS moved faster, but the U.N. was harder for an
individual government to manipulate.[45]

One sees here why the United Nations and the Organization of American States were viewed with such foreboding by the Junta and with such
hope by the Argentinian relatives. The process was relentless and ponderous. Here it was, gathering momentum just as the Junta was arguing that

normality was returning to the country. Delaying the IACHR inquiry for a year now looked like a serious miscalculation, because it had lengthened the period reviewed by the report and made it even less acceptable that sixty-four disappearances took place in 1979.[46]

Underneath the bravado, there is a note of resignation about Washington Pastor's memo to Videla. It was almost as if he spotted the writing on the wall. He put it like this: "It will be very useful to take whatever measure is possible in respect to the disappearances, which shows that in spite of everything the government will continue to guarantee internal juridical order and fulfill our political aims."[47]

This convoluted language could be interpreted in one of two ways: as encouragement to continue the dirty war, or to put an end to it. In the event, the mass killing effectively came to an end and the disappearances tailed off in the last quarter of 1979. The Junta had too much on its hands at home and abroad to risk continuing its policy of political murder. It had taken three long years, but Patricia Derian's long campaign was finally bearing fruit. The next challenge facing the Junta lay in Geneva.[48]

14. Martínez Prepares

It was time for the climax to Argentina's long campaign in the United Nations. Gabriel Martínez knew it. He knew that the forthcoming session of the U.N. Human Rights Commission, beginning in Geneva on February 1 1980, would see his strategy vindicated or in ruins. The sense of tingling anticipation emerges clearly from his cables back to Buenos Aires.

Martínez was by now a key player in Argentina's diplomatic high command and his cables show a man steadily gaining in self-confidence, with responsibilities far exceeding those normally expected of an ambassador in Geneva. It was proof of Martínez's own stock and also of the importance attached by the Junta to the United Nations.

On December 18 1979 Martínez and nine other ambassadors arrived in Buenos Aires for the council of war on human rights. The meeting opened at 10:00 A.M. in the Green Room at the Foreign Ministry with an address by Foreign Minister Pastor. Over the next two days each of the ten ambassadors reviewed the state of the human rights campaign in his host country. At 5:00 P.M. on Wednesday December 20, the meeting resumed in the cabinet room at Government House, where each ambassador delivered another fifteen-minute briefing to President Jorge Videla. This would have been the crowning moment of Gabriel Martínez's career and it is easy to imagine the pride that this intensely egotistical man would have felt in the presence of his president. He would have prepared to return to Geneva with a renewed sense of commitment.[1]

The script for the upcoming session of the Commission was carefully drafted at this December summit. Martínez's strategy, of using the private 1503 procedure in order to muzzle any public debate, was endorsed. He then began work on drafting a response to the confidential communications, which would have to be answered in full if his strategy were to succeed. President Videla signed presidential decree 310, designating Enrique Ros, Argentina's ambassador to the U.N. in New York, as head of the delegation in Geneva, with Gabriel Martínez as his alternate. Three ministries—Foreign, Interior, and Justice—were instructed to bear the expenses of keeping the delegation in Geneva for forty-five days, and to provide an additional fifteen hundred dollars as an entertainment allowance for the two ambassadors.

Nothing else was left to chance. On February 18 1980, the Foreign Ministry sent a note to the Ministry of the Interior, strongly advising it not to reply to a Swedish government protest about the disappearance of Dagmar Hagelin until after the Commission. The note warned that there could be "possible negative effects" on Argentina's position if the reply were made public in Sweden beforehand.[2] Poring over their documents, Enrique Ros and Gabriel Martínez then flew in through the thick winter fog that lay like a blanket over Geneva, to head off the Western offensive.

Argentina Exploits the Grain Embargo

Argentinian Foreign Ministry documents written at the beginning of 1980 reflect the dramatic change in the international climate that had occurred since the last Commission meeting. The Soviet Union had invaded Afghanistan and President Carter, in retaliation, had declared a grain embargo against the Soviet Union. Vietnam had invaded Kampuchea. Central America was exploding. In Teheran, American diplomats had been seized by Iranian revolutionary guards. There was growing tension in the Persian Gulf between Iran and Iraq.

That a decisive shift had occurred in the global balance of power was apparent in Buenos Aires. Suddenly the invasion of Afghanistan had handed the Junta the leverage it needed in Washington. It was clear that the U.S. grain embargo would only work if other major grain exporters, principally Australia and Argentina, were to follow suit. On January 24, General Andrew Goodpaster, a former Supreme Allied Commander in Europe, arrived in Buenos Aires to ask for help.

This was a major boost for the Junta. An American general was back in Argentina! Not, as one Buenos Aires newspaper put it, a "Department of State careerist," but a real live general. In concrete terms, it must be said, Goodpaster's visit achieved little. The Argentinians refused to join the grain embargo, although they promised not to exploit it commercially. In return, Goodpaster offered a modest program of military cooperation.[3] Symbolically, however, Goodpaster's visit was momentous. Finally, the Junta could throw off the shackles of 502B. Argentina was again deemed important to American security—vitally important. The Junta was exuberant. Fate had dealt a lucky card. It mattered not that the stench of war was again in the air. What mattered was the prospect of rehabilitation, and Argentina's readmission to the "free world": "Our non-adhesion to the grain embargo . . . coming on top of a gradual increase in trade with the Soviet Union over the decade has provided the most effective means to force a change in U.S. human rights policy towards Argentina," crowed one memo. "This shows the extent to which the government of Argentina can turn the global rivalry between the two superpowers to its own advantage without abandoning its natural allies."[4]

These words were written in the second half of 1980. It is as if a magic wand has been waved. Suddenly, after four years as an ugly sister, the Junta is again desirable. Romance is in the air. But not, it must be stressed, with the Russians. The Junta is playing two suitors against each other, but the hand it yearns for is American.

Much would subsequently be made of the Junta's relationship with the Russians, but the facts are somewhat less than dramatic. When the U.S. stopped selling arms to Argentina in 1978 its place was taken not by the Soviet Union but by France and West Germany. Soviet military penetration into Argentina was limited to one week-long visit by General Ivan Jacovich Braiko that began on August 21 1979. The following month, a low-ranking Argentinian general visited Moscow. The exchange produced much talk of "fraternization," but very little of substance.[5]

Even the Junta's defiance of the U.S. grain embargo was more a matter of necessity than a snub to the United States. Martínez de Hoz had borrowed so much that Argentina could not have joined the grain embargo even if it had wanted to. It was far from a two-way street: in 1980, the value of Argentina's exports to the Soviet Union was thirty-six times greater than its imports. Thus, when Yuri Fokin, the Secretary General of the Soviet Foreign Ministry, ended a week-long visit to the Argentina on August 1 1980, newspapers stressed the trade imbalance rather than any burgeoning military alliance.

The one area where the two nations—the USSR and Argentina—shared a common concern was human rights. Both were feeling the chill of international disapproval, and both huddled together for warmth and consolation in the United Nations. This fact, too, featured in Fokin's talks, as Claus Ruser made clear in a cable back to Washington from the U.S. embassy in Buenos Aires.[6] But the alliance extended no further than the United Nations. In regional bodies the situation was very different.

Within the Conference on Security and Cooperation in Europe, for example, the Soviet Union was able to trade off human rights against disarmament. No such option was open to Argentina in the OAS.[7]

With the exception of human rights, the relationship between the Soviet Union and Argentina never really flourished—even after the Russian invasion of Afghanistan. (In December 1981 the Soviet Union vetoed the Junta's candidate for Secretary General of the United Nations.) What changed, in fact, was not so much the actual relationship as the way it was perceived in Washington. The invasion of Afghanistan divided the world anew into East and West—the world that Carter himself had disdained when he spoke in 1977 of an "inordinate fear of Communism." Here was Kissinger's world where every event outside the Soviet bloc was a legitimate American security concern. This all-encompassing definition of U.S. security was one thing Carter had hoped to challenge. In the end he embraced it.

During 1980, the Junta gleefully ignored the grain embargo and broke its promise to Goodpaster. In 1978, Argentina exported 1.4 million tons to the Soviet Union. In 1980 the figure jumped to 7.6 million, and within six months of Goodpaster's visit the Junta had signed a five-year export agreement with Moscow.[8] Washington watched and agonized. The mood in the United States in 1980 was so nervous that the slightest hint of closer relations between Argentina and the Soviet Union was bound to seem threatening. The Junta realized this and became adept at twisting the knife, with a hint here, a gesture there. It was enough to throw the Carter Administration into a frenzy. At the same time, however, the Junta did nothing seriously to jeopardize its relationship with Washington.[9]

Derian's Decline

Another bonus for the Junta was the apparent decline in Patt Derian's fortunes, as security concerns began to replace Carter's early zeal on behalf of human rights. Even before the Soviet invasion of Afghanistan and the Iranian hostage crisis, the outlook was sufficiently dispiriting for Jeane Kirkpatrick—a registered Democrat like Derian—to argue that Carter's human rights policy had undermined U.S. allies, notably in Iran and Nicaragua, and opened the way to regimes that were considerably more hostile.[10]

By the beginning of the election year of 1980, Jeane Kirkpatrick's thesis seemed prophetic. The Soviets had invaded Afghanistan, the Iranians had invaded the U.S. embassy in Teheran, and Carter had acquired the unfortunate label of a "flip-flop" president. Everywhere, it seemed, American allies were under pressure and Communism was on the rampage. In the U.S. Donald Fraser had failed in his attempt to win election to the Senate and had left Washington, taking some of the steam out of the congressional drive on human rights. (Fraser's key aide, John Salzberg, joined Derian's staff in the human rights bureau.) Robert Drinan had been told by the Vatican to choose between God and mammon, opted for God, and resigned his seat in Congress. Jimmy Carter himself began to act as though human rights was a luxury that he could not afford. Carter would devote almost no space to the subject in his memoirs.[11]

Derian herself disagrees that the Carter Administration abandoned human rights. From the start she had seen her job as twofold: first, to present the human rights facts dispassionately and let others weigh them against U.S. security; second, to build an institutional base that would survive her. By 1979, she insists, the record was one of success. As her office grew in bureaucratic "standing" and as the rough edges were smoothed out, there was less friction and less controversy spilling over into the press. The annual human rights reports had grown in stature and usefulness, and the wrath of America's allies was slightly appeased in 1979, when they were extended to all countries in the world, not simply those that received American aid. (This left one nation exempt from the exacting review—the United States.)

Derian's main concern was the way her bureau unwittingly contributed towards Carter's image of indecisiveness—the image that helped to lose him the 1980 election. Even after a formal mechanism was set up to balance human rights against other considerations (the Inter-Agency Group on Human Rights and Foreign Assistance, or Christopher group), each case was decided on individual merits instead of precedent or even policy. One regular participant recalls ruefully that decisions could go either way, depending on the persuasiveness of the case, the current mood in Congress, even the vacation roster. The whole thing was terribly haphazard. This, agrees Derian, was unfortunate.

Even Derian does not deny that it was an uphill fight after the Allis Chalmers controversy. On June 14 1980 the State Department forwarded to President Carter the results of an interagency review which effectively recommended an end to the Argentinian arms embargo. Patt Derian went public and threatened to resign. In July word came through that an Argentinian officer was to be invited to join instructors at Fort Gulick in Panama. The resumption of full relations was only prevented by the Junta's decision to support a particularly brutal coup in Bolivia in July. Reports began to arrive that Argentinian military personnel were torturing detained Bolivian legislators. Old habits, it appeared, died hard. At this even the Junta's supporters at ARA like John Bushnell accepted defeat.[12]

Asia was even more difficult. After the Soviet invasion of Afghanistan, Pakistan suddenly became a vital U.S. ally, and Zbigniew Brzezinski headed off to Pakistan to laud President Zia ul-Haq, who had recently hanged Zulfikar Ali Bhutto, his democratically elected predecessor. Brzezinski offered American military aid and posed for photographers at the Khyber Pass looking down the barrel of a gun at Russian soldiers. Within days Derian was off to Pakistan trying to reassert some balance. The visit got off to a poor start when Zia met her with the words: "So you're the wife of Hodding Carter?" It was only partially redeemed when Bhutto's wife and daughter were released from detention shortly afterward.

Derian remembers hours of grueling arguments over aid for South Korea—arguments that her office usually lost. She insisted that it was possible to distinguish between the presence of 50,000 American troops on the frontier, which was necessary for South Korean security, and the provision of shock batons to the South Korean police, which was not. She also argued that the United States could exert far more leverage on the regime to improve human rights. Repressive regimes, she insisted, made lousy allies. She did manage to ensure that when Jimmy Carter went to South Korea he took a full briefing book with him, and Carter obliged by delivering a tough lecture to President Park. But she also remembers the fiasco over Kim Dae Jung, who was kidnapped from his hotel in Japan, shipped back to South Korea, and sentenced to death. Some of the frustration still spills out in conversation. "We were floppy, pathetic."[13]

Like so many others, she stumbled badly over El Salvador. Between 1977 and 1979, Derian's staff used all possible avenues under U.S. legislation to oppose security aid going to El Salvador's corrupt and brutal military regime. On October 23 1979 young officers seized power in El Salvador in an effort to break the mold of repression. The civilians and military joined up to form a government, but the left-wing civilians fit in uneasily. Instead of helping to forge a broad coalition, the Carter Administration encouraged the exclusion of the left, which withdrew in January

1980 to link up with the guerrillas. Carter then increased the stakes, and proposed $5.7 million dollars in military aid to El Salvador's military regime.

When this news came through, the Archbishop of San Salvador, Oscar Romero, raised his voice in anguished protest. Romero was the focal point for the human rights movement in the country, and in November 1979 he had presented the Junta with a list of one hundred seventy-six missing people and demanded an explanation.[14] His was a powerful voice, and on February 17 he used his pulpit to warn that the delivery of American aid "instead of promoting greater justice and peace in El Salvador will without doubt sharpen the injustice and repression."[15] On March 24 the warning struck home with terrible force when Romero himself was gunned down while celebrating mass.

It was clear that the death squads were connected to the security forces: clear to Romero, clear to the human rights groups, clear to the U.S. ambassador in San Salvador Robert White. Yet the notion of a moderate center squeezed by men of violence on the right and the left in El Salvador was carefully nurtured by the Carter Administration in the latter part of 1980. The reason was that, for aid to be justified under 502B, El Salvador's government had to be absolved from responsibility for the killings.[16]

Precisely because they were licensed to kill, the killers stepped up their murderous work. On the morning of November 27 1980 more than one hundred armed men forced their way into an office in the San José Externales high school, where five members of the left-wing civilian coalition (Frente Democrático Revolucionario) were holding a press conference. The five men were dragged out, and their tortured bodies were later found alongside a highway. With that callous and brutal act, all hope of reconciling El Salvador's squabbling political factions vanished permanently. The sense of shock at the U.S. embassy gave way to gallows humor. The weekly analysis of political killings, previously called "violence week in review," was renamed "grimgram."

Worse was to come. On December 4, the bodies of four American churchwomen were dug up from shallow graves near the road to El Salvador's new airport. The following day President Carter suspended the aid package. It was decided that aid would not be resumed until the violence by the security forces had fallen and the outrage thoroughly investigated. Yet, relatives of the murdered Americans found themselves faced with baffling bureaucratic indifference and even told to pay for the bodies to be flown home.[17] In El Salvador itself the government refused to follow up clues that pointed to the killers' identities.

In spite of this, an unusual meeting was held at the State Department on the morning of December 31 1980 under the chairmanship of Secretary of State Edmund Muskie. It decided that military aid to El Salvador should be resumed, even though none of the U.S. conditions had been met. Patt Derian was pointedly not invited to the meeting. It was a final painful reminder of her loss of influence within the State Department.[18]

In El Salvador, the last few months of 1980 ushered in an orgy of blood-letting that would do irreparable damage to that sad little country and the reputation of the United States. Ronald Reagan would simply pick up where Jimmy Carter left off. His officials would maintain the fiction of a beleaguered center struggling to combat terror from the right and left and use this to justify military aid. They would say that they were picking up where Carter left off, and in this they would be largely correct.

Martínez Weighs the Future

By the end of 1979, Carter's policy toward the United Nations had also come full circle. The value of the U.N. to Carter had long been clear. The U.N. offered a forum for promoting human rights without risking American jobs, enraging American allies, or inviting the charge of interference. In spite of this, Carter's term in office will be remembered for two blunders which severely weakened multilateral human rights procedures.

On November 5 1975 Henry Kissinger had written to the International Labor Organization in Geneva to protest against its "politicized" attacks on Israel and indifference to human rights abuses in Eastern Europe. Kissinger had given the ILO two years to get its house in order. By a dreadful irony, the deadline for U.S. withdrawal—November 5 1977—fell one month after Carter had signed the three major human rights treaties at U.N. headquarters in New York.

Kissinger's charges against the ILO were manifestly unfair and clearly calculated to appease the wrath of the U.S. Jewish lobby over a controversial resolution equating Zionism with racism that was passed in November 1975 by the General Assembly—an entirely separate body from the ILO. The ILO was pro-Western in its outlook and composition, and it had not ignored abuses in Eastern Europe. Worse, the United States had itself shown almost no interest in ratifying the ILO conventions that it was using to criticize the Soviets. The ILO itself, as we have seen, offered valuable support to Argentina's beleaguered trade unions. But the agency had a powerful foe in George Meany, the AFL-CIO chief who had always thought the ILO "soft" on Eastern Europe. Carter owed Meany a debt for support in his election campaign and, overriding the advice of Cyrus Vance, he pulled the United States out of the ILO in 1977. The decision crippled the ILO financially and excluded the United States from some vibrant human rights debate in the ILO, not least over Poland and the USSR. For a government that believed in the U.N. and human rights, it was a devastating self-inflicted wound.[19]

The second major disappointment occurred when the three international human rights conventions that Carter had signed with a flourish in 1977 came before the Senate for advice and consent. Like all international law, the conventions contained ambiguities that had been exploited by conservative critics in the United States, but Carter evidently calculated that any loss of sovereignty to the United States would be outweighed by the boost to international human rights law from participation by the United States. Besides, the United States had less to fear than most. Yet it was four more months before Carter sent the conventions up to the Senate. The reason for the delay soon became clear. Lawyers at the State Department had insisted on a thicket of legal reservations designed to meet the most minute, unworthy suspicions.

To make matters worse, the Senate did not get around to formally considering the treaties until November 14 1979, ten days after the American hostages were taken in Iran. This traumatic incident underlined Iran's contempt for the fragile consensus that supports international law, and suddenly, the skepticism of American conservatives seemed less eccentric. By now Carter's political capital was fast ebbing away, and he was not going to squander it on marginal causes. The conventions returned to the shelves to collect dust.

It was another serious reversal for Derian. Her office was now preparing human rights reports on every country in the world except the United States, and her human rights campaign was invoking laws which the United States itself was unwilling to ratify. If the United States was unwilling to submit its own vaunted system to U.N. scrutiny, how could it possibly demand that the Junta in Argentina follow suit?[20]

From Buenos Aires, all this looked very promising. U.S. policy in the United Nations and on human rights had lost all momentum. The pros-

pects for a vigorous American initiative on disappearances at the forthcoming U.N. Human Rights Commission meeting in Geneva appeared to
be receding fast. From his narrower perspective in Geneva, Gabriel Martínez was much less optimistic. The previous year, 1979, he had appealed
to the Nonaligned, particularly Yugoslavia, to head off Western pressure.
That, as he warned in a cable back to Buenos Aires, would now be more
difficult.[21] The crises in Afghanistan and Kampuchea and the turmoil in
the Persian Gulf and Central America had placed great strain on the Nonaligned Movement that were bound to weaken its ability to take a unified
position on disappearances at the United Nations. Martínez had also relied
on help from the Soviets, but the Soviets had been savagely criticized by
the Nonaligned over Afghanistan and were now on the defensive.

In fact, concluded Martínez, there was only one regional bloc that enjoyed cohesion, and this was the Western group under the leadership of
the United States. The invasion of Afghanistan had breathed new life and
new purpose into the Western group. This was ominous for Argentina.

It was, as always, an astute assessment from Martínez. It also acknowledged that different factors were at play in Geneva from those in Washington and Buenos Aires, and that they threatened to deprive Argentina of
weapons that had served it well between 1976 and 1979. In addition, Martínez had generated enormous personal resentment by his intimidating
tactics, and this too would tend to offset any benefits to Argentina from
the global shift. In a sense, Martínez's tactics had backfired. They had won
the Junta valuable breathing space, but they had also increased the chances
of the United Nations deliberately ignoring the fact that disappearances
had almost stopped.

The situation facing the Argentinian delegation was thus less than
promising. By the same token, it was not nearly so gloomy for the American delegation as it might have appeared in Washington. Added to this,
Congress had called on the American delegation to take action on the
disappearances. Don Bonker—Fraser's successor as chairman of the House
Subcommittee on International Organizations and Human Rights—had
made a personal commitment to the issue. Even though Carter seemed to
be turning his back on human rights, the situation was still ripe for
the right kind of American delegate to the forthcoming Human Rights
Commission.

15. Shestack Breaks the U.N. Jinx

Very few Americans who had served as their country's delegate to the United Nations Human Rights Commission had made a lasting impression, and even fewer had enjoyed it. This was hardly surprising because the post called for a rare mixture of attributes: knowledge of the labyrinthine U.N. procedures, a way with people, concrete objectives, extraordinary stamina, optimism, a rhino-thick skin, and an ability to spot the irrelevant. Jerome Shestack, Carter's nominee to the 1980 session, possessed most, if not all, of these qualities.

A partner in one of the largest Philadelphia law firms, Shestack was also president of the International League for Human Rights, a New York-based human rights organization that had assiduously monitored the uneven progress of the U.N. since 1945.[1] His connection to the League provided Shestack with knowledge of the U.N. and clear objectives. As a lawyer he believed that the U.N. had done a reasonable job in drafting standards, but as an activist he spotted the need for something more. Like Patt Derian, he thought the disappearances were the nearest thing to sheer evil since the Holocaust. He also had very little time for quiet diplomacy. If anyone would see through Martínez's game, it was Jerry Shestack. He was easily the most formidable opponent to confront the Argentinian since Theo van Boven.

Shestack was helped by an impish sense of humor and strong streak of sentimentality. One of his efforts, "Political Prisoner," went: "Nights that are years, / dark, full of fears, / nightmares and jeers, / dreams that are tears. / Torture to rend / men that can't bend / time does not end / days without end / stifle my cry / justice a lie / silent I die / world: tell me why." Shestack didn't expect prizes for that, but the career diplomats at the U.S. mission in Geneva were impressed. Back in Washington, Juan Méndez, a defense lawyer who had been imprisoned by Isabel Perón's government, kept a copy on his wall.

Shestack was a life-long Democrat who had served as a campaign manager for vice-presidential candidate Sargent Shriver in the abortive 1972 campaign. He spotted Jimmy Carter's potential before it was fashionable, met with him in Philadelphia, and started his fundraising campaign. Like Patt Derian he had good contacts with the Carter Administration and knew Cyrus Vance, Warren Christopher, and William Maynes—who had all taken senior posts in the State Department. He was offered the job of U.N. Commission delegate in 1977, but turned it down because of the commitment in time.

Shestack remained on close personal terms with the triumvirate, and in October 1979 he received a call from Walter Mondale asking if he would accept the post for the forthcoming 1980 Commission session. Shestack accepted and Jimmy Carter announced his appointment on December 10—International Human Rights Day. In just nine days' time, Martínez would be briefing President Jorge Videla in Buenos Aires.

Shestack threw himself into his new job as completely as his Argentinian counterparts. He loved cables. He would stay up until midnight drafting, and watch fascinated as the cable disappeared into the scrambling machine to be instantly decoded in Washington. The next day he might be reading reactions from ten different embassies. He used to compare it to flicking a switch: suddenly, you could light up a huge network of embassies around the world. He would return to Washington deeply impressed with his country's foreign service.

Many of those he came into contact with in Geneva found him too blunt. His relations with Theo van Boven were never warm. Shestack had admired van Boven from a distance, but when they met in person he found van Boven dour and cautious. He did not know the pressure that van Boven was under from the Argentinians and the Soviets, and van Boven never took the time to tell him. As a result, van Boven appeared to Shestack as the stereotypical U.N. bureaucrat. Van Boven, in return, viewed Shestack as a loose cannon.[2]

Shestack quickly appreciated, like Martínez, that the Commission's composition would prove decisive, but instead of lamenting the existence of regional blocs as Jeane Kirkpatrick would do, Shestack tried to turn them to the advantage of the United States. Hitherto there had been relatively little formal coordination among the Western nations on the Commission, in spite of their common interests. In 1980 the number of Western seats had increased to eleven, including Japan. They began to meet at 9:00 A.M. at the spacious West German mission in Geneva to go over plans for the day. They took on the name "Western European and Others Group" (WEOG for short).

Shestack also realized the importance of rewarding delegates who sup-
ported U.S. positions. He was particularly taken by Agha Hilaly from
Pakistan, a melancholy silver-haired diplomat who had helped to arrange
Kissinger's secret trip to China while serving as Pakistan's ambassador in
Washington. After Hilaly helped to push through a resolution criticizing
the Soviet invasion in Afghanistan, Shestack cabled Washington suggest-
ing that President Zia ul-Haq be told and thanked. Mohamed al-Jabiri of
Iraq was another delegate who seemed to have a mind of his own.

Although he was a Jew, Shestack was quickly subjected to blasts of anti-
Israeli rhetoric at the Commission. He felt personally that the Israeli oc-
cupation on the West Bank was relatively humane, but at the same time he
accepted that the Palestinians had a cause for grievance. When Theo van
Boven introduced him to the PLO representative, a cultivated man named
Daced Barakat, Shestack proposed further meetings. But the memory of
Andy Young's resignation over a meeting with PLO delegates was still
fresh in Washington, and he was quickly told not to go any further.[3]

Shestack refused to be dispirited. He also remained undaunted by the
ominous climate created by the Soviet invasion of Afghanistan and the
exile of Andrei Sakharov to Gorki. The case of Sakharov was particularly
distressing, because the Russian's human rights monitoring committee
was affiliated with Shestack's League. Shestack had phoned Sakharov
shortly before his exile.

Sakharov had been banished a few days before the Commission session
began, and it was too late for Shestack to receive any formal instructions,
so he raised the issue with other Western delegates on his own initiative.
What could be done? There was little optimism because individual cases
were traditionally handled in the confidential 1503 procedure, never in
public. Well, insisted Shestack, tradition had better damn well change.
Mark Colville, the British delegate, came up with an idea. Why not start
with a telegram of concern to the Soviet government? The rest agreed.
Shestack was given a free rein by Washington, and for two exhilarating
days it was a case of the tail wagging the dog. The debate grew heated,
with the Soviets furiously insisting that it was an "internal issue." The row
spilled out into the press and gave a healthy impression of an active Commission and a committed American delegation.

Eventually, the deadlock was broken when the Iraqi delegate Mohamed
al-Jabiri suggested that the issue be postponed and brought up again later
in the session. Al-Jabiri's proposal was accepted by fifteen to thirteen, with
Argentina one of the countries that supported the Soviets. When it resur-

faced, Shestack had to settle for a compromise resolution to defer consideration of Sakharov until the 1981 session. Nonetheless, he had achieved his first objective by getting the case of Sakharov publicly discussed twice and put on the U.N. agenda. Al-Jabiri's initiative had come as a surprise because he had already delivered some dour and predictable statements on Israel. Shestack took note.[4]

Shestack Clashes with Martínez

In a way, everything else was a dress rehearsal for Argentina. There was a sense of inevitability about the looming clash between Martínez and Shestack. Technically, it was Enrique Ros who was Shestack's opposite number as head of the Argentina delegation. But Martínez was his spiritual foe. Martínez was the man who had plotted for four long years to prevent any U.N. action on the disappearances, the man who had humiliated three successive American delegations. Shestack inherited three years of accumulated frustration from his predecessors. He had a score to settle.

Unlike Martínez, Shestack did not benefit from clear and unequivocal instructions on the issue of disappearances. Patt Derian and Congressman Don Bonker (Fraser's successor as Chairman of the House Subcommittee on Human Rights) wanted to maintain the pressure on Argentina. But the powerful ARA regional bureau felt that the Junta had paid its dues by admitting the IACHR the previous year. Disappearances were on the decline. No more could be asked. In addition, there was Argentina's strategic importance. One week earlier, generals Goodpaster and Videla had reviewed the Commission during their talks in Argentina. There is little doubt that Videla asked for a softer U.S. line in Geneva and no reason to suspect that the Goodpaster was unsympathetic.[5] One immediate result: Shestack was instructed not to initiate or sponsor anything critical of Argentina.

Shestack and his team, on the other hand, were strongly in favor of keeping up the pressure. The U.S. delegation included Roberta Cohen, who had directed the International League before joining Derian's staff, and Millard Arnold, a young black lawyer from the Washington-based Lawyers' Committee for Civil Rights. The U.S. ambassador in Geneva, Gerald Helman, was a career diplomat who had been appointed by Carter and had earned the reputation of being diligent, sympathetic, and well-informed. Frank Sieverts, Helman's human rights deputy, had also worked at the State Department under Derian, where he prepared the annual human rights reports before moving to Geneva. This was a team prepared to back Shestack up to the hilt if it came to a clash.

Helman was the first to cross swords with Argentina. He met with Martínez and warned that any strong-arm tactics would backfire. One week into the Commission session the NGOs held a meeting on the disappearances at which they publicized a new Amnesty report disclosing startling details about sixteen secret detention centers in Argentina.[6] The meeting also served to whip up enthusiasm for the Commission debate on disappearances that loomed ahead. Nineteen delegations, including Algeria and Iraq, attended. It might have taken four years to get there, but in 1980 the issue of disappearances was white hot in the United Nations.

Once again, under the glowering winter sky of Geneva, tense negotiations got under way in the U.N. Commission. Once again, they were watched anxiously from the sidelines by representatives of the Mothers of the Plaza de Mayo. The Western delegations were now taking advantage of their regular meetings at the West German mission in Geneva to try to plan a common strategy on disappearances. It was horrendously difficult. They could not even agree on how to define "a disappeared person."

Eventually, the issue passed by default to the French, who had come to Geneva with a prepared resolution. The French clung tenaciously to their 1979 proposal for a group of three independent experts who would act on behalf of the U.N. Secretary General, consult with relatives, prepare detailed proposals, and "take appropriate action." Argentina was not mentioned by name, but in U.N. terms it was a tough proposal. Unfortunately, like so many concoctions of the Quai d'Orsay, while pure in logic and elegant of phrase it was also totally unworkable. Quite apart from anything else, the French concept of a disappearance appeared to cover people who were missing as well as kidnapped. The French added the word "enforced," which helped, and "involuntary," which did not. (The difference between a disappearance that was involuntary and one that was enforced escaped everyone except the French.) It was all rather unsatisfactory, but characteristically the French refused to budge.

Gabriel Martínez's first goal, as we have seen, was to permit a review of the confidential 1503 communications but ensure that the case of Argentina remained "under review," or under wraps, for another year. On January 28 Martínez and Ros presented a ninety-two page response to a preliminary group of five Commission delegates which was headed by Mohamed al-Jabiri, the Iraqi.[7] These five played the same role as the five subcommissioners who drew up the initial blacklist at the summer session of the Sub-Commission. They reviewed the Sub-Commission list of gross viola-tors and decided to recommend that the case against Malawi be made public because Malawi had failed to reply. They also reviewed Javier Pérez de Cuéllar's controversial visit to Uruguay the previous month. After Mohamed al-Jabiri read out Miguel Angel Estrella's damning letter, they paid a barbed compliment to Pérez de Cuéllar, expressing gratitude for the way he had "presented the Uruguayan government's point of view," and decided to ask the U.N. Secretary General to pursue his efforts the next year. This move neatly sidestepped the problem of whether to rebuke Pérez de Cuéllar or drop the case. Carlos Giumbruno, the Uruguayan delegate who wanted the case dropped, was furious.

Next came Argentina. The five thanked the Junta for "cooperating," but suggested that much more information was required on the question of "disappeared persons who appeared to have been kidnapped by agents of the government, or with the connivance of the government." It put seven questions to Martínez and Ros and hinted that if they were not answered, the case could be made public the following year. Martínez's grand plan was in serious jeopardy.[8]

When this recommendation was discussed in private by the full Com-mission, the Brazilians intervened on Argentina's side and suggested that the seven questions be softened. Shestack was unhappy with this and pro-posed a series of four supplementary questions that had the reverse effect. The meeting ran over lunch and into the afternoon as Shestack's proposals were examined one by one and dropped. The final resolution simply asked for information about "disappeared" persons, and dropped the reference to "agents of the government."

Shestack learned soon afterward that Martínez had complained angrily to the Foreign Ministry in Buenos Aires over his intervention and that this had immediately been communicated to Washington. It alarmed officials in the ARA bureau, who immediately assumed that Shestack was exceed-ing his instructions. Martínez had also reported that he had seen Shestack "lobbying" with the Cuban delegation. In fact, Shestack had been talking to the Cubans about a large and lurid pamphlet that Martínez was circu-lating. This showed pictures of people mutilated by terrorist bombs and alleged that the terrorists had been supported by Marxists abroad. She-stack found it ironic that Martínez was aligning Argentina with the Soviet Union in the Commission, and pointed out the contradiction to the Cu-ban delegation. Cuba was harboring Argentinian guerrillas at the time.

The upshot of this exchange was that the 1503 procedure did, eventually, play into Argentina's hands, thus vindicating Martínez's strategy. This was a grave snub to the relatives waiting in the corridor outside. It was now more vital than ever to produce something worthwhile from the public debate.

On February 22, at the end of the third week, word came through that the Argentinians had rejected the French draft and were pressing a weaker proposal in Western capitals. (Ros and Martínez had, in fact, cabled the text of the French proposal back to Buenos Aires and had been curtly informed that it was unacceptable.)[9] Shestack proposed a division of labor, which should have by all rights have backfired in a human rights body opposed to neocolonialism, but which had the merit of being extremely practical. He suggested that the Western countries lobby their former colonies on the Commission. Britain was assigned Nigeria and Ghana; France took the Ivory Coast and Senegal. Holland was given Peru and Colombia, and the United States took on the job of wooing a group of governments that received American aid: Egypt, Pakistan, Costa Rica, Panama, and the Philippines. Someone found that Zambia was still unassigned, so the United States took on Zambia as well. Shestack flipped the magic switch and illuminated the arteries of American diplomacy.

Back in the Zambian capital of Lusaka, Alick Mpengula, director of international organizations in the Zambian Foreign Ministry, was in a quandary. He would love to help, but he had no way of getting in touch with the Zambian delegation on the Commission in Geneva, Zambia being too poor to afford a separate mission. He couldn't even put through a telex message to the Palace of Nations in Geneva because the one operator in his office who knew the telex number was on vacation. Gerald Helman was asked if he could loan the services of an American telex and help put the Zambian delegate in Geneva in touch with his own government.

The Egyptians then passed over the Argentinian draft proposal. The Argentinians wanted to postpone the issue for another year, and they knew it would be unacceptable to the Western delegations. They exuded confidence that the West would be defeated in a straight vote because they, not the West, had the support of the Nonaligned. This was a bluff, as it had been the previous year. Argentina was a virtual pariah among the Nonaligned delegations and Martínez knew it. On February 18, he was approached by Waleed Sadi, the Jordanian ambassador in Geneva and current Chairman of the Commission. Sadi, a cheerful, curly-haired man, told Martínez that he had been personally been approached by Argentinian relatives of disappeared persons and asked to intervene with Martínez. He said he would send over a list of names the following day.[10] Sadi was an influential ambassador. He could not have issued a clearer rebuke, nor given clearer proof of Argentina's isolation.

The Group is Established

By now, Martínez was engaged in a major covert operation against his critics. Following his complaints against Shestack, officials in the U.S. State Department suddenly began to have doubts. Worried that Shestack was letting his enthusiasm run away with him, ARA Assistant Secretary of State William Bowdler proposed sending his senior deputy, John Bushnell, to Geneva. Shestack wrote out a blistering cable threatening to quit, which Ambassador Helman toned down and redrafted. On March 5, apparently reacting to the reports from Buenos Aires, Claus Ruser telephoned Helman and asked him obliquely whether Shestack was following his instructions. Shestack was furious and cabled William Maynes and Warren Christopher to protest.

Anyone who had been on the receiving end of Martínez's threats over the previous four years would not have been surprised. It was all part of a familiar game plan. Martínez had identified five governments that were playing a key role in the negotiations. He warned the Dutch that Argentina would cancel a two-billion-dollar contract and close down Argentina's agricultural mission in the Hague if the Dutch persevered. The British were warned to expect a tougher position from Argentina in talks that were under way on the disputed Falkland Islands. The French were told they could sell their arms elsewhere. Senegal's delegate Kéba M'baye was told that Argentina would stop selling Senegal grain. Such a threat would be taken very seriously in an African country.

But it was the Iraqi, Mohamed al-Jabiri, who most provoked the Argentinian. Later, al-Jabiri would tell Shestack that Martínez had complained to the Iraqi delegation. Al-Jabiri was, recalled Shestack, "always giving out signals." But what kind of signals? If he was acting independently, then al-Jabiri was playing a very dangerous game. He had now provoked the Soviet Union (over Sakharov), Argentina, and Uruguay.

By now, the normally stolid Commission was heaving and bucking. Two separate drafts on disappearances—French and Argentinian—were circulating. The Western delegations were unhappy with the French proposal but unable to agree on an alternative, so it was the French text that was set before the Commission on February 25. The Nonaligned delegations were unwilling to side with Argentina, but favored something weaker than the French proposal. A group of young Western diplomats sat down over coffee with M'baye, al-Jabiri, and the Yugoslavians in an attempt to hammer out a compromise. But as in 1979, time was running out. Small groups of delegates were meeting and dissolving in the circular conference room. Conference Room 17 was finally looking used, untidy, lived-in.

Then crisis struck. The group of Nonaligned delegations broke from cover, while M'baye unexpectedly introduced a new text. Shestack smelled treachery, and mounted a feverish attempt to regain the initiative. He turned angrily against his young Western colleagues and tried to persuade M'baye to withdraw his text. Meanwhile, British and Canadian delegates met with Martínez and Ros, who rejected the French draft. The session lasted all of two minutes.

It looked to many observers as if the Western delegations had once again blundered, and the mood in the Western trenches grew scrappy. The time limit for entering new resolutions had passed, and the only alternative was to take the Nonaligned text and incorporate as many Western ideas as possible. Once again, the Iraqi Mohamed al-Jabiri came to the rescue with a compromise that looked acceptable: a group comprising five members of the Commission that would last for one year year initially, to examine (in deference to Gallic pride) "enforced or involuntary" disappearances.

Shestack now tried to ensure that such a group be empowered to review individual cases, take evidence from individuals, and consult NGOs that did not have consultative status with the U.N. As the clock ticked by, one was reminded of a strange contradiction: the U.N. was so profligate with words that the Palace of Nations consumed one thousand tons of paper a year.[11] Here, however, the future of the U.N.'s human rights machinery hung on the difference between just two words—"cases" and "situations." The difference was critical. "Cases" would permit the group to press the Junta about victims like Mónica Mignone and Dagmar Hagelin. "Situations" would not.

Shestack dug in his heels, and al-Jabiri agreed. But other Nonaligned delegations were unhappy. The vote was only hours away. David Weissbrodt and David Krämer, two American lawyers who were observing the proceedings, later conveyed the frantic atmosphere: "Delegates stepped up the pace, searching each other out, yelling, cajoling and pleading." [12] There had been nothing like it before. The scene was more like the New York Stock Exchange than a U.N. conference, only more was at stake.

Shestack then proposed alternative wording. What about "questions relating to disappearances" instead of "cases?" It was vaguer, but it could leave the door open to consideration of individuals—if, that is, the group itself so decided. Al-Jabiri returned to his shuttle diplomacy and persuaded the Nonaligned to accept the new formula. It now remained to be seen whether Argentina would also accept or whether it would cast a no vote, thus signaling a refusal to work with the new group.

The die was finally cast on the evening of February 29 1980. There was no time to introduce the new amendment in writing, so this was done verbally from the floor. Al-Jabiri—by now the dominant actor in the drama—stood up to introduce the change, followed by the Algerian and Nigerian delegates. It was a powerful display of Nonaligned solidarity and it went against Argentina, although Argentina's friends tried one last ploy. Carlos Giumbruno, the Uruguayan, suggested that governments should have the chance to "reply" to any charges leveled by the proposed group. Giumbruno conceded that he had not worked out the precise wording, but suggested a recess. His intention was to spin out the debate and prevent any agreement. Yet another crisis.

Al-Jabiri stepped forward and asked Giumbruno to withdraw his proposal. Waleed Sadi, the Jordanian chairman, agreed. Of course, he said, the honorable delegate from Uruguay was free to persist with an amendment, but he strongly suggested against it. Looking at Sadi, with his muscular build and pugilist's face, made it clear he meant what he said. Giumbruno evidently sensed the antagonism, and withdrew his amendment.

There was a long moment of silence, almost as if the Commission was pausing to consider the fateful decision it was about to take. "Do I have a request for a vote?" asked Sadi, to an almost audible intake of breath from the chamber. Sadi allowed no time for second thoughts, and he walloped his gavel against the wooden desk. For once, even Martínez had remained silent. The proposal had been accepted without a vote. Suddenly, the tension broke. Shestack and other Western delegates turned to each other in open relief. Upstairs in the gallery, relatives of the disappeared persons started weeping. Theo van Boven felt as though a cloud had lifted. The four-year jinx had been broken.

Argentina's Disillusionment

After the Commission meeting, Gabriel Martínez stood back to survey the battlefield. On April 8 1980 he drafted a long aide-mémoire for his foreign minister, blaming his defeat in Geneva on the disarray in the Nonaligned Movement. He had particularly harsh words to say about Jerry Shestack:

> The U.S. delegate stood out for his aggressivity and his constant activism in relation to the case of Argentina. Indeed, his activities do not appear consistent with the expressed willingness of the U.S. for closer relations that we have heard at other meetings, and at the bilateral level. Mr. Shestack has proved that his government is keen to seek closer relations with us . . . without sacrificing its approach on human rights towards us in the international organizations.[13]

Jerry Shestack returned home to acclaim and criticism. During the Commission, Congressman Don Bonker had spent a few days in Geneva. On March 31 he wrote a glowing letter to Secretary of State Cyrus Vance. "From all accounts . . . our delegation was rated by some the best in recent memory. This was a remarkable accomplishment given the tense and uncertain international situation. A large share of our success was due to Jerry Shestack."[14] Bonker added that Iraq's role in winning over the Nonaligned nations also deserved special mention. This was fair: al-Jabiri had indeed played an important role in turning the tide.

In concrete terms Sakharov was still in Gorki, the Soviets were still in Afghanistan, Mónica Mignone was still unaccounted for. But Shestack allowed no doubts to intrude when he appeared before Bonker's subcommittee on April 29. Exuding rugged optimism, he simply insisted that this had been the best session ever—for the Commission, for the United States, and for human rights. No one disagreed because no one wanted to and so, in a sense, it became true. It was proof of the power of positive thinking.[15] Shestack had done more than show that the United States took the U.N. seriously. He had used the Commission to save lives and set up new machinery, instead of pandering openly to U.S. foreign policy goals. This showed a confidence in the U.N. and its human rights machinery that could only be profoundly invigorating.

Once home, however, Shestack found himself exposed once again to the Carter Administration's ambivalence toward Argentina. The ARA bureau was so angered by his performance in Geneva that it refused to attend the delegate's traditional briefing at the State Department, and on April 9

Shestack made a special visit to ARA to defend his stand on Argentina in Geneva. He pointed to Argentina's pattern of voting against the U.S. on Sakharov, on the Camp David agreement, on Kampuchean refugees, on the Soviet invasion in Afghanistan, on religious intolerance. There should, he said, be no apologizing for the tough stand he had taken on disappearances.[16]

In June, Shestack received word that the interagency policy review was proposing a renewal of relations with Argentina, and he added his own protest to that of Patt Derian, citing Argentina's performance in Geneva. On June 5, Warren Christopher promised Shestack that no firm decision would be taken until Videla had stepped down as chief of state. At the same time, Christopher did not hide the fact that options were being reviewed for rewarding Argentina for the "modest recent progress" in improving human rights.[17] As we have seen, any chance of a change in U.S. policy was killed by the Junta's involvement in the Bolivian coup.

Like Patt Derian and Theo van Boven, Jerry Shestack was to be thoroughly vindicated by Argentina's transition to democracy. When a disappointed Jimmy Carter left office he sent a short note to Shestack that now sits on a dresser next to a priceless collection of Charles Dickens novels. It reads: "Your service as our nation's representative on the U.N. Commission merits special attention." Shestack liked that. He had left Geneva poorer by the eight thousand Swiss francs of his own money that he had spent on diplomatic receptions, but he had had the time of his life.[18]

16. The Chairman Disappears

Immediately after Argentina's reverse at the 1980 Human Rights Commission, Gabriel Martínez received a blunt cable from the Foreign Ministry in Buenos Aires telling him to remain vigilant in "confronting terrorism at the international level" and to lobby Western governments in order to thwart Marxism.[1] It was, under the circumstances, astonishingly insensitive and it must have left the irrepressible Martínez even more despondent. "We must profoundly re-examine our strategy," he replied in an April 9 1980 memorandum. "Our margin for maneuver in the diplomatic field is now more narrow than ever."[2]

It was, without any doubt, the lowest point yet in Martínez's long campaign within the United Nations. Instead of blocking the public debate, he had been forced to acquiesce in the creation of an entirely new public U.N. inquiry. Such had been the pressure and the overwhelming distaste for the Junta's policy of disappearances that even Argentina had been unable to vote against the decision. Martínez would now be forced to work with the new group or undermine it. Either way, he would have to move fast.

Membership of the group was settled during the Commission. Each of the five regions was entitled to contribute a candidate. The West decided on Mark Colville, a peer who headed the British delegation. Ivan Tosevski, a cautious Yugoslavian law professor, was chosen by the East Europeans. Mohamed al-Jabiri was rewarded for his efforts by being offered the Asian seat and the chairmanship. The Latin Americans appointed Luis Varela from Costa Rica, and the African place on the group was taken by Kwadwo Nyamekye, an affable Ghanaian diplomat.[3]

The overriding concern was whether the Commission had settled for second best by setting up a group on disappearances instead of an inquiry on Argentina, as it had done over Chile. But there were other more practical problems. It was not clear how independent the five members would be. Nor was it clear whether they would want to hear directly from organizations like the Mothers, which did not enjoy "consultative status" with the United Nations. Gabriel Martínez would argue they could not. He would also insist that the new group was not entitled to review individual cases, because they fell under the purview of 1503. Jerry Shestack and Theo van Boven were equally determined that the group would have to break with U.N. tradition, gather information where it wanted, and review individual cases. Otherwise, Martínez would succeed in his grand strategy and keep individual cases within the confidential 1503 procedure. This was to be the key issue in the uneasy months that lay ahead.

The task of shaping the work of the new group now fell to Theo van Boven. Gabriel Martínez had sensed the threat from van Boven when he had launched his intimidating campaign against the Dutchman three years earlier, and van Boven now showed that Martínez had been right. Van Boven set to his task with relish. He found money for a computer, which was almost unknown in the U.N. in those days, and appointed one of his most trusted officials, Tom McCarthy, to service the group. During the Commission, van Boven and McCarthy met with representatives of Amnesty International, the International Commission of Jurists, and the World Council of Churches. Van Boven assured them that the group would investigate individual cases and also accept submissions from organizations like the Mothers which had no formal relationship with the United Nations.

How should the group respond to new disappearances? The experience of the Red Cross and Amnesty had shown that the worst torture occurs in the first few hours of a victim's kidnapping, which meant that the group was going to have to move fast if it was going to save lives. The resolution had spoken only generally of the need to "deal effectively and expeditiously" with this. It was agreed that when a new case was reported, McCarthy would first check the allegation with key NGOs and then contact the chairman of the group, Mohamed al-Jabiri, before intervening directly with the government concerned.

Other problems remained. Van Boven would have to find two hundred thousand dollars from his budget and other staff to work with McCarthy. The group was only scheduled to last one year. It would be impossible to hire full-time staff in this time, so van Boven began advertising for temporary staff members who were familiar with Latin America and spoke Spanish. He hired a Chilean named Antonio Fortín Cabezas, one of three brothers who had all been prominent in Allende's government before the coup in 1973. Antonio himself had fled to Argentina, where he had struck up a close friendship with Augusto Conte MacDonell and Emilio Mignone. It never occurred to van Boven that this could compromise Fortín's work, and he saw no reason to make concessions for Martínez. He also gave a six-month contract to a young woman named Nathalie Müller. Van Boven did not find out until later that her father had been the representative of the U.N. High Commissioner for Refugees in Buenos Aires during the terrifying months following the coup.

Many of the uncertainties were thus ironed out by van Boven well before the five members of the group met in June. Van Boven and McCarthy began to prepare for the June meeting, confident that the group's future was secure. How wrong they were.

The first hint of a crisis came late in March. Mohamed al-Jabiri telephoned van Boven from Madrid, where he served as Iraq's ambassador. Al-Jabiri sounded nervous. He told van Boven that he was going to be transferred back to Iraq and he asked if van Boven could contact Baghdad and request his presence at the meeting of the U.N.'s Economic and Social Council in May. Van Boven quickly complied. But the Iraqi did not appear at the ECOSOC meeting, and a Western delegate hinted to van Boven that al-Jabiri was in deep trouble with the Iraqi dictator Saddam Hussein. Soon after he returned to Geneva from the ECOSOC meeting, van Boven received a frantic telephone call from al-Jabiri's wife in Madrid. The woman was almost incoherent. Her husband had been recalled to Iraq and she had not heard from him. Where could he be? Alive? Dead? In some jail in Baghdad? Van Boven remembers his feeling of incredulity. The first chairman of the U.N.'s new working group on disappearances had himself disappeared.

There was no explanation for al-Jabiri's plight, although the Iraqi had made some powerful enemies at the U.N. Commission, including—of course—Gabriel Martínez. When the story of al-Jabiri's disappearance surfaced in a newspaper, Martínez filed away a copy with key sections carefully underlined.[4]

Van Boven now embarked on a frantic scramble to save al-Jabiri's life, and in so doing almost certainly exceeded his authority. He contacted a senior Iraqi diplomat who was present in Geneva and told him bluntly that he would protest to U.N. Secretary General Kurt Waldheim if he received no news. A week or so later van Boven received a brief handwritten note from al-Jabiri saying he was retiring from government on a pension and would not be able to take up his position as chairman of the group.

Van Boven's staff compared the letter with a sample of the man's handwriting and concluded it was genuine. But they also noticed that the letter was addressed to "Theodor Ban Boven." When van Boven subsequently showed the letter to Mark Colville, the British member of the group, Colville remarked that the Iraqi would surely have known the correct spelling of van Boven's name. Was this a disguised plea for help from a doomed man? It was a grim possibility, but there was nothing more van Boven could do without inviting an angry charge that he was "interfering" in Iraq's internal affairs. Waleed Sadi, the Jordanian president of the 1980 session of the Commission, took al-Jabiri's place on the Working Group for the June meeting. The chairmanship passed to Kwadwo Nyamekye, the Ghanaian. Al-Jabiri himself survived, quite possibly thanks to van Boven's efforts. Jerry Shestack also intervened on the Iraqi's behalf.[5]

Mark Colville Takes Over

During the June meeting Mark Colville, the British member, took over al-Jabiri's mantle as the dominant member of the group, and at the end of the year he assumed the chairmanship when Nyamekye was appointed van Boven's deputy at the Division. It was the first time in memory that a Briton had assumed such a prominent role in a U.N. human rights investigation.

As a barrister, businessman, and British peer, Mark Colville was ideally placed to handle the principal challenge facing the U.N. group on disappearances, namely, talking to governments. He had succeeded to the impressive title "Viscount Colville of Culross" at the age of twelve, after his father was killed in active service in the Second World War. During the early 1970s, Colville served for two years as a Minister of State at the Home Office—Britain's equivalent of Interior Ministry—in the Conservative government of Edward Heath. His responsibilities included prisons and complaints against the police, and he remembers some of the cases as being awkward: "You had to be aware of the public interest without discouraging the police." Around this time, the government of Ireland was preparing to take Britain to the European court in Strasbourg over charges of having mistreated prisoners in Northern Ireland. Colville was utterly convinced of the rightness of the British case.

He was surprised when he was asked to lead the British delegation on the U.N. Human Rights Commission in 1979, but like Shestack he had friends in high places. Margaret Thatcher had formed a new Conservative government in Britain and the new British Foreign Secretary, Lord Peter

Carrington, was Colville's cousin. Colville himself had no idea what to expect from the Commission, but he quickly mastered the procedural rules. He forged a close friendship with Jerry Shestack, which was surprising because although both men were lawyers they were also totally different in personality and philosophy. Shestack was a self-made man on the liberal wing of the American political spectrum who felt the need to question authority. Colville was a right-wing aristocrat who believed in authority—passionately.

He cut an odd figure in the United Nations. He had a rich, plummy voice and always seemed to be wearing a crumpled suit, with trousers that were a shade too short. The cuffs flapped anxiously about his calves as he strode rapidly around the Commission, head thrust forward. He could inject more feeling (usually it was disdain) into the routine opening of a statement—"Thank you Mr. Chairman"—than any other delegate. He treated every word with exaggerated care. The whole effect was a caricature and one that was staggeringly out of place in the Commission, no less than ten of whose members were former British colonies.

But there was nothing lightweight about Colville. Indeed, he turned out to be one of the sturdiest delegates on the Commission. He was slightly shy at first, like a schoolboy determined not to let the side down, but soon the snickering turned to admiration. On occasions he even took the discussion too seriously, and whenever this happened it provided the Commission with some badly needed theater. On one occasion he rose furiously to an uninhibited attack against Western decadence by the old Soviet delegate Valerian Zorin, who lashed out impetuously at the plight of homosexuals in Holland, Catholics in Northern Ireland, and Indians in North America.

Colville had known that Britain would be attacked over Northern Ireland and he had gone to the trouble of visiting Belfast the previous December. It had been a full day. He had visited the grimy Catholic estates to the north of Belfast and talked to community workers, so he was well prepared to reply to Zorin. It was a powerful statement, delivered with conviction, and marred only by an impromptu comment before the interpreters had a chance to turn off the microphones. Colville's colleagues insisted it was "Try that one on for size," but others thought they heard something more unlordly. Colville manfully apologized when he heard the titters of laughter and realized what had happened.

He was a surprising choice for the new U.N. Working Group on Disappearances but an inspired one at the same time. No one doubted his capacity for hard work. Above all, as a former government minister he would be able to understand, and talk to, governments. No one said so in so many ways, but his aristocratic pedigree was also certain to appeal to the snob in Gabriel Martínez. Martínez was the kind of man who would relish the challenge. Here was someone sophisticated, not like that Iraqi peasant al-Jabiri or that Jordanian bruiser Waleed Sadi. Like many of his fellow countrymen, Martínez had a basic contempt for the developing countries. What better test of his skills than to cross swords with a British lord? Rapiers, of course, not broadswords.

The Group Confronts Martínez

Once they had recovered from the shock of losing al-Jabiri, the group started to get down to work. They quickly rubber-stamped van Boven's decision to handle individual cases and adopted several criteria for a case's admissibility. First, it had to fit the agreed definition—an "enforced or involuntary disappearance." Second, there had to be clear evidence of security officials being involved. Third, all domestic remedies, such as habeas corpus, had to have been exhausted. In restrospect, says Mark Colville, the undertaking was audacious. "We were criticizing governments for their treatment of their own citizens." Did this mean interference—in violation of the U.N. Charter? Colville did not think so at the time.

The confrontation with Argentina came sooner than expected. The Junta protested loudly at the U.N. about "interference" in its internal affairs when NGOs protested the killing, but thought nothing about sending a stream of assassination squads into neighboring countries to murder Argentinian refugees and suspected "subversives."[6] Most of these escapades ended in failure, but they did not stop the Junta from launching a major operation in Peru. On June 6 1980 eight Argentinian officers arrived in Lima under the command of a "Colonel Ronald Rocha," acompanied by an Argentinian prisoner named Federico Frías Alberga who was apparently taken along to help identify four Argentinians who had sought asylum in Peru. The four included Noemí Esther de Molfino, aged fifty-four, one of the Mothers. On June 11 Frías Alberga tried to escape. One of the guards chased him, struck him on the head with a pistol, and took him to a clinic, where Alberga told the doctor that he had been brought from Argentina and that he wanted political asylum in Peru. He was then taken to a Peruvian police station.[7]

On June 12, newspapers reported that five Argentinian refugees in Peru had disappeared. The U.N. Working Group on Disappearances had been meeting for three days, and was discussing at this very moment how to respond to new disappearances. Van Boven confirmed the newspaper accounts with human rights groups, and sent over a note to Martínez at the Argentinian mission requesting information. He was careful to quote from the newspapers.[8]

The mystery deepened after the body of Noemí de Molfino was found in an apartment in Madrid on July 12. The apartment, at 37 Calle Tutor, had been rented out by Julio César Ramírez, another of the five. The Argentinian embassy in Madrid put out a communiqué claiming that Molfino had died of natural causes. Argentinian papers then reported that two sets of fingerprints, one belonging to Ramírez, the other to a "Luís Almirón," were found at the apartment in Madrid. Both men, they said, had been expelled from Peru with Molfino.

CADHU, the exiled Argentinian human rights group, responded by holding a press conference in Madrid to claim that Molfino had been secretly taken by Argentinian security officials from Peru and killed in Madrid.[9] Claus Ruser, who had by now left ARA for the U.S. embassy in Buenos Aires, reserved judgment. In an August 23 human rights round-up cable, he noted that Ramírez had used the name of "Almirón" as an alias. How could there be two sets of fingerprints for the same person? How indeed? "The plot thickens," wrote Ruser.[10] Although the Argentinian squad had evidently acted in concert with Peruvian officials, the affair caused a chill in relations between Peru and Argentina.[11] The incident also proved hideously embarrassing for the Spanish.

At this distance, it is more difficult than ever to pin down the precise details of this murky case, but it is known that Federico Frías Alberga and Julia Acabel were never seen again. Van Boven learned from the Office of the U.N. High Commissioner for Refugees (UNHCR) that the Junta had been planning a major campaign to eliminate some two hundred prominent exiles abroad, but that it was aborted because of the furor caused by the Molfino case. If this was indeed true, the new Working Group on Disappearances had played its part. It was helping to save lives.

Tension Among the Mothers

The establishment of the U.N. group was perfectly timed to support and encourage the Argentinian relatives. They were no longer fearful and isolated. By 1980, they had grown out of all recognition into a powerful, vengeful movement with impressive international connections. They were also hungry for contacts abroad and access into the United Nations.

They had been constantly and consistently underestimated by the Junta. On September 12 1979, while the IACHR was still in Argentina, the Junta had issued a decree (#22068) stating that any "desaparecido" who did not reappear within ninety days would be considered legally dead. The decree, which was drafted by Mario Amadeo, Argentina's representative on the U.N. Sub-Commission, was presented as a way of settling the relatives' financial and legal worries and allowing them to claim life insurance. But it was greeted by a torrent of protest. It was clear that the Junta was trying to bury the issue once and for all. The authorities would be able to declare a person dead against the wishes of a relative, and also quietly to kill anyone still alive in centers like the ESMA. Emilio Mignone described it as "a final solution—like Hitler's." The Junta was taken aback by the reaction. Although the decree remained on the statute books, it was hardly used.[12]

In 1980 the relatives' movement still revolved around the Mothers of the Plaza de Mayo. During the 1978 World Cup soccer championship tournament, more foreign journalists had attended their weekly Thursday vigil than the soccer matches. Each time they were jostled by the police it was avidly recorded and reported abroad. Their white scarves and matronly appearance had become a symbol of resistance to Argentina's military rulers.

For the Mothers, 1978 to 1980 were years of growing international recognition and internal consolidation. They began taking to the road, paying their own way. The money started to trickle in. West German students sold seventy liters of blood and raised enough money for a small peace prize which was given to the Mothers. Twenty-five influential women in Holland started a solidarity group and helped to raise money for another peace prize, worth thousands of guilders, which was presented to the Mothers. Dutch churches gave twenty thousand dollars, the Norwegian parliament thirty-four thousand dollars.[13]

In August 1979, the Mothers formed themselves into a nonprofit association, and the following year they purchased an old, rambling house on the Calle Uruguay, near the Plaza de Mayo, which they called "la casa de Madres" (the Mothers' house). It was in a state of permanent if cheerful chaos. In 1980, the Mothers agreed on a loose form of administration and set up a "directiva" (council) of eleven, with Hebe de Bonafini as president. De Bonafini had succeeded the unlucky Azucena, who had disappeared in 1978, as the dominant personality in the movement. De Bonafini herself had lost two sons, both presumed guerillas, but she was completely indifferent to their politics. All she wanted was their return alive—"aparición con vida." She had a tenacious, uncompromising personality and she was afraid of no one. They were admirable qualities in 1979 and 1980, when the relatives were still being bullied in spite of semi-official protection from the U.S. embassy.[14]

Their numbers had grown dramatically from fourteen in April 1977 to five thousand in 1980, but in spite of the expansion they still clung to the magic formula. They still met on Thursday in the Plaza de Mayo. Donning the white scarves was a reaffirmation of purpose, an act of faith—an extension of the "denuncia." Many of the women started to embroider their scarves with elaborate designs and patterns, bearing the names of their disappeared relatives and the date of the crime. Following the march, they would walk on to their "casa," arms linked, deep in conversation. Once at the casa, they would pass away the evening talking and drinking tea. Occasionally, there would be films or talks by visitors. In one meeting room, the walls were covered by a mosaic of tiny passport pictures of their disappeared children.

They served many functions, these gatherings. They stoked the coals of resentment at the Junta and kept alive the desire for revenge. By drawing comfort and consolation from each other, the Mothers created their own "women's movement." Yet, they continued to reject the label of "feminists." Their goal was to recover their children, and it was a goal they shared with their husbands and countless other Argentinian men. Like the movement, it was simple, straightforward, and single-minded.

Between 1976 and 1980, the years of danger, this single-mindedness had welded the Mothers into a highly effective group. But in 1980 the danger passed. The Junta stopped using disappearances, tried to shift the emphasis toward national reconciliation, and pointed to "improvement." There could be no "improvement" for the parents who had split up or fallen into deep depression because they blamed each other for the loss of their children. Yet the shift presented the Mothers with a new challenge. It meant uncovering the secrets of the dirty war. Was their provocative style the best way of achieving the goal?

The new challenge caused the first major split in the movement. In November 1980, five parents arrived at the U.S. embassy in Buenos Aires for a discussion with Ambassador Harry Shlaudeman. They found Shlaudeman sympathetic. In a revealing cable, he wrote:

There seemed to be something of a division on the critical question of whether or not hope remains that any of these missing young people could surface again alive. Two of the women expressed what sounded like genuine conviction that large numbers of prisoners are being held in clandestine centers and that their missing relatives may well be among them. However, one mother said flatly that the disappeared are gone for good.

Within the U.S. embassy itself, views differed over the all-important question. While most believed that the disappeared were dead, five "desaparecidos" had emerged unexpectedly from a secret center in August 1979, only to disappear a second time. Some of the ESMA survivors had equally strange stories to recount.[15] Whatever the tensions in their movement, Shlaudeman had no doubt of the Mothers' impact:

> Those who encourage the Mothers and other relatives can be faulted for cruelty. But clearly, [their] persistence in calling for an accounting has a substantial effect on the military. . . . The government's maneuvers in the OAS General Assembly strike me as signs of considerable strain and even fear within the armed forces.[16]

To some extent, the Mothers were already prisoners of their success when this was written. They were a one-goal movement, yet the nearer they came to that goal, the greater the likelihood that it would reveal their children to have died. How would they be able to face the truth, and still survive as an organization? Or, if they refused to face the facts, how would they retain their credibilty? Would they have the maturity to face such dilemmas?

The Grandmothers Begin to Obtain Results

The Grandmothers of the Plaza de Mayo faced a totally different set of problems. Their aim was the recovery of 180 infants who had disappeared with their parents or had been born in captivity. While each month that passed made it less likely that the parents were alive, the evidence that the infants had survived and been adopted multiplied. After emerging from the same relatives' movement as the Mothers back in 1977, the Grandmothers were now on a very different course. Their goal was more practical than that of the Mothers, and their chances of success improved further in 1980 as the killing came to an end.[17]

They began to receive money and information from midwives, janitors, or former detainees who had witnessed births inside centers like the ESMA. The Grandmothers would scour public records for birth certificates looking for the telltale signs: a certificate filed late, or the signature of a military physician. If a name seemed promising, the Grandmother in question would try to discover the identity of the child's adoptive parents. If they turned out to be retired police or senior military personnel, she could well be on the right track. In 1977 they identified thirteen missing infants. By 1980, the figure had risen to over 150. On March 19 1980, they registered their first success when they found seven-year-old Tatiana Britos and her sister Laura. Tatiana had been four and Laura just two months old when they were kidnapped with their parents in October 1977. They had been adopted by a military family. The Grandmothers were on the trail.[18]

Emilio Mignone's efforts to determine the whereabouts of his daughter Mónica had been as fruitless as Hebe de Bonafini's, and by the end of 1978 he was feeling the need for a new, more aggressive approach. The Permanent Assembly remained a prestigious and influential source of information for groups abroad, but its approach was limited to publishing lists of the disappeared. Even the Assembly's use of the word "desaparecido" appeared insufficient.

In the summer of 1979 Mignone established a new human rights organization known as the Center for Legal and Social Studies, with encouragement from a Washington public interest group of the same name and a grant of $40,000 from USAID.[19] Mignone was joined at CELS by two other fathers who had suffered, José Westercamp and Augusto Conte MacDonell. (MacDonell's son had disappeared while doing military service; Westercamp's son had been detained under PEN for five years.) The three set themselves the goal of trying to rejuvenate Argentina's moribund legal process, particularly the system of habeas corpus. CELS began to take on individual cases where there was evidence of involvement by the security forces, including those of the two French nuns and Dagmar Hagelin. CELS also coined the term "detenido-desaparecido," which implied complicity by the government security forces.

Mignone had formidable contacts abroad and he used them to the limit in extending his campaign against the Junta. During a trip to Europe he met Alejandro Artucio, the Uruguayan defense lawyer and former political prisoner who had joined the International Commission of Jurists in Geneva. Artucio asked whether Mignone would be interested in affiliating CELS with the ICJ. Mignone realized it would give him access to the world of the international organizations in Geneva and some measure of protection, so he happily accepted. He also affiliated CELS to Jerry Shestack's International League for Human Rights in New York. By 1980 Mignone had become the best-known human rights lawyer in Argentina, snapping at the heels of Argentina's military leaders. Outside the country, his reputation was growing.[20]

The Relatives in Europe

As the Argentinian relatives turned their attention outward they converged with an ever-growing pool of vengeful exiles. Between 1976 and 1980, groups and boycotts came and went. CADHU's office in Washington was closed down after it was investigated by the Justice Department, while Rodolfo Matarollo, who had caused such a blazing controversy at the U.N. in 1976 and 1977, withdrew from CADHU's Paris branch after an internal dispute. But it ceased to matter. The international human rights campaign against the Junta had been transformed by the testimony and perseverance of hundreds of individuals who had no official connection with the guerrillas.

Two of the most persistent exiles were Raul and Valentina Nughes, whose fourteen-year-old son Angel had disappeared on the evening of August 11 1976. Angel was being driven home from school by a teacher in the small town of Alberdi, in the province of Tucuman, when the road was blocked by a red Chevrolet. Two men got out, punched the teacher and pulled the screaming boy out by his hair. He was bundled into the other car and driven off.[21]

Soon afterward Raul and Valentina Nughes fled to Bolivia and sought asylum in Switzerland, with help from the office of the U.N. High Commissioner for Refugees. As soon as they arrived, they began to spend their meager refugee allowance on "a committee for the freeing of Angel Nughes." Every Thursday they traveled 150 kilometers from Bern to unroll a large banner in front of the United Nations in Geneva asking: "Where is our son?"[22] The Nugheses struck a chord in the insular Swiss, and served as a reminder that five Swiss citizens had also disappeared in Argentina. Solidarity committees were formed for Angel Nughes and one of the five, Alexei Jaccard. Every first Thursday of the month Swiss groups held a vigil outside the offices of the Argentinian airline Aerolineas to protest against the disappearances. The Swiss government was not allowed to forget that

Swiss companies were doing brisk business in Argentina and that Swiss banks were underwriting the Junta's debts. Switzerland's human rights activists had found a cause.

The same chemistry was at work throughout Europe and the United States, as support groups emerged from the foundation that had been laid by CADHU. Within Latin America, the process was even more explosive. The Argentinian Mothers had inspired relatives in other countries where disappearances had become a feature of the political landscape and as in Argentina, the search for the "desaparecidos" was being conducted by the mothers of the families.[23] Women from the different countries began to realize that they had something in common and the idea of a Latin American association emerged naturally in 1979, when two Latin American human rights bodies, one in Venezuela and the other in Costa Rica, put up the money for a meeting in Costa Rica. This lead to the creation of the Federation of Families of Disappeared Persons and Political Prisoners (FEDEFAM).

In the Latin American context FEDEFAM was a remarkable creature—almost as remarkable as the Mothers within Argentina. Relatives of disappeared persons had found a common cause that cut across some of the most fiercely defended frontiers in the world. They came from countries which in some cases (Chile and Argentina, El Salvador and Honduras) were almost at war. They were, to a large extent, women in a man's world—challenging the authoritarian assumptions and petty nationalism that had constantly hindered Latin America's progress.

FEDEFAM's first president, Lidia Galletti, was a member of the Mothers "directiva," but ironically it was left to a European male to provide the continuity and perseverance necessary to weld FEDEFAM into an international organization. Patrick Rice had himself been detained and tortured in Argentina in 1976 and was released only after the intervention of the Irish ambassador.[24] He set himself up in a small office in Caracas with a borrowed typewriter and a volunteer secretary. In time, FEDEFAM would help to internationalize the disappearances—acting as a magnet to relatives throughout Latin America, and encouraging them to make a concerted appeal to the U.N.[25]

By the summer of 1980, with the creation of FEDEFAM still a year away, the establishment of the new U.N. Working Group on Disappearances was looking like an inspired move, instead of the compromise it had seemed after the Commission in February. The group would be ideally constituted to complement the painstaking detective work that now faced the Argentinian groups. It could also encourage relatives and human rights groups in other countries of Latin America—nowhere more so than in Central America, where disappearances had reached epidemic proportions.

17. The Dialogue Starts, the Disease Spreads

It had been a long, hot summer in Geneva and some of the drowsiness still hung in the air. The trees in the park were losing their luster. Tourists strolled around the Palace of Nations and tossed the occasional coin into the water fountain. Out on Lake Leman, wind tugged at the sails. Beyond, snow glistened on Mont Blanc. It was September 1980, and Geneva had never seemed more gracious and more relaxed. But behind this tranquil scene history was being made. The five members of the new U.N. Working Group on Disappearances were meeting with relatives and with Ambassador Gabriel Martínez. It was the first time that the United Nations had talked so directly to victims and violators.

By now the disease of disappearances had spread far beyond Argentina. The crisis was continent-wide and so was the group of witnesses who arrived at the Palace of Nations in Geneva. Here were Emilio Mignone and a group of Mothers from Argentina; Marianella García Villas and Roberto Cuéllar, who headed the two main independent human rights groups in El Salvador; Julia Esquivel from Guatemala; José Estéban González, the foremost human rights activist in Nicaragua.[1] These were remarkable people—neurotic, suspicious, obsessive and highly intelligent. They had lived for years in the shadow of death and recorded acts of extreme barbarity. They had been abused, labeled "subversive," threatened, and shot at. Yet they had bounced back, armed with nothing more than persistence and a desire to get at the truth. With these weapons they had unsettled some of the most brutal regimes to exist since the Second World War. Now—finally—they had a chance to tell their story directly to the United Nations. And a remarkable story it was.

In 1979, according to the Catholic Church, 1,792 people died from political violence in El Salvador.[2] In 1980, as Salvadoran society disintegrated, the figure rose to 11,895. Hundreds disappeared, and there was even less doubt about their fate than in Argentina as corpses started to turn up at preordained spots. The most notorious dumping ground was a strip of black lava twenty-five miles from San Salvador known as El Playón. One or two open spots were accessible from the road, and here in 1979 the killers started adding bodies to the garbage. By the time officals came to investigate, the dogs and vultures had satiated themselves on the corpses. Of the four hundred bodies found on El Playón betwen 1979 and 1980, only fifteen could be identified. Most were buried in a little graveyard next to the lava, with a primitive cross that bore a single laconic word— "desconocido" (unknown). It was El Salvador's equivalent to "nomen nescio."

Most locals gave El Playón a wide berth, but Marianella García Villas spent many hours combing the black, jagged rock.[3] García Villas was president of El Salvador's independent human rights commission (CDHES). She had been born in 1948, studied law and philosophy, and joined the Christian Democrats. Between 1974 and 1976 she was the only woman deputy to serve in the Salvadoran Assembly. She then split from the Christian Democrats and teamed up with six lawyers to form and run the CDHES from offices in an unfashionable part of town.

Wherever possible, García Villas and her colleagues tried to photograph the corpses. She knew that her critics would attack her "political motivation," but that they could not argue with the photo of a shattered body lying on El Playón. In 1979, the Commission hired a photographer. When people came by the office to report a disappearance, they used to scan the photos. Once an identification was made, the relative's testimony was taken and rounded off with a shaky signature.

Some of the photos clearly confirmed the complicity of the security forces. One memorable sequence of pictures showed Manuel Alfredo Velásquez Toledo and Humberto Bazzaglia Recinos being arrested by national guardsmen and handed over to a death squad. Their bodies were dug up from shallow graves shortly afterward.[4] By 1980, the photograph had become the single most powerful weapon at the disposal of El Salvador's human rights groups, and García Villas's commission possessed a grim and terrifying record of death in El Salvador. In some of the photos, the eyes were still open and the victim seemed startlingly alive; in others, the eyes were closed and the lips drawn open in a snarl. Sometimes the familiar shape of the head had exploded under the impact of a bullet, looking like an impressionist painting.

It is impossible to exaggerate the impact of these photos. Visitors arrived in El Salvador with their imagination already in turmoil, and they left Marianella García Villas's commission feeling nauseous and timid. The streets seemed sinister. Taxis were chosen with trepidation. It was days before the images receded. El Salvador seemed doom-laden. In September 1980 García Villas arrived in Geneva, visited van Boven in his office and showed him her photos of tortured, broken corpses. "I found them quite disgusting," he later recalled.

Parallel to García Villas's commission, Roberto Cuéllar and a group of lawyers at the Church Legal Aid Service ("Socorro Juridico") explored legal avenues.[5] As in Argentina, their work revolved around the "denuncia," and as in Argentina the word "denunciation" did not begin to convey the psychological importance of the act. Following a disappearance, the only recourse open to a relative was to tell everything they knew. It provided an essential release from the tension. In Argentina the relatives did it by walking round the Plaza de Mayo. In El Salvador, they went to Roberto Cuéllar and Marianella García Villas.

By taking the time to listen, Roberto and Marianella acted as confessors, psychologists, and law court rolled into one. Once a case was entered in the files at Roberto's legal aid office or Marianella's commission it then became part of a wider "denuncia" by Archbishop Oscar Romero. Every Sunday, he would stand in the pulpit of the cavernous, ugly cathedral and deliver a precise and detailed account of the previous week's terror, to the accompaniment of murmurs from the congregation. Some time later the homily would reappear in printed form at the archdiocese and be transmitted on the local Jesuit-run radio station.

If El Salvador's human rights movement was one of the most influential on the continent, it was also one of most endangered. On April 1979 the car that Marianella García Villas was driving in was struck by machine gun bullets. On March 13 1980, the offices of her commission were damaged by a bomb. Over at the legal aid office, Roberto Cuéllar was shielded from such attacks by his association with the Church. That changed dramatically on March 23 1980 when Romero was shot down while saying mass in a small chapel near the college.[6] He died in an ambulance. By the time Roberto Cuéllar arrived at the hospital, all he could do was squeeze Romero's hand in a final gesture of affection. The two men had grown close in the three years. Many conservatives in the Church accused Romero of being a divisive influence and saw his identification with the poor as subversive. But Roberto Cuéllar remembers him as a man of infinite compassion.

On May 11 1980, seven shadowy right-wing groups met and formed themselves into an umbrella organization called "the secret army of anti-Communism." The event was marked by the circulation of a long communiqué that echoed the same fascist language of "cleansing" and "antibodies" used by the Argentinian Junta. And as in Argentina, working for human rights was seen as part of the disease. The communiqué described Romero, Marianella, and Roberto as "enemies of the people."[7]

As the danger grew, Roberto and Marianella turned outside for help and protection. Marianella was invited to affiliate her commission with the International Federation of Human Rights, based in Paris. The World Council of Churches in Geneva helped Roberto's legal aid group. Over the next troubled years the WCC would contribute twenty thousand dollars a year, help publish its weekly bulletins, and pay for Roberto to attend the U.N. Human Rights Commission in Geneva.

These links gave Marianella and Roberto access to the U.N. Human Rights Commission, but it was of little use as long as the Commission was examining its own bureaucratic entrails, wondering whether or not to criticize El Salvador in public. Roberto and Marianella were impatient for a more direct way of addressing the United Nations, and the new U.N. Working Group on Disappearances was only too happy to oblige. Theo van Boven was aware that the inquiry would only be as effective as the information it received, and the quality of this information was outstandingly good. Between March and September 1980, the paths of the Working Group and the embattled Salvadorans thus converged giddily.

During the September meeting, Roberto Cuéllar enjoyed Geneva, but Marianella García Villas seemed lonely and preoccupied. She was self-conscious about her poor skin and isolated by her lack of English and French, and she made no effort to share in the camaraderie. At the same time, she made a memorable contribution. The Mothers, even Emilio Mignone, put their case to the Group as victims, but García Villas put hers dispassionately, like a lawyer. She said something that seemed trivial at the time but which remained with van Boven long afterward: "Bullets cannot stop people, people must stop bullets. Every individual is precious to us." It summed up van Boven's own mood as the working group approached the end of its first year. Mark Colville's recollection of García Villas was of a very brave, very well-informed, and very serious young woman. He brushes aside the suggestion that she was politically motivated. "If you got involved in human rights in El Salvador you were bound to have political views. But I wouldn't have thought she was a political activist."[8]

José González Takes on the Sandinistas

Just before the September meeting, Tom McCarthy received a telephone call from Miami from José Esteban González, the coordinator of the independent Nicaraguan Human Rights Commission. He wanted to attend the meeting.[9]

José Esteban González had experienced a bewildering personal upheaval. He had set up the commission with a group of friends on April 20 1977 and turned it into a credible and effective organization, monitoring the brutality of Somoza's National Guard and sending the details out to the OAS, the United Nations, Amnesty, and the International Commission of Jurists. As his stock grew within Nicaragua, so did the risks. In April a car came cruising past the office late one evening. Unknown gunmen opened fire just as he was leaving, but he was unhurt.

It was strikingly similar to the work being done in El Salvador by Marianella, and José shared a sense of common purpose with other groups working against right-wing military regimes. To human rights organizations in Europe and North America, he was a heroic figure. Opposing Somoza was in vogue and the money came easily.[10] "I was," he says rather wistfully, "a star."

Then, during the 1979 revolution, it all went sour. González spent the turbulent weeks in Venezuela, where, according to newspaper reports, he tried to use his contacts with Venezuela's Christian Democratic President to maneuver himself into a centrist provisional government, along the lines advocated by the United States. It was, to the Sandinistas, an act of rank treachery.[11] González vehemently denies this, but he returned home after the triumph of the revolution excluded from power and deeply resentful. His commission had closed during the frantic weeks of June and July, but in August the doors were again opened. To José González, it was business as usual—except that the Sandinistas were now the target.

His former Sandinista friends were at first incredulous and then furious. The new government was making a massive effort to play by the rules: it had ratified the American Human Rights Convention and invited the IACHR to visit. It needed help to get the country back on its feet, not criticism. In the eyes of the Sandinistas, José González was now an enemy of the Nicaraguan revolution.

Late in July, he received information that disappearances had occurred in the small town of Grenada. González followed up and uncovered what to him seemed like a clear case of complicity by the Sandinistas.[12] González had heard that the U.N. Working Group on Disappearances would be holding a meeting with witnesses in Geneva in September 1980. He prepared a large dossier in which he claimed that 785 disappearances had been reported to his commission since the revolution; ninety-three, he said, had occurred in the first nine months of 1980. Hundreds of detainees had been tortured. Throughout the summer of 1980 González worked on this explosive report. Then, on the day before he was due to leave for Geneva, he had a very unpleasant surprise.

On September 12 1980 Sergio Ramírez Mercado and Rafael Córdova Rivas, two members of Nicaragua's ruling Junta, appeared before journalists. They were in an exultant mood. The first independent analysis of human rights under the Sandinistas was about to be released and, claimed Ramírez, it gave them a clean bill of health.[13] The report had been prepared by none other than the Geneva-based International Commission of Jurists which had encouraged José González during his lonely fight against Somoza. This, said the two Sandinistas, proved what they had been saying all along—González's supposedly "independent" commission was only interested in making "politically motivated" attacks against the new government, not in human rights.

It was a body blow for González. The ICJ report had been written by Alejandro Artucio, the former Uruguayan defense lawyer, and Heleno Fragoso, the vice-president of the Brazilian Bar Association, who had visited Argentina for the ICJ in 1975. Artucio had been impressed by Nicaragua. He had arrived in Managua on April 8 1980 to find a group of naive revolutionaries gamely trying to reconstruct a devastated nation and meet the requirements of justice at the same time. It was, he would later say, impossible not to be moved and sympathetic.[14]

Artucio knew that disappearances had occurred in the immediate aftermath of the June revolution, but were they deliberate acts perpetrated by the Sandinistas, as González claimed, or local scores settled in the aftermath of a brutal civil war? Artucio spent several hours at González's commission but was not convinced. Indeed, he was put off by González. The man clearly had a chip on his shoulder and some kind of political axe to grind against the Sandinistas. When Artucio's ICJ report was released, it praised the Sandinistas and contained no reference to disappearances. Worse was to come. The ICJ put its worries about the Sandinista system of justice—and they turned out to be numerous—into a separate confidential report for the Sandinistas alone.[15]

A bitter José González then flew off to Geneva feeling as Gabriel Martínez had felt in 1977—that Niall MacDermot's Commission of Jurists was "politically motivated." Here, to González, was the unkindest cut of all. As soon as he arrived in Geneva in September 1980 he went over to ICJ and angrily demanded an explanation from Artucio and MacDermot. Why had they not published the second report on the Sandinista tribunals? Why had they ignored his evidence on disappearances? How had they let themselves be manipulated by the Sandinistas? Artucio and MacDermot were incredulous. They concluded that José González was a troublemaker. For his part, González concluded that the ICJ was guilty of employing double standards. He was determined to bring it to the attention of the U.N. Working Group on Disappearances.

José González was easily the most awkward witness to come before the group. Inside Nicaragua he was seen as "politically motivated" by the Sandinistas. Outside the country, his personal reputation and working methodology were very much in question. Among the human rights community, there was much sympathy for the Sandinistas who had overthrown Somoza, and a feeling that they should be given some breathing space to develop a political middle ground between East and West. If the U.N. group sided with González, it might offend its natural friends among the NGOs, but to dismiss him could open the way to the charge of American conservatives that it was soft on the "totalitarian" Sandinistas. It was a horrible dilemma.

González cared not at all. He unveiled his grievances against Alejandro Artucio and the International Commission of Jurists—highly respected in Geneva—and demanded that the U.N. group take his side. González accused Artucio of double standards. He stated bluntly that he had registered 785 disappearances by the Sandinistas. Given Nicaragua's recent ordeal, the group was inclined to agree with Artucio. Mark Colville, the British member, certainly had a good deal of sympathy for the problems facing the Sandinistas. "The entire government had been housed on the first floor of a hotel under heavy fire. We decided there was no point in asking questions about Somoza."[16] There were other, practical considerations: at this early stage the group wanted to encourage governments to cooperate. The previous month, the Sandinistas had proferred an invitation to the O A S. A U.N. visit could establish an important precedent.

They quickly narrowed González's dossier down to seventy cases, but even these seemed borderline. They felt it would be next to impossible to establish the facts, let alone determine whether the Sandinistas should be held responsible. One thing was certain: there was no way that the disappearances in Nicaragua under dubious circumstances could be remotely compared to the systematic, government-inspired carnage in El Salvador. Besides which, González was a prickly, difficult, fellow.

This fact carried absolutely no weight with Theo van Boven. Most of the best human rights groups were lead by irritating people, but that was what made them effective. Van Boven insisted that González's information be handled in exactly the same way as the rest. Colville and his four colleagues looked hard and long at the seventy cases. They found that eight had occurred in June 1979 and seventeen in July. Another seventeen were reported in August, five in September, and five in October. Of the ninety-three cases registered in the first eight months of 1980, only six fitted the group's criteria. The group thus sided with Artucio. It agreed that the disappearances were largely a product of the civil war and that they had tapered off dramatically as soon as the Sandinistas consolidated control. Nonetheless, the list was dispatched to the Sandinistas for an explanation.[17]

The Group Takes Up Guatemala

Julia Esquivel, who represented Guatemala's human rights community at the September 1980 meeting, had been bruised too many times to take people at their face value. As a result, like so many human rights activists, she seemed to have a permanent chip on her shoulder. She had studied theology in a village near Geneva in the early 1970s. That brought her into contact with the World Council of Churches. On return to Guatemala, she plunged into an exhausting schedule that took her up into the rocky hinterland of the country and back to the dirty slums of Guatemala City. In the interior, she tried to encourage Indian cooperatives, explaining that pooling their resources offered the best chance of mastering the grudging land.[18]

The largest and richest nation in Central America, Guatemala had been deeply troubled ever since June 1954 when the CIA had orchestrated the overthrow of democratically elected Jacobo Arbenz Guzmán. Arbenz's fall was followed by twenty years of army rule which gave civilian politicians three unenviable options: stay out of politics; follow their political instincts and risk death; join the military and serve the detested doctrine of state security. It was a terrifying period, marked by bursts of frenzied mass murder, and it also marked the first recorded cases of disappearances in

Latin America. After twenty-eight members of the Communist party disappeared, a relatives group was established. It was disbanded after its legal
adviser, Edmundo Guerra Theilheimer, was shot by police on March 10
1967, while sitting at his desk.[19] In 1970 a state of siege was declared, and
another two thousand Guatemalans died in less than six months. Nineteen
seventy-six was another year of massacre and murder. Then, in July 1978,
former Defense Minister Romeo Lucas García took over as president and
the killing escalated again.[20]

This was a horror story that rarely hit the headlines. For most of the
outside world, Guatemala remained an exotic, isolated country of jungles,
banana plantations, and Mayan ruins. It broke into the news briefly in
1976, when an earthquake ripped through the shantytowns perched on the
slopes around Guatemala City and killed twenty-two thousand people.
Otherwise, the turmoil that lay just beneath the surface failed to spark
international imagination or outrage.

Indians account for seventy percent of Guatemala's population, and
they had suffered from systematic repression since the time of the Spanish
conquistadors. Most lived in the highland provinces of El Quiché and
Chemaltenango. There, in poor villages, one in every ten children died at
birth, and most of those that survived were infected with parasites and
tuberculosis. Malnutrition was widespread, health and education services
nonexistent. Peasants who owned less than one acre of land had to provide
proof that they had worked more than one hundred days for wages in the
year; otherwise they were liable to work on estates, without pay. It came
close to a form of slavery. There was little color in this drab existence,
except for the brightly patterned native costumes—and even these had
been used by the Spanish as a method of identification and for controlling
movement between villages. Repression against the Indians caused recruits to flock to two determined guerrilla organizations. The armed forces
responded with ferocity.[21]

During the 1970s, Julia Esquivel was the most outspoken human rights
activist in Guatemala. It was an uphill battle, but immensely rewarding.
She preached a bit, talked a lot, and railed constantly against the injustice.
There was a lot of what Latin Americans termed "conscientisación," and a
lot of what others would call "liberation theology." Julia Esquivel saw it
as a matter of survival, but Guatemala's military, schooled in the doctrine
of state security, saw it as subversive.

In 1970 Esquivel began to edit a monthly selection of poetry, quotations
from the bible, and essays called *Diálogo*. Written in dense and often in-

comprehensible prose and illustrated with drawings of poor Indians and agonized, angular crucifixions, it hardly seemed "subversive." It only sold fifteen hundred copies a month. Yet its impact on brutalized Guatemalan society was considerable. The generals knew that she posed a danger. They sent soldiers to the union headquarters where *Diálogo* was being printed, to smash up the printing presses. Esquivel was in a cold fury for the rest of the day. The next day seven policemen came up to her in the street with machine guns. She began to yell and scream—more in anger than in fear. People came running out of banks and shops and found the little woman hopping around on the pavement, while the seven goons tried to grab her.

They seized her camera. "Give it back," she shouted. "Is the government so poor it can't afford a camera?" They replied that they wanted the film. She ripped it out and threw it at them. They slunk off into the crowds. It had been quite a scene. But it was clearly time for her to adopt a lower profile. Her name appeared on a mysterious death threat that began to circulate, signed (as in El Salvador) by "the secret anti-Communist army." Cars circled by her house. On February 17 1980 she slipped out of sight after handing over the editorship of *Diálogo* to a Jesuit priest named Luís Pellecer.[22]

By now, Guatemala had made history at the United Nations. On January 25 1979, Alberto Fuentes Mohr, the unoffical leader of Guatemala's small group of opposition deputies, had been assassinated in the center of Guatemala City. Fuentes Mohr was an experienced politician who had worked at the Palace of Nations in Geneva during a spell in self-imposed exile. The U.N. Human Rights Commission met in the same building shortly after his death and decided to send a cable of concern to the Guatemalan authorities. The regime replied that it repudiated this "unspeakable crime." Three months later, Fuentes Mohr's successors in the Christian Democratic party were killed. There was thus a logic to the appearance of the name of Guatemala on the agenda at the 1980 as a "gross violator"—but in public. It was one of a small handful of cases that had gone straight into public without first passing through the confidential 1503 blacklist. The privilege was richly deserved: more than two thousand Guatemalans died or disappeared during 1979 alone.[23]

Yet, given the circumstances, the Commission's 1980 resolution on Guatemala was offensively mild.[24] Julia Esquivel was determined that the new U.N. Working Group on Disappearances take a very different line. She had been almost constantly on the road since slipping out of Guatemala on February 17: Brazil, Australia, France, and finally Switzerland. She arrived in Geneva just as the Working Group was preparing to meet. She took to Theo van Boven immediately, which was less than surprising. Both were serious and religious. Esquivel offered to prepare a list of disappeared persons in Guatemala and present them to the U.N. group. She told the group that three thousand Guatemalans had disappeared between January and August.[25]

Julia Esquivel did not take to Mark Colville. She remembers him as skeptical and bullying. She told the group there was no possibility of habeas corpus in Guatemala. "Madam, are you saying there are no lawyers in Guatemala?" asked Colville in an offended tone. Julia replied that fifty lawyers had been killed in the country. She was also thinking of sixteen-year-old Jolanda Aguilar Urizar, who had been arrested personally by the chief of police and repeatedly raped by his officials. Julia Esquivel had herself submitted forty separate cases of habeas corpus on the girl's behalf, made a recording of the mother's testimony, and sent the cassette all over the world.

Part of their difference was cultural. Like so many upper class Englishmen, Colville mixed haughtiness and banter. This grated on Esquivel, who had spent much of the last ten years confronting haughty men in Guatemala. He remembers her as dour, suspicious, lacking in warmth, and impervious to charm. The relationship never really developed.

Showdown with Martínez

During the three months leading up to the September meeting, the group's relationship with Gabriel Martínez had grown increasingly fraught, and on September 15 he came over to the Palace and launched into a ninety-minute tirade that Mark Colville later decribed as "a bloody nightmare." Martínez, he says, "ranted and raved." During this meeting, Martínez also demanded that Antonio Fortín, the Chilean exile whom van Boven had hired to service the group, leave the room. Van Boven was tempted to refuse, but he thought there was no point in needlessly provoking Martínez and Fortín slipped out.

Martínez continued to insist that the group could not handle individual cases. In one long letter on December 8, he insisted that Argentina would only cooperate "at the level of generalities."[26] This was bluntly rejected by the group. When Colville later met with the American ambassador Gerald Helman he would describe it as "complete rubbish."

Martínez's performance was so belligerent that van Boven and McCarthy had serious doubts whether he was even sending their inquiries back to Buenos Aires. These doubts were to persist for the next three years. Foreign Ministry files of this period show that Martínez transmitted all of the sixty-seven queries put to him by the group in 1980 back to Buenos Aires, together with the names of the disappeared.[27] After the September meeting he received a two-page note that began with an urgent message: "This information is for the exclusive use of Ambassador Gabriel Martínez. Once used it is to be destroyed." There was no call for such melodrama. Typical of the note was the entry on Federico Frías Alberga, one of the Argentinians who had disappeared in Lima. All it said was: "His place of residence could be Peru."

This situation raises an important question. Was Martínez being kept in the dark by his own government—as he would imply when he gave testimony before the 1985 trial? The answer to this is no. Foreign Ministry officials were not aware of the details of specific abductions but Martínez was one of the privileged few who was privy to the broad outlines of the campaign. His close friend Tomás de Anchorena, the ambassador in Paris, even lost a colleague, Elena Holmberg, to the killing. Martínez declined to share the sparse information he received with the U.N. group, because to have done otherwise would have been to admit that it was entitled to take up individual cases.[28]

The group helped to save at least one more life in Argentina before the end of the year. Osvaldo Jauretche, a journalist, took his children to school on October 8 1980 in Buenos Aires and failed to return home. Armed men searched his house later the same day. On October 14, the U.N. group appealed to Martínez. On October 21 Jauretche reappeared and issued an ambiguous statement saying that he had been the victim of an "incidental relationship with a leader of an extremist organization." Claus Ruser, from the U.S. embassy in Buenos Aires, cabled Washington that "human rights activists here are convinced that Jauretche was seized by some element of the security forces. We are inclined to agree. It is hard to imagine that if he were a knowing participant in some plan to embarrass the government he would surface himself in Argentina, given the very high risks he would run."[29] Quite probably, the Junta weighed the speedy protest from the U.N. and decided to let Jauretche go free.[30]

The U.N. group had less success in El Salvador. On October 3 1980, shortly after Marianella García Villas testified before the group in Geneva, María Magdalena Henríquez, her closest friend in the human rights commission in San Salvador, was kidnapped by a group of men while shopping near her house and bundled into a Cherokee van. The following day her body was found with four bullets in the back. She had been raped. On October 7 while commission members watched the remains of their former colleague being exhumed, a group of policemen arrived and started interrogating them. On October 25, Ramon Valladares, a secretary at the commission, was shot dead while he was leaving his house. Shortly afterward, García Villas left for Mexico City to establish a commission branch office in exile.[31]

In spite of this, it had been a good year at the United Nations in Geneva, and Theo van Boven felt elated at the progress of the U.N. disappearances group. After the September meeting Theo van Boven and his wife Ann-Marie hosted a party. It was a fun evening with plenty of laughter, although Marienella García Villas looked sad and out of place. Perhaps she had a premonition of the tragedy that was about to befall her friend in San Salvador. Her counterpart from Nicaragua, the prickly José Estéban González, didn't turn up.

18. The Pressure Pays Off

The case against Argentina's military rulers would not come to a court of law until 1985, but by December 1980, when the five members of the U.N. Working Group on Disappearances met to prepare their first report, the United Nations had compiled one of the most exhaustively documented cases prepared against a government since the Nuremberg trials. Fittingly, the most decisive testimony had come directly from the ESMA concentration camp—from its torturers as well as its victims.

The freewheeling days of kidnap and murder at the ESMA had effectively ended with Admiral Emilio Massera's withdrawal from the Junta in September 1978. Rear Admiral Rubén "Dolphin" Chamorro, his close colleague and commander of the ESMA, then fought a rear-guard action to preserve the cherished GT 3/32 unit and secure diplomatic postings for its star performers. On June 14 1979 Chamorro himself was posted to Argentina's embassy in Pretoria, South Africa, as military attaché. He was followed by Alfredo "Angel" Astiz, Jorge "Puma" Perren, and Jorge "Tiger" Acosta. Jorge Vildoza, Alberto González Menotti, and Victor Cardo were all posted to the Argentinian Embassy in London. Four GT 3/32 members went to Spain, and one to Bolivia.[1]

Meanwhile a handful of their former victims had arrived in Europe—dispirited, guilt-ridden, and still bearing the physical and psychological wounds of torture. How and why they were allowed to survive is still a mystery. On December 18 1978 Ana María Martí was moved out of the ESMA and reunited with her two children. She found them seriously disturbed from having spent months detained with pimps and seeing men savagely beaten. She was then handed her passport, driven to an airport, and put on board a plane bound for Spain with her children and her ESMA cellmate Sara Solarz de Osatinsky.

Both women were warned not to talk about their experiences, but they ignored the warning and plotted revenge. They spent the next nine months with another released detainee, María Lillía de Pirles, reliving the nightmare—recalling every incident, every face, and every damning fact. From the numbers they had been given they concluded that 4,726 Argentinians were detained at the ESMA between 1976 and 1979 and that less than a hundred had survived. The three released their report at a press conference at the French National Assembly on October 12 1979. It caused an uproar throughout Europe and remains one of the most striking documents on the dirty war.[2]

By 1979, the ESMA authorities concluded that Carlos Muñoz, who had worked on information in the school, was sufficiently "recuperated" to be allowed home to spend Christmas with his family. But he was released on parole, and an ESMA official accompanied him and sat at the dinner table. There was not much conversation.[3] Miriam Lewin de García continued to work for Massera after leaving the ESMA in January 1979. She too was later allowed to leave the country, in spite of the trail of broken promises. Before she left, Alfredo Astiz gave her his address in Mar del Plata and told her to write if she needed help.[4]

Norma Susana Burgos had left Buenos Aires on January 25 1979 for Spain with a ticket costing $706 paid for by the navy, and an extra $107.50 to cover excess baggage. She too broke her promise and continued on to Sweden. On December 13, she sat down in the office of Hans Danelius, who headed the legal department in the Swedish Foreign Ministry, and recalled how she had seen her young Swedish friend Dagmar Hagelin inside the ESMA, chained to a bed, with the bullet wound inflicted on her by Alfredo Astiz clearly visible.[5]

Danelius took down this testimony with mixed emotions. Dagmar Hagelin's ordeal had become an obsesson for him, as it had for many Swedes, but Burgos's arrival in Sweden had greatly increased the chance that he might do something about it. In 1977, shortly after Hagelin's abduction, Danelius had presented a draft convention on torture to the U.N. Human Rights Commission in the hope of filling the gap in international human rights laws noted earlier. The Swedish draft called for torture to be declared a criminal offense and for torturers to be punished. In 1980, armed with the testimony of Norma Susana Burgos, Danelius could be more certain that torturers like Astiz could be identified, and proof obtained.

There remained the practical problem of arrest, but even that was beginning to look less insuperable. Early in May 1980, after the Burgos testimony was published in Sweden, an enterprising Swedish journalist located Astiz and Chamorro in Pretoria and questioned Chamorro about

Dagmar Hagelin. Chamorro described the girl as a "terrorist," provoking fresh outrage in Sweden. One cable from the U.S. embassy in Buenos Aires noted aptly: "Astiz's current notoriety must send chills through other Argentine military men who fear an eventual Nuremberg in Argentina. The ESMA remained the Argentine navy's major detention and interrogation center and the last stop for many of the disappeared."[6] A year later, a South African paper would expose Astiz and Chamorro and their roles at the ESMA; Astiz would be asked to leave.[7]

Here was proof not only that the torturers were known, but that they could be found in foreign countries. On June 30 1980, Judge Irving Kaufman, a U.S. federal appeals court judge, gave another major boost to Danelius's torture convention when he allowed a Paraguayan doctor, Joel Filártiga, to sue a former Paraguayan police official who had tortured Filártiga's son to death. The novelty of this landmark case was that it allowed U.S. courts to hear a case that had occurred on foreign soil, involved foreign nationals, and found that torture violated customary (i.e., non-treaty) international law.[8] In legal terms, this gave teeth to the concept known as "universal jurisdiction," which was a key element in the Swedish draft torture convention. It was a warning to the Argentinian torturers, particularly Alfredo Astiz. The Angel was now internationally notorious.

The U.N. Presents Its Case Against the Junta

Critics of the United Nations often underestimate the importance of reports. In the U.N., the written word has less immediate impact than a verbal protest, but carries more weight. Unlike one of Gabriel Martínez's searing insults, the pain starts as a dull ache. It then grows as the report is translated into several official languages; presented before the Human Rights Commission, ECOSOC, and the General Assembly; used by journalists who are too lazy to attend meetings; sent to 157 different governments; lodged in filing cabinets; and scanned by diligent researchers at the International Commission of Jurists and Amnesty International. Here is something solid and tangible that can be used, reused, and thumbed through hundreds of times. It is, potentially, a formidable weapon, as the five members of the U.N. Working Group on Disappearances knew when they met in Geneva to draft their first report.

They had reviewed over 13,000 disappearances during the past nine months, but felt able to confirm just 2,300 in fifteen countries.[9] Argentina was difficult. On the one hand, they had to avoid the impression of "selectively" singling out Argentina for criticism; on the other, they had to produce something of use to the relatives of the disappeared. They also had to strike a balance between publicity and confidentiality. The result was an artful compromise. The report mentioned that five hundred cases had been carefully chosen as representative, but without naming names, and tried to meet Martínez halfway on the all-important issue of individual cases.[10]

Overall, however, the section on Argentina was devastating. It named sixteen clandestine detention centers.[11] Even if the disappearances had slowed in Argentina, it warned, there could be no question of any "improvement" until the disappearances had been explained. This was exactly what Emilio Mignone and the Mothers were saying in Argentina. On balance, the report presented a sober, if limited, review of the case as it stood against Argentina in 1980. It was sober enough to warrant inclusion in the records of a March 1981 U.S. congressional hearing on Argentina.[12]

Here was yet another key moment in the long and bitter confrontation between Gabriel Martínez and Theo van Boven. Argentina was finally charged with disappearances, in a public U.N. document. The issue for Gabriel Martínez was not "selectivity." He was indifferent to what the report said or did not say about Nicaragua or the Soviet Union. His concern was simply that the group was now bearing down on the Junta just as the Junta was loftily calling for national reconciliation.

His worst fears were now being realized. Martínez had spent two years keeping Argentina off the confidential 1503 blacklist. When that redoubt fell, he retreated in good order and began funneling all the charges against Argentina into the confidential procedure, hoping to use its secrecy as his next line of defense. The Working Group on Disappearances had driven a wedge into this strategy. It was taking evidence from human rights groups, some of which did not have formal affiliation with the United Nations, and giving it the written stamp of approval. In a month, the report would be reviewed by the U.N. Human Rights Commission. Martínez was in trouble. Hints of his frustration, and his intense anger at Theo van Boven, found their way back to Buenos Aires and into cables from the U.S. embassy. One cable even charges that van Boven was meeting with Montoneros.[13]

The Charge of Selectivity

By December 1980, when the Working Group sat down to draft their report, Ronald Reagan had won the election and the charge of "selectivity" that would be leveled against the United Nations by Jeane Kirkpatrick was just below the surface. The group's report would be the first real test of this charge.

Of the fifteen governments accused of disappearances, nine were Latin American military regimes and twelve had ties to the United States. Only one—Ethiopia—could be described as "totalitarian." Nicaragua appeared on the list alongside Argentina and El Salvador, even though the Inter-American Commission on Human Rights visited Nicaragua in October 1980 and agreed with Alejandro Artucio that the Sandinistas could not be held responsible for the disappearances that had occurred in June 1979 just after the civil war.[14]

This might have been an argument for the U.N. group to ignore José González's charges, but once again it had no effect on Theo van Boven. González was a lone figure trying to hold his government to its own laws, and to have ignored this would have discredited the group. González's September testimony was printed in full, together with harsh words about the International Commission of Jurists. The official Sandinista reply, trying to set the record straight, was published as a separate document, ensuring that it would be read by far fewer people.[15] This bestowed legitimacy on González and infuriated the Sandinistas.[16] They wanted support from the United Nations, not criticism. One case, six cases, sixty, six hundred cases—it was all the same. They angrily withdrew an invitation to the group to visit Nicaragua. The group was paying a price for remaining evenhanded, but van Boven was determined to avoid the charge of selectivity.[17]

He did not altogether succeed. It was impossible to ignore the report's bias against right-wing regimes, particularly Argentina, and against Latin America. What accounted for this? The principal reason, noted earlier, was that disappearances (like torture) were very much a product of Latin American dictatorships, that is of "authoritarian" regimes. "Totalitarian" regimes were responsible for much heartache and broken spirit, but there is no record of political kidnapping and clandestine murder in the Soviet bloc.[18]

There were other reasons for the surface bias against Latin America, one being that if there was no one to submit evidence to the group, there was no evidence. As a result, the report noted that twenty-two disappearances occurred on the island of East Timor following the 1975 invasion by Indonesian troops. This was clearly an underestimate, but no one had stayed to record this bleak episode. Throughout much of Asia and black Africa, human rights monitors were almost nonexistent. This was why Uganda did not appear in the report.

In Latin America, however, human rights groups were effective and vigilant. American neoconservatives would see this as proof of the relative tolerance of Latin American "authoritarian" regimes.[19] Such a conclusion was highly questionable. In Uruguay, dissent had been stamped out far more thoroughly and ruthlessly than in most countries of Eastern Europe. In El Salvador, Brazil, and Chile, human rights work would have been entirely extinguished had it not been for the resilience of the Roman Catholic Church. In Argentina, the fact that Emilio Mignone and the Mothers were gaining in confidence by 1980 was not due to tolerance by the Junta. This was a country where over a hundred defense lawyers had disappeared and died, and a major attempt to stamp out the Mothers at the end of 1977 had failed by a whisker. Mignone and the Mothers had their own resilience and the pressure from abroad to thank for their survival.

Did these limitations discredit the little that was achieved by the Working Group in its first report? Surely not. It could hardly be described as "politicized." Indeed, given the enormity of the crime, the report was absurdly conservative. (Far more than five hundred people had disappeared in Argentina.) The group did not pass judgment, issue rebukes, or even express concern—in sharp contrast to the U.N.'s strident tone towards Chile, South Africa, and Israel. Its toughest language was reserved for governments that refused to answer, not those who had killed and murdered.

In spite of all these facts, an era ended with this report. Thirty-five years of taboo came tumbling down. The group had intervened to save lives. It had named governments, bypassed confidentiality, and taken information from people because they had suffered and not because they had been given "consultative status." It had concentrated the U.N.'s limited energies on the paramount evil, namely violence by governments. Finally, by taking up a theme as opposed to a country, it had also broken the mold of discriminatory, single-country probes on Israel, South Africa, and Chile, and made the U.N. less "selective."

The whole effect was profoundly invigorating. Even the ramshackle 1503 procedure—so manipulated by Martínez, so debased by Javier Pérez de Cuéllar—felt the wind of change. No fewer than seventeen governments were placed on the confidential 1503 blacklist of "gross violators" during a bizarre session of the U.N. Sub-Commission in August 1980. The Soviet member, Vsefolod Sofinsky, had just been expelled from New Zealand, where he was ambassador, on a charge of spying. The Swiss held up his visa, which delayed his arrival in Geneva and ensured that he was not present to cast his veto at the all-important first stage of vetting communications. Emboldened, his four colleagues placed over twenty governments—including those of East Germany, Japan, and the United States—on their blacklist. Eventually, the Sub-Commission trimmed the list slightly, taking out the United States. But the names of East Germany and Japan remained. It was the first time that an Eastern European country had been formally accused of "gross violations" in the U.N.'s thirty-five-year history.[20]

When Ronald Reagan was elected President in November 1980, the U.N.'s human rights machinery had never been less "selective." Six governments were publicly accused of "gross violations," seventeen were on the confidential 1503 blacklist, and another fifteen had been charged by the U.N. Working Group on Disappearances. One sixth of the entire U.N. membership was under some kind of U.N. human rights investigation.[21] This testified to a dramatic expansion since 1967 and indicated a healthy willingness by the organization to criticize its own membership, including Eastern Europe. It was certainly a more courageous record than that of the U.S., which had not formally accused a single government of "gross violations" under the 502B legislation.

If the United Nations was "selective" at the close of 1980, it lay in omissions rather than inclusions. Among the more vicious regimes that deserved, but had escaped, censure were Turkey, Iran under Khomeini, Iraq, Syria, and Pakistan. The two regions that escaped entirely were North America and Western Europe, even though their treatment of migrant workers, ethnic minorities and indigenous groups clearly deserved closer scrutiny by the U.N.

But "selectivity," as it would be defined by Jeane Kirkpatrick, meant a bias against Latin America.[22] Latin America contributed eight of the seventeen governments on the confidential blacklist, nine of the fourteen accused of disappearances, and three of the privileged six which were subject to public inquiries. There were reasons for this, as we have seen: under Theo van Boven, the U.N. was beginning to concentrate its energies on torture, disappearances, and other violations of the "right to life." Chile, Argentina, El Salvador, Guatemala, and Uruguay stood out because they were clearly guilty as charged.

Did the exclusion of some names discredit the inclusion of these Latin American regimes? Jeane Kirkpatrick said yes, Theo van Boven said no. He was convinced that the disappearances inquiry had made the U.N. less "selective" than ever.

The Carter Administration agreed. Even the ARA bureau in the State Department—a fierce defender of the Junta—agreed that the disappearances group might prove very useful to its client. One August 1980 ARA memorandum argued that the United States should support an extension of the group past 1981, and even urged that it visit Argentina.[23] Gerald Helman, the U.S. ambassador in Geneva, was another strong supporter. In a January 1981 cable to Washington he wrote that thematic inquiries would assure "more even-handed and less politicized treatment of human rights issues in the U.N."[24] Three months earlier, Helman had met with Mark Colville for a briefing. Colville was so enthusiastic that he suggested the group might even try to get the American hostages released from Iran. Colville also told Helman bluntly of the general resentment felt toward Gabriel Martínez and urged that the U.S. government put some diplomatic pressure on Argentina.

Helman was so receptive that he even suggested that the Carter Administration consider opposing loans to Argentina in the World Bank and other international institutions. (U.S. policy at the time was abstention.) He also suggested that the U.S. show its gratitude toward Nicaragua and Mexico for having invited the group to visit. These views were unfashionable in Washington in the twilight of Jimmy Carter's administration, and by the end of November, following the election of Ronald Reagan, they would appear heretical. Yet, Helman evidently had no reason to doubt that the group's life would be extended for another year and that the new administration would remain steadfast in its support of an inquiry that the U.S. had worked to create.

Change at the White House

On the surface, Ronald Reagan's sweeping election victory over Jimmy Carter on November 4 1980 was greeted with jubilation in Argentina. According to one *New York Times* editorial, "They toasted the news with champagne. . . . They saw the change in American policy literally as a hunting license."[25] It had been clear for several months that a major shift would occur in American human rights policy if Reagan was elected, and that it would favor the Junta. "There has been sparse public comment by members of the government or armed forces," cabled U.S. Ambassador Shlaudeman from Buenos Aires. "However, Argentina military officers have not hestitated to express to mission officers their pleasure at the results."[26]

It was hardly surprising. Ronald Reagan had long admired the Junta and supported its stand against "subversion." In one 1978 column he had lashed out at Patt Derian:

> There is an old Indian proverb: "before I criticize a man, may I walk a mile in his moccasins." Patricia Derian and her minions at Mr. Carter's human rights office apparently have never heard of it. If they had, they might not be making such a mess of our relations with the planet's seventh largest country, Argentina, a nation with which we should be close friends. . . . Ms. Derian, would you care to try on a new pair of moccasins?[27]

Reagan's election removed Derian from the political scene, but this was not enough to allay the doubts. Even as opinion polls in the U.S. were predicting a Reagan landslide, cable traffic in and out of the Foreign Ministry in Buenos Aires remained apprehensive rather than elated. In the last week of October, one senior ministry official gave a speech to the staff in which he warned: "In the event that the November 4 elections turn out to be a triumph for the Republican candidate, that may not guarantee us a change. On the contrary, it may result in a hardening of attitude among the 'liberals' who want to win their great battle before being deprived of the presidency or the Department of State."[28]

Why such pessimism? Probably because, like most Argentinian diplomats, the author of these words had been conditioned by four appallingly difficult years to expect the worst, and he probably had little reason to expect a dramatic improvement following a Reagan victory. There would clearly be some immediate gains, particularly if the new administration succeeded in getting the 1978 embargo on U.S. arms sales repealed. On the other hand, international opinion had been hardened, conditioned by the lies: no one had believed the Junta when it denied it was killing its critics—why should anyone believe it when it claimed an "improvement?"

The isolation gnawed and throbbed, like a slow ache that could not be ignored.[29] Three years earlier, in 1977, one internal memorandum had predicted that the Carter Administration would switch the focus of its human rights campaign from bilateral confrontation to the international organizations as it began to meet domestic resentment. This proved to be prescient. Even as Jimmy Carter was struggling in 1980 to project greater sensitivity to America's security interests, U.S. representatives in the OAS and U.N. were increasing the pressure. "They want us to swallow our bitter medicine," was how one memo described it.[30] In the United Nations, Jerry Shestack's intervention had proved particularly deadly.

When one Argentinian Foreign Ministry official drew up his balance sheet late in October, he rounded it off with the following warning: "Public opinion in the West has been saturated when it comes to human rights in Argentina, and this has benefited the government. However, we can predict adverse consequences from the machinery now in place in the international organizations. To counter this, we will need decisive support from the other countries."[31] This was a significant comment. It showed again that the very qualities that rendered the U.N. an object of contempt in the West—the delay in acting, the ponderous bureaucracy—made it an object of acute concern in Argentina.

The 1980 Nobel Peace Prize Goes to an Argentinian

Shortly after these words were written, on October 13 1980, an elderly Norwegian professor, John Sanness, stood up in Oslo to announce the identity of the latest Nobel Peace Prize winner. It was Adolfo Pérez Esquivel, the Argentinian sculptor and pacifist who headed the Peace and Justice Commission and had spent fifteen months in a detention center for his human rights work. It was the ultimate accolade for Argentina's human rights movement and the ultimate public rebuke for the Junta.[32]

Pérez Esquivel had been chosen from a field of seventy-one candidates that included Jimmy Carter. Within Argentina's human rights movement he was a lesser figure than Emilio Mignone or Hebe de Bonafini, and he made no effort to project his own personality. One article described him "a backroom man with long dishevelled hair, a committee organizer not a charismatic public leader." One immediate effect of the award was to make him a rich man. Ironically, under a law passed by the Junta in 1977, any living Argentinian laureate was entitled to receive the salary of a Supreme Court justice ($2,000 a month). Now, the award had gone to one of the Junta's critics.[33] The Nobel committee rubbed salt into the wound by comparing him to the 1975 laureate Andrei Sakharov. "Pérez Esquivel," said the communiqué, "is among those Argentinians who have shone a light in the darkness."

Pérez Esquivel's own reaction was shy, pleased disbelief. He announced he would donate ten percent of the $212,000 prize money to the Mothers of the Plaza de Mayo. The public abuse from the government and Church was quick and predictable, but in private the Junta's reaction was close to panic. Concluded one Foreign Ministry analysis: "The decision of the Nobel Peace committee is further proof of the intensity of the international campaign. It also creates a situation in which Argentina and the Soviet Union are placed in the same boat. Sakharov and Pérez Esquivel are symbolic figures who have been projected from anonymity to international prominence by the prize. This serves to unite both governments and subject them to the same criticism."[34]

This revealing comment featured in a secret memorandum written less than two weeks before Ronald Reagan's victory. By drawing a precise parallel between Argentina and the Soviet Union, it shows the irrelevance of the distinction between "totalitarian" and "authoritarian" regimes that would underpin Mr. Reagan's human rights policy. As seen from Buenos Aires in October 1980, both governments, so different in so many ways, were in the dock for the same reason—consistently violating human rights.

Three weeks later, the Junta returned to the fray and won a victory when the OAS annual Assembly decided not to pass a resolution criticizing Argentina by name. During the Carter Administration it had become traditional that every country that was the subject of a special IACHR report also be featured in an OAS Assembly resolution. But in the year that followed the IACHR mission to Argentina, the Junta had mounted a diplomatic offensive and warned repeatedly that Argentina would withdraw from the OAS if such a resolution was passed. This was probably bluff, but it was effective bluff.[35] The Junta toughed it out and it paid dividends. Instead of passing a resolution critical of Argentina, the OAS Assembly agreed on an umbrella formula which merely endorsed the two special IACHR missions during the previous year—to Argentina and Haiti. It also referred to human rights violations in several other countries and thanked Argentina for cooperating.[36]

The Argentinians were also helped by the fact that many career officers at the State Department, particularly those in regional bureaus, were trying to curry favor with the incoming Reagan Administration. When

Adolfo Pérez Esquivel visited Washington in October, shortly after receiving the Nobel award, officials in the ARA bureau tried to prevent him from seeing Deputy Secretary of State Warren Christopher. Derian's office intervened, and the meeting went ahead. The ARA was successful in getting a reference to disappearances taken out of the State Department's annual 1981 human rights report, and ARA officials lobbied discreetly on behalf of Argentina at the OAS Assembly.

Yet the OAS result was not an undiluted triumph. Observing the debate from the embassy in Buenos Aires, newly arrived Ambassador Shlaudeman and his ever-skeptical associate Claus Ruser were unsure about what lay ahead. Wrote Shlaudeman: "The government did not escape unscathed. The human rights chapter may not be closed after all." [37] Ruser agreed. In another cable he suggested that the Junta's prime consideration was to "assure the officer corps that it will be protected from international pressure to make an accounting for the past." It was not at all clear, he concluded, whether "this key audience is convinced." [38] Indeed it was not.

The Reckoning

Patt Derian had started receiving death threats from Argentina in 1978, and by the end of 1980 she was still under the protection of State Department security. It seemed a fitting comment on her efforts to moderate the cruelty of the Junta. It seemed as if she, not Videla, was under siege.

To the Junta, Derian remained a detested figure to the very end. But she had many admirers in Argentina. "Certainly her influence was considerable here," wrote James Neilson in the *Buenos Aires Herald* in late 1980:

> When she took office, the Argentine authorities treated those suspected of being their foes with contemptuous cruelty. But today, three years after Mrs. Derian began her work, a semblance of legality has been restored. Is it a mere coincidence that this improvement took place when Mrs. Derian was in office? Scorned and despised as she may be in military messes and well-furnished living rooms, Mrs Derian will be remembered with gratitude in thousands of less exalted places. When precious few cared a jot for the fate of individual Argentines she cared and cared deeply. [39]

It was ironic that it should be left to Argentinians to defend Derian. Friend or foe, they realized that she had remained unswervingly loyal to American ideals and a rock of consistency in Carter's otherwise slithering foreign policy. Back home, it was different. More than anyone else,

Derian epitomized the aggressive, counterproductive side of Carter's human rights policy. By the end of 1980, it was widely assumed that she had lost America jobs, undermined U.S. allies, and failed even to save lives. Following Ronald Reagan's ascendancy, this view would become orthodox.

The most influential and damaging attack came in an article by another registered Democrat, Jeane Kirkpatrick. "Dictatorships and Double Standards," which was published in the November 1979 issue of *Commentary*, did not mention Derian by name. In addition, it focused on Nicaragua and Iran rather than Argentina. Nonetheless, the article amounted to a withering analysis of Carter's overall human rights policy and of Derian's highly public approach to gross violations like the disappearances. As we shall see, it was also to provide a rationale for Ronald Reagan's own human rights policy.[40]

The underlying thesis of the article is that by pressing "authoritarian" regimes over human rights, the Carter Administration caused their downfall and so damaged U.S. security. This may or may not have been the case with the Shah of Iran and Anastasio Somoza of Nicaragua, but it was certainly not with Argentina. The relationship between the U.S. and Argentina survived the difficult years of 1977 to 1979 to the detriment of neither Argentina's security nor the security of the United States, and the Junta made a series of friendly gestures towards the U.S. to offset its refusal to join the grain embargo against the Soviet Union. As one senior Foreign Ministry official pointed out in a speech to his colleagues late in 1980, Argentina was the only major Latin American nation to boycott the Moscow Olympic Games and support the U.S. in demanding that the PLO be denied observer status in the International Monetary Fund.[41] The Junta also voted against Cuba and Vietnam in the World Food Program and withdrew its ambassador from Iran following the hostage crisis. The well-publicized "alliance" with the Soviet Union—as we have seen—went no further than grain sales, and even then Argentina's trade surplus was deeply resented by the Soviets.

The second charge against Derian was that she had failed to save lives. This was concisely, if scornfully put by Ernest Lefever, who was designated by Mr. Reagan to fill Derian's post. During his nomination hearings in May 1981 Lefever suggested that Derian had played a "Sir Galahad role," hogging the limelight but achieving nothing that could not have been achieved by "quiet diplomacy."[42]

How justified was this accustation? In September 1980, Claus Ruser, at the U.S. embassy in Buenos Aires, summarized what he termed the "tactic of disappearances." Ruser had vigorously criticized Jerry Shestack's hard line on Argentina at the U.N. Human Rights Commission in February. Now, in September, he was struck by the fact that disappearances were still occurring—twenty-four were reported in 1980—in spite of the damage to Argentina's image abroad.

"This does not reflect simple bloody-mindedness by unthinking military men," he wrote. "If it did the problem might be more soluble." Ruser's own explanation, noted earlier, was that Argentina's military was committed to the "tactic" because of its awesome effectiveness and the need to spread responsibility to all ranks. Given this fact, wrote Ruser, there was little the U.S. could do, by either public censure or quiet diplomacy: "We obviously can do little to affect the terrorists' choice of whether or not to continue their struggle. Our ability to influence the government's decision on tactics it will use in this war is not much greater."[43]

Curiously, Ruser knew better than most that U.S. pressure was indeed effective. On August 28 1980 a young woman named Edith Bona disappeared. According to Ruser's cabled account, an embassy official contacted a senior member of Videla's staff and "noted that we had to be concerned for humanitarian reasons and for the effect of such practices on U.S.-Argentina relations." Six days later, the embassy learned that Edith Bona had been handed over to a civilian judge to be tried on a charge of possessing explosives. "It is probable that the embassy's intervention in this case moved the GOA [Government of Argentina] in positive direction," cabled Ruser, with understandable satisfaction.[44] At the time Derian was still Assistant Secretary of State for Human Rights and there was no reason to think Carter would lose the election.

Up to this point it had been an article of faith from Videla downward through the ranks of government that the problem was simply one of presentation. Toward the end of 1980, the façade cracked. After four years of self-delusion, Argentina's diplomats stopped telling their military masters what they wanted to hear. It was not that surprising. The diplomats had suffered extraordinary abuse. Their government had been accused of horrific crimes. They had been inundated with protests about Dagmar Hagelin and the two French nuns. Their once-proud foreign service had been compromised. Their country's reputation was in tatters.

At the end of the summer, an official in the Argentinian Foreign Ministry sat down and drew up a balance sheet:

> The government of Argentina has a number of options if it wants to stamp its control on the situation once and for all. These are: a) PEN detainees

must be tried, freed, or given the right to leave the country; b) measures must be taken to explain the fate of the disappeared persons; c) there must be no new actions which constitute a violation of human rights; d) constitutional government must be restored. Taken in the context of the first three proposals, it is this last measure which will permit a return to a full and normal international relations for Argentina.[45]

This statement went further than merely calling for an end to the policy of disappearances. It called for a restoration of democracy. After four stormy years, the Junta was finally hearing the truth from its own Foreign Ministry: Argentina would only rejoin the family of nations when the disappearances stopped and the Junta surrendered the power it had illegally seized in 1976. The killers were finally on the run. Four years of pressure had indeed paid off.

IV

The Reagan Years

19. The Neoconservative Revolution

In mid-December 1980 Patricia Derian and Jeane Kirkpatrick were interviewed for a CBS television program. Their disagreement about the crisis in El Salvador was sufficiently noteworthy for it to be recorded by Philip Geyelin, the newspaper columnist:

> Measuring her words, and speaking in level tones was Georgetown University political scientist Jeane Kirkpatrick: "If we are confronted with the choice between offering assistance to a moderately repressive autocratic government which is also friendly to the United States, and permitting it to be over-run by a Cuban-trained, Cuban-armed, Cuban-sponsored insurgency we would assist the moderate autocracy."

> The response from Patricia Derian was, well, explosive: "What the hell is moderately repressive—that you only torture half the people, and that you only do summary executions now and then?"

It was, concluded the columnist, an "arresting and richly rewarding exchange—arresting in its emotional intensity and revealing in what it suggests about a profound change in American foreign policy."[1]

Under Ronald Reagan, U.S. foreign policy was indeed about to change. The broad outlines had emerged during the election campaign. By the time Reagan took the oath of office on January 18 1981, it was clear that the Cold War was officially back. Too much ground had been lost to the Soviet Union—the "Evil Empire" as Reagan would describe it. Fire would now be met with fire, and the "Brezhnev doctrine" met with the "Reagan doctrine." Instead of waiting fearfully for the next blow to fall, the United States would seize the initiative—challenge Soviet satellite governments and even the legitimacy of the Soviet Union itself. In one of its first major foreign policy decisions, the administration announced that it would seek repeal of the 1975 Clark Amendment, which had banned the delivery of U.S. aid to the UNITA rebels seeking to overthrow the government of Angola.[2]

If foes were to be treated like foes, allies would be treated like allies. Argentina's President-elect Roberto Viola received an early invitation to the White House. In February 1981, the Reagan Administration issued an order to U.S. representatives in the World Bank and other international financial institutions to stop opposing loans to Argentina, Chile, Uruguay, and Paraguay. Soon afterward, it announced that it would ask Congress to repeal the 1978 Humphrey-Kennedy amendment that banned all U.S. military sales and security aid to Argentina.

Even South Africa, so long a pariah, was offered the olive branch. In 1980, Chester Crocker, who was at Georgetown University's Center for Strategic and International Studies, had used the magazine *Foreign Affairs* to argue for a policy of "constructive engagement" with South Africa as a way of encouraging internal reforms.[3] Crocker was appointed an Assistant Secretary of State in the Reagan Administration and told to follow his own advice.

Central America was where the line was to be drawn. El Salvador's right-wing regime would be supported against the left-wing insurgents, while neighboring Nicaragua would become the first test case of the new "Reagan doctrine." The Sandinistas would be denied the seventy-five million dollars of U.S. aid promised to Nicaragua by Carter, treated like enemies of democracy, and pressured to stop aiding the Salvadoran guerrillas. By the end of 1981 the CIA was training Nicaraguan contras. By 1983, it was mining Nicaraguan harbors.[4]

The problem was that Nicaragua's security forces did not—as the Inter-American Commission on Human Rights made clear in its 1981 report—kidnap, torture, and kill unarmed civilians like their counterparts in El Salvador. Nor did they practice institutionalized racism like South Africa. In short, it was clear that Reagan's foreign policy agenda was fundamentally at odds with human rights as it had been defined by the United Nations and practiced by Patricia Derian and Theo van Boven.[5]

This left the new administration with two options. Either human rights had to be expunged from the political landscape and the clock turned back to the early 1970s, or human rights had to be radically redefined. Reagan attempted both. He proposed a conservative activist, Ernest Lefever, to fill Derian's shoes as Assistant Secretary of State for Human Rights. Lefever was so opposed to Derian's approach that in 1979 he had even proposed abolishing her post. Now he was filling it. There could be no clearer indication of President Reagan's determination to break with the past. An early decision was also taken to reverse Carter's policy toward Argentina, bilaterally and in the United Nations. As Alexander Haig was to put it in his memoirs: "We told Argentina that it had heard its last public lecture from the United States on human rights."[6]

At the same time, the new administration turned to Jeane Kirkpatrick for a rationale of its new policy, and a redefinition of human rights. She provided both by elaborating on the distinction between "authoritarian" and "totalitarian" regimes.

Dictatorships and Double Standards

The story of how a college professor who was a registered Democrat transformed this theory into a Republican foreign policy is a dramatic one. No less dramatic is the almost obsessive way her ideas were embraced by the Reagan Administration.

Jeane Kirkpatrick was born Jeane Jordan in Oklahoma, where her father was an oil driller. After graduating from Barnard College, she attended Columbia University and wrote her master's thesis on the British fascist Oswald Moseley. She then moved to Washington to work on East European refugees under Evron Kirkpatrick, who had managed Hubert Humphrey's campaign for mayor of Minneapolis in 1945 and remained one of Humphrey's closest political confidants. After studying in France, she returned to work at the State Department with Chinese who had been captured during the Korean War but refused to be repatriated. She married Evron Kirkpatrick the same year.[7]

She was one of the earliest "neoconservatives." This was a group of Democrats who were liberal on domestic issues but hawkish on foreign affairs, particularly on the Soviet Union. They grew increasingly disenchanted by the liberal drift of the Democratic Party in the post-Vietnam years, under first George McGovern and subsequently Jimmy Carter. Many remained registered Democrats while campaigning for Ronald Reagan because however hawkish they might have been on foreign policy, they still clung to the ideals of the New Deal.[8] Jeane Kirkpatrick played an active role in the conservative wing of Democratic politics through the early 1970s. She helped to form the Coalition for a Democratic Majority in 1972 and was active in the Committee on the Present Danger. Both groups advocated a more muscular policy towards the Soviet Union. By 1976 she was firmly ensconced in the ranks of the neoconservatives, and she voted for Gerald Ford against Carter.[9]

Her first major statement on "authoritarian" regimes came in her book on Peronist Argentina, published in 1971.[10] This established her as an expert on Argentinian politics, and nine years later, early in 1979, she again came into contact with Argentina when she participated in the controversial seminar on Argentina at Georgetown University.[11] During 1979 she pulled her thoughts on U.S. foreign policy together and published them in the November 1979 issue of *Commentary* under the title of "Dictatorships and Double Standards."[12] It was to launch her political career and underpin President Reagan's foreign policy.

The underlying premise of this article is that Carter's human rights policy had undermined U.S. security. How? First, by ignoring the realities of life under authoritarian regimes that are neither democratic like the United States, nor "totalitarian" like the Soviet Union. The rulers of such regimes are often autocrats who have a highly personalized style and control every aspect of government. This means that once their authority is challenged, as it was by Carter's human rights policy, society unravels and the ruler is replaced by a regime that is invariably more hostile to U.S. interests.[13]

Another dire consequence is that any prospect of eventual democracy is snuffed out, because however brutal the traditional ruler he does leave traditional life undisturbed. This preserves the seeds of dissent and leaves open the possibility of an eventual evolution into democracy. In the "totalitarian" regime, by contrast, the state has taken over religion, expression, work, and family. There is no chance of individual expression nor of change. Dissenters are simply spat out.[14]

Kirkpatrick illustrated this thesis by looking at Iran and Nicaragua, where two autocratic American friends had recently been deposed by revolution. The Shah of Iran and Anastasio Somoza emerge as relatively appealing figures in her article: the Shah is described as "dashing," Somoza as "tenacious." Somoza even had his children educated in the United States.

Carter's human rights policy, wrote Kirkpatrick, was based on a fundamental misreading of "traditional societies" like Iran and Nicaragua. What is life like in this distant combat zone? Nasty, brutish, and short—but passive. People accept their lot, however dreadful it may appear to the well-meaning American liberal: "because the miseries of traditional life are familiar they are bearable to ordinary people . . . who learn to cope, as children born to untouchables in India acquire the skills and attitudes necessary for survival in the miserable roles they are destined to fill." [15] In such a context, any attempt to impose democracy is doomed.

Carter's second mistake was to ignore the fact that the Third World is really a bleak world of Soviet mischief-making in which the United States cannot afford to relax its guard for an instant. Carter had only betrayed his naiveté when he had talked of an "inordinate fear of Communism." Wrote Kirkpatrick: "So what if the deep historical forces at work in such diverse places as Iran, the Horn of Africa, South East Asia, Central America and the United Nations look a lot like Russians and Cubans?"

From a human rights perspective, the most noticeable fact about this article is that it is not about human rights. Jeane Kirkpatrick offers no suggestions about what, if anything, the United States or United Nations should do about torture or disappearances—the kind of physical violence that was a trademark of "authoritarian" military rulers. Nothing is said in the article about human rights, except to downplay such violations. Somoza and the Shah, writes Kirkpatrick, "sometimes invoked martial law to arrest, imprison, and occasionally, it was alleged, torture their opponents." This was an unorthodox view. Only "occasionally" and only "alleged"? That was certainly not the view of Amnesty International, the International Commission of Jurists, the U.N., the Red Cross, the OAS, or even the U.S. State Department—all of whom documented widespread abuse by one or both regimes. [16]

But "Dictatorships and Double Standards" was principally about U.S. security, not human rights. It was a plea for restraint and inaction, and a plea against "interference," the rewards being a gradual evolution to democracy and firm friendship from a loyal ally.

Many articles were written disputing the article's distinction between "totalitarian" and "authoritarian" regimes and its claim that authoritarian regimes revolve around individual autocrats. In March 1981 Tom Farer, who had visited Argentina in 1979 as a member of the IACHR, pointed out that most of Latin America's military regimes, like the Argentinian Junta, were "bureaucratic/authoritarian," in which names at the top changed without any perceptible shift in the patterns of power. At most, only two rulers in Latin America—Stroessner in Paraguay and Duvalier in Haiti—fit Kirkpatrick's description of the traditional ruler. Farer also pointed out that half the nations of Latin America and the Caribbean were democratic and concluded: "The eccentricity of Kirkpatrick's account may raise doubts about her competence for public service." [17]

But such impertinence had little impact. Jeane Kirkpatrick's star was beginning to rise in the political firmament, and by 1980, as we have seen, her article was beginning to look prophetic. The Soviet Union had invaded Afghanistan, Vietnam had invaded Kampuchea, Central America was in turmoil, and the U.S. embassy in Teheran had been sacked by a mob. Carter himself was scrambling to regain the initiative. Huge refugee movements were under way from such "totalitarian" states as Vietnam, Cuba, Cambodia, and Ethiopia. Everywhere, it seemed, Communism was on the march. Even the 502B legislation had come unstuck. What was the point of a law denying aid to countries that were guilty of a "consistent pattern of gross violations" if the U.S. was not willing to pin the label on anyone? All of the contradictions, present since 502B was drafted in 1974, were now out in the open.

Kirkpatrick's article became a kind of bible for other neoconservatives who had been frozen out by Carter, as well as for Republican party foreign policy specialists. Later in 1980, five conservative Latin American specialists echoed Kirkpatrick's warning about Communist subversion in Latin America and the threat this posed to U.S. security. Their report, for the Council for Inter-American Security, proved highly influential during the transition, and its authors subsequently gained senior foreign policy posts in the Reagan Administration.[18]

"Dictatorships and Double Standards" thus meshed perfectly with Ronald Reagan's emerging foreign policy, particularly as it concerned troubled Central America. El Salvador the ally was under attack from left-wing guerrillas, while Nicaragua the enemy was drifting into the Soviet camp. Both developments had to be reversed in the interests of U.S. security. Now, thanks to Jeane Kirkpatrick, Nicaragua could be called a "totalitarian" state and blamed for exporting revolution, while the regime in El Salvador could be described as "authoritarian" evolving into a democracy. True, there was the violence in El Salvador, but Kirkpatrick had made it clear that killing, like poverty, was a product of such "traditional" societies. It became an article of faith during the Reagan Administration that violence in El Salvador was "routine," as the U.S. embassy in San Salvador would describe it in a 1982 "grimgram."[19]

Richard Allen, one of Ronald Reagan's foreign policy advisors, read Kirkpatrick's article and passed it to the candidate. Reagan—himself a former Democrat—was impressed. Allen introduced Kirkpatrick to Reagan, and they sat next to each other at a dinner given by the conservative columnist George Will. Reagan and Kirkpatrick, so the legend goes, got on famously. She joined his foreign policy team and played the role of the television journalist Barbara Walters when his team prepared Reagan for his television debate with Jimmy Carter.[20] After Reagan won the election, she was appointed to replace Donald McHenry as U.S. ambassador to the United Nations. She was also given a seat in the Cabinet and began to attend meetings of the National Security Council, which was unprecedented.

Elaborating the Theory

Ronald Reagan's foreign policy was hostile to human rights because, as we have seen, U.S. allies like El Salvador and Argentina had engaged in systematic violence against their own civilians. Kirkpatrick's next major article addressed this problem head on. In December 1980, she delivered a paper at the annual public policy seminar of the American Enterprise Institute, where she and her husband were resident scholars. The paper was entitled "The Hobbes Problem: Order, Authority and Legitimacy in Central America." She described the problem thus: "How to establish order and authority in a society where there is none."[21] This paper was later subsumed into an article which appeared in *Commentary* in January 1981.[22] The combined effect was to build on the thesis of the "Dictatorships" article, by downplaying the murder and mayhem in El Salvador and playing up the subversive nature of the Sandinista regime in Nicaragua.

The Hobbes paper is about the breakdown of society in Central America, particularly in El Salvador. Yet it draws such a close parallel with Argentina under Perón—a vastly more sophisticated society—that one can safely assume its thesis applies to all "authoritarian" regimes, traditional or otherwise. Argentina under Perón, Kirkpatrick had written in 1971, suffered from a "legitimacy gap": "No procedure was recognized as the legitimate route to power. . . . No group had sufficient authority to win widespread allegiance to any given decision process."[23] Now, in December 1980, she wrote about Central American politics: "No procedure is recognized as the legitimate route to power; no one has sufficient authority to win definitive allegiance to any given decision process."[24]

Such was the lack of any tradition of political legitimacy, wrote Kirkpatrick, that violence was not only routine but accepted: "El Salvador's political culture . . . emphasizes strength and machismo. . . . Competition, courage, honor, shrewdness, assertiveness, a capacity for risk and recklessness, and a certain 'manly' disregard for safety are valued." She even had praise for General Hernández Martínez, who was responsible for a nation-wide orgy of bloodletting in 1932 that is still known as "la matanza" (slaughter). So terrifying was his reputation that the general's name had already been taken by one of the death squads that had just driven Roberto Cuéllar and Marianella García Villas into exile. The general was, conceded Kirkpatrick, ruthless: "It is said that 30,000 people lost their lives." But, she said, this made him a "hero": "To many Salvadorans the violence of this repression seems less important than the fact of restored order and the thirteen years of civil peace that ensued."[25]

One of the central arguments of this paper appears to be the following. In El Salvador, in 1980, "legitimacy" came with power, no matter how that power was acquired nor how bloody the process: "Where there is no legitimacy, there is no authority. There is only power, and the habit of obedience to whoever successfully claims the power of government. Under these circumstances, a government's status depends, even more than usually, on its capacity to govern, to secure obedience, to punish those who disobey—in sum, to maintain order." Here was the solution to Hobbes's dilemma of how to establish authority in a society where there is none.

What happened in this miserable, damaged society could be of no concern to the well-meaning liberal from North America or Western Europe, because this was traditional Third World society where Western standards did not apply. In El Salvador, everything was more or less in balance until Jimmy Carter, "armed with an optimistic, deterministic theory of social change," encouraged the coup of October 1979 and started to impose foreign concepts like land reform and human rights. Under the pressure, traditional society began to unravel. Nine thousand people lost their lives in the following year, including the four American churchwomen.[26]

Two bold claims are made here. First, in a society that lacks political legitimacy, the use of force by a government against its own people is not only to be expected but is a legitimate way to establish authority.[27] Once this is accepted, those in power can employ any means to retain control, no matter how violent. Second, any challenge to their authority—no matter how well-meaning—is subversion and even terrorism.[28]

These views were even more at odds with traditional thinking on human rights and international human rights law than the earlier article.[29] The vision of Third World society and social change was equally challenging. Working to improve the lot of the poor was a goal not just of many American churches, but also U.S. government programs like USAID and the Peace Corps. Here it was seen as a "subversive" challenge to traditional rulers and a threat to U.S. security. Here were the early death squads being likened to chivalrous rogues and mass slaughter credited with creating thirteen years of "civil peace." What sort of peace was enjoyed by those 30,000 families during those thirteen years? The same sort of "peace," one imagines, that was enjoyed by Emilio and Angélica Mignone, and the other relatives of the disappeared. It was a bold thesis to put forward less than a month after four American churchwomen had been murdered in El Salvador.

Then there was Nicaragua. By January 1981, in Kirkpatrick's writings, the ousted dictator Anastasio Somoza had been canonized. No longer simply "tenacious," he had become a bluff and effervescent Latino like Gabriel Martínez—"a West Point graduate with an American wife and an expansive appetite for women and alcohol." [30] The Sandinistas, in contrast, were irredeemably "totalitarian." Even their nationwide literacy program (which was acclaimed by UNICEF, the OAS, and International Commission of Jurists) was portrayed as an attempt to extend "the junta's reach further into the minds of Nicaragua's people as well as into the countryside." [31]

Called upon to justify support for the regime in El Salvador, Kirkpatrick had picked up the gauntlet with characteristic vigor. She had also taken a step toward redefining human rights, and playing down the importance of the right to life and freedom from violence. These had been replaced by a different, more sinister kind of "violence"—the violence of "subversion" which slips like a thief in the night across frontiers, eroding support for "authoritarian" regimes. Yet there were risks. Almost immediately, it landed her in a dispute over the four murdered churchwomen.

Furor over the Churchwomen

On December 16 1980, Jeane Kirkpatrick was interviewed at an airport in Florida by John Hall of the Media General News service. The four American churchwomen had been murdered in El Salvador on December 2, and the Carter Administration had responded by suspending aid to the government. [32] Kirkpatrick was asked about the nuns. She replied:

> I think it's meaningful to ask, Do you think the government was responsible? The answer is unequivocal. No I don't think the government was

responsible. The nuns were not just nuns. The nuns were also political activists. We ought to be a little more clear about this than we actually are. They were political activists on behalf of the Frente [the guerrilla movement] and somebody who is using violence to oppose the Frente killed these nuns. I don't have any doubt about that and I don't think those people are in control of the government. . . . The death squads are not agents of the Salvadoran government.[33]

Every comment on El Salvador was being scrutinized in the shocked aftermath of the nuns' murder. Whether and how to support the regime in El Salvador would be the most urgent decision facing the incoming Reagan Administration. The issue was white-hot with emotion. Yet Kirkpatrick's remarks might still have gone unnoticed when they appeared in the *Tampa Tribune* of December 25 1980, if the article had not been spotted by the Lawyers Committee for Human Rights, in New York, a public interest group that had been asked by the relatives of the nuns to take up the case. The lawyers telephoned Kirkpatrick's office and were told she had been misquoted. They then contacted John Hall, the journalist, who was quite unaware of the fuss he had caused. No, he said, he did not think he had kept the tape, but he would call back. He called back to say he had found the tape and could confirm the quotation.[34]

Shortly afterward Alexander Haig, Mr. Reagan's Secretary of State-designate, told a congressional hearing that the four nuns had apparently been shot while trying to run a roadblock, thus implying once again that they were more than just nuns. Haig's comments surprised even the FBI team that had been sent to El Salvador by the Carter Administration to investigate the case. Later he qualified it.[35]

The identities of the killers were discovered by the U.S. embassy in San Salvador within weeks of the outrage. On the evening of December 2 1980, five members of the Salvadoran National Guard had changed out of their uniforms before flagging down the van and killing the churchwomen. They were still on duty. The orders were given by Sub-Sergeant Luís Colindres Alemán. The five were arrested on April 26 1981. Kirkpatrick had been wrong; this death squad had indeed been part of the security forces.[36] But she did not retract her essential charge against the nuns. As a result, the wound festered and helped create an intimidating aura about her. It even caused misgivings among some close friends. Michael Novak, a devout Catholic, later said he had been shaken when he read her comments. Like other friends, however, he refrained from referring to the controversy, aware of the anguish it caused her.[37]

But there was also anguish within the families of the four American churchwomen. They wrote to newspapers and spoke at congressional hearings, and their anger grew as the Salvadoran authorities refused to bring the killers to justice. On one occasion, the brother of Jean Donovan, one of the four dead women, happened to be traveling to Washington on the same plane as Kirkpatrick. He approached her seat with the intention of talking to her; according to him, she refused even to speak to him.[38]

How did she allow it to get this far? During an interview with the author in late 1983, Kirkpatrick grew quiet and withdrawn when she was asked about the affair:

> I'm very bitter about this whole case. I believe there has been a strange unwillingness on the part of a good many people to accept what I clearly meant. . . . I was speaking as a political scientist about the problem of politicization and polarization of a society. . . . Activities and persons who are totally removed from what would be conceived of as political roles normally become sucked into this process. . . . The nuns, because they were teaching in an area that was largely inhabited by guerrillas, were perceived as political activists, sucked into the process as it were, and shot. There you are, that's the beginning and the end of it. I don't believe there are any grounds for anyone to be offended by that. . . . For some quite extraordinary reason, people have not been willing to accept my very straightforward . . . comment. I find this a very deeply disturbing experience.[39]

This explanation was consistent with Kirkpatrick's view that the Church had become an agent of radical change and even subversion in Latin America, and it was widely held among American conservatives. Ernest Lefever, himself a former lay preacher and conscientious objector, was also crossing swords with American churches over their advocacy of social change in developing countries. He too was approached by Michael Donovan, brother of one of the dead churchwomen. According to Donovan, Lefever replied with a remark about "nuns hiding machine guns for the guerrillas" in El Salvador.[40]

But did the neoconservatives draw no distinction between avowed radicals and churchworkers who went to countries like El Salvador to feed, clothe, and support refugees? Their writing suggested not, and that they viewed such work as a challenge to authority, as "subversive." The four American nuns had contributed towards the disintegration of Salvadoran society and paid the price.

This is why the whole episode caused such incredulity. Kirkpatrick held strong views, and she had made them known. She thought she had spoken as a detached political scientist, but American human rights groups and missionaries, aware of her views, assumed she was speaking as an ambassador-designate. In the absence of any statement of outrage, they could only assume that, in an effort to overturn Jimmy Carter's legacy, Ronald Reagan and his senior advisors were trying to turn human rights upside down by exonerating the killers and denigrating their victims. This, they argued, could only encourage the killers in El Salvador.[41]

The next squall blew in from South Africa. On March 15, Kirkpatrick met with the chief of South Africa's military intelligence, Lieutenant General P. W. van der Westerhuizen, at her office in New York.[42] It had been standing policy since 1965 that there was to be no official U.S. contact with any member of the South African military above the rank of brigadier—just as it was policy that there was to be no official contact with the PLO. When Kirkpatrick's predecessor Andy Young had met with the PLO privately, he had lost his job.

When Kirkpatrick's meeting with the general came to light on March 23, she first said she had been unaware of his real identity and that the meeting had been part of her general policy of trying to see as many people as possible and understand all points of view. Black congressmen called for her dismissal and she was closely quizzed about the meeting at congressional hearings, but she remained unrepentant. She said that the policy on South African contacts was "ambiguous" and under review, and she pointed out that there was no such ban on contacts with Chinese and Soviet military. Why, she implied, should she act "selectively" toward South Africa? She adamantly refused to accept that a private discussion with a senior South African officer sent any kind of a "political" signal. She had merely been collecting views, informing herself about her new job.[43]

This was the academic not the politician speaking, but it was disingenuous. Any meeting between a U.S. ambassador and a South African delegation in March 1981—two months after the South Africans had wrecked a U.N. conference on Namibia—was bound to send out a political signal, and it could only be viewed as friendly. As with human rights, there could be no neutrality when it came to apartheid.[44]

The Redefinition of Human Rights

By now what had started as a *Commentary* article had evolved into a neoconservative policy that subordinated human rights to U.S. security. "Totalitarian" subversion posed a greater threat to U.S. security than "authoritarian" disappearances, and the respective abuses had to be graded accordingly. In March, Secretary of State Alexander Haig told an audience of foreign policy experts: "We should distinguish between the deprivation of national rights through aggression and the deprivation of personal rights through oppression." Regrettably, said Haig, Soviet-inspired aggression took priority. "It is a recurrent tragedy of the human condition—and foreign policy—that the choice of a lesser evil is still very evil." [45]

Neoconservative philosophers used their skills to elevate "totalitarian" violations to a higher plane than "authoritarian" violations. In one April 8 1981 article, Irving Kristol described torture as "so fundamentally obnoxious as to be always and anywhere unacceptable to us." But, he wrote, "the right to emigrate is the most basic of all individual rights since it tends automatically to set limits to what an authoritarian or totalitarian regime can do." The previous year, it may be recalled, Judge Irving Kaufman had said precisely the opposite while deciding that torture in Paraguay was an "international crime" that could be heard before U.S. courts. [46]

Ernest Lefever, Reagan's choice to succeed Patricia Derian, had described torture as in the "Iberian tradition." In a later conversation with the author he went further and maintained that torture and detention were not even violations of a right, let alone a fundamental right. Torture, he explained, is a "tactic" used to deprive people of such rights as freedom of worship, which is fundamental because it affects a person's soul. Lefever had also written that the idea of universal standards in human rights was dangerous to the United States. As we have seen, it was widely agreed among neoconservatives that political rights were seen as little more than goals in "authoritarian" Latin America. [47]

How should the Reagan Administration respond to torture and disappearances by its allies? The answer was by "quiet diplomacy" so as not to disturb the progress to democracy. Totalitarian regimes like the Soviet Union, Nicaragua, and Cuba, which practiced egregious violations and exported subversion, however, should be met with public censure and even (as it would turn out) military force. Kirkpatrick defended the merits of quiet diplomacy in an appearance on May 12 before the House Subcommittee on Foreign Operations. [48]

At first sight there was great plausibility to all this when applied to Argentina. The disappearances had slowed and Argentina's President-elect Roberto Viola was promising democracy. On August 28 1980 the U.S. embassy in Buenos Aires had successfully practiced "quiet diplomacy" when Edith Bona disappeared and almost certainly saved the woman's life.

Looked at more closely, however, the new neoconservative philosophy

was totally inappropriate to Argentina, as well as being profoundly subversive to human rights as a whole. "Quiet diplomacy" and "public pressure" had never been mutually exclusive. For either to be effective, both
were required. This was the lesson to be learned from the U.N.'s lamentable 1503 procedure. One reason for its failure to prevent torture in Uruguay and other "authoritarian" regimes was that the threat of publicity
was never employed. Similarly, Patt Derian's crusade had never been as
loud and public as Lefever and others suggested. (Her sinister meeting
with Massera at the ESMA would only emerge at Massera's trial by an
Argentinian court, in 1985.)

At the start of 1981 the challenge in Argentina was not simply to stop
the killing and nudge the government toward democracy. It was accountability. Somehow the killers would have to be brought to justice. This was
clear to career diplomats at the State Department. In a confidential January
19 briefing paper, Renée Joyner, at the human rights bureau, wrote: "We
recognize that eventually there will have to be some kind of accounting
and that the issue will not simply go away."[49]

What kind of response did this situation call for from the United States?
Clearly, a judicious mixture of public and private pressure. To strike the
right balance without undermining the alliance with Argentina and jeop-
ardizing U.S. interests would not be easy. On the other hand a total absence of public criticism would be interpreted as approval for Argentina's
military rulers. That could delay the transition to democracy and would
certainly do nothing to ease the anguish of the Argentinian relatives. The
question at the start of 1981 was not simply whether Ronald Reagan's foreign policy would allow for sufficient flexibility. It was whether the incoming administration even cared enough to face the dilemma.

A rugged political fight thus began to unfold in the United States at the
beginning of 1981 over human rights, just as it had at the outset of the
Carter Administration in 1977. It was just a matter of time before the Reagan Administration began to impose its views on the United Nations and
challenge the new U.N. Working Group on Disappearances—which had
itself challenged so many U.S. allies in Latin America.

20. The Carrier Changes Course

One of Jeane Kirkpatrick's first tasks was to recommend a U.S. delegate for the U.N. Human Rights Commission, with a session due to begin in Geneva on February 1 1981—thirteen days after Reagan's inauguration. She suggested Michael Novak, a friend and colleague at the American Enterprise Institute. Richard Schifter, another close friend, was asked to serve as Novak's deputy and alternate. This would be the first opportunity for the outside world to judge the new administration's human rights policy. Much was at stake.

There were great expectations, and great skepticism. Novak would later recall how he read articles on the plane to Geneva that talked of the "de-emphasis in human rights" under Reagan. Upon arriving in Geneva he found himself the subject of intense curiosity: "I felt like the first live Reaganite in captivity." The Danish ambassador hosted a dinner for the Western delegates on the eve of the Commission and Novak was peppered with queries. He decided that it was a disadvantage to be representing a Republican administration. "Democrats," he later wrote, "seem to be understood to be on the right side of history while Republicans are imagined to represent the bastion of reaction."[1]

At the same time, Novak assured his diplomatic audience that they would notice very little change in this administration's policy. "A great nation," he said, "changes its foreign policy like an aircraft carrier—a degree at a time." There would be, said Novak, no dramatic change. He was, of course, wrong. The aircraft carrier was already shifting hard to starboard, and as Jeane Kirkpatrick had already discovered over El Salvador, there were shoals everywhere.

Novak's first problem was that, like many American neoconservatives, he knew very little about the United Nations. His second problem was that he did not have concrete instructions from the new administration. Before leaving Washington, he had asked his friend Jeane Kirkpatrick what she expected of him. As he recalls it, she said: "Michael, the most important thing is to represent our ideas on human rights. That's what I want you to do. I want you to be friendly. . . . I want you to be clear that you don't condone any offense of human rights by anybody."[2] There were, he says, no other instructions.

Michael Novak was totally unsuited for a bruising, six-week political meeting like the U.N. Human Rights Commission. He had planned originally to become a priest and had studied in Rome, but left the seminary shortly before ordination. He then turned into a political hippie—opposing the war in Vietnam, visiting war resisters in Paris, teaching with the left-wing Mexican guru Ivan Illich (with whom he would come to disagree violently). Eventually he joined the disastrous 1972 Democratic campaign as a speechwriter for vice-presidential candidate Sargent Shriver. In 1973, after the McGovern fiasco—"we lost dreadfully"—Novak joined other neoconservatives in the Coalition for a Democratic Majority. He remained a Democrat, but says that he was an early member of the "ABC [Anyone But Carter] club."

When one asks for Novak's biography from the American Enterprise Institute in Washington, one learns that he has not just written ten books, but ten "philosophical" books, which have not just appeared, but have appeared in "every major Western language." The U.S. mission in Geneva issued a similar curriculum vitae in January 1981. It began with the words: "Michael Novak is a theologian and journalist." This stamped him immediately as otherworldly and in love with words. He would amply confirm this during his spell as delegate on the Commission.

He loved the florid, rolling phrase. His first speech before the Commission in February 1981 was on the subject of Israel, but he took the opportunity to congratulate the Brazilian chairman, Carlos Calero Rodrigues: "First my congratulations to our new chairman for his election, but also for the brisk and affable competence he has already shown. May the brevity of my congratulations permit a leap of soul to soul."[3] This must have been a novel sensation for Calero Rodrigues, a wizened Brazilian diplomat, but he was given no time to enjoy it. Novak finished his statement on an enigmatic note: "Mr. Chairman, my delegation is delighted to work with you in this assembly; depressingly ugly as its proceedings often seem. We well know that pearls come from oysters, silk from worms, butterflies from caterpillars, and great human vision from poor human clay."[4]

Back in the United States, Novak's political reputation rested on his forceful criticism of liberation theology and of the Catholic Church's involvement in the antinuclear campaign, but he still could not shake off the image of being a slight oddity.[5] Many of his former liberal friends looked on Novak with affectionate bemusement. Patt Derian called him "a sweet guy with nutty constructs."

Nutty constructs may not have mattered in domestic American politics, but they mattered enormously in the U.N. Commission. Novak was a writer and a thinker, not a politician, and he recoiled from the harsh words that are the essence of any political body. He wilted when the Arabs pitched into Israel. He hated the "emotional violence" of these attacks, as he later put it. It remained with him like a nightmare long after he had left Geneva. After a week he wrote a letter to Kirkpatrick, lamenting his plight: "Jeane, what have you let me in for?"

Why was he so surprised? He had worked on that 1972 presidential campaign of dirty tricks and smears. He knew that people were dying in the Middle East, that bombs were being dropped on refugee camps, rockets launched at kibbutzim. Real bombs, real rockets, real people underneath. Jerry Shestack, a Jew, had at least understood that Israel generated powerful passions and tried to salvage something from the wreckage by proposing a meeting with the PLO. When this failed, he shrugged and moved on. Novak, a Christian, railed about the ugliness but took no initiatives because he was primed in advance to be appalled at the "selectivity" of the U.N. attack on Israel. This was an article of faith with American neoconservatives, and they were delighted at Novak's statement on the Middle East.[6]

Then there was South Africa. Surely apartheid was sufficiently loathed for it to merit a concise expression of displeasure? Not from Novak. A year later he would have the following to say about South Africa's downtrodden blacks: "A black man is as free as a white man, as gifted, as talented. His loves are as passionate. His mind seeks truth with the same avidity. His conscience is as immortal."[7]

Novak was so in love with the spoken word, and so indifferent to U.N. procedure, that he unwittingly imperiled the important 1980 decision to place East Germany on the confidential 1503 blacklist. This was a vital test case for the Reagan Administration. It was proof that the U.N. was not biased in favor of the Socialist countries and it reaffirmed U.N. support for the right to emigrate—a right that Irving Kristol would call "the most basic of all individual rights."[8]

On February 27 1981, the Commission decided in a private session by nineteen votes to fourteen to keep the case of East Germany under review for a further year. Michael Novak then proceeded majestically to jeopardize this decision by disclosing it to a Swiss newspaper. Like Gabriel Martínez, the Soviets missed nothing and they pounced gleefully. Valerian Zorin, the Soviet delegate, lectured Novak sternly and proposed that the Commission express concern at his "politically motivated" disclosure. Novak asked Zorin whether he was trying to read his mind, but Zorin wasn't that ambitious. Eventually, under urging from Argentina and Uruguay—both of them on the 1503 blacklist—the Soviets withdrew their proposal and East Germany remained on the blacklist.[9] But this had been a grave misjudgment by Novak.

This whole episode—Novak's blunder and the U.N.'s decision to indict East Germany—was completely ignored by American neoconservatives. A month later, Kristol would write loftily: "I regard it as nothing less than a scandal that our representatives to the U.N. have, over the years, deliberately ignored this issue [the right to emigrate] presumably for fear of offending Soviet sensibilities." Yet the fact that East Germany was under indictment for a "consistent pattern of gross violations" was public knowledge even if the details of the charge were confidential. Kristol evidently neither knew nor cared.[10]

The second American blunder in 1981 was to lose the resolution on Andrei Sakharov's exile in Gorki.[11] Sakharov, it will be recalled, was on the agenda because of the combined efforts of Jerry Shestack and Mohamed al-Jabiri the previous year. Now the Soviets came up with a standard procedural ploy and proposed a resolution criticizing the treatment of blacks in Miami. Syria and Jordan then proposed counterresolutions criticizing each other, and toward the end of the session the Yugoslavians proposed a single motion to take no action on any of the four resolutions.

Richard Schifter, Novak's deputy, was handling East European issues. Schifter would succeed Novak in 1983 and prove to be one of the most effective U.S. delegates ever appointed, but on this occasion—in the view of most observers—he was betrayed by lack of experience. Instead of fighting the Yugoslavian move and tabling counterproposals, the American team was unprepared and the Yugoslavians won. U.S. human rights experts present in the room were struck by the speed with which Nonaligned delegations hurried to support the Yugoslavian compromise, clearly worried at Reagan's cold war rhetoric and suspicious of any American proposal on human rights in the Soviet Union.[12] Shestack, in sharp contrast, had won them around on Sakharov because of his impartial approach to the disappearances.

These two blunders by the U.S. team showed how the new administration's negative approach to human rights would backfire in the U.N. It also showed the insincerity of the neoconservatives' charge of "selectivity" against the United Nations. Sakharov and East Germany had been on the Commission agenda, and Mr Reagan's team had done everything to dislodge both. It was not the U.N. that was "selective" and "politically motivated." It was simply that the Reagan Adminstration had shot itself in the foot.

Novak and the Disappearances

Like Jerry Shestack before him, Michael Novak now had to confront Gabriel Martínez. This would be the sixth year that American delegates had run the gauntlet of his taunts and goads, only this time there would be wider principles at stake. Reagan's human rights policy, and the U.S. approach to the U.N., were very much under scrutiny. Once again Argentina was to become a lightening rod of a new administration's foreign policy.

By a strange quirk of fate, both Richard Schifter and Michael Novak knew what it meant for loved ones to disappear. Schifter had been born in Austria and in the mid-1930s he left his homeland for the United States. He never saw his parents again, and later assumed they had perished in the Holocaust.[13] Michael Novak also knew the horror of a disappearance. In 1964 his younger brother Richard had vanished while serving as a Catholic priest in East Pakistan. Years later Novak learned that Father Richard had been crossing a river when he was accosted and killed by a group of young bandits.

Novak sympathized with the Argentinian Mothers he met in Geneva at the 1981 Commission, but it did not prevent him from championing the government that had killed and tortured their relatives. Novak knew that the Reagan Administration wanted to make a new start with Argentina, but he faced a problem: how could this be reconciled with U.S. support for the U.N. Working Group on Disappearances which his predecessor, Jerry Shestack, had helped to establish?[14] This would have been a severe test of any administration, let alone one that had been in office barely two weeks.[15] There was also potential friction between the Reagan-appointed neoconservatives who saw "danger" in the U.N. and human rights, and career foreign service officers who had been won over by Carter's human rights policy.

The issues, however, were well known. On January 29, Renée Joyner, one of Ernest Lefever's aides at the human rights bureau, had drafted a memo predicting that Argentina would try to muzzle the U.N. group, and urged that this should be resisted by the U.S. delegation. As a "first priority," she wrote, the U.S. delegation should express "energetic support" for extending the group and seek "firm assurances" from Argentina that it would cooperate with the U.N. group on future disappearances.[16] This advice was ignored. In mid-February the delegation in Geneva received instructions fom Washington: if the Commission agreed by consensus to extend the working group, then the United States should join it. If the negotiations broke down, the United States should side with Argentina—even if this meant breaking with Britain and France.

By this time, the key decisionmakers in Washington had evidently decided that the U.N. Working Group on Disappearances fit the pattern of a "selective" U.N. body that was biased against American allies. During his Senate hearings two months later, Ernest Lefever would observe:

> The U.S. delegation was concerned about the selectivity of the issues being addressed by the Commission, and was reluctant to single out one issue over another, particularly one issue that pertained largely to one country. Our delegation to the Commission also was interested in broadening the agenda to include issues in addition to disappearances. I recommended adding internal exile under brutal conditions.[17]

This was not the opinion of Gerald Helman, the U.S. ambassador in Geneva. Ronald Reagan's election had left Helman in an uncomfortable position. He was a career diplomat, but he had spent much of the previous year nurturing the U.N. disappearances group against the attacks of Gabriel Martínez. At one stage he had even proposed opposing loans to Argentina in international institutions because of Martínez's refusal to cooperate. Helman must have been viewed with misgivings by the new administration, and the feeling was probably mutual. In spite of this, he would be forced to orchestrate the new administration's policy on disappearances in Geneva, because of Novak's inexperience.[18]

In January, just before the Commission opened, Helman sent a detailed memorandum to Alexander Haig. The Commission, he said, afforded "excellent opportunities to advance U.S. interests, strengthen cooperation with our allies . . . and contribute to the development of more effective multilateral human rights institutions." He singled out the disappearances working group. This, he wrote, "would assure more even-handed and less politicized treatment of human rights issues in the U.N."[19]

This cable showed that at least one senior U.S. diplomat realized that the group could prove extremely useful to the United States. This was confirmed on February 26, when the Commission began to debate the group's report. The loudest complaints came from Argentina, the Soviet Union, and Nicaragua. President Reagan's confidants should have realized that the group had tried to be evenhanded with its information and that even the "totalitarians" felt threatened.[20] Helman's cables also made it clear, as he put it, that there was no "desire to target Argentina or any special animosity towards that country."[21]

But the prevailing ideology in Washington was unaffected with such nuances. The U.N. was "dangerous." U.S. policy on the disappearances group such as it was, had been spelled out: support a consensus if consensus could be reached, vote with Argentina if it couldn't.

Haig cabled the delegation in Geneva to ask whether the debate could be postponed, to allow time to study the group's report. Helman took the idea to the chairman, Calero Rodrigues of Brazil, who rejected it out of hand. There were no further instructions, and before long Helman's cables began to show signs of desperation. He was aware of the growing resentment of the French and British. It would, he wrote, be hard to remain silent much longer. "We have thus far kept our counsels. . . . We recognize that this decision poses difficult choices for Washington, engaged as it is in a thorough review of U.S.-Latin American and human rights policies . . . we would appreciate instructions by Tuesday, February 17."[22] But by February 17, the instructions had still not arrived and it was time for the debate.

Martínez Attacks

Well aware that the carrier of U.S. foreign policy was changing course, Gabriel Martínez began to step up his war of nerves in the U.N. and fired off a series of notes to senior U.N. administrators warning about the possibility of Argentinian "terrorists" infiltrating the Human Rights Commission. This was clearly aimed at the Mothers and other relatives, who planned to attend the Commission in force. The U.N. took no action, but it heightened the mood of tension.[23]

A familiar pattern now began to unfold. France tabled a straightforward resolution proposing the extension of the disappearances group for another year. Martínez began to lobby behind the scenes in support of a weaker investigation that would work in private and refuse to handle individual cases. This proposal was discussed at a meeting of Western delegations and, as Helman cabled back to Washington, rejected out of hand after Mark Colville, chairman of the group, had warned that it would mean "the destruction of the group." Helman waited for Martínez to react, but the Argentinian let the matter quietly fall—somewhat to Helman's surprise.[24]

Speaking first, Gabriel Martínez then proceeded to unleash one of the most malicious statements ever delivered before the Commission. He spoke for ninety minutes, barely glancing at the notes that he had jotted down on a yellow legal pad. He had written in short, staccato jabs of the pencil—the way he spoke. It was a numbing tirade that would have done credit to an East European commissar. Of course no one had disappeared in Argentina! They had either gone into hiding or were terrorists who had been killed by other terrorists. Terrorists, terrorists, Martínez kept repeating the word until nerves screamed out in protest. Raul and Valentina Nughes were watching, puzzled and frightened, from the visitors' gallery. Angel, their son, had been fourteen years old when he was pulled screaming into a car by his hair and driven away to torture. Had he been a terrorist? Most sinister was the way Martínez repeated the lie. Students of totalitarianism would have recognized the technique, and it was anything but haphazard. Alexander Haig had declared terrorism the first enemy of American foreign policy. Martínez was simply picking up his cue.

Martínez then turned to his vendetta against Theo van Boven, and accused van Boven of hiring terrorists to service the group. This was clearly a reference to Antonio Fortín, the Chilean exile. It was an outrageous charge, but Martínez also knew that one way to cripple the group would be to cripple its secretariat. If Martínez had been challenged, he probably would have yielded. But no one came to van Boven's defense. Martínez duly took note. It was left to van Boven to snap back an angry reply. The hatred between the two men was almost visible.[25]

Two observers remained strangely silent through this exchange. One was Mark Colville, who had worked with van Boven and must have known better than anyone that Fortín was no terrorist. Yet he stayed in his seat. Why? Colville was certainly keen to win Martínez's cooperation, but per-

haps he also sensed a subtle shift in the mood of the Commission. Martínez was no longer the detested outsider. With the change in U.S. policy
toward Argentina, he had gained in confidence and stature. Colville was
beginning to hedge his bets.[26]

Surely this was also a moment for Michael Novak to intervene? Novak
would later tell a congressional subcommittee that he believed in "human
rights institutions." Well, here, in the form of the working group, was
an institution worth saving. Martínez, in contrast, was bent on destruction, as Novak would later acknowledge in an interview. "He could cause
trouble at the drop of a hat. This was a man who did mad things for
purposes I doubt anyone knows, not even himself. It seemed to me exhibitionism. Sometimes he was just clearly causing mischief."[27]

But of course it was not that way. Martínez was simply doing what he
had done for six years—intimidating his enemies. The sudden shift in
American policy had handed him an unexpected bonus, and to judge from
what now transpired, Michael Novak was willing to help. Novak had been
told to side with Argentina in the event of a vote, and he had prepared a
statement with this possibility in mind. "We recognize in Argentina," he
wrote, "one of the world's advanced civilizations; a religious culture, a
proud institutional tradition." Then, the now familiar complaint—that the
U.N. was oblivious to the distinction between "totalitarian" and "authoritarian": "The freer nations of Latin America seem to be disproportionately
singled out for blame while the totalitarian states of that region and elsewhere escape blame. . . . Totalitarian states loathe liberal ideals. . . . The
very freedoms of Argentina result in its being held to a standard which
societies with lesser liberties escape."[28]

This full-blooded apology for a government that had murdered thousands of its own citizens revealed, once again, the basic insincerity of the
American charges against the U.N. and the complete irrelevance of the
distinction between "authoritarian" and "totalitarian." The issue at hand
was how to strengthen the working group. Novak was set on making the
task harder. By singling out Argentina this statement—had it been delivered—would have made the group out to be more "selective" than it actually was.

This was pointed out by Ambassador Gerald Helman, whose task it
was to cable Novak's draft statement back to Washington for clearance.
Helman added his own dry observation, that Novak's draft might "err by
mentioning Argentina too prominently." By now, there must have been a

yawning gulf between the two men. Novak's draft was never delivered, whether because of Helman's comments or because consensus was achieved is unclear. It was, however, leaked to Jerry Shestack by worried officials in the State Department.[29]

Gabriel Martínez may have sensed Novak's goodwill toward his government, because he dug in his heels. On February 24, two days before a vote was scheduled, negotiations broke down over whether the working group should consider individual communications. A vote now seemed inevitable. Thanks to Gerald Helman, it was avoided. Helman was by now a lonely figure, isolated from his nominal chief on the delegation—Michael Novak—and out of sympathy with his political masters in Washington. Try as he might, he had failed to convey the mood of the debate in Geneva and the frustration felt by America's allies, the French and British. He had not even been able to extract clear instructions. The State Department had told him to press for consensus; he had replied that on issues like confidentiality and individual communications there could be none, and that to concede would be to emasculate the working group. This, evidently, was not what Alexander Haig wanted to hear.

Helman was in an invidious position. When a newspaper article criticized the shift in American policy, Helman reprimanded the author, but more in sorrow than anger.[30]

In the absence of clearcut instructions, Helman took it on himself to confront Martínez and insist that the stalling come to an end. Six months later, Novak would tell a congressional subcommittee that Helman had "twice sought and received permission to go directly to Martínez and express keen displeasure that the U.S. would feel if consensus was not reached."[31] It was the only hint of any American pressure on Martínez at the Commission, and Novak himself would not have made such a move. He was noticeably cool toward Helman in this testimony, and noticeably warm toward Martínez in his testimony at the Lefever hearings.[32] Yet Helman's comments probably convinced Martínez that there had to be a limit to his blackmail and on the morning of February 26 a resolution was finally passed extending the working group for another year.

It was at once clear that Martínez had extracted a major concession. According to the resolution, the U.N. Working Group on Disappearances would henceforth "observe United Nations standards and practices regarding the receipt of communications, their transmittal to governments and their evaluation." "Established U.N. practice," as we have seen, meant handling all individual communications in private. This was a major breakthrough for Martínez—his first since the group had been established a year earlier.

Novak's Verdict

Shortly after the vote, Michael Novak delivered a spectacularly insensitive statement about disappearances. It had been drafted by Ernest Lefever, and complained again about the "selectivity" of the United Nations: "The Human Rights Commission has as yet no other similar working group looking into other serious human rights abuses in the world, like penal labor camps, the abuse of mental hospitals for political purposes and political exile under brutal conditions. We do not go far enough when we single out this one category of human rights violations." Then the familiar distinction: "In non-totalitarian societies information on abuses is quite readily available. In closed totalitarian societies, such information is difficult to obtain. The unfortunate result is that we spend more time criticizing those countries that are partly free."[33]

Inevitably, it was this issue, not the vote, that made the news in the United States. In a March 4 1981 memorandum to Walter Stoessel, Elliott Abrams noted that Novak had drawn attention to "the lack of working groups on labor camps, political exile and psychiatric commitment." On March 25 1981, Abrams recommended to Secretary of State Haig that Novak and Schifter be rewarded with a letter of appreciation for having handled the Commission "with skill and a sensitive appreciation of the President's view on international human rights." Haig obliged and the letters were sent.

On April 28 1981, Novak himself went on the record to claim that he had kept alive the one tradition that makes the U.S. a "shining city on the hill"—a profound and forthright concern for human rights everywhere.[34] Six months later, Novak gave a glowing account of his role in the disappearances debate before Don Bonker's subcommittee: "On no issue," he said, "were we more jubilant." Novak went on to record that Michael Newlin, the Deputy Assistant Secretary for International Organizations, expressly "thanked me for brilliant tactical maneuvering over 15 days."

There was no stopping Novak. In case anyone missed the point, a collection of his and Schifter's statements to the Commission was published by the Foundation for Democratic Education at a cost of one dollar. The man primarily responsible for preventing collapse, Gerald Helman, was shamefully treated. He remained in Geneva only as long as it took to re-place him with a California millionaire who had made a fortune from selling clothes and had helped to fund Reagan's election campaign. Hel-man was banished to the darker recesses of the State Department before reemerging on the U.S. delegation to a U.N. conference on outer space.

With each stage, the facts about the debate in Geneva receded. More ominous, the U.S. obsession with "selectivity" in the U.N. was now be-coming a self-fulfilling prophecy. The obvious way to make the U.N. less "selective" was to establish more working groups, but that would only be achieved by strengthening the pioneering U.N. Working Group on Dis-appearances and standing up to the threats of Martínez. American actions at this Commission had had the reverse effect: they had encouraged Mar-tínez and weakened the group. Someone would pay. That someone was to be the long-suffering Emilio Mignone.

Mignone's Ordeal

On February 27 1981—one day after the U.N. Working Group on Disap-pearances was extended for another year—Emilio Mignone's frustrating search for his missing daughter resulted in a second terrifying encounter with the military in Argentina.

Mignone was at home when he received a garbled telephone call saying that the offices of his agency CELS (the Center for Legal and Social Stud-ies) were being raided by police. He got in his car and drove down the few blocks where, sure enough, he found lights blazing in the building and police cars parked along the street. Trying not to arouse suspicion, he drove slowly back to his apartment. As he drew up, he noticed cars parked outside without lights. Gun-carrying police surrounded him as soon as he got out and forced him into the elevator. Mignone's son Javier had a friend staying with him and the sight of his father being brought in at gunpoint revived the fearful memories of Mónica's kidnapping that dreadful night in May 1976.[35]

"Are you going to cause my father to disappear?" asked the boy.

"No," came the reply. "He's too well known." But the group that had taken his sister had said something like that four years ago. The intruders conducted a brief search of the apartment before bundling Mignone out.

It had been a major operation. Six other members of the CELS staff had been arrested, the offices had been ransacked, files and boxes overturned, and hundreds of documents seized. The following day, Augusto Conte MacDonell was also arrested.[36] The captives were held for seven days in tiny, stuffy cells. It was uncomfortable but not sinister in the way that Mónica Mignone's detention would have been. Mignone quickly realized they were not going to be secretly murdered as soon as he emerged from the van at the courthouse, filthy, unshaven, and blinking in the sunlight, to find four hundred people demonstrating noisily on their behalf.

In the context of the past horror in Argentina and the current horror in Central America, this was a minor episode. Yet it had quickly escalated into an international cause célèbre. A bitingly critical editorial in the *New York Times* suggested that the Reagan Administration had—by its lack of a human rights policy—emboldened the Junta to arrest Mignone and his friends. "By standing mute the Reagan Administration says it doesn't really care. It is a shaming silence."[37]

Administration officials, however, were not standing mute. They were practicing "quiet diplomacy" to get the seven released. The State Department had been peppered with protests the day after the arrests, and Secretary of State Haig cabled Ambassador Shlaudeman with instructions to approach the Argentinian government "at the highest level" to express concern.[38] Embassy officials then contacted the Argentinian Foreign Ministry and President Videla's office, warning that the incident was having a "very strong impact" in the United States, and that it could even harm Argentina's case at the U.N. Human Rights Commission, which still had two weeks to run.[39]

The Reagan Administration had spotted the danger and it was now trying to put discreet pressure on its Argentinian ally without implying any criticism or "interference." Another cable from Washington, drafted by acting Assistant Secretary of State for Inter-American Affairs John Bushnell, asked Shlaudeman to express "deep concern," but "in private and without publicity."[40] After lodging his protest, Schlaudeman mumbled a "no comment" as journalists peppered him with questions at the entrance to the embassy.

The actual case against Mignone and the others ended on a note of farce. The investigating judge who had ordered their arrest, Martin Anzoátegui, was well known as a critic of the human rights groups. (Anzoátegui was the same judge who had ordered six thousand files confiscated from the office of the Human Rights League in August 1979, just prior to the IACHR visit.) His case against Mignone was based on a 1974 security law passed by Isabel Perón. In court, however, he produced just two documents from the hundreds collected at the CELS offices and his questioning was halfhearted. Under Argentinian law, arresting officers must make a full inventory of any documents that are taken. This Mignone's captors had failed to do—as Mignone himself pointed out. On May 13 1981 the case against him and the other defendants was dropped.

Martínez Strikes Again

Why had Mignone been arrested in the first place? One long analysis from Ambassador Shlaudeman portrayed it as another warning by army hard-liners to President-designate Roberto Viola against any political relaxation. Shlaudeman pointed out that the hard-liners had used Judge Anzoátegui for just such a purpose in 1979, before the IACHR arrived.[41] By the time Shlaudeman visited Videla for a discussion on March 4 he was convinced that this was the explanation. Sources at the Foreign Ministry, he cabled, viewed the arrests as a "disaster." Hardliners, however, were gleefully portraying them as an example of judicial independence by Judge Anzoátegui of the kind long advocated by the United States.[42]

One important reason for Mignone's arrest that went totally unnoticed in the United States was the Junta's growing concern at the U.N. Working Group on Disappearances. It was clearly no coincidence that Mignone was arrested the day after the vote was taken in Geneva to extend the group, and during his police interrogation, Mignone found himself repeatedly queried about his September 1980 testimony to the group. This showed that Gabriel Martínez was involved. By having Mignone picked up, Martínez was warning the group to draw back from investigating the disappearances in Argentina. He was also trying to intimidate one of its principal informants.

The group rose to the challenge. On March 2, three days after Mignone's arrest, Mark Colville delivered a stern note of protest to Martínez in Geneva: "As you know Dr. Mignone met with the group and transmitted to it information on reported enforced or involuntary disappearances in your country. This gives us particular cause to request from your government any information it might wish to submit on the arrest of Dr. Emilio Mignone."[43] This must have been a shock to Martínez, but he parried it the following day with a brilliant thrust by demanding full details of what Mignone had said in September.[44] Colville could not have complied without further endangering Mignone. The dilemma was resolved two days later when Mignone was released—quite possibly as a result of the group's protest.

Gabriel Martínez must have realized that he had not succeeded in muzzling the group, and that as long as van Boven was in place he probably never would. On April 16 1981 he sent a gloomy cable back to Buenos Aires, noting that: "So far from putting an end to the debate [on disappearances] in the Commission, one can perceive a marked increase in the level of disappointment shown by European papers at the results obtained." Novak's performance, he continued, had served to convince European opinion that Reagan was "de-emphasizing" human rights.[45] Clearly, it was only a matter of time before he clashed again with van Boven.

None of this was reported in the United States, where the debate continued to center around the implications of Mignone's arrest and release for Mr. Reagan's human rights policy. After Mignone's release, a *New York Times* reporter wrote from Buenos Aires: "Mr. Mignone . . . and other human rights leaders here say that in some ways the Reagan administration was more effective in getting the arrested human rights leaders . . . released than the Carter administration might have been . . ."[46] On April 28 the irrepressible Michael Novak portrayed Mignone's release as a triumph for "quiet diplomacy."[47]

This was not what Mignone had meant at all, and he tried to set the record straight in a letter to the *New York Times*.[48] The letter was never published. Michael Novak plowed ahead, turned U.S. "quiet diplomacy" into a public event, and claimed part of the credit himself. Appearing before Don Bonker's subcommittee in November, he said:

> We do hear from time to time of a real person released from prison through our efforts or of a single family re-united. In particular State Department officials have stopped me in the corridor from time to time to say that thanks in part to our work, hard cases upon which they have been working for months or years have suddenly been cleared by governments concerned. . . . Mr. Mignone . . . has written expressly to Ambassador Kirkpatrick to thank her for human rights benefits that have flowed to Argentina from our new relationship there.[49]

This could not have been further from the truth. When Novak had arrived in Geneva the U.N.'s human rights machinery was tougher, less biased, than it had ever been. By the time he left, only six weeks later, it was tottering. Novak himself had wrought fearful damage.[50] For human rights victims in general the U.N. was once again a "dangerous place," although Emilio Mignone did at least seem a little stronger. He had been personally adopted by Michael Novak and the Reagan Administration. This, presumably, would bring him some protection. After challenging Gabriel Martínez, he would need it.

The U.N. Working Group on Disappearances now faced another difficult year ahead in its dialogue with the Argentinian Junta. Its members now had to decide how to "observe established U.N. practice" in handling the communications that were pouring in from the relatives in Argentina. Should they be treated confidentially, like the discredited 1503 procedure? The group sought van Boven's opinion. He told them to ignore the resolution and continue as they had done over the previous year. Encouraged, they began to prepare for their next encounter with Martínez in New York on May 18 1981.

21. Lefever's Calvary

Two weeks after Emilio Mignone was released from jail, General Roberto Viola, President-designate of Argentina, arrived in the United States. Like the outgoing President, Jorge Videla, Viola was viewed as a "moderate" in the lineup of military chiefs. On March 17, he met with a group of senators at the Capitol. Later in the day, Senator Claiborne Pell issued a short but dramatic press release: "I am delighted that at a Senate coffee today for members of the visiting Argentine delegation, President-designate Viola stated that his government will publish a list of all those known by the government to have disappeared and to have died over Argentina's past several years of internal turmoil."[1]

If this was to be believed, then a breakthrough was indeed in the offing. Within hours, however, journalists accompanying Viola were given a different account. There were no plans to publish a list of the disappeared. Even if a list were eventually published, said Viola, there would be no investigation of the role of the military: "A victorious army is not investigated. If the Reich's troops had won the last world war the tribunal would have been held not in Nuremberg but in Virginia."[2] This sinister comment provoked the following reaction from James Neilson in the *Buenos Aires Herald*: "Viola after all is supposed to be a moderate, and if moderates think the only thing the Nazis did wrong is lose, the normal mind will find it hard to imagine what the view of the hardliners must be."[3]

Viola left behind him some red faces on Capitol Hill, but the Reagan Administration was determined to forge ahead, and on March 20 John Bushnell told a House subcommittee that the plan was to lift the 1978 embargo on military sales to Argentina. Bushnell—Jerry Shestack's former adversary—had been named acting Assistant Secretary for Inter-American Affairs. On April 1, the House held further hearings to consider the administration's proposal.[4] These were the first hearings specifically on Argentina since 1976 and, like the earlier session, they helped concentrate minds on the wider issues at stake.

The hearings were carefully monitored at the Argentinian embassy in Washington by Ambassador Aja Espil and his staff, and on April 9 1981 Aja Espil sent an optimistic assessment back to Buenos Aires which was forwarded to Martínez in Geneva: "The majority of the legislators have conceded that human rights have improved during 1980/1981, even if the liberals are fighting to maintain the embargo. Second, optimism has been aroused by the visit of President Viola, and there is a general feeling in Congress that his administration will lead to a progressive normalization of political life in Argentina."[5]

On May 14, Aja Espil's optimism seemed born out when the full House Committee on Foreign Affairs rejected a proposal by Democrats to resume arms sales only if President Reagan certified that an explanation had been given on the disappeared. In a lengthy cable analyzing the vote, the Argentinian embassy expressed the view that intensive lobbying by the administration had helped convince wavering Republicans and won over at least three Democrats, thus swinging the vote in favor of Argentina. John Bushnell's presence, it said, had proved decisive. Bushnell had pointed out that no disappearances had been reported since August 1980 and said that other nations, including Israel, had taken advantage of the arms embargo to sell over two billion dollars worth of arms to Argentina since 1978.[6]

Following this session, an official from the Argentinian embassy phoned Bushnell and thanked him for his "timely intervention." According to a cable drafted by the official, Bushnell told him that he thought the Reagan Administration would win the battle, but warned that the "ultraliberals" were counting on the presence in America of the Argentinian newspaper publisher Jacobo Timerman to help maintain the arms embargo. After being released in 1979, Jacobo Timerman had written a powerful book (*Prisoner Without a Name, Cell Without a Number*) about his experience as a disappeared person and charged his kidnappers with anti-Semitism.[7] Aja Espil was aware of the threat, and he noted in his cable that several congressmen had already picked up Timerman's charge.

It was left to Gabriel Martínez in Geneva to set this modest gain in perspective. Martínez was still smarting from defeat at the U.N. Human Rights Commission, and in a bleak April 16 cable he once again gave vent to his deep frustration. From a European perspective, wrote Martínez, General Viola's visit to the United States had turned into a public relations disaster:

> European critics have taken statements by General Viola out of context . . .
> to attribute to him the intention of publishing a list of disappeared persons.

They try to nullify the positive declarations made by the Reagan Administration on the situation in Argentina and the future of bilateral relations.
They insist on the marked lack of interest of the administration in matters
of human rights, citing as an example the nomination of Ernest Lefever as
Assistant Secretary of State for Human Rights.[8]

Martínez was right to be worried. Outside the United States, there was
considerable skepticism about the change in U.S. human rights policy.
Meanwhile, within the United States itself, the honeymoon period was
over. Human rights groups were gearing up for the fight of their lives.
They were preparing to challenge Reagan's nomination of Ernest Lefever
to Patt Derian's sensitive post.

Lefever Agonistes

Ernest Lefever had languished on the fringes of the Democratic party,
gloomily predicting disaster, until the accession of Ronald Reagan to the
presidency brought him sudden, unexpected respectability.[9]

Lefever had begun his political life as a liberal. He graduated from Yale
Divinity School and became an ordained Protestant minister. During the
Second World War he was a pacifist, and he helped relocate Japanese
Americans who had been detained in camps after Pearl Harbor. Subse-
quently, however, he underwent a profound conversion and abandoned
pacifism for fervent anti-Communism. After working briefly for Hubert
Humphrey, Lefever went to Georgetown University as a lecturer, and then
to the Brookings Institution. In 1976 he set up his own think tank, the
Ethics and Public Policy Center, which was affiliated with Georgetown
University before becoming fully independent in 1979. Throughout the
1970s, Lefever found himself in almost constant conflict with the Geneva-
based World Council of Churches, which represented 400 million Protes-
tants, and its American affiliate, the National Council of Churches.[10]

Lefever was a quirky figure, rather like Michael Novak, although a less
elegant writer and a more abrasive personality. Outside his own circle, his
writings attracted less attention than they probably deserved. This quickly
changed when he was nominated to succeed Patricia Derian. It was a clear
sign of Mr. Reagan's determination to expunge human rights from his
political agenda, and—failing that—to subordinate it to U.S. security.

Lefever was not, of course, the only fox who was put in charge of the
chickens by Reagan, but he was surely the first who had called for his own

post to be abolished. On July 12 1979, in testimony before Don Bonker's subcommittee, he had stated:

> In a formal and legal sense the U.S. government has no responsibility—and certainly no authority—to promote human rights in other sovereign states. . . . In my view, the United States should remove from the statute books all clauses that establish a human rights standard or condition that must be met by another sovereign government before our government transacts normal business with it, unless specifically waived by the President. It should not be necessary for any friendly state to pass a human rights test before we extend normal trade relations, sell arms or provide economic or security assistance.[11]

Statements like this ensured that Lefever's appearance before the Senate Foreign Relations Committee in 1981 would serve as a rallying call to conservatives and liberals alike. Lefever's abrasive personality added spice to the hearing, and helped to turn it into an event of high political drama.

Most hearings on new presidential nominations attract attention because they offer insights into administration policy, but no one was prepared for the excitement generated by the Lefever hearings. It was standing room only in Room 1202 of the Dirksen Senate Office Building, when the hearings began at 10:05 A.M. on the morning of May 18. Senator Charles Percy, the chairman, opened the proceedings with a short statement. What the audience did not know was that Lefever had already committed one blunder. Angered by the extent of his critics' organization, he had suggested that it was some kind of "Communist conspiracy." At least that was what Percy had understood him to say. Lefever asked whether the chairman had heard him correctly, not knowing that Percy was hard of hearing and sensitive about it. Percy was furious.

It was, without doubt, an intimidating ordeal for Lefever. At times the questions sounded more like a criminal interrogation than an exchange of views. The senators were blunt, unsympathetic, and even impertinent—as when Lefever was asked to explain why his own brother had described him as unqualified for the post. There were moments of laughter, but not many. Reading the report of the proceedings, one almost feels Lefever praying for it to end.

Yet he was his own worst enemy. Throughout the first two days he kept adding fuel to the fire, irritating committee members. Instead of respect, he conveyed disdain. He made no concessions to the occasion, no attempt to ingratiate himself. Even Republican senators began to entertain doubts. Where others would have dodged the troubling issues, Lefever made them more prominent. During a discussion about apartheid, he spoke sympathetically of white South Africa, and described black Africa in offensive terms: "illiterate Bantu," "primitive tribes," and "a female continent inviting penetration." Then came a startling disclosure. Lefever had received funding from a government front organization, the South African Foreign Affairs Association, that had been set up to discredit foes of apartheid, including the World Council of Churches.[12]

Each issue, large and small, turned into a black mark against Lefever and the Reagan Administration. Other neoconservatives like Jeane Kirkpatrick were making out a convincing intellectual case for the distinction between "totalitarian" and "authoritarian" regimes, but it called for more subtle exponents than Ernest Lefever. Lefever trivialized it by describing the Soviet Union as "a conspiracy masquerading as a state"—and repeating his contention that torture in Chile had been routine, in the "Iberian tradition."

He admitted that he had "goofed" in calling for the repeal of U.S. human rights legislation back in 1979, but he stubbornly refused to commit himself to retaining those same laws. He also stuck to his position on the key question of "interference." In his writings he had argued against "playing God," and he was far from being the sole exponent of this view, but he allowed himself to be sidetracked disastrously into implying that he would not even have protested the Holocaust. This presumably was not true—Lefever had visited the concentration camps of Buchenwald and Dachau after the war—but the implication was immensely damaging.

He also allowed himself to get carried away, and hurt, by his fierce distrust of church radicals. This too was neoconservative orthodoxy, but once again Lefever managed to wound himself instead of his opponents. He criticized a church-led boycott of Nestle that was aimed at preventing the sale of baby foods in the Third World. But the disclosure that Nestle had made a sizeable contribution to his own center completely undermined his case.[13]

The memory of the four American churchwomen who had been murdered in El Salvador four months earlier was still fresh in the minds of committee members and the audience. Shortly before the hearing, Michael Donovan, the brother of one of the four women, had told of an interview in which Lefever had accused the nuns of hiding machine guns for the insurgents in El Salvador. Lefever denied making the comment, but he did tell the committee—echoing his friend Jeane Kirkpatrick—that it was "inappropriate for missionaries to go to foreign countries and then actively engage in civil strife against the government."[14] Yet in 1980 Lefever had suggested that missionaries and nuns could be recruited by the CIA.

Lefever and Argentina

It was the disappearances in Argentina that helped to seal Lefever's fate and summed up the manifold contradictions in his nomination. Again and again Lefever was asked how he could remain silent in the face of such a crime. Again and again the parallel was drawn between Argentina and Nazi Germany. What difference did it make to the thousands of disappeared persons and victims of torture whether Argentina was an "authoritarian" or "totalitarian" regime? By what standard did Lefever judge the global aspirations of the Soviet Union more "egregious" than the killing of ten thousand Argentinians? One by one, the unanswered questions about Reagan's human rights policy came crowding in on the hapless Lefever.

Lefever himself had taken up the post of Assistant Secretary—prior to his confirmation—just as the issue of disappearances was about to be discussed at the U.N. Human Rights Commission in Geneva. Questioned about this by Senators Claiborne Pell of Rhode Island and Paul Tsongas of Massachusetts, Lefever unveiled a dismal tale of muddle and deception. On his first day at work, he said, he had arrived to find that there was no policy on whether to side with the French or the Argentinians over the U.N. Working Group on Disappearances: "I did not hit the ground running on that one. I hit the ground crawling. . . . I was astounded that we had no position of our own. I said do you mean we went into an important international forum without our own position? That we are going to have to decide between taking the French and Argentine position?"[15]

The answer was yes. A decision had to be made and, as we have seen, that decision was to side with Argentina in the event that negotiations collapsed. Yet, said Lefever, his own role in actually formulating this position was "minimal." The formulation had been done by Jeane Kirkpatrick and Elliott Abrams, the Assistant Secretary of State for International Organizations. Pressed by Pell, Lefever denied that he had drafted the instruction to Novak to side with Martínez if the negotiations in Geneva fell through.

Elsewhere in his testimony, however, Lefever gave a very different impression and suggested that he had played a significant role in this policy decision. And why not? The administration was anything but reticent about its support for the Junta. But the real surprise was to come during the second part of Lefever's hearing, on June 4. Jerry Shestack had been told by a contact inside the State Department who was deeply unhappy with the change in U.S. policy that Lefever had sent instructions to Geneva. Shestack informed Senator Claiborne Pell. After persistent questioning, Lefever admitted that his name had appeared on an important cable that left Washington for Geneva with the instructions to Novak on how to vote if the negotiations broke down.

Lefever's explanation went as follows. He had been in his office for only a few days when Elliott Abrams, "who had operational responsibility for this issue," telephoned for a general chat about the considerations involved in the issue. "I did not recommend any specific line of action," continued Lefever. "Not long thereafter, two key documents were drafted, an action memorandum and a telegram instructing our delegation in Geneva. I participated in the drafting of neither, nor did I clear either. However my name was erroneously carried as one of the drafters of the telegram. The original copy of the telegram maintained in the Department bears no written initials . . ."[16]

Lefever also said that subsequently he only participated "peripherally in the preparation of tactical instructions" to the US delegation in Geneva. Yet he drafted the key passage in Novak's damaging February 26 statement, regretting the fact that the U.N. was not investigating "totalitarian" abuses like psychiatric detention. This was more than a "peripheral" involvement. In terms of bureaucratic muddling and buck passing, the episode certainly equaled anything that happened during Patricia Derian's stormy tenure.

Timerman Appears

At this stage fate dealt Lefever a desperately unlucky blow. By an unhappy coincidence, Jacobo Timerman's passionate account of torture and anti-Semitism in Argentina had just been published. Timerman arrived in the United States just as Lefever's inquisition began.

In a way, it was appropriate that their paths should cross. Lefever and Timerman were at opposite poles of the human rights debate, but they were curiously similar. Both had spent their working lives thinking and writing about ideas. Both were obstinate, passionate, impetuous. *Prisoner Without a Name, Cell Without a Number* had been written in one exhausting session and it was a cry of pain rather than a reasoned analysis—one reason, according to friends, why it left so many important questions unanswered. Lefever was similar in that once he had an idea, he clung to it stubbornly. To their friends these were attractive characteristics. To critics they were deeply irritating.

Jacobo Timerman had been the publisher and editor of the newspaper *La Opinión* in Buenos Aires until he was kidnapped in April 1977. He spent one year in a secret detention center where he was humiliated and tortured by the head of the Buenos Aires police force, General Ramón Camps. His wife immediately filed a habeas corpus petition for his release. When the case eventually reached the Supreme Court, the Court was informed that Timerman was no longer under the jursidiction of the military, but still remained in detention.

By now the case was an international cause célèbre, thanks in part to the efforts of Patt Derian on Timerman's behalf. On July 20 1978 the Court decided that the state of siege was insufficient justification for keeping Timerman detained. Timerman, however, remained under house arrest. On September 17 1979 the Court decided this was unconstitutional. By now the case had caused a rift within the armed forces. Videla theatened to resign if the Court was defied. Timerman was stripped of his citizenship and sent into exile. It was one of only two habeas corpus petitions out of thousands of "desaparecidos" to result in a release.

Like Ernest Lefever, Jacobo Timerman quickly became a symbol. His book was more than a dramatic account of what it meant to be tortured. It was proof of the irrelevance of the distinction between totalitarian and authoritarian regimes, and the limits to "quiet diplomacy." By raising the specter of anti-Semitism among his captors, the book also underlined the parallel between Nazi Germany and modern Argentina. The Junta was already associated with fascism and concentration camps.

Behind Timerman's arrest lay a complex story. For several years, Timerman had had a business association with David Graiver, a financier and former minister. Graiver was under investigation for the collapse of two U.S. banks (including one owned by himself) when he died mysteriously in a plane crash in Mexico in August 1976. In April 1977, Timerman learned from Graiver's widow that his former partner had laundered money for the Montoneros. Two weeks later he was arrested. The reason given by the Ministry of the Interior was his association with Graiver. None of this was mentioned in Timerman's book, but Timerman himself had never been formally charged with a crime in Argentina, which suggested that his interrogators had failed to establish a connection with Graiver.[17]

Timerman's publisher at Random House, Robert Bernstein, was due to speak in the capacity of Chairman of the U.S. Helsinki Watch human rights group at the Lefever hearings. According to subsequent newspaper accounts, Bernstein asked Tsongas whether Timerman could attend the hearings. Tsongas willingly found a seat for him. Claiborne Pell was the first committee member who specifically referred to Timerman's book during the hearing. Timerman wrote that his conditions improved after Patt Derian had intervened on his behalf. Would Lefever intervene in a similar way? Lefever gave another insensitive reply: "I believe my job is to help sensitize the entire foreign policy establishment to the concern for human rights rather than play a Sir Galahad role going around the world on personal missions."[18] This did not go down well.

There is an unwritten rule in Congress that foreigners never testify before the Senate Foreign Relations Committee. That evening, Timerman dined with two of Lefever's critics on the Committee, Senators Pell and Tsongas, together with two congressmen who were also fiercely opposed to Lefever's nomination, Don Bonker and Tom Harkin. According to two columnists, "Tsongas [said] there was no discussion of using Timerman as a weapon against Lefever, but that as a politician he immediately perceived the force of his personality."[19] The following morning, Tsongas announced Timerman's presence in the room. Chairman Percy invited Timerman to stand, which he did to thunderous applause. It was, wrote one observer, "The most powerful moment in the whole hearings—the appearance of someone who gave no testimony, but bore witness simply by his presence."

Timerman indeed had plenty to say. He held an impromptu press conference in the hall, and told reporters that "silent diplomacy is silence; quiet diplomacy is surrender." It was, observed another journalist, a "motto for critics of the Reagan administration."[20] It also put the final nail in Lefever's coffin, and to this day Lefever remains bitterly angry. He told the author that Senator Percy had refused to allow a Vietnamese refugee family that he and his wife had sponsored to testify on his behalf, on the grounds that they were foreigners.

The episode also troubled some commentators who felt that Timerman had manipulated the committee by making his point while managing to escape embarrassing questions about the reason for his arrest—his connection with Graiver. Timerman appeared before an editorial meeting at the *New York Times*. William Buckley, the conservative columnist, wrote that he surprised his audience with the "virulence of his attacks on Kirkpatrick, and the state of Israel, which he characterized as well advanced along the road to fascism." [21] According to friends of Timerman, this too was very much in character. Timerman had deep misgivings about the government of Menachem Begin, and in a subsequent book he would describe the role of Ariel Sharon in Israel's invasion of Lebanon as profoundly anti-democratic.

Lefever's supporters persevered. Jeane Kirkpatrick organized a small dinner for Timerman. According to columnist William Buckley, who attended, Timerman put on another ungracious, temperamental display. Enough was enough. Now the gloves came off. On May 29, during a recess in the Lefever hearings, Irving Kristol wrote a long column in the *Wall Street Journal* which accused Timerman of covering up his connection with Graiver.[22] Two days later Buckley himself reported that Simon Weisenthal, the Nazi-hunter, had questioned Timerman's integrity during an April 26 interview with a Uruguayan journalist.[23] Weisenthal was quoted as saying that Timerman was a "leftist" who had exaggerated the extent and nature of anti-Semitism in Argentina and had hindered Weisenthal's hunt for Josef Mengele, the Nazi camp doctor, with premature disclosures. This was very damaging. Weisenthal was lionized by Jews in America.

But it was too late to rescue Ernest Lefever. At 10:13 on the morning of June 5, Lefever's ordeal came to an ignominious end, when the Senate Foreign Relations Committee voted against him, by thirteen to four. The Reagan Administration could have persisted, but the fight clearly had been lost and shortly afterward Lefever withdrew from the nomination. It was a bitter personal blow to Lefever and a major political defeat for Ronald Reagan.[24]

Lefever himself had been a dreadful ambassador for his and the administration's views. He had been abrasive, maladroit, politically naive, and often plain silly. Under careful questioning, the neoconservative thesis that had so dazzled candidate Reagan had unraveled. It now stood revealed as intellectually flawed, heartless, and fundamentally at odds with American values. The facts were now embarrassingly clear. Any distinction between "authoritarian" and "totalitarian" regimes had little to do with human rights. Indeed, the Reagan Administration appeared to have no human rights policy. Its charges against Patt Derian—and the United Nations—could not be taken seriously.

Whatever Lefever's own personal feelings, his rebuff could not be described as "politicized." It had been a bipartisan decision, underlining the fact that America's remarkable human rights apparatus was not the product of an opportunistic Democratic president or a few motivated individuals like Donald Fraser and Patt Derian. It was, rather, the product of something that transcended party politics: a commitment to the promotion of basic democratic values outside the confines of the United States. That commitment could only be tempered and strengthened by the Lefever hearings. Once Ronald Reagan recovered from his anger over the fiasco, even he might find it useful.

Anti-Semitism in Argentina

The news of Lefever's defeat was greeted with profound dismay at the Argentinian embassy in Washington. "It must be analyzed not as an isolated incident," wrote Ambassador Aja Espil in a secret June 13 cable, "but in conjunction with a resurgence in the campaign against the Argentinian government, exacerbated by the publicity over Timerman and his book." There followed an astute appraisal of the political mood in Washington. Aja Espil predicted that the liberals would take heart, and that the administration's policy of not criticizing "authoritarian regimes of the right" would be severely weakened. The liberals in both houses would redouble their efforts to ensure that the Junta be held to some conditions in return for lifting the arms embargo. The most likely condition was the publication of a list of disappeared persons.[25]

"Anti-Semitism," warned Aja Espil, "continues to be the decisive factor that could influence the lifting of sanctions against our country." There was still much to play for, and plenty of reasons to keep up the pressure on Jacobo Timerman.

The Timerman affair had caused anguished soul-searching among Argentina's three-hundred-thousand-strong Jewish community. This was the kind of publicity they dreaded. Any scrutiny of the Jewish role in an insecure society like Argentina was bound to uncover compromises. If they failed to acknowledge Timerman's ordeal they would be accused of timidly siding with a detested regime; but to side with Timerman publicly would be to invite certain reprisals. They turned in irritation against the man who had forced them into a corner. Timerman was not particularly popular. He was not an Orthodox Jew, and many recalled his initial support for the military takeover in 1976. Now, after kicking up the hornet's nest, he had escaped to Israel and left others to face the consequences. To cap it all, he was starting to criticize the government of Israel, which had accepted him with open arms, and to take issue with heroes like Simon Weisenthal. This, as Claus Ruser noted in an October 1980 cable from the U.S. embassy in Buenos Aires, had put Argentina's Jewish community at odds with the former editor.[26]

There was, of course, the uncomfortable facts of Timerman's torture, the anti-Semitic sneers of his captors, and the large number of Jews (proportionate to the community) that had disappeared. But most chose to accept a distinction drawn by Aja Espil in his cables: that there had been "scattered acts" of anti-Semitism, but nothing systematic or government-inspired. The message coming in from Claus Ruser at the U.S. embassy in Buenos Aires actually pointed in the other direction. In one long October 1980 analysis Ruser wrote: "The evidence that the government through omission tolerates a level of overt active anti-Semitism within its ranks is unblinkable."[27] Moreover, Ruser's cables were also recording regular acts of abuse, such as defacement against synagogues, which—rather like the disappearances—could not have happened without the acquiescence of the authorities.

Most agreed that this fell far short of Timerman's suggestion that a new Holocaust was afoot in Argentina. One of his defenders, columnist Anthony Lewis, wrote: "When he compares Argentina to Nazi Germany, Mr. Timerman may well be exaggerating—no outsider can be sure. My impression is that he was not so sensitive to the danger before he was imprisoned, that in his book he expresses the anguish of a Jew confronting for the first time the consequences of his birth."[28]

Like Ernest Lefever, Jacobo Timerman was now paying for his outspokenness by being exposed to a campaign of denigration and innuendo. On June 14 Simon Weisenthal stated that he had not, in fact, criticized Timerman, as reported first in the Uruguayan newspaper, second by the American embassy in Montevideo, third by Carl Gershman, Kirkpatrick's assistant at the U.S. mission in New York, and finally by William Buckley in his May 31 column. Gershman remained unrepentant and Buckley was reported to have made no effort to check the quotations with Weisenthal himself. Three days later, Aja Espil's lobbying appeared to pay dividends when the columnists Evans and Novak published a damaging account of Timerman's role at the Lefever hearings. This provoked an angry response from liberal columnists.[29]

Up until this point the Argentinian Junta had maintained a dignified silence, relying on the embassy in Washington and allies at the State Department to refute Timerman. In mid-summer, the façade cracked after a devastating television debate hosted by Bill Moyers. Timerman was not present, but several other protagonists, including Patt Derian and Ernest Lefever, participated. In the audience were Timerman's son Hector and Hebe de Bonafini from the Mothers of the Plaza de Mayo, who was in the United States to receive a human rights prize. Argentina's diplomats concluded gloomily that the show had done far more damage to the Junta than to Timerman: "The tone of the program was obviously biased in favor of Timerman," cabled an official from the Argentinian mission in New York. Patt Derian was particularly "aggressive," and young Hector Timerman also intervened from the audience to compare the detention center of La Perla to Auschwitz.[30]

This thoroughly alarmed the Junta. On July 3 Foreign Minister Oscar Camilión called in Claus Ruser at the U.S. embassy in Buenos Aires, and complained bitterly about Hector Timerman's comments.[31] By alleging the existence of concentration camps, Camilión said, both the Timermans were lying and following the example of Joseph Goebbels: "slander, slander and something will stick."

The Junta also released transcripts of Timerman's interrogation, which suggested that he had been questioned about his connection with David Graiver. Timerman's reaction when asked about this in Tel Aviv was understandably weary. It seemed incredible that he was being tried again in the press.[32] But the trial continued. William Buckley returned to it on July 25. Mark Falcoff returned to the affair in *Commentary*.[33] It was an undignified campaign—but then Lefever's friends complained that Lefever too had suffered. As for the central issue—whether the Junta was encouraging anti-Semitism—both sides stuck to their arguments.

The upshot of these frantic weeks was a legislative compromise. Congress agreed to the administration's request to lift the 1978 Kennedy-Humphrey ban on arms sales to Argentina. In return, it inserted several conditions into the International Security and Development Act, which President Reagan signed into law on December 29 1981. A total of four governments were written into the bill: Argentina, Nicaragua, El Salvador, and Chile. In the case of Argentina, Reagan was asked to issue a presidential certification that a "significant" improvement had taken place in human rights. This would have to include an accounting for the disappeared persons and the release or trial of the PEN prisoners held without charges. Only then could arms sales proceed.[34]

Meanwhile, the level of activity in the demoralized Human Rights Bureau fell off and effectively stopped. Lefever's desk was occupied by Stephen Palmer, a caretaker diplomat. Rudderless and paralyzed, Patt Derian's dynamic little ship drifted into Washington's hot and humid summer.

22. Abrams Recoups

After Ernest Lefever's withdrawal, the post of Assistant Secretary of State for Human Rights was to remain vacant for the next five months. This was a product of confusion as well as pique. The Reagan Administration was under a legal obligation to implement a policy it detested, and it was at a loss how to react.[1]

Under the compromise reached with Congress over the disappearances in Argentina at the end of 1981, the administration would have to certify that the disappearances had been explained before U.S. arms sales could be resumed. This went straight to the heart of the debate inside Argentina itself. The other requirement, proof of an "improvement," was less straightforward. Had an "improvement" taken place because disappearances had all but stopped? From one point of view, yes—but from the perspective of relatives like Emilio Mignone, clearly not. Each passing day that the Junta failed to provide an explanation prolonged the agony.

Ronald Reagan, as it happened, had a uniquely effective way to monitor any improvements anywhere in the world, in the form of U.S. embassies. Each year they submitted reports to the State Department which were revised and published. After Ernest Lefever's withdrawal this inspired nothing but dread. How could these reports be compiled without criticizing America's allies? How, indeed, could Derian's vacant post be filled without doing similar damage? One thing was certain—it would be a brave individual who took on such a challenge. In the summer of 1981, the human rights bureau seemed a sure graveyard for anyone with political ambitions.

Some, but not many, at the State Department were addressing the problem. On June 12 1981 John McClaughry, a senior policy adviser at the White House, drafted a four-page memorandum to Deputy Secretary of State William Clark. "In the wake of the Lefever withdrawal," he wrote, "I sense that our policy on human rights is being rethought. I have thus put on paper some ideas about designing a new policy."

McClaughry suggested that the policy should revolve around the right
to own property which, he said, could be used to promote free enterprise
in the Soviet Union. Some of his other ideas were more unorthodox. They
included the establishment of a "World Council of Elders"—fifteen to
twenty internationally known people who would travel around the world
free of charge mediating conflicts and setting a good example by the fru-
gality of their lifestyle. They would, suggested McClaughry, be required
to live a life of simplicity in "phrontisteries" (defined as places of se-
clusion). McClaughry allowed that this might seem far-fetched, but he
pointed out that history was replete with people with the right qualifications. They included Jesus, Marcus Aurelius, Effendi Shogun, Confucius,
and Robert E. Lee. This was fairly odd, but it did at least suggest that
someone at least was wondering how human rights could be harnessed to
serve President Reagan's foreign policy.[2]

Five months passed before the deadlock was broken. Elliott Abrams,
the thirty-three-year-old Assistant Secretary of State for International Organizations, waited patiently through the dog days of summer and then
put in a bid for the human rights post. It was a calculated political gamble
by an ambitious young politician. Abrams was frustrated with his current
post, which offered few opportunities for political advancement or exposure. The United Nations was not taken seriously enough, and whatever
limited political capital it generated was going to Ambassador Kirkpatrick
in New York.

Jeane Kirkpatrick had helped introduce Abrams to the Reagan team,
but their relationship then soured. The two posts had always overlapped,
and Abrams now found himself squeezed out from policy-making and
overshadowed by Kirkpatrick's powerful personality. She picked the representatives to important U.N. meetings and formulated human rights
policy. Abrams was marginalized, and his staff made no secret of the fact
that he resented it.

Pondering the lessons from the Lefever fiasco, Abrams apparently realized, like McClaughry, that human rights could not be expunged from
America's foreign policy agenda. Neither Congress nor the American public would accept that. There was another alternative: turn it to advantage.
Turn it against the "totalitarian" Soviet Union—the "Evil Empire."

There were, it is true, risks. The Lefever hearings had polarized the
human rights debate, and liberals and conservatives were totally at odds
over how to handle American allies who practiced torture and disappear-

ances. It would require a clever balancing act to reconcile the two positions and satisfy both camps. Abrams, however, was well-placed to try, because his short working life had been spent straddling liberal and conservative positions. He had won degrees at Harvard and the London School of Economics and practiced law in New York before arriving in Washington to work as assistant legal counsel for a Senate committee. Between 1975 and 1979 he worked on the staffs of three Democratic Senators—Hubert Humphrey, Daniel Moynihan, and Henry Jackson—and joined the conservative wing of the Democratic party. In 1980 he joined Ronald Reagan's campaign and spoke out on Reagan's behalf before Jewish groups.

This put him in the mainstream of the neoconservatives who were now molding Reagan's foreign policy. Abrams's position was further cemented by his marriage to the daughter of Midge Decter, one of the co-editors of *Commentary* magazine. It was the perfect career. Abrams had no obvious faults. He was young and smart. He was not encumbered by connections to unsavory multinational companies or an irascible personality, like Ernest Lefever. Most important, he was far more of a political animal than the other neoconservatives who had come from think tanks and universities. Abrams's work at the Senate had given him a sixth sense about where to dig in and where to yield gracefully. If anything marred this impressive record, it was the opportunism. That and a certain hubris. One profile in the magazine *Mother Jones* ran an illustration of a young Abrams with slicked-back hair and a slight sneer, who looked remarkably like a young Elvis Presley. He was the smartest kid on the block, and he acted like it.[3]

After the Lefever fiasco, Deputy Secretary of State William Clark asked his director of policy planning, Paul Wolfowitz, to look for a replacement. Wolfowitz drew in Abrams, a friend, and Abrams spotted an opportunity. He put his ideas down on paper and sent them to Richard Kennedy, Assistant Secretary of State for Management, who passed them on to Secretary of State Alexander Haig on October 27. The memo included a recommendation that Abrams himself be appointed to the post vacated by Lefever and the human rights bureau invigorated. On October 30, Ronald Reagan announced Abrams's nomination. On November 5 1981 the memo appeared in the *New York Times,* after being leaked. It was generally assumed that Abrams himself was responsible for the leak.[4]

On November 17 1981 Abrams went before the Senate Foreign Relations Committee, which endorsed him unanimously. The hearing was short and totally free from the rancor that had poisoned Lefever's appearance. The senators were charmed, relieved, and grateful: they wanted to bury the hatchet with the White House and put the memory of Lefever behind them. On December 10, International Human Rights Day, Abrams was sworn into his new office. He had accomplished the first part of his agenda in brilliant style.

Abrams Changes Course

Now came phase two, putting Abrams's philosophy into practice. It was set out in the much-publicized memo which began with the challenging words: "Human rights is at the core of our foreign policy." This was eye-catching and constructive. Human rights was then set in the Cold War context. The main target was to be the Soviet Union—the evil empire which was fundamentally at odds with the very concept of human rights.[5] On the other hand, Americans would only be persuaded by this if U.S. allies were also occasionally criticized: "At the very least we will have to speak honestly about our friends' human rights violations." All the resources of the State Department, particularly the annual Country Practices reports, should be geared to this "two-track" approach.[6]

This was a subtle document, carefully drafted to appeal to both liberals and conservatives. The liberals would be reassured by Abrams's evident desire to strengthen the human rights bureau and the annual reports. In addition, they would welcome his willingness to criticize American allies and avoid the distinction between "totalitarian" and "authoritarian" regimes, which had provoked so much controversy during the year. (In an interview following his Senate hearing, Abrams accepted the distinction—he was no apostate—but at the same time he suggested that its "utility in foreign policy-making is limited.")

Abrams's conservative allies, meanwhile, would have welcomed the memo's full-blooded attack on the Soviet Union. Reading between the lines they would have concluded that Abrams still planned to practice "quiet diplomacy" with authoritarian regimes and publicly reprimand totalitarian ones. But this was presented as pragmatic rather than ideological: U.S. leverage with right-wing rulers would be dissipated by public denunciation. Another message that would have reassured the conservatives was the memo's curt rejection of "economic rights." It was a tenet of the neoconservatives that economic rights did not exist. "Calling them rights,"

said the memo, "confuses the issue of liberty with that of wealth and implies that government has an equally central role in both."[7]

Like Abrams's own career up to this point, the memo placed a heavy
emphasis on staking out positions that made political sense. It recommended against issuing licenses for crime-control equipment like CS gas
and police batons "in questionable cases" because such equipment could
easily be purchased elsewhere. It would waste political capital and dissi-
pate energy. Abrams was a pragmatist.

As soon as he took up his new post, Abrams encountered Patt Derian's
long shadow. Initially, it grated. During interviews he would accept Derian's terminology of "winning" and "losing" and acknowledge that she had
given the office its political clout, but he also resented being constantly
measured against her and there was no love lost between them. More significant was the difference in the way Abrams viewed his new duties. He
had no intention of acting like an advocate, holding out for a human rights
issue when he knew it was a lost cause. Not for him Derian's exhausting
guerrilla warfare with the ARA regional bureau over arms sales. Nor
would he impale himself on an ideological stake, as Ernest Lefever might
have done. Abrams would himself balance the political risks against advantages, and act accordingly.

Secretary of State Alexander Haig had abolished the Christopher group
that was set up in 1977 to weigh human rights and security concerns, and
replaced it by regular low-level meetings where everything was resolved
amicably.[8] There was very little debate and no disagreement, because
Abrams and his staff had already balanced out the human rights considerations against security or economy. Between 1981 and 1983, only one
issue, to Abrams's knowledge, slipped through. (This was a proposal to
sell cattle prods to South Africa. The Commerce Department had over-
looked the possibility of them being used in crowd control.) That apart,
there were no disputes, and no fratricidal squabbles spilling out into
the press.

Here was a radically new, highly political, vision of the human rights
post. It was all part of a calculated game plan, the outline of which would
only gradually become clear during 1982. On the one hand, Abrams made
concessions. The most important was not to certify improvements in
Chile. In a 1983 interview he described the law requiring certification as "a
bad statute," and argued that Pinochet had indeed made significant improvements, but what he had not done was bring to justice the killers of
Ronni Moffitt and Orlando Letelier, as required by U.S. law.[9] Abrams's

acute political antennae told him that recommending certification for Chile would embroil him in a damaging confrontation with Congress. In this, he disagreed with Thomas Enders, the Assistant Secretary of State for Inter-American Affairs.

Equally popular with liberals was Abrams's positive response to an appeal from black Congressmen on behalf of Ethiopian asylum-seekers who were due to be deported from the United States. The human rights bureau had the job of reviewing individual refugee appeals. The fact that the Ethiopians had sought asylum in the United States reminded the world that Marxist regimes produced refugees, which was another important neoconservative tenet. Abrams recommended that they stay and this won him praise from the Black Congressional Caucus. When the Commerce Department proposed to give an export license for shock batons to the South Korean riot police, Abrams objected on the grounds that he had outlined in the memo: it did not make political sense.

All of this won Abrams political credit with the liberals and made it harder for them to attack the central thrust of his strategy, which was to play a decisive role in implementing Ronald Reagan's Central American policy. This would involve defending the disreputable regimes in El Salvador and Guatemala and criticizing the regime in Nicaragua. As part of this, refugees from El Salvador were to be termed "economic migrants" and refused entry to the United States, while those who fled from the left-wing regime in Nicaragua were—to a large extent—deemed genuine "political" refugees.

It was a calculated risk. The rewards, if Abrams could carry it off, would be enormous. He would gain the gratitude of conservatives for taking on a thankless task and reinforce his credentials as a loyal team player. On the other hand, Abrams was preparing to use his office, and the annual human rights reports, to defend the death squads, ensure their supply of arms from the United States, and turn refugees away from the land that prided itself on admitting victims of repression. This was indeed a breathtaking gamble.

By the time the human rights groups had collected their wits and perceived his strategy, Abrams had a head start. They clashed over El Salvador almost immediately. When the Americas Watch and American Civil Liberties Union (ACLU) issued a highly critical report on U.S. policies in El Salvador, Abrams asked one of his officials, Dale Shaffer, for an analysis. Shaffer reported on February 4 1982 that he had found nothing basically wrong with the content of the report, but described it as "fruit from a poisoned tree" because its contributors were "politically motivated." They included some leading American NGOs as well as the Salvadorans Roberto Cuéllar and Marianella García Villas. It was the same approach that Gabriel Martínez had employed in Geneva: when you can't fault the message, impugn the motives of the messenger.[10]

This set the tone for a rugged three-year campaign by Abrams to impugn the motives of El Salvador's beleaguered human rights advocates, which, in the view of his critics, greatly increased the dangers they ran. His office also took the lead in refusing to grant asylum to Salvadorans arriving in the United States and in defending their deportation back to El Salvador. This policy was underway when Abrams arrived in the office and had already provoked two official protests from the office of the U.N. High Commissioner for Refugees in 1981, but Abrams took up the fight with gusto.[11]

The State Department's annual human rights reports quickly became a powerful weapon in Abrams's new strategy and when the 1981 report emerged, readers found some subtle, but significant, changes. First, "economic rights" had been expunged from the reports altogether—in keeping with the conservative view that such "rights" did not exist. Second, the concept of political rights had been diluted and broadened, with the apparent aim of easing pressure on U.S. allies like Argentina.

Under Patricia Derian, the bureau had drawn a distinction between the right to be free from government violence and the right to enjoy civil liberties. The fact that the Soviet Union violated civil liberties but did not generally practice killing and disappearances was awkward for the neoconservatives. Abrams's solution, ever-pragmatic, was to retain Derian's distinction but expand the right to be free from violence to include "killing"—a broad concept which could equally be applied to guerrillas and so dilute criticism of regimes like the Argentinian Junta.[12] As we shall see, this seemingly innocent adjustment was to prove an important weapon in Abrams's armory when it came to Argentina.

When Charles Maechling, a former State Department official, angrily accused Abrams of "definitional confusion," Abrams shot back that the "invisible terror of a police state" like the Soviet Union posed its own kind of threat.[13] It was clear by now that the reports would be turned to the broad goal of embarrassing the Soviet Union and defending U.S. allies, but that it would be done with subtlety and intelligence. The human rights NGOs faced a far more formidable opponent than Ernest Lefever.

What did Abrams's strategy promise for the United Nations? The answer—an all-out campaign to indict the Soviet Union and its allies.[14] Moreover, Abrams and his colleagues would probably be less restrained in the U.N. than at home. They no doubt realized, as Carter had done, that promoting human rights in international organizations carried few political risks.

Controversy in Buenos Aires

Meanwhile, it had also been a busy six months for the new American ambassador at the United Nations. On August 1 Jeane Kirkpatrick arrived in Buenos Aires on the second leg of a tour of Latin America. According to one State Department cable, she had told the Argentinians in advance that she was particularly interested in "human rights" and "the role of Latin American nations in the U.N."[15] The visit turned out to be highly controversial.

Before she arrived, the Mothers of the Plaza de Mayo prepared a long letter for Kirkpatrick, asking for a meeting. This was a difficult time for the Mothers. Shortly before, their president and vice-president, Hebe de Bonafini and María Antokoletz, had been arrested at Buenos Aires airport when they returned from the United States. It had been an eventful trip. They had received a ten-thousand-dollar human rights prize, participated in the inauguration of an American support group headed by Patt Derian, and spoken out loudly in the Moyers television debate over Timerman and anti-Semitism. One article about them had left little doubt about their views. It was entitled "Argentina Called Especially Cruel to Jews."[16]

These activities were carefully monitored by Argentinian diplomats in the United States and cabled back to Buenos Aires so it was hardly surprising that the two women were picked up when they returned.[17] Aware of the risk, Americas Watch had asked the U.S. embassy in Buenos Aires to meet the two women at the airport. This was not done. The Mothers never received a reply to their letter to Kirkpatrick, much less an interview with the ambassador. Here indeed was a contrast with Patt Derian, who had gone out of her way to visit them in 1977. Although 1977 was a more perilous year than 1981, the Mothers' quest still required considerable courage.

When Americas Watch protested, it was told that the letter had been "misrouted" inside the embassy. This was certain to be interpreted as a sign of disapproval for the Mothers and as support for the Junta, and

Kirkpatrick encouraged this interpretation at a press conference in Buenos Aires. According to one newspaper report, she "sidestepped" questions about the disappeared persons, but said that the governments of Argentina, Chile, and Uruguay had "more elements of constitutionalism" in them than many other countries.[18] She did, by all accounts, show her hosts the rough edge of her tongue at a private meeting in the American club, where she is said to have insisted that torture and disappearances were not acceptable to the Reagan Administration. In public, however, she declined to give any details beyond saying that she had raised the issue of some nine hundred PEN political detainees.

Jeane Kirkpatrick herself refuses to accept that not seeing the Mothers was in itself a political statement. In a later interview, she told the author:

> I was [there] for 48 hours, not much of which I slept. . . . I was absolutely booked. . . . I don't think I had more than five minutes of give in the schedule. . . . I followed the advice of the State Department and the U.S. embassy. They made my schedule. . . . The Mothers, I was informed myself, had not asked for an appointment with me at all until the day that I was there, and even then did not do so in a systematic orderly fashion. . . [No] public figure is in a position to interrupt the course of activities we are committed to, which invariably involve keeping people waiting.[19]

At the same time, she appears to have remained personally detached from the immense trauma that the Mothers and other relatives were suffering. Patt Derian had admired their courage, identified with them as a woman, and liked the way they operated in a country of machismo. But Jeane Kirkpatrick did not, apparently, view these as virtues. As she said in the interview, "I don't know them. I have never met them. I will tell you this. If it is true, as alleged, that there were childen, small children taken from families that were Montoneros, whomever, and relocated elsewhere . . . no contact and no records . . . I think that's simply despicable. . . . This as I understand it is what they are principally concerned with. I would be wholly sympathetic to their cause, I should say wholly."[20]

By the time of this interview, late 1983, it was well-established that most of the disappeared had no direct connection with left-wing guerrillas. But Kirkpatrick would not, apparently, deviate from her longstanding views. As she had made clear in her writing, Kirkpatrick profoundly disapproved of those who had presumed to challenge those in power—and the Mothers, like the four American churchwomen in El Salvador, had challenged authority and been "politicized." Here was another example of the unswerving consistency which was much admired by some and much disliked by others.

From Buenos Aires Kirkpatrick went to Pinochet's Chile, only to create more resentment among the human rights community. Jaime Castillo, president of the Chilean Human Rights Commission had contacted the U.S. embassy in Santiago and asked for a meeting with her. When her delegation heard of this, they were dismayed. They decided instead that the wife of Kirkpatrick's Cuban-born deputy José Sorzano would meet with Castillo. The ambassador herself left Chile on August 9 without seeing Castillo. In the early hours of August 11, Castillo and three other prominent human rights activists in Chile were arrested and expelled. Kirkpatrick's office issued no statement of regret at what had happened.[21]

Jaime Castillo never publicly blamed Jeane Kirkpatrick for having caused his exile. But the human rights community did blame her and the clamor grew as she refused to offer any explanation or expression of remorse. Later in the year she received Castillo at her office in New York in a private meeting. The mood, according to one participant, was uneasy on both sides. But Kirkpatrick graciously apologized for any possible connection between her visit and his exile, and the two had another meeting during the U.N. General Assembly later in the year. When it came to "quiet diplomacy," she was clearly effective. The problem was that the outside world never got to hear of it.

Whatever her intentions, this sequence once again showed Jeane Kirkpatrick distancing herself from critics of the regime in power while conveying strong support for the actual rulers—even someone as discredited as Augusto Pinochet. Relations between the United States and Chile had been profoundly strained since 1976, when Orlando Letelier and Ronni Moffitt were blown up in Washington on the instigation of the Chilean secret police. During her stay in Santiago, Kirkpatrick was quoted as saying that the investigation was solved, which it certainly was not, and that the U.S. desired to normalize relations with Chile.[22]

Both Kirkpatrick's interventions in Chile—on behalf of Pinochet and against Castillo—had unintended results. Such was the outcry over Castillo's exile that all senior officials who traveled to Chile were henceforth instructed to look in on his Commission. According to U.S. human rights groups, the controversy also helped to insure that the prohibition on U.S. aid to Chile was not repealed.

On her way back to the United States, at a stop-over in Peru, Mrs. Kirkpatrick was again caught off balance in an interview. She was asked about the crisis in Central America and was quoted as making the following comment about Costa Rica, long regarded as one of the most stable countries in Latin America because it had no army: "Their economy is weak, and we can help them with some training for their police."[23] This remark caused a storm in Costa Rica which was in the throes of a general election campaign. The American ambassador in Costa Rica, Francis Macneil, was forced to explain that the "United States has no interest in the militarization of Costa Rica." Jeane Kirkpatrick to this day insists that she was misquoted. "Your question is living proof that the misquotation lives on," she told the author in a 1983 interview.

Analyzing this series of incidents through the first six months of 1981, one perceives the same neoconservative ideology at work that sunk Ernest Lefever. Here was Jeane Kirkpatrick expressing support for the governments of South Africa, Chile, and Argentina; criticizing churchpeople working for social change; and showing a profound lack of sympathy for human rights groups. She was no less pugnacious than Lefever and her theories aroused almost as much hostility from liberal academics and newspapers.[24] But Lefever was ignominiously bundled out of office, while Kirkpatrick grew in political stature throughout 1981. The contrast was indeed striking.

The human rights groups perceived a powerful foe in Kirkpatrick, but they were powerless. On May 21 1982, the committee of the Americas Watch met at the publishing headquarters of Random House to review a dossier on Jeane Kirkpatrick prepared by executive director Aryeh Neier. It ran to nine pages, and reviewed twelve separate controversies generated by the ambassador during the previous fifteen months. It was an unusual dossier and an unusual meeting, but Neier was aware that a personal attack against such a prominent individual could undermine the broader campaign against Reagan's human rights policy: "Although the dossier is damning," he wrote, "personally I oppose now calling for Kirkpatrick's resignation. In my view it would not advance our cause and might make it more difficult for us to influence the Reagan administration." The meeting reluctantly agreed.[25]

Why was Kirkpatrick so invincible? One possible answer was her striking success at the United Nations. The tongue-lashings she delivered at U.N. meetings were overwhelmingly popular with Americans. They had launched her on an impressive political career and left her many critics far behind, even though she was employing in the U.N. the same arguments that had now been discredited by the Lefever hearings.

Kirkpatrick's dominance at the end of 1981 and the elevation of Elliott Abrams to the Bureau of Human Rights left some United Nations initiatives and officials looking very exposed. Two stood out. One was Theo van Boven, Director of the U.N. Division of Human Rights. The other was his creation, the U.N. Working Group on Disappearances. Both had adopted a high profile, and both had challenged Latin American regimes. From the perspective of the Reagan Administration, both posed a danger.

23. The Knives Sharpen

Until the U.N. Human Rights Commission session in February 1981, Theo van Boven had seemed surefooted and confident. He had taken risks, but they had paid off. After the Commission he lost his sense of balance completely. Suddenly he seemed accident-prone and clumsy. It was the same high-wire act, but the safety net was no longer there.[1]

On April 1 1981, two weeks after the Commission had ended, van Boven gave an interview with a Swiss newspaper, the *Illustré* of Lausanne. Van Boven used it to express his concern at Ronald Reagan's human rights policy. He attacked what he termed Reagan's "primitive view" that everything in the world must be viewed in East-West terms, and he praised former President Carter's "honesty." He said that it had taken so long to get Argentina on the U.N.'s blacklist because the Soviets had been afraid that it might damage trade relations between the two countries. Van Boven ended with a lament: "We are all prisoners of the U.N. system and its limits. Frankly, I have grave doubts about my role."

It was a disastrous interview. He believed it all deeply and it was all true. He was tense and frustrated, following Martínez's attack on him in the Commission, and he had every reason to be concerned at Reagan's human rights policy. The outlet he chose was obscure. But Martínez was by now perched hungrily on his shoulder waiting to snap up any indiscretion. And van Boven was indiscreet. His reference to an alliance between the Argentinians and Soviets in the confidential 1503 procedure would obviously lend credence to Martínez's earlier accusation that van Boven had been the source of newspaper leaks.

It took the Argentinians less than a month to react. On May 1 Juan Carlos Beltramino, Argentina's representative to the Economic and Social Council (ECOSOC), stood up in New York to deliver a withering attack on van Boven and denounce "the arrogance of this international civil servant who in his view thinks the only honest people are former President Carter and himself."[2]

Up on the thirty-eighth floor of the U.N. headquarters, Under Secretary General William Buffum caught a whiff of the row and asked van Boven if he wanted him to speak out in his defense. Van Boven said no, and no other delegation followed Beltramino's lead. Some even defended van Boven vigorously. But twelve days later the Argentinian mission at the U.N. followed up with a ponderous, overly formal note to Kurt Waldheim that effectively called for van Boven's dismissal: "I have been instructed by my government to request you to be good enough in this unfortunate situation to inform it of any measures which you may take with regard to the behavior of the director of Human Rights, Mr. Theo van Boven."[3]

This incident has to be put in some perspective. In the first place, however indiscreet van Boven may have been, many U.N. officials have said far worse in years gone by and escaped without a word of censure. Short of physical assault, senior U.N. officials can get away with almost anything. Moreover, Michael Novak had committed a massive breach of confidentiality just one month earlier by disclosing that East Germany was on the U.N. blacklist. Third, one does not expect the ambassador of an important country to while away his working hours thumbing through copies of the Lausanne *TV Times*.

But Argentina's Junta was no ordinary government and Martínez was no ordinary ambassador. Mignone's arrest two months earlier had shown that his reach extended well beyond Geneva, and van Boven was naive not to take greater precautions. His interview had given Martínez further ammunition to use against the U.N. secretariat and the disappearances working group. Van Boven had played straight into his enemy's hands.

Martínez Coopts Colville

Gabriel Martínez had bounced back quickly from his depression following the 1981 U.N. Human Rights Commission session. He had work to do. The working group was preparing to take up the disappearances of infants. This would stretch Martínez's talents to the fullest because few aspects of the disappearances had evoked such anger. The group had been established just as the Argentinian Grandmothers were preparing to take their campaign to the outside world, and during 1981 they presented it with seventy-seven cases out of the one hundred ten they had on their files. Each case was carefully documented. Roughly two-thirds of the children had been born in captivity, the rest kidnapped along with their parents.

On May 15 1981 Mark Colville, the British chairman of the U.N. group, explained to Western diplomats in New York why the issue had been singled out. As Ambassador Kirkpatrick cabled to Washington, "The working group has taken the approach with Argentina of first inquiring about infant children of women who disappeared, as well as unborn babies of pregnant women who disappeared, since they cannot possibly be accused of being terrorists."[4]

Once again, the threat to Martínez was clear and unambiguous, and he redoubled his efforts to undermine the U.N. group. Colville and van Boven held the key to success or failure. Van Boven was a committed foe, an "enemy of Argentina," as Martínez had described him in cables. But what of Colville? Perhaps he could be turned? Martínez began to apply his formidable talents to winning over the English lord.

The two men had sparred with each other during the previous year. But during 1981, Colville underwent a subtle change of attitude. He began to put greater stock on "dialogue" and in winning the cooperation of governments, particularly Argentina. From now on, it would be a duet rather a duel. Colville was too much of a politician not to realize the way the wind was blowing. With Carter in power there had never been any doubt of U.S. commitment to the group, but now that could no longer be taken for granted. Colville must have known that most of the governments being challenged by the group were seen as allies by Washington, and he evidently decided it was time to pay greater heed to them.

Martínez had a golden opportunity. He only had to play the game and appear to cooperate without conceding anything of substance, and he stood a good chance of giving his military masters in Buenos Aires another year's breathing space. With a little luck, he might even turn the working group to his advantage, as he had done with the confidential 1503 U.N. procedure.

Instead of acting like a thug, Martínez started to flatter Colville and show him exaggerated respect. Initially, Colville would snort impatiently and try to shrug him off—he knew that Martínez was not someone to be seen talking to. But Martínez relished his sinister reputation. Purring, he would draw closer. Colville would shy away like a thoroughbred. To onlookers, it looked rather like a primitive mating ritual.

The ground was being laid for what would turn into a close friendship. Colville knew that Martínez was a rogue but he was also beginning to appreciate the man's qualities as a stubborn, effective defender of his government's interests. He would later describe the Argentinian as "a tough man who ruled his mission with a rod of iron." But Colville rather liked that. "He did a very good job of defending an undefensible position. Like a front-line advocate he handled it with some skill."[5] This appealed to the barrister in Colville. Defending an unpopular cause was something all successful lawyers have to do, besides which Colville was also impressed by the evil of terrorism. He had held office as a junior minister in the British government when the IRA campaign was at its worst in Ulster.

Following its extension in February 1981, the disappearances group thus began to pull in two different directions. On the one hand it toughened its line. On May 27 Colville sent a detailed dossier to Martínez, together with a covering note describing the problem of the infants as a "particularly acute humanitarian problem," and asking the Argentinians to investigate it as a "matter of urgency."[6] In September 1981, the Grandmothers submitted a dossier of forty-nine cases of pregnant women who had disappeared. This went straight over to Martínez, together with photocopies of another 150 cases. Martínez would have found this very difficult to ignore.

At the same time, however, Colville's friendship with Martínez was blossoming. At the end of an otherwise severe letter in September, Colville scribbled a short PS: "I much look forward to our lunch on 14th September. C of C." The two were beginning to meet socially. Colville was convinced that this would persuade Martínez to release information. He would later tell his colleagues on the group that Martínez had started to let slip tantalizing tidbits—on condition that Colville kept them to himself. Martínez was stealthily edging the group into confidentiality.

Yet Colville's confidence was unshakable. He stubbornly shut his eyes to the evidence of Martínez's sinister role. Relatives who came to testify before the U.N. group in September 1981 even spotted an ESMA torturer, known only as "Cortez," in Martínez's contingent.[7] The group was told of this, but Colville did nothing. All the while, Martínez never said anything that shed light on the fate of the disappeared persons or the role of the military. Colville was allowing himself to be hoodwinked.

Martínez Tries to Undermine the Working Group

Martínez's campaign against the U.N. group on disappearances now changed direction. He had tried and failed to get it voted out of existence at the Human Rights Commission in February. Now he embarked on an elaborate plan to achieve the same result by depriving it of staff and money.

There were two noticeable facts about the U.N. staff who serviced the disappearances group. The first was the preponderance of Spanish-speakers, particularly from Latin America. The second was that all but one—Tom McCarthy—were on short-term contracts. This was because the group had only been extended for one year at a time.[8] Without its staff the group would grind to a halt. Martínez realized this and set out to exploit it.

He had already accused one of van Boven's officials, Antonio Fortín, of being a terrorist. In May 1981 van Boven was suddenly informed that the contracts of Fortín and Nathalie Müller (the young Swiss woman whose father had worked for the UNHCR in Argentina) would expire on June 30. Van Boven contacted Jay Long, Buffum's assistant at the United Nations in New York, and asked for help. Long suceeded in getting Fortín's contract extended until December 30. Müller was less lucky; her contract ran out.

That is where it stood as of September 24 1981, when the U.N. office in Geneva routinely informed the local Chilean mission that Fortín's contract had been extended for another six months. Almost two months later, on November 19, well into the 1981 session of the U.N. General Assembly, Manuel Trucco, the Chilean ambassador in New York, called on William Buffum and protested vehemently. Trucco also recalled Argentina's complaint against van Boven at the ECOSOC meeting in May.[9] The Chileans had picked up their cue. The two dictatorships were almost at war over the Beagle Channel in the South Atlantic, which both claimed, but here in the United Nations they had discovered a common enemy in a Dutch U.N. official.

The Chileans had as much reason as the Argentinians to detest van Boven. He had been an enthusiastic member of the U.N. group that had visited Chile in 1978 and had masterminded its excruciatingly detailed report, complete with its macabre centerfold of torture wounds. Van Boven must have seemed, to the Chileans, like a man with an obsession. But why had they suddenly followed the lead taken by Martínez and the Argentinians in attacking van Boven personally? Trucco's statement was noteworthy for its confident, almost arrogant tone. So long the pariah in the U.N., the Chileans would not have dared present such a demand, or expected to see it acted on, between 1973 and 1980. The fact that they were doing it now and in this manner can only be put down to two things—the tacit sympathy of the Reagan Administration and a growing sense of solidarity among Latin American governments.

Little by little, Gabriel Martínez was cleverly building his case against Theo van Boven, and chipping away at the foundation of the U.N. Working Group on Disappearances. He now moved stealthily in for the kill behind the cover of the U.S. desire to curb U.N. bureaucracy.[10]

Every year the General Assembly reviews the U.N.'s budget in three stages. The first takes place at a private meeting of the Advisory Committee on Administration and Budgetary Questions (ACABQ). The two subsequent reviews occur in the Fifth Committee of the General Assembly and in the General Assembly plenary. Each successive stage rubber-stamps the previous one, and as the process advances it becomes progressively harder to reverse decisions.

When the U.N.'s human rights budget came up for discussion in the ACABQ, the Argentinians innocently proposed a cut of $54,900. This, as it happened, was the exact amount required to finance the Working Group on Disappearances for another year and also the U.N. investigation into Chile. The proposal was accepted by the ACABQ in private debate, with support from the United States. Once again, crisis.

The aim of the Argentinians was transparent. Van Boven would have to find the $54,900 from his regular budget, which would be difficult but not impossible given that his annual budget was $5 million. Much more important, van Boven would have to find two officials with permanent U.N. contracts to replace Fortín and Müller, whose salary came out of the $54,900. Given the U.N.'s ponderous hiring procedures, that could be impossible in the time available.

Van Boven was in Washington meeting Elliott Abrams when the ACABQ decision was taken. When he heard the news on returning to Washington, van Boven frantically began lobbying to have the decision reversed. Denmark came to the rescue in the Fifth Committee and proposed that the $54,900 be reinstated. The Soviets and their allies abstained. They loathed the disappearances group, but they wanted the U.N. to continue investigating Chile. Even so, the Danish proposal only just scraped through, by twenty-nine to twenty-four votes with forty abstentions. Alone of the Western states Canada, the United States, and Turkey voted against the proposal.[11] Canada subsequently reversed its decision; the United States did not. It was around this time that Michael Novak was telling Don Bonker's congressional subcommittee "with full and glad candor" that the establishment of the U.N. disappearances group was one of the U.N.'s proudest achievements.[12]

It seems inconceivable that the Reagan Administration did not spot the political implications of the Argentinian proposal. Here was a political action by the United States disguised as a cost-cutting exercise—and another friendly gesture to Argentina's military rulers.

The Noose Tightens Around van Boven

If Theo van Boven was aware of growing pressure then, it did not show as he went about his business in the General Assembly in late 1981. He appeared, and was, relaxed. There were no sign of panic or compromise. He never moved to lobby or call in political dues among governments which might have been useful in a crisis. It was not his style. The fact was, of course, that for all his fascination with Latin America and his intense relationship with the human rights groups, he was singularly bereft of friends among Latin American governments. This was not surprising. He had, after all, chosen to identify with their critics.

Van Boven was now dangerously isolated and an object of suspicion not just to the powerful Argentinians but to most governments on the continent. They began to close ranks against him. In addition to Chile and Argentina, Uruguay detested van Boven for his role in toughening Javier Pérez de Cuéllar's 1979 report. The regime of El Salvador was also hostile. El Salvador was now under pressure from the United Nations on two fronts: a U.N. rapporteur, and the U.N. Working Group on Disappearances. By December 1981 the group had inquired from the government about 302 disappearances. Only three had been explained.[13]

The Reagan Administration had cause to be alarmed at this because it knew how vulnerable the Salvadoran regime was to the charge of violating human rights. On November 14 1981, officials from the U.S. embassy in San Salvador visited the volcanic lava bed at El Playón and found six fresh bodies being devoured by vultures, as well as the remains of thirty other corpses, many with bullet holes in the back of the skull.[14] In Geneva, meanwhile, U.S. diplomats were horrified to learn that the disappearances group had received word that a quality meats plant was being used to grind up the bodies of the disappeared in El Salvador.[15]

But it was the military regime in Guatemala that next picked up Argentina's vendetta against Theo van Boven. Van Boven's personal involvement with this unhappy Central American country had become almost as intense as his interest in Argentina, and the crimes of both governments were matched only by their determination to prevent any inquiry by the

United Nations. In March 1981 van Boven had been asked by the Human Rights Commission to find an investigator acceptable to the Guatemalans. He had proposed an eminent Ecuadoran lawyer, Julio Prado Vallejo. Guatemala's ambassador, Eduardo Castillo Arriolla, rejected his candidacy and complained that Guatemala was the "victim of an international conspiracy." In fact Vallejo's credentials were impeccable. The Guatemalans were stalling.[16]

Van Boven's search was then complicated by a strange episode. Julia Esquivel's successor as editor of the magazine *Diálogo*, the Jesuit priest Luís Eduardo Pellecer Faena, had disappeared in July. He then reappeared quite unexpectedly on September 30 at a press conference arranged by the government in Guatemala City. Pellecer made an extraordinary confession. He said that he had worked for the Guatemalan guerrillas and that he had engineered his own kidnapping to avoid being drafted by them into military service. He said that the army had kept him in hiding for 122 days. "I give humble apologies to the people of Guatemala," he said. No questions were allowed and Pellecer was whisked away.

The Guatemalan government videotaped the press conference and sent copies around the world. Former friends of Pellecer noticed immediately that he seemed dazed and aggressive. The film arrived in Geneva just as the U.N. Working Group on Disappearances was meeting in September 1981. Mark Colville recalls watching it with his four colleagues on the group and U.N. officials. "We didn't believe a word of it," he said later.

It was a common reaction. Outside Guatemala, the feeling grew that Pellecer had been kidnapped by the government, brainwashed in a secret jail, and then released. But inside the country, as the U.S. embassy in Guatemala City reported in cables, the reaction was that Pellecer was telling the truth. If so, this was a spectacular example of left-wing subversion by the Church in Central America, and equally spectacular confirmation of the suspicions of Jeane Kirkpatrick and Ernest Lefever. The facts are still hard to verify, but in 1981 the affair was clearly a major blow to the human rights groups and it vastly complicated van Boven's efforts to find someone to investigate human rights in Guatemala.[17]

The task passed to Kurt Waldheim, the U.N. Secretary General. But Waldheim was fighting an uphill battle to win reelection for an unprecedented third term, and never one to relish a challenge, he passed the buck to Under Secretary General William Buffum. Buffum was equally uneasy, so he turned to his colleague, Under Secretary General for Political Affairs Diego Cordovez, from Ecuador. Cordovez had organized the 1978 meeting at which Argentina had tried to muzzle the NGOs and he was a close friend of Eduardo Castillo Arriolla, Guatemala's ambassador at the United Nations.

Van Boven now stuck his neck out yet again. He visited Maryknoll, the Catholic foreign missionary society, and was warned that Pellecer might commit suicide. Van Boven put this to Buffum and suggested that Pellecer had been coerced into making his televised confession. He asked that Pellecer be allowed to come to Geneva, and wrote to Arriolla at the Guatemalan mission in New York. There was no reply. In November 1981 van Boven met with Cordovez in Buffum's office and pressed him to help find an investigator for Guatemala. Cordovez turned him down brusquely: "As long as you are head of the Human Rights Division there's no chance," said Cordovez testily. "You have ruined relations with Latin America."

Cordovez later apologized to van Boven, but by the beginning of December 1981 van Boven was no nearer finding someone acceptable to the Guatemalans, and this filtered down to the floor of the General Assembly. Van Boven was determined to try to put some pressure on the Guatemalans, and started to canvass for sponsors for a resolution. This was risky, but someone had to do something. Three years had passed since the U.N.'s first expression of concern over the brutal murder of Alberto Fuentes Mohr, and there was still no sign of cooperation from Guatemala.

The U.S. Assault

Van Boven's lobbying at the General Assembly may well have brought him to the attention of Ambassador Kirkpatrick. The two had never met in person, but van Boven was well known to the Reagan Administration. Earlier in the year in February, ambassador Henry Cohen had visited Western Europe to firm up support for the Reagan Administration's policies in Central America and found van Boven deeply skeptical. This was put down to van Boven's left-wing sympathies.[18]

By the end of 1981, van Boven and Kirkpatrick were on a collision course over Latin America. It was Kirkpatrick's first General Assembly, and it climaxed a tumultuous year in which the Reagan Administration had launched a massive preemptive strike against the U.N. system. Instead of the traditional American delegate—sympathetic and well-informed even while casting a "no" vote—participants at U.N. meetings found themselves facing a new breed, fiercely ideological and fiercely suspicious of any international commitment. Predatory Reagan appointees moved through the still waters of U.N. meetings, carving into resolutions and upsetting compromises reached by previous U.S. administrations.

One early casualty was a U.N. plan to negotiate an end to South Africa's illegal occupation of Namibia. The U.N. plan had been enthusiastically backed by the Carter Administration, and in January 1981 all the parties to the conflict met in Geneva to work out the final arrangements. Emboldened by the prospect of "constructive engagement" with the United States, the South Africans pulled the rug from the U.N. plan. Eight long years would pass before the Reagan Administration would help to negotiate a settlement to Namibia, claiming a foreign policy triumph. The truth was very different. U.S. policy had helped to ensure much unnecessary bloodshed.[19]

The assault went on. Over the months that followed in 1981, the Reagan Administration demanded sweeping changes in an ambitious U.N. treaty that extended international law to the world's seas; cast the sole vote against a World Health Organization proposal (to curb the promotion of baby foods) that was aimed at preventing infant mortality; proposed cuts of thirty-two million dollars in U.S. voluntary contributions to such agencies as UNICEF, the U.N. Development Program, and the OAS—all of which had served the U.S. well; unilaterally decided to delay assessed dues to the U.N. and fifteen major agencies, thereby causing a hideous cash-flow crisis; withdrew U.S. funding from the International Development Association, which gives soft loans to the Least Developed Countries.[20]

Many of these decisions actually ran counter to the advice of U.S. government officials. But the fact was that an activist United Nations, and strong international law, stood in the way of President Reagan's domestic and foreign goals. Once again, the U.N. had to be being portrayed as "dangerous" to the United States. It had to be humbled, marginalized, discredited.

The U.S. mission in New York took on the task with gusto. During 1981, Kirkpatrick compared the U.N. to "death and taxes," and described it as a place "where moral outrage is distributed like violence in a protection racket" and a place "which breeds conflict tension, exacerbation and polarization," where the United States is "ignored, deplored, despised and reviled."[21]

Every speech she made—even the way she delivered them—bespoke hostility. When addressing a U.N. meeting she spoke slowly and deliberately, as if throwing down a challenge. A profile that appeared in *Life* in

April 1981, entitled "Call Her Madam and Color Her Tough," showed her standing in the General Assembly, hands on hips, grinning confidently. One read later that she had winced at the photo and caption, but she certainly did little to discourage the image.[22]

No doubts were allowed to creep into the U.S. mission. Career diplomats who were most likely to stress continuity with Carter policies and plead for the U.N. were excluded from the inner circle of policymakers and replaced by a phalanx of tough-minded neoconservatives to whom the U.N. was just one more theater in the Cold War.[23] They looked across First Avenue at the United Nations building, looked across the sea of yellow taxis—and saw danger.

These months were to set the tone for American policy in the United Nations during Reagan's two terms in office. By deliberately accentuating the negative, Kirkpatrick and her team primed American opinion to look on the U.N. as "politicized," "selective," and biased against the U.S. and its allies. Should the U.S. withdraw from the U.N.? She never put the question directly and refused to answer it in interviews. Yet she repeatedly insisted that it be asked. And asked it was. During 1981, the conservative Heritage Foundation canvassed its supporters. Would they be willing to support a series of hard-hitting reports on the United Nations? The response was an enthusiastic yes. Burton Pines, a former *Time* bureau chief, was appointed to head the project. Its first researcher was a former Rumanian television child star, Juliana Pilón.[24]

Pilón's family had not been driven from Rumania—she told the author that her father ran a travel agency and still visited Rumania regularly—but she brought the refugee's gratitude and patriotism to her new work, together with a very sharp mind. Her first paper took its cue from Kirkpatrick and ended by posing a question: "Is the U.S. benefiting from its U.N. membership given the paralysis of the Security Council and the anti-American, anti-Western, anti-industrial, anti-Capitalist majority in the General Assembly?"[25] It was quite clear what Pilón's own answer would be.

Over the next four years the Heritage Foundation would link up with influential legislators and key staffers on Capitol Hill who were deeply hostile to international organizations. Together they would take the U.N. out of the right-wing fringe of American politics and force it onto center stage. Their aim was crude: to win U.S. veto power on the budget, cut U.N. spending, increase the number of Americans in the secretariat, and turn the U.N. into an instrument of raw pressure on the Soviet Union.[26] In 1987 they finally achieved their goal. Long after it had imposed zero growth and cut its costs, the U.N. found itself pushed to the brink of bankruptcy by the Reagan Adminstration's inability to control the U.S. budget. The U.N. was humbled and discredited—just when the U.S. was becoming aware of its potential. It was a disastrous episode—hypocritical, unjustified and totally irresponsible.[27]

Jeane Kirkpatrick had made human rights her own issue within the Reagan Administration and it was inevitable that human rights would dominate her 1981 assault on the United Nations. On November 24 she delivered a fiery attack on U.N. "selectivity" before the General Assembly. The U.N., she said, had been silent when three million Cambodians died under Pol Pot. Silent when a quarter of a million Ugandans died under Idi Amin. Silent on political detention in Cuba. Silent on the confinement of Sakharov to Gorki. Yet, it had criticized Latin America mercilessly:

> No aspect of United Nations affairs has been more perverted by the politicization of the last decade than have its human rights activities. In Geneva and in New York, human rights has become a bludgeon to be wielded by the strong against the weak, by the majority against the isolated, by the blocs against the unorganized. . . . The activities of the United Nations with respect to Latin America offer a particularly egregious example of moral hypocrisy. Four countries of Latin America were condemned: El Salvador, Guatemala, Chile and Bolivia. . . . Doubtless, some of these countries, some of these governments are guilty as charged. But the moral standing of their judges is undermined by their studious unconcern with the much larger violations of human liberty elsewhere in Latin America, by the government of Cuba.

The ambassador ended her address with the following words: "Nothing less than the moral integrity of the United Nations is at issue in our deliberations here. Nothing less than the commitment of this organization to its own reason for being is at stake."[28] She had turned the tables in a startling fashion. It was not the death squads and torturers that were on trial, so much as the United Nations. The only thing was that her analysis was demonstrably wrong. The U.N.'s human rights machinery had never been more effective.[29]

Kirkpatrick warned that, until the United Nations rediscovered its commitment, the United States would vote in support of the Latin American regimes, no matter how repugnant their deeds. This the United States proceeded to do in a succession of votes on behalf of Guatemala, Chile, and El Salvador.

Yet there was nothing remotely "politicized" about these resolutions.

Quite the contrary. Resolution 36/435 on Guatemala was innocuous—unworthily so. It simply "took note" of second-hand material pulled together by van Boven's office and asked the Secretary General to continue his efforts to establish direct contacts with the government. The resolution on Chile was also tame: it merely proposed the extension of the U.N. inquiry for another year. But Carl Gershman, Kirkpatrick's assistant, complained that the latest report did not acknowledge "improvements" that had taken place in Chile. (Pinochet was evidently encouraged by this expression of U.S. support because shortly afterwards, on December 10 1981, International Human Rights Day, security forces in Chile rounded up seven dissidents and tortured them. This prompted an angry protest by American human rights groups.) [30]

As for El Salvador, the U.N. would surely have lost all credibility if it had not expressed some concern after a year in which 16,276 people had died from political violence. By the end of 1981, Roberto Cuéllar and Marianella García Villas had both fled into exile after threats against their lives.

It was little wonder that commentators talked of U.S. support for dictators, and little wonder the Latin Americans flaunted their sense of solidarity. By now the climate was extraordinarily charged. The Security Council was trying to elect a successor to U.N. Secretary General Kurt Waldheim. The lackluster Waldheim was clinging on, hoping for a third term, but there were other hats in the ring. One of them belonged to van Boven's old rival Javier Pérez de Cuéllar of Peru.

Van Boven Goes to Nicaragua

This, if ever, was a time for van Boven to keep a low profile. True to form, he did not. Instead, he promptly went off to attend a highly political seminar on racism in Nicaragua, where he became embroiled in a huge anti-American rally. It was precisely the kind of incident needed to tip the Reagan Administration from irritation into outright hostility.

To a large extent, van Boven was cornered into visiting Managua. The U.N. Human Rights Division was obliged to hold the seminar in Latin America, and Nicaragua was the only government that made an offer to host it. Van Boven rationalized it quite easily.[31] He had detested Somoza and he sympathized with the Nicaraguan revolution. He strongly disapproved of the U.S. policy. (It was around this time that President Reagan authorized the CIA to assist the contras.) Perhaps his presence would help relieve their growing sense of isolation.

But the Sandinistas repaid van Boven for his trust as they were to repay Pope John Paul II on his trip to Central America in 1983. If van Boven had taken a personal risk in attending this seminar, they did not reward him for it. If his exposed position demanded that they act with restraint and dignity, they ignored it. Instead, they gleefully and gratefully used van Boven for raw propaganda. He was interviewed as soon as he arrived and asked what he thought about Nicaragua's human rights record. He chose his words carefully, saying that he was glad the Nicaraguans had allowed the IACHR to visit. The local press interpreted this as ringing praise for the Sandinistas. Within hours a cable had arrived from Buffum's office in New York, asking for clarification.

Van Boven realized by now that he was trapped, but he persevered. Two days later, a Nicaraguan soldier burst into the hotel room where one member of the U.N. team, a Polish woman, was sleeping and made a search. That prompted an angry protest from van Boven and he threatened to pull out the whole team. He went to José Esteban González's independent human rights commission as a gesture of encouragement. González had fled the country by now and the commission was under some pressure. The office was run-down and ramshackle, but van Boven collected the latest reports. He also urged the Sandinistas to admit the U.N. Working Group on Disappearances. They turned him down flat.

It was van Boven's own way of trying to remain objective, but the gesture was in vain. Just after the racism conference ended, he received a vaguely worded invitation to attend "some kind of closing ceremony." Van Boven and two assistants were picked up and driven out of town. It was only when they arrived in the huge floodlit field, thronged with Nicaraguan soldiers, that they realized the purpose of the rally. It was to be addressed by the veteran revolutionary Tomás Borge, Luis Echeverría Alvarez (the former Mexican president)—and Theo van Boven.

Van Boven was invited up to the podium. He scribbled down some notes on the back of his invitation card. One of the things he remembers saying is that the Western media "distort"—innocuous enough had it not come from the senior U.N. human rights official in Nicaragua, 1981. Here, on a hot Nicaraguan evening in front of three thousand Sandinista troops, van Boven killed off his promising U.N. career.

Van Boven later said that to have pulled out of the ceremony would have further isolated the Sandinistas and shown the U.N. as biased and cowardly. All of which was no doubt true. But this was Nicaragua. Once again, though, van Boven showed himself remarkably unconcerned once he had made a fateful decision. His assistant, Bertie Ramcharam, recalls him as totally composed when they arrived at the field for the rally. At the same time, van Boven knew instinctively that the incident would hurt him as soon as he heard Borge's ringing denunciation of American imperialism. The atmosphere was charged and tense: some members of the local diplomatic corps were present, looking highly uncomfortable. The Argentinian ambassador was heard to refer to van Boven's "nest of communist vipers."

When he returned to Geneva, van Boven found his office bombarded with requests for clarification. There were four queries from William Buffum. The American mission in Geneva also showed itself extremely interested. Was it true, as reported, that several participants had pulled out in disgust at the anti-American tone? It was not.

Pérez de Cuéllar Triumphs

Van Boven's own fate was conclusively sealed when Kurt Waldheim finally failed in his undignified attempt to win a third term. Instead, the General Assembly chose van Boven's old foe, Javier Pérez de Cuéllar, after one of the most bitter and prolonged elections in the history of the United Nations.

The system requires all five permament members of the U.N. Security Council (China, the U.S., the U.S.S.R., Britain, and France) to vote for the new Secretary General; this requirement had killed the chances of Waldheim and Salim Salim, Tanzania's Foreign Minister, who were vetoed by China and the United States respectively. After six weeks and sixteen inconclusive ballots, it was time to look for compromise candidates. Three front-runners emerged—Pérez de Cuéllar; Argentina's ambassador to London, Carlos Ortíz de Rosas; and Prince Sadruddin Aga Khan, the former U.N. High Commissioner for Refugees.[32]

Pérez de Cuéllar campaigned for the post against a background of some personal difficulty. He had resigned from his U.N. post earlier in the year and returned to Peru, fully expecting to be nominated ambassador to Brazil. But democracy had returned to Peru, and Pérez de Cuéllar's past returned to haunt him. Vice President Javier Alva Orlandini opposed his nomination on the grounds that Pérez de Cuéllar had officiated at the swearing-in of the military regime that had overthrown the elected president, Belaunde Terry, in 1968. Pérez de Cuéllar was rejected in a secret ballot by the Peruvian senate. It was a jarring reverse. According to one cable from the U.S. embassy in Lima, Pérez de Cuéllar was "temporarily crushed," although his public reaction was "dignified and measured."[33]

Unlike his rivals who lobbied personally in New York, Pérez de Cuéllar remained at home in Peru and left his campaign to Emilio de Olivares. Olivares had served in the Peruvian diplomatic service. Olivares mounted a persistent but low-key lobby. The United States, apparently, had reservations until the last minute. One December cable enigmatically described Pérez de Cuéllar as "damaged goods."[34]

He survived, nonetheless. On December 10 the Security Council accepted Pérez de Cuéllar as the next U.N. Secretary General by ten votes to one with four absentions. Sadruddin Aga Khan found himself in the appalling position of having been promised more votes than Pérez de Cuéllar but being blocked by a Soviet veto. Carlos Ortíz de Rosas, from Argentina, fell foul of the disappearances: France vetoed his candidacy because of the Junta's record in human rights. The Soviet Union also vetoed the Argentinian, revealing once more how lukewarm was the alliance between the two nations.[35]

On December 15, Pérez de Cuéllar was elected to a round of applause from a General Assembly that had grown weary of the lobbying and Waldheim's undignified attempts to remain in office. Pérez de Cuéllar inherited a salary of $158,340, a hospitality allowance of $24,000, and a rent-free townhouse in Manhattan.

The consensus was that the new U.N. Secretary General was a thoroughly decent, thoroughly experienced diplomat, but not a man of human rights. Throughout his many diplomatic assignments—trying to negotiate a Soviet withdrawal from Afghanistan, swearing in a Peruvian military regime, visiting Uruguay's notorious Liberty jail—Pérez de Cuéllar had shown infinite understanding of the regime, no matter how ruthless or illegal. Pérez de Cuéllar dealt with the facts before him. He was neutral. This put him at odds with his human rights chief, Theo van Boven, who had criticized Pérez de Cuéllar after his disastrous trip to Paraguay and Uruguay in 1979. Pérez de Cuéllar had let it be known that he had never forgiven the Dutchman.

Whatever Pérez de Cuéllar's personal views, he publicly committed himself to restoring the morale of the U.N. secretariat and bolstering its independence. On January 12, shortly after taking up his office, he made a stirring pledge to U.N. staff members in New York: "I perceive the strengthening of the secretariat as the first order of business. I am determined to do my utmost to preserve and defend the independence and international character of the secretariat and to resist any attempts that tend to erode that principle."[36]

This was a reassuring message to the U.N. staff, and Pérez de Cuéllar followed it up with the imaginative appointment of Leila Doss, from Egypt, to head the highly sensitive department of U.N. personnel. In public, at least, the U.N. secretariat seemed about to enjoy something of a rejuvenation, its independence strengthened.

24. The Dictators Triumph

Storm clouds hung heavy and glowering over the U.N. Human Rights Commission that opened in Geneva on February 1 1982, and they were blowing from East to West. Less than two months earlier, on December 12 1981, the Polish government had declared martial law. Lech Walesa, head of the Solidarity union and symbol of change in Eastern Europe, was detained near the Russian frontier. Hundreds of Solidarity supporters had been rounded up and several killed during a disturbance at a mine.[1]

If the human rights debate at the end of 1981 had been less passionate, it might have been possible to put the Polish crisis into some kind of context. In terms of deaths, repression, and mistreatment of prisoners it was certainly less vicious than Argentina's dirty war.[2] Yet there was another dimension to the Polish crisis that removed it from the East-West context. There was a decency about Walesa, and an exuberance about Solidarity, that gave the Polish union an extraordinary international appeal. In addition, international law had been flouted, and a union snuffed out. The International Labor Organization's labor conventions and the International Covenant on Civil and Political Rights (neither of which had the U.S. ratified) both protected the right to form independent trade unions. It mattered not whether the "context" was socialist or capitalist.

Western governments quickly began to review their options, and attention turned to the forthcoming session of the U.N. Human Rights Commission in Geneva. The United States was still smarting from the failure of the Sakharov resolution the previous year and indignant about the perceived "selectivity" of U.N. attacks on Latin America. Very well, Poland would be the test. Michael Novak, who had been reappointed U.S. delegate, put it like this at a briefing on the eve of the Commission:

> The government of Poland has declared war upon its own people and terrorized and abused the rights of some 36 million persons. That's a lot of persons to have a diminished number of human rights in a year. Now that

happened just seven weeks ago, and it makes us very, very sad. The Human
Rights Commission would lose all self-respect if it did not confront this
urgent, immediate and systematic abuse of an entire population.[3]

It was vintage Novak. One was reminded of Patt Derian's description
of him as "a sweet guy with nutty constructs." Yet the prospects for the
U.N. were anything but sweet. The U.N. was on trial yet again. The Commission would be found guilty by the Reagan Administration of "double
standards" if it failed to act on Poland. It would also be found guilty by
the United States—of "double standards"—if it took action on the sixteen
thousand people who had died from political violence in El Salvador during 1981! The stage was set for another tumultuous session.

Van Boven's Announcement

Overriding everything for Theo van Boven at this moment were images
of death and cruelty in Guatemala. Reports were emerging that were almost too beastly to recount—stories of crucifixion and disemboweling, of
indiscriminate savagery against the Indians. The stories were coming from
reliable NGOs, but could not be confirmed or refuted by the U.N. because
Guatemala was still conducting its astute diplomatic campaign to avoid
any U.N. investigation.

In October 1981, during the General Assembly, the regime of General
Lucas García had turned its full fury against the Indian population in the
highland provinces, particularly El Quiché. This was the area of poor,
impoverished villages where Julia Esquivel had toiled. Now, from exile in
Europe, she began to hear of massacres by the Guatemalan armed forces.
The news was vague but terrifying, and it threw her into turmoil.

In January Esquivel arrived at van Boven's office with an Indian catechist from the Catchikel Indian tribal group and a Guatemalan nun. The
catechist had just returned from the area. She recounted how the army
and air force had systematically moved against Indian villages, bombing,
shooting, killing. Women had fallen, crushing their babies in the panic.
The meeting was attended by van Boven and three of his staff members:
Bruna Molina, Tom McCarthy, and Augusto Willemsen Diaz. Willemsen
Diaz and McCarthy had both accompanied van Boven to Chile in 1978 and
Diaz translated the catechist's story. Julia Esquivel thinks that van Boven
sat on his chair with his head in his hands. Bruna Molina is sure he wept.
Van Boven himself has forgotten.

He was, however, extraordinarily moved by the testimony. There would be many similar allegations in the months to come. According to some church sources, the Guatemalans had even fitted devices to the bottom of their helicopters that were capable of spotting the brightly colored clothes of Indians through the forest. Ironically, van Boven's contact with the regime in Geneva, the Guatemalan ambassador, was the sister of the author of this butchery, President Lucas García.[4]

Events were now rapidly moving out of van Boven's control. He was well into preparations for the Commission session, due to open on February 1 1982. Traditionally, the director of the U.N. Human Rights Division delivers the opening statement. In the past it had been a bland address, full of the usual U.N. jargon about "organs being seized" but very little about torture and disappearances, and certainly no mention of governments by name. This year, van Boven decided it would be different. During the General Assembly in New York, he instructed his Guyanese assistant, Bertie Ramcharam, to draft a statement on political killings, and told him to name names.

Van Boven was in a determined mood. Thousands of murders had been committed in El Salvador and Guatemala. Guatemala had not cooperated with the U.N., and yet it was clear that the killings were the work of government security forces. According to Amnesty International, the killers were even working out of the presidential palace.[5] In Iran the regime of the Ayatollah Khomeini seemed crazed by the taste of blood. Throughout the world, thousands of people were being carved up, beheaded, blown apart, mutilated, and tortured by the forces of law and order—in the name of national security and other fascist doctrines. Yet thanks to Gabriel Martínez the Argentinian Mothers had a hard time even getting past U.N. security officials and into the building. This, in van Boven's view, was not a time to be talking about conventions and organs. He felt as Kirkpatrick had the previous September, although for opposite reasons: nothing less than the moral integrity of the United Nations was at stake.

Ramcharam drafted a statement referring to six regimes which he put in inverted commas: Kampuchea, Uganda under Idi Amin, Chile, Iran, El Salvador, and Guatemala. Van Boven took the inverted commas out and added several other touches, including one dramatic reference to mass graves and "unidentified bodies floating down rivers clothed in native dress" in Guatemala. This came directly from powerful firsthand testimony by the Guatemalan nun, Sister Petronila, who had survived one of the highland massacres.

On the morning of Monday February 1, van Boven delivered his address before the Commission, denouncing "mass killings, genocide, political liquidation, torture, summary executions, disappearances." He was nervous and the Commission was unusually attentive.

Later the same day, Ambassador Kirkpatrick and one of her senior deputies, Theodore Papendorp, crossed First Avenue in New York and made their way up to the office of Javier Pérez de Cuéllar, the new U.N. Secretary General. There were four people present: Pérez de Cuéllar, Papendorp, Kirkpatrick, and Emilio de Olivares, Pérez de Cuéllar's executive assistant. Olivares kept a record for the U.N. Kirkpatrick, he wrote, expressed "dissatisfaction" at van Boven, whereupon Pérez de Cuéllar "immediately said his [van Boven's] contract would not be extended."[6]

Eight days later, on February 8 1982, Theo van Boven announced that his contract was not being renewed—that he had been dismissed—because of "policy differences" with the new Secretary General Javier Pérez de Cuéllar. Gabriel Martínez had triumphed.

The Background

The circumstances surrounding Theo van Boven's final speech are without precedent in the history of the United Nations. It is not normal for the director's opening statement to be distributed before his actual address, but this one was, and by Thursday morning it was prominently displayed in press bureaus with an angry red "embargo" slashed across the top.[7] According to one U.N. official who worked closely with van Boven during this period, the Guatamalan ambassador in Geneva, Ana María Lucas de Rivera, informed Gabriel Martínez and the Guatemalan ambassador in New York, who called on Pérez de Cuéllar. On Friday evening, van Boven received a phone call from Jay Long, William Buffum's assistant, requesting that the full text of the speech be sent through immediately to New York.

The following day, Saturday, van Boven was working at the United Nations when his wife, Ann-Marie, received a call at home from Jay Long. Was Theo in? She referred him to the U.N. When he got through, Jay Long told van Boven that the speech was far too lengthy, and he suggested that van Boven remove all references to individual countries. Van Boven snapped back a refusal and insisted on talking to his superior, Buffum.

Van Boven's recollection is of two "very unpleasant conversations" with Buffum. Buffum said he was calling on instructions of the Secretary General, who wanted the government names omitted. Van Boven was adamant. He pointed out that the speech had already been distributed, so any change in the text would excite comment. He threatened to resign. Buffum hung up. The following day, Sunday, Buffum phoned again. According to a secret February 17 memorandum prepared by Buffum for Pérez de Cuéllar, Buffum suggested a general statement giving priority to cases "involving the loss of human lives."[8]

Van Boven turned him down. "I'm sitting here dealing with these people, receiving exiles from Uganda, El Salvador," he said. Buffum was resentful at the implication. He pointed out that the U.N. also had responsibilities in New York and complained that van Boven's draft statement was "selective" because it made no reference to killing by terrorists. This echo of Kirkpatrick's complaint was another sign of how cowed the U.N. secretariat had been by the American assault. Van Boven was exasperated. Terrorists, he said, don't pretend to uphold the law or defend Western civilization. Again, he threatened to resign. Buffum advised against it, saying that it would be bad for van Boven's career. Then he lost his temper. "This is not the first time you've disobeyed orders!" he shouted into the phone.

The conversation finally ended on a happier note, and an hour later Buffum rang back to say that Pérez de Cuéllar had given permission for van Boven to make the statement—as long as he made it clear they were his own personal views.[9]

The official U.N. position on van Boven's dismissal was explained by François Guiliani, Pérez de Cuéllar's spokesman, who accused van Boven of "speaking out of turn." This was clearly not the case, even if van Boven's address had persuaded his many foes to make their move. The six governments he mentioned had all been the subject of public U.N. inquiries, and van Boven's job was to give an overview of his Division's work at the start of each Commission. The real reason for his dismissal was rather more simple. Van Boven, by now, had run out of friends.

Most of the Latin Americans, of course, had long hated him. According to one report, Pérez de Cuéllar (or his tactician Olivares) had agreed to dismiss van Boven during his election campaign in exchange for Latin support.[10] Following this deal, Gabriel Martínez coordinated the search to find a Latin American successor to van Boven, and by the time of van Boven's statement, the search was well under way throughout Latin America. This fact emerges clearly from a cable from Hector Gross Espiell, a Uruguayan diplomat, that reached Martínez in Geneva just hours after van Boven had spoken. Gross Espiell cabled that he already approached an Ecuadoran lawyer, Martínez Cobo, but been turned down. Espiell suggested that they approach Pérez de Cuéllar "to see what possibilities exist."[11]

U.S. disillusionment with van Boven had been building for some time, and his indiscreet comment about President Reagan in the disastrous April 1981 interview had evidently been deeply resented. William Buffum wrote in the secret February 17 memorandum to Javier Pérez de Cuéllar:

Over the past year van Boven became increasingly outspoken and indiscreet in his comments about the positions of member states on human rights. This was, for example, very evident in an interview he gave the Swiss magazine *Illustré* on 1 April 1981 when he permitted himself to be quoted criticizing the government of Argentina. . . . The government of Argentina lodged a formal complaint. He also criticized President Reagan by name, claiming he was less interested in human rights than President Carter and that American policy shifted from the human factor to the power factor with a narrow base which misjudged world realities. The U.S. later made clear it would not be sorry to see van Boven replaced.[12]

The Soviets, too, had always detested van Boven. They were opposed to an activist U.N. secretariat as a matter of principle, and they resented his refusal to hire Soviets for the sensitive vetting of individual 1503 communications.

Perhaps van Boven could have survived had he not lost the support of his superiors. By now, he had personally alienated four key figures in the U.N. hierarchy: Javier Pérez de Cuéllar, William Buffum, Jay Long, and Diego Cordovez. Van Boven's relationship with Pérez de Cuéllar had never recovered from the aftermath of Pérez's mission to Uruguay's Liberty jail in December 1979. William Buffum was different. Right until the end, van Boven had looked on Buffum as a friend. Until the final, fateful telephone conversation, Buffum had never rebuked van Boven and always urged him to stick it out. Buffum's secret February 17 memorandum to Pérez took a very different line. It implied that van Boven had been a constant source of irritation. This was nasty and dishonest.

Yet, in retrospect, van Boven felt no personal bitterness toward Buffum. He realized that Buffum's shoulders were neither broad enough, nor his convictions strong enough, to defend van Boven against so many powerful enemies. To this day van Boven accepts, somewhat sadly, that his own refusal to compromise forced Buffum to make a difficult choice—between regimes like the Junta in Argentina that had murdered thousands and Buffum's obstreperous Dutch colleague.

Buffum had no choice. He was a creature of the United Nations, dedicated to upholding the sovereignty of its member governments. His February 17 memo to Pérez de Cuéllar described Argentina and Chile in tones of respect and admiration instead of contempt. Their relentless pressure against van Boven and the Argentinian relatives of the disappeared—one of the most sinister campaigns ever launched against an international civil servant—appeared to Buffum entirely reasonable.

Novak Tries to Recover

Van Boven announced his dismissal to the Human Rights Commission on Monday, February 8. Alerted by rumors in the papers, the television cameras were rolling as he spoke.[13] Van Boven's wife Ann-Marie was sitting at the back, choking back tears. Several delegations—notably Senegal—recovered quickly from their shock and made dignified statements expressing surprise, regret, and affection for van Boven. But neither Michael Novak of the United States nor Lord Colville of Britain said a word. Not a word of shock or regret, nor thanks for the work done. Their silence was deafening.

Gabriel Martínez, van Boven's old foe, left no doubt about how he felt. Looking like a cat that had just fallen into a bowl of cream, Martínez suggested that if van Boven had been speaking in a personal capacity, he no longer represented the U.N. Secretary General and should leave immediately instead of even waiting for the end of the Commission session. Martínez was so keen that van Boven should personally hear this final insult that he asked one of his colleagues to go and call van Boven from his office.

Michael Novak quickly realized how much sentiment had been stirred up by the affair. At a meeting of the Western delegations on February 11 he heard that an all-party protest would be introduced in the Dutch parliament. According to an account cabled back to Washington, the meeting also heard that the Latin Americans had made a concentrated démarche to have van Boven dismissed. Someone—probably Novak—said he doubted that "Latin pressure alone" could have produced the decision.[14] The meeting took seriously Martínez's suggestion that van Boven leave immediately: it was one more sign of how he had rattled the West.

Unlikely as it seemed, the dismissal of a middle-ranking U.N. official had mushroomed into a full-blooded international cause célèbre. Like Jacobo Timerman and Ernest Lefever, Theo van Boven had become a symbol of wider issues—in this case, of U.N. officials prepared to stand up for their ideals. Unlike the Reagan Administration, most Western Europeans still wanted to believe in the U.N. Novak was evidently unprepared for this. As he observed in a cable to Washington: "There is some speculation that thru lack of US comment US may have responsibility." By midday Novak realized that he had to say something, so he convened an impromptu press conference. This was Novak's cabled account:

> Replying to press at noon in crowded palais, US rep Novak praised Theo van Boven after the announcement Feb 10 for his integrity, idealism, and organizational skills and gave opinion it would be hard to find a better successor. . . . Finally, by 1300 Geneva time, US rep reached amb Kirkpatrick in NY and learned of her surprise at van Boven announcement..Confirmed her "good, cordial" relations with van Boven and respect for the prerogative of SYG to make his own appointments. . . . In response questions US rep Novak noted special bonds between van Boven and himself often remarked by van Boven—scholarly and religious interests approx same age same emphasis on people rather than resolutions.[15]

Novak went on to ask the State Department for "some words of praise for van Boven," preferably stronger than the lukewarm comments that were being issued from Pérez de Cuéllar's office.

Nicholas Platt, at the Bureau of International Organizations, contacted Elliott Abrams at the Human Rights Bureau: "Mike has asked us to underscore van Boven's good points in reacting to any inquiries, suggesting his ideals, integrity and capacity to organize among his fine qualities. . . . Parenthetically, Jeane Kirkpatrick told Mike that she was surprised by the announcement."[16]

Michael Novak was apparently ignorant of his government's efforts to see van Boven replaced. In spite of this, no one believed a word of what he said at his two press briefings. Ronald Reagan's assault on the U.N. had astonished people in Europe and they knew how exposed it had left van Boven. Novak's belated praise increased the sense of anger and made American policy seem even less credible.

Martínez Redux

On February 17 1982, a week after the announcement of Theo van Boven's dismissal, Gabriel Martínez hosted a lunch for delegates from the U.N. Human Rights Commission. We do not know what Martínez served his distinguished visitors, but we do know that he was at his most charming as he moved around, chatting, putting people at their ease and calming their jangled nerves. The first two weeks of the Commission had been unusually tense, and Martínez was largely responsible for the tension. But now he was playing his other role, that of the polished diplomat. His fellow delegates probably welcomed the respite. They had no stomach for confrontation.

Just before lunch Martínez offered a toast. It was vintage Martínez—breathtakingly insincere. He paid his visitors the compliment of delivering it in English:

> Ladies and Gentlemen, In the first place, I wish to express my deep appreciation for your presence in [sic] this lunch that I wanted to offer as a token of friendship and goodwill. We are all here in pursuance of one common goal; the fostering of the respect of human rights all over the world. "Think positive," the Anglo Saxons say. If we think positive and try to place ourselves in the other people's problems, maybe our approach to their difficulties will contribute to a better outcome.

Martínez was so proud of his eloquence that he cabled the text to Buenos Aires.[17]

The lunch marked an astonishing turnaround in the personal fortunes of the stocky Argentinian diplomat. After two years of virtual ostracism he was once again a figure of respect. His savage campaign against van Boven had paid off. Martínez had once again imposed his will on the United Nations.

He had not, however, been able to prevent the U.N. Working Group on Disappearances from issuing another extremely damaging report. The group was able to confirm that the kidnappings had more or less ceased in Argentina: eight people had disappeared in 1981 and seven of them had subsequently reappeared. But if Martínez expected a compliment for this "improvement" he was gravely disappointed. The group chided the Junta for again refusing to divulge any information and warned that the "structure" which had lead to disappearances—unmarked cars, secret detention camps—was still very much in place. Most of all, it wanted the disappearances explained.[18]

It was the fate of the missing infants—a tragedy to which the Junta had no real answer—that kept the issue well to the fore, and Emilio Mignone who kept up the pressure. Six months earlier, Mignone had told the U.N. group that Argentina's juvenile judges could and should be encouraged to investigate the infants' fate.[19] His testimony was circulated round the Amnesty International network in the United States, with the suggestion that it be sent in the standard "courteously worded" Amnesty letter to Argentinian judges.[20] Once again, Martínez was reminded of Mignone's persistence. Mignone represented the one remaining obstacle to his hopes of crippling the group. Somehow, he had to be muzzled.

The previous year, in February 1981, Martínez had tried to muzzle Mignone in Buenos Aires by using his testimony at the U.N. against him. This time, it was to be the other way round: Martínez would use Mignone's activism at home to muzzle him in the United Nations. On January 5 1982 Mignone had given a press conference in Buenos Aires to denounce two of the eight disappearances that had occurred during 1981. Shortly after this press conference, one of the two men, Daniel di Bernardo reappeared alive. Mignone's response was, naturally, relief that the young man's life had probably been saved by his intervention. He remained pessimistic about the other victim, Gerardo Brugo Marco, and with good reason. The man never reappeared.

The Junta was furious and charged Mignone and four other human rights activists under a security law (#14034) which made it an offense for Argentinians to demand sanctions against their own governmment. On February 11 1982, Mignone appeared before federal judge Norberto Giletta for the second time in a year. The charge was quickly dropped. Mignone left for Geneva, where he was due to deliver a statement before the U.N. Human Rights Commission on behalf of the International Commission of Jurists.[21]

In Geneva, Ambassador Gabriel Martínez had been kept informed of this sequence of events. Martínez went for the throat, and history began to repeat itself. In a way, nothing had changed. Five years earlier, in 1977, Martínez had tried to muzzle the International Commission of Jurists when it invited Rodolfo Matarollo to speak. Now he returned to the attack against the ICJ, ignoring the fact that Mignone's group CELS was, unlike Matarollo, formally affiliated to the ICJ and that Mignone himself had been virtually adopted by the Reagan Administration the previous year. Aware that Mignone was due to speak, Martínez suddenly interrupted the debate to demand that all representatives of the NGOs identify themselves before speaking. It was quite unprecedented, but no one objected.

The first speaker was Nigel Rodley, the head of Amnesty International's legal section. Rodley has a solid British accent: "My name is Nigel Rodley, and I work for Amnesty International . . ." Next on the list was the International Commission of Jurists. People held their breath. They knew what was coming. Even before Mignone had even opened his mouth, Martínez's dry voice was barking out a protest.[22] Sometimes, the Commission can produce a dry nervous mood, when the snap of a pencil or the tumble of a briefcase makes people jump. At moments like these, silence seems ominous and no one seems in control. Here was one such moment. As with the exchange the previous year between Martínez and van Boven, the tension was heightened by the hint of personal hatred between Emilio Mignone and the Argentinian ambassador.

The two men made a striking physical contrast. Mignone, with his loose tie and sad expression, seemed out of place in Conference Room 17. Martínez, smooth and elegant, seemed in his element. Neither impression was entirely accurate: Mignone was considerably shrewder than he looked and Martínez was as adroit at retreat as attack. But Mignone was close to breaking. For five years he had lived with a nightmare, struggling with the memory of his daughter being taken off at dawn. He had visited morgues, watched secret graves being dug up, and been repeatedly rebuffed by people in uniform. Obsessed and desperate, he had brought his grief to the United Nations.

Now he found himself once again exposed. The rules were stacked against him. In front of him was Gabriel Martínez, who had been playing this game for six years. Mignone was aware that all eyes were on him. But were they sympathetic, curious, or maybe even hostile?

At moments like this in the movies, the hero steps out of a crowd and confronts the bully. The occasion seemed tailor-made for Michael Novak. After all, had he not used Mignone's own release from prison to show how enlightened President Reagan's human rights policy was? Novak said nothing. Two years later in a private interview he would excuse himself by saying that Martínez had been acting as a loose cannon, with no particular purpose.[23] But of course Martínez had a purpose. He had not wavered since his confrontation with Matarollo six years earlier. Surely Novak knew what that purpose was? He had deplored the "emotional violence" of the attacks against Israel in the Commission. Surely he could see that Martínez's hatred of Mignone was, if anything, palpable? Still, Novak didn't intervene.

Niall MacDermot of the International Commission of Jurists was now under greater pressure than at any other time in his long and illustrious career. Instead of yielding, he stoutly chose to stand his ground and insist that Mignone would speak on the Jurists' behalf. The meeting went into recess for several hours, and during the break Colville approached Mac-Dermot. Perhaps he was going to help his fellow British barrister? Perhaps he felt that this time Martínez had gone too far, and that Mignone was now in need of defense? Not at all. Colville could be seen angrily trying to persuade MacDermot to change his mind. He was desperately worried that Martínez, affronted, would vote against the extension of the working group. MacDermot refused to budge.

By the time the session resumed, the shock had worn off and Mac-Dermot had managed to lobby with sympathetic delegates, several of whom plucked up courage to confront Martínez. The tide began to turn and eventually Mignone was allowed to speak. He started nervously. He then delivered an intensely personal statement, speaking not as the director of a legal aid office in Buenos Aires, but as a father who had seen his daughter taken away before his eyes: "I, too, am a victim of this indiscriminate repression. On May 14 1976 one of my children Mónica—who was then 24—was arrested defenseless in my home, in my presence, in the presence of my wife and Mónica's brothers and sisters, by officials of the armed forces . . ."[24]

A daughter's life snuffed out. A father's life wrecked. This put human rights on a different plane altogether. One observer remembers his feeling of indignation: instead of listening to Mignone humbly and praying that the same fate never befell them, they acted as if they were doing him a favor. There was a sigh of relief when Mignone finished. He had been close to tears, and no one likes it when a man breaks down in public. Too undignified. Too emotional. Quite out of place in the United Nations. Poor Mignone. He had expected a lot from the United Nations, but when the moment of truth finally arrived, he found out that it was indeed "a dangerous place." After the debate was over, Gabriel Martínez sent one of his colleagues to Mignone with a short message. It read: "No hard feelings, I hope."[25]

Shortly afterwards, Martínez aimed one last thrust at van Boven during the confidential 1503 debate, accusing his opponent of having leaked confidential material to the press. Van Boven, by now free of restraint, snapped back an angry reply. Martínez stood up and stalked from the room.[26]

The Farewell

A week after the end of the Commission session, Theo van Boven's friends organized a concert at the University of Geneva. Topping the bill was the Argentinian pianist Miguel Angel Estrella, whose detention in Uruguay's Liberty jail had caused such distrust between van Boven and Javier Pérez de Cuéllar. Estrella swooped and soared over the piano before embracing van Boven with equal feeling. There were other contributors from tormented countries—folk singers from El Salvador, Chile, and Guatemala.

The audience were young and excited. They spilled into the aisles, wearing long hair and duffel coats, just as an earlier generation had done in the turbulent 1960s. Many had never seen van Boven in person, but they had read a lot about him in the local press and sensed he stood for something they approved of. What it was, though, was hard to fathom. Instead of obliging his audience with a furious assault on the governments and superiors who had killed his career, van Boven gave a tedious speech. There were no disclosures, but plenty of talk about "organs" and "standard-setting." It was the sort of speech that had made him the despair of journalists, and it showed that he remained, to the end, a loyal servant of the United Nations.

But this young audience would have forgiven him anything. They shouted encouragement when he spoke about "standards." They stood and roared when he raised his hands above his head. They stomped and clapped as he embraced Estrella. They cheered lustily as his wife Ann-Marie joined him on the stage and the two waved farewell. It was a revealing moment. There was, in that audience, a sense that the United Nations had again betrayed its own ideals.

Soon afterward, van Boven left for Holland with his family, many memories, and three prized possessions. One was a thick manila folder containing five years of threatening notes from Gabriel Martínez, another a series of small embroideries that had been given to him during his trip to Chile by relatives of disappeared persons. The third was the first two reports of his precious Working Group on Disappeared Persons, beautifully bound, and initialed by his staff.

V

Uneasy Transition

25. The Angel's Wings are Clipped

The final and most extraordinary phase of the U.N.'s long confrontation with Argentina opened in the last week of March 1982 on a string of wind-swept islands in the South Atlantic, just as Theo van Boven was cleaning out his files and preparing to leave Geneva.

Appropriately enough, one of the men who launched the Falklands (Malvinas) war between Britain and Argentina was well known to van Boven and the relatives of the disappeared. He was none other than Lieu-tenant Alfredo Astiz, who had served so diligently behind the white-washed walls of the ESMA concentration camp. On the evening of March 25 1982 Astiz disembarked with a contingent of Argentinian marines from a navy vessel at the small port of Leith, on the South Georgia islands. A week later, Argentinian troops landed in force on the Falkland Islands, some 800 miles to the west. Astiz and his troops raised the blue and white Argentinian flag over the South Georgias, which they renamed "Isla San Pedro." Astiz the Angel (as he had been known in the ESMA) was finally fighting a real war.[1]

He could not guess at the time how momentous the invasion would turn out to be. Within three months, the Junta's dream of indefinite mili-tary rule would be shattered, Astiz himself would be known internation-ally as a torturer, the Argentinian relatives would be facing a new and frustrating challenge, and the United Nations would be handed an un-precedented chance to ease Latin America's transition to democracy.

The war in the South Atlantic was a product of desperation. Argentina's rulers had fought their dirty war with cold efficiency but bungled the busi-ness of government. After several years of mismanagement by Alfredo Martínez de Hoz, "the Wizard," Argentina's economy was in ruins. The country owed $35.6 billion in foreign debts, companies were going broke, the currency had collapsed, wages had fallen, and inflation was rampant. For the first time since 1976, Argentina's cowed labor unions were showing signs of protest.[2]

The first casualty was President Roberto Viola. On December 22 1981, after serving less than a year, Viola was pushed aside and replaced as president by General Leopoldo Galtieri, the army Commander in Chief.[3] Galtieri was surrounded by crisis on every side, yet he gave the impression that if anyone could salvage the dream of indefinite military rule, it was he. From his curly gray hair to his shining boots, he seemed born to authority.

In November 1981, Galtieri visited Washington and took a first confident step in an entirely new campaign to shore up the regime. Galtieri held a luncheon at the Argentinian embassy in Washington. Among the visitors were U.S. Secretary of Defense Caspar Weinberger, National Security Advisor Richard Allen, and Assistant Secretary of State for Inter-American Affairs Thomas Enders. Galtieri promised his distinguished guests that Argentina would join the United States in its hemispheric crusade against Communism, particularly in Central America. Weinberger and Allen called him "magnificent."[4]

Galtieri returned to Argentina dazzled by his reception. Acting on the advice of his army attaché in Washington, General Mallea Gil, he began to distance Argentina from the Nonaligned Movement. Argentina's ambassadors were withdrawn from Cuba and Nicaragua and plans were drawn up to invite Weinberger and other senior U.S. government officials to Buenos Aires.[5]

At the same time, Galtieri intensified Argentina's involvement in Central America. Argentina had been playing an independent role in the crisis since 1979, but with the accession of President Reagan it took on the role of an American proxy. The Reagan Administration was legally forbidden from direct military involvement in either El Salvador or Nicaragua, so Argentina filled the gap by training Nicaraguan contras and instructing Salvadoran security forces in the techniques of "interrogation." On December 31 1981 a former Nicaraguan National Guardsmen, William Baltodano, crossed into Nicaragua from Honduras with sixteen other Nicaraguan "contras." He was captured and confessed that he had met with Argentinian army commanders in Buenos Aires, who had given him $50,000 to buy arms.[6]

Argentina's military rulers were even more willing to be coopted into U.S. strategic plans for the South Atlantic. Throughout 1981, the United States consistently raised the specter of Soviet naval incursions into the area and even encouraged the possibility of a South Atlantic treaty organization, similar to NATO. Even South Africa, it was suggested, would be a welcome participant.[7] Such reports were officially denied when they appeared in the press, but one Argentinian author, Horacio Verbitsky, has argued convincingly that Galtieri and his colleagues took them very seriously. By the end of 1981, writes Verbitksy, "the ideological circle had closed," and the South Atlantic and Central America were linked by the common threat of Communist "subversion." So vehement was U.S. distrust of this twin menace that Galtieri concluded that the Reagan Administration would not object if Argentina acted on a long-standing dispute and seized the Falkland Islands from its NATO ally, Britain.[8]

Galtieri's Gamble

Argentina and Britain had been at loggerheads over the Malvinas/Falklands since 1833, when the islands were occupied by Britain. In 1964 the United Nations classified the Falklands as "non-self governing," which cast doubts on the legitimacy of British sovereignty. The problem with this was that some eighteen hundred settlers lived on the islands, and all of them were staunchly loyal to Britain.[9]

Talks began between Britain and Argentina in 1964 and continued sporadically thereafter—punctuated by bursts of Argentinian bellicosity and long periods of British procrastination. In 1977 an Argentinian invasion of the islands was preempted only when Britain sent a submarine to the area.[10] In 1977, as we have seen, the Montoneros put out a series of pamphlets advocating the seizure of the islands, which tallied so exactly with the strategic designs of Admiral Massera that the navy personnel at the ESMA thought the Montoneros had a mole in the navy high command. Massera asked Admiral Jorge Isaac Anaya, who was commander of the fleet at the time, to look into it. Massera himself resigned from the Junta in 1978, and the plan was shelved.[11]

In the summer of 1981, it resurfaced. Gualter Allara, the former Deputy Foreign Minister, was now serving as Argentina's naval attaché in London, and he concluded that the British government of Prime Minister Margaret Thatcher had neither the resources nor the stomach for an armed confrontation in the South Atlantic. This he communicated to Admiral Juan Lombardo, chief of staff of the Argentinian navy. Lombardo was himself under pressure from the human rights groups and he spotted an opportunity to salvage some of the navy's ravaged reputation.[12]

Lombardo put the idea to his chief, Admiral Jorge Anaya, who had now ascended to the Junta. It was brief and simple: first, test the resolve of the British on the distant South Georgia islands, and second—if Britain failed to react—invade the Malvinas. Anaya had no love for Britain and he liked the plan. At a lunch with Galtieri on December 9 1981 he promised his support for Galtieri's palace putsch against Viola on condition that Galtieri agree to the seizure of the Malvinas. Galtieri readily agreed. The Junta desperately needed a boost, and the Malvinas was the one issue that united all shades of opinion in Argentina. Calculating that the United States would not object and that Britain would not resist, Galtieri told Anaya to work on the plan. Admiral Lombardo had it ready within two weeks. On January 13 1981, it was presented to the air force. The die had been cast.[13]

British and Argentinian diplomats met in New York on February 26 for yet another inconclusive meeting, and two weeks later the first phase of Lombardo's plan went into operation. On March 11 Constantino Davidoff, an Argentinian scrap merchant, arrived at South Georgia with forty-three men to dismantle an old whaling station. Instead of reporting to the British authorities on the island for a visa, Davidoff's party hoisted an Argentinian flag, thus deliberately challenging the British ownership of the islands.

The reaction in far-off Britain was mirth mixed with outrage, but it evidently convinced the Junta that Allara had been right and that Britain would not fight. Instead, Britain's Foreign Secretary, Lord Carrington, appealed to the United States to send a vessel and take the Argentinians off. The U.S. embassy in Buenos Aires was strongly against the idea, which U.S. Ambassador Harry Shlaudeman felt would compromise U.S. neutrality. The American attitude, combined with Britain's apparent unwillingness to act, would have emboldened Galtieri still further.[14]

Davidoff sailed from South Georgia two days later, leaving a handful of men on the island. Two days later, under cover of night, the transport ship *Bahía Paraíso* slipped into Leith harbor carrying 150 Argentinian troops under the command of Lieutenant Alfredo Astiz.[15]

In Buenos Aires itself, any wavering doubts that Galtieri might have harbored about the invasion were almost certainly swept aside by a wave of domestic protest. On March 18, the Mothers of the Plaza de Mayo mounted the largest ever Thursday vigil to protest the disappearance and death of Ana María Martínez, three months pregnant. Galtieri replied by announcing that eighty prisoners were being released, whereupon Emilio Mignone pointed out that most had already been freed. Two days later came the announcement that political parties would be legalized toward the middle of the year, provided they acted "responsibly." The political parties replied robustly by refusing to accept any conditions.[16]

On March 31, thousands of people swarmed into the center of Buenos Aires for what would prove to be the largest and most violent demonstration mounted in six years. In a direct challenge to the Junta the protest was summoned by the outlawed General Confederation of Labor. When the fracas had died down, scores of people had been injured and fifteen hundred arrested. They included all the Confederation leaders, five Mothers, and the son of Nobel Prize winner Adolfo Pérez Esquivel. Galtieri was now cornered. The invasion of the Falklands was his last chance to unify the country and hold his critics at bay.[17]

The Role of the United States

Did the Reagan Administration encourage the invasion of the Falklands? The question was repeatedly asked during and after the war. On January 24 1982 Jesús Iglesias Rouco, an influential Argentinian columnist who was close to Argentina's Foreign Minister, wrote in *La Prensa*: "The U.S. would support all acts leading to the restitution [of the Falklands] including military action." On March 3 another front-page article in *La Prensa* presented Argentina's recovery of the islands as consistent with the U.S. strategy in the South Atlantic toward the Soviet Union. It said that the Reagan Administration had expressed "understanding" of Argentina's position on the Falklands.[18]

No author has uncovered any evidence to show that the Reagan Administration directly encouraged the invasion, but it is far less clear whether the U.S. actively warned the Argentinians against such a drastic move. Indeed, it is hard not to conclude that Galtieri had been encouraged by the endless succession of friendly signals. "The Junta thought they had Washington in their hip pocket, no matter what they did. And that belief was critical in their decision to gobble up the Falklands," wrote Anthony Lewis in one scathing article.[19]

Lewis was particularly offended by an official dinner at the Argentinian embassy in Washington on the evening of April 2 1982—the night of the invasion. It was attended by Jeane Kirkpatrick and several other senior administration figures, including Assistant Secretary of State Thomas Enders and Deputy Secretary of State Walter Stoessel. The timing was extraordinary, and the presence of such a senior contingent was later taken to indicate sympathy for the Argentinian invasion. Kirkpatrick herself added fuel to the fire a few days later in a television discussion at which she pointedly declined to describe the Argentinian operation as "aggression" on the grounds that Argentina claimed sovereignty to the islands.[20]

Kirkpatrick angered the British over this dinner, but at least one British account of the war has given her the benefit of the doubt. According to the *London Sunday Times*, the timing of the dinner had been accidental. Kirkpatrick was offered several dates by the Argentinians and chose the last. There was debate within the Reagan Administration about canceling the invitation, but it was decided that such a snub would compromise any prospect of the United States mediating in the dispute. At this time, the full weight of U.S. diplomacy was geared toward avoiding any hint of favoritism.[21] As a result, wrote the *Sunday Times* team, "many of the Americans present felt they had been set up."[22] Once the actual fighting began, the Reagan Administration would find it even harder to remain neutral.

Over human rights, however, the administration showed outright approval of the Junta. Before the 1978 embargo on U.S. arms sales to Argentina could be lifted, the administration had to certify that human rights had "improved." Here was an opportunity for the new Assistant Secretary of State, Elliott Abrams. In the famous memo that had secured him the post, Abrams had argued that the annual State Department reports be "turned to our policy goals." Now Abrams used them to exonerate Argentina.[23]

The reaction in Buenos Aires was jubilant. "Human Rights Improves in Argentina, According to the U.S.," ran one headline.[24] The paper was right. The report was highly complimentary to Argentina, and on March 2 1982 Secretary of State Alexander Haig used it to argue strongly for a resumption of U.S. aid to Argentina before a congressional committee. The administration proposed a token amount of fifty thousand dollars in military aid to Argentina and Chile for the next fiscal year. Elliott Abrams had fired his opening shots in his information war. Had there really been an "improvement" in human rights? Not for Emilio Mignone and the other relatives—as long as the Junta refused to offer any explanation.

Alfredo Astiz, Angel on the Run

This is not the place to retrace the story of the Falklands war, but it is important to note the extent and nature of the support for the Junta.

Initially Galtieri's gamble appeared to be paying off. Galtieri himself basked in popular approval and his early appearances from the presidential balcony were triumphant.[25] The General Confederation of Labor announced it had put aside its differences with the government and was supporting Argentina's historic claim to the "Malvinas" (Falklands). Even the human rights protests were muted. Mignone and the Mothers still spoke out against the Junta, but the Thursday vigils were smaller.

Gradually, however, the mood changed as the British fleet drew closer, and with it the prospect of war. The occupation of the islands was costing Argentina half a million dollars a day and eating into the country's depleted reserves. Union leaders started to distance themselves from the Junta while continuing to support the cause. Galtieri's first assumption, that the British would not respond, proved a grave mistake. His second collapsed when Alexander Haig's shuttle diplomacy failed, and the United States sided with Britain. At 5:00 A.M. on June 14, after two months of increasingly bloody conflict, the Argentinian high command announced that a ceasefire had gone into effect on the islands.[26] The war had been lost, and with it the military's grand design of holding power indefinitely.

Throughout the crisis, Kirkpatrick tried to maintain a position of neutrality. This showed remarkable conviction and consistency, but it won her few friends. Secretary of State Haig was irked and so were the British.[27] Perhaps even she was dismayed by the vehemence of the anti-American feeling that emerged in Latin America once the United States threw in its lot with Britain, and the warmth with which the "authoritarian" Argentinian Junta embraced "totalitarian" Nicaragua and Cuba. In her earlier 1971 book on Perón she had accurately noted that Argentinian nationalism defined itself partly in terms of distrust of the United States.[28] The same was true throughout much of Latin America. Whatever friendship had grown up between the Junta and the Reagan Adminstration was, it appeared, only skin-deep.[29]

The war was a clear refutation of any notion that "authoritarian" regimes made for good allies. Patricia Derian had downplayed Argentina's security importance to the United States, while the Reagan Administration had gone to the other extreme and exaggerated it. Of the two, Reagan's approach had backfired more spectacularly. Galtieri and his colleagues had forced the United States to choose between its closest European ally and Latin America. It was an unenviable choice which evidently caused particular anguish to Kirkpatrick, but given the importance of the NATO alliance to the Reagan Administration there was really no choice at all.

When it came to the war itself, Argentina's military collapsed igno-miniously. After six years of kidnapping and torturing unarmed civilians, it had no spirit for fighting a real enemy. Indeed, it was perhaps symbolic that the branch of the armed forces which performed most valiantly in the war against Britain—the air force—had been least involved in the dirty war against Argentinians. The dirty war against imaginary subversion had turned Argentina into a pathetic, unreliable ally.

There was something particularly apt in the photo which flashed around the world on April 26. It showed a disheveled, bearded Lieutenant Alfredo Astiz surrendering to British forces on South Georgia. Astiz and his men had given up with barely a fight. When Ana María Martí saw the photo in a Swiss paper, she felt weak at the knees. Martí, as readers will recall, had been abducted by Astiz and tortured at the ESMA. Suddenly the memories of terror and torment came flashing back, and with them the image of Astiz "the Angel" boasting of his prowess at kidnapping un-armed women. Now, at last, the Angel's wings were clipped.

Astiz Invigorates the U.N. Torture Convention

Astiz's capture had one entirely unpredictable consequence. It all but res-cued the U.N.'s faltering attempts to draft a new convention outlawing torture. To recap briefly, there was, it will be recalled, no international convention on torture in existence when the dirty war broke out in Argen-tina in 1976. In 1977 Sweden proposed to fill the gap with a new conven-tion making torture an international crime. The Swedish draft called on states either to prosecute torturers or to extradite them, a system known as "universal jurisdiction." Although this formula was used by other con-ventions on hijacking and hostage-taking, it presented three obvious prac-tical problems: first, whether torturers could be identified; second, how to find proof against them; and third, physically how to arrest them.

Between 1977 and April 1982, as we have seen, the actions of Lieutenant Alfredo Astiz suggested that none of these three obstacles was insur-mountable. Astiz's role at the ESMA had been kidnapping as opposed to interrogation, but he had enough blood on his hands to warrant question-ing under the new convention on torture. Survivors had emerged from the ESMA to testify that Astiz had shot and wounded Dagmar Hagelin and that he had killed at least one other ESMA detainee. By May 1980, when he was traced to Argentina's embassy in South Africa, Astiz was well known outside his own country, particularly in Sweden. The first and second requirements of universal jurisdiction were thus met: torturers could be identified and witnesses found to testity against them. By taking up a post in South Africa, Astiz had shown that torturers could find themselves on foreign soil where it might be easier to arrest them. In South Africa he was able to benefit from diplomatic immunity—although his presence proved an embarrassment even to racist South Africa, which discreetly asked him to leave.[30]

Here is where the situation stood in March 1982, when the U.N. Human Rights Commission met in Geneva to review Sweden's draft torture convention. Five years had passed since Hans Danelius of Sweden's Foreign Ministry had first presented his draft, but there was still no agreement on the key issue of universal jurisdiction. Gabriel Martínez mounted a furious attack against Danelius's draft during the Commission meeting, and he had powerful backing from the Soviet Union, India, and Cuba—none of which wanted to strengthen the U.N.'s powers of investigation. Even Britain and Australia still harbored doubts about whether universal jusridiction could be made to work.[31] The group operated by consensus and the discussion was postponed for yet another year. It was one of Martínez's less publicized victories, but an important one, nonetheless.

Within three months the tables had turned dramatically. Alfredo Astiz found himself not only far from home but in enemy hands. Once again, Sweden and France relived the anguish of 1977, and Hans Danelius had the immense satisfaction of applying to Britain for Astiz's extradition. Once again, it seemed, Astiz had unwittingly breathed life into Danelius's torture convention. Would the government of Margaret Thatcher rise to the challenge?

For a time, it appeared as though it would. Britain repatriated all 190 prisoners captured on South Georgia except for Alfredo Astiz, who was taken by boat to Britain and confined in a military police barracks north of London. There he was questioned on two separate occasions, not by the Swedes or the French, but by a senior British police officer, who put a series of questions to Astiz relating to the two nuns and Dagmar Hagelin. Astiz refused to answer beyond giving his name and rank, as required under the Geneva Conventions. The file on the exchange, such as it was, was dispatched to the Swedish and French governments. On June 10 1982, Astiz was repatriated to Argentina. Four days later, the Argentinian forces surrendered on the Falklands.

Astiz was saved on this occasion not by diplomatic immunity but by the Geneva Conventions, which forbid prisoners from being interrogated, mistreated, or transferred to a third country during a conflict. Britain was acutely aware of the need to abide by the Conventions to prevent any reprisals by Argentina against British prisoners. Were there not other possibilities? Why had Britain itself not prosecuted Astiz on grounds that torture was a crime under international law or, failing that, allowed Dagmar's relatives to file a civil suit against Astiz similar to the one filed in the United States by the Filártigas against the Paraguayan police who had tortured their son to death? At least one lawyer from the Red Cross was of the opinion that this might well have worked—and that it might have set a major precedent for international, and British, law.[32]

So the Angel slipped through the net yet again, after demonstrating both the need for, and the viability of, the new U.N. convention on torture. This left one final avenue open to the relatives of his victims. What would happen once military rule ended in Argentina—as now seemed inevitable after the Falklands/Malvinas conflict? If Argentina's next civilian government was to prosecute military personnel for their actions during the dirty war, then the international campaign against torture would receive a huge boost.

The possibility could not be discounted. Argentinian relatives filed charges against Astiz in a Buenos Aires court. His ordeal was evidently far from over.

26. The Unplugging

They called it "el destape" (the unplugging). Following the Falklands/
Malvinas war, all the emotion that had been bottled up through six long
years of military rule exploded and the human rights campaign entered a
new and decisive phase. The relatives had lived with the disappearances
for six years. Now the cause was taken up by Argentina's nascent political
parties, as a symbol of their determination to restore democracy. Argentina reverberated with demands for accountability—even as the actual killing receded further into the past. This the Reagan Administration could
not, or would not, accept. While Argentinians were recalling Nuremberg,
Elliott Abrams was talking of an "improvement."

On July 17 1982 the Interior Ministry lifted an eight-year ban on political
rallies. The following day it made an even more important concession and
recognized political parties. The same day, five thousand people gathered
in a boxing stadium to hear an address by Raúl Alfonsín, of the Radical
party. Alfonsín was described by one foreign reporter as a "55-year-old
leftist firebrand with a long face and a drooping moustache."[1] The next
few months would reveal Alfonsín to be a shrewd and pragmatic politician
as well as a standard-bearer for the human rights groups. A lawyer by
profession, he had defended political detainees and served as a member of
the board of the Permanent Assembly of Human Rights.

Discredited and disunited, the military twisted and turned in an effort
to control the manner and timetable for a return to civilian rule. It was a
period of bitter recrimination within the armed forces. Leopoldo Galtieri
resigned as president and army commander in chief on June 17. Alfredo
St. Jean, the Interior Minister, replaced him for a month before handing
power over on July 1 1982 to retired Major General Reynaldo Bignone.
Bignone had served as the Secretary to the presidential palace following
the 1976 coup, and he too had an unsavory association with the dirty war.[2]
Within three months of the war, all the officers responsible for the Malvinas disaster had resigned or been dismissed, and the war itself was the

subject of an inquiry. But the army still kept a grip on the Junta and the government, and a hardliner, General Cristino Nicolaides, was appointed the new army commander.[3]

Bignone faced crisis on every side. A new emergency economic program quickly collapsed. Argentina required four billion dollars to cover repayments on its debt in 1982, but its reserves had been drained by the Falklands war and held just 3.5 billion. The central bank kept announcing new rates of exchange, but none succeeded in staunching the hemorrhage of capital out of the country. Bignone conceded the need for wage increases in an effort to mollify the angry unions, but inflation promptly gobbled up the gains, prompting new demands.[4]

The human rights groups were even harder to satisfy. On August 10 the Junta dug in its heels. General Carlos Cerda, the under secretary at the Ministry of the Interior and the army's legal counsel, announced that there would be no list of disappeared persons published and no explanation. Instead, suggested Cerda, the armed forces intended to declare an amnesty before transferring power to the civilians. This was to be the first of several attempts by the military during 1982 and 1983 to exonerate itself, and it was immediately rejected.[5] The army and political parties had already agreed on the formula for political registration and an amnesty for the armed forces was not part of the package. Led by Emilio Mignone's CELS and the Mothers, the human rights groups stiffened the resolve of the political parties.

On September 30 1982 another tragedy accelerated the process and brought Argentina face to face once more with the dirty war. The relatives of Elena Holmberg, the diplomat from the Paris "pilot center" who had been murdered around Christmas 1978, reopened the case. Gregorio Dupont was the first witness at the inquiry, and he testified about how Holmberg had told him of Massera's meetings with the Montoneros in Paris shortly before she was killed by navy officers. A week later Gregorio's brother Marcelo, an advertising executive with four children, disappeared. Marcelo's body turned up shortly afterward. He had been thrown from the top of a building.

Gregorio initially thought that Massera, whose political ambitions still burned, had had Marcelo killed to intimidate Gregorio from disclosing further details. He later found out that his brother was killed by the 601 army intelligence unit, in an apparent attempt further to undermine Massera's political ambitions and make Massera a scapegoat for the dirty war. Massera himself just had time to sue Gregorio Dupont for slander before he was ordered to jail by a judge on a charge of having murdered his lover's husband. Shortly afterward, his connections with the Italian P 2 lodge emerged.[6]

The killing of Marcelo Dupont rekindled the fury of the relatives. On October 5, 7,000 people defied a government ban and swarmed into the Plaza de Mayo. It was called the "march for life," and among its organizers were the two Catholic bishops, Jaime de Nevares and Jorge Novak, who had defied the Church hierarchy and supported the human rights groups during the dark days.

Searching the Graveyards

By now, one issue more than any other summed up the dilemma and anguish of the relatives: the discovery of mass graves. The case of Miguel Angel Sosa started it off. Miguel had disappeared on May 25 1976. His family submitted several habeas corpus petitions, all to no avail. In February 1981, the Interior Ministry unexpectedly wrote saying that Miguel had been found dead two days after his reported disappearance, and that his body could be found in a small cemetery known as Grand Bourg, some eighteen miles west of Buenos Aires.[7]

Emilio Mignone's CELS had taken on the Sosa case, and Mignone himself was still looking for any clues about the fate of his own daughter Mónica, so he went with Sosa's brother to examine the court records of the case. They found an autopsy report, which stated that Miguel had been tortured and shot in the head at close range, together with a letter from the investigating judge to Miguel's family which had—according to the file—been sent to the wrong address and returned to the judge. This story was impossible to believe. Clearly, the investigating judge had either colluded with or been intimidated by the military.

Mignone urged the Sosa family to go public, but they held back and applied instead to have the body exhumed. After months of legal wrangling, permission finally came through. Mignone and the Sosas went to the cemetery to watch the grisly remains being dug up. They had been packed into a cardboard box alongside three other corpses. There was no gravestone, simply a notice carrying the letters "N.N.," short for "nomen nescio" (name unknown).

During the search among the graves, Mignone noticed a small handwritten note stating that if the anonymous bodies were not claimed, they would be removed. It was not the only disturbing discovery. Mignone and the Sosas were told by local inhabitants that throughout 1976 and 1977 army trucks used to pull up at night and unload what they assumed were bodies. The main army base of Campo de Mayo, a notorious concentration camp, was nearby. Mignone concluded that there could be as many as 400 bodies buried in the Grand Bourg cemetery. Although these were victims of army squads, not the navy, it gave him a terrible sense of the fate of his own daughter. At this point the Sosas agreed to publicize their case.

On October 22 Mignone, Augusto Conte MacDonell, and four parents held a press conference at the headquarters of the Permanent Assembly to announce the discovery. The four hundred bodies, said Mignone, appeared to have been buried in cardboard coffins in eighty-eight separate graves. When the Mothers held their next Thursday vigil in the Plaza de Mayo, they were joined by a huge throng. The chief of police held up the traffic and the Mothers were publicly applauded. After six years of vilification, they were suddenly being recognized. Plagued by self-doubt and desperate for proof that someone had resisted the Junta during the dark days, Argentinians turned to the crazy Mothers. It had taken a mass grave to bring their fellow countrymen to their senses.[8]

The discovery of the grave led to a major confrontation between the human rights movement and Argentina's judges, prompting Mignone to warn that judges as well as soldiers could expect to face charges once civilian rule was restored. The effect of the disclosures on the Mothers was profound and traumatic. Most of the relatives knew in their hearts that their children were dead, in spite of the Mothers' slogan—"aparición con vida, castigo a los culpables" (appearance alive, punishment to the guilty). Rene Epelbaum, who lost three children, remembers the feeling. Part of her cried out to know the truth, however ghastly; another part shrank from facing it, hoping against hope that they could still be alive. Least of all did she want to face the ultimate horror of seeing her strong sons as grinning skulls.[9]

Many mothers, like Rene Epelbaum, had good reasons for not visiting the cemeteries. They knew that the corpses had been mutilated or were far too decomposed to be identifiable. In addition, most of the disappeared persons had been too young to have full medical records, and this too made identification difficult. In the rare case that a body could be identified, the relatives were called to a police station, shown a few bones, and asked to sign a receipt. It was casually and cruelly done, like so many of their encounters with officialdom, and the Mothers—a determined bunch—wanted none of it. Some of their fellow countrymen suspected that they didn't want to face the truth. But in early 1983, as the Mothers led the exhilarating charge to democracy, it hardly seemed to matter.

The discovery of the graves also triggered off yet another wave of hostility against the Junta abroad. Two hundred and eighty-nine people with Italian nationality had disappeared in Argentina and Italians began to ask why their government had raised no protest. Spain let it be known that 164 Spanish nationals had disappeared. West Germany published its own figure (48) as did Brazil (9) and Peru (6). In Uruguay, where 123 people had disappeared, a protest by eighty Mothers was broken up by police.[10] At the end of January, Congressman Michael Barnes, chairman of the House Subcommittee on Latin American Affairs, visited Argentina, met with human rights groups, and announced that he was still opposed to a resumption of American military aid. The pressure was growing. Retribution was slow in coming, but it was coming nonetheless.

Each challenge by the relatives was met with threats and intimidation. On August 24 1982 fifteen armed men forced their way into the house where the vice-president of the Mothers, María Antokoletz, was living. Antokoletz was away at the time, but she found crude threats painted on the walls when she returned. Anti-Semitic slogans appeared on walls in the Jewish quarter. When a journalist exposed the campaign in her radio show, she herself received telephone threats.

On November 17, the army chief of staff Edgardo Calvi gave his blessing to the harassment by declaring that the Mothers were "financed by terrorists." Five Mothers immediately found their walls covered by threatening notices, and Emilio Mignone found that someone had used a spray can on the wall of his building, accusing Mónica of being a terrorist. He immediately asked a judge to subpoena General Calvi. On December 5, two of Mignone's colleagues at CELS received threatening phone calls warning that there were two graves reserved for them in a cemetery. On January 1, a phony bomb was placed in the doorway of Pérez Esquivel's Justice and Peace Service. A week later Edgardo Pimentel, president of the Permanent Assembly, announced that threats had been made against his two-year-old grandson. Abroad, Amnesty International launched a special "harassment action."[11]

The few months that followed the war left the military more detested, more despised, than ever before. The five main political parties had formed a single group to negotiate with the military. They agreed to delay the holding of elections until October 1983, and the actual transition until February 1984, but refused to promise the military an amnesty in advance. It all combined to create an unsettling atmosphere. The unions declared the first general strike under military rule on December 7 1982. Three days later, ten thousand people joined the Mothers for a protest. A week later a huge rally by the political parties attracted one hundred thousand, and a demonstrator was killed by the police.[12] On Christmas Eve, 1982, Argentina was still a deeply troubled nation, as it had been five years earlier following the kidnapping of the twelve Mothers at the Church of the Holy Cross. The one word that was on no one's lips was "improvement."

The U.S. Sides with the Junta

During the Falklands war, the Reagan Administration set aside its plans to resume arms sales to Argentina. Taking Britain's side in the conflict had involved a total freeze on even the spare parts that were already in the pipeline. When this restriction was lifted on September 29 1982, it was time to reconsider the wider 1978 arms embargo. In spite of the upheavals in Argentina itself, the issue in Washington was still whether Argentina complied with the conditions of the 1981 law. Had human rights improved? Had there been sufficient progress in accounting for the disappearances?

Early in February 1983, Elliott Abrams answered with a decisive yes for the second successive year. The annual State Department country report on Argentina included the following sentence: "The Argentine government has received approximately 6,000 requests for information on the whereabouts of disappeared persons and is believed to have provided information to family members on the deaths and in some instances the location of the remains of the disappeared in about 1,450 cases."[13] This suggested that one fifth of the disappearances had indeed been accounted for, and that one of the two crucial conditions was well on the way to being met. But was it true?

All the information coming out of Argentina suggested that the exact reverse was the case, and that the military was making plans to ensure that the information would never come out, even after the return to civilian rule. The possibility of a Nuremberg trial was being widely mentioned in the press, and the soldiers were worried. General Carlos Cerda, the army's legal counsel, had let it be known that a decree was being prepared to prevent any investigation into the disappearances. On November 13 1982, the army proposed what it termed a fifteen-point "concertación" (agree-ment) with the political parties. This too insisted there should be no in-vestigation after the elections. The parties, which had set up a single group to negotiate with the military, flatly rejected the demand.[14]

It was against this background that the U.S. State Department report appeared, claiming that the Junta had accounted for 1,450 disappearances. It was immediately spotted and challenged by the human rights groups. By now the system was fine-tuned. Juan Méndez, a lawyer who had been illegally detained under PEN during the rule of Isabel Perón and who now represented Americas Watch on Capitol Hill, contacted his office in New York and Emilio Mignone in Buenos Aires. Aryeh Neier, the executive director of Americas Watch, appeared before the Foreign Relations Com-mittee on March 16 1983 to deliver a blistering rebuke to Abrams's human rights bureau, and Emilio Mignone's CELS began a study to discover exactly how many families had indeed been informed.

Mignone selected 1,100 cases of disappearances from the 4,464 in the files of the Permanent Assembly and sent a detailed questionnaire to all the families. Somewhat to his surprise, he received 607 answers. Of these, only eighteen families (three percent) said they had been contacted, and of the eighteen only two said they had been able to recover any remains. None had been told what had happened to their child. Mignone produced an impressive document—factual, detailed, and well argued. Mignone's daughter Isabel translated it into English, performing one last small service for her disappeared sister Mónica.[15]

How and why had the human rights bureau made such a blunder? The material on Argentina was prepared at the U.S. embassy in Buenos Aires by John Bushnell, the former ARA official who had fought Jerry Shestack and Patt Derian over the disappearances and had consistently expressed sympathy for the Junta. Throughout the congressional hearings in 1981, Bushnell had pleaded for a resumption of U.S. military aid to Argentina, loyally keeping the Argentinian embassy informed of the political currents. Bushnell was considered so sympathetic to the Junta that when he re-placed Claus Ruser at the U.S. embassy in Buenos Aires in the final stages of the Falklands war, the move was presented by one paper as an attempt by the Reagan Administration to "appease" Argentina for siding with Britain.[16]

Emilio Mignone recalls several strange conversations with John Bush-nell during 1982 and 1983. Bushnell said how worried the military were about their safety and the possibility of acts of vengeance against their

families—this at a time when Mignone and the relatives were being subjected to a campaign of intimidation. The mood and the personnel at the
U.S. embassy in 1982 were totally out of sympathy with the relatives and
their desire for accountability. Instead, the embassy struggled to present
the best possible case for the Junta and to keep embarrassing disclosures
to a minimum. It was assumed that no good would come of it if the
military were harassed.

As a result, the embassy even inadvertently turned its back on three
young Americans—Jon Pirmín Azorena, Billy Lee Hunt and Toni Agatina
Motta—who had disappeared. When the Falklands war erupted, most of
the embassy staff in Buenos Aires were evacuated to Montevideo and
thousands of documents were destroyed to prevent a repeat of the Iranian
hostage crisis. Among the documents was the list of disappeared persons
compiled by Tex Harris and Blanca Vollenweider in 1977 and 1978. That
list contained the names of Azorena and Hunt. (Toni Agatina Motta disappeared in 1980.) [17]

Throughout 1982 the U.S. embassy denied that any Americans had disappeared during the dirty war. It was not until May 19 1983, after the
consulate requested information from the State Department in Washington and was sent a copy of the old files on Hunt and Azorena, that the
embassy finally reversed its position and confirmed the three disappearances. [18] After reviewing the files, Ambassador Shlaudeman was able to
confirm in a cable: "The three cases are sensitive because of possible involvement of Argentina police and military forces." [19]

Bushnell's 1983 country report on Argentina was full of subtle distor-
tions intended to show the Junta in the best possible light: little phrases,
such as "disappeared persons had been killed at the hands of terrorist
groups," which were hard to disprove, hard to spot. This was the language
of clientism, not human rights. Emilio Mignone's friends in New York
had initiated an exhaustive analysis of the reports the previous year and
found them subtly slanted towards "allies" of the United States like Argentina and El Salvador and slanted against left-wing foes like Nicaragua. [20]
The distinction between "totalitarian" and "authoritarian" had not disappeared with Abrams completely, after all. Yet in the case of Argentina it
made no sense. What could the United States achieve by identifying with
a discredited military regime that was about to surrender power except
resentment among the civilians who would take over?

What the U.S. attitude probably did was prolong Argentina's agony
and encourage the Junta to dig in its heels. On April 28 1983, aware that

Argentina's political parties would not agree to an amnesty, the Junta be-gan to lay the groundwork for its own amnesty with the publication of "the final document on the military junta on the struggle against subver-sion and terrorism." "God," observed the document portentously, "will be the final judge." It then repeated the old lies, greatly exaggerating the threat from the revolutionary groups. Of the twenty-five thousand subver-sives, it claimed, fifteen thousand were combatants. There was no apology, no expression of regret for the carnage.[21]

Adolfo Pérez Esquivel, the Nobel Prize winner, broke off a hunger fast to lead 25,000 people on a protest march. In Rome, the Pope spoke to fifty thousand pilgrims about the tragedy of the disappeared in Argentina, while the Vatican newspaper complained that the "final document" had raised "new and, if possible, more anguishing questions." Sandro Pertini, the Italian president, sent a cable to the Junta protesting against the "chill-ing cynicism" of the document. The Junta portrayed Pertini as an emotional old man before replying formally that he had interfered in Argentina's internal affairs. Pertini kept up the correspondence with a letter saying that "all mankind should feel offended." At the same time, the Italian Foreign Ministry warned Argentina that it might break off relations unless the Junta changed its tune.[22]

The Reagan Administration stayed silent for three weeks before issuing a muted statement on May 17:

> We share the sense of disappointment others have expressed that an occasion has been lost to begin the resolution of this question. It is an issue which the Argentines themselves must resolve. We have consistently encouraged the authorities to provide as complete a report as possible on the fate of the disappeared.

"That simpering comment," protested liberal columnist Anthony Lewis, "was the logical result of the Jeane Kirkpatrick theory that now informs U.S. human rights policy: that we should be more tolerant of 'authori-tarian' than of 'totalitarian,' i.e., communist, governments. The theory has been applied with special care to Argentina."[23]

The Relatives Triumph

The Mothers of the Plaza de Mayo watched all these events with a certain detachment. They had never asked for favors from the outside world. If the U.S. Government was going to side with them, so much the better; if the United States felt more comfortable siding with the generals, so be it. With the enemy cornered, it made even less difference. With branches all over Latin America, and support groups across Europe, the Mothers had changed beyond all recognition from the small group of fourteen frightened women who had made their way to the Plaza de Mayo in 1977.

Visitors to the "casa de las madres" on the Calle Uruguay still came away with an impression of disorganization. They would find groups of elderly women standing around, absentmindedly cleaning cups or wiping the sink while they denounced the latest political scandal. No one seemed to know where the money came from but there was clearly no shortage, and according to one estimate the income in 1983 reached almost half a million dollars. Some of it came from the 5,000 members, most of it from a seemingly endless series of human rights prizes and foreign donations.

By 1983, they had grown into a rich and powerful conglomerate with impeccable international connections. The Mothers had been constantly traveling for six years, feeding foreign journalists with quotable quotes and goading the armed forces. The stocky figure of Hebe de Bonafini and the white scarves had come to personify Argentina's restless, uncompromising, human rights movement. Each concession by the Junta and each discovery of a secret grave only served to vindicate their long struggle.

As a result, when Hebe de Bonafini and María Antokoletz arrived in Europe early in 1983 they were received like heads of state. In Madrid they met Felipe González Márquez, the Spanish prime minister. Then it was on to Paris for a session with President Mitterrand, who recalled that he himself had protested outside the Argentinian embassy while he was a deputy. Then it was on to Rome for an audience with Italian president Sandro Pertini and the Pope. In each capital they handed over a list of nationals from that country who had disappeared in Argentina.

It was the Mothers' fourth meeting with Pertini, and the third time they had met with the Pope. They told Pertini that the disappearances simply had to be explained before the transition to democracy. Argentina's new constitutional government should not, they insisted, be expected to inherit such a dreadful legacy. The international pressure had to be maintained. They were equally forthright with the Pope. The two women bluntly returned to one of their favorite themes—that they had been betrayed by the Catholic Church in Argentina. The Pope was taken aback, but it was not the first time he had heard the complaint. María Antokoletz continued on to West Berlin to open an exhibition on Argentina, while

Hebe de Bonafini returned in triumph to Argentina. She was greeted at the airport by over a hundred Mothers wearing white scarves. It had been an extraordinary three weeks. Outside their own country, the Mothers were now being treated like heads of state, their every word recorded by respectful journalists; Argentina's diplomats, in contrast, found it hard to get past secretaries.

In Argentina it was different. Indeed, it was hard to tell whether the Mothers' weekly Thursday vigils did more to unsettle or to uplift Argentinians. On balance, with the Junta giving ground, the effect was probably uplifting; but everyone was aware that the Mothers would not withdraw obligingly from the scene after the Junta went. "If the problem of disappearances is not solved, the next constitutional government will find them a formidable pressure group," predicted one newspaper profile.

They presented an uncompromising front as the October elections drew closer. Other groups, less secure and with broader concerns than just human rights, found them arrogant and irritating. After one Thursday vigil the Mothers streamed over to the headquarters of the labor federation and began to taunt the unionists over their ambivalent attitude toward the disappearances. Some goons descended and started to beat up the women with sticks.[24] It was an ugly confrontation between two allies, but it was also symptomatic of the brittle mood in Buenos Aires as the elections drew nearer. The air was full of talk of another coup. There had been sporadic acts of political violence throughout the year, and another disappearance—that of Rubén Alberto Alvarez—was reported on September 17.

Overshadowing all was the escalating tension between the politicial parties and the military. In September 1983, with elections just over a month away, the military made a third desperate attempt to head off any investigation into the disappearances, by publishing a so-called pacification law nullifying all penal actions against terrorists and military. Since the terrorists were mostly dead, the military was effectively exonerating itself of the atrocities. Once again, like the April "final document," it was resoundingly rejected.[25]

So, inevitably, the disappearances became the dominant issue as elections drew closer. The firmest and most uncompromising position was taken by Raúl Alfonsín, the candidate of the Radical party. Carrying a copy of the 1853 constitution on the hustings, Alfonsín fought a vigorous campaign against his Peronist rival and emerged the clear winner with 52 percent of the vote. His triumph was helped by his unswerving position on disappearances, the dominant issue of the campaign. He had rejected the military's self-amnesty from the start and promised to restore respect for human rights. His own record suggested he would stick to the promise. The rival Peronists, in contrast, suffered from the fact that Isabel Perón had imposed the state of siege in 1974 and turned a blind eye to disappearances by the Triple A death squads. In addition, the Peronists seemed unsure about whether to prosecute the military or accommodate them.

Alfonsín's election victory brought out a sense of elation and release in Argentina which had foreign correspondents burbling sentimentally about lovers holding hands in the parks and spring in the air. On December 9, the U.S. Congress finally agreed to lift the 1978 arms embargo,[26] and the Mothers of the Plaza de Mayo called out ten thousand sympathizers for their last protest march against the military. The following day, December 10 1983 Alfonsín was inaugurated president. It was thirty-five years to the day since the adoption of the U.N.'s Universal Declaration of Human Rights.

The newly elected Chamber of Deputies had the immense satisfaction of abolishing the Junta's self-amnesty as its first official act. Upstairs in the gallery, the Mothers watched and applauded, still wearing their white scarves. The doubts would come later.

27. Betrayal in Geneva

As 1982 gave way to 1983, and the relatives of the disappeared closed in on the military Junta that had killed their children, the one place they expected support was at the United Nations and its pioneering Working Group on Disappearances.

The group had been established early in 1980 when the Junta was at its most confident. Throughout the next two difficult years, it had kept faith with the relatives and they had responded by making it one of the best-informed and most effective operations in the U.N. Now the Junta was crumbling and the relatives were moving in for the kill. Few crimes in history had received more publicity than the disappearances, nor generated more anger. The U.N. group had confronted Gabriel Martínez and perfected its working procedures. Now, surely, was the time to support the demand for accountability and to help take some of the anguish out of Argentina's transition to democracy. Now, surely, was the time for the United Nations to apply some pressure to the Junta.

As in previous years, the first all-important clue about the group's intentions would come in its latest report, and February 1983 found the relatives back at the Palace of Nations, draped over sofas, waiting for the publication. It was reminiscent of September 1980 when the relatives had come to Geneva for the first time.[1] Here was Patrick Rice, the tall Irish priest who served as the coordinator of FEDEFAM, the Latin American federation of relatives. By now FEDEFAM had affiliates in ten countries of Latin America and support groups throughout Western Europe.

Here, too, were Hebe de Bonafini and María Antokoletz from the Argentinian Mothers, half-way through their European tour. And here was María de Mariani from the Argentinian Grandmothers, still looking resolute and still wearing a tweed suit and no-nonsense bonnet. De Mariani's granddaughter, Clara, would now be approaching her seventh birthday, and her grandmother was determined that the U.N. group should continue to press the Junta. Emilio Mignone from CELS had important work back in Argentina, but he had not given up entirely on the U.N. after his bruising encounter with Gabriel Martínez. Mignone sent a detailed communication to the group on June 7 1982.

While the Argentinian relatives found themselves stronger and more confident than ever at the start of 1983, it was a very different story elsewhere on the continent. By now the epidemic of disappearances had spread far beyond Argentina. FEDEFAM's literature claimed that no less than ninety thousand people had disappeared in thirteen different Latin American countries. This startling statistic bore little resemblance to official estimates, but that was no reason to dismiss it out of hand. Official estimates, when they existed, were always far too low.

One new vistor to Geneva was Ramón Custodio, a doctor from Honduras who had set up an independent human rights commission in Tegucigalpa. Custodio had monitored an ominous increase in disappearances, from ten in 1981 to twenty-five in 1982. Roberto Cuéllar, from El Salvador's "Socorro Juridico" (Legal Aid), was also there, denouncing the latest outrage in El Salvador with characteristic intensity. But Marianella García Villas, from the independent Salvadoran Human Rights Commission (CDHES) was absent. She had slipped back into El Salvador to investigate charges that the army was using chemical weapons against civilian populations, ignoring the warnings of friends that it might prove very dangerous. She was expected in Geneva before the end of the U.N. Human Rights Commission.

This was the first time in Geneva for Rosario de Ibarra, an attractive talkative middle-aged woman from Mexico. On April 19 1975 her son had been picked up off the streets by Mexican police in plain clothes. He would be twenty-eight years old today. "I don't want to hate anyone," she explained, before making it plain that she did. She had already caused acute embarrassment to the government in Mexico by standing for president on a platform of human rights. She was a natural choice to head the Mexico chapter of FEDEFAM.

Juan Salazar had come to Geneva to represent relatives of the hundreds of people who disappeared in Chile following the 1973 coup. Salazar was a retired railway worker, with the calluses still on his hands, still searching for a missing son. And here, gazing out at the Alps was another new face. Twenty-five-year-old Zenaida Velásquez, from Honduras, did not speak English and was new to the peculiar business of human rights lobbying. She was still reeling from the shock of losing her young brother, who had been taken off his motorcycle in downtown Tegucigalpa and had subsequently disappeared. She was shy and out of place in Geneva. The older women were protective toward her, fending off questions and buy-ing her coffee. Under normal circumstances, they would have had little in common with her except language, but here in Geneva they shared the same grief and the same goal.

It was another decisive moment in Gabriel Martínez's long war against the United Nations. Would he now be forced to give ground like his mili-tary masters back in Buenos Aires? The answer was no. When the relatives opened the new report they found one crucial omission and two damaging admissions.[2]

First the omission: the written appendices that contained the relatives' oral testimony had been dropped. The significance of this would have been hard to explain to the Reagan Administration, which complained about the cost of paperwork in the United Nations. Yet written reports, as has been noticed above, carry a value far beyond their monetary cost.[3] Here, to the besieged relatives, was a clear statement of their government's mis-deeds. Here was tangible proof that they had taken their own campaign to the United Nations and that the United Nations had responded. Here was something that would be thumbed through, brought out at branch meetings of FEDEFAM in San Salvador, Ayacucho, or Medellín. These U.N. reports acted like glue. They had unified a human rights movement across Latin America and linked it to friends outside. Without the written appendices, the U.N. Working Group on Disappearances had lost much of its value.

And the admissions? By 1983, the U.N. group had submitted 1,377 dis-appearances to Martínez. Not one case had been explained. When it pre-sented Martínez with a fresh batch of seven hundred cases in December 1982, Martínez had told the group that they were being investigated and the relatives "informed" of the results. When the U.S. State Department had made a similar claim it had been challenged and exposed, but the U.N. group took Martínez at face value. Instead of continuing to support the relatives during their moment of triumph, the group had thrown in its lot with the discredited Junta. It was a strange and tragic decision, and the first signal that Theo van Boven's dismissal would hurt the United Nations and human rights.

Kurt Herndl Sides with the Junta

U.N. Secretary General Javier Pérez de Cuéllar had moved quickly to choose a successor to Theo van Boven on February 18 1982. Kurt Herndl, from Austria, had already served in the U.N. between 1969 and 1977, spending the last two years in Waldheim's entourage. His task on return- ing to the Austrian foreign service was to defend his government against citizen complaints before the European Court of Human Rights. This he did with some success, taking on ten cases and losing only one, and it left him with an instinctive sympathy for governments and a corresponding suspicion of individuals who challenged their authority. This was precisely what Pérez de Cuéllar was seeking in van Boven's successor. Herndl would not rock the boat. He was—like his Austrian nationality—"neutral."[4]

There was just one shadow on the record. Herndl's departure from the U.N. in 1977 was made less painful by a "golden handshake." Given that his leaving was seen as being in the interests of the U.N., some asked what had changed in 1982 when he was reinstated. Others considered that he should repay the money. This did not happen. There is no sug- gestion of any impropriety by Herndl, but there was some grumbling among some of his colleagues, who felt that all this jarred with the new Secretary General's desire to improve staff morale and tighten up staff procedures.

It was not all that surprising. Pérez de Cuéllar had set a strange example by promoting the man who had masterminded his campaign, Emilio de Olivares, to the post of his executive assistant through two senior staff levels in considerably less time than his U.N. service justified. This was pointed out by the staff's advisory Appointments and Promotions Board. Technically, Pérez de Cuéllar was not bound by seniority rules in choosing his assistant, but this could only be discouraging to other lesser mortals. Olivares, who was highly autocratic, effectively usurped staffing policy. He once suggested to the U.N. personnel office that a brother of Vice- President George Bush might play a role in the U.N. Personnel's reaction was that this would be highly inappropriate. In the event, a firm with Bush on the board was hired to advise on the U.N.'s insurance plans.

Theo van Boven had worked himself to the bone through four years, snatching a week of holiday here and there, but Kurt Herndl delayed his arrival in Geneva for almost four months—compromising preparations for the 1982 session of the U.N. Sub-Commission. When he finally arrived, Herndl was the object of curiosity and some resentment among journalists who had known and liked van Boven. They even pounced on the infor- mation that Herndl had accepted a box of Jaffa grapefruit from the local Israeli mission. Israel was on the U.N.'s list of "desperados," and this was a gesture that could have irritated Arab delegations.

This trivial episode appeared in the papers, because like most neutral people Herndl gave journalists nothing more substantial to write about. Indeed, he kept such a low profile during his first few months in Geneva that no one was sure he even existed. When he finally emerged to give the traditional press conference before the 1983 Human Rights Commission, the audience was struck by his bizarre phraseology. Herndl talked with a rapt expression on his face about "advisory services," and "clearing-houses." "Standards" was his favorite word: it seemed to excite an almost mystical fervor. But real life—and death—was not allowed to intrude. The era of U.N. jargon was back, but with a purpose. Herndl used it as a smokescreen, to avoid taking a position critical of governments.

Herndl was chosen because—unlike van Boven—his personality and nationality appeared neutral. But as van Boven had shown, U.N. officials could not remain neutral when it came to human rights. They were either for governments or for their victims. Herndl, like Javier Pérez de Cuéllar, was a man of government.[5] As a result, a profound shift now began to take place. After four years of close alliance, the U.N. human rights secretariat began to confront NGOs over disappearances—just when the relatives in Argentina were at last turning the tide against the Junta.

Herndl soon signaled his intention to disengage from the battlefield. He insisted that he wanted to maintain an "open door," but some NGOs usually found it shut in their face or Herndl disinclined to talk seriously. The irritating procedural rules of yesteryear began to resurface. Documents would be returned with a request that they be shortened by two hundred words, or mysteriously held up for several days, appearing too late to be useful in the item under debate. They were all little skirmishes, but they added up to a larger war. When Hebe de Bonafini and María Antokoletz, the two Mothers, arrived in Geneva in February 1983, Herndl refused to see them, pleading pressure of other work. During this trip, they met the Pope, two presidents, and a prime minister, but they found the door of the U.N. secretariat barred to them. A local Swiss newspaper published a damaging article. Herndl saw the Mothers the following day, but without any enthusiasm.

Other U.N. officials, more junior, took their lead from the new U.N. human rights chief. By February 1983—four years after the brutal murder of the Guatemalan politician Alberto Fuentes Mohr—the U.N. had still not found anyone to investigate human rights in unhappy Guatemala. Herndl compounded the failure and produced a three-page document for the 1983 U.N. Human Rights Commission that simply listed the documents submitted to the U.N. over the previous twelve months. The U.N. information office then rubbed salt in the wound with a dreadful blunder. Delegates at the 1983 Commission learned from a U.N. press release that a U.N. rapporteur had finally been appointed to investigate human rights in Guatemala. His name was Alberto Fuentes Mohr. The next day a newspaper reported that the U.N. had apppointed a dead man to head its Guatemala inquiry.[6]

U.N. information officials were angry and embarrassed, but they had only themselves to blame. An Algerian official with no experience or interest in human rights had been asked to compile the release. He had worked from something that landed on his desk bearing the name "Fuentes Mohr" without reading it. If he had, he would have realized that the document was an appeal to the U.N. from the son of the murdered Guatemalan politician.[7] Such a bizarre mistake might not have occurred if Herndl's office had conveyed commitment to human rights instead of "neutrality," and of course it played straight into the hands of the Guatemalan regime. Jeane Kirkpatrick's charge that the U.N. was involved in a "politicized" attack on Guatemala was totally wrong. It was the exact reverse. There was no attack at all.

Colville Surrenders to Martínez

Mark Colville, the aristrocratic British chairman of the U.N. Working Group on Disappearances, was another self-proclaimed "neutral." But Colville's "neutrality" was even more of a fiction than Herndl's. He had been totally charmed by Gabriel Martínez.

During 1982, Colville told anyone who cared to listen that it was time to steer the U.N. group toward more tranquil waters, but in fact, under his captaincy, the group was beginning to acquire an openly political role. The days when Colville had considered Martínez a scoundrel were long gone. Their friendship had even survived the war between Britain and Argentina, which had destroyed the political career of Colville's cousin Peter Carrington. During the war, Martínez spearheaded a virulent campaign against Britain in the U.N., fighting a rear-guard action against British economic sanctions and appealing to the innate hatred of colonialism among other developing countries. It was, as usual, brilliantly done, and more than one British delegate was seen stalking out of a meeting, flushed and humiliated.

Mark Colville, however, never wavered. He chuckles at the recollection of one loud argument, during the war, at a luxurious golf club which was a favorite watering hole. The two discussed the respective merits of their positions—in English. Here, once again, was Martínez pluckily defending an impossible position. Colville was entranced.

Colville found it easy to rationalize. If the working group was going to survive, let alone make any headway in uncovering the dark secrets of Argentina's dirty war, then Martínez's cooperation would be indispensable. Colville said this so often that everyone assumed it to be true, and the more that the two men were seen in each other's company, the easier it became to assume that Argentina was indeed cooperating. Yet a review of Martínez's "dialogue" with the U.N. group during the critical months of 1982 shows that he did the exact reverse. He stonewalled.

Following the tumultuous session of the U.N. Human Rights Commission in February 1982, Martínez changed the direction of his strategy. With van Boven gone, the U.N. secretariat cowed, and Colville coopted, all he had to do was to appear to cooperate without yielding any information whatsoever. In this he apparently had the full approval of the Reagan Administration. Michael Novak, as Martínez cabled back to Buenos Aires, had publicly complimented Argentina for "cooperating" with the U.N.[8] In fact, the full extent of Martínez's "cooperation" had been to attend the group's meetings and harangue its members.

On the surface, at least, the group maintained the pressure. During 1982 it asked the Junta to explain no less than 637 disappearances, bringing to 1,337 the total number transmitted since 1980. This was only one quarter of the number on the files of the Permanent Assembly in Buenos Aires, yet it still amounted to an extraordinary challenge by the U.N. against a member government. When it met Martínez in December 1982, the group asked him about the wave of attacks on human rights groups in Argentina. It had also pressed for further information on the missing infants, citing six more cases that it had received from Argentinian Grandmothers.[9]

But by now Martínez knew from Colville that there would be no annexes, and thus no written testimony in the next report. On September 15 he wrote a long letter to Colville praising the group's "discretion." His confidence must have increased further when, on November 4 1982 he received an extraordinary note from Colville. The note announced that the group was sending over files on another one hundred eighty disappearances and asked for information on another three infants and thirteen women "who were reportedly pregnant at the time of disappearance." But

Colville completely undermined the effect with a scribbled PS: "1. I have already thanked you verbally for our delicious lunch at the golf club but would wish formally to do so again. 2 thank you for the information . . . about sr Dupont . . . C o C." This last comment, referred, presumably, to the assassination of Marcelo Dupont, which had just occurred in Argentina. But whatever Colville learned from Martínez about this controversial killing he did not share it with his colleagues on the group or with Tom McCarthy, his principal U.N. aide. Quiet diplomacy was once again at work.[10]

Martínez must have been encouraged by this letter. Whatever pressure he felt from the group would have been more than offset by the knowledge that he had a friend in its chairman. This allowed him to brush off the group's efforts to locate the disappeared infants. Argentinian Foreign Ministry files show that on September 28 1982 Martínez received a reply from Buenos Aires to his request for information on the six disappeared infants. Two of the six, Humberto Ernesto and Elena Noemí Francisetti, had disappeared with their mother María. The Foreign Ministry note pointed out that their father, Renato Colauti, had not married their mother and that together with his "well-known connection with terrorist activity," this made it impossible to say whether the two children had been forcibly abducted or spirited away by their parents.[11]

Martínez repeated this in a December 2 letter to the U.N. group, and added his own chilling personal touch: "In the notes of the working group there is mention of cases of children who could hypothetically have been born from women supposedly pregnant at the moment of their presumed disappearance. . . . Even if we accept the hypothesis that the person in question was pregnant at the moment of her presumed disappearance, we could not possibly conclude that in general these cases resulted in a birth." It was as if Martínez was writing of objects, to be crushed and broken, not flesh and blood. These comments were entirely of his own invention. It shows very clearly how he refined what he received from Buenos Aires— on his own initiative.[12]

It was all lies, of course. Shortly afterward, on February 28, María de Mariani, president of the Grandmothers, held a press conference in Geneva to announce that her organization had located five infants adopted by military families, including little Elena Noemí and her brother Humberto.[13] So they had not, after all, been "spirited away" by their "terrorist" parents, as Martínez had claimed. De Mariani then asked Colville that the U.N. group put pressure on the Junta to have the infants returned to their grandparents. This would not happen. At this point, the Grandmothers also lost any illusions about the United Nations.[14]

This explains why the group's third report lacked the all-important appendices, but contained its two shocking admissions. Each of those 1,337 disappearances registered by the group had been as brutal and traumatic as the kidnapping of Mónica Mignone. Not one had been solved, not a single infant located as a result of the boxes of files that had been sent over to the Argentinian mission in Geneva.

Whatever Colville might claim, Martínez had not "cooperated." He had remained a loyal and diligent servant of Argentina's military rulers right up to the end. Yet the U.N. group had made no effort to confront Martínez, and it compounded this failure by omitting the appendices. Martínez's lies would at least have been exposed if they had been public. Gone indeed were the heady days of 1980, when Colville had suggested that the new group might intervene on behalf of the American hostages in Teheran.

Gabriel Martínez had bounced back in spectacular style. On January 19 1983 he wrote a letter to Kurt Herndl. Herndl had just been promoted to the level of U.N. Assistant Secretary General by Javier Pérez de Cuéllar. "My sincere congratulations," purred Martínez. "You are carrying out your task with brilliance and efficiency."[15] From the Junta's viewpoint, this was undoubtedly true.

28. The Politicized United Nations

By siding with Gabriel Martínez, Mark Colville took a far-reaching political gamble. Like Elliott Abrams, Colville was convinced that human rights could only flourish in a Western-style democracy, founded on multiparty elections. At the same time, he concluded that the transition from dictatorship to democracy would only be jeopardized by humiliating the military and demanding a strict accounting for their past crimes. Not only could this make them more reluctant to surrender power, but it would make them an unreliable, embittered, partner in government.

This was a perfectly respectable position. While it was clear that any nation which has suffered from an immense trauma must somehow expiate the past, history offered no standard formula for how to achieve this—least of all when the trauma has been caused by a nation's own soldiers. Nazi Germany offered the clearest example. But the Nuremberg trials were imposed on a defeated Germany by the victorious Allies, and they probably proved more cathartic for the Allies, who had failed the Jews, than for the Germans. More relevant to Argentina, perhaps, was the decision by the Allies to free thousands of Nazi criminals, on the argument that postwar Germany could not tolerate a massive witchhunt.[1]

What position should the United Nations take? Argentina's own human rights groups and their friends abroad were adamant that the killers had to be punished and justice seen to be done if Argentinian democracy was to take root. On this reading, the U.N.'s role should be to present the human rights facts dispassionately, as Patricia Derian had done at the U.S. State Department, and leave it to the politicians to weigh what action to take.

There was one precedent. In 1980, Fernando Volio Jiménez, a former Costa Rican foreign minister, had visited Equatorial Guinea, the West African country, for the U.N. Human Rights Commission. The dictator Macias Nguema had just been overthrown and the country was totally devastated. Volio recommended an imaginative package whereby the U.N.

would provide a program of relief aid on condition that the country's new rulers held elections and introduced democracy. But Volio had no advice on whether or not to prosecute Nguema, who was duly tried and sentenced to death.[2]

Colville took Volio's approach a huge—even fateful—step further. He decided that the best role for the U.N.'s human rights machinery would be to act as a political mediator and absolve Argentina's military from past crimes in the interests of democracy. This dictated his strategy not just toward Argentina, but toward Guatemala as well. During 1985 Colville's approach became official U.N. policy. In the language of the Reagan Administration, this meant "politicizing" the U.N. This was rich in irony, remembering the tongue-lashing that Emilio Mignone and the International Commission of Jurists had received from Colville's friend Gabriel Martínez for their "politically motivated" statements in Geneva.

Colville dropped hints of political ambitions throughout 1982. Theo van Boven recalls a final session with the disappearances group before he left Geneva. Colville, he says, gave the group details of discussions he had held in London with Roberto Molteni, who was Gabriel Martínez's right-hand man in Geneva until he was transferred to London. These discussions concerned the Falklands war. Colville gave the impression that Molteni had told Buenos Aires that he—Colville—could be a useful intermediary. This, implied Colville, was one further reason for keeping the lines of communication open to Buenos Aires. One diplomat who worked with Colville on the Commission finds the idea fantastic. But it would have fitted Martínez's strategy of appealing to Colville's vanity.

After setting himself the political goal, Colville began to rearrange the facts. He grew increasingly skeptical of the information being presented by NGOs, even Amnesty International. Back in 1980, he said in a 1984 interview, "we swallowed anything." Gradually, however, he began to look more carefully at the evidence. He had been skeptical from the start about Julia Esquivel's information on Guatemala, which he later described as "sensationally inaccurate and distorted." By 1983 he was convinced that many of the allegations from the human rights groups were fabricated. He showed little concern at the danger they faced—dangers that were dramatically illustrated in March 1983 when Marianella García Villas, president of the Salvadoran Human Rights Commission, was killed by the Salvadoran army during a fact-finding investigation inside a guerrilla zone. (Colville had admired her when she gave evidence to the disappearances group in 1980.)[3] He chose to ignore the fact that the policy of disappearances had been designed to avoid leaving traces, and that this made the furnishing of proof almost impossible. Colville wanted facts that would stand up in court. When the relatives failed to produce, he grew suspicious.

In the process Colville effectively sacrificed the U.N. group that he had striven so hard to build. Blind, toothless, deaf, and dumb, it was starting to resemble one of those strange U.N. bureaucratic animals from the early 1970s. It was now impossible to tell who had furnished the group with its information. The group never passed judgments. Cases were "kept under review" year after year as in the confidental 1503 procedure. (At least, in the 1503 procedure, there was the theoretical possibility of a case going public.) "Cooperation" was the key: praise was reserved for governments like El Salvador and Argentina, which had sent their ambassadors to talk, even though they lied.

If a government invited the group to visit, as Mexico did, it could find itself rewarded by being struck off the list. Mexican relatives had accused the government of causing the disappearance of seventy people. Colville was astonished when the Mexicans handed him a list of three hundred names—before the group had even made a formal complaint. This was above and beyond the call of duty. Colville was so eager to encourage this frankness that he proposed the investigation into Mexico be terminated. He was much tougher on the left-wing Sandinistas.[4]

After shaking the United Nations out of thirty-five years of torpor, the U.N. Working Group on Disappearances—the "jewel in the crown" as Michael Novak had described it—had become a tool in the hands of the killers, instead of their victims.

Colville's friend, Gabriel Martínez, was not present at the U.N. Human Rights Commission in February 1983 to witness the fruits of his labor. It was one thing to play the loyal diplomat in private, but quite another to do it in public. Martínez now began to prepare to retire from the scene and portray himself as someone who had only been acting under orders. Chameleonlike, he slipped into the role as easily as the others he had played.

But there was still unfinished business to attend to. He returned to Geneva in August when the U.N. Sub-Commission met and again drew up the 1503 blacklist. Argentina's name had been on the list since 1979 and Martínez now used the forthcoming transition to democracy to argue it off. Just before Argentina's case was due to be reviewed, he hosted another of his excellent lunches for twenty-three of the twenty-six subcommissioners. The three not invited were his fiercest critics—the subcommissioners from Britain, France, and Belgium. It was obviously a good lunch, because that same afternoon the Sub-Commission agreed to drop Argentina from the blacklist by a vote of 10 to 7. Vsefolod Sofinsky, the Soviet who had done so much to support the Junta in the past, again voted on its behalf.[5]

Like so much else the U.N. did on Argentina in 1983, this action was totally unwarranted. The Junta had threatened, stalled and stonewalled for seven years. It had done nothing to "cooperate." Here was a gesture from the U.N. that could only have encouraged the Junta to dig in its heels, and sure enough it was only a few days later (on September 23) that the Junta passed the "pacification law" absolving the security forces from responsibility and forbidding any civilian investigation into the dirty war. As we have seen, this law threw the election debate into a turmoil. Gabriel Martínez had performed yet another valuable service to his military masters.

Betrayal in Guatemala

In 1983, Mark Colville decided to apply his political talents to helping yet another tortured Latin American country emerge from dictatorship. For four years, Guatemala's military regimes had successfully avoided any U.N. investigation. By February 1983, however, there could be no more procrastinating. The Guatemalans surveyed the field for a U.N. investigator, or rapporteur, and proposed the name of Mark Colville.[6]

Colville was flattered and surprised. During 1981 and 1982, while he was Chairman, the U.N. Working Group on Disappearances had received terrifying information about Guatemala from Julia Esquivel. Guatemala was almost at war with Britain over the former British colony of Belize. But President Efraín Ríos Montt, the latest in a series of Guatemalan dictators, had evidently weighed up the risk. Colville appeared to have an open mind, and it had not been closed by Guatemala's refusal to cooperate with his group over the disappearances. Given their close contacts with Gabriel Martínez, the Guatemalans would also have known that Colville had grown increasingly sympathetic toward governments and increasingly suspicious of their critics. All of this was promising. Gabriel Martínez had been able to manipulate Colville and appealed to his evident desire to play the role of a political intermediary. Why not Ríos Montt?

It is easy to imagine the excitement Mark Colville must have felt when he arrived in Guatemala City on June 25 1983. The journey from the airport would have taken him past the barrios and seedy side streets where army patrols and death squads had prowled. He had heard about it from Julia Esquivel's testimony to the U.N. Working Group on Disappearances. Now he was seeing it at first hand.

Later, in a 1984 interview, Colville would agree that the Guatemalan army under Lucas García and his successor Ríos Montt had acted in a "completely uncivilized manner." But this was not reflected in the reports that Colville wrote for the U.N. Human Rights Commission following visits to the country in 1983 and 1984. Why? The first reason was that Ríos Montt was himself deposed in yet another coup on August 8 1983 by his Defense Minister, Oscar Mejía Víctores. Colville reasoned that there was little to be gained from criticizing a regime that had already fallen. Nor did he feel comfortable about publicly excoriating the man who now held power, even though Mejía Víctores (as defense minister) had been an architect of the killing under Ríos Montt. Colville would need his "cooperation" as badly as he had needed that of Gabriel Martínez.

So Colville decided to wipe the slate clean and ignore the murder of several thousand Guatemalans. In the event, he would not blame the Guatemalan army for a single specifically named massacre between 1983 and 1985. As a result, three of this century's most bloodthirsty dictators—Lucas García, Ríos Montt and Mejía Víctores—would escape virtually without censure.[7]

Human rights groups were dumbfounded. Late in 1983 Colville met with Aryeh Neier, executive director of the Americas Watch office in New York. The meeting ended with Colville convinced that Neier was a self-serving polemicist and Neier convinced that Colville saw himself as a political mediator instead of a human rights rapporteur. This was to be the first of several bitter confrontations between Colville and human rights activists.[8]

During a subsequent visit to Guatemala, Colville perfected his methodology. He was familiar with the charge—massacre and murder. Now he wanted proof, and he decided to go after it himself. In March 1984 Colville learned that one hundred villagers had been reported massacred by the army at a small village named Santiago Ixcán. The news came out in *Enfoprensa*, a bulletin put out by Guatemalan exiles in Mexico, and its source was said to be a survivor of the massacre named Marcela Velásquez. This was hard on Santiago Ixcán but a stroke of luck for Colville, because he had visited the very same village the previous year.

Colville put Santiago Ixcán at the top of his list, and on a hot summer's day in August 1984 he returned by army helicopter to the hamlet. The helicopter made one broad sweep around the village before landing, during which Colville noticed no signs of major damage. On landing, his suspicions hardened. There had, said the villagers, been an incident on February 14 when an outpost of civil defense guards had been attacked by guerrillas who were beaten off. But nobody from the village had been killed or wounded, no one was missing, and no army unit was stationed at the village. Most important, no one knew Marcela Velásquez, the source of the report.

Colville concluded that the alleged massacre had never taken place, and this conclusion featured prominently in his report to the 1985 session of the U.N. Human Rights Commission.[9] He investigated another five alleged massacres and reached the same conclusion about them all. This was devastating for the Guatemalan human rights groups, although they took some time to realize it. Here was an English lord, appointed by the U.N., calling them liars. The tiny hamlet of Santiago Ixcán had become their Waterloo.

In fact, there was another side to the story of Santiago Ixcán which suggested that a massacre might indeed have taken place. This should have made Colville pause, but he ignored it completely.[10] The fact was that Colville was no more "neutral" in Guatemala than he had been when reviewing the disappearances in Argentina with Martínez. He went to the country with preconceived, highly political ideas: the guerrillas were subversive terrorists, while the military regime was battling manfully to introduce democracy. Colville's report on his visit makes it absolutely clear than he had decided to take the government's side and play a political role in supporting multiparty elections.[11]

This position vitiated his inquiry. Although his eagerness to get at the facts was admirable, his detective work was biased from the outset. Colville put all his considerable energy into trying to disprove the charges against the army. Those he could not disprove he ignored. Colville did learn of several authentic massacres, and even visited one village where twenty-five civilians had died. Colville was accompanied on the trip by a British television crew. He told the local military commander what had happened and was satisfied when the commander looked gratifyingly sheepish. But the massacre itself did not feature in his report. Instead, it was merely described as one of several "grave charges" which Colville promised to follow up, but never did. When the British television producer asked for the tape of Colville's conversation with the military official, which he had not been able to film, Colville refused to let him have it.[12]

Colville and the Disappearances

Colville turned into a vigorous supporter of the government's rural "pacification" program, under which ninety thousand Guatemalan peasants were drafted into civil defense patrols and placed in fortified villages. This had provoked a chorus of alarm among human rights groups, which warned that those peasants who joined up would be fair game for the guerrillas, while those who balked would be considered fair game by the army. Colville considered forcible recruitment justified by the threat from the guerrillas. In one interview he even compared the Guatemalan patrols to Britain's volunteer Home Guard during the Second World War.

Yet he turned a blind eye to what was perhaps the most unacceptable abuse of all—the disappearances. The most convincing proof of disappearances in Guatemala was, of course, the work of the U.N. group that Colville himself had chaired. Disappearances, as we have seen, had begun in Guatemala in the 1960s. A short-lived relatives' association collapsed on March 10 1967 when its legal adviser was shot at his desk by police. During the regimes of General Lucas García and Ríos Montt, the disease spread again.[13]

By the time Colville first visited Guatemala, in June 1983, the U.N. group had transmitted 1,050 cases to the government of Guatemala—the third largest case load after Argentina and El Salvador. The Guatemalans had reacted with contempt and furnished the U.N. group with precisely four replies.[14] This was an abominable record, both in terms of the crime itself and also the government's reaction. Rios Montt had refused to talk to the group, and so did his successor Mejía Victores—even during the initial year (1983) that Colville wore his two hats as chairman of the group and U.N. rapporteur.

Colville thus arrived in Guatemala in the summer of 1983 uniquely informed about the problem and the government's obstinacy. The issue of disappearances was not raised in Colville's first meeting with Ríos Montt on June 27, but the following day he did question the minister of labor about the highly-publicized disappearance of Lucrecia Orellana, a labor lawyer, from a hotel. The minister replied blandly that the government was not interested in having people disappear. The following day, June 29, Colville had a sobering encounter with the rector of San Carlos University, who told him that thirty-seven students and professors had disappeared from his university. He said he had approached the authorities about Ms. Orellana, but had received no reply.

Colville presented the government with a sample list of people from

San Carlos University who had disappeared. On July 4, during a second meeting with President Ríos Montt, he expressed concern that some of the disappeared were being held under the special tribunals. Ríos Montt brushed aside the remark with the kind of outrageous claim that Colville had heard many times during his spell as chairman of the disappearances group. There were, said Ríos Montt, no missing people in Guatemala. They had all been released, and some now even worked for the government. Colville made no effort to challenge this during the interview, and he devoted almost no space to the disappearances in his report. Nor did he pass judgment on Ríos Montt's absurd claim in the report, beyond suggesting that the disappeared in Guatemala were "politically-motivated subversives" and that governments had plenty of experience in dealing with such miscreants without murdering them.[15]

By the time Colville returned in November, Ríos Montt had fallen and Colville found himself facing a new head of state, General Mejía Victores, whose own sister had just been released unharmed after being held captive by the guerrillas. Colville asked him about the disappeared, and the general replied that none were being held by the army. The tribunals were now abolished, but the disappeared had not emerged. This confirmed what Colville must have known—that he had been lied to by Ríos Montt and his ministers.

Mejía Víctores then told Colville that he favored the "Argentinian solution," under which a "desaparecido" could be declared dead after ninety days. Colville did not respond, nor did he refer to this staggering suggestion in his next report. Instead, wrote Colville, he had been given the explanation advanced so often by Gabriel Martínez—that the disappeared were "subversives" who had gone underground. Colville did at least express skepticism about this in his report.[16]

On June 5 1984 three mothers of disappeared Guatemalans who had been fruitlessly combing the morgues and police stations met by chance at a church meeting and heard a cassette produced by the Salvadoran mothers. The three decided to form the "Grupo Apoyo Mutuo" (Mutual Support Group, or GAM). Within a week twenty-five relatives had joined. This was a major event. After all the years of killing, Guatemala at last had a functioning human rights group.[17] On August 13 Colville met with one hundred twenty-six relatives of disappeared at the hotel El Dorado. They asked him to remain in the country until their relatives were located. Colville said this was not within his mandate, but he referred to the meeting in his November 1984 report to the General Assembly.

Two months later, in January 1985, he arrived in Guatemala for yet another visit. In light of the recent formation of the GAM, and his own knowledge, the report that appeared in local newspapers seemed scarcely credible. Colville, it stated, had told deputies at the Constituent Assembly that disappearances in Guatemala were "a thing of the past." Colville scrambled to retrieve the situation. He claimed he had been misquoted. He had visited the Assembly, where relatives were causing "a frightful din" with a loudspeaker, as he would later put it in an interview. At the same time, deputies were pressing round, asking for his advice about the new constitution. He shouted that he would have to arrange two meetings: one with the deputies and the other with the relatives who were concerned with disappearances that had happened in the past. A reporter had understood Colville to be saying that disappearances had stopped, which they certainly had not.[18]

But even if he had been misquoted, Colville never took the initiative with the relatives. Given his intimate knowledge of the crime and the pressure on the relatives, one might have expected him to be hammering on their door. Why did he not insist that they be given protection and threaten the wrath of the U.N. if anything happened to their leaders? "I knew they would come to me," he said airily in a 1985 interview. The relatives did send him a letter, and later, when he returned again to update his report, they presented him with thirty new cases that had occurred since October.

According to an account cabled back to Washington from the U.S. embassy, Colville told the relatives that "at least some of the disappearances had been arranged by persons who sought to embarrass the government, and had joined the guerrillas."[19] He later said that he had found no evidence of secret jails. By now, Colville's open support for the regime was beginning to worry even Guatemala's Church leaders (who were relatively conservative). According to the U.S. embassy cable, the archbishop told a press conference that he did not share Colville's optimism.

Throughout this period, Colville made no effort to apply his investigating zeal to the disappearances, as he had done to disproving allegations against the army. Moreover, in 1985 he decided to suspend any investigation into the disappearances on the grounds that they were being covered by the U.N. group. In so doing, Colville took a unilateral decision to redefine his mandate: the U.N. Human Rights Commission had asked him to inquire about disappearances. Here, once again, was Colville straining to understand the government's position and bury the evidence. Why? Because Guatemala, like Argentina, had to be nudged toward democracy.[20]

Toward this goal Colville brought all the qualities of his English up-bringing—stubbornness, pride, devotion to the task at hand. In the pro-cess he became a full-blooded apologist for the Guatemalan government and the most "politicized" human rights investigator ever appointed by the United Nations. Kirkpatrick had inveighed against "politicization" in the U.N., but Colville was now turning the charge on its head—voicing support for a U.S. ally, challenging prickly human rights groups, and ad-vocating elections. His reports would be used by the State Department to justify a renewal of arms sales to Guatemala and even to send Guatemalan asylum-seekers back to Guatemala. Inevitably, they also paved the way for a suspension of the U.N. inquiry into gross violations in Guatemala in 1987, even though the torture and disappearances had continued under democracy.[21]

All this might have made the United Nations seem less "dangerous" to the Reagan Administration, but it did not look that way to the Guatema-lan relatives of the disappeared. Early in 1985 the Mutual Support Group in Guatemala sent a huge dossier to the U.N.'s human rights secretariat in Geneva. Such was the lack of commitment under Kurt Herndl that no-one even felt able to sign for the registered package, so the package was sent to a courier firm in Geneva for return to Guatemala City. Luckily, one of the firm's employees suspected that it might fall into the wrong hands in Guatemala and contacted the Geneva office of Pax Christi. Adrian Zoller, of Pax Christi, took charge of the package and directed it to the U.N. Working Group on Disappearances.[22]

Shortly afterward, Héctor Gómez Calixto, one of GAM's six directors in Guatemala, disappeared. His body was found with the tongue cut out. Rosario Godoy Alfaro de Cuevas, another member of the six, was then found dead in a car with her brother and three-year-old son. (Cuevas had been one of the relatives who had met with Colville on August 13 1984.) A third director of GAM had already left the country, and a fourth resigned out of fear. After just a year in existence, only two of the six original GAM founding members were confident enough to continue the work.[23] Col-ville's reluctance to demand guarantees on their behalf had almost certainly increased the dangers, and when he returned for his next visit in Septem-ber 1985 the relatives refused even to meet with him. "The GAM position," cabled the U.S. ambassador, "has become one of absolute refusal and bitter criticism. They describe the Colville visit as tragic and counter-productive and accuse Colville of covering up for the government and peddling the government line on disappearances."[24]

So the relatives of Guatemala's disappeared passed their verdict on Colville's efforts. Colville himself could claim that his political mediation had been successful. He prided himself on having persuaded Guatemala to recognize the independence of Belize, and in having helped to persuade Mejía Victores to hand over power to the civilians. Yet he did nothing to make the civilians' job any easier. President Vinicio Cerezo, Guatemala's democratically elected president, inherited a tormented society. So many deaths, so much horror—and no accounting. The elections that Colville had helped to nurture merely papered over the wounds and gave a veneer of normality. They did not heal Guatemala's wounds.

But the United Nations might have helped to heal the wounds in Argentina and Guatemala if it had honored its mandate and presented the human rights facts dispassionately and honestly. This would at least have given the democrats and relatives in both countries a common point of reference, and reduced the likelihood of confrontation. Instead, the relationship between these two groups, former allies during dictatorship, quickly soured. Ominously, the preconditions of disappearance and murder in the interior of Guatemala remained.[25]

The Relatives Render Their Verdict

On February 24 1984, five women and one tall bearded man delivered their verdict on the U.N. Working Group on Disappearances. They unfurled a handmade banner outside Conference Room 17 where the U.N. Human Rights Commission was meeting, and announced that they were going on a hunger strike for the 90,000 people who had disappeared in Latin America. The six were all from the executive committee of FEDEFAM, the Latin American relatives' organization. Patrick Rice was the only male.[26]

This was an impressive group. They had stood up to some of the most murderous regimes in the world, yet they were nervous as they unfurled their banner. They knew that Room 17 was "neutral" once more, and that they were once again the enemy. This was the United Nations of yesteryear—the world of conformity and anonymous gray suits. Sensing trouble, U.N. guards bore down, and a small knot of journalists quickly gathered. They were joined by Assistant Secretary General Kurt Herndl looking hot and irritated. "This is silly!" he exclaimed, before noticing the journalists. Herndl then listened without any visible emotion as Rice told him that FEDEFAM would give the United Nations three months to start acting on their information. They had run out of patience. The six then went on a hunger strike in a nearby church before leaving Geneva in disgust. Three months later, true to their word, they stopped sending information to the group they had helped to establish.

Two months after the FEDEFAM demonstration, two more players in our story found themselves badly let down by the U.N. group. On May 2 1984, Andrei Sakharov, the Soviet scientist, began a hunger strike in Gorki where he had been exiled in 1980. Within two weeks all contact between the Sakharovs and Moscow had been cut and Western papers were suggesting he had died. Sakharov's human rights monitoring group in Moscow was affiliated to the International League for Human Rights based in New York, and readers may recall that Jerry Shestack, the President of the League, had pressed the Soviets about Sakharov when he served as the U.S. delegate on the U.N. Human Rights Commission in 1980. Shestack had also played a major role in creating the U.N. disappearances group.

The group was, as it happens, preparing to meet in New York when news of Sakharov's disappearance came through. It was highly unlikely that Sakharov had disappeared and been secretly murdered, like the Argentinian "desaparecidos," but Shestack seized the opportunity and appealed to the U.N. group on behalf of Sakharov.[27]

The U.S. State Department spotted a chance to embarrass the Soviet Union. Echoing the language of early 1981, a report in the daily bulletin put out by the U.S. Information Service observed: "The U.N. Working Group was established in 1980 to deal with disappearances in Latin America." (This was not true: the mandate was disappearances worldwide.) "This is the first time the Group is considering a case concerning the plight of a Soviet citizen." By turning the Sakharov case into a public East-West confrontation, the United States quickly destroyed any chance of a successful U.N. move, although the group did decide to appeal to the Soviets "on humanitarian grounds" and delegated their chairman, Ivan Tosevski from Yugoslavia, to make the approach. But Tosevski was so appalled by the publicity that he did not even mention Sakharov during his visit to the Soviet mission, and shortly afterward, at the 1985 session of the Human Rights Commission in Geneva, the angry Soviets succeeded in opposing a proposal to extend the group for two years. The one-year extension left it vulnerable to attacks against its funding and staff of the kind leveled by Gabriel Martínez in 1981.

The temporary collapse of the group in 1983 was almost as significant as its creation had been in 1980. The importance of the group had been to concentrate the U.N.'s limited energies on the core problem of violence by governments and to open the way to "thematic" investigations instead of the "selective" probes on individual countries. But its success had hinged on its ability to confront and work independently of governments, and to avoid politics.

By surrendering to the Argentinian Junta, the group set a precedent that tainted the entire U.N. human rights fact-finding apparatus. Between 1983 and 1986, rapporteurs investigated El Salvador, Suriname, Guatemala, Equatorial Guinea, Haiti, Chile, and Uruguay for the Human Rights Commission. All these nations had been labeled "gross violators" by the Commission, yet almost without exception these rapporteurs saw their task as mediation rather than criticism—as the reestablishment of democracy rather than support for embattled relatives and other victims. One exception was a 1985 report on Afghanistan by Felix Ermacora, the Austrian professor who had visited Chile with Theo van Boven in 1978. Ermacora angrily criticized Soviet-inspired abuses in 1985, but he too softened his criticism measurably after being admitted to Afghanistan in 1986.[28]

One distinguished victim of this process was Kurt Herndl, who had succeeded van Boven in 1982 as director of the Human Rights Division. Instead of defending his own program during the U.N.'s severe financial crisis of 1986/87, Herndl took the initiative in proposing cuts that led to the cancellation of the 1986 session of the Sub-Commission, and probably would have killed off that body altogether had it not been for the furious reaction of NGOs. Rather like Ernest Lefever, Herndl managed to give the impression that he viewed his own job as redundant, and Pérez de Cuéllar duly responded. Herndl's post was abolished and Herndl himself was dismissed in 1987. This placed the day-to-day running of the U.N.'s human rights machinery more directly under the management of U.N. headquarters in New York, and of the Secretary General.

This was a small step backward in the wider crisis of the U.N. but a giant reverse for human rights. Pérez de Cuéllar was not only by nature sympathetic to governments, as he had shown in Uruguay in 1979. He was not going to permit the U.N.'s human rights machinery to compromise his otherwise laudable efforts at mediation in Central America, Afghanistan, and the Persian Gulf.[29]

With this action, the vision of 1948 vanished. The founders of the United Nations had realized that human rights meant challenge and exposure of governments. They also realized, as noted earlier, that this would be impossible for an organization of governments without a secretariat that was strong, committed, and independent. That goal had seemed attainable under van Boven. Now it was lost. The era of revival had been short-lived. The U.N.'s human rights machinery was working with, instead of against, governments—slipping back into bureaucratic torpor and "neutrality." This was as grave a betrayal as any in the U.N.'s forty-year history.[30]

Democratic Argentina Passes Its Verdict

On February 27 1984 Argentina's new Foreign Minister, Dante Caputo, rose before the U.N. Human Rights Commission in Geneva to deliver his verdict on the U.N.'s efforts on behalf of the disappeared. Short and bespectacled, Foreign Minister Caputo seemed out of place among the nylon suits, neutral faces, and opaque vocabulary. A thirty-nine-year-old professor of political science, Caputo was one of Alfonsín's closest personal advisers. He had studied at Tufts University and the Sorbonne, and had married the French official who handled human rights at the French embassy in Buenos Aires. No one could have been more different from the bombastic Gabriel Martínez. Caputo was thoughtful—even meek. If this was the face of democratic Argentina, it was attractive. Certainly, within the family of nations, Argentina would be easier to live with. One immediate beneficiary was Sweden's draft torture convention, which would be adopted by the U.N. General Asembly later in the year.[31]

After so long supporting Argentina's military regime, the Commission quickly changed its colors and embraced democracy. It was effortlessly done with a round of deferential applause for Foreign Minister Caputo. Suddenly, the slate was wiped clean. Did those delegates not feel any twinges of remorse? Did they not think back to Gabriel Martínez's countless interventions, and the way they had passively submitted to his long tirades? Did they not recall his brutal attacks on Niall MacDermot, Theo van Boven, and Emilio Mignone? The way he had made fools of them in the private 1503 sessions?

Did they not recall Martínez arguing that the disappeared persons had taken refuge abroad, and that any killing was justified by terrorism? They had long known that this was a lie and now they heard it from Argentina's own Foreign Minister. Caputo began with the words: "By fighting the devil with the devil's own weapons, Argentina became hell." Did they not feel any shame? If so, it did not show. Instead, they congratulated Argentina on its new-found freedom and tried to bury the past, just as the Junta had done. At this moment, Argentina exposed the United Nations more comprehensively than any of Jeane Kirkpatrick's biting statements.

Caputo delivered a kinder verdict on the U.N. Commission than it deserved. He did not stand up, like the uncompromising Hebe de Bonafini in the Plaza de Mayo, to remind the delegates of their weakness and make them squirm. Instead, he generously thanked the Commission for the "invaluable co-operation" and "demonstrations of solidarity." There was no point in being needlessly provocative—that was not Alfonsín's style. More important, Alfonsín too was preparing to make compromises.

Gabriel Martínez was not present for Caputo's statement. His place at the head of the Argentinian delegation was taken by Hugo Bianchi, a broad-shouldered career diplomat. Bianchi sat beside Caputo, basking in the acclaim. But Bianchi had served as ambassador to Sweden, and it was he who had received Sweden's protest at the murder of Dagmar Hagelin and transmitted the Junta's reply. None of Argentina's diplomats who had served the Junta was entirely blameless. But Caputo realized that diplomacy would have to continue to function. He was as pragmatic as his friend and chief, Raúl Alfonsín.[32]

This was unsatisfying. One accepted that Argentina needed Alfonsín. Wounds had to be healed, and life had to go on. At the same time, this was too comfortable. Perhaps Hebe de Bonafini would have brought people to their senses. Perhaps the Commission needed someone in the gallery, wearing a white scarf and mouthing "betrayal" behind the thick glass partition. The United Nations could no more plead innocence than could Gabriel Martínez.

Martínez himself resigned from the diplomatic service and slipped back into civilian life in Argentina. He was not quite finished with the U.N. Later in 1984 he was invited back to the U.N. headquarters in Vienna to participate in a round table on trade. It was not enough that he had destroyed the career of a senior U.N. official and damaged the fragile U.N. human rights machinery; he had to be rewarded for it—by the U.N.[33]

29. Alfonsín's Compromise

If human rights had proved to be the midwife of Argentinian democracy, human rights also presented democracy with its single greatest dilemma.

The task confronting Raúl Alfonsín was different from the one that had confronted Mark Colville. Alfonsín's concerns ranged wider than human rights. He had to govern a nation that owed forty-five billion dollars and had suffered a humiliating defeat in war—a defeat, moreover, that was attested to by the presence of British troops on the nearby Malvinas. Overshadowing all was the bitterness between the armed forces and the human rights groups. While the demoralized military was prepared to give Alfonsín its support, it would not tolerate a witchhunt. The relatives, on the other hand, were implacable. They wanted "aparición con vida, castigo a los culpables," and there was plenty to keep them indignant. In the three weeks that followed Alfonsín's inauguration, 238 bodies were recovered from burial sites across the country. The dirty war was beginning to yield up its secrets.

Alfonsín had won power on a human rights platform, but once in power he treated human rights like the political problem it undoubtedly was, and showed himself ready to compromise in order to ensure the wider goal of securing democracy for Argentina. Alfonsín moved swiftly and decisively. Before the confetti had been swept up off the streets, he had presented his fellow countrymen with a carefully constructed political package, aimed at punishing the military without inviting another coup.

Jaime Malamud-Goti, one of Alfonsín's closest advisers, would later recall how he struggled for months before the election to find a suitable formula. He was up against the all-important fact noted by Claus Ruser from the U.S. embassy in 1980: hundreds of officers in the armed forces had been involved to some degree, yet it was clearly impractical to prosecute them all.[1]

At his inauguration on December 10 1983, Alfonsín promised to prosecute both military and guerrilla leaders who had "sowed terror, pain and death throughout Argentine society." On December 13, he ordered the trial of the nine members of the three juntas that had ruled Argentina between 1976 and 1983, and the same day he called for the arrest and trial of seven Montonero leaders, starting with Mario Firmenich. On December 15 Alfonsín announced the creation of an independent commission (CONADEP) to investigate the disappearances under the charge of Ernesto Sabato, one of Argentina's foremost authors. A separate law, 280/84, ordered the trial of the notorious former police chief of Buenos Aires province, General Ramón Camps.

The most controversial element in Alfonsín's package was a modification in Argentina's code of military justice, to allow for any cases arising from the dirty war to be judged by the military, not by civilian courts. If, after six months, the Supreme Council of the armed forces had taken no action in a prosecution, it could then pass to the civilian court of appeals. The 1984 law was generally assumed to have strengthened the excuse of acting under orders, or "due obedience." Before 1984, Argentina's penal and military codes allowed the plea in limited circumstances. The 1984 law broadened this by giving judges discretion to decide whether it applied—while making an exception for "atrocious acts." President Alfonsín argued that it also fixed a hierarchy of responsibility: senior officers who gave the orders, middle-ranking officers who committed excesses, and junior officials who followed orders. This justified prosecuting the nine former commanders, but it also expanded the plea of due obedience.

The main justification for the reform, as Emilio Mignone pointed out in an article, was political rather than legal. Alfonsín had to punish some, but not all, of Argentina's military personnel. If, on balance, the package seemed unduly favorable to the military, it was in the hope that the armed forces would accept that the dirty war had been a mistake and prove to be more respectful of democracy.[2] That would help Alfonsín reduce the military's role in civilian life.

Did the reforms open the way to the plea of "due obedience" by lower-ranking officers like Alfredo Astiz, who had pulled the trigger and applied the cattle-prod, and done it with gusto? Had Alfonsín, the democrat, undermined the Nuremberg principles and international law? It seemed so, as the weeks passed. By the end of the first six-month period, the armed forces Supreme Council had not even taken testimony from the nine accused Junta members, let alone passed judgment. The Council raised hopes by ordering the detention of retired Admiral Rubén Chamorro, the director of the ESMA, who was forced to return from South Africa.

It also upheld the government's decree 280/84 ordering the arrest of Ramón Camps. This apart, there was little to show.

In July 1984 the civilian federal appeals court gave the Council a further ninety days. By August, only two Junta members—Videla and Agosti—had been interrogated. The federal court fixed October 11 as the new deadline. The Council responded with a brief flurry of activity, ordering the arrest of General Benjamín Menéndez, the former head of the First Army Corps, and Admiral Massera. It then lapsed into inactivity once again before announcing that it would not proceed with the trial of the nine Junta members. There was an immediate outcry, following which the Supreme Council members resigned in protest. The federal court of appeals acted quickly to pick up the case against the nine, five of whom were placed in detention and the other four told to ready themselves. Prosecutor Strassera and his staff began to prepare for a long trial.[3]

So far, Alfonsín's gamble was failing. Argentina's military hierarchy was prepared to prosecute the former commanders for the humiliating defeat on the Malvinas but not for the dirty war.[4] Over human rights, the military had closed ranks and thrown down a challenge to the new democracy. The First Army Corps maintained a special "museum of subversion," featuring weapons and literature used by guerrillas during the 1970s.[5]

Much was now hanging on the trial of the nine. Equally important was the independent commission on the disappearances (CONADEP). As the military showed itself increasingly reluctant to apologize for the dirty war, CONADEP's work assumed increasing importance for the survivors and their relatives. Midway through 1984, CONADEP published its findings in a small stout book, with a blood-red cover and the words "Nunca Mas" (never again) slashed in white like a wound across the cover.

Nunca Más, the Unlikely Best Seller

From the start, CONADEP found itself in a difficult position. The human rights groups had wanted a fully fledged parliamentary commission with power to subpoena witnesses. Instead, they got an advisory panel that would merely review the facts and send any criminal cases to the courts. Adolfo Pérez Esquivel and Augusto Conte MacDonell both refused to join CONADEP, and Emilio Mignone turned down a request to give legal advice. It was a vote of no confidence from the human rights community.[6]

In spite of this, for nine months CONADEP kept up an exhausting pace to honor its mandate, working initially from the list of some six thousand disappearances registered by the Permanent Assembly on Human Rights and building it up as new evidence came in. The secretariat drew up a file of 3,500 photographs of disappeared people—just as Marianella García Villas's colleagues had done at the independent Human Rights Commission in San Salvador. Anyone claiming to have information about a "desaparecido," was invited to find the person in the file. The secretariat then tried to check a claim against other testimony and follow it up with an on-site investigation.[7]

On some days, they took in over one hundred "denuncias." Catalina Martin, a lawyer for CONADEP, recalls how witnesses broke down and wept. Others screwed up their eyes, clenched their hands, and remained silent for minutes while they summoned up the courage to go on. The strain proved too much for four CONADEP officials, who resigned. Several others were so shaken that they sought psychiatric help. Yet, as always, the "denuncia" proved immensely cathartic—even for those relatives or survivors who had spoken out before. The lesson had been driven home many times, from El Salvador to Argentina: a "denuncia" meant more than information. By the end, CONADEP registered 8,960 names of disappeared persons. The list included 172 infants, 160 adolescents between the ages of thirteen and eighteen, and 52 people aged beween fifty-five and seventy-seven years old.[8]

Argentina's military accepted CONADEP as part of Alfonsín's political compromise, but did so with bad grace and undisguised hostility. On March 9 1984 a CONADEP team set out to inspect the ESMA school, where so many Argentinians had been tortured and murdered. They were accompanied by six former detainees. One of the six, Carlos Muñoz, had gained access to many damaging secrets while working in the ESMA documentation department, and CONADEP was keen to verify as much of his testimony as possible. Before departure, he and the other former detainees were asked to make sketches of as much as they could remember of the ESMA.

The ESMA was functioning normally when they arrived, and they found Captain González, the director, cool but cooperative. The CONADEP party split up and Muñoz immediately directed his group to the ground floor and basement where Ana María Martí, Juan Gasparini, and Mónica Mignone had been tortured. The officers protested that this was a restricted area, but the tour was allowed to go on after they had signed a paper of authorization. The CONADEP team entered the "golden room" on the ground floor, where the abductions had been planned, then went down to the basement where Muñoz had worked in the laboratory next to the torture room. Finally, they climbed up to the "capucha" (hood) on the third floor where the two men had been kept chained and blindfolded.

The other four former detainees then went over the same route and confirmed what Muñoz had said. All the instruments of torture had been removed, and what was formerly the torture room in the basement was now full of filing cabinets, but there were marks on the floor which appeared to correspond to torture benches. All the detainees remarked on the fact that the elevator between the basement and ground floor, together with other incriminating evidence, had been removed. It was an eerie experience for everyone involved, and it brought to mind a similar visit by Theo van Boven and the U.N. team during the trip to Chile in July 1978. Van Boven had visited the Villa Grimaldi, the former Chilean torture center. Ironically, his guide had also been a former detainee named Muñoz.[9]

Argentina's 1984 inquiry into the misdeeds of its own military at the ESMA was brief and deeply resented. The CONADEP team snatched some photos, one of which was reproduced in the report. It showed a member of the team sitting under the long sloping roof of the "capucha" (hood) where Juan Gasparini had spent almost a year constantly chained.[10] There were no chains now, of course, just bare boards. But imagination filled in the details. By 1985 the ESMA was as familiar to Argentinians as the presidential palace. The amateurishness of the photo seemed appropriate. It summed up the distrust of the military and the pressures that CONADEP was under.

CONADEP received no shortage of evidence from the victims, but none from their tormentors.[11] Forty-four of the most notorious officers, from Astiz to Galtieri, were asked to testify. None replied. Not one serving officer volunteered information. Eventually, CONADEP did compile a list of 1,351 names of security officers directly implicated by witnesses. A furious debate then ensued within CONADEP about whether it should be published. In the end, caution won out and only forty names were sent to the Ministry of Justice for possible prosecution. (The full list of the 1,351 names was published in 1985 in a local magazine.) Coming on top of the initial disappointment about the CONADEP composition and terms of reference, this was devastating for the relatives. The Mothers also protested at CONADEP's determination to identify the corpses appearing in clandestine graves—or, failing that, to pronounce the "desaparecidos" dead. The Mothers did not want to know, and they took exception to CONADEP's determination to solve the mystery.[12]

So, ultimately, CONADEP managed to infuriate both the relatives and the military. It was yet another sign that there could be no meeting of the minds between these two bitter enemies, and yet another warning to Alfonsín. At the same time, CONADEP was also the first essential step toward healing wounds. *Nunca Más* was an unlikely best-seller. It was unevenly written, badly organized, and lacked even the normal accouterments of indexes and footnotes. Its five hundred pages provided only snatches of the fifty thousand pages of evidence received by CONADEP. Its analysis of fairly common themes, such as the doctrine of national security, was shallow. It left unanswered many of the questions that CONADEP had asked, beginning with the most important one: Where were the disappeared persons? It conceded that many more Argentinians had disappeared than the 8,960 names on its list, but offered no other estimates.

In spite of all this, *Nunca Más* caught the mood of Argentina in the second half of 1984. For most Argentinians, who wanted to face the past, but feared for the future, CONADEP succeeded. *Nunca Más* became a best-seller overnight, and within weeks of appearing on the book-stands it had sold over two hundred thousand copies. However much of a compromise, it was an act of great confidence by Argentina's young democracy—a five hundred-page "denuncia" of authoritarian military rule.

It also answered, eloquently, many of the questions posed earlier by this story. Yes, a single standard of behavior can be expected from all governments when it comes to the "right to life," integrity of the person, and legal protection. Yes, these rights are as important in the "authoritarian" Latin American context as they are in a Western democracy. No, they cannot be tossed aside—even under an assault from terrorism. When that happens, said *Nunca Más*, the terrorists have won and civilization has lost.[13]

Democracy's Verdict on the Dirty War

The CONADEP commission had made it easier for Julio César Strassera to prosecute the nine former military commanders. It had sifted through the information and identified the issues. During the four months of 1985, as he slowly built his case, Strassera would gratefully call many of the CONADEP witnesses to testify. He would have the advantage of being able to subpoena witnesses, including former and serving military officers.

The mood when the trial opened on April 22 was tense. 80,000 Argentinians collected outside the gray courthouse, and U.S. embassy cables acknowledged that the trial would climax what one cable termed the "extremely delicate and emotional issues" that had split Argentina since the Junta stepped down. How Alfonsín's government handled the trial, predicted the cable, could have profound implications for Argentina's democracy.[14]

Whatever difficulties Strassera would have normally faced in prosecuting his country's former military rulers, they were made immeasurably more difficult by the fact that the trial was part of a complex political compromise. Strassera's problem was simple: in order to prosecute successfully, he would have to show that these nine individuals were responsible for the thousands of disappearances and countless acts of robbery and torture—even though (with the possible exception of Massera) none of the nine had ever personally pulled the trigger.[15] The long-term implications of this were equally striking: if Strassera succeeded, he might reinforce the concept of "due obedience" and allow the actual killers to walk free. At the outset of the trial, in April 1985, this left the nine military commanders looking very much like scapegoats.

Former President Jorge Videla was convinced he would not get a fair trial and refused the services of a defense lawyer. Videla's complaint was the same one he had leveled against the human rights groups back in 1976 and 1977—that the trial was "politically motivated." The court designated Juan Carlos Tavares, the public Defender, as Videla's lawyer. But he too would maintain throughout that the trial was a show trial, and that its witnesses were too "politically motivated" to be credible.

Videla was right in one respect. An unprecedented amount of effort and money—not to mention public expectation—had been directed at securing his indictment and those of his eight co-defendants. Cases before the federal appeals court in Argentina are normally decided on the basis of written evidence. This one was to be oral.[16] In addition, an enterprising publishing firm had decided to bring out a weekly paper on the trial. *El Diario del Juicio* contained the latest developments, verbatim accounts of key testimony, and some excellent interviews. It was hard for Argentina to remain ignorant of the trial, even if it had wanted to. This, too, was part of Alfonsín's intention—another way of healing the wounds.

Strassera knew, like everyone else, that the judicial system was itself on trial. Alfonsín wanted a functioning judiciary, not a humiliated one, and he had already promoted several lower-ranking judges who, in the eyes of the Mothers, had collaborated with the dictators. The six members of the federal appeals court who would render a verdict on the nine were not as compromised as most, but none of them had gone out on a limb to challenge military rule.

Even Strassera himself had made compromises. He had been named to the rank of judge by none other than President Jorge Videla—the man he would now be prosecuting. Did this not make Strassera an accomplice? When pressed in one interview Strassera replied: "I served the law, not the dictatorship. I swore to defend the constitution. When presented with a habeas corpus, I made what inquiries I could, but never got results. What could I do? Raid the ESMA? Justice was handcuffed."[17] On the whole, the public was prepared to accept this at face value and to judge Strassera on his performance at the trial. They knew that many in the Argentinian legal profession, with the exception of Emilio Mignone, had made compromises over the past ten years.

Strassera's aim was twofold: establish the complicity and responsibility of the nine and demolish the notion of a "dirty war" in which any response to terrorism was justified. He put it like this: "Either there was no war and we find ourselves faced with acts of common criminality, or there was a war, in which case we are faced with war crimes." As we have seen, Strassera's strategy was to choose 709 individual disappearances and use them as the basis for his case against the nine.[18]

After Strassera's summary on September 18 1985, defense lawyers for the nine defendants replied. True to form, Massera delivered his own final plea in what one U.S. diplomat described as a "booming voice." It was a predictable mixture of arrogance and bathos—of the "history will judge me" variety. The defense lawyers argued that the commanders had merely responded to Isabel Perón's 1975 invitation to "annihilate" terrorism, and extended the state of siege she imposed. They maintained, chillingly, that terrorism justified any and every response, no matter how cruel. One lawyer described the Montoneros and ERP guerrillas as "bastards who do not deserve to live on this earth." "Moderation in warfare is stupidity," argued another. "The death of innocents was the inevitable price of war," claimed Massera's lawyer. The armed forces were "ready to rise again and wipe out the enemy," warned Massera himself, in his booming voice. The opinion at the U.S. embassy, which monitored the trial, was that the six judges would not be intimidated by such bombast. One cable to Washington predicted stiff sentences for all nine, with the possible exceptions of Graffigna and Lami Dozo from the air force.[19]

The court then recessed while the six judges retired to consider the case. They returned to render a sentence that was, like everything else in the trial, enormously lengthy. Each element in Strassera's argument was analyzed, and a separate verdict passed on each of the 709 individual cases. On December 9, court president Carlos Arslanian finally announced the verdict. Videla and Massera—life imprisonment; Viola—seventeen years; Lambruschini—eight years; Agosti—four and a half years; Graffigna, Galtieri, Lami Dozo, Anaya—freedom.

One member of the audience did not stay long enough to hear the final verdict. Hebe de Bonafini, president of the Mothers of the Plaza de Mayo, arrived in the public gallery wearing the white scarf she had worn through countless marches in the Plaza de Mayo and at the United Nations. Wearing the scarf was a political gesture, and she was told that the session could not begin until she took it off. Eventually, she agreed. Then, at eighteen minutes past six, aware of the direction that the sentencing was taking, she donned it again. The court president stopped talking and asked her to choose between the scarf and the trial. Hebe de Bonafini chose the scarf, turned her back on the trial, and left the hall.

Many shared Hebe de Bonafini's acute disappointment. How could the judges have been so lenient? The answer was, they had no choice. They had to deal with the 709 cases presented by Strassera, which immediately limited the scope of the charge. There was, further, the underlying ambiguity of the charge. Leopoldo Galtieri was on trial as President and Junta member, not as commander of the Second Army Corps in Rosario. Galtieri walked out a free man because his membership in the Junta only began at the end of 1981 by which time the killing had slowed. He could still be charged by the armed forces Supreme Council, but even that slim possibility would vanish if there was an amnesty.[20]

The message for international law was also less than reassuring. Six months earlier, the United Nations had finally adopted an international convention that would not allow torturers to plead they were acting on orders. Alfredo Astiz, as we have seen, had given the convention repeated boosts. Now, it seemed, Argentina's first democratic president had imperiled this progress by giving Astiz the chance to plead "due obedience." Would the trial judgment strengthen or weaken such a plea?

The six judges delivered a carefully nuanced verdict. In one way they did indeed confirm the plea of due obedience by stating that the nine commanders were "criminally responsible for criminal deeds which their subordinates committed in carrying out orders." At the same time the judges asked the Supreme Council of the armed forces to "investigate criminal acts by their subordinates, including regional and subregional commanders and others who had operational responsibility." In addition, said a U.S. embassy cable, the judges distinguished between acting on orders and performing "unwarranted" or "excessive" acts like rape and torture. This left open the possibility that many other military officers could still face prosecution.[21]

By now, the government had taken the political decision that human rights trials would come to an end. On October 28 1985 President Alfonsín reportedly met with the heads of the armed services and made the pledge. The question of how this would be achieved was not, however, answered for another year. On December 24 1986 Alfonsín called a special session of Congress and passed a law putting a "punto final" (full stop) to any prosecutions not brought within sixty days. The human rights groups then worked frantically to bring charges, and by the time the law took effect, almost four hundred former officers, including forty generals, eight admirals and two former presidents, still faced charges.

But Alfonsín was coming under brutal pressure by the humiliated military to declare an amnesty. In April 1987, army units under the leadership of Colonel Aldo Rico staged an insurrection and demanded a total amnesty. On April 19 1987, Alfonsín made a dramatic visit to talk to Rico and the rebellion collapsed. But Alfonsín paid a price. Two months later, on June 5 1987, he effectively yielded to the demands of the insurgents and passed a new law expanding the concept of "due obedience," which covered virtually all the crimes committed during the dirty war and amounted to a total amnesty.[22] Alfonsín's long balancing act aimed at healing the national trauma without humiliating the military was finally over. It would be left to his Peronist successor, Carlos Menem, to bring the curtain down on the final act.

What was left after the 1985 trial of the nine, apart from an inevitable sense of anti climax? The answer was yet another ringing denunciation of military rule and a boost for the rule of law. By avoiding a witch-hunt, Prosecutor Strassera and the six judges had ensured that the trial would not be dismissed as a "politically motivated" gesture by a fickle judiciary serving a new master.

"Few expected life sentences and equally few expected four of the nine accused to be freed," cabled U.S. ambassador Frank Ortiz from Buenos Aires. "In one sense the decision is one more dramatic demonstration, if any more were needed . . . of judicial independence in democratic Argentina."[24] This could not but strengthen democracy and restore credit to Argentina's judicial system. But would the gain be wiped out by the sense of frustration and anger felt by those who had suffered?

30. The Denuncia

In spite of Hebe de Bonafini's protest, the trial of the nine military commanders offered hundreds of relatives, former detainees, and even foreigners the opportunity to make their own personal "denuncia." Many seized the chance gratefully.

By 1985 Theo van Boven had still not recovered from the sense of betrayal that followed his dismissal from the United Nations three years earlier. The Dutch government had offered him a humiliatingly minor diplomatic posting. Apparently, van Boven was too outspoken even for his own people. He resigned from the foreign service and took up work as a law professor at the University of Limburg in Maastricht, in the south of Holland. But his wife and two children pined for their friends in Geneva, and as he thumbed through the yellowing files, van Boven yearned for the chance to make his own "denuncia" against Argentina's military rulers and his old foe Gabriel Martínez.[1]

In 1985 the chance came. Van Boven received a phone call in Holland from Leandro Despouy, an Argentinian lawyer who had been in exile in France and had returned to work in the Foreign Ministry. Despouy asked whether van Boven would be prepared to testify for the prosecution at the forthcoming trial in Buenos Aires. Van Boven accepted. He briefed himself on the plane by rereading his old correspondence with Martínez and the first two volumes of the report of the U.N. Working Group on Disappearances. He was determined that Martínez should be exposed. He had lived with the obsession for three years. Now it was time for him to exorcise some of the ghosts.

Once on the witness stand, van Boven quickly realized that this was no show trial. He found himself vigorously cross-examined by defense lawyers who even objected when he made reference to some notes he had prepared on the plane. Most of the cross-talk between the lawyers and judges was in Spanish. This he found extremely confusing. He still did not speak Spanish.

Gradually, the shadowy figure of Gabriel Martínez began to emerge under Strassera's questioning. Between 1976 and 1982, the diplomatic debates in Geneva had seemed distant and unrelated to Argentinians. Martínez had evidently counted on this and hoped to slip back into civilian life, but now he was being drawn snarling from obscurity. Van Boven recalled his 1977 war of memos with Martínez. He also suggested that Martínez had not sent back all the information to Buenos Aires, acting instead on his own initiative—which, as we have seen, was partly true. The packed courtroom listened in attentive silence. They were hungry for any information about the dirty war, particularly on far-off skirmishes that had gone completely unreported.

One of the lawyers for former President Roberto Viola asked van Boven whether he had any hostility toward Martínez. "He is not someone I like," replied van Boven. Never one to mince words, he then recalled the way Martínez had talked of the terrorists as being "non-socials"— language which, said van Boven, was reminiscent of Hitler.[2] This drew heated protests from the defense lawyers. Van Boven had kinder words to say about two other Argentinians. One was Mario Amadeo, the former member of the U.N. Sub-Commission. Van Boven recalled how Amadeo had intervened on behalf of the parents of Graciela Geuna, the young woman released from the camp of La Perla. The other was Lucio García del Solar, who had served at Argentina's embassy in New York in December 1981 during van Boven's desperate attempts to salvage money for the U.N. Working Group on Disappearances. Del Solar had told van Boven that he was troubled by the reports of disappearances.

Van Boven stepped down from the box after four and a half hours of exhausting testimony. He had to wait for another thirty minutes in the judges' chambers while the lawyers argued about whether he needed to remain in Argentina and confront Martínez directly. Eventually, it was decided that it would not be necessary. It was just as well, because van Boven was expected in Geneva for a meeting on human rights in Afghanistan. He felt deeply about the cruelties inflicted by the Soviet presence in that small country. Indeed, he had never really been as obsessed with Latin America as the Reagan Administration claimed.

Argentinian newspapers made much of van Boven's appearance, and the cameras followed his slightly disheveled figure around until he left the country. The papers made one serious mistake by confusing the name of Martínez with García del Solar, thus labeling poor del Solar (Argentina's then ambassador in Washington) as an accomplice to the terror. Van

Boven, it seemed, had not lost his knack for accidentally tripping people up. But he passed through Geneva on his way back to Holland looking relaxed.[3] It was clear to friends that he had gone some way in ridding himself of an old obsession.

Patt Derian was another with ghosts to exorcise. She had already been invited to Buenos Aires for President Alfonsín's inauguration in 1983 and had eclipsed Vice-President George Bush, who represented President Reagan. It was hardly surprising. Derian had suffered much personal abuse from American neoconservatives, but Argentinians remembered the way she had pleaded for the relatives in their darkest hour. It was appreciated. Now her unrelenting criticism of Massera and Videla was being vindicated by Alfonsín's decision to put them on trial, and she had a chance to use it in the service of law.

She arrived at the courthouse on June 13 1985 with her husband Hodding Carter and two American secret servicemen, her every move avidly recorded by the local newspapers. She could have taken a shortcut into the courtroom but, noted one paper, she chose the route taken by the normal spectators as a "small gesture of respect for the law." The breathless coverage noted that her dress was blue and voluminous and that she answered with a "laconic yes" when asked if she would tell the whole truth. She spoke with a "thick voice, excellent diction, quick rhythm, and care in the selection of adjectives." The mood was very different from the one that had prevailed in Buenos Aires in 1977 when she had first visited the country. Then, she had come as a villain and had been followed around by three cars full of heavily armed goons. Now she came as a heroine: "If we had listened to her voice, we might be living in a different, better country," said one paper wistfully.[4]

Videla and Massera, both of whom she had last seen in very different circumstances six years earlier, were not in court when she testified. All the defense lawyers except one—Videla's court-appointed Dr. Tavares—stood up and walked out in protest. As one cable from the U.S. embassy noted, they explained that they needed coffee.[5]

Derian's testimony gave her an opportunity to answer many of the charges that had been made against Carter's human rights policy by Jeane Kirkpatrick and others. Was there "political motivation" in the vehemence of her criticism of the Junta? No, replied Derian. "It was impossible to ignore the detailed information coming in about the disappearances— from the relatives, from human rights groups like Amnesty, and from the U.S. embassy itself. Human rights was U.S. government policy." Was it

"selective" in the way it had singled out Argentina and ignored other violators? No. "Hundreds of thousands of people were unjustly persecuted
around the world, but the resources of the U.S. were stetched thin, and it
concentrated its efforts where they were most effective."[6]

The most important question facing the trial was whether the military
commanders could be held responsible for the actions of more junior officers. Derian was asked about this. Had not Videla told her in 1977, while
they were sitting on his couch, that he was "sad" about the excesses, and
blamed them on lower-ranking officials? Did this not imply that Videla
was either not in control or not aware of what was happening? On this
all-important point Derian was able to make a decisive contribution. She
recalled her meeting with Admiral Emilio Massera at the ESMA on August 10 1977. There was absolute silence as she told the court how she had
finally confronted Massera with the fact that torture was almost certainly
being practiced on the floor below. The observing American diplomat
caught the drama in a later cable back to Washington: "In a moment that
caught the gallery's attention, Derian related that Massera had smiled
broadly in response to this statement. He then made a washing hands
motion while asking if she remembered the story of Pontius Pilate."[7] Patt
Derian had been waiting a long time to get the memory of that exchange
out of her system. Now it would help to put Massera behind bars for life.

Strassera asked the U.S. government to allow Tex Harris, who had handled human rights at the U.S. embassy in 1977, to testify. This was turned
down by the State Department. Strassera received a more surprising rejection from Amnesty International when he requested the presence of Patricia Feeney, the Amnesty researcher who had accompanied the mission to
Buenos Aires in 1976. Feeney was in Buenos Aires during the trial, but
Amnesty stuck to the letter of its official policy. There was nothing to add
to official reports. Or was it, rather, that Feeney's appearance would be
interpreted as a "political" act? Whatever the reason, here was Amnesty
International being cautious yet again. It was the very reason why the
Junta had failed to prove "political motivation" following Amnesty's dev-
astating 1976 mission.

John Bushnell was one American who did attend the trial—although
as an observer, not a witness. Bushnell, as we have seen, had been one of
Argentina's most articulate defenders at the ARA bureau during its bureaucratic war with Derian in 1977 and 1978. He had served briefly as the
acting Assistant Secretary of State for Inter-American Affairs in early 1981
and had argued before Congress for a resumption of military aid to Ar-

gentina. In 1983 Bushnell had drafted the controversial section of the State Department report claiming that 1,450 disappearances had been solved.[8]

Now, in May 1985, he evidently had changed his mind. As a senior diplomat at the U.S. embassy in Buenos Aires, he attended one eight-hour session of the trial and came away highly impressed by both the orderly atmosphere and the emotional impact of the disclosures: "With each day's testimony adding a new dimension to the public awareness of the widespread human rights violations of the 1970s there appears to be a growing consensus that the military Juntas cannot escape political responsibility for this tragic chapter in Argentina's history."[9] He had not always thought that way.

Tom Farer, the former president of the Inter-American Commission on Human Rights, ignored a cable from his former colleagues at the IACHR asking him not to testify. The IACHR's visit to Argentina in 1979 had been one of the most visible products of Derian's long campaign, and Farer himself had helped to ensure that the clandestine graves were fully reviewed in the mission report. With the IACHR visit, the disappearances slowed dramatically. One diplomat from the U.S. embassy who watched Farer testify seven years later was impressed. In a cable he described Farer as "careful, precise and respectful." The most striking aspect of the testimony, he reported, was Farer's explanation of the OAS human rights system:

> Farer emphasized that the IACHR understood that in Latin America there had been times where governments had to suspend certain rights . . . to maintain peace and order. Farer also emphasized, however, that there were three rights that could not be suspended: the right to life; the right to personal security; the right to due process of law.

"The prosecution was probably delighted," concluded the American observer. The defense was less than delighted. Its parting question to Farer was whether U.S. troops had committed human rights violations in Vietnam. The judges said Farer did not need to answer.[10]

Emilio Mignone also gave impressive testimony. Nine years after his daughter's kidnapping, Mignone was still able to recall in extraordinary detail the type of pistol carried by the intruders, the exact time he had gone to the police station, and his subsequent conversations with senior government officials. His meetings with Massera also stood out, as they had for Derian. He remembered the way Massera had described Videla as a "son of a bitch" and his own reply to Massera: "At least we can agree about something, Admiral."[11] Mignone felt better after testifying, much better. Like van Boven and Derian, this final "denuncia" had been immensely satisfying. It was some small consolation for the years of abuse and harassment.

Martínez the Chameleon

Gabriel Martínez, the man who had tried to prevent Mignone from testifying at the United Nations in 1982, gave a characteristic performance when he appeared before the court—unctuous one moment, haughty the next. Up to now, no one had questioned his unsavory past. Now it all started to return—all those years of tenacious infighting in the marble corridors of the Palace of Nations in far-off Geneva.

By another satisfying irony, one of those who was present to watch Martínez testify in 1985 was none other than Rodolfo Matarollo, the former ERP sympathizer whose presence in Geneva in the summer of 1976 had so provoked Martínez. Some thirty former guerrillas faced arrest if they returned to Argentina, but Matarollo was not among them. Indeed, he was now a professor and journalist. Democratic Argentina thus rendered its verdict on the fierce debate over Matarollo's credentials, which Martínez had used to try and muzzle NGOs at the United Nations. Matarollo now derived great satisfaction from seeing Gabriel Martínez wriggling under Strassera's sharp questions. After ten years, the roles had been reversed.[12]

True to form, Martínez adopted an astute strategy. He evidently assumed that the judges knew and cared little about the complexities of the U.N. human rights machinery which he had mastered so completely. He tried to confuse them with the convoluted U.N. jargon like "organs" and "standards." But Strassera was prepared. He knew that 116 files from the Argentinian mission in Geneva—seven hundred kilos of material—were neatly stacked in an adjacent room.[13] He asked Martínez why it had mattered, this far-off, wordy, debate in the United Nations? Martínez gave a revealing answer that echoed the memos prepared by his colleagues in the Foreign Ministry during 1977 and 1978: "When sanctions are taken by the U.N. it can affect a country's negotiating power, prestige, and commercial interests." His own aim, said Martínez, had been to prevent such sanctions.

Had the Junta ever clarified any of the cases forwarded to it by the U.N. Working Group on Disappearances? Martínez reacted cautiously. He was treading on eggs, and he probably knew it. "It depends, Mr. President, on what you mean by 'clarify.' If you mean by that did the person reappear alive, or was the corpse identified, I have to say very few." He was contemptuously dismissive about the U.N. Group on Disappearances which he had so skillfully manipulated: "Its information was lousy. Sometimes you'd get asked about just a single name—say 'Gonzales'—without anything else."[14] This was not the impression he had given his friend Mark Colville.

These Argentinian judges proved harder to trick than the United Nations, or Colville had been. Strassera had done his homework. Did Martínez recall, he asked, that 1977 meeting of the Sub-Commission, at which the others had complained about Martínez practicing "terrorism" in the United Nations? Martínez could only reply yes and hope Strassera did not follow up. Did Martínez remember Theo van Boven, who had said some rather hurtful things about Martínez in this very court not two weeks earlier? Because he was pleading diplomatic neutrality, Martínez could not afford to betray any personal feelings and he parried the question with a splendidly haughty answer: "What were my relations with van Boven? The sort you'd expect between an ambassador and a low-ranking U.N. official."

Yet Martínez was not quizzed as harshly as he might have been because he was not on trial. Strassera's aim was to show that so many complaints had arrived from the United Nations that the Junta members in Buenos Aires could not have pleaded ignorance—an important fact in establishing their responsibility. This meant taking Martínez at face value and accepting that he had loyally channeled all the information back to Buenos Aires like any dutiful diplomat. It meant ignoring the fanatical, destructive way in which he had supported the policy of disappearances. It meant allowing Martínez, like the junior officers, to plead "due obedience" to orders. It meant exonerating Argentina's diplomacy. It meant yet another compromise, yet another scoundrel set free.

After betraying the Junta that he had served so loyally, Martínez slipped back to his civilian job with a large company, where his diplomatic contacts must have proved invaluable. His son even secured a job in the presidential palace.

The Angel Goes Free

By now Lieutenant Alfredo Astiz was also probably sleeping a little easier. Astiz returned from his brief spell in a British jail in June 1982 like a hero, not a villain. He was awarded a medal, and he resumed working for the navy intelligence.

Dagmar Hagelin's father Ragnar was determined that the Angel should not escape, and he initiated a charge against Astiz for murder, with help from Mignone's CELS. The case went before Judge Miguel del Castillo, who ordered Astiz put in jail while he decided how to proceed. The day, appropriately, was December 10 1984—the same day that the U.N. General Assembly adopted the final draft of the new convention against torture that Astiz himself had helped to invigorate. The coincidence in dates between Astiz's arrest and the adoption of the convention was noted in a magazine article by Rodolfo Matarollo.[15]

Astiz, however, was to be one of the many beneficiaries of Raúl Alfonsín's political balancing act. The navy was aware that if Astiz was prosecuted the same fate would befall the entire GT 3/32 group which had worked from the ESMA. The navy high command informed the government that this could well provoke a navy revolt, and demanded that the case be handed over to the armed forces Supreme Council as required by the 1983 revision of the military justice code. Astiz was released from house detention after eighty-six relatively comfortable days.

Within forty-eight hours the Supreme Council had quashed the arrest warrant. The Council then acquitted Astiz on the grounds that he had already been investigated by the military in 1981 and cleared. Shortly before taking over as the navy's new commander in chief, Admiral Ramón Arosa offered a startling opinion: because of his age and rank Astiz could not possibly have taken "life and death decisions" in the war against subversion.[16]

Astiz's case was so provocative, and the evidence against him so well documented, that the government could not stand idly by. Yet it was tied by its own laws that required that six months pass before Astiz's case could be returned to the civilian courts. CELS lawyers appealed to the (civilian) Supreme Court, which recognized the validity of the armed forces' Supreme Council's ruling. It had no alternative. CELS lawyers would now have to wait six months before appealing the case before a civilian court. It would be a race against time: the trial of the nine commanders was well under way, and it looked likely to confirm that lower-ranking officers could plead due obedience.

Now promoted, Astiz returned to active service on the aircraft carrier *25 de Mayo* like a conquering hero. When Angel Fragelli and Alejandro Yanonne stated publicly that Astiz had participated in the kidnapping of Dagmar Hagelin, they were put under arrest on the orders of Judge Miguel Pons for harassing the unfortunate young navy lieutenant.

Eventually Mignone appealed, and the case against Astiz was heard before the Buenos Aires federal court of appeals, which had tried the nine commanders. Astiz refused to appear at an identification line-up. When ordered to appear, he wore a navy uniform. The court took up the case and decided that it could not charge Astiz with murder because Dagmar's body had never been found. It did charge him with false arrest but decided that the case was covered by the statute of limitations. In June 1987, all charges were dropped against Astiz and nineteen other ESMA operatives under the "due obedience" law. Those acquitted including Jorge "Tiger" Acosta, who is thought to have killed Dagmar. Alfredo Astiz thus became a symbol of the military's impunity under democracy, just as he had been a symbol of its cruelty under dictatorship.[17]

Dagmar's father Ragnar Hagelin watched this sequence of events with some despair, as he continued his increasingly forlorn search for Dagmar. Earlier in 1984 he had gone to Mar del Plata and visited a house which had reportedly been used as a detention center by the navy. Ragnar found the house deserted, but noticed the initials "D. H." carved in a tree in a garden. It was tantalizing but he could take it no further.[18]

By a quirk of fate, Alfredo Astiz was on leave at the time at Mar del Plata, where his family owned a cabin at an exclusive local bathing resort. A magazine had published photos of Astiz at the beach looking relaxed, paunchy, and bronzed, in the company of several pretty girls. It was, wrote Hagelin later, the face of a man "who has no moral debts to pay." One can imagine his feelings. Here, cavorting on the beach, was the man who had shot and kidnapped his daughter, the man he had pursued for six years. How he must have wanted to confront Astiz. But this was Astiz's territory. "I just didn't have that kind of courage," wrote Hagelin.

No wonder he shrank back. It cannot have been the fear of being knocked down by Astiz or arrested for harassment that terrified Hagelin. Like all the relatives, he had plenty of that kind of courage. No, it must have been the fear felt by the Mothers when standing at a graveside—the fear of facing the truth. Hagelin probably knew that those handsome blue eyes of Alfredo Astiz held the same secrets as a clandestine grave.

So he held back. But how would he live with the knowledge that Astiz was free, while his own daughter was dead? How could he—and Argentina—live with the pain?

Aftermath: Buenos Aires, September 1985. Relatives in Limbo

Near the Plaza de Mayo, in the "casa de las madres," a whole wall is covered by hundreds of tiny passport-size photos of the "desaparecidos." For the Mothers of the Plaza de Mayo, their children never really disappeared. Yet the mood in the "casa" is subdued. The trial and the CONADEP commission have produced plenty of villains, but few heroes. Signs of compromise are everywhere. Argentina's hunger for revenge has been replaced by a yearning for democracy.

Democracy has stranded the relatives. Their long and lonely campaign has been vindicated, and their courage—never in doubt—is now officially recognized. But the period of gratitude felt by their fellow countrymen has been brief. Hebe de Bonafini's action at the trial has been deeply unpopular. It suggests that the Mothers of the Plaza de Mayo want vengeance at all costs, and that they will harass democracy as they had harassed the dictatorship. Admiration has turned to resentment.

The problem facing the relatives is that the enemy is no longer exposed and easy to identify. In addition, with the advent of democracy, the objectives of the human rights groups have begun to diverge. As a result, they have begun to lose their cohesion.

Emilio Mignone's organization, CELS, emerged from the dictatorship with the most impressive reputation. Not only did it conduct a conventional human rights campaign—putting out publications, lobbying, and feeding information to outside groups like Amnesty—it also took cases to the law courts, filed habeas corpus submissions, and tried to identify the dead.

President Alfonsín's political package gave CELS further practical objectives. It was CELS which took up the case against Alfredo Astiz in 1981 and CELS that recovered the case again in 1985 after it had gone full circle. CELS is well placed to take up such cases. With the exception of Prosecutor Strassera, it probably possesses the fullest collection of documents on the dictatorship in Argentina. The practical nature of CELS's work and the personal prestige of Emilio Mignone means that it has generally escaped the charge of being "politically motivated," even though two of its leading lawyers, Luis Zamora and Marcelo Parrilli, were both senior in the Movimiento al Socialismo (MAS), a Trotskyite organization.

By the end of 1985 CELS faces a financial crisis. Most of its money has come from the Ford Foundation and been earmarked for specific publications, but by the end of 1985—with democracy established in Argentina—Ford is reviewing its grant and the CELS staff are racking their brains for fund-raising ideas that will not detract from their ability to take cases before the courts. Administration is another headache. Augusto Conte MacDonell has won a seat in the Congress, and this means that much of the day-to-day running of the organization falls on Emilio Mignone. Mignone is, by now, physically and emotionally exhausted. He always threw everything into his work, whether it was confronting Gabriel Martínez in the U.N. Human Rights Commission, giving advice to grief-stricken parents, or marching in solidarity with the Mothers. Mignone is not a young man, and the years have taken their toll. One member of his CELS board, Alfredo Galletti, committed suicide. For him, the strain was too much, the wait too long.

The final, and most serious, threat is political. Mignone knows that amnesty for the military will deprive CELS of its principal raison d'etre. The trial of his foes finds this formidable campaigner tired and withdrawn, and his organization groping.

*   *   *

The Grandmothers of the Plaza de Mayo, in contrast, are growing in confidence. By 1985, the number of infants they are seeking has risen to 182. They have managed to locate thirty and return some to their grandparents. It has been a long and often heartbreaking search. But at least they knew from the start that the infants were probably alive.

The Grandmothers have received a boost from the presence of Dr. Clyde Snow, an emiment American forensic anthropologist. Snow first arrives in June 1984 at the invitation of CONADEP to advise on how to identify the unknown dead. Judges have started to exhume bodies, but in an appallingly haphazard manner. Snow carefully performs one exhumation in which he examines the remains of an entire family of five, the Lanouscous, who are known to have died. Only four skeletons have been found. A fifth tiny coffin is empty. Snow concludes that five-month-old Matilde Lanouscou was not buried with her parents and two siblings, and should be assumed to be still alive. Here is a ray of hope in an otherwise ghastly story. Matilde's name enters the Grandmothers' files.[1]

Once the Grandmothers know that an infant is still alive, they face the problem of location. This is the most difficult part. They have spent hundreds of hours scanning registries of birth certificates, looking for discrepancies in dates or a suspicious certificate signed by a military doctor. They have advertised widely and relied heavily on phone calls. A curious neighbor might have noticed that a new child has suddenly appeared with the family next door. "You know, they never said anything . . ."

Once an infant has been found, the search is far from over. How can the grandmothers persuade a judge to give the child back to the grandparents? How can the child be told the facts of what happened to his or her real parents? Suppose the new adoptive parents are also totally unaware of what happened? Suppose they have provided a loving family? Should that now be shattered to satisfy the needs—perhaps even the urge for revenge—of an old woman? It is the kind of dilemma so delicately and movingly portrayed in the film *The Official Story*. Yet the Grandmothers remain stubborn and uncompromising. They want their grandchildren back, and by the end of 1985 several have been successfully returned with no obviously harmful side-effects. Once again, science has helped. In the case of Paula Logares, Mary-Claire King, a noted American geneticist, employs blood tests to prove the link between the little girl and her grandmother. This, too, is a first.[2]

Each success story is picked up by magazines and avidly devoured by Argentinians. In spite of their stubbornness, the Grandmothers seem more in tune with democratic Argentina than the Mothers. Perhaps because their goals are concrete. Perhaps because out of so much death, they are uncovering life.

*   *   *

While Clyde Snow's detective work in identifying the unknown dead has brought hope to the Grandmothers, it has brought despair and anger to the Mothers of the Plaza de Mayo. From the start, the Mothers have opposed exhumations and the identification of the corpses. Some hold out the faint hope that their children might still be alive, others prefer the memory of the living to the sight of the dead. All know that once their child is identified they can no longer belong to the Mothers group which had brought them so much comfort. Identifying the unknown dead will spell the end of the Mothers.

When Clyde Snow arrives in the Parque cemetery at Mar del Plata in March 1985 he finds himself embroiled in a deeply upsetting quarrel. Three "desaparecidos," two women and a man, have been buried in the cemetery. It is known that one is Liliana Pereyra (an ESMA victim) and Liliana's mother wants the body exhumed. But all three bodies have to be brought up before Liliana can be identified. One of the other bodies is thought to be that of a young man named Torti. Torti's sister has applied to a judge to have the body exhumed, but his mother vigorously disagrees and she has contacted the Mothers' president Hebe de Bonafini. De Bonafini arrives at the cemetery with a group of other Mothers and physically prevents the exhumation from taking place. "We don't want people killed by decree," she insists, in her typically aggressive manner. "We won't accept scientists or anthropologists from no matter where coming to tell us that our sons are a bag of bones."[3]

Eventually, the exhumation proceeds and Snow is able to confirm from the skeleton that Liliana Pereyra delivered a baby before she died. There is no sign of a dead infant. This confirms the testimony of Ana María Martí, who recalls seeing Liliana in the ESMA in the advanced stages of pregnancy. It is doubly important. The uncertainty has finally ended for Liliana's mother, and the Grandmothers can add another case to their files. But the Mothers face more turmoil.

It is understandable. The killers know the psychological importance of identification. On November 13 1984 Beatriz Rubenstein and her husband, parents of a young disappeared woman, received a macabre package. It contained a skull, several bones, and a letter from a "Commander Condor": "Señora, as a culmination of your incessant search for your daughter Patricia, we have decided to send you a part of what is left of her. . . . Patricia Huchansky de Simón was condemned to death by shooting for treason, and active collaboration with the Montonero killers." A forensic scientist later examined the bones and found that they belonged to a male. It had been, apparently, a cruel hoax.

In spite of this, the way Hebe de Bonafini halted the exhumation in Mar del Plata is unpopular, even among the Mothers' sympathizers. There is a feeling that the time has come to face the truth, however unpleasant, and that by such actions, the Mothers are simply prolonging Argentina's agony.

By the end of 1985, a major split has developed between the Mothers and their erstwhile allies. Eduardo Rabossi, secretary of CONADEP and one of Alfonsín's closest political advisers, feels they are conducting a left-wing political campaign aimed at destabilizing Alfonsín's regime. When Rabossi and Alfonsín visit Paris on a state visit, they are picketed by several protesters demonstrating on behalf of the Mothers. It is embarrassing for Alfonsín, and his French hosts ask if he wants the protesters cleared away. Alfonsín says no, and shrugs it off, but Rabossi fumes.

Outside Argentina, however, the Mothers are still feted and revered: it is almost as if their supporters abroad share the Mothers' fear of losing a cause. But inside Argentina they are an uncomfortable reminder of a past that most people want to forget. The Mothers are not "politically motivated"; they simply refuse to adapt. They have always been a single-issue group with a single slogan: "aparición con vida y castigo a los culpables." Always uncompromising and simplistic, both in their aims and their methods. That has been the appeal of the movement and the reason why it posed such a threat to the dictatorship. As the torturers—"los culpables"—have slipped off the hook, the Mothers have turned their anger against the government.[4]

They publish an effective monthly newspaper which features a rogues' gallery of former torturers, denounces the "fascism" of the middle class, and inveighs agdanst the "collaboration" of the Church and judiciary. Every headline screams "no compromise." As the Mothers subject Alfonsín's political platform to pitiless scrutiny and expose his compromises, he becomes understandably angry. So do other Argentinians. Hebe de Bonafini has turned from a plucky heroine into a harsh demagogue. Why can the Mothers not accept that their children are dead and start helping to build a better future? Why not harness their energy to a better cause than raking over old coals and prolonging the agony? Gazing around the Mothers' headquarters, it seems just a matter of time before they become irrelevant.

Then your eyes fall on that remarkable mosaic of tiny photos on the wall. There is a portrait of Mónica Mignone. It is an attractive, intelligent face, with thick dark hair and that distinctive Argentinian mixture of Mediterranean and Latin American features. Whatever battles were raging on the streets when this photo was taken, Mónica seems at peace with herself. Some of us tense up when we face the camera lens, but Mónica apparently relaxed. Argentina has been described as "a man on the defensive," but looking at this face the possibilities seem endless. It's impossible to believe that Mónica has disappeared, unthinkable that she could be dead.

Appendices

Appendix 1. The 1982 Dismissal of Theo van Boven

Chronology of the author's FOIA requests

On May 30 1984, the author put in a FOIA request to the U.S. State Department on Theo van Boven's dismissal. On June 24 1985, the State Department released several documents, including cable 01760 from Geneva, which implied that the Reagan administration was surprised at van Boven's dismissal (see page 327).

In 1986, during an interview with a senior U.N. official, I was given a copy of William Buffum's confidential memo to Javier Pérez de Cuéllar (see page 414), and shown a note for the file written by Emilio de Olivares about a February 1 1982 meeting between Pérez de Cuéllar and Jeane Kirkpatrick at which Ambassador Kirkpatrick expressed "dissatisfaction" with van Boven. Unlike the earlier cable, both these documents suggested U.S. involvement in van Boven's dismissal. The U.N. official refused to give me a copy of the Olivares memo on the grounds that this would be a breach of confidence, and that Olivares himself had since died.

On the basis of this information, I put in another FOIA request to the State Department on December 2 1986, requesting specific information about Kirkpatrick's meeting with Javier Pérez de Cuéllar. On January 2 1988, John Burke informed my lawyer, Stephen Feingold, that the department had discovered two responsive documents. One could be released subject to extensive excisions, the other was being withheld in its entirety. The material released described the February 1 meeting as "the first extensive discussion on U.N. secretariat staffing" to take place between Mrs. Kirkpatrick and Pérez de Cuéllar, but did not mention van Boven.

Feingold appealed for the release of the material withheld on March 10 1988, arguing that the Reagan Administration itself had turned the effectiveness of the U.N. secretariat into an issue of legitimate national and international interest. It thus could not withhold information on grounds of "national defense and foreign policy."

On June 9 1988 the State Department informed Feingold that an appeals panel had rejected our appeal and decided to continue to withhold the material. It added that the material withheld from the one document that had been partially released contained no reference to van Boven. This clearly implied that the second document did refer to van Boven.

On July 20 1988 Feingold filed a suit for release of the second document with the U.S. district court sitting in Massachusetts.

On October 20 1988 Eugene Bovis from the State Department wrote to Feingold and myself saying that a further search of U.S. mission files in New York had produced another four memoranda about the February 1 meeting. Three dealt with "diverse U.N. political problems" and were not responsive to our request. The fourth was being withheld because its disclosure could damage U.S. national security. The implication, clearly, was that the fourth document referred to van Boven.

It was now clear that that there were two documents on the February 1 meeting which referred to van Boven, both of which were denied to us.

On October 26 Pratt Byrd, the acting deputy director of the State Department Review Center, responded to Feingold's suit with an affidavit, justifying the decision to withhold these two documents. Pratt Byrd gave a brief description of the two documents:

(a) Document one was a February 2 1982 cable from the U.S. mission in New York to U.S. Secretary of State Haig. According to Byrd, the first paragraph referred to comments about van Boven that were "exclusively" made by Pérez de Cuéllar. Releasing this, he said, would damage U.S. relations with foreign governments. Information provided by foreign governments or international organizations to the United States is deemed confidential.

(b) Document two was entitled U003, and dated February 19 1982. Byrd's affidavit described it as follows:

Memorandum of Conversation (part I of V) dated February 19 1982. Subject: UN Secretariat staffing. Participants: UN: The Secretary General, Mr. Emilio de Olivares. US: Ambassador Kirkpatrick, Mr. Theodore Papendorp. Date and Place: February 1982, the Secretary General's office. Three pages classified CONFIDENTIAL RDS/ 2/1/2002.

According to Byrd this memorandum consisted of eight paragraphs "only one of which relates to the Division of Human Rights and its then-director Mr. Theodore [sic] van Boven. This paragraph provides basically the same information as does Document 1 . . . though in memorandum rather than telegraphic format.

"[This memorandum] contains foreign government information (i.e., the remarks of the U.N. Secretary General) and remarks of Ambassador Kirkpatrick, the release of which would cause damage to U.S. foreign relations and thereby to national security." On the basis of Byrd's affidavit, Assistant U.S. Attorney Peter Gelhaar moved to have the case dismissed.

Feingold and I had hoped that our FOIA request would confirm or deny what I had learned from the Olivares memo—namely, that Ambassador Kirkpatrick had expressed "dissatisfaction" with van Boven. We now knew that the first document would be withheld because it contained a record of the comments of a non-U.S. official (Pérez de Cuéllar). The second document (U003) was not absolutely protected because it contained Ambassador Kirkpatrick's own comments to Pérez de Cuéllar. We knew that it referred to van Boven, but this in itself did not suggest criticism or "dissatisfaction."

If Feingold appealed for the release of U003, there was a chance that we would lose on the grounds that releasing Kirkpatrick's comments about van Boven would damage national security. If, however, we could learn more about why document U003 was being withheld, we might learn enough to corroborate Olivares's memo. Feingold told Gelhaar that if he would supply us with more information, we would drop the case. Gelhaar agreed, and on January 19 1988 Byrd drafted a supplementary affidavit on U003. He had the following to say about the February 1 discussion:

> Although the remarks of Ambassador Kirkpatrick might be comprehensible when segregated from those of the Secretary General her comments, along with other publicly known events, provide clues as to the comments of the Secretary General de Cuéllar. However, even if completely segregable, comments made by Ambassador Kirkpatrick about U.N. officials, if released, would exacerbate the relationships between American officials and the U.N. officials with whom they work and possibly with the nations from which these officials come. This would seriously affect the ability of U.S. representatives to work effectively in the U.N., thereby causing harm to our foreign relations. These comments, therefore, remain properly classified.

We could only assume from this that there were two reasons for withholding the paragraph in U003 that referred to van Boven. The first was that it was inconsistent with the cables already released to me in which Ambassador Kirkpatrick was quoted as expressing surprise at the news of van Boven's dismissal. Second was the admission that her comments would "exacerbate" relations between American and U.N. officials. This seemed sufficient to confirm Olivares's description of the February 1 meeting, and on January 27 1989 Feingold dismissed the action.

February 17 1982 Memo from William Buffum
to Javier Pérez de Cuéllar About Theo van Boven

The Secretary-General   17 February 1982

CONFIDENTIAL

William B. Buffum

The Chef de Cabinet indicated you wished to have a summary of the van Boven case which follows:

Theodorus van Boven, 48 years old, was appointed Director of the Division of Human Rights in Geneva 1 May 1977 on secondment from the Government of the Netherlands. His initial two-year contract was extended an additional three years on 1 May 1979.

Van Boven has been a dedicated, energetic and conscientious official. He approaches his work seriously but does so in an exceptionally independent spirit. He said on several occasions that he finds it difficult to work within a. bureaucratic structure where he is subject to directions from above. It was essentially for this reason he advised us last fall he was looking for employment elsewhere after his current contract expires on 30 April 1982. He sought re-employment with the Dutch Government but was informed at the time that no appropriate position was vacant in The Hague. He was also looking for an appointment to the faculty of a university. Failing to find such outside employment, he had hoped his present contract would be extended until he could find a new job.

Over the past year, van Boven became increasingly outspoken and indiscreet in his comments about the positions of Member States on human rights. This was, for example, very evident in an interview he gave the Swiss magazine *Illustré* on 1 April 1981 where he permitted himself to be quoted criticizing the Government of Argentina, which he said was able to prevent its case from being placed on the Human Rights Commission agenda because of its friendship with the USSR and the USA. The Government of Argentina lodged a formal complaint. He also criticized President Reagan by name, claming he was less interested in human rights than President Carter, and that American policy shifted from the human factor to the power factor with a narrow base which misjudged world realities. The US later made clear it would not be sorry to see van Boven replaced.

We also received numerous complaints from the Government of Chile alleging van Boven was biased against them and favouring opponents of the régime.

All these complaints were brought to van Boven's attention. He was explicitly cautioned to observe the limits incumbent on any international civil servant by refraining from public statements offensive to Member States, and most particularly when his statements were not submitted for prior approval and went far beyond what the Secretary-General himself would say under similar circumstances.

Over a period of time, some of the Governments involved in the UN Human Rights investigations refused to co-operate with van Boven and chose to work out the necessary arrangements with New York Headquarters rather than Geneva.

In the case of his address to the opening session of the present Human Rights Commission meeting, on 1 February 1982, an advance copy of which was given to the press, he singled out a number of Member States, mostly from Latin America, for particular criticism. A copy was made available to Headquarters in New York only after we requested it. Van Boven was advised his text would be considered offensive by Member States since he was selective in those which he chose to criticize, and unbalanced by ignoring the causes why human rights are occasionally suppressed by Governments when they face insurrection, guerrilla warfare or widespread terrorist activities. His response was to say he would not change a single word.

We then offered to address a personal message from the Secretary-General to the Commission dealing with the same theme which van Boven wished to emphasize, namely, priority attention should be given to cases involving loss of human lives. The thought was that such a message would make van Boven's statement redundant and give him a face-saving way out. He rejected this solution, saying he would not read the message but would merely appear before the Commission to announce he was leaving his job because UN Headquarters wished to censor his statement.

As an exceptional measure to avoid a public scene, van Boven was then told if he wished to deliver his text, he could do so provided he made clear that it represented his personal views. He did so.

With less than three months remaining in his contract, it was agreed for compassionate reasons to tell him now his contract would not be renewed. This was done in a "no distribution" cable to Cottafavi. Immediately on being informed of the contents, van Boven took the floor in the Human

Rights Commission and announced this would be his last session as Director since he had major policy differences with the leadership of the Organization in New York. He then proceeded to give another uncleared speech developing his views in detail on highly controversial subjects such as the establishment of the position of a High Commissioner for Human Rights. The USSR immediately denounced him for doing so. While a number of countries, especially Western Europeans, praised him for his courage and expressed regret at this impending departure, Argentina openly expressed pleasure he was leaving.

In short, by persistant public statements of views not compatible with his status as an international civil servant and his rejection of Headquarters guidance he alienated a large number of Governments and seriously reduced his effectiveness in dealing with the human rights problems for which he is responsible.

Extract from Martínez's September 13 1979 cable calling to "weaken" van Boven and exploit the confidentiality of 1503

SECRETO

TELEGRAMA EXPEDIDO A CANCILLERIA
Ginebra,   13 setiembre de 1979

Nro.   1972/1973.-

mis 1923/5 y 1947/9 respecto tratamiento por comision derechos humanos "caso argentina" trasmitido por subcomision expertos (tramite privado) y propuestas sobre desaparecidos (debate publico) se indican seguidamente algunas posibles alternativas y cur sos de accion:

(iii) respecto secretaria division derechos humanos: utilizacion al maximo de la prerrogativa que implica ser miembros de la comision, especialmente respecto a acceso informacion reservada, tramite dado a la misma, etc. en lo que hace al personal de la division y particularmente su director (enemigo declarado de nuestro . . .

pais) mantener una posicion de critica activa, a fin de debilitar su gravitacion o prestigio frente a otros miembros, aprovechan do la personalidad del senor van boven y los problemas internos que vive actualmente su servicio a raiz irregularidades en la division o denuncias contra funcionarios, incluyendo el subdirector pierre sanon, que se ventilan actualmente a nivel de la secretaria general naciones unidas y con repercucion en la prensa. pro yecto de nota transmitido mi 1960 apunta en dicha direccion.

2) el problema de las desapariciones: este asunto debera ser re examinado en profundidad a la luz de eventuales acciones o nuevas medidas que puedan ser intentadas por los paises occidentales en la proxima asamblea general, partiendo quizas del examen de los informes de la comision o de la subcomision por parte de la tercera comision, la cual fue origen de la resolucion 33/173. empero, cabe pensar que nuestra accion en la comision de dere chos humanos deberia procurar: (i) impedir la creacion del grupo de expertos propuesto por la subcomision o, de no ser posible, limitar al maximo su mandato, y (ii) asegurar el cumplimiento pleno del procedimiento fijado por la resolucion 1503 en el tramite de las comunicaciones. dado que el "caso argentino", o al menos las comunicaciones en que se sustenta, alude fundamentalmente al problema desapariciones, su mante-

nimiento dentro del marco de los mecanismos contemplados en la resolucion 1503 (mi telex 1947/9 punto (iv), alternativas b) y c)), nos ayudara a
evitar la repeticion del debate publico de casos individuales, impidiendo
tambien la participacion testimonial de las ong cuando se trate este tema.

1309 1800 martinez

Appendix 2. Liberty Jail, Uruguay, December 1979

Extract from Javier Pérez de Cuéllar's Report, December 1979

	Distr. RESTRICTED*
UNITED NATIONS E C O N O M I C A N D S O C I A L C O U N C I L	E/CN.4/R.50/Add.2 14 February 1980 Original: ENGLISH/SPANISH

COMMISSION ON HUMAN RIGHTS
Thirty-sixth session

STUDY OF SITUATIONS WHICH REVEAL A CONSISTENT PATTERN OF GROSS VIOLATIONS OF HUMAN RIGHTS AS PROVIDED IN COMMISSION RESOLUTION 8 (XXIII) AND ECONOMIC AND SOCIAL COUNCIL RESOLUTIONS 1235 (XLII) AND 1503 (XLVIII)

*Report prepared by the Secretary-General pursuant to
Commission on Human Rights resolution 15 (XXXIV)*

The present document contains the reports of the Secretary-General on his direct contacts with the Governments of Paraguay and Uruguay, pursuant to the confidential decisions relating to these countries, adopted by the Commission on Human Rights at its thirty-fifth session under Economic and Social Council resolution 1503 (XLVIII).

---

* All persons handling this document are requested to respect and observe its confidential nature.

GE.80-10608

. . .

E/CN.4/R.50/Add.2
page 10

As for the trials of detainees, the authorities gave their assurance that they always acted within the constitutional and legal framework prescribed by Parliament, and particularly the Security Act. The procedure provided for in that Act, which continues to be applied, requires that the arrested person be brought before the competent Examining Military Judge within 10 days. The Government therefore rejects the charge that the prisoners are held incommunicado for months without being brought before a judge. It explained that if they had not been brought before a judge they would have invoked the right of habeas corpus under the Constitution (articles 12, 17, 23 and 30 of the Constitution). It stated that only three out of a thousand detainees had invoked that right. The constitutional principle of the right of defence was also respected, according to the authorities. Once the trial began, the prisoner had the right to designate his own defence counsel from among members of the national bar association and, if he did not do so, he could be assisted by counsel appointed *ex officio*. Defence counsel had access to all the records, and could seek and produce any kind of evidence to clarify the position of the defendant. The Uruguayan authorities, and chiefly those immediately concerned, gave their assurance that all trials proceeded normally, and they offered to take steps to ensure that they went forward as expeditiously as possible, subject to the procedure prescribed by law.

The authorities most strongly denied that any ill treatment or torture of prisoners, either before the trial or during their stay in prison, had been tolerated.

With regard to prison conditions and the treatment of prisoners, Mr. Pérez de Cuéllar was able to pay a *lengthy* visit to the two houses of detention, the Establicimiento Militar de Reclusion No. 1, situated near a place called Libertad, hence its name "Carcel de Libertad," which is a prison exclusively for men, and the Establicimiento Militar de Reclusion No. 2, known as "Punta de Rieles", which is exclusively for women and both of which only house prisoners on trial for the offence of subversion. It was made quite clear that those prisons did not house any common criminals who had not committed offences against State security. Mr. Pérez de Cuéllar was able to observe that the prison conditions were extremely reasonable as regards hygiene (cleanliness, lighting and ventilation), neatness, food and medical services. He was able to see that normal arrangements were made for recreation and outdoor activities. He visited special reading rooms, music rooms and workshops for the teaching or practice of handicrafts, such as carpentry, printing, weaving, upholstering, mechanics and bookbinding. The prisoners can hear radio programmes, national and international news reports, and information on and broadcasts of sports events. The guards are armed only with wooden truncheons for purposes of self defence. He was told that visits to prisoners were normal and regular, and he himself was able to observe the presence of relatives waiting to pay such visits. As regards correspondence, including parcels and foodstuffs, he was assured that they were of the kind allowed in any detention centre.

As for the physical condition of the detainees, Mr. Pérez de Cuéllar found that they all appeared healthy. Among the many prisoners whom he was able to meet, were Messrs. Altessor, Estrella, Massera and Turcanski, whose cases are known internationally.

In December 1979 the Uruguayan Government made an arrangement with the Committee of the International Red Cross whereby delegations from that organization could see persons imprisoned for offences detrimental to the nation or "related situations" in detention centres, and could freely converse with them, without witnesses or time-limits, and were permitted to make suggestions to the prison governor. After the visits they make a report, to be submitted to the Government of Uruguay. A further set of visits may be considered after a further arrangement is made with the authorities.

4. The authorities interviewed made repeated references to the campaign being waged outside the country about the trial conditions and pressure on prisoners in Uruguay. They feel that this campaign is being engineered by exiled or fugitive opposition politicians, with the support of foreign political groups interested in projecting an image of inhuman repression in Uruguay. They consider that these persons and those groups are abusing the good faith of international organizations concerned with the protection of human rights. Mr. Pérez de Cuéllar was shown numerous documents which the authorities considered to provide proof of this manipulation of the campaign against the Uruguayan Government.

Conclusions

The Uruguayan Government considers that Uruguay has been the object of widespread sedition aimed at destroying its democratic structure and that the authors of this campaign used criminal methods to achieve their purpose and still have not completely given up the struggle to defeat it.

The Uruguayan Government considers that in its fight against sedition it has invariably adhered to the Constitution and the law.

The Uruguayan Government is aware of the concern caused by this struggle and attributes it to a concerted campaign mounted abroad by its expatriate opponents and by Marxist-Leninist elements and organizations whose good faith has been abused by such persons.

The Uruguayan Government expresses its continuing concern to ensure that human rights are protected in the course of its anti-subversive activities.

The Uruguayan Government, according to the personal observations of the representative of the Secretary-General, is holding persons arrested for offences detrimental to the nation and related offences under normal detention conditions.

Extracts from the Report on Liberty Jail by Jean-François Labarthe, ICRC

[Page 8 of the original]

Whenever a prisoner moves out of his cell, he has to keep his hands behind his back and his eyes fixed directly in front of him. A glance over his shoulder or up to the floor above, and he will forfeit his walking hour for several days, which means being confined in his 9' by 6' cell, 24 hours a day. The prisoner becomes a walking number.

Visits take place in a windowed booth with a telephone. At the close, the prisoner and his visitor may, if they wish, enjoy a moment's kiss through a tiny opening in the window.

The child who comes to visit (once a month) leaves his or her mother behind the barbed wire perimeter to meet his or her prisoner father in a pretty garden arranged specially for childen's visits (sandboxes, slides, swings, etc.) The visit, which takes place on a bench, will be stopped as soon as the father makes an affectionate gesture. The punishment will be one or two months of disciplinary cell, with no visits. On the other hand, if the father makes no such gesture, he will be able to meet his child during 9 hours every year. In any event, following each visit the child is interrogated by a guard.

The glass booths devised for visitors are also used by lawyers, who are officially appointed by the military junta; the telephones used make recording of the conversation possible. The freedom to express himself in writing is "forgotten" by the prisoner: almost all of his letters are seized by the censor.

The prisoner gradually loses contact with his family and his friends. A system of two-way communication between prosecution and defense is quite active.

The fact that physical exercise in the cell is forbidden, and prisoners are not allowed to lie down on the cot during the day, causes irreversible physical damage which can result, after some time in prison, in paralysis or atrophy of certain limbs.

[Page 9 of the original]

Sometimes a prisoner in a double cell is mentally ill. During one of his crazes, he may be gently reinterrogated by the prison psychologist, and he may unwillingly give away information about his single cellmate. The authorities may then take advantage of the situation to resume the questioning of the latter and possibly add several years of imprisonment to his already long sentence.

When this mentally ill prisoner is returned to his cell, racked with guilt, he may attempt suicide. But the administration is there to stop him through constant surveillance, since it does not want this type of "escape" either. About 10% of the prisoners are listed by the authorities as mentally ill, and tens of thousands of tranquilizers are handed out each month. Under prison conditions, the inmates' medical needs are barely related to ordinary treatment, and are geared to a different purpose.

Newspapers and radios are banned. The library only includes books predating the French Revolution; one would say that book publishing stopped for ever at that time.

.   .   .

For all of the prisoner, the tension and insecurity effects did not start at the prison doors; they had started earlier, at the time of the interrogation. They have all been tortured, kept in secret places of detention, questioned, all of them without exception, between 1971 and 1979. All of them have spent weeks, months, sometimes more than a year, in military units. In some units, prisoners are tortured with electrodes, in others they are suspended by their arms previously tied behind their back or kept with their heads under water until suffocation, not to mention other similar refinements. Then, other military units take these prisoners for "recovery" and get them "back into shape". Once they are presentable, the soldiers put them into the prison. Some of the prisoners seen at "Libertad" had been sent back to military units for second or third interrogation.

[Page 10 of the original]

.   .   .

Does this type of imprisonment entail serious consequences for the prisoner? If so, what are those consequences?

Deprivation of freedom is, in itself, the most painful of frustrations, and restrictions imposed by the authorities upon the prisoner's movements and upon his will are a hindrance or a check to the satisfaction of his most basic needs. The deprivation of movement for one who has legs, like the deprivation of a limb or of one of the sense organs, results in a frustration of greater or lesser significance leading the prisoner to a reaction the seriousness of which will depend particularly upon:

- the importance of the particular need in terms of intensity;
- the person's tolerance for this frustration, and its duration;
- the defense mechanisms of the prisoner.

The prisoners we met no longer express any needs. They manage by trying to mask their pain and their fear of showing a deteriorated personality to a sympathetic interviewer. They tell the delegates of an anguished and impoverished life, of a silent isolation from persons and of psychological disturbances.

The prisoner is never free to hide, because security requires the constant opening of cell windows and doors and may monitor the performance of everyone's most private functions.

Among other liberties which the prisoners of "Libertad" are deprived of, one should not forget the freedom to speak, to whistle, to sing (the rules impose silence), the choice of one's friends, the freedom to write, to look where one wants upon leaving the cell.

[Page 11 of the original]

The prisoner thus feels acutely the differences between detention and oppression. The combined effect of the suppression of visits and censoring, as we have seen, leaves the prisoner alone with his prisonmates. He loses his identity as a man and receives in turn the mere identity of a prisoner and his number. He can choose neither his uniform nor his haircut. He is not free to get up, to walk, to shower, to shave or to let his beard grow. He must work with no pay; his shoes and his denture belong to the institution; if he breaks his glasses, he is punished, and then deprived of them for a long time; he is kept day and night under lock and key in his concrete cage; he cannot even call the guard.

In the course of the interviews, the prisoners reveal, as such as state explicitly, that they have a minimum of contacts with their cellmates and with inanimate objects. This lack of sensory stimulation manifests itself in a loss of interest in the environment on the part of the prisoner. He only speaks of himself. His responses are highly emotional. His anguish manifests itself in psychosomatic disturbances. He loses the thread of his sentence and describes his hallucinations.* One prisoner, victim of a neurosis, spoke of having lived in his cell for several months with his father and sister "who had both been dead for a long time", until the prison doctor started to medicate him. Since that day, this prisoner cannot stand living any more. He could live with his neurosis. He had got used to the prison. With this added input of medicines, his condition has collapsed into a psychosis.

---

*   It is interesting to note from a recent study conducted among the inmates of a prison that the mental health of the prisoners improves noticeably if there are relations with others and a possible "adjustment" to the realities of daily life.

Does a doctor have the freedom to prescribe and to maintain confidentiality in his relations with prisoner patients in the context of "Libertad"? One thing is certain: that military power takes precedence over medical power, and that the former exclusive power is overwhelming for the imprisoned person.

The prisoner sinks into the quicksand of a robot's alienating life, where everything is done according to a bell ring, a sign, a whistle and a nod.

[Page 12 of the original]

The administration of "Libertad" fears riots, escapes and suicides. It knows that with the excessive deprivation of liberty, it is driving prisoners, through deep emotional disturbances, to the point of suicide, murder or a psychotic state. In addition to this impoverishment due, in large part, to sensory and social deprivation (tiny concrete cell, banging of the steel doors, solitude, absence of contacts, etc.), the prisoner is unceasingly harassed, provoked and punished. He must live through periods of increasing discipline, followed by periods of relaxation of restraints.

The tension in the prison can be felt and seen. The insecurity of prisoners used to be hounded shoots nevertheless up during simulated escapes staged by the guards shooting from their watchtwers at dummy stand-ins for the prisoners, while misleading information is broadcast throughout the prison on loudspeakers. Certain sentences are very long; punishment seems out of proportion to the crimes charged, whether actually committed or not. At the end of the sentence, if the prisoner, or rather his family, cannot raise the money to reimburse the cost of board and lodging at "Libertad" (which may amount to several thousands of dollars), the prisoner will not be released.

The prisoner thinks more about what he may not do than about what he is entitled to do; he is not allowed to use his skills; corrective action is always based on fear or deprivation.

Being differential, the treatment of prisoners at "Libertad" leads to divisions, tensions and competitions among the prisoners in the midst of their misery. The prisoner has two options:

- he can try to settle down in this environment as a reaction;
- he can try to commit suicide, or drug himself with medications.

. . .

[Page 13 of the original]

First conclusion:

- "I will pull out your eyes and put them in the place of mine; you will
- pull out my eyes and put them in the place of yours. Thus, you will
- look at me through my eyes, and I through yours."

L. Binswanger

This text is on the wall above the desk of the prison psychologist at "Libertad".

Appendix 3. September 1980 Cable from the U.S. Embassy in Buenos Aires on "The Tactic of Disappearances"

Department of State **TELEGRAM**

TAZT'C

CONFIDENTIAL

CONFIDENTIAL

AN: D800460-0026

PAGE 01   BUENOS 07745 01 OF 02 261400Z
ACTION SS-30

INFO OCT-01 ADS-00 SSO-00 /031 W
------------------016260 261418Z /42
O R 260900Z SEP 80
FM AMEMBASSY BUENOS AIRES
TO SECSTATE WASHDC IMMEDIATE 6889
INFO USMISSION GENEVA
AMEMBASSY LIMA
AMEMBASSY ROME
USMISSION USUN NEW YORK

C O N F I D E N T I A L SECTION 1 OF 2 BUENOS AIRES 7745

EXDIS

ROME FOR VATICAN OFFICE
DEPT PLS PASS USCINCSO FOR INTAFF

E.O. 12065: GDS 9/19/86 (RUSER, CLAUS W.)
TAGS: SHUM PINT AR
SUBJECT: THE TACTIC OF DISAPPEARANCE

REF: BUENOS AIRES 7578

   C - ENTIRE TEXT.

2. SUMMARY: DISAPPEARANCE IS STILL THE STANDARD TACTIC
FOR THE ARGENTINE SECURITY FORCES IN DEALING WITH CAPTURED
TERRORISTS. THE MILITARY'S COMMITMENT TO THIS METHOD IS
PROFOUNDLY ROOTED IN ELEMENTS THAT RANGE FROM EFFECTIVE-
NESS THROUGH EXPEDIENCY TO CULTURAL BIAS. WE DOUBT WHETHER
INTERNATIONAL SANCTIONS AND OPPROBRIUM WILL, IN THEMSELVES, CAUSE
THE GOVERNMENT TO CHANGE THE TACTIC AND GRANT CAPTURED TERROR-
ISTS DUE PROCESS. GETTING THE AUTHORITIES TO ABANDON THIS
TACTIC WILL BE AN UPHILL BATTLE. WE MUST TRY.
THE VATICAN MAY BE THE MOST EFFECTIVE ADVOCATE IN THIS
CONFIDENTIAL
CONFIDENTIAL

PAGE 02   BUENOS 07745 01 OF 02 261400Z

EFFORT WHICH SHOULD TRY TO CONVINCE THE LEADERSHIP THAT

CONFIDENTIAL

CONFIDENTIAL

THERE ARE OTHER WAYS TO DEAL WITH THE PROBLEM--ESPECIALLY
THROUGH THE ESTABLISHMENT OF MILITARY COURTS. END SUMMARY.

3. THOUGH DRASTICALLY REDUCED IN NUMBERS FROM PREVIOUS
LEVELS, DISAPPEARANCE CONTINUES TO BE THE STANDARD TACTIC
FOR THE ARGENTINE SECURITY FORCES IN DEALING WITH PEOPLE
THEY BELIEVE TO BE MEMBERS OF TERRORIST ORGANIZATIONS.
DISAPPEARANCE IS A EUPHEMISM FOR THE UNACKNOWLEDGED DETEN-
TION OF AN INDIVIDUAL BY SECURITY FORCES. BASED ON EVERY-
THING WE KNOW, WE BELIEVE THAT DETAINEES ARE USUALLY
TORTURED AS PART OF INTERROGATION AND EVENTUALLY EXECUTED
WITHOUT ANY SEMBLANCE OF DUE PROCESS. AS WE UNDERSTAND
IT, THE CURRENT GUIDELINES FOR THE SECURITY FORCES ARE TO
USE THIS PROCEDURE ONLY AGAINST ACTIVE MEMBERS OF TERROR-
IST ORGANIZATIONS. THE RESULT HAS BEEN THAT VIRTUALLY
ALL OF THOSE WHO DISAPPEARED THIS YEAR HAVE PROBABLY
BEEN MONTONEROS.

4. THE ARGENTINE SECURITY FORCES WON THE "DIRTY WAR"
AGAINST THE TERRORISTS TWO YEARS AGO. SINCE THAT TIME THE
MONTONEROS HAVE BEEN ABLE TO CARRY OUT ONLY ISOLATED, IF
OCCASIONALLY SPECTACULAR, ACTS FOR WHICH THE TERRORIST
ACTORS HAVE OFTEN EVENTUALLY PAID WITH THEIR LIVES.
THUS, EVEN IF ONE WERE TO CONCEDE THE CASE BEFORE, NECESSITY HARDLY
CAN BE INVOKED BY THE MILITARY TO JUSTIFY THE USE OF DISAPPEAR-
ANCE AS A COUNTER-INSURGENCY TECHNIQUE. ON THE OTHER
HAND, THE CONTINUED USE OF DISAPPEARANCE HAS A VERY HIGH
INTERNATIONAL POLITICAL COST FOR THE GOVERNMENT. IT IS
ON THE DEFENSIVE IN INTERNATIONAL ORGANIZATIONS. RELATIONS
WITH THE UNITED STATES CONTINUE TO BE STRAINED BY THE
ISSUE. THE PROBABLE INVOLVEMENT OF ARGENTINE SECURITY
FORCES IN THE DISAPPEARANCE OF THREE ARGENTINE MONTONEROS
CONFIDENTIAL
CONFIDENTIAL

PAGE 03   BUENOS 07745 01 OF 02 261400Z

IN PERU FORCED PRESIDENT VIDELA TO CANCEL A TRIP TO LIMA
THAT HE WISHED TO MAKE TO SYMBOLICALLY
EXPRESS HIS GOVERNMENT'S DEMOCRATIC INTENTION.
AT THE POLITICAL LEVEL IN THIS GOVERNMENT, OUR CONTACTS,
EVEN AMONG THE MILITARY, RECOGNIZE THESE COSTS AND EXPRESS
THE HOPE THAT EVENTUALLY DISAPPEARANCES WILL CEASE.

5. BUT THEY DON'T.THIS UNWILLINGNESS DOES NOT REFLECT
SIMPLE BLOODY-MINDEDNESS BY UNTHINKING MILITARY MEN. IF
IT DID THE PROBLEM MIGHT BE MORE SOLUABLE. RATHER THE

CONFIDENTIAL

CONFIDENTIAL

ARGENTINES HAVE RECORSE TO DISAPPEARANCE BECAUSE:

--IT WORKED. MORAL AND LONG TERM POLITICAL COSTS APPEAR
LESS IMPORTANT THAN SECURITY CONSIDERATIONS TO THE GOA.
ARGENTINE SECURITY FORCES DEFEATED ONE OF THE LARGEST
TERRORIST ASSAULTS ON A MODERN SOCIETY USING THIS
TACTIC. THE EXPERIENCE OF WEST GERMANY AND THE UNITED
STATES IN USING THE LAW TO MEET A TERRORIST THREAT MAKES
LITTLE IMPRESSION HERE SINCE THE MILITARY ACCURATELY
EVALUATE THE THREAT THAT THEY BESTED AS BEING MUCH LARGER
THAN THE ONE THE UNITED STATES AND THE FRG FACED. RATHER,
ARGENTINES INVOKE ITALY'S CONTINUING TORMENT AS WHAT
THEY MIGHT HAVE FACED IF THEY HAD STUCK TO THE LAW.

--IT CONTINUES TO BE EFFECTIVE. DISAPPEARED PRISONERS YIELD
UP INFORMATION UNDER TORTURE. DISAPPEARED PREISONERS CAN
BE TURNED AGAINST THEIR FORMER COMRADES. DISAPPEARED
PRISIONERS ARE BELIEVED TO BE A FRIGHTENING EXAMPLE THAT
INHIBITS THE MONTONEROS' ABILITY TO RECRUIT NEW PERSONNEL.

NOTE BY OC/T: NOT PASSED ABOVE ADDRESSEE.

CONFIDENTIAL

CONFIDENTIAL

CONFIDENTIAL

CONFIDENTIAL

PAGE 01   BUENOS 07745 02 OF 02 2613462
ACTION SS-30

INFO OCT-01 ADS-00 SSO-00 /031 W
------------------016125 2614322 /40
O R 260900Z SEP 8C
FM AMEMBASSY BUENOS AIRES
TO SECSTATE WASHDC IMMEDIATE 6890
INFO USMISSION GENEVA
AMEMBASSY LIMA
AMEMBASSY ROME
USMISSION USUN NEW YORK

C O N F I D E N T I A L SECTION 2 OF 2 BUENOS AIRES 7745

EXDIS

ROME FOR VATICAN OFFICE
DEPT PLS PASS USCINCSO FOR INTAFF

--THE MILITARY ARE UNWILLING TO USE CIVILIAN COURTS TO
PUNISH ACTIVE TERRORISTS. THEY ARGUE THAT THE COURTS
WOULD SIMPLY LET THE TERRORISTS GO. IN VIEW OF THE
STIFF SENTENCES HANDED OUT RECENTLY TO TERRORISTS
CAPTURED IN EARLIER YEARS, THIS ARGUMENT IS NOT CONVINCING.
WE BELIEVE THAT THE PROBLEM IS FOUNDED FIRST IN THE
INABILITY OF THE MILITARY TO PRODUCE EVIDENCE FOR USE
IN THE COURTS AGAINST MEN AND WOMEN FANATICALLY DEDICATED
TO THEIR CAUSE--OTHER THAN THAT EXTRACTED FROM THE
DETAINEES UNDER TORTURE. SECONDLY, THE SECURITY SERVICES
ARE UNWILLING TO SURRENDER THEIR COMPLETE CONTROL OVER
THE DETAINEES.

--THE MILITARY DOES NOT HAVE FULL CONFIDENCE IN THE FUTURE.
THEORETICALLY A SYSTEM OF MILITARY JUSTICE WOULD
HANDLE THE TERRORISTS, METING OUT CAPITAL SENTENCES IF
THAT WERE TO ITS TASTES. HOWEVER, FOR SUCH A SYSTEM
TO WORK, THERE WOULD HAVE TO BE OFFICERS OF RECORD WHO
CONFIDENTIAL
CONFIDENTIAL

PAGE 02   BUENOS 07745 02 OF 02 2613462

IN THE FUTURE COULD BE HELD ACCOUNTABLE FOR THEIR
ACTIONS. AS ONE MAN, HIMSELF A MEMBER OF ONE OF THE MAJOR

CONFIDENTIAL

CONFIDENTIAL

SECURITY FORCES, TOLD US, THERE IS VIRTUALLY NO
ARGENTINE OFFICER WHO WANTS TO HAVE HIS NAME ON RECORD
AS ORDERING THE EXECUTION OF A TERRORIST. UNDER THE
CURRENT SYSTEM, THE MILITARY ARE RESPONSIBLE AS AN
INSTITUTION BUT THE INDIVIDUAL IS FREE FROM ACCOUNTABILITY.

--AT BEST, THE RULE OF LAW IS A WEAK AND FRAGILE CONCEPT IN
ARGENTINA. THE MILITARY DOES NOT OPERATE IN A VACUUM AND ITS
DISREGARD FOR THE PRINCIPLES OF DUE PROCESS REFLECT
WIDESPREAD ATTITUDES IN THIS SOCIETY. ARGENTINES WHO
.ENUINELY BELIEVE IN THE RULE OF LAW, SOME IN THE GOVERN-
MENT AND OTHERS OPPOSING IT, REMAIN A MINORITY.
--FORCING THE SECURITY FORCES TO ABNADON THE TACTIC WOJLD
INVOLVE CONFRONTATION BETWEEN THE POLITICAL LEVEL OF
THE GOVERNMENT AND VERY POWERFUL ELEMENTSIN THE SECURITY
FORCES. THE POTENTIAL COSTS OF SUCH A CONFRONTATION MAKE
IT A VERY UNATTRACTIVE ALTERNATIVE TO A GOVERNMENT WHICH
MUST COUNT ON A MILITARY INSTITUTION THAT IS MORE OR
LESS UNIFIED.

--INTERNATIONAL SANCTIONS AND OPINION ARE GIVEN LESS
WEIGHT BY THE MILITARY THAN THE NEED TO CLEAN UP THE
REMANANTS OF THE ANTI-TERRORIST WAR. THEY WILL NOT
EASILY CHANGE THEIR TACTICS TO MOLLIFY CRITICISM.

6. THE USE OF DISAPPEARANCE IS NOW RESTRICTED, WE BELIEVE,
TO ACTIVE TERRORISTS. THUS, THE EXTENT TO WHICH DISAPPEAR-
ANCES OCCUR DEPSNDS SOLELY ON THE NUMBER OF MONTONEROS WHO
E ACTIVE AND GET CAUGHT. AS THE NUMBER OF ACTIVE
MONTONEROS HAS DECLINED, SO HAVE THE NUMBER OF DISAPPEARANCES.
THIS TREND WILL CONTINUE IF THE NUMBER OF ACTIVE MONTONEROS
CONFIDENTIAL
CONFIDENTIAL

PAGE 03   BUENOS 07745 02 OF 02 2613462

CONTINUES TO DROP, BUT DISAPPEARANCE AS AN ACCEPTABLE TACTIC
WILL NOT END SOON.

7. AS THE WAR BETWEEN THE TERRORISTS AND THE SECURITY FORCES
GOES ON, HUMANITARIAN VALUES AND US RELATIONS WITH THIS
COUNTRY ARE CAUST IN A CROSSFIRE. WE OBVIOUSLY CAN DO
LITTLE TO AFFECT THE TERRORISTS' CHOICE OF WHETHER OR NOT
TO CONTINUE THEIR STRUGGLE. OUR ABILITY TO INFLUENCE THE
GOVERNMENT'S DECISION ON TACTICS IT WILL USE IN THIS WAR
IS NOT MUCH GREATER. IT WILL REMAIN DIFFICULT FOR US TO ARGUE
AGAINST ARGENTINE "SUCCESS" IN ITS UNDELCARFD WAR AGAINST

CONFIDENTIAL

CONFIDENTIAL

TERRORISM AND PARA-MILITARY GUERRILLA ACTIVITIES. BUT WE
BELIEVE THAT DESPITE THE OBSTACLES WE MUST MAKE THE EFFORT.
WE SHOULD:

--MAKE IT CLEAR TO GOA OPINION MAKERS THAT WHILE WE HAVE
NO SYMPATHY FOR THE TERRORISTS WE CANNOT CONDONE EXTRA-
LEGAL ACTIONS GAINST THEM. SO LONG AS THE GOVERNMENT
CONTINUES TO EMPLOY SUCH TACTICS THERE WILL BE AN
IMPORTANT IMPEDIMENT TONORMAL RELATIONS.

--ENCOURAGE THE GOVERNMENT TC PONDER SERIOUSLY HOW THIS
POLICY IMPEDES ITS EFFORTS TO MAKE ARGENTINA A RESPECTED
MEMBER OF THE WESTERN FAMILY OF NATIONS.

--STIMULATE THE GOVERNMENT TO THINK ABOUT ALTERNATIVES TO
THE TACTIC OF DISAPPEARANCE. WE BELIEVE THAT THE ESTABLISH-
MENT OF AN EFFECTIVE SYSTEM OF MILITARY JUSTICE MAY BE
THE BEST ANSWER. IF THE MILITARY COULD BE SHAKEN OUT OF
THEIR BELIEF THAT DEATH IS THE ONLY REASONABLE PUNISHMENT
FOR TERRORISTS, THE ARMED FORCES MIGHT SEE ADVANTAGES
IN USING THE MILITARY COURTS. THE BRAZILIANS RELIED ON
THEM DURING THEIR SUCCESSFUL BOUT WITH TERRORISTS. THIS
EXAMPLE MIGHT HELP CONVINCE THE ARGENTINES THAT THEY
SHOULD SERIOUSLY CONSIDER THIS ALTERNATIVE.

CONFIDENTIAL
CONFIDENTIAL

PAGE 04   BUENOS 07745 02 OF 02 2613462

--ENCOURAGE THE VATICAN AND POSSIBLY THE ARGENTINE CHURCH
TO INTERVENE WITH THE ARGENTINE AUTHORITIES. THE
PAPAL NUNCIO HERE UNDERSTANDS THE ISSUES AND IS ALREADY
INVOLVED IN TRYING TO GET THE GOA TO EXAMINE THE MORALITY
AND WISDOM OF THE TACTIC OF DISAPPEARANCE (SEPTEL). THE
CHURCH AND THE POPE HAVE FAR MORE INFLUENCE HERE THAN
THE USG AND CAN BE THE MOST EFFECTIVE ADVOCATES OF A
FULL RETURN TO THE RULE OF LAW. WE WILL OF COURSE
CONTINUE TO FOSTER RETHINKING OF THE POLICY OF DISAPPEAR-
ANCES WITHIN THE MILITARY AND THE GOVERNMENT.
RUSER

CONFIDENTIAL

CONFIDENTIAL

Appendix 4. Extracts from the Speech Michael Novak Planned to Deliver to the U.N. Human Rights Commission, February 1981

ACTION HR COPY

LIMITED OFFICIAL USE
Department of State

INCOMING
TELEGRAM

PAGE 01   GENEVA 01656 01 OF 02 181801Z   4813
ACTION 10-15

INFO OCT-01   ADS-00   AID-07   INR-10   EUR-12   SS-15   AF-10
      CIAE-00 EA-10   DODE-00 H-01   NEA-06   MSCE-00 ARA-16
      HSAE-00 SSO-00   NA-06   L-03   CSCE-04 TRSE-00 PM-07
      PA-01   INRE-00 ICAE-00 SP-02   SPRS-02 /128 W
      ------------------387453 181921Z /50

O 181750Z FEB 81
FM USMISSION GENEVA
TO SECSTATE WASHDC IMMEDIATE 4458
INFO AMEMBASSY BUENOS AIRES
USMISSION USUN NEW YORK

LIMITED OFFICIAL USE SECTION 01 OF 02 GENEVA 01656

E.O. 12065: N/A
TAGS: SHUM, UHHRC, AR
SUBJECT: UN HUMAN RIGHTS COMMISSION: PROPOSED U.S. EXPLA-
-        NATION OF VOTE ON DISAPPEARANCES - ARGENTINA
-        (ITEM 10B)

1. WE TRANSMIT HEREWITH PROPOSED DRAFT OF EXPLANATION OF
VOTE FOR USE IN CONNECTION WITH AGENDA ITEM 10B (DISAPPEAR-
ANCES) ON ARGENTINA TO BE DELIVERED BY USREP NOVAK
THURSDAY, FEBRUARY 19. DEPARTMENT SHOULD NOTE THAT THIS
DRAFT MAY NOT BE NEEDED, SINCE ARGENTINE REP MARTINEZ
HAS TOLD USDEL PRIVATELY THAT HE WOULD LIKE TO SEEK
CONSENSUS (AS WAS ACHIEVED LAST YEAR). ARGENTINA WILL
TRY TO NEGOTIATE ONE OR TWO CHANGES IN THE FRENCH
RESOLUTION, SAYS MARTINEZ, BUT STILL HOPES FOR CONSENSUS.
FINALLY, PROPOSED USDEL DRAFT MAY ERR BY MENTIONING
ARGENTINA TOO PROMINENTLY, SINCE FRENCH RESOLUTION IS
COUCHED IN GENERAL TERMS, AS ARE ARGENTINE EFFORTS TO
AMEND IT.

2. TEXT OF STATEMENT FOLLOWS.
BEGIN TEXT:

MR. CHAIRMAN, WITH THIS VOTE MY DELEGATION WISHES TO
EXPRESS A NEW GENERAL ORIENTATION TOWARD THE IMPORTANT
QUESTION OF DISAPPEARANCES.

THIS NEW ORIENTATION REFLECTS FIVE PRINCIPLES.
LET ME BEGIN BY STATING EACH SUCCINCTLY. THEN WE MAY
ELABORATE ON SEVERAL OF THEM. THE FIVE PRINCIPLES ARE:

1. CONDONE NO ABUSE OF HUMAN RIGHTS ANYWHERE.
2. UNDERSTAND THE FULL CONTEXT OF EACH ABUSE.
3. AVOID DOUBLE STANDARDS.
4. DISTINGUISH BETWEEN LIBERAL, AUTHORITARIAN AND
    TOTALITARIAN SOCIETIES.
5. LOOK TO THE FUTURE.

LET ME EXPLAIN EACH IN TURN.

FIRST, CONCERNING ARGENTINA OR ANY OTHER STATE, WE
CONDONE NO ABUSE OF HUMAN RIGHTS--PAST, PRESENT, OR
FUTURE. WE RECOGNIZE IN ARGENTINA ONE OF THE WORLD'S
ADVANCED CIVILIZATIONS; A RELIGIOUS CULTURE, A PROUD
INSTITUTIONAL TRADITION. NOT LONG AGO THE PRESIDENT
OF ARGENTINA DESCRIBED THE YEARS 1976-1977--YEARS OF
STRUGGLE AGAINST TERROR AND GUERRILLA WAR--AS ONE OF
THE DARKEST PERIODS OF ARGENTINE HISTORY. WE CONDONE
NOTHING.

SECONDLY, WE UNDERSTAND THE FULL CONTEXT OF THE
"DISAPPEARANCES" OF 1976-1977. ARGENTINA WAS EXPERI-
ENCING GUERRILLA WARFARE; DAILY ACTS OF TERROR; MURDER

AND BOMBINGS WHICH IN CERTAIN WEEKS CLAIMED HUNDREDS
OF LIVES. SUCH TERROR ALSO TOOK INDIVIDUAL LIVES,
SUCH TERROR ALSO TO
CAUSED SORROW TO FAMILIES, OCCURRED OUTSIDE DUE PROCESS,
AND VIOLATED BASIC HUMAN RIGHTS. WHOEVER CONDEMNS
DISAPPEARANCES WITHOUT CONDEMNING THIS TERROR ATTEMPTS
TO CLAP WITH ONE HAND. NEITHER FORM OF VIOLENCE
EXCUSES THE OTHER. DISAPPEARANCES DO NOT EXCUSE
TERROR. TERROR DOES NOT EXCUSE DISAPPEARANCES. MY
DELEGATION CONDEMNS BOTH. WE ALSO CONDEMN THOSE NATIONS,
WHOEVER THEY ARE, WHO INCITE, TRAIN, SUPPLY, AND
COORDINATE TERRORISTS IN OTHER LANDS. TOO OFTEN IN
THIS ASSEMBLY, THESE ASSASSINS OF THE HUMAN RIGHTS OF
OTHERS ESCAPE THE GLARE OF EXACT ATTENTION. THEIR AIM
IS TO DESTROY INSTITUTIONS OF HUMAN RIGHTS IN OTHER
NATIONS, SO AS TO BRING THOSE OTHER NATIONS INTO
PUBLIC DISGRACE. MY DELEGATION CALLS ON THIS COMMIS-
SION NOT TO REWARD THIS TACTIC.

THIRDLY, MY DELEGATION WISHES TO AVOID JUDGING
OTHER NATIONS ACCORDING TO A DOUBLE STANDARD. IT HAS
NOT ESCAPED OUR ATTENTION THAT THE FREER NATIONS OF
LATIN AMERICA SEEM TO BE DISPROPORTIONATELY SINGLED OUT
FOR BLAME, WHILE THE TOTALITARIAN STATES OF THAT
REGION AND ELSEWHERE DISPROPORTIONATELY ESCAPE BLAME.
MR. CHAIRMAN, THE REASON WHY THIS IS SO IS STRUCTURAL
AND SIMPLE. THE MORE HIGHLY DEVELOPED A NATION'S
INSTITUTIONS OF HUMAN RIGHTS, THE MORE READILY ITS
ABUSES ARE CITED. THE LESS DEVELOPED A NATION'S
INSTITUTIONS OF HUMAN RIGHTS, THE FEWER THE OPPOR-
TUNITIES AVAILABLE TO ITS CITIZENS OR TO OUTSIDE
INTERNATIONAL ORGANIZATIONS TO OPERATE FREELY AND TO
REFER CASES TO THIS COMMISSION. MR. CHAIRMAN, THIS

ACTION
COPY

LIMITED OFFICIAL USE
Department of State

INCOMING
TELEGRAM

```
PAGE 01        GENEVA  01656  02 OF 02  181802Z                    4741
ACTION IO-15

INFO  OCT-01   ADS-00   AID-07   INR-10   EUR-12   SS-15    AF-10
      CIAE-00  EA-10    DODE-00  H-01     NEA-06   ·NSCE-00  ARA-16
      NSAE-00· SSO-00   HA-06    L-03     CSCE-04  TRSE-00  PM-07
      PA-01    INRE-00  ICAE-00  SP-02    SPRS-02  /128 W
      ------------------307461  181823Z  /40

O 181750Z FEB 81
FM USMISSION GENEVA
TO SECSTATE WASHDC IMMEDIATE 4459
INFO AMEMBASSY BUENOS AIRES
USMISSION USUN NEW YORK
```

LIMITED OFFICIAL USE SECTION 02 OF 02 GENEVA 01656

STRUCTURAL FLAW, THROUGH NO ONE'S FAULT, IMPOSES A
PERVERSE INCENTIVE. IT ASSIGNS BLAME BY INVERSE
PROPORTION. THE WORST VIOLATORS ARE SELDOM CITED.
THE LESSER VIOLATORS ARE GIVEN MAXIMAL ATTENTION.
SUCH A STRUCTURE DISCOURAGES MODERATE, OPEN REGIMES
AND ENCOURAGES TOTAL CLOSURE IN SELF-DEFENSE.

THIS POINT, MR. CHAIRMAN, LEADS MY DELEGATION TO
STRESS THE CRUCIAL DIFFERENCE BETWEEN LIBERAL, AUTHORI-
TARIAN, AND TOTALITARIAN SOCIETIES. SOMETIMES, THIS
COMMISSION PROCEEDS AS IF IT EMBRACED, AS A SINGLE
STANDARD, THE IDEALS OF THE RELATIVELY FEW LIBERAL
STATES. ACTUALLY, HOWEVER, SOME STATES REPRESENTED
AT THE UNITED NATIONS ARE TOTALITARIAN. SUCH TOTALI-
TAIAN STATES LOATHE LIBERAL IDEALS. THEIR OWN IDEAL
IS TOTAL CONTROL OVER THEIR CITIZENRY...OVER POLITICAL
PARTIES, CHURCHES, LABOR UNIONS, THE MEDIA, THE ARMY,
THE SECRET POLICE, EVEN OVER THE PUBLIC SPEECH AND
PRIVATE THOUGHTS OF EVERY INDIVIDUAL. TOTALITARIAN
STATES OFTEN CLAIM TO BE DEMOCRATIC, TO BE IN FAVOR
OF LIBERATION, AND EVEN TO BE CHAMPIONS OF HUMAN RIGHTS.
IN OUR VIEW, MR. CHAIRMAN, THIS IS DOUBLESPEAK. TOTALI-
TARIAN SOCIETIES ARE, IN OUR VIEW, SLAVE STATES. THEIR
VISION OF "HUMAN RIGHTS" IS WHAT WE MEAN BY THE ABSENCE
OF HUMAN RIGHTS.
MR. CHAIRMAN, A LIBERAL SOCIETY IS NEITHER·TOTALI-
TARIAN NOR AUTHORITARIAN. YET MY DELEGATION NOTES THAT,
UNLIKE TOTALITARIAN STATES, AUTHORITARIAN STATES PERMIT
VARYING DEGREES OF FREEDOM OF ASSOCIATION AND VARYING
DEGREES OF FREEDOM OF SPEECH. IN ARGENTINA, FOR EXAMPLE,
MANY FREE INSTITUTIONS THRIVE. THERE ARE MANY SOURCES
OF DISSENT, CRITICISM, AND INDEPENDENT INQUIRY. THERE
ARE CONSIDERABLE FREEDOMS AVAILABLE TO THOSE WHO ACCUSE
THE GOVERNMENT OF WRONGDOING. MY DELEGATION APPLAUDS
ARGENTINA, FOR THESE FREEDOMS. AND WE NOTE ITS IRONIC
EFFECT. THE VERY FREEDOMS OF ARGENTINA RESULT IN ITS
BEING HELD TO A STANDARD WHICH SOCIETIES WITH LESSER
LIBERTIES ESCAPE.

FINALLY, MR CHAIRMAN, MY DELEGATION NOTES THE
RECORD OF IMPROVEMENT IN ARGENTINA CITED BY THE WORKING
GROUP. OUR NEW GOVERNMENT DESIRES TO FACE THE FUTURE.
DISAPPEARANCES HAVE BEEN REDUCED; WE HOPE THAT NO MORE
WILL OCCUR. FOR HUMANITARIAN REASONS, OUR GOVERNMENT
STANDS READY TO INTERCEDE IN INDIVIDUAL CASES. OUR
EMPHASIS WILL BE UPON PREVENTING DISAPPEARANCES IN
THE FUTURE.

END TEXT. HELMAN

LIMITED OFFICIAL USE

Appendix 5. 1235 and 1503 — Two Resolutions That Changed the United Nations

Resolution 1235 and public debate

Resolution 1235 of the Economic and Social Council (ECOSOC), passed on June 6 1967, authorized the U.N. Human Rights Commission and its Sub-Commission to review communications arriving at the U.N. for "information relevant to gross violations of human rights and fundamental freedoms as exemplified by the policy of apartheid as practiced in the Republic of South Africa and the Territory of South West Africa (Namibia) under the direct responsibility of the United Nations and now illegally occupied by the Government of South Africa and racial discrimination as practiced notably in Southern Rhodesia." Resolution 1235 also authorized the Commission and Sub-Commission to "make a thorough study of situations which reveal a consistent pattern of violations of human rights" like apartheid.

Six months later, the Sub-Commission publicly reviewed allegations of torture in Greece and Haiti and forwarded the names of both governments to the 1968 Commission session, which took no action but did not rebuke the Sub-Commission. This was a breakthrough, but how far would it go? The Soviet Union had always rejected any move to turn the U.N. Human Rights Commission into a tribunal or court, but at the same time was happy to join the chorus of criticism against South Africa and colonialism. Resolution 1235 posed a dilemma for the Soviet Union, because while it strengthened the U.N.'s human rights machinery—something the Soviet Union did not want—it also offered a chance to embarrass the West and criticize right-wing dictatorships. The Soviets therefore voted in favor of 1235, which has formed the basis for public criticism of gross violations ever since.

Resolution 1503 and private debate

On May 27 1970, ECOSOC passed resolution 1503, setting up an elaborate procedure for reviewing communications for "particular situations which appear to reveal a consistent pattern of gross and reliably attested violations of human rights." Resolution 1503 was a compromise because it encompassed three unrelated goals. First, to act on individual communications—something the U.N. had never managed to do (see Chapter 7, note 22). Second, to continue the move begun under Resolution 1235 to indict individual governments and extend the U.N.'s concern beyond South Africa. Third, to encourage a dialogue with governments. To this end, it was decided that the entire 1503 procedure would be kept confidential.

The Soviet Union decided that even this was too strong. At the start of the 1503 procedure, Soviet delegates routinely register their formal rejection of the process—and then participate with gusto. In spite of this, the U.N. makes an extraordinary concession to the Soviet Union. One of the five subcommissioners who perform the initial review of communications is from the East European group. Traditionally, the Soviet subcommissioner reserves the privilege for himself. The U.N. secretariat arranges the communications according to the articles of the Universal Declaration. In order to placate the Soviet Union, the Soviet delegate is traditionally given communications alleging violations of the right to leave (Article 13), thus allowing him to reject most of the complaints relevant to the Soviet Union.

The early years of 1503 (1971–1975) were not promising. (For a full review of the treatment of Greece under 1503, see Lillich and Newman, eds., *International Human Rights: Problems of Law and Policy*, pp. 316–87.) During these four years some fifteen governments were placed on the 1503 blacklist by the Sub-Commission or Commission, but names slipped off the list without any visible improvements having been made and not once did the U.N. go public as a way of protest. This suggested that gross violators had little to fear.

The case of Idi Amin's Uganda led to a more ominous conclusion— that 1503 might actually prove useful to violators, by offering them a confidential refuge from public criticism. On May 27 1974 the International Commission of Jurists submitted a long and detailed communication to the United Nations on Uganda, alleging that 75,000 people had been murdered during Amin's three and a half years in power—a rate of slaughter surpassed only by the shadowy Khmer Rouge in Cambodia. The name of Uganda was placed on the Commission's 1503 blacklist in March 1975, but African delegations were unwilling to act because Amin was the president of the OAU, and they closed ranks. Uganda's name was struck off.

The evidence against Amin, however, was impossible to ignore, and when the Commission met a year later in March 1976, it had before it an urgent request from the Sub-Commission for swift action. Amin sent one of his most intelligent ministers, Justice Minister Godfrey Lule, to answer the charges during the confidential session. Lule proved to be an impressive witness and the Commission again decided to keep Uganda under review for another year. The Commission soon had cause to regret this decision. Instead of going back to Uganda, Lule sought asylum in Britain. When the Sub-Commission met in Geneva in August 1977 he appeared unexpectedly to tell the stunned group that he had lied to the Commission just three months earlier. When this statement came before the Commission in March 1978 it was received in an embarrassed silence. There was no case to be argued, and everyone knew it. The chairman of the 1978 Commission was Kéba M'baye, the Chief Justice of Senegal and one of Africa's most distinguished lawyers. M'baye demanded that Amin receive an envoy from the Commission. A U.N. representative, a Nigerian judge, arrived in the summer of 1978 just as Tanzanian troops invaded the country. The U.N. thus arrived too late, and its attempts at quiet diplomacy received another setback.

Authors are constrained from writing about 1503 for the simple reason that it is confidential. In *Petitioning the United Nations*, pp. 39–75, Ton Zuijdwijk sifted the available documents and produced a useful chronological account of the 1503 procedure between 1972 and 1978, and of subsequent developments in the procedure. Howard Tolley's *The U.N. Commission on Human Rights* picks up where Zuijdwijk left off, and reviews the 1503 procedure up to 1987. But even these two authors are constrained by the 1503 confidentiality. As far as Argentina goes, I feel no such constraints given the Junta's own cynical manipulation of 1503, and the fact that President Alfonsín opened the 1503 file in 1984. In general my personal view is that confidentiality has not persuaded governments to cooperate with the U.N. The larger thesis of this book is that 1503 has become truly dangerous to human rights—and that it offers a useful refuge to repressive regimes.

Appendix 6. Non-Governmental Organizations and the United Nations Human Rights Machinery—An Uneasy Partnership

On June 21 1946 the U.N.'s Economic and Social Council (ECOSOC) established relatively liberal guidelines for granting accreditation, known as "consultative status," to NGOs. These made no reference to "politically motivated" attacks against governments but did state that organizations "discredited by past collaboration in fascist activities" should not be admitted (Records of ECOSOC. E/43/Rev 2, July 1 1946). NGOs would be allowed to refer to human rights violations in written and oral statements.

From the start, the idea of allowing NGOs to participate in the U.N.'s human rights work was bound to prove more amenable to Western governments, which respect (in theory) the right to dissent, than governments from Eastern Europe or the Third World.

In 1952 the rules were tightened, and NGOs were forbidden from circulating communications alleging violations by governments.

By 1966, 206 NGOs had U.N. status, and all but sixty of them were based in the United States. In 1966 ECOSOC began a two-year review of NGOs with status after complaints by the Soviet and Arab governments, which found NGOs too forthright. The 206 NGOs were asked to fill in a questionnaire. Forty failed to reply and were disqualified. Only one of the remaining 166 NGOs—the Coordinating Board of Jewish Organizations—was rejected. Several major human rights organizations were reconfirmed during the review (Amnesty by 8 votes against 4, the International Commission of Jurists by 9 to 0, with 2 abstentions).

The review culminated on May 23 1968 with the passage of resolution 1296, setting out different categories of NGO, depending on their work. Category 1: Organizations such as the International Committee of the Red Cross and the Interparliamentary Union, which have "considerable membership" and broad connection with the work of ECOSOC and its subsidiary bodies. Category 2: organizations like Amnesty which have special expertise in one area of ECOSOC work (e.g., human rights). Category 3 (also known as "roster"): groups which can make "occasional and useful contributions."

Resolution 1296, which is still in force, grants each category different privileges. Category 1 NGOs can propose items for the agenda and give oral and written statements. Written statements, which are circulated by the U.N. secretariat, cannot be longer than two thousand words. Category 2 NGOs can speak and submit written statements of no more than 1,500 words. Roster NGOs can submit written statements, but not speak.

Resolution 1296 has governed the granting of NGO status ever since. For an NGO to qualify, its work has to be in conformity with the "spirit, purposes and principles of the U.N. Charter." It has to have international membership and international goals. It has to be financially independent. (Governments can help financially, but any contributions have to be openly declared.) The NGO has to have a "democratic" system of organization (president, policy making assembly, etc.). Resolution 1296 also states that an NGO can have its status suspended or withdrawn if it "clearly abuses its status by systematically engaging in unsubstantiated or politically motivated acts against States Members of the United Nations contrary to and incompatible with the principles of the Charter."

Precisely what this requirement meant was not spelled out in 1968, and it was clearly open to abuse by governments. During the early 1970s, the rules grew more restrictive. NGOs were to be allowed to speak once on an agenda item and for no longer than ten minutes. They were not allowed the right of reply, even if they had been criticized by a government. NGO statements would only be heard after members of the Commission and observer governments had spoken. These procedural restrictions can be extremely burdensome. There may be over twenty items on the agenda of the U.N. Human Rights Commission, but the chances are that an NGO only has sufficient manpower, interest, and resources to contribute to one. The upshot is that a group like the Federation of Latin American Relatives (FEDEFAM) might bring relatives from several different countries to Geneva for the Commission, but only deliver one ten-minute statement during the whole six weeks on one agenda item.

After Mrs. Allende spoke at the Commission in 1974, other NGOs took heart and challenged the restrictive rules of resolution 1296. In 1975 Homer Jack named seven governments and accused them of religious intolerance. The reaction of the Commission was fury. It adjourned and met behind closed doors. The counter-attack was led by Mohamed Gangi, from Iran, and Sergei Smirnov, from the Soviet Union. Neither government had any interest in seeing the U.N. made more open.

This confrontation gave rise to yet another restrictive resolution. On May 5 1975 ECOSOC passed resolution 1919, forbidding NGOs from naming governments that were subject to the confidential 1503 process. This was responsible for the nonsensical episode involving Paraguay described in Chapter 7. Paraguay was on the 1503 blacklist, but because the case was confidential NGOs did not know whether the charge involved mistreatment of the Ache Indians in Paraguay or torture resulting from Paraguay's permanent state of siege. Patrick Montgomery, from the Anti-Slavery Society, referred carefully to a small land-locked country in Latin America, was forced to name the country and then ruled out of order! Here was an early example of the way in which the 1503 procedure shielded violators and a foretaste of what lay ahead.

Resolution 1919 applied not just to oral statements, but also to written submissions. Theo van Boven, the incoming Director of the U.N. Human Rights Division, interpreted the rule liberally, with the result that between 1977 and 1982 NGOs were allowed to circulate written statements on virtually any government which had been the subject of a U.N. human rights resolution.

It was not until 1978 that the Commission finally published the list of governments that it had considered under the 1503 procedure, and even then it only did so in order not to single out Uganda. (The Commission had decided to send a mission to Uganda, but the Commission Chairman, Kéba M'baye from Senegal, was unwilling to mention a fellow African nation without mentioning the other governments on the 1503 blacklist, so he mentioned all seven.)

References: Weissbrodt, "The Contribution of International Nongovernmental Organizations to the Protection of Human Rights"; Lifskovsky, "The U.N. Reviews its NGO System"; The *Human Rights Reporter*, published by the Harvard-based Human Rights Internet, offers the best regular coverage of the pressures on human rights NGOs, inside and outside the United Nations.

Appendix 7. The Human Rights Machinery of the Organization of American States

In 1890 American states met in Washington for the first time and created the International American Conference. The Ninth International Conference, which met in Bogota in 1948, adopted the Charter of the Organization of American States, subsequently amended by the protocol of Buenos Aires in 1967. During the Second World War, the Inter-American Conference was preoccupied by the need to plan a common defense, and this led to the creation of the Inter-American Defense Board in Washington in 1942. Argentina's overt sympathies with fascism caused incessant controversy. The coup which toppled the government of President Ramón Castillo in 1943 in Argentina was widely viewed as a pro-Axis coup, and the U.S. led efforts to isolate Argentina both during the war and afterward. (Europe was forbidden from making purchases from Argentina with Marshall Plan funds.) Eventually, Argentina was admitted to the OAS.

There are five separate elements to the OAS human rights machinery. By 1977 and 1978 the machinery was spread so broadly that it covered governments like Argentina, which had taken pains to keep its legal obligations to a minimum.

(a) *The OAS Charter*. The Charter contains broad provisions on human rights, but these were not considered to impose obligations on governments until 1967, when a protocol was adopted in Buenos Aires. The protocol also recognized the normative character of the 1948 American Declaration (see below) as a standard for judging the actions of all OAS member states. What this meant in practice was that a government like Argentina's, which had not ratified the American Convention on Human Rights (see below) could still be charged with violations of the Declaration by the Inter-American Commission on Human Rights (IACHR), the system's investigating arm. At the time of writing (1989), all the thirty-three nations of North and South America, and the Caribbean, are members. Cuba does not participate.

(b) *The American Declaration on the Rights and Duties of Man* was adopted at Bogota in May 1948. The Declaration affirms the importance of individual rights and freedoms and was the first international instrument of its kind. As was the case with the Universal Declaration of Human Rights, adopted some months later, there was not sufficient agreement to make it legally binding.

(c) *The American Convention on Human Rights* was adopted in 1969 at San José, Costa Rica, and entered into force in July 1978. The Convention is similar to the International Covenant on Civil and Political rights in that it embraces the same single standards (right to life, security of person, etc.). It lays the same heavy stress on freedom from torture and the right to judicial protection; and attempts the same balancing act in allowing for the suspension of some rights during emergencies (of which there have been many in Latin America) while attempting to keep these within reasonable limits. The American Convention is longer and more ambitious than its European equivalent or the International Covenant. (It contains 82 articles.) Another significant difference lies in the fact that it assumes that life begins at conception.

Implementing the Convention presents its own problems, because there exist huge cultural, political, and economic disparities within the OAS membership. But there is still a far greater sense of common identity and common history within the Americas than exists among the over 160 members of the United Nations. This makes it harder for OAS members to dismiss the American Human Rights Convention as a "Western creation," the perennial complaint of repressive regimes within the United Nations. As of 1989, the Convention had been signed by twenty-two member nations of the OAS, and ratified by twenty. The United States and Chile have signed, but not ratified.

(d) *The Inter-American Commission on Human Rights* (IACHR) was established in 1960 and incorporated into the OAS in 1967. It comprises seven independent experts who are chosen in an individual capacity by the OAS General Assembly and serve for a term of four years. The presidency rotates, and in 1978 it was held by Andres Aguilar, an eminent Venezuelan international lawyer. The IACHR is serviced by a unit within the OAS secretariat, which has headquarters in Washington. It has broad power to investigate and report on human rights violations throughout the entire OAS system, not simply in countries which have ratified the American Convention. In addition, it can receive complaints not just from individuals (as with the European system) but from any NGO legally recognized by an OAS member state. Its reports are not confidential, like the reports of U.N. rapporteurs who work under the 1503 procedure. During the 1960s, for instance, it issued hard-hitting reports on Cuba, Haiti, and the Dominican Republic, although it was refused access by all three governments.

One of the first on-site visits occurred in 1977 in Panama, prior to which a formula for such visits was agreed upon. The IACHR would insist on interviewing whomsoever it wanted, and in absolute privacy; its visits would be publicized in advance, and it would have access to jails. This made the IACHR altogether more effective at fact-finding than the U.N., and thus more menacing to governments like the Argentinian Junta in 1977. It was hardly surprising that it was viewed as "left-wing" in Buenos Aires. This, after all, was the standard smear for any human rights group which took its work seriously.

(e) *The Inter-American Court* comprises seven judges. The first elections took place in May 1979, a year after the American Convention entered into force, and the court was installed in San José in June 1979.

The court acts on the basis of complaints by the IACHR. It can issue advisory opinions, which are not binding, and it can issue binding judgments in cases where the defending government has accepted its compulsory jurisdiction. As of writing (1989) nine governments, all from Latin America, had accepted the court's compulsory jurisdiction. Argentina accepted in 1984.

So far, only one country has been actually charged. This was Honduras, which was charged by the IACHR of responsibility for the disappearance of four individuals. Three separate cases were heard. On July 29 1988, the court found the government of Honduras guilty of violating the rights to life, personal liberty, and humane treatment in the disappearance of Manfredo Velásquez Rodríguez. On January 20 1989, it found against Honduras over the disappearance of Saúl Gordínez Cruz. On March 15 1989, the court found itself unable to render a verdict over the disappearance of two Costa Ricans, Francisco Garbi and Yolanda Soliz Corrales, in Honduras. On July 21 1989, the court ordered the government of Honduras to pay 650,000 lempiras (roughly $325,000) to the family of Gordínez Cruz, and 850,000 lempiras to the family of Velázquez Rodríguez.

These judgments are considered exceptionally important, both in establishing disappearances as a crime under international law and in cementing the court's compulsory jurisdiction. But they were also costly. Miguel Angel Pavón Sálazar, president of the independent Honduran human rights commission, was shot dead on January 14 1987, after testifying before the court. For disappearances and international law in 1976, see Chapter 7, note 19.

See Buergenthal, "Inter-American System for the Protection of Human Rights," in Human Rights in International Law—Legal and Policy Issues, ed. Meron. See also OAS, *Basic Documents Pertaining to Human Rights in the Inter-American System.*

Notes

Prologue

1. The trial was, of course, the major news event of 1985 in Argentina and was widely covered. Much of the material for this chapter, and for Chapter 30, comes from an excellent newspaper devoted exclusively to the trial, *El Diario del Juicio* (*Record of the Trial*) which ran from May 1985 to January 1986 and offered a lively mixture of reports, editorials, and verbatim records of the most important testimony.
2. For the background and implications of the trial, see Chapter 30. The full text of Strassera's charge was published in several Argentinian newspapers and magazines. This chapter draws on the version which appeared in *La Semana* on September 19 1985.
3. *Diario del Juicio* 15, September 3 1985. Viola's expletive was noted by an observer from the U.S. embassy in Buenos Aires who was attending the trial, and cabled back to Washington (FOIA cable 04734).
4. *Diario del Juicio* 15.
5. Strassera was appointed judge by former President Videla, one of the nine men he was prosecuting. This was alluded to in one profile (*Somos,* September 27 1985). See Chapter 30 passim for the trial and its background.
6. *Diario del Juicio* 13, August 20 1985.

Chapter 1. Mónica Disappears

1. This account of Mónica Mignone's abduction is taken from the author's interviews with her father Emilio and her elder sister Isabel, the judges' written sentence at the 1985 trial, and Emilio's testimony at the trial on July 15 1985. Mónica's case (no. 190) was one of the 709 chosen by the prosecution. It was also registered (no. 2209) by the Inter-American Commission on Human Rights (IACHR).
2. "For Mrs. Perón the Burden of High Office was Just Too Great" (*New York Times,* March 25 1976).
3. The cycle of military coups in Argentina began in 1930 with the overthrow of President Hipólito Yrigoyen by General José Uriburu. Civilian rule was restored after one year. In 1943, President Ramón Castillo was overthrown by a coup that was partly masterminded by Colonel Juan Perón. Perón himself was subsequently elected President in 1946, reelected in 1951, and overthrown in 1955.

Arturo Frondizi, the next civilian President, served between 1958 and 1962 before being overthrown. A civilian government was allowed to regain power under president Arturo Illia in 1963, but was bundled out of office in 1966 by General Juan Carlos Onganía, a hard-line anti-Marxist whose regime was the first in Argentina to adhere to the doctrine of national security (see below, note 21). Juan Perón was reelected to a third term in 1973. He died on July 1 1974, and was succeeded by Maria Estela (Isabel) Martínez de Perón, his third wife. See below, note 8.

4. Habeas corpus, a writ used to test the legality of someone's detention, first developed in seventeenth-century England. "Amparo" originated in Mexico in 1840 and now exists in roughly twenty Latin American countries. Its scope is broader than habeas corpus in that it covers constitutional rights other than the right against illegal detention.

For Argentina's legal system see Garro, "The Role of the Argentine Judiciary in Controlling Governmental Action Under a State of Siege"; Mignone et al., "Dictatorship on Trial"; Amnesty International, *The State of Siege and Political Imprisonment in Argentina;* OAS, *Report on the Situation of Human Rights in Argentina,* pp. 224–31 (habeas corpus) and p. 232 (amparo); Berman and Clark, "State Terrorism: Disappearances."

Under Article 23 of the Argentinian constitution, a state of siege can be declared by Congress "in the event of internal disorder or foreign attack endangering the operation of the constitution." (If a state of siege is declared by a President during a congressional recess, it has to be confirmed or suspended by Congress). Congress itself cannot be suspended. During the state of siege the President has the power to detain and move people unless they choose to leave the country, but not to punish them.

5. Prior to 1984 Argentina's system of military justice strictly enforced the gulf between civilian and military life. Wrote Emilio Mignone: "The military judiciary, as an integral part of the armed forces, consists of active or retired high-ranking officers deeply imbued with a sense of strict hierarchy and discipline and with an aggressive esprit de corps" (Mignone et al., "Dictatorship on Trial," p. 130). In 1984, as part of a complicated political package, President Alfonsín reformed the military justice code in such a way as to allow the plea of "due obedience" for certain crimes committed in the dirty war. With this, according to Mignone, military jurisdiction encroached still further into civilian jurisdiction. (See below, Chapter 30, notes 1, 2, and 21.)

6. The Supreme Court was purged five times: in 1946, 1955, 1966, 1973 and 1976 (Garro, "Role of the Argentine Judiciary," p. 314).

7. See, e.g., Naipul, *The Return of Eva Perón.*

8. Kirkpatrick, *Leader and Vanguard in Mass Society: A study of Perónist Argentina.* Between 1939 and 1941, Colonel Juan Perón served as Argentina's military attaché in Italy, where he developed an admiration for Mussolini's style of fascism. Perón returned to Argentina and played a key role in the military coup which overthrew President Ramón Castillo in 1943. He then built a political base from organized labor, with help from his charismatic second wife Eva, and won the presidential elections in 1946 and 1951. In 1955 Perón was himself

overthrown by an army coup and exiled to Spain, whence he kept his movement alive. Perón returned from Spain in 1972 for a brief visit to lay the groundwork for a triumphal return to power the following year. His stalking-horse, Héctor Cámpora, served as President for forty-nine days in 1973, before stepping aside to allow elections, which Perón carried in a landslide on October 17.

9. *Leader and Vanguard,* p. 77.
10. Ibid., p. 47.
11. Ernest Lefever made the comment before the House Foreign Affairs Committee in August 1974. He was questioned about it at his own hearings for the post of Assistant Secretary of State for Human Rights on May 18 1981 ("Nomination of Ernest W. Lefever." Hearings before the Senate Committee on Foreign Relations, May 18, 19; June 4, 5, 1981, p. 170). For more on the Lefever hearings see below, Chapter 21.
12. Wiarda, ed., *Human Rights and U.S. Human Rights Policy,* p. 34. Wiarda's description of political rights in Latin America as "goals" is ironic. One neoconservative argument against "economic rights" (education, housing, etc.) is precisely that they are government "goals" whose attainment cannot be guaranteed, whereas political rights can be claimed by all individuals of their governments irrespective of a country's level of economic development. See below, Chapter 22, note 6.
13. The 1976 coup in Argentina brought all but two of the larger South American countries under military rule. The two democracies were Colombia and Venezuela.
14. See, e.g., Institute for Policy Studies, *The Southern Connection.* Lernoux, *Cry of the People,* amounts to one long denunciation of the U.S. role in Latin America. Andersen, "The Military Obstacles to Latin Democracy," is also critical. Andersen maintains that the U.S. has been as lukewarm in encouraging Latin American democracy as it was in supporting dictatorship.
15. According to critics of U.S. policy in Latin America, the doctrine of national security originated at Fort Gulick in the Panama Canal Zone, where the U.S. trained thousands of Latin American servicemen and police officials in the not-so-gentle techniques of counterinsurgency. The doctrine was reinforced by the Inter-American Defense system based in Washington. The Inter-American Defense Board was set up in 1942 by American foreign ministers to prepare against any invasion of the continent by the Germans and Japanese. After the war, it developed into the permanent security wing of the Organization of American States.

Supporters of the Inter-American system say it has kept the continent relatively free from open war but critics have portrayed it as a U.S. conspiracy to indoctrinate future Latin American military leaders in the evils of "subversion," the effect of which has been to weaken democracy. "The U.S. role in militarizing the continent and its continued influence over the situation are widely taken for granted among theoreticians of both the right and left," wrote Joanne Omang ("Latin American Left, Right Say U.S. Militarized Continent").

The U.S. has also developed a series of bilateral military agreements with

Latin American governments. On May 10 1964 the U.S. and Argentina signed an agreement that cemented military ties between the two nations and laid the basis for close cooperation. This military alliance came under great strain during the Carter Administration, when Congress cut off U.S. security assistance to Argentina. See below, Chapter 13.

16. José Zalaquett, a lawyer who was expelled from Chile in 1975 and joined the staff of Amnesty International, has defined the doctrine of national security as follows:

> In its essentials, the national security doctrine regards domestic political struggles as an expression of a basic East-West conflict and sees Marxist penetration and insurgency as an all-pervading presence of a new type of enemy fighting a new type of war. Civilians are also warriors, ideas a different form of weapon. Democracy and politics cannot lead the fight against Marxism (indeed they often pave the way). Neither can they coordinate all national resources effectively so as to achieve modernization and economic development, pillars of a modern notion of national security. This can only be done by the professionals of national security, the military. Since the war on Marxism is an insidious one, unorthodox methods are called for, including torture and extermination of irredeemable political activists

(from the Aspen Institute conference paper *State Crimes: Punishment or Pardon*).

17. "We Don't Cause Latin America's Troubles—Latin Culture Does." Harrison worked for USAID between 1962 and 1981.

18. Mignone was rewarded by Perón for his loyalty with a senior post in the provincial Ministry of Education at the age of twenty-seven. He resigned and went into law practice when Perón confronted the Church. For five years, between 1962 and 1967, Mignone worked on education at the headquarters of the Organization of American States in Washington before returning to Argentina. In 1969 he took the post of Deputy Minister of Education under the military regime of General Juan Carlos Onganía. Later, he would regret the decision bitterly. Throughout, Mignone remained under the spell of Perón. He was one of the many faithful followers who made the pilgrimage to Perón in his exile in Spain and accompanied Perón home to Argentina from Rome in November 1972. In 1973, after Perón was again elected President, Mignone was appointed rector of a new experimental university at Lujan, near the capital.

19. Figures from Rock, *Argentina 1516–1987*, pp. 283ff; Munck, *Argentina*, pp. 207–19.

20. Mignone has written a book about the Church's dubious role in the dirty war, *Iglesia y Dictadura*, translated and reprinted in English as *Witness to the Truth*. For the Church's collaboration with the Junta between 1976 and 1983, and its importance to Argentina's human rights movement, see below Chapter 4, notes 11ff.

21. It is well established that categorizing detainees as "Communists" or "subversives" makes it easier for torturers to dehumanize their victims, swallow their doubts, and resist the strain. Greek military personnel who tortured during the reign of the colonels were given daily lectures on "national ethical educa-

tion" and taught that prisoners were "worms" and "Communists" that had to be "crushed." (Gibson and Haritos-Fatouros, "The Education of a Torturer.")

For a highly critical account of the doctrine of national security in Argentina see Frontalini and Caiati, *El Mito de la Guerra Sucia* (hereafter *El Mito*), p. 50ff. The CONADEP commission set up by President Alfonsín in 1983 also had harsh comments about the doctrine of national security (CONADEP, *Nunca Mas*, pp. 473–76). Robert Cox, former editor of the *Buenos Aires Herald*, thinks that the Junta's commitment to the doctrine has been greatly exaggerated by analysts like Emilio Mignone in their need to make sense of the military's campaign of murder. Cox's own opinion is that the campaign was more chaotic and lacking in overall motivation.

22. *Leader and Vanguard*, p. 71.

23. *Leader and Vanguard*, p. 222.

24. Andrew Graham-Yooll's *Portrait of an Exile* captures the mood of this period brilliantly. Argentina's left-wing guerrillas were inspired by a concoction of Peronism, Marxism, and Cuban-style revolution. The Montoneros, one of several groups, formed during the 1960s from the extreme left wing of the Peronist movement. Following their sensational murder of Aramburu in 1970, most of the leadership was wiped out. They regrouped under the leadership of Mario Firmenich, who had been a right-wing Catholic activist before embracing radical left-wing politics. Two other guerrilla groups that had already formed at the left wing of the Peronist party, the Revolutionary Armed Forces (FAR), and the Peronist Armed Forces (FAP), merged with the Montoneros to create a potentially formidable urban guerrilla movement. See Gasparini, *Montoneros: Final de Cuentas (The Montoneros: The Final Reckoning)*.

The second main grouping, the Revolutionary Army of the People (ERP), began as part of the international Trotskyite movement. It then broke this link in favor of the Cuban model of revolution and began a nationwide campaign in the late 1960s before concentrating its limited energies on regions that seemed ripe for revolution. Its first major target would be the impoverished province of Tucumán, where the once-thriving sugar industry had collapsed.

One detailed chronology of terrorist actions can be found in Government of Argentina, *Evolución de la Delincuencia Terrorista en la Argentina (Evolution of Terrorism in Argentina)*, published by the Junta in November 1979 to counter the adverse impact of the visit of the Inter-American Commission on Human Rights. The document does not identify those responsible for the acts of terrorism.

25. On February 14, ERP leaders met with guerrilla leaders from Chile and Uruguay and announced the creation of a coordinating body (Junta Coordinadora Revolucionaria).

26. Gasparini, *Montoneros: The Final Reckoning*, p. 80.

27. Estimates from Gasparini, op. cit. Andersen's claim that Firmenich was recruited rests on some convincing detective work he conducted while reporting for *Newsweek* and the *Washington Post* in Argentina. On June 20 1975, Firmenich gave a famous "press conference" at which he handed kidnap victim Jorge

Born over to journalists. Andersen later discovered that the house was used as a safe house by Argentina's state intelligence service. Firmenich himself was extradited from Brazil in 1984 and sentenced to a long term in jail. He has yet to speak out. (Andersen, "Argentina's Dirty Secrets.")

28. Figures from *El Mito de la Guerra Sucia*, pp. 57–74.

29. According to the Junta's 1979 report, *Evolution of Terrorism*, sixteen Montoneros were killed in the attack. Newspapers put the total force of guerrillas at between 50 and 180 (*El Mito*, p. 65).

30. The action which triggered the October 6 decrees was the decision by the ERP to execute sixteen army officers in retaliation for the execution of sixteen captured ERP guerrillas who had surrendered. The text of the three October decrees (2770, 2771, and 2772) was published in full in *Diario del Juicio* (November 19 1985). No. 2770 created a Council for Internal Security and a Council of Defense; 2771 placed all provincial forces under executive power; and 2772 gave the armed forces the green light to operate throughout Argentina.

Although kept under the overall control of the civilian government, the three services were left to organize themselves internally. They were allowed to detain and interrogate suspects, but not torture them or hold them clandestinely. After the initial period of detention, prisoners were supposed to be handed over to the civilian courts for trial or placed in executive detention (PEN). There was another important provision. The overall offensive against subversion was supposed to achieve its objective by the end of 1975 and be transformed into a civilian police operation by the end of the following year.

31. The judges at the 1985 trial included in their written verdict a list of twenty anti-terrorist laws passed by President Isabel Perón. For a 1975 analysis of the laws see the report prepared for the International Commission of Jurists by Dr. Heleno Fragoso in March 1975, *The Situation of Defense Lawyers in Argentina* (PEN figures from *Nunca Más*, p. 408.)

32. Gasparini, *Montoneros*, p. 138.

33. From a memorandum marked "Secret," in the author's files. The author of the memo presumably had no reason to exaggerate, or diminish, the success of the armed forces' antiterrorist campaign prior to the coup.

34. These figures were presented to the 1985 trial by Eduardo Rabossi. CONADEP recorded 19 disappearances in 1973, 50 in 1974, 359 in 1975, and 549 in the first three months of 1976 (Trial Sentence, Ch. 6). This was almost as many people as had been killed by left-wing terrorists in the previous five years (687). Between 1973 and 1975 relatives submitted 1,089 requests for habeas corpus, inquiring into the whereabouts of family members who had disappeared.

35. Grondona tried to report his kidnapping to the police, but found them "uninterested." He had better luck with an official from the U.S. embassy who took him out to lunch, listened sympathetically, and cabled a dramatic account of the affair back to Washington (FOIA Cable 05298, August 1976).

36. Fragoso, *The Situation of Defense Lawyers*.

37. Guzetti's comment was reported in *La Opinión*, October 3 1976, and quoted by Strassera in his prosecution summary (p. iii) and *El Mito*, p. 21.

38. *Nunca Más*, p. 99, and Alipio Paoletti, in *Madres* (*Mothers*), issue no. 4 (March 4 1985).

39. Massera served on Argentina's delegation to the Inter-American Defense Board and was trained at Fort McNair, the Inter-American Defense College.

40. Cardozo was fated to fall victim to one of the most outrageous attacks of the entire dirty war. On June 16 1976 Ana María González, a Montonero, took advantage of her friendship with Cardozo's daughter to slip into the house and place a powerful bomb under Cardozo's bed. Cardozo, by now chief of the federal police, was killed. Some think that Ana María González was killed in a shootout a year later, others that she was held at the ESMA.

41. Fernández served in the federal police before working as bodyguard of General Harguindeguy, the Junta's first Interior Minister. He left the country in 1980. On January 4 1983 he gave his testimony in Madrid to the Argentine Human Rights Commission (CADHU), formed by exiles (Douglas Grant Mine, "Argentina Accused of Gulag Operation"; Isabel Hilton, "Death Squad Secrets Revealed ").

Fernández also testified that in May 1976, shortly after the coup, retired senior army officers were invited to a meeting to review the plan with army chiefs and asked to cast a vote. Out of the fifty-three generals, only three voted against but they agreed to go along with the majority. According to Simpson and Bennet (*The Disappeared*, p. 62), one of the three dissenting generals was Roberto Viola. Details of the meeting remain sketchy. It could not be confirmed by the prosecution team at the 1985 trial for the simple reason that almost all documents pertaining to the dirty war had been destroyed.

Chapter 2. The War Begins

1. Videla was an infantry officer whose elevation to army Commander in Chief had broken a tradition of dominance by the cavalry. His appointment was announced in August 1975.

2. *New York Times*, March 25 1975.

3. From Robert Cox's testimony at the trial, April 26 1985.

4. The armed forces decided on a collegial system, in order to avoid any concentration of power by one individual or service such as had marked the rule of the highly autocratic General Juan Carlos Onganía. It was agreed that the three service chiefs and the president would form a Junta that would rule for a period of approximately three years before stepping down and handing power over to a new Junta. In the event, Videla doubled as army commander and president in the first Junta, and served until 1980—well after the other two members of the first Junta had stepped down.

Nevertheless, the collegial system was maintained; this fact, combined with Videla's lack of personal charisma, gave the regime a completely different flavor from personalized autocracies like Somoza's Nicaragua or Duvalier's Haiti, in which one individual exercised absolute power. Political scientists coined the label of "bureaucratic/authoritarian" to describe regimes like the Argentinian Junta. Wrote Tom Farer in 1981: "In these authoritarian countries, the names at the top can and generally do change without any shifts in the pattern of wealth and political power. Formidable institutions are in control, usually the armed forces . . . and these institutions work within a complicated setting of interest groups . . . all struggling to influence the regime's economic and social policies" ("Reagan's Latin America").

5. Agosti had taken part as a young pilot in an abortive 1951 uprising against Juan Perón and had sought exile in Uruguay. He had served as Air Attaché in Washington in 1972 and was appointed air force Commander in Chief after helping Videla to put down the abortive coup in December 1975.

6. Massera's defense lawyers made much of his spectacular rise through the ranks during the trial. Massera's first command was the training vessel, the *Liberty*.

7. The disclosure of the P 2 in Italy in 1982 almost toppled the Italian government. A special inquiry was subsequently held in Argentina to investigate the extent of Gelli's operation in the country, and it emerged that Gelli owned the building where Massera established his new Social Democracy party (see below, Chapter 5, note 26ff.). Gelli first met Juan Perón in Spain. When Perón returned to Argentina, Gelli was a guest at his inauguration. Shortly afterwards Perón appointed Gelli a special economic councillor at the embassy in Rome. General Carlos Suárez Mason, chief of the First Army Corps, was also on Gelli's P 2 list.

8. The press office was headed by Captain Pérez Froio, who visited the ESMA concentration camp frequently. Among the other navy officers who worked in both the ESMA and the Foreign Ministry press office were González Menotti and Miguel Benazzi (from the testimony of Ana María Martí, pp. 16ff).

9. From Gregorio Dupont's testimony to the trial, August 9 1985, and an interview with the author. Dupont bears no grudge against Allara, who played an important part in launching the invasion of the Falklands. In 1982, Allara unexpectedly called a press conference to announce that Dupont's abrupt departure from the diplomatic corps had not been due to incompetence.

10. In 1982, Dupont's brother Marcelo disappeared and was found murdered. Initially, Gregorio thought Massera was responsible. This turned out not to be the case. See below, Chapter 26, note 6.

11. The Junta replaced the constitution by the "Statute for the Process of National Reorganization," published on March 31 1976. By this, the Junta assumed the right to enact laws and even amend the constitution. It also assumed the authority to exercise the three powers, judicial, legislative and executive. The legislative powers of Congress, which was dissolved, passed to a nine-man legislative military committee. See International Commission of Jurists, *States of Emergency: Their Impact on Human Rights*, pp. 3–30. For the Junta's decrees, and their dubious legality, see OAS, *Report on the Situation of Human Rights in Argentina*, pp. 13ff.

12. For a concise summary of the measures taken against habeas corpus, amparo and the right of option, see Amnesty International, *State of Siege*.

13. *Nunca Más*, pp. 416–24.

14. From Ragnar Hagelin's testimony at the trial, July 17 1985.
15. Habeas corpus figures from *Nunca Más*, pp. 400ff.

    For a detailed account of the Timerman case and its legal implications, see Garro, "Role of the Argentine Judiciary," p. 332 and OAS, *Report of the Situation of Human Rights in Argentina*, p. 231. See below, Chapter 21 for the political aftermath of the Timerman case.

    There were many cases that proved the complicity of the judges. Norma Susana Burgos was abducted on January 25 1977. Her family submitted a habeas corpus writ on her behalf. A judge made a peremptory inquiry and was told that the navy knew nothing of her whereabouts. He pursued it no further. A year later, after spending a year in the ESMA (navy mechanics school) Norma left with a plane ticket paid for by the navy. A copy of Norma's ticket and her parents' futile habeas corpus request were published in *Diario del Juicio*. Norma herself went on to Sweden, where she provided information about the explosive kidnapping of Dagmar Hagelin. (See below, Chapter 18, note 5.)

16. For the discovery of Miguel Angel's grave and those of other unidentified dead, see below, Chapter 26, note 7. According to the judge's file, the letter to Angel Sosa's family was sent to the wrong address and returned to the court. This was clearly a lie, because the family's correct address was in the file. Miguel Angel was buried in a tomb in the small, isolated Grand Bourg cemetery some 18 miles west of Buenos Aires under a wooden cross bearing the words "nomen nescio" (name unknown). Emilio Mignone agreed to take up the case for the family, and to submit a writ of habeas corpus. Three years later it would lead Mignone to the discovery of mass graves at the Grand Bourg.

17. *Nunca Mas*, p. 244.

18. "There are certain juridical norms that do not apply in this case. For example the right of habeas corpus. This type of struggle requires secrecy. No one should know who has captured whom. A cloud of silence should exist over all." (General Tomás Sánchez de Bustamente, as quoted by *La Capital*, a Rosario newspaper, on June 14 1980.)

19. In 1975, workers had taken over a large ACINDAR factory in the town of Constitución, and announced they were establishing a workers' cooperative. The government of Isabel Perón sent in the troops. Martínez de Hoz ordered the workforce of 5,000 to be photographed for new identity cards which were then handed to the police to help them track down troublemakers. Hundreds of people were detained, and some disappeared. It was a shameful episode which did much to rob Isabel Perón of her traditional support among the unions. Martínez de Hoz would be bitterly criticized by the CONADEP for his role, even though the incident took place well before the coup (*Nunca Más*, p. 386; also quoted by Roberto Martinez in the *Mothers* paper, no. 4, March 4 1985).

    For a detailed account of the Junta's measures against the unions, see Munck, *Argentina: From Anarchism to Peronism*, pp. 207–19; OAS, *Report on the Situation of Human Rights in Argentina*, pp. 239–44; *Nunca Más*, pp. 375–87.

20. See below, note 26 for CONADEP's estimate of the number of workers who disappeared.
21. Foster, "After the Terror."
22. *Miami News,* Oct 20 1978, p. 13.
23. Figures from the March 24 1977 open letter by Rodolfo Walsh, the well-known Argentinian journalist (see note 24).
24. Details of Walsh's letter and its transmission to Patricia Derian, were cabled by the U.S. embassy in Buenos Aires to Washington (FOIA cable 02663, April 1977). Rodolfo Walsh's March 24 letter was translated and published by CADHU, the Argentine Human Rights Commission. As head of the Montonero intelligence service (he was known as "Professor Neurus") Walsh had been the brain behind some of their more daring operations and had provided Firmenich with advance warning of the coup (a warning that Firmenich had ignored). Thereafter Walsh grew disillusioned with Firmenich's mindless campaign of violence.
25. The International Labor Organization took up the repression of Argentinian unionists in 1977 and issued a strong rebuke in February 1978 (see below Chapter 11, note 1).

    In May 1978 the French passed over a list of 1,142 disappeared workers to the U.S. embassy. U.S. Ambassador Raul Castro cabled Washington (FOIA cable 03563) that the majority were assumed to be shop stewards. FOIA Cable 02677 from the U.S. embassy in Buenos Aires (April 1978) makes it clear that the aim of the disappearances was to quash strikes: "The labor sector naturally has been an area of high priority to the security forces. . . . Under this government's security laws, strikes are tantamount to subversion and are subject to heavy penalties."
26. *Nunca Más,* p. 375.
27. From the summary by prosecutor Strassera at the 1985 trial, p. vi.
28. *Nunca Más,* p. 329. A similar operation occurred during the "night of the ties," when a group of defense lawyers were picked up in the city of Mar del Plata for no other apparent reason than that they were labor lawyers.
29. María Hourcadie de Francese's chauffeur, stepson, and his son (a navy officer) also disappeared.
30. The family's story is told in *Nunca Más,* pp. 344ff.
31. This diplomat asked to remain anonymous.
32. Emilio Mignone conducted his own survey in the small town of Luján, where thirteen families reported disappearances to the local authorities, and found another thirteen who had not put in a report because they were afraid or had no hopes of an explanation. This, concluded Mignone, would be even more likely to happen in the interior of the country. On November 27 1982 CLAMOR (Comité de Defensa de Derechos Humanos en el Cono Sur), based in São Paulo, issued a report listing 7,791 disappearances in Argentina.
33. The first Night and Fog decree was issued by General Wilhelm Keitel on December 7 1941 (Amnesty USA, *Disappearances: A Workbook,* p. 2). For the Guatemalan disappearances in the 1960s and the short-lived attempt by the Guatemalan relatives to set up a support group see below, Chapter 17, note 19.

For the United Nations account of the missing in Chile see the report of the 1978 U.N. mission to Chile (A/33/331, October 25 1978), pp. 114–33.

34. FOIA cable 7578 (September 1980) from the U.S. embassy in Buenos Aires to Washington. For the text see Appendix 3.

35. It is the author's contention that violence, in the form of torture and disappearance, was very much a product of right-wing "authoritarian" military rule, while abuses of civil liberties were associated with "totalitarian" regimes. International law considered the former more heinous, which is one reason why American neoconservatives had to redefine human rights. See below, Chapter 19.

36. This was certainly the impression of outsiders. On April 17 1977, Joanne Omang, writing in the *Washington Post*, concluded that left wing terrorism was "completely annihilated."

37. *Nunca Más*, p. 227.

Chapter 3. Torture at the ESMA

1. The role of the navy mechanics school (ESMA) in the disappearances has been thoroughly documented. Several survivors testified before the CONADEP commission and the 1985 trial of the generals. They included: Miriam Lewin de García; Victor Basterra, who falsified documents of detainees and took photos of detainees; Carlos Muñoz, who handled audiovisuals at the ESMA; and Thelma Jara de Cabezas, secretary of one of the eight human rights groups, who was herself abducted in 1979. In addition to their testimony, I have also drawn on Prosecutor Strassera's summary against the former Junta members, particularly Admiral Massera; the judges' sentence, delivered on December 9 1985; *La Pista Suiza* (*The Swiss Trail*) and *Montoneros: Final de Cuentas* (*Montoneros: The Final Reckoning*), two books by Juan Gasparini (another ESMA survivor); *Madres* (*Mothers*), the monthly newspaper of the Mothers, particularly issue no. 9 (August 1985); *Nunca Más*, report of the CONADEP commission, which sent a team to the ESMA in 1984 (pp. 126–43); and the written testimony of Ana María Martí (see below note 10).

2. From Emilio Mignone's testimony at the trial.

3. According to (retired) Captain Jorge Busico, who took part in the February operation, the police were contacted in advance and asked to clear the area. The target was Dr. Pedro Eladio Vázquez. Busico was frozen out after he expressed surprise at the clandestine nature of the operation, and transferred from the ESMA soon afterwards (*Diario del Juicio* 9, July 23 1985).

4. Following the 1976 coup, five counter-intelligence task forces ("Grupos de Tarea") were set up by the services. GT 1 and GT 2 worked under army intelligence, GT 3 under the navy, and GT 4 under the air force. GT 5 worked under the State Intelligence Service (*Nunca Más*, p. 257).

5. Suárez Mason's 1978 proposal was produced by the Argentinian government of President Alfonsín in 1988 to support a request for Suárez Mason's extradition from the United States. It is one of the few military documents not to

have been destroyed. The arrangements for making daily reports and declaring "free zones" with the help of the local police first emerged in 1980 when Amnesty International published the testimony of Oscar González and Horacio Cid de la Paz, two detainees who were held in five camps before their escape (Amnesty International, *Testimony on Secret Detention Camps in Argentina*). See below, Chapter 15 note 6.

Carlos Suárez Mason fled from Argentina in 1983 and entered the U.S. on a forged passport. President Alfonsín's government charged him with forty three murders and applied for his extradition. Horacio Martínez-Baca, who was tortured while detained by soldiers under the command of Suárez Mason, sought twenty million dollars in damages against the former general. He was awarded twenty-one million dollars, and Suárez Mason was sent back to Argentina in 1988. (For an excellent account of Suárez Mason's spell in a U.S. jail see Camille Peri, "Getting to Know the Lord of Life and Death.")

6. The navy's task group (GT 3) was divided into eleven regional units along the lines of an earlier counterintelligence plan known as PLACINTARA 75 (Plan de capacidades internas de la armada), drawn up on November 21 1975 after Isabel Perón's call to "annihilate" terrorism. The third unit, or task force, covered the capital Buenos Aires and was nominally under the command of Admiral Oscar Montes (subsequently named Foreign Minister). It was further subdivided into task groups, one of which (GT 3/32) was headquartered at the ESMA. The GT 3/32 was thus only one element in the navy's intelligence-gathering operation, but it quickly grew to be the most important. It comprised three distinct units. "Operations" performed the actual kidnapping. "Intelligence" interrogated the prisoners and identified new targets. "Logistics" handled administration and disposed of booty collected during the raids.

7. *Madres* 9 (August 1985) gives a list of the ESMA operatives and their noms de guerre. Vantman and Radice married and had three children. Radice, a former civilian, continued to work for Massera when he retired from the navy. He gave testimony, with great reluctance, at the trial on July 9 1985.

8. The birth of Hilda Dunda's baby was noted in Ana María Martí's report. See below, note 10.

9. From Strassera's summary at the 1985 trial, p. 4.

10. This account is based on the author's interviews with Ana María Martí, who was detained at the ESMA school between March 28 1977 and December 19 1978, and the report that Ana María prepared with two other detainees after her arrival in Europe. (For more on the report and its impact, see below, Chapter 18, note 2.)

Martí, a militant Peronist, has been accused of having permitted her house to be used to plan a terrorist attack, but there is no evidence that she herself was a terrorist nor even an active Montonero. Her written evidence at the 1985 trial was taken under oath by Ambassador Juan Carlos Katzenstein at the Argentinian embassy in Berne, Switzerland, on July 30 1985.

11. *Buenos Aires Herald*, November 15 1982. During forty-five years of study, Pedace found that while the "picana" does not leave a visible scar on the outer

skin, it does deform skin cells on inner layers, turning them into an oblong shape.

12. Father Rice's story is told in full in the OAS *Report on the Situation of Human Rights in Argentina*, pp. 209ff.

13. Carlos Muñoz gave testimony to the CONADEP and at the 1985 trial.

14. The routine nature of the torture at the ESMA and other centers was confirmed by Claus Ruser's September 1980 cable from the U.S. embassy in Buenos Aires: "Based on everything we know, we believe that detainees are usually tortured as part of interrogation. . . ." (Appendix 3).

15. Torres also gave evidence to the CONADEP (*Nunca Más*, p. 137).

16. Tincho's real name was Emilio Bonazzola, and he deserted to the Montoneros from the army. After the injection, a guard told him that he was wanted by another GT. He occupied a cubicle next to Juan Gasparini before being taken away to his death. Norma Susana Burgos wrote out her recollections of the ESMA in written testimony in Sweden on December 13 1979 (see below, Chapter 18, note 5). She also testified to the CONADEP.

17. This was widely known as early as 1977. In his March 24 open letter, Rodolfo Walsh wrote that one of the corpses was that of a fifteen-year-old boy, Floreal Avellaneda, who was found with his hands and feet tied and his anus torn. See above, Chapter 2, note 24.

18. *Nunca Más*, p. 137.

19. Ana María Martí's children were detained with common criminals for several months before being released. They left Argentina with their mother. See below, Chapter 18, note 2.

20. Sara Osatinsky's story was a terrible one. Her husband Marcos, a Montonero leader, was captured. He succeeded in getting his captors to suspend torturing in exchange for a promise that the Montoneros would suspend operations for a month. Unaware of the deal, the ERP tried to storm the police station and free him. In revenge the military tied Osatinsky to two cars and pulled him along a road until he died. Sara Osatinsky's two sons both died in the dirty war. She herself was abducted on May 14 1977. An army officer visited her at the ESMA with the sole purpose of telling her how her husband had died.

21. Ana María Martí's report, pp. 1–7.

22. The following account is taken mainly from the author's interviews with Martí and Juan Gasparini, and from Gasparini's book *La Pista Suiza*.

23. Using the name of "Dr. Paz," Juan Gasparini is reported to have acted as an intermediary between the Montoneros and David Graiver, a well-known Argentinian financier who invested Montonero ransom money before he died in 1976 in a plane crash in Mexico. (For Graiver's connections with Jacobo Timerman see below, Chapter 21, notes 17ff.) Gasparini's own ordeal was another example of the extraordinary cruelty of the armed forces. On January 10 1977 Gasparini was sucked up ("chupado") by an ESMA patrol near his house. His sole act of resistance was to bite one of his captors, Lieutenant González Menotti. (González Menotti was to take a special delight in tormenting Gasparini during captivity.) They took him, still groggy from torture, off to his house,

and told him to summon his wife through the buzzer. Gasparini refused, whereupon several officers opened fire without warning through the windows and door, fatally wounding his wife and a visiting friend. Gasparini recounted his capture and ordeal at the ESMA in *Montoneros,* pp. 101ff.

24. In *La Pista Suiza* Gasparini gives a riveting account of the evening's entertainment. Astiz was the only officer present at the ESMA. He called for the guard to come and unlock Gasparini's shackles. Teeth gleaming in the dim light, Astiz told the guard not to bother noting it down in the book. "I'll take care of prisoner 774." "Where are you taking me?" asked Gasparini. "We're going to piss off and have fun," replied Astiz as the guard unlocked the chains. They walked out to Astiz's blue Falcon and headed off to La Paz, a well-known cafe, where Astiz ordered cognac after cognac and talked and talked about friends in common, about work, about rugby, about literature, about the war against subversion, about his letter to Margaret Thatcher.

25. González Menotti was posted to London, where he was exposed by a television program in 1981. (See below, Chapter 18, note 1.)

26. Gasparini's conclusions suggest that Astiz should not, in fact, have been able to benefit from President Alfonsín's 1986 decision to allow the plea of "due obedience." (See below, Chapter 30.)

According to Gasparini, Astiz almost found the real fight he craved when he took part in an expedition to recapture Lennox, Picton, and Nueva, three small islands in the Beagle Channel, which were also claimed by Chile. The expedition landed under cover of dark, but the Pope offered to mediate at almost exactly the same time and the Argentinian party managed to slip away undetected. See below, Chapter 5, note 27 for the startling claim that the ESMA prisoners may have helped to persuade the navy to recapture the Falklands from Britain by force.

27. This account of Dagmar Hagelin's abduction is taken from Ragnar Hagelin's testimony at the trial (July 17 1985), and his moving book *Mi Hija Dagmar.*

28. Norma Susana Burgos gave her testimony to a senior official at the Swedish Foreign Ministry on December 13 1979. It is reprinted in *Mi Hija Dagmar,* pp. 198–204.

Chapter 4. The Relatives Resist

1. This exchange is taken from Emilio Mignone's testimony at the 1985 trial.
2. For the full text of the Court's ruling, see OAS, *Report on the Situation of Human Rights in Argentina,* pp. 122–24.
3. In 1979 Emilio Mignone teamed up with two other parents and formed the Center for Legal and Social Studies. See below, Chapter 16, note 19.
4. Thelma Jara de Cabezas disappeared in 1979 on the eve of the arrival of the IACHR in Argentina. She survived and gave testimony at the 1985 trial. See below, Chapter 13, note 36.
5. This account of the foundation of the Mothers is drawn from the author's interviews with René Epelbaum, María Adela Gard de Antokoletz, and other

Mothers. For an analysis of the Argentinian Mothers' role in Latin America's human rights movement, and a comparison with the mothers of desaparecidos in Chile and Guatemala, see Schirmer, "Those Who Die for Life Cannot Be Called Dead."

6. Daniel Antokoletz, a defense lawyer, was an expert in refugee law. He had been preparing a large dossier for an Amnesty International mission. He disappeared the day before the team arrived on November 6 1976.

7. Bousquet remained a staunch friend of the Mothers, and dedicated the profits of his book (*Las Locas de la Plaza de Mayo*) to their organization.

8. It is also worth noting that young women like Ana María Martí and Mónica Mignone were encouraged to pursue professions and were also highly political. (Witness the high percentage of women among the disappeared persons.) Argentina had a woman member of the Supreme Court in the 1960s and a woman President (Isabel Perón). But none of this translated into broad political involvement by Argentinian women at the federal or provincial levels.

9. Harguindeguy was a close personal friend of Colonel Guillermo Ramírez, a senior Uruguayan intelligence officer, and the two were suspected by the Mothers of coordinating the operation which led to the death in Buenos Aires of the two well-known Uruguayan exiles, Zelmar Michelini and Héctor Gutiérrez Ruiz. (See below, Chapter 5, note 4.) Harguindeguy told the trial on August 14 1985 that Ramírez was godfather to one of his children, but denied the charge of kidnapping.

10. The case of Clara Anahi Mariani is described in OAS, *Report on the Situation of Human Rights in Argentina*, pp. 59–62, and in the Grandmothers' reports.

11. Hesayne's April 24 1977 letter to Harguindeguy was published in *Diario del Juicio* on December 17 1985. The Church's collaboration with the dictatorship between 1976 and 1983 is still widely discussed in Argentina and has been extensively covered (*Nunca Más*, pp. 259–63; Emilio Mignone, *Witness to the Truth;* Jimmy Burns, "The Church in Argentina" and "A Church That Failed"; *Iglesia y Dictadura, El Periodista*). Several leading Church members were criticized by the CONADEP commission and during the trial. But official criticism of the Church under Alfonsín has been muted, in line with the policy of compromise.

12. Pio Laghi, the papal nuncio, was on close terms with many critics of the Junta including Robert Cox and Emilio Mignone, and as the Pope's ambassador in Catholic Argentina, he had considerable influence. In April 1980 a fierce argument broke out about Laghi's role after the release of Juan Martín, a young man who arrived in Europe after spending three years inside secret detention centers and who claimed to have seen Pio Laghi at a camp in Tucumán. Pio Laghi himself denied ever meeting Martín, although he did say he had celebrated mass on one occasion in Northern Argentina. Emilio Mignone questioned Pio Laghi and took his side after discovering several inconsistencies in Martín's testimony. Others, like Robert Cox, also sprang to Laghi's defense.

There is no doubt that Laghi made many discreet inquiries on behalf of the disappeared. The Interior Ministry file on Dagmar Hagelin refers to two dated September 28 1979 and June 4 1980. One internal 1980 Foreign Ministry memorandum complains that Laghi made "comments about Argentina's internal affairs on several occasions." (Both documents in the author's possession.)

13. Hebe de Bonafini's encounter in the church was described in *Iglesia y Dictadura.*

14. For sources on Pérez Esquivel's arrest and his award of the 1980 Nobel Peace Prize, see below, Chapter 18, notes 32ff.

15. The disappearance of the two French nuns was one of the most notorious and well-documented events of the dirty war. See OAS, *Report on the Situation of Human Rights in Argentina,* p. 102; *Nunca Más,* p. 387; the testimony of Ana María Martí, pp. 8–11; Gasparini, *La Pista Suiza,* pp. 127–55.

16. *Madres* 2 (February 1985) ran an affectionate tribute to Azucena.

17. For the text of the letter and an analysis see Gasparini, *La Pista Suiza,* pp. 132–33.

18. FOIA cable 00482, December 1977.

19. Gasparini, *La Pista Suiza,* pp. 127ff.

20. For Massera's attempt to explain away the nuns' deaths to French President Giscard d'Estaing, see below, Chapter 5, note 32.

Chapter 5. The Truth Comes Out

1. The 1951 Convention on the Status of Refugees defines a refugee as someone with a "well-founded fear of persecution" and is the bedrock of international refugee protection. By 1976, only three hundred Latin Americans had been granted formal refugee asylum by Argentina, but another eleven thousand were accepted as de facto refugees by the office of the U.N. High Commissioner for Refugees (UNHCR) established on December 30 1950. The UNHCR moved 5,500 refugees out of Argentina following the 1976 coup and budgeted $4.3 million for Latin America in 1977; $2.9 million were earmarked for Argentina. (These figures, presented at the 1977 session of the U.N. Human Rights Commission, are taken from document E/CN 4/1230, February 7 1977.)

2. From a September 6 1976 briefing paper by Amnesty International (NS 193/76). The paper put the number of Latin American exiles living in Argentina at one hundred thousand and listed the names of thirty-nine Uruguayans killed or abducted in Argentina.

3. Military rule in Uruguay effectively began in 1968, following the emergence of the Tupamaros. (See below, Chapter 10 for the dialogue between the United Nations and Uruguay's military rulers.)

4. The kidnappings of Gutiérrez Ruiz and Michelini were recorded in an open letter to President Videla by Wilson Ferreira Aldunate, another prominent Uruguayan exile in Buenos Aires, before he sought refuge at a Western embassy. It was clear that Gutiérrez Ruiz and Michelini were killed by Argentinian authorities because the two other victims found in the car, a man and his wife, had been abducted a week earlier with their three infant children. The children were delivered to a Buenos Aires hospital alive two weeks later.

5. Enrique Rodríguez Larreta, a journalist who survived this action later told

Philippe Labreveux, the correspondent in Argentina for *Le Monde,* that he and the other Uruguayans were tortured in Buenos Aires, taken to the Buenos Aires airport, loaded into a waiting Uruguayan Air Force plane, and flown across the river Plate to Uruguay. On arrival, a Uruguayan officer told them: "We saved your lives. If we hadn't intervened, the Argentines would have sent you up to play the harp with St. Peter." Labreveux's article ran in *Le Monde* on April 9 1977. Labreveux himself was forced to leave Argentina with his Argentinian wife Irene, also a journalist, after threats to his life. He subsequently joined the UNHCR.

6. Foreigners who disappeared included 304 Italians, 164 Spaniards, 48 West Germans, 10 Brazilians, 36 French (including the two French nuns), 6 Swiss, 6 Peruvians, 3 Americans, and a Swede (Dagmar Hagelin). Statistics from the judges' written sentence at the close of the trial, January 1986.

7. Technically, under article 4 of the 1930 Hague Convention, Dagmar Hagelin had no right to Swedish diplomatic protection while residing in the country of her second nationality, Argentina. One October 1977 cable from the U.S. embassy in Stockholm (FOIA 04214) notes this fact and says that the Swedes were relieved that it had not yet been raised by the Argentines. The account of the meeting between Ragnar Hagelin, Guzetti, and Ambassador Kollberg comes from Ragnar's testimony to the trial, July 17 1985.

8. FOIA cable 01106 (March 1977) from the U.S. embassy in Stockholm. The comment about deteriorating relations comes from Foreign Ministry memo B in the author's possession (p. 18).

9. Ragnar Hagelin, *Mi Hija Dagmar,* p. 11.

10. CADHU was set up in 1975 by several members of the "Partido Revolucionaria de los Obreros Argentinos" (Argentinian Revolutionary Workers Party). In 1976, after two of the founding members disappeared, the remaining founders (including Eduardo Duhalde and Gustavo Roca) moved CADHU and themselves abroad. Lidia Galletti, mother of one of the two disappeared, was an early member of the Mothers. Her husband served on the board of CELS (the Center for Legal and Social Studies) until he committed suicide.

11. For a published account of the growth of the Argentinian guerrillas and Matarollo's alleged involvement and international contacts, see "Latin America's Terrorist International."

12. Rodolfo Matarollo was the only permanent member on the boards of CAIS and CADHU according to "Latin America's Terrorist International."

13. This testimony had considerable impact back in Buenos Aires. Jacobo Timerman, the newspaper editor, read it and wrote to Congressman Donald Fraser, the Subcommittee chairman, lamenting the "obvious partiality" of Garzón Maceda and Roca. Timerman asked to appear before the Subcommittee to set the record straight. Fraser replied with a lofty refusal. The text of Timerman's letter and Fraser's reply were printed in Timerman's paper *Opinión* on December 9 1976.

14. CADHU raised $9,800 in the first five months from churches and individual donations (CADHU press release, April 15 1977). Olga Talamante's account of being tortured was published in "Human Rights in Argentina." (Hearings

before the Subcommittee of International Organizations, September 28, 29 1976.)

15. From an undated Foreign Ministry file in the author's possession.

16. Ibid. The file also contains a file on Lucio Garzón Maceda which gives details of his background as a labor lawyer and political activist but says nothing about terrorist activities.

17. Fragoso's report, *The Situation of Defense Lawyers in Argentina,* was published by the ICJ from Geneva in March 1975. Sinigaglia's death was noted in a follow-up ICJ report on the judiciary in Argentina, April 1978.

18. The thirty-five-page Burson Marsteller report, entitled "Improving the International Image of Argentina," was obtained and made public by the U.S. section of Amnesty International. A copy is in the possession of the author. According to the columnist Jack Anderson, the Junta paid Burson Marstellar $1.2 million ("The Art of Making Bad Look Good").

19. An advertisement in the *Wall Street Journal* of September 25 1978 stated: "Government actions under the state of emergency are always under the surveillance of the judicial system." For an angry response see Freund, "The Law and Human Rights in Argentina." Freund coordinated the highly effective campaign on behalf of Argentinian detainees by the U.S. section of Amnesty International.

20. Under the 1938 law on foreign registration Lofredo and Talamante were required to show they were employed by a foreign power or cease making political statements. Neither was possible in the case of CADHU, which claimed to be headquartered in Argentina. The author put in a FOIA request on this case to the Justice Department. The response shows that someone tipped off the department during the debate on Capitol Hill about cutting off arms sales to Argentina. Under a settlement agreed upon with the department, Lofredo and Talamante agreed to write to all the lawmakers they had contacted and apologize. This action did not make much difference. U.S. security aid to Argentina stopped in September 1978. (See below, Chapter 13, notes 6ff.)

21. Verbitsky, *La Ultima Batalla,* p. 58. The Washington-based Council on Hemispheric Affairs (COHA) denounced the seminar as Junta propaganda in a May 4 1979 press release.

22. For the pilot center see *Nunca Más,* pp. 142–43; Amnesty International external report (AMR 13/28/82); the testimony of Ana María Marti, pp. 16–20.

23. De Anchorena was a businessman with close ties to the army chiefs, and his June 1976 appointment to the embassy in Paris, the European center for Argentinian exiles, was a measure of their confidence in him. He gave testimony at the trial on August 11 1985. Other witnesses who testified about the pilot center and Elena Holmberg at the trial were Gregorio Dupont and Sylvia Aguila de Harcourt, who worked with Holmberg in Paris.

24. Elena Holmberg was a niece of General Alejandro Lanusse, President of Argentina between 1970 and 1973, and a fierce anti-Peronist. Between 1953 and 1955 she ferried messages to opponents of Perón in refuge in Uruguay, for which she was briefly jailed. After Perón's ouster in 1955 she sat on a commission that investigated corruption under Perón's rule. During this period she developed a friendship with many middle-ranking military officers.

25. Gonzales was a police officer who had tortured at the ESMA, while Captain Perren had headed the GT 3/32 operations (kidnapping) unit. The group placed bogus appeals in newspapers under the name of "Federico Volpi," with the address of "PO Box 16, Bella Vista," and sent letters purporting to come from Mothers of disappeared persons.

26. The West German frontier police were suspicious enough to take a photocopy of Astiz's false passport together with Yon's, who was traveling under his true identity. In spite of this, the French continued to allow Yon to operate for another year out of Paris. The escapades of Astiz and Yon were recorded in a detailed report by the International Federation of Human Rights, December 1982.

27. *La Ultima Batalla*, pp. 48–57. According to Verbitsky, a series of Montonero tracts began to arrive at newspaper offices in Buenos Aires late in 1976. They argued that instead of promoting the doctrine of national security and killing Argentinians, the armed forces should realize that Argentina's real security problems lay in its territorial disputes with Brazil, Chile, and Britain. This coincided with Massera's own change of strategy. Massera was breaking with the Junta and trying to forge a civilian political party. To stand any chance of success he needed to embrace a nationalist cause. According to Verbitsky, Massera's idea in 1975 had been to negotiate an alliance with Britain and the United States under which Argentina would concede de facto ownership of the Malvinas (including oil rights) to British companies and base facilities to the U.S. in return for recognition of Argentinian sovereignty. By the end of 1976, however, the navy was once again reviewing military options; the Montoneros' tracts tallied so closely with these events that several prisoners at the ESMA were closely interrogated about whether the Montoneros had a mole in the navy high command. Juan Gasparini downplays Verbitsky's theory. As he recalls it, the Malvinas was just one of many issues discussed by the detainees.

28. Several "ministaff," out and out collaborators, were allowed out of the ESMA to sleep at their homes, and they were deeply hated by other prisoners. Others, like Ana María Marti and Juan Gasparini, who were spared and worked at the ESMA without embracing the navy's philosophy, were known as "staff." They had nothing but loathing for their navy captors, but they were not prepared to turn down the chance to live. Juan Gasparini rationalizes his decision with the thought that he may have helped to persuade Jorge "Tiger" Acosta to call off a campaign of kidnapping against deputies suspected of being left-wing sympathizers (related in Gasparini's *Montoneros*, p. 111). In spite of this, some human rights groups still view the ESMA survivors as collaborators.

29. Miriam Lewin prepared a daily press review for Massera. After being released from the ESMA on January 10 1979, she worked briefly at 3696 Zapiola Street, where much of the ESMA booty was stored. It is thought that all of the files on ESMA prisoners together with the war booty were transferred to 3696 Zapiola Street, which was owned by Radice's parents. Selling off the stolen property was entrusted to one of Radice's cousins who lived opposite.

30. Mignone recorded his second conversation with Massera and had it published in *DIAL*, a Latin American newsletter. Massera later told him that his Junta colleagues had been so furious that they had disciplined him for eight days

after sending him before the "tribunal de honor." Mignone recalled his third
meeting with Massera at the 1985 trial.

31. Gasparini, *Montoneros,* p. 109. See below, Chapter 27, note 6, for the death of
Marcelo Dupont and the connection with the Holmberg killing.

32. Giscard d'Estaing released Massera's note on September 4 1985 for use at Massera's trial. Giscard wrote that he had "expressed disappointment" to Massera
at their 1978 meeting. But Giscard's government continued to sell arms to
the Junta and allowed Antonio Pernía, one of the nuns' killers, to operate on
French soil.

33. Massera's invitation came from Roger Fontaine, who directed the Latin
American Department at the Georgetown Center for Strategic Studies. The
journalist was Mario del Carril, a Georgetown professor and journalist who
had planned to cover Massera's address for the *Buenos Aires Herald.* Massera
warned del Carril not to write about his split with Videla. Massera had already
tried to intimidate Robert Cox, the *Herald* editor, in Buenos Aires. (From
Cox's testimony at the 1985 trial.)

34. Silvia de Harcourt, who served as Holmberg's secretary at the pilot center in
Paris, told the 1985 trial that she learned from Americo Muñoz (the chauffeur
to the naval military attaché) that he had driven Firmenich and Vaca Narvaja
(another leading Montonero) to the Hôtel Intercontinental in Paris for a
meeting with Massera. Muñoz told Cecilia Sanchez, who in turn told Silvia de
Harcourt. De Harcourt was ready to believe anything. Her brother had been
shot in the head by an assassin at point-blank range in a crowded street in
Buenos Aires.

35. Juan Gasparini thinks that Elena Holmberg was killed because she heard about
the misuse of funds at the pilot center while having a love affair with Antonio
"the Rat" Pernía.

36. In 1982, while trying to track down the killers of his brother, Gregorio Dupont
unwittingly uncovered further proof of Massera's meetings with Firmenich.
He visited Italy and met officials from the parliamentary commission investigating Licio Gelli's P 2 lodge. Gelli's diary contained a scheduled meeting with
Firmenich and Massera in the Italian town of Arezzo.

37. See below, Chapter 26, note 6 for the story of Marcelo Dupont's murder.

38.   The aims of the contract with Burson Marsteller were known by the Western media
before the agency could even start work on improving the image of the government of
Argentina. This undermined its impact and credibility. Later, the center for press and
information [pilot center] was set up in Paris. Quite apart from the serious lack of
coordination caused by placing it outside the normal channels, the inexperience of those
who worked in it meant that their counter-offensive was almost non-existent (from
Memo B in the author's possession, p. 59).

Chapter 6. Amnesty's Fraught Visit

1. Bishop Moure's letter was reproduced in the Mothers' paper *Madres,* March 5
1985. Becerra was one of 242 PEN prisoners in Argentina for whom Amnesty
campaigned between 1976 and 1983.

The material for this chapter is drawn from memoranda, interviews, and newspaper clippings collected by the author in Argentina and from Amnesty documents. For two widely different accounts of Amnesty, one sympathetic, the other critical, see Cosmas Desmond, *Persecution East and West* (critical) and Jonathan Power, *Against Oblivion* (sympathetic).

2. From the Amnesty International 1977 *Report of the Mission to Argentina*.

3. Amnesty's mandate has been enlarged to include torture and the death penalty. In December 1972 Amnesty launched a worldwide campaign against torture. This campaign raised one million signatures and inspired a United Nations declaration against torture that was adopted by the U.N. General Assembly in 1975.

4. See, for example, the November 21 1982 newsletter put out by Marketa Freund, coordinator of Amnesty's Argentina action program in the United States.

5. Desmond, *Persecution East and West*. As well as being a subtle indictment of Amnesty's apolitical approach, Desmond's book offers an excellent critique of the fragility of international human rights law.

6. Amnesty's international secretariat prizes its collection of angry government comments and occasionally publishes them. Generally speaking, newspapers that have set out to expose Amnesty's "left-wing" bias have failed dismally. See, for example, the first issue of the French magazine *Confidentiel* (Winter 1979).

7. From Foreign Ministry memo A, in the author's possession, p. 27.

8. I have tried to recreate the Amnesty visit as it was viewed in Argentina in 1976—which should not imply that I in any way sympathize with this view. I have drawn on the following newspapers: *Opinión* (November 9, 11, 12 1976); *Nación* (November 10, 13, 16 1976); Telam, the Argentinian press agency, (November 10 1976); *Prensa Libre* (November 11, 12 1976); *Buenos Aires Herald* (November 13 1976); *Le Monde* (18 November 1976); *Siete Dias* (November 19 1976).

9. A total of eighty-four journalists were to disappear in the dirty war (*Nunca Más* pp. 367–74).

10. Circular cable 142 was sent to Argentinian embassies in Europe by the Foreign Ministry describing the arrangements for the Amnesty visit, including the meeting with Allara (in the author's possession).

11. *Report of the Mission to Argentina*.

12. From Foreign Ministry memo A, in the author's possession. The Argentina embassy in London issued a four-page press release denouncing the report as "hearsay."

13. Three years later, in 1980, a Foreign Ministry official would describe the decision to admit the Amnesty team and other human rights inquiries as a colossal blunder: "If the government thought [the Amnesty visit] useful, or controllable, it had a misjudged or incomplete picture of the mood outside the country." The Junta was consistent in its hostility to Amnesty during the years that followed. Of the six confidential communications on Argentina submitted under the UN's 1503 procedure between 1977 and 1979, Amnesty's was the only one that the Junta declined to answer. (See below, Chapter 15, note 7.)

Chapter 7. A Dangerous Place

1. José María Sert, a well-known Catalonian artist, was posted to the Spanish mission to the Vatican after his defection to the fascists.

   The League of Nations and Human Rights. The covenant establishing the League of Nations did not refer specifically to human rights, but human rights was very much on the League's agenda. The League set up a system for protecting the minorities that were left stranded by the reordering of Europe's frontiers after the First World War. Under this plan, individuals were allowed to lodge complaints to the League's Assembly. The League also gave several governments the task of mandating territories previously occupied by Turkey and Germany. These governments were supposed to promote a wide range of what would come to be known as human rights, including racial equality. Progress was monitored by a special Mandates Commission, which reported to the League Council.

   The 1926 Convention against Slavery was the first legally binding international human rights treaty and it owed its existence in part to a long international campaign by the first international human rights nongovernmental organization (NGO), the London-based Anti-Slavery Society. (The Society was created in 1825 by William Wilberforce, the British politician who led the fight for the abolition of slavery in Britain.) In addition, it was during the time of the League that the international community first recognized that refugees require special international protection. See Brookings Institution, *The United Nations and Human Rights*, pp. 8–13; James Avery Joyce, "Broken Star"; F. P. Walters, "The League of Nations."

2. The principal goal of the U.N. Charter is to prevent war, and the preamble of the Charter makes it clear that violations of human rights are seen as a threat to peace. Article 55c reads: "The United Nations shall promote . . . universal respect for, and observance of, human rights and fundamental freedoms for all without distinction as to race, sex, language and religion." Article 2(7), on the other hand, reads as follows: "Nothing contained in the present Charter shall authorize the United Nations to intervene in matters which are essentially within the domestic jurisdiction of any state."

3. For the full text of the Universal Declaration and all other conventions see United Nations, *A Compilation of International Instruments*.

4. Drafting the Declaration between 1946 and 1948 was a race against time to reconcile the two competing ideologies of East and West before the Cold War set in and made consensus impossible. For a first-hand account see John Humphrey, *The Great Adventure: Human Rights and the United Nations* (Humphrey was the first director of the U.N. human rights secretariat and author of the earliest draft); Howard Tolley, Jr., *The U.N. Commission on Human Rights*, provides a thorough account of the various stages of drafting, culminating in the December 10 1948 vote. During the 1948 General Assembly, eighty sessions were taken up on drafting the Declaration and no less than thirteen hundred separate votes taken.

   The original intention was to complement the Declaration with a legally binding treaty, but this proved politically impossible because of the differences between East and West. Instead, the two categories of rights in the Declaration were incorporated into two separate legally binding covenants. The International Covenant on Civil and Political Rights and the International Covenant on Economic, Social and Cultural Rights were both adopted by the General Assembly on December 16 1966. The Covenant on Civil and Political Rights became law on March 23 1976, when thirty five states ratified. The Covenant on Economic, Social and Cultural Rights became law on January 3 1976.

5. *International Herald Tribune,* December 8 1984. The term "Newspeak" was coined by George Orwell in his novel *1984* to indicate verbal obfuscation. The teachers' rebuke was ironic because when the State Department did use the word "killing," this too was seen as a form of verbal Newspeak by human rights activists. (See below, Chapter 22, note 12.)

6. Seven Islamic states voted in favor of the Declaration and Pakistan openly disputed Saudi Arabia's interpretation. In spite of this, the controversy over the compatibility between Islamic law and the Declaration revived in 1983 when the Iranian government threatened to withdraw from the Declaration on grounds that it was "Judeo-Christian." For the Iranian argument and the U.N. counterargument see the 1988 report by Reynaldo Galindo Pohl, the U.N. rapporteur on human rights in Iran (U.N. document E/CN.4/1988/24, January 25 1988).

   The Soviet Union. One action which caused particular fury in the United States was the February 15 1947 refusal of the Soviet government to allow Russian women to marry foreigners, and its subsequent refusal to allow Russians wives to leave with their foreign husbands. (See Brookings Institution, *The United Nations and Human Rights,* pp. 159ff.) Soviet concerns at the U.N. turning into a tribunal had been expressed by Andrei Vishinsky, the chief Soviet delegate to the U.N. General Assembly, in the *New York Times Magazine* in 1946.

7. Eddison Zvobgo, who was to become the Minister of Justice of Zimbabwe, charged that the Universal Declaration was a Western attempt to impose free enterprise and capitalism on the rest of the world, outlaw single-party systems, and universalize Western-style multiparty elections. Zvobgo is quoted by Cosmas Desmond in *Persecution East and West,* p. 67. A large part of Desmond's book is spent arguing that Zvobgo was correct. For the counterargument, that the Universal Declaration has stood the test of time, see Philip Alston, "The Universal Declaration at 35: Western and Passé or Alive and Universal?"

8. As of 1989, the list of international human rights instruments (including legally binding conventions, declarations, and recommendations) stood at no less than sixty-seven. The list, and the full texts, can be found in the U.N. publication *Human Rights: A Compilation of International Instruments.*

   By 1976 the ILO had sponsored one hundred fifty conventions and another one hundred sixty-eight recommendations. While the majority established technical standards, some covered human rights. The most important is Convention 87, which allows for freedom of association (the right to form independent labor unions) and is monitored by a special committee of the ILO's Governing Body. A group of independent legal experts review the application of all ILO conventions for the annual ILO conference. The ILO is widely respected, and was an object of great suspicion to the Argentinian Junta. (See below, note 39 and Chapter 11, note 1.) However, on November 5 1975, U.S. Secretary of State Henry Kissinger served notice of U.S. withdrawal from the ILO. (See below, Chapter 14, note 19.)

By 1989, UNESCO has adopted twenty-six conventions, twenty-six recommendations, and five declarations in the four areas with which it is concerned: education, science, culture, and information. Individuals and groups can submit complaints, which are then examined by a committee that meets every six months. In 1978 UNESCO received eighty-eight communications. (Figures from "Evaluation of the [UNESCO] Human Rights Procedures," 23rd General Conference, 23 C/17, October 8 1985.) For UNESCO's dealings with the Argentinian Junta, see below Chapter 11, note 1.

The European human rights system, based in Strasbourg, France, is the oldest and most cohesive regional system in existence. It comprises a convention, commission, and court. (See Rosalyn Higgins, "The European Convention on Human Rights.") For two controversial cases against Britain and Greece that went to the European Court see the Amnesty International *Report on Torture,* pp. 79–113, case studies B and C.

The OAS. For the OAS and its human rights machinery, particularly the Inter-American Commission on Human Rights (IACHR), see below, Chapter 13, note 21, and Appendix 7.

9. This was one reason why the International Covenant on Civil and Political Rights imposed no legal obligations on the Argentinian Junta.

Almost all the major conventions suffer from ambiguous definitions that are imposed by governments at early stages of drafting. Thus, there is no mention of "political groups" in the definition of genocide in the convention adopted on December 8 1948. (As a result, it is unclear whether the massacre of a million Cambodians by the Pol Pot regime would constitute "genocide" under the convention.) The 1976 U.N. convention against apartheid describes apartheid as a punishable crime, yet states airily that "international criminal responsibility shall apply irrespective of the motive involved." For Western legal systems, built on the concept of *mens rei* (motive) this is a major flaw.

10. International law in 1976 imposed little pressure on governments to outlaw torture, in spite of the fact that torture was (together with slavery) recognized as a universal evil. Torture was prohibited by no fewer than seven international instruments (and was also an offense under criminal law in most countries). But many of these instruments were not legally binding, while those that were binding were carefully avoided by most governments which practiced torture. In addition, there was no universally agreed definition. The other problem was the lack of any implementation procedures.

The seven instruments were the Universal Declaration of Human Rights; the four Geneva conventions of 1949; the International Covenant on Civil and Political Rights; the 1975 U.N. Declaration on the Protection of all Persons from Torture and other Cruel, Inhuman or Degrading Treatment or Punishment; the European Human Rights Convention; the American Human Rights Convention; the 1957 Standard Mininum Rules for the Treatment of Prisoners. To these have since been added the African Charter on Human and Peoples' Rights (1981); the U.N. Code of Conduct of Law Enforcement Officials (1979); the U.N. Principles of Medical Ethics (1982); the 1987 U.N. Convention against torture; and the 1989 European Convention against torture.

There was widespread, almost universal, outrage at the torture being applied by the military regimes of Greece, Brazil, Uruguay, South Vietnam, and Chile. Amnesty International launched a campaign against torture in 1972 and raised a million signatures; this led to the adoption of the 1975 declaration against torture by the U.N. General Assembly. But the U.N. declined to name, let alone challenge, governments which practiced torture. This fact, together with the spread of torture as an instrument of state policy during the 1970s, weakened Amnesty's global campaign, and it was hardly surprising that a 1974 global survey by Amnesty found torture practiced in no less than sixty-one countries. (The follow-up report, *Torture in the Eighties,* concluded that the number of countries had risen to sixty-six.) All this pointed to the need for a new, legally binding convention specifically outlawing torture.

See Nigel Rodley, *The Treatment of Prisoners Under International Law,* pp. 17–43; the 1975 Amnesty *Report on Torture,* pp. 70–105; Robert Drinan, *Cry of the Oppressed,* pp. 49–57. For four case studies of international action against torture, see Jonathan Power, *Against Oblivion,* pp. 59–70.

11. The international campaign against torture might have had more success by 1976 if the U.N. had been able to develop the concept of an "international crime." By 1976 there were three different elements:

Laws of war. Humanitarian law, in the form of the Geneva Conventions, had attempted to protect noncombatants caught in war. Violations were termed "war crimes."

Crimes against humanity. The tribunals established after the Second World War by the Allies to prosecute Japanese and Nazi leaders agreed that there is a higher law that takes precedence over man's laws. They also rejected the time-honored plea of the war criminal—that he was only acting under orders. On the other hand, the tribunals also acknowledged that without discipline an army will quickly collapse and that orders have to be obeyed. Justice Jackson observed in one ruling that a soldier who is ordered to take part in a firing squad is not chargeable, "even if the death is unjust" (cited in Robert Drinan, *Cry of the Oppressed,* pp. 166ff.). See below, Chapter 30, for how democratic Argentina attempted to reconcile these two principles.

The Nuremberg and Tokyo trials were legally questionable because they were imposed by the victors on the vanquished, and the U.N. General Assembly asked the International Law Commission to draft a set of legal principles based on Nuremberg. This was achieved in 1950. Principle 6 contains three separate categories of "international crime": crimes against peace; war crimes; and crimes against humanity. Principle 4 states that the fact that someone acted under orders ("due obedience") does not relieve him or her from responsibility. This progress came to an abrupt halt when the U.N. tried to expand on Principle 6 and draft a "Code of Offenses Against the Peace and Security of Mankind." It was agreed that "aggression" should feature, but it proved impossible to agree on a definition until 1974.

    Universal jurisdiction. During the 1970s, four anti-terrorist conventions were adopted calling on states to prosecute or extradite violators. These were the 1970 Hague Convention on Hijacking; the 1971 Montreal Convention on Aircraft Sabotage; the 1973 U.N. Convention on the Protection of Diplomats; the 1979 U.N. Convention on the Taking of Hostages. For further background see the message of President Reagan to the Senate of May 20 1988 transmitting the U.N. Convention Against Torture. 100th Congress, second session. Treaty Doc. 100–20, U.S. Government Printing Office.

    The Swedish government was determined that torture should be clearly defined as a punishable crime under international law. Regimes like the Argentinian Junta were equally determined to oppose this. (See below, Chapters 18, 24, and 25, passim.)

12. The most comprehensive account of the U.S. reluctance to join international human rights treaties is found in the report of the 1979 Senate hearings on the four major international conventions that were signed by President Carter in 1977. ("International Human Rights Treaties," Hearings before the Senate Committee on Foreign Relations, November 1979.) Two NGOs provide a good political analysis: Amnesty International USA, in its 1989 campaign to force U.S. ratification of the Torture Convention, *Ratification Now,* and Lawyers Committee for Human Rights, *Project 88.* See also Drinan, *Cry of the Oppressed,* pp. 61–69.

13. Address to the University of Georgia Law School April 30 1977 (reprinted in David Newsom, ed., *The Diplomacy of Human Rights,* pp. 207–212).

    The right to "life, liberty and security of the person" is found in Article 3 of the Universal Declaration. Similar language is found in the International Covenant on Civil and Political Rights, the European Convention, and the American Convention. Most international lawyers would agree with Yoram Dinstein, who writes that "the human right to life is entrenched in customary international law" (Dinstein, "The Right to Life, Physical Integrity, and Liberty," pp. 114–37). On the other hand, the actual interpretation of the right has been complicated by its association with abortion, euthanasia, nuclear war and the death penalty—all of which are viewed as a violation of the right to life by various bodies of opinion.

14. Article 4 of the International Covenant on Civil and Political Rights allows states to suspend certain rights and liberties (including the right to leave) in "time of public emergency which threatens the life of the nation." No exceptions are allowed to the following rights: life; freedom from torture and slavery; arbitrary detention; the right to a legal identity; freedom of thought, religion and conscience. The escape clause allowed by Article 4 has been endlessly exploited by military governments like the Junta—first to impose a state of siege under an often flimsy legal pretext and second to justify massive detention. The definitive work was published by the International Commission

of Jurists in 1983 and contains fifteen case studies, including Argentina (*States of Emergency: Their Impact on Human Rights*).

15. Kaufman, "A Legal Remedy For International Torture?" (Judge Kaufman was responsible for the landmark Filártiga decision on torture. See below Chapter 18, note 8 and Chapter 25, note 32.)

16. "Human beings, unlike oysters, frequently reveal their emotions. And they are prolific at discovering new 'rights'," wrote the columnist George Will in one 1978 article ("A Right to Health"). Another attack on the concept of economic rights can be found in the memo which secured Elliott Abrams the post of Assistant Secretary of State for Human Rights in October 1981: "Calling them rights confuses the issue of liberty with that of wealth and implies that government has an equally central role in both" (see below Chapter 22, notes 4ff.).

17. The State Department's 1977 *Country Reports on Human Rights Practices for 1977* distinguished three categories of rights: freedom from governmental violation of the integrity of the person; the right to civil and political liberties; and the right to fulfillment of vital, basic needs such as food, education, shelter and health care. It did, however, agree that a government's ability to meet these basic needs would depend on its level of development. (This was also accepted by the International Covenant on Economic and Social Rights.) The text of Roosevelt's two addresses to Congress are quoted in Brookings Institution, *The United Nations and Human Rights,* p. 14.

18. Female circumcision, like child labor, straddles the line between social practice and human rights abuse. (For a detailed article on female circumcision and human rights see *Human Rights Quarterly,* 1989, vol. 1.) Similarly, while many find stoning and the use of the death penalty both repugnant, international human rights law does not cover legally sanctioned forms of punishment. It does outlaw "cruel, inhuman, degrading treatment or punishment," but without defining it.

19. The U.N. Working Group on Enforced or Involuntary Disappearances included a list of the international laws violated by disappearances in its first report (E/CN.4/1435, January 26 1981, pp. 79–81). See also Nigel Rodley's "The Treatment of Prisoners under International Law," pp. 191–218.

   The clearest legal statement that disappearances represents a violation of international law is to be found in the series of decisions by the Inter-American Court of Human Rights against the government of Honduras. See Appendix 7.

20. The establishment of an international criminal court is still opposed by Eastern Europe. Canvassed for their opinion by the U.N. Human Rights Division in 1981 as to whether such a court could help put teeth in the U.N. convention against apartheid, the Soviet Union replied curtly that such an idea was "unrealistic" (E/CN.4/AC 22/1982/WP 3, November 30 1981).

21. The Human Rights Committee held its first meeting in March 1977, and continued thereafter to alternate between New York and Geneva. From the author's own experience as a reporter it suffered, at least initially, from three serious obstacles: first, the limited participation allowed to NGOs; second, the general lack of interest and understanding among journalists; third, paper-

work. States which ratify the International Covenant on Civil and Political Rights are required to report regularly to the Committee and this imposes a huge administrative burden. As of June 1 1986, no fewer than 460 state reports on the four main conventions were overdue ("Chaos Threatens U.N. Treaties," from Human Rights Internet, *Report of the 1988 Session of the Commission on Human Rights,* p. 106).

22. The U.N. Charter made no provision for individuals to petition the U.N. on human rights, and the first session of the Commission in 1947 decided to take no action on the hundreds of communications arriving at the U.N. In 1969 a group of Soviet citizens tried to hand in a petition at the U.N. office in Moscow. The Soviet government protested, and on October 29 1969 U Thant ordered all 51 U.N. information offices not to accept petitions.

In 1970, ECOSOC passed Resolution 1503, setting up a confidential procedure for reviewing individual communications that indicated a "systematic pattern of gross violations" (Appendix 5). Meanwhile, an optional protocol, allowing individuals to submit complaints against their governments to the Human Rights Committee, was added to the International Covenant on Civil and Political Rights. Not surprisingly, the only governments which joined were those that had little to fear. Uruguay was one striking exception. (For the Committee's important decision on the case of Professor Luís Massera, see below Chapter 11, note 14; for the Committee's findings between 1976 and 1980 see U.N., *Selected Decisions Under the Optional Protocol.*)

23. The Commission is comprised of governments elected by ECOSOC for a three-year term. Each of the five regional groups is guaranteed a set number of seats, and the Commission has been progressively enlarged from its original membership of eighteen. Currently, it stands at forty-three. The Commission's agenda is reviewed the previous summer by the twenty-six-member Sub-Commission, which is supposedly independent. The same issues are then reviewed by ECOSOC, and again by the U.N. General Assembly—which meets a full eighteen months after the Sub-Commission. The system is profoundly bureaucratic, incredibly difficult for outsiders to follow, and crippled by its own innate lethargy—all of which plays into the hands of governments. At the center of this galaxy sits the Commission—bloated, wordy, and ponderous, but still the main focus for the U.N.'s human rights work.

Howard Tolley, Jr.'s *The U.N. Commission on Human Rights,* is essential reading for students of this strange body.

24. See above, note 22, and Appendix 5.

25. The U.N. was on a collision course with South Africa from the moment the South African government enacted the 1946 Asiatic Land Tenure and Indian Representation Act, restricting the freedom of Indians in South Africa to trade and residence. India's delegation brought the issue up at the first session of the U.N. Human Rights Commission (summary records of the 1947 session, E/CN.4/SR 1, January 28 1947). In 1962 the General Assembly set up an eighteen-nation committee on apartheid and in 1967 the Human Rights Commission nominated six delegates to a working group on Southern Africa that has been extended regularly ever since. It has never visited South Africa and is

viewed as biased by South Africa, but given the evil of apartheid it is hard to see how the U.N. could have acted differently and still retained its self-respect. This is not, however, to say that the U.N.'s elaborate, expensive anti-apartheid machinery has had much impact. (For details of the U.N.'s actions against apartheid see U.N., *United Nations Action in the Field of Human Rights*, pp. 76–94.)

26. Israel, like South Africa, has refused any dialogue with the U.N. Committee on Israeli Practices on the grounds that it is inherently biased, but this position obscures the question whether there has been a legitimate human rights problem in the occupied territories that justifies U.N. concern. Most would say there is. According to the U.N. and the International Committee of the Red Cross, the building of Jewish settlements on Arab lands, the demolition of Arab houses, and the expulsion of Palestinian "agitators" are all contrary to the Fourth Geneva Convention protecting civilians under occupation. The U.N. has also repeatedly argued that the Palestinians have a right to "self-determination." In addition, Israel's treatment of Palestinian detainees prior to the current Palestinian "intifada" (uprising), caused periodic waves of concern. (See, e.g., *Report and Recommendations of an Amnesty International Mission to the Government of the State of Israel*.) Israel's response to the current Palestinian uprising, of course, has evoked widespread indignation.

   For a hostile analysis of the U.N. Committee on Israeli Practices and its alleged "politicization" as well as a sympathetic interpretation of Israel's actions on the West Bank, see Allan Gerson, "Israel, the West Bank and International Law," pp. 151–59.

27. By allowing the United Nations to take public and private action against governments which were guilty of a "consistent pattern of gross violations of human rights," resolutions 1503 and 1235 changed the face of the U.N. human rights machinery. See Appendix 5.

28. International Commission of Jurists, *Final Report of the Mission to Chile, April 1974*.

29. The coup in Chile had a dramatic impact on the United Nations. By taking action, the Commission expanded the U.N.'s action against "gross violations" beyond apartheid and colonialism to include detention, torture, and disappearance; opened the way for NGOs to participate directly in the work of the Commission; and ensured that the Soviet Union was finally co-opted into the U.N.'s human rights work.

   Six months after the coup, Allende's widow, Hortensia Allende, was allowed to address the 1974 session of the U.N. Human Rights Commission for the Women's International Democratic Federation. It was the first time the representative of an NGO had criticized a government without being accused of making a "politically motivated attack." On March 1 1974, the Soviets supported a proposal to send a telegram to Pinochet expressing concern on behalf of five well-known detainees, including the trade union leader Luis Corvalán. The momentum petered out, however, and it was not until the following year, 1975, that the U.N. working group, comprising five delegates, was established. Three years would pass before the group finally visited Chile in 1978 for what was to prove a trailblazing visit. For two good factual accounts see the preface to the report of the UN 1978 visit to Chile (A/33/331, October 25 1978, pp. 1–4) and Lillich and Newman, eds., *International Human Rights: Problems of Law and Policy*, pp. 263–315. Judge Frank Newman, one of the two editors, was part of the Amnesty International team that visited Chile after the coup.

30. No fewer than seventeen out of the thirty-two governments on the 1977 Commission appeared in the 1975 Amnesty International *Report on Torture*. Even accepting that the Third World wanted to embarrass the West and retaliate for the West's lack of enthusiasm toward sanctions against South Africa, it has to be said that the election of Idi Amin's Uganda to the Commission was an extraordinary expression of contempt for human rights.

31. For more on the role of the U.N. secretariat, and the difficulty in ensuring its independence, see below Chapter 10, note 4.

32. Forty-two NGOs attended the 1945 San Francisco Conference. By 1976, 377 were affiliated to ECOSOC. Although this was a dramatic increase, the rules governing NGO participation in the U.N. had grown more, not less, restrictive over the years, seriously hindering their ability to act as a bridge between the U.N. and the outside world. See Appendix 6.

33. A U.S. congressional inquiry found the name of the ICJ among some two hundred recipients of CIA funding, and this emerged in press accounts. Philip Agee, *Inside the Company: CIA Diary*, contains the full list.

34. This confrontation at the 1975 Commission lead ECOSOC to pass another resolution (#1919) which further restricted the participation of NGOs in the U.N.'s work. See Appendix 6.

35. For the human rights provisions in the OAS Charter, see Appendix 7.

36. This list of Argentina's international legal obligations comes from the judges' written summary at the 1985 trial.

37. From memo C in the author's possession, p. 36. The Vienna Convention on Consular Relations entered into force March 19 1967.

38. Ibid., pp. 17, 37.

39. The ILO Governing Body committee that oversees freedom of association took up the case of Argentina in November 1976 (see the 160th report of the ILO Governing Body, pars. 394–444). The Argentinian member of the committee, Antonio Jakasa Vitaic, was to pay dearly for his participation (see below Chapter 8, note 10). For UNESCO's action on the disappearances, see below Chapter 11, note 1.

40. For a review of the U.N.'s use of economic sanctions in the protection of human rights, see Lillich and Newman, eds., *International Human Rights: Problems of Law and Policy*, pp. 415–20.

41. On the 502B legislation and other related U.S. laws, see below Chapter 12, passim.

42. One 1979 U.N. report by Abdelwahab Boudiba from Tunisia estimated that one million Cambodians died under Pol Pot (E/CN.4/1335, February 1979). The U.N. kept Uganda under review after Amin left the country in 1978 under an item known as "advisory services," which was a mixture of carrot (technical aid) and stick (criticism). Equatorial Guinea was also kept under review under

the advisory services program after the fall and execution of the dictator Macías Nguema in 1980. (See below, Chapter 28, note 2.)

Chapter 8. The Godfather

1. I tried several times to interview Ambassador Martínez between 1977 and 1983, but each time he refused even though he made use of the articles I wrote in his campaign against the U.N. secretariat. (See below, Chapter 24, note 26.)
2. From U.N. press release CR 98 (May 30 1974).
3. On September 12 1974 the General Agreement on Tariffs and Trade (GATT) launched a series of negotiations known as the "Tokyo Round," aimed at reducing tariffs and revitalizing world trade. Gabriel Martínez was to establish a formidable reputation at the GATT between 1974 and 1982. UNCTAD was established in 1964 with the aim of helping to spur economic development in the Third World. During the 1970s, UNCTAD served as the cockpit for efforts by the Third World to restructure world trade, increase aid, and implement a "new international economic order." One of UNCTAD's aims was debt relief, something else that was of obvious interest to Argentina.
4. "An Argentine Atom Bomb for Libya?" An account of the Libyan-Argentinian trade deal is to be found in Jimmy Burns, *The Land that Lost its Heroes,* pp. 55–60. The Argentinian wheat rotted and the Libyan oil arrived in Buenos Aires mixed with sea water. Nonetheless, the two governments remained on friendly terms and Argentina purchased arms from Libya during the 1982 Malvinas/Falklands war. The information that Martínez accompanied López Rega to Libya comes from Emilio Mignone, with whom Martínez was to clash at the U.N. in 1982. (See below, Chapter 24.)
5. From Memo C in the author's possession, p. 7.
6. Details of the reorganization were given by Gabriel Martínez in his testimony at the 1985 trial. For contacts between the U.S. Embassy and the Foreign Ministry over disappearances, see below, Chapter 13, note 8. After several career officers declined to head the new human rights department at the Foreign Ministry, the post eventually went to Juan Arlia, who supported the Junta almost as fanatically as did Gabriel Martínez in Geneva. Arlia was one of only a handful of career diplomats compelled to retire by the government of Raúl Alfonsín in 1983.
7. Details from a copy of the Hagelin Interior Ministry file, in the author's possession.
8. From Memo C in the author's possession, pp. 37 and 38. The task that faced Argentina's ambassadors—to gain time—is stated on both pages for emphasis.
9. Gabriel Martínez's files contained a complete list of names of Argentinian citizens in Geneva. Martínez also knew how to flatter. On December 22 1978 he wrote to Ghulam Allana, the Pakistani chairman of the U.N. working group on Chile, expressing regret that Allana had not been put forward for a U.N. human rights prize for his work on Chile: "This being the 30th Anniversary of the Declaration, it was without doubt the right moment for the organiza-

tion to recognize your great merits and your constant struggle for the protection of human rights." At first sight, this was a very strange letter, given that Martínez was spending much of his waking time trying to ensure that the U.N. did not establish a similar investigation on Argentina. The point was that Allana was powerful in the U.N. and could prove to be an important ally when it came to Argentina. Allana also knew Shariffuddin Pirzada, a prominent Pakistani lawyer and future Pakistani Minister of Justice, who was elected to the Sub-Commission in 1976. Pirzada, as we shall see, was to play a crucial role in keeping Argentina's name off the 1503 blacklist of "gross violators" (see below Chapter 9, notes 12ff). Martínez was careful about those he chose to flatter.

10. "Cortez" was spotted by Juan Gasparini, an ESMA survivor, in the U.N. cafeteria in 1981. Graciela Fernández Meijide, secretary of the Permanent Assembly and a staff member on the CONADEP commission, referred to the incident during her testimony in the trial on May 30 1985. Antonio Jakasa Vitaic's name appears in the 1984 CONADEP list of disappeared.

According to Ana María Martí, a special ESMA assassination squad traveled to Geneva in June 1977 in the hope of killing Gonzalo Chavez, a member of the Montonero labor committee who was in Geneva for the ILO's summer conference. The attempt failed. In March 1981 two Argentinian security officers, Rubén Bufano and Luís Martínez, were arrested by the Swiss police in Geneva when they attempted to pick up the ransom for a Uruguayan banker being held in Buenos Aires. They were subsequently extradited to Argentina at the request of the Alfonsín government. Juan Gasparini is convinced that these operations were carried out by independent cells that would have had no contact with the Argentinian diplomats in Geneva, but Theo van Boven is equally convinced that Martínez was part of Argentina's large and well-oiled European intelligence network. Given that ESMA torturers were subsequently posted to embassies in London, Paris, and Madrid it seems quite possible.

11. Cable from Martínez dated August 28 1976, in the author's possession.

12. The text of the resolution is found in U.N. document E/CN/ 4.Sub 2/L649, August 26 1976. It was adopted by 8 votes to 1, with 8 abstentions.

13. From Prince Sadruddin Aga Khan's opening statement to the UNHCR Executive Committee on October 4 1976 (A/AC.96/534). Martínez's reply from p. 10 of the summary record (A/AC.96/SR 274).

14. From a secret October 5 1976 cable (3936) from Oscar Sanguinetti in the Department of International Organizations at the Foreign Ministry. Sanguinetti's three-page cable is a reply to queries from Martínez about four refugees, whose deaths had provoked expressions of alarm: Gutiérrez Ruiz, Michelini, Enriquez Espinoza (a Chilean), and Regina Marcondes (from Brazil).

15. From Memo C, in the author's possession, p. 29.

Chapter 9. The Junta Counterattacks

1. Alejandro Artucio was a leading defense lawyer in Uruguay before he was arrested in June 1972 under the state of emergency. He disappeared for seven

months and was then taken before a judge who dismissed the case against him. The military took no notice and detained Artucio in the notorious Liberty jail for another year. Artucio was eventually put on a plane to France, and made to pay for his ticket as a final indignity. Niall MacDermot visited Uruguay in 1974 when Artucio was in jail. As a former defense lawyer himself, MacDermot was very much in sympathy with Artucio, and when he learned that Artucio had been released and was in Paris doing odd jobs, he invited him to Geneva for an interview. MacDermot queried Artucio closely about his connections with the left-wing Tupomaro guerrillas, some of whom Artucio had represented in court. Satisfied that Artucio's contacts were entirely professional, MacDermot offered him the post of Latin American specialist at the ICJ.

2. The author spent several hours with Niall MacDermot in preparation for this book.

The full story of the MacDermots' ordeal at the hands of British intelligence is told by David Leigh in *The Wilson Plot*. For a brief but useful analysis of the ICJ's CIA connection see Lars Schoultz, *Human Rights and United States Policy Toward Latin America* pp 85–86.

3. McGeorge Bundy, National Security Assistant to Presidents Kennedy and Johnson, made a grant of $500,000 to the ICJ at the end of the 1960s as President of the Ford Foundation. (MacDermot assumes it was partly to make amends for the damage caused by the ICJ connection with the CIA.) Only $9,000 remained when MacDermot took over. MacDermot persuaded Roy Jenkins, the British Home Secretary, to make a grant of 20,000 pounds. After MacDermot took over from MacBride, the ICJ ran on a shoestring budget for several years.

4. MacDermot also encouraged debate on such controversial topics as Islam and human rights, and the right to development. But his most important contribution to broadening the human rights debate was to hire lawyers from the Third World—including Alejandro Artucio—to work at the ICJ headquarters in Geneva.

5. Fragoso's report, *The Situation of Defense Lawyers in Argentina,* was published by the ICJ in March 1975 (see above, Chapter 5, note 17). In 1979, Fragoso visited Nicaragua with Artucio for the ICJ. Together they wrote a controversial report (Artucio and Fragoso, *Human Rights in Nicaragua: Yesterday and Today;* see below, Chapter 17, notes 13ff).

6. De Richter was another diplomat who supported the Junta with something close to fanaticism, but she was also a reminder that many Argentinian diplomats bore personal scars. One of her relatives, a serviceman, was crippled in a terrorist attack. Partly as a result, she was treated with some sympathy by the incoming Alfonsín government. At the time of writing she is serving as Argentinian consul in the town of Antofagasta in the north of Chile.

7. Craig Williamson's espionage was one of the major scandals that hit the Geneva NGOs in the 1970s. Williamson was deputy director of the International University Exchange Fund (IUEF) when he drafted the statement on Argentina for the Human Rights Commission (E/CN.4/ NGO/202). The statement listed the names of Uruguayans who had disappeared in Argentina and other details that were being widely publicized by 1977. But Argentina invoked

the restrictive 1975 resolution 1919 (see Appendix 6) and insisted that any information on individuals should fall under the confidential 1503 procedure. Williamson won great credibility when his statement was attacked by Martínez—the ultimate accolade for a human rights group in the late 1970s—and this helped him disguise his identity as a valued and trusted member of the South African intelligence service. The IUEF was chosen because it funded scholarships in Europe for Namibian and Latin American refugees. Its own funding came largely from Swedish Social Democrats.

Williamson was eventually exposed by a South African who defected to Britain. Williamson himself escaped from Switzerland just ahead of the Swiss police and was rewarded with a medal in South Africa. The IUEF subsequently collapsed after a long and lingering attempt to stay afloat. The author covered these events for the *London Guardian,* which broke the story of Williamson's espionage.

Diego Cordovez was the director of the ECOSOC secretariat when he issued his directive to NGOs on May 26 1977. Cordovez was to rise high in the U.N. As Under Secretary General for Political Affairs he would help to negotiate a Soviet withdrawal from Afghanistan.

8. Copies of MacDermot's correspondence with Martínez in the author's possession.

9. After the meeting, the Argentinian team drafted a nine-page note marked "Secret," which is in the author's possession. The complaint about Matarollo's connection with the provincial government is erased from page 9, but is still visible. It reads: "This information is not available to this observer delegation and was certainly not known by the officials who wrote the note for the U.N. committee."

10. Paragraph (iv) c, of a secret memorandum dated March 26 1979, in the author's possession.

11. Jewish NGOs would probably maintain that the politicization of the committee began in 1969, when the Arabs and East Europeans succeeded in getting a Jewish NGO (the Coordinating Board of Jewish Organizations) stripped of its accreditation. Governmental pressure on the committee increased following the disclosure that the International Commission of Jurists had unwittingly received CIA funds. But the 1978 assault by Argentina confirmed this trend, and during the 1980s the committee grew increasingly unwilling to admit NGOs that took a strong position in criticizing governments. The London-based Minority Rights Group and the New York-based Lawyers Committee for Human Rights have both found themselves repeatedly blocked.

12. The twenty-six subcommissioners, while independent, were nominated by their governments and elected by the Commission for three-year terms. For many years the Sub-Commission suffered from an identity crisis about its work, which often seemed to duplicate that of its parent Commission, until the creation of the 1503 procedure in 1970 enstrusted it with a task—drawing up the preliminary "blacklist" of gross violators—that was both important and complementary to the work of the Commission. In addition, as NGOs began to flex their muscles, they began to see great potential in the fact that the subcommissioners were nominally independent from governments. Subcom-

missioners responded. In 1976 they still had another two years of the term to run and so were not intimidated by the prospect of lobbying for reelection. Gabriel Martínez was well aware of the threat. On May 29 1978 he drafted a long account of the background of the Sub-Commission and its work, dwelling on the 1503 procedure. For a history of the Sub-Commission see Howard Tolley, Jr., *The U.N. Commission on Human Rights,* pp. 163–86.

13. Beverly Carter, a journalist by profession, was the senior black diplomat in the U.S. foreign service when, as ambassador to Tanzania, he fell afoul of Secretary of State Henry Kissinger over a hostage incident in Zaire. Three Stanford University students were taken hostage by opponents of Mobutu's regime in Zaire. Carter intervened and negotiated their release, incurring the wrath of Mobutu and Kissinger, who was opposed to any negotiation with terrorists. Carter was slated to be the next U.S. ambassador to Denmark, but Kissinger opposed his nomination. Carter was assigned instead to Liberia, which he found fascinating. Much respected by colleagues and human rights lobbyists, he died in 1982.

14. The exchange between Martínez and Cassese was recorded in the Sub-Commission summary records (E/CN.4/Sub.2/SR 785 and 786). In his March 26 1979 analysis to Buenos Aires, Martínez complained that Cassese had "launched a particularly serious attack with respect to violations in Argentina. The French expert followed suit. Faced by the energetic reaction of the Argentinian observer [Martínez himself] the experts from Britain and Belgium rallied to their side, and demanded a closed meeting."

    It is hard at this distance to convey the sinister aura that surrounded this incident and the menace that Martínez managed to convey. Two days after the debate, the author was contacted by a worried Antonio Cassese. Could they arrange a meeting, say at Geneva's railroad station later that night? The author agreed, but with some hesitation. Was this not slightly melodramatic? No, insisted Cassese, before hanging up. So the meeting went ahead in the shadows of Geneva station. When the story of Martínez's maneuvers came out in the *London Guardian* the following morning, Ben Whitaker, the English subcommissioner (who has an impish sense of humor), passed it over to Martínez. Martínez read the article with enormous amusement.

15. A copy of Martínez's letter to U.N. Secretary General Kurt Waldheim questioning the legal validity of Martínez's expulsion from the Sub-Commission is in the author's possession.

16. From cable 266 S/79, in the author's possession.

17. This allows the Soviet subcommissioner to reject most of the complaints from East European Jews and other dissidents. See below Chapter 18, note 20 and Appendix 5.

18. These figures are from a source—not in the U.N. secretariat—who asked for anonymity. The figures for 1977 were: 18,842 communications sent on to 36 governments, 129 replies.

19. The case of Uganda under Idi Amin, one of this century's most brutal dictators, offered vivid proof that the 1503 procedure was not living up to the hopes of its creators. See Appendix 5.

20. See above, Chapter 7, note 38.

21. The three communications came from Amnesty International; the International Federation of Human Rights; and the Women's International Democratic Federation (information from cable 878/79, from Gabriel Martínez, in the author's possession).

22. The 1503 voting on Argentina was published by the author in an article in the *London Guardian* (September 5 1977).

23. For more on the economic relations between Argentina and the Soviet Union, see below Chapter 14, notes 3ff. The Argentinian Junta and Somoza enjoyed close relations. In 1977 Admiral Emilio Massera and Roberto Viola, the army chief of staff, visited Managua and gave Somoza 10 million dollars of credit to arm the Nicaraguan National Guard.

24. Mario Amadeo, who died in 1983, remains a deeply equivocal figure for many Argentinians. His major claim to fame is that he saved Juan Perón from a nasty accident when Perón was leaving on a launch for exile in Paraguay following his ouster in 1955. Perón slipped and was about to tumble into the water when Amadeo offered his hand. Many of Perón's foes never forgave him. Amadeo's own daughter married into a family that was so virulently right-wing that they refused to let Amadeo visit his grandchildren on the grounds that he was too liberal.

    Amadeo was certainly more humane than Gabriel Martínez. When Graciela Geuna, a young woman who had survived the center of La Perla, in Córdoba, came to Geneva to give testimony her parents in Argentina received threats. Theo van Boven told Amadeo, who promised to help, and the threats stopped. On the other hand, Amadeo willingly helped the Junta project a more sympathetic image abroad. He attended the seminar at Georgetown University in January 1979 which was denounced by human rights activists as propaganda. Amadeo was also the principal author of the highly controversial September 1979 law (22068) which allowed the government to declare any desaparecido dead who did not reappear within ninety days. (See below, Chapter 16, note 12.)

    Martínez makes it clear in one long cable that Amadeo's election to the Sub-Commission was no accident, but rather the result of energetic Argentinian lobbying: "Not only have we managed to obtain the election of an Argentinian expert but we saw to it that those who were most energetic against us (the Italian and Belgian) were not re-elected" (from cable 266 S/79, March 26 1979, in the author's files).

25. Amadeo's bizarre claim that disappearances were happening in New York is from paragraph 13 of the summary record of the debate (E/CN.4/Sub.2/SR 820).

    In a September 9 1979 cable to Foreign Minister Carlos Washington Pastor, Martínez stated that the U.N. had sent 13,124 communications to 61 governments. Thirty-nine governments had replied with 235 replies (from cable 878/79 in the author's possession). In the same cable, Martínez informed Foreign Minister Pastor that the U.N. secretariat had summarized sixty communications on Argentina for the Sub-Commission. Three were eventually chosen as representative, from the Women's International Democratic Federation, Amnesty International, and the International Federation of Human Rights. In

August 1979 the Sub-Commission added three more to the list from a group of "exiled lawyers in France" (including Rodolfo Matarollo), the World Christian Democratic Union, and the Lawyers Committee for Human Rights.

Throughout 1977 and 1978 Martínez worked feverishly to prevent these even being discussed. On August 7 1978 he wrote a thirteen-page letter to Waldheim complaining that one of the communications came from CADHU and was written by "delinquent terrorists" like Matarollo. This letter (in the author's possession) was quite improper, not just because it ignored the fact that the Sub-Commission was supposed to be independent from the rest of the U.N. system, but also because the identity of communicants is supposed to be irrelevant.

26. *Le Monde,* September 13 1978.

27. From page 2 of Martínez's March 26 1979 memo to Foreign Minister Pastor.

Chapter 10. Martínez Against the U.N. Middleman

1. The material for this chapter comes from personal interviews with Theo van Boven, from van Boven's personal files which he shared with the author, and from Argentinian government files. A compilation of van Boven's speeches and statements was printed in 1982 (*People Matter: Views on International Human Rights Policy*).

2. The challenge of creating an international secretariat that is efficient and honest as well as genuinely international was first attempted, with some success, under the League of Nations. Approximately half the professional posts in the U.N. are divided among U.N. member governments. In 1978, 505 of the 2,677 posts at U.N. headquarters in New York were filled by Americans. Twenty nations were not represented at all ("U.S. Participation in International Organizations and Programs." Report of a House Committee on Foreign Affairs Staff Mission, October 6–November 11 1978). The U.N. uses levels of U.S. government pay as a standard.

    The Human Rights Division, or secretariat, should not be confused with the Human Rights Commission, the body of forty-three governments which meets every year in Geneva for six weeks. The independent Sub-Commission on Prevention of Discrimination and Protection of Minorities also meets annually in Geneva and reports to the Commission. (See above, Chapter 9, note 12.) Quite separate, again, is the Human Rights Committee, set up to monitor the 1976 International Covenant on Civil and Political Rights. (See above, Chapter 7, note 4.)

3. See below, Chapter 23, notes 20ff. for the background to these programs and the Reagan Administration's reaction.

4. This was particularly serious for the U.N. Human Rights Division, when faced by a formidable political foe like Gabriel Martínez. Under pressure from the Soviet Union, which did not want human rights given too high a profile, Kurt Waldheim refused several American requests to upgrade the human rights secretariat from a Division to a Center (like disarmament), a move

which would have greatly increased its political authority. Van Boven's rank as Director, accordingly, was only D2. While this was a senior post—there were eighty D2s in the UN in 1977—it was not senior enough to withstand a major political assault.

The U.N. human rights chain of command begins with the Secretary General, who has considerable discretionary power to use his "good offices." Waldheim's lack of commitment to human rights tended to increase the power of his deputies. In 1976 responsibility for the Human Rights Division lay with the Assistant Secretary General for Political and General Assembly Affairs. Traditionally an American post, this was held by William Buffum. Buffum had held a series of middle-ranking jobs in the American diplomatic service, including the post of vice-consul in Stuttgart, before moving to the United Nations.

The human rights specialist on Buffum's staff was another American. Jay Long was an intense, chain-smoking former diplomat who had served in Haiti in the U.S. diplomatic service before joining the U.N. He had a Machiavellian reputation for working the system and (as he told the author in an interview) was deeply unhappy when Waldheim ordered the Human Rights Division moved out of New York to Geneva on June 15 1974. In 1977 a third American diplomat, Donald Fitzpatrick, arrived as Buffum's special assistant. This left human rights at the U.N. headquarters in the hands of three Americans who were by and large more preoccupied with the risks than with the opportunities. This did not matter between 1977 and 1980, when the Carter Administration was supportive of the U.N., but it became critical after Ronald Reagan became president.

5. For an expression of doubt by van Boven, see Bernard Nossiter, "U.N. Rights Body has Poor History of Biased Reports." Nossiter describes van Boven as "a shrewd Dutch lawyer who is candid enough to voice doubts about his task," and suggests that van Boven saw his task as reforming the U.N.'s ramshackle human rights machinery. In fact, the doubts were probably less on van Boven's side than on Nossiter's. Nossiter's reporting betrayed a distinct lack of sympathy for the U.N.

6. Hammarskjöld's address, "The International Service in Law and Fact" is reprinted in Kay ed., *The United Nations Political System*.

7. Quoted in *People Matter,* pp. 40–49.

8. From Article 100 of the U.N. Charter. Van Boven collected his staff together the day he started work and read them this passage. Articles 97–101 cover the duties and responsibilities of the U.N. secretariat. In 1977 the U.N. Human Rights Division was representative of the overall U.N. secretariat. The forty-seven professionals came from no fewer than thirty nationalities, and they included five Americans, three Soviets and one East German.

9. On May 7 1979 Arnaud de Borchgrave charged in *Newsweek* that Yuri Rechetov, a Soviet official in the U.N. Division was sending details about confidential 1503 communications back to Moscow. This was almost certainly untrue. Several years earlier, Jakob Moller, the Icelandic head of the communications unit, had been a magistrate in Iceland when Rechetov (then a diplomat at the

Soviet embassy in Reykjavik) was caught red-handed dumping electronic devices into a lake. Moller went on to join the U.N. Human Rights Division in Geneva, like Rechetov. Moller was head of the U.N. communications unit in 1977, knew exactly what the Russians were up to, and guarded his 1503 files like a mother hen. Van Boven backed him up loyally.

This is not to say that the Russians did not abuse the system. One unpleasant little incident occurred in 1978 when a Soviet official in the U.N. information service took umbrage at an anti-Soviet resolution in a mock debate in a U.N. room by some Swiss students. The official, Eugene Kissalev, telephoned the Soviet ambassador, who demanded that the students be expelled. (This incident was reported by the author in the *International Herald Tribune*.) For other Soviet U.N. staffing horror stories, see the 1985 report by the U.S. Senate Select Committee on Intelligence, "Soviet Presence in the U.N. Secretariat."

10. Luigi Cottafavi was cruelly caricatured by Arnaud de Borchgrave in his novel, *The Spike*. Cottafavi was a political appointee and notoriously unwilling to stand up to governments.

11. This information comes from van Boven's personal file.

12. From an interview with the author.

13. Van Boven's letter on the Cardenas case and Martínez's reply are both in the author's possession. It was far from unprecedented for senior U.N. officials to exercise "good offices" on behalf of human rights victims. In 1979, U.N officials asked the U.S. mission in New York to help find Esther Ballestrino de Cariaga, a Paraguayan refugee who was kidnapped in Argentina together with the French nuns in December 1977 (FOIA cable 02190 from USUN).

14. From an interview with the author.

15. Cable dated March 26 1979, p. 5, in the author's possession.

16. For the background and significance of the U.N. action on Chile see above, Chapter 7. For the build-up and background to the 1978 U.N. visit to Chile see the mission report ("Protection of Human Rights in Chile: Report of the Secretary General," A/33/331, October 25 1978). The report is certainly one of the fullest, most informative U.N. reports ever written and is essential reading for anyone interested in Chile and the United Nations. The Chileans demanded that Ghulam Allana, the Pakistani head of the working group, should not participate in the mission. In the event, only three members of the group made the trip: Abdoulaye Dieye, a high court judge from Senegal; Felix Ermacora, an Austrian law professor; and Mariam Kamara, a nurse from Sierre Leone. Van Boven took three of his most trusted aides: Tom McCarthy, an American who had worked at the OAS; Myrta Teitelbaum, an Argentinian; and Augusto Willemsen Diaz, from Guatemala.

They did not go unprepared. Van Boven and McCarthy had had three years in which to plot out the terrain, and they knew exactly what questions to ask. During the 1978 Commission meeting they had met secretly with a staff member from the Chilean human rights group, the Vicariate of Santiago, (set up by the Catholic Church in 1975), who flew up from Chile and stayed in a French hotel just across the Swiss border so as not to arouse suspicions.

17. Ermacora was an indefatigable member of the U.N. human rights circuit, the

author of countless books and articles, a former U.N. Commission chairman, and a member of the U.N. working groups on South Africa and Chile. He also made no secret of his right-wing political views. He had written a thesis on the dispute between Austria and Italy over the Tyrol, and served in the German army on the Eastern front during the Second World War. He represented a right-wing party in the Austrian parliament and believed in the re-unification of Germany. None of this mattered to anyone until 1984, when Ermacora agreed to take on the sensitive task of reporting on Afghanistan. The Soviets deluged the Commission with lurid accounts of his right-wing views and war record.

18. The mission report contains a chapter on the visit to the Villa Grimaldi which is riveting reading when compared to normal U.N. standards (A/33/331, annex XXXII). The photo of Muñoz Muñoz standing in front of the blue tiles appeared in the February 24 1978 edition of *La Tercera* and two other papers. Three other prisoners were pictured with him.

19. The wounds caused to Muñoz by torture were illustrated with a diagram on p. 101 of the mission report (A/33/331). This, too, was a first: official U.N. conference documents never carry illustrations.

20. These figures come from Amnesty International briefing paper AMR 22/13/88, *Chile Briefing* Amnesty draws on figures of the Vicariate of Solidarity. The independent Chilean Human Rights Commission puts the number of disappeared at over 1500.

21. For one of the fullest accounts of the problem of the disappeared in Chile see A/33/331, pp. 114–33.

22. See annex LXXXIII of A/33/331 for the full text of the Chilean reply.

23. Referring to the "institutionalization of Chile" in his March 26 1979 round-up cable, Martínez wrote: "Evidently, it is the Chilean case that our 'Western friends' would like to compare to the situation in Argentina" (from the author's files).

24. Theo van Boven returned to Chile in December 1978 for a conference organized by Cardinal Enrique Silva to celebrate the thirtieth anniversary of the Universal Declaration of Human Rights. Niall MacDermot from the International Commission of Jurists was also present. Van Boven was personally presented with the founding statutes of a new Chilean Human Rights Commission by Jaime Castillo, a former Minister of Justice under President Eduardo Frei (see below, Chapter 22, note 21). Van Boven was again reminded of the courage of these people and the trust they placed in him. It further stiffened his resolve.

Chapter 11. The Junta's Bluff

1. The UNESCO Committee on Recommendations began a session in Paris on September 10 1979. According to a cable from the U.S. embassy in Paris, a proposal to send a UNESCO mission of inquiry to Argentina was actively considered. Theo van Boven wrote from Geneva urging action (FOIA cable

27628). The ILO Governing Body first accused the Junta of violating ILO Convention 87, on freedom of association, in 1977 (see above, Chapter 7, note 8). In May 1978 the ILO asked the Junta for an explanation of the large number of disappeared and detained trade unionists. ILO protests continued regularly thereafter, although the agency never set up a special commission on Argentina as it did on Poland following the 1981 declaration of martial law.

2. Martínez gave a detailed account of the lobbying from Argentina's perspective and of his successful appeal to the Nonaligned delegations in a March 26 1979 cable (no. 266 S/79).

3. From Memo B in the author's possession. As was noted above in Chapter 2, Admiral Massera had personally taken the lead in promoting closer ties with South Africa, ignoring protests from career diplomats like Gregorio Dupont.

4. In his March 26 1979 cable, Martínez observes that "confusion reigned in the Commission" after the U.S. rejected the compromise.

5. "Once more our observer delegation was able to avoid the institutionalization of the 'Argentinian case' at the level of the Commission and Sub-Commission," wrote Martínez in his March 26 1979 cable following the Commission.

6. "The U.S. delegation deeply regrets inaction on this item this year. It appears that the intended strategy of appeasing Argentina did not succeed in gaining support from other delegations," wrote Ambassador Vanden Heuvel from Geneva to Washington (FOIA cable 04523, March 1979).

7. Paragraph IV (c) in Martínez's March 26 1979 cable.

8. These figures are taken from p. 3 of Martínez's September 8 1979 cable (no. 878/79).

9. Noted in Martínez's September 11 1979 cable (no. 1947).

10. Martínez noted in his September 6 1979 cable (no. 1925) that the absence of the Soviet and Pakistani experts from the session of the whole Sub-Commission meant that the item was introduced by Beverly Carter, who was hostile to Argentina.

11. Cable 1925, par. 4 (iii). Martínez assessed the risks and benefits of his startling U-turn in cable 1929. On balance, he wrote, he had chosen the right course in allowing the name of Argentina on to the 1503 blacklist:

> Weighing the adverse results of this session one can cite:—The institutionalization of the Argentinian case under the 1503 procedure; and the setting in motion of further international action following on from the 1978 General Assembly resolution.
>
> On the other hand, there are mitigating circumstances, at least as far as concerns public, open action at the level of the international organizations:—The fact that the 1503 procedure is confidential at the Sub-Commission level, and cannot be referred to officially at the forthcoming session of the Commission; that the decision does not recommend any of the various possible courses of action allowed for under 1503 [i.e., a mission of inquiry]; the fact that the disappearances are being discussed under the general rubric of "serious situations"—something that applies to numerous countries of the world.

12. Uruguay was known as the "Switzerland of Latin America" because its form of government employed a system of rotating presidents similar to Switzerland. It then became synonymous with political tranquility.

The key dates in Uruguay's descent into military rule are as follows: November 1967: a state of emergency is declared in response to the Tupamaros' increasingly successful campaign among impoverished sugar farmers; September 9 1971: the government hands the fight against terrorism over to the armed forces after a mass escape by Tupamaros from jail; April 14 1972: a "state of internal war" is declared; June 27 1973: a coup d'état by the army.

A good summary of the effect of military rule in Uruguay can be found in International Commission of Jurists, *States of Emergency—Their Impact on Human Rights,* pp. 337–70. The chapter on Uruguay was written by Alejandro Artucio, the defense lawyer who was arrested, tortured, and detained in Liberty Jail. (See above, Chapter 9, note 1.) The principal source for conditions in Liberty jail is a 1982 report prepared by the Justice and Peace Service, run by Father Pérez Aguirre in Montevideo ("Informe sobre el establecimiento militár de reclusión EMR—1. Libertad").

13. Estrella's family appealed to the U.N. Human Rights Committee, which found against the Uruguayan regime. For a legal analysis of Estrella's detention and treatment see Nigel Rodley, *The Treatment of Prisoners Under International Law* pp. 81–83.

14. The Committee's finding in favor of Professor Luís Massera can be found in its 1979 report to the U.N. General Assembly (A/34/40). Uruguay ratified the Covenant (on April 1 1970), and the Optional Protocol, and so was bound by both procedures when they entered into force on March 23 1976. It remains a mystery why Uruguay's military did not withdraw from the Covenant and Optional Protocol. (Nigel Rodley analyzes four decision on Uruguay by the Human Rights Committee in *The Treatment of Prisoners Under International Law,* pp. 79–83.)

15. Javier Pérez de Cuéllar's report on his mission, and details of contacts with the government, can be found in U.N. document E/CN.4/R 50/ Add 2., February 14 1980.

16. For more on this incident and Pérez de Cuéllar's diplomatic background see below, Chapter 23, notes 32ff.

17. See Appendix 2 for extracts from Pérez de Cuéllar's report.

18. See Appendix 2 for extracts from Labarthe's report.

Behind the daily routine of insult, reprimand, and cruelty in Liberty jail lay one fundamental assumption. What made men like Estrella and Massera "subversive" was their sense of social responsibility. This meant they had to be rendered asocial. The prisoners were most vulnerable when it came to contact with their family. A man's strongest bonds are with his family, so those bonds had to be destroyed. If family visits were the only thing that kept him sane, then they could just as well drive him insane.

The prisoners were allowed to send two letters a week, but the letters were opened by the camp censor, photocopied, and scanned for hints of the prisoner's weakness. Prisoners were forbidden to include any signs of affection in their letters. Some prisoners wrote every week, but only one or two of their letters arrived each year. Alejandro Artucio sent a birthday card to one of his daughters. A few days later it was returned. The reason given was that he had written "happy birthday" in capital letters.

Every month, children under thirteen were allowed to spend time with their fathers in a special area of the prison garden which was equipped with hammocks, swings, and slides. The other parent was left outside the barbed wire perimeter. As soon as the father made an affectionate gesture, armed soldiers moved in to break up the visit and the prisoner was sentenced to one or two months without visits. Following each visit, the child was interrogated by a guard. The aim was to sever the bonds between father and child. One prisoner, Beto Rolando, gave a ring to his daughter. That small gesture earned him 100 days of solitary confinement. He emerged mad.

The brain behind this ghoulish regime was a civilian psychologist named Dolcey Britos Puíg, who began working at Liberty jail in 1973, compiling profiles on each prisoner and supervising the experimental use of new psychotropic drugs. Britos kept the following sign above his desk at the jail: "I will pull out your eyes and put them in place of mine; you will pull out my eyes and put them in place of yours. Thus, you will look at me through my eyes, and I through yours." He had absolute power over the daily routine in Liberty, and the prisoners were terrified of him.

19. See Appendix 2 for extracts from Labarthe's report.

The all-Swiss International Committee of the Red Cross was set up in 1864 to oversee the first Geneva Convention, which protected wounded in war. In addition to its formal role of keeper of the Geneva Conventions, the ICRC also plays a major role in the protection of human rights through its prison visits. Since the Second World War, ICRC delegates have visited an estimated 250,000 political prisoners in seventy-five different countries. Such visits are not based on any formal legal undertaking by the governments concerned, and are allowed on the understanding that the ICRC will not publicize what its delegates find in the jails. In return, the ICRC insists on seeing prisoners in private and returning for a follow-up visit.

Following the leak of Labarthe's report the Uruguayan regime immediately halted Red Cross visits to Liberty Jail. They only resumed in 1983. The Red Cross never found out precisely who leaked the report. According to one rumor it originated with the local Red Cross branch in Venezuela.

20. Estrella's first (February 25 1980) note read:

Contrary to what may have been stated, I was never visited by the United Nations official Mr. Pérez de Cuéllar. From what I could gather after my liberation it was probably someone who went to the prison one day and whom I caught sight of as he was being escorted by military officials in charge of the prison. That person, however, had no verbal contact with me or to my knowledge with any other of my prison comrades.

In July 1981 Estrella prepared a second, longer, statement about his detention for the Human Rights Committee, in which he elaborated on the visit to Liberty prison by Pérez de Cuéllar. (Both statements in the author's files.)

21. Van Boven was not the only one to express concern at Pérez de Cuéllar's performance. Roberta Cohen, Deputy Assistant Secretary of State at the time of the event, recalled the details in a 1982 memo to Patricia Derian:

Although Pérez de Cuéllar had substantial latitude and discretion he interpreted his mandate in the narrowest possible way. Thus, his report was flimsy in length and content. (He did visit a prisoner or two in Uruguay but I am told his performance was shabby—he didn't really talk to them.) Our delegation was appalled. In addition, many other HRC members considered de Cuéllar's reports scandalous. (Nobody said so publicly, but everyone openly talked about it.)

During his visit to Montevideo—he was accompanied by Carlos Giumbruno—Javier Pérez de Cuéllar never made any attempt to contact Father Pérez Aguirre, the plucky Jesuit priest who ran the Justice and Peace Office in Montevideo and who had been arrested and harassed for his human rights work. The U.N. "information" office in Montevideo was uninformed about his visit, and Pérez de Cuéllar did not meet with any relatives of the detainees. In short, his visit was a political act in support of an unscrupulous regime.

How much was due to Pérez de Cuéllar himself and how much to the actual 1503 procedure? The blame, probably, should be equally apportioned. Javier Pérez de Cuéllar had shown himself to be inherently sympathetic to governments and the doctrine of national security. But it had been a mistake for the Commission to entrust the choice of envoy to the U.N. Secretary General instead of grasping the nettle and appointing its own envoy. Kurt Waldheim had a wider mandate than human rights and could not afford to make value judgments about a regime. A human rights investigator, on the other hand, could not afford not to.

Nor was Pérez de Cuéllar helped by the erratic way that the 1503 procedure had evolved over the previous ten years. There was no set formula such as that followed by the Red Cross for talking to prisoners without witnesses or returning for a follow-up visit to check against reprisals. It would have helped enormously if Pérez de Cuéllar and William Buffum had insisted on such an agreement, as van Boven had done before visiting Chile in 1978.

The Uruguay episode showed, once again, that because publicity was the ultimate sanction of 1503, the Commission was naturally unwilling to use it. "Keeping the dialogue going" became an end in itself and far more important than the actual violations. "Dialogue," to the U.N., meant "cooperating," and cooperation brought its reward: the case stayed confidential. If it felt under any pressure, an astute government could always introduce minor changes and present them as "improvements." There was endless room to maneuver for clever diplomats who knew the rules, like Gabriel Martínez and Carlos Giumbruno.

22. In his March 26 1979 cable to Buenos Aires (p. 16, par. c), Martínez states that Uruguay is "illustrative" of the advantages of the 1503 procedure.

23. For extracts from Martínez's September 13 1979 cable, see Appendix 1.

24. Martínez hints that he had a "mole" among van Boven's staff in a September 8 1979 cable (878/79): "The Division of Human Rights is totally sympathetic to those parties which are against us, and this is an attitude that one finds not just with the Director (Theo van Boven) but also his immediate subordinates. There is one exception—and this has allowed us to count on some indispensable information concerning the issues which are of concern to us." Given that Sanón had tried to mediate between van Boven and Martínez and was friendly with the Argentinian, it is conceivable that he was the mole.

25. The report of the U.N. inquiry into the Sanón affair is still a closely guarded secret.

Chapter 12. Derian Into the Lion's Den

1. The material for this chapter comes principally from interviews with Patricia Derian and Derian's testimony at the 1985 trial in Buenos Aires as recorded by *Diario del Juicio*. For an affectionate profile of Patricia Derian, see Raymond Bonner, *Waltzing with a Dictator,* pp. 179 ff. Bonner also wrote sympathetically about Derian and her bureaucratic travails in his book about El Salvador, *Weakness and Deceit* (pp. 41 ff).

2. Jimmy Carter wrote of the connection between international human rights, the Vietnam war and the civil rights movement in his memoirs (*Keeping Faith: Memoirs of a President,* pp. 141–51).

3. As Robert Ingersoll, then Assistant Secretary of State for East Asian Affairs, explained in a letter to Congressman Thomas Morgan on June 27 1974 (cited in Stephen Cohen, "Conditioning U.S. Security Assistance on Human Rights Practices," p. 250).

4. For a chronology of the principal U.S. human rights laws between 1973 and 1978 see "Pertinent U.S. Legislation" (Appendix D in Newsom ed., *Diplomacy and Human Rights,* pp. 223–35).

5. International Commission of Jurists, *Final Report of Mission to Chile.* For the 1973 subcommittee hearings see "International Protection of Human Rights. The Work of the International Organizations and the Role of U.S. Foreign Policy" (Subcommittee on International Organizations and Movements, House Committee on Foreign Affairs, 93rd Congress, First Session). The subcommittee report was entitled "Human Rights in the World Community: A Call for U.S. Leadership."

6. "Nomination of Henry Kissinger," Hearings Before the Senate Committee on Foreign Relations. 93rd Congress, First Session, 1973.

7. "US Blocks Rights Data on Nations Getting Arms." For a careful account of Henry Kissinger's approach to human rights see David Weissbrodt, "Human Rights Legislation and U.S. Foreign Policy."

8. Lars Schoultz, *Human Rights and United States Policy Toward Latin America* p. 185. For the administration's justification, see "Chile: The Status of Human Rights and Its Relationship to U.S. Economic Assistance Programs" (Hearings Before the Subcommittee on International Organizations, April 29, May 5 1976).

9. The 1976 Senate measure turning 502B into mandatory legislation was sponsored by Senators Hubert Humphrey and Alan Cranston.

10. Jeane Kirkpatrick, "Dictatorships and Double Standards." See below, Chapter 19, passim.

   In one lecture after leaving office that anticipated Kirkpatrick's argument, Henry Kissinger said:

   While human rights must be an essential component of our foreign policy, to pursue it effectively over the long term we must take the measure of the dangers and dilemmas along the way. The ultimate irony would be a posture of resignation toward totalitarian states and harassment of those who would be our friends and who have every prospect of evolving in a more humane direction (Arthur P. Salomon Lecture).

11. By 1976, as we have seen, three nations had been publicly indicted by the U.N.

for "gross violations" under resolution 1235 (South Africa, Israel, and Chile). Another sixteen had been indicted between 1971 and 1976 under the private 1503 procedure. In his September 1977 lecture, Kissinger denounced "the hypocritical double standard increasingly prevalent in the United Nations where petty tyrannies berate us for our alleged moral shortcomings."

12. John Salzberg, who worked on the staff of Fraser's subcommittee, recalls one breakfast meeting with Senator Alan Cranston and Fraser at which the three struggled to find the right wording for the 502B amendment. Salzberg had written a thesis about the U.N.'s 1503 procedure, and was able to come up with its formula: "a consistent pattern of gross violations." Thus, not only did 502B and 1503 look alike on paper, they were closely related. (Salzberg has written on his work with Fraser. See, e.g., Newsom, ed., *The Diplomacy of Human Rights,* pp. 13–21)

13. Address by Leonard Garment to the American Jewish Congress, April 1 1976.

14. See above, Chapter 5 note 13. Timerman's letter and Fraser's reply were printed in Timerman's newspaper, *La Opinión,* on November 9 1976. In his letter, Fraser denied reports circulating in Argentina that his subcommittee had also received testimony from Rodolfo Puiggros, a Montonero leader.

15. The State Department received a barrage of inquiries after Raymundo Gleyzer, a well-known Argentinian filmmaker, disappeared. In July 1976 Kissinger cabled the embassy in Buenos Aires asking for information (FOIA cable 184787, July 1976).

16. For Kissinger's meeting with Guzetti see Martin Andersen, "Kissinger and the Dirty War."

17. *Detroit Free Press,* January 7 1977. The six reports—covering Argentina, Haiti, Peru, Indonesia, Iran, and the Philippines—were requested by the House International Relations Committee. The remaining country reports—there were eighty-two in all—were released by the State Department on April 25 1977. The State Department insisted that while the six governments had indeed violated human rights as defined by 502B, they should not be denied aid for security reasons (*New York Times,* January 2 1977). Robert Drinan criticized the report on Argentina in the House of Representatives on January 19 1977.

18. Patt Derian's appointment alarmed many seasoned foreign policy experts. Morris Abram, a former U.S. ambassador at the U.N., would recall being "dumbfounded." Abram described Derian as "a civil rights activist from Mississippi whose dedication, though laudable, hardly qualified her for the sophisticated complexities of international human rights" ("U.S. Participation in the United Nations." Hearings before the House Committee of Foreign Affairs, April 22 1982. p.40.)

19. When Derian's office prepared its first annual report on human rights in countries receiving U.S. aid, readers found three separate categories of rights, in the following order: first, the right to be free from governmental violations of the integrity of the person; second, the right to fulfillment of vital needs like food; and third, the right to enjoy civil and political liberties (*Country Reports on Human Rights Practices for 1977,* U.S. Department of State, February 1978). Derian gave a concise account of the bureau's view in "Human Rights and American Foreign Policy."

20. *Chronica,* August 11 1977.

21. *Buenos Aires Herald,* June 3 1980.

22. "Dictatorships and Double Standards." Much has been written about whether the United States "interfered" in the internal affairs of countries like Argentina, but very little about whether U.S. human rights policy represented interference in the work of the multilateral development banks, particularly the World Bank, which is not supposed to take political considerations into account in allocating aid. Under section 701 of the 1977 International Financial Institutions Act, U.S. executive directors in international financial institutions were required to vote against or abstain on all projects in countries whose governments were guilty of gross violations of human rights. In one unpublished 1989 paper, Ibrahim Shihata, the World Bank's legal counsel, suggested that the prohibition against raising political issues applied to the executive directors (who represent governments). However, he also conceded that there was no way to challenge a director's vote ("The World Bank and Human Rights: An Analysis of the Legal Issues and the Record of Achievements"). Between 1977 and 1981 the United States voted against 110 MDB loans to 16 countries on human rights grounds. 28 were directed against Argentina. In July 1981 the Reagan Administration announced that section 701 no longer applied to Argentina.

23. This philosophy, and its apparent indifference to U.S. security needs, was denounced by Kirkpatrick in "U.S. Security and Latin America."

24. Carter spoke to the Permanent Council of the OAS on May 9 1977. On June 1 1977 he signed the American Convention on Human Rights. Carter signed the International Covenant on Civil and Political Rights and the International Covenant on Economic and Social Rights, together with the racism convention (CERD) on October 5 1977, the day after the Helsinki review conference opened in Belgrade. On February 23 1978 the Carter Administration submitted the three treaties to the Senate. The Senate Foreign Relations Committee did not get around to a review until November 14 1979. For a useful chronology see Senator Pell's written statement for the 1979 hearings "International Human Rights Treaties," (Senate Committee on Foreign Relations, November 1979), pp. 60–64. See above, Chapter 7, note 12.

During the hearings, Patricia Derian argued that U.S. ratification would strengthen the treaties:

Ratification would emphasize our determination to work for a world in which the rights enjoyed by our own citizens are universally respected. . . . In countries where citizens have few domestic remedies for human rights abuses they can point to these international standards. Today dissidents throughout the world are monitoring their own governments' compliance with this body of international law for the protection of human rights. It is cited by wall posters in China, on manifestos of Soviet dissidents, and by families of disappeared in Latin America. ("International Human Rights Treaties," Hearings, pp. 33–34.)

25. From Memo C in the author's possesion, p. 15.

26. Ibid., p. 9.

27. Ibid., p. 2.

28. Patricia Derian recalled her meeting with Massera when she testified at his 1985

trial in Buenos Aires. It helped to put him behind bars for life. (See below, Chapter 30, note 7.)

Chapter 13. The Allis Chalmers Controversy

1. The position of the Chancellery should be to respond in a way that will be consistent with our previously stated position, but . . . without generating an escalating confrontation which will harm our relations in any substantial way. We must not exalt this question, or inflame public opinion, and must strive to keep our remaining areas of contact with the United States intact (Memo C in the author's possession, p. 12).

2. Vance made his announcement before the appropriations subcommittee of the Senate Foreign Operations Committee on February 24 1977. The other three governments which spurned U.S. security aid for 1978 were Brazil, El Salvador and Guatemala. Brazil went so far as to terminate the joint Brazil-U.S. Military Commission.

3. There is a double standard in the way the U.S. interprets its national interest without taking into account the interests of a friendly nation. This implies that the U.S. accepts that its own security is a goal of its foreign policy, but does not accept that Argentina's security can be a valid goal of the policy pursued by the Argentinian government (Memo A in the author's possession, p. 37).

   Another memo observes: "Exceptions to this human rights crusade were made for Iran, the Philippines, South Korea, Brazil. But Argentina was not given an exception, and some sectors of the Democratic administration feel that Argentina is an excellent example to show to the rest of the world the impact of the new policy" (Memo C, p. 10). This was justified: one communiqué put out by CAHDU, the independent Argentininian human rights commission in Washington, was headed: "Campaign Materials for Stopping U.S. Military Aid to Dictatorships. Argentina: A Test Case."

4. The Inter-Agency Task Force, also known as the Christopher group, comprised representatives from all the State Department Bureaus, the Treasury, Defense, Commerce, and Labor Departments, the National Security Council, and the U.S. Agency for International Development (USAID). It was suspended in 1981 after Reagan took office.

5. For a detailed account of the bureaucratic struggle, see Stephen Cohen, "Conditioning U.S. Security Assistance in Human Rights Practices," pp. 256–64.

6. From a CADHU fact sheet, produced by CADHU's Washington office, May 1977.

7. William Hallman, the political counselor, remembers Blanca Vollenweider as "a sweet white-haired little Swiss lady" who personally thought most of the disappeared were hippies and leftists, in spite of her admirable work with Harris.

8. Mrs. Carter asked the embassy to inquire about Ruben Nestor Antonanzas, and Tex Harris raised the case at his October 31 and November 9 meetings with the Foreign Office Human Rights Working Group (FOIA cable 08459). Many of the communications from the United States concerned Jews because,

during the huge wave of Jewish emigration from Eastern Europe at the turn of the century, thousands of families split with some going to North America and the others to Argentina. Many of the Jewish families that suffered in Argentina thus had close relatives in the United States.

9. Stockman inquired of the embassy on behalf of Ignacio Ikonicoff and María Bedoyan (FOIA cable 01265, February 1979).

10. In 1982, the U.S. embassy in Buenos Aires lost the files on the disappearance of Hunt and Azorena. (See below, Chapter 26, notes 17ff.)

11. Castro's quote comes from FOIA cable 04971.

12. Argentinian Foreign Ministry circular telegram 152, in the author's possession. The Argentinian cable implictly blamed Tex Harris for the fact that the "distorted" story about the list was widely reported in the American press.

Piecing together this story from U.S. government cables, there is some truth to the Argentinian account. It is clear that the United States wanted to make a major impact with the famous list while at the same time disclaiming responsibility for it. The list itself was drawn up by the Argentine Information Service Center in New York and passed to Patricia Derian by the highly respected Washington Office on Latin America. It was not checked by the U.S. embassy in Buenos Aires or the State Department. In spite of this, Derian's office thought the list sufficiently significant to be handed over during Vance's November 21 1977 visit to Buenos Aires.

Vance did so willingly. According to FOIA cable 282685 he raised the list at a meeting with Admiral Massera and again in a November 21 1977 meeting with Foreign Minister Montes. On November 26 the U.S. embassy followed up with a short aide-mémoire to the Foreign Ministry. Castro managed to dilute the impact of all this at his November 29 press briefing, when— according to the Argentinian cable—he denied that Vance had handed over the list personally. The U.S. embassy was further embarrassed when the local correspondent for the London *Times,* Andrew Tarnowski, told embassy officials that he had analyzed 687 names on the list and found that 20 percent were detained before the takeover and that no dates were given for 39 percent (FOIA cable 09834) Tarnowski's article was harshly criticized by Amnesty International in a letter to the *Times* and Tarnowski later told embassy officials that he had been accused of receiving $20,000 from Burson Marsteller (FOIA cable 09748).

Still, Vance continued to place stock in the famous list. In December 1977 Warren Christopher cabled the embassy and repeated Vance's earlier request that the Junta give the list early and serious consideration (FOIA cable 296710).

13. The EXIM Bank offers loans, guarantees, and insurance to U.S. exporters, and on October 27 1977 it was brought within the scope of U.S. human rights legislation. The amendment required the EXIM bank to consult with the Secretary of State about human rights in the recipient country before agreeing to support a project. E Systems is based in Garland, Texas. According to FOIA cable 05596 from Ambassador Castro, a joint Argentinian-Paraguayan mission which toured Europe seeking finance for the Yacyreta project was well received

by European bankers. "EXIM financing [is] not crucial to the project," concluded Castro.

15. In one cable to Castro (FOIA 162533), Cyrus Vance observed: "Any prospect that we might have considered EXIM bank financing apart from human rights matters was eliminated by insistence that the Government of Argentina looked upon restrictions on EXIM financing as political act and clearly sought approval of such financing as indication of U.S. acceptance."

16. William Hallman told the author that he recalls the incident of the letter as follows. Hallman got wind that Harris was preparing to send an explosive informal official letter back to Washington. Hallman told Harris that the back-channel procedure had been intended as a device of last resort instead of a way of influencing policy in Washington, and that particularly sensitive issues should be thoroughly discussed in the embassy first. He asked Harris to reconsider. Harris, who is described as a "strong personality" by Hallman, refused. Hallman then informed Chaplin, who told Hallman to retrieve Harris's letter from the registry. Hallman refused, considering this would have been a serious breach of Harris's rights. Hallman never told Harris about this. As a result he was regarded with some suspicion by both Derian and Chaplin, who described Hallman as "unreliable" in his efficiency report, thus probably damning his chances of ever making ambassador. Hallman looks back on his term in Argentina, and the way he was squeezed between two stubborn personalities, Chaplin and Harris, with some bitterness. He was posted to El Salvador from Buenos Aires in late 1979. Shortly after he arrived, a rocket blasted the conference room at the U.S. embassy. Three weeks later, the four American churchwomen were shot.

17. Castro commented on his meeting with U.S. businessmen in FOIA cable 05596: "The publicity and resentment over EXIM's refusal to do business with Argentina is considerable. The way the story broke in Washington as an exchange of letters added to Argentina's ire over what it considers peremptory treatment by the U.S."

18. Young's cable was quoted by Evans and Novak in "Human Rights Zeal that Costs U.S. Jobs".

19. The law on EXIM credit was amended to read as follows: "Only in cases where the President determines that such action would be in the national interest and would clearly and importantly advance U.S. foreign policy goals, should the EXIM deny applications for credit for non-financial or non-commercial reasons."

20. Newsom insisted on four specific conditions when he met with Allara on June 23. These were: a) The issuance of an invitation to the Inter-American Commission on Human Rights; b) prisoner release (Newsom said that the United States was ready to accept some of the 3,000 PEN detainees, as long as they had no terrorist background); c) a halt to torture and disappearances; and d) the provision of information to the relatives (FOIA cable 161509 from Buenos Aires).

21. For the OAS and its human rights machinery, see Appendix 7.

22. FOIA cable 06425, August 1978.

23. "Terrorism was the most noticable absentee at this Assembly," complained the author of Memo C (p. 26). The Argentinian argument, according to the memo, was that by "stressing persistent and systematic violations, international law tended to favor the terrorist and penalize the government." Argentina proposed a resolution to this effect which was accepted by 11 governments—9 of them dictatorships—but this was short of an absolute majority (as required by the OAS charter) and the proposal was defeated. A more traditional U.S.-inspired resolution urging governments to cooperate with the IACHR was accepted.

    The notion that international law ignored violations by terrorists emerges repeatedly in Argentinian documents and was one of Gabriel Martínez's constant laments from Geneva. The argument was answered at some length by the IACHR in its 1980 report on Argentina (see below, note 40).

24. The OAS Secretary General, Alejandro Orfila, had been appointed Argentinian ambassador to the U.S. by Juan Perón. As OAS Secretary General, Orfila played an important role in helping to ease pressure on the Junta, although he had some anxious moments in 1978 when he was summoned to the Argentinian embassy in Washington and questioned for a whole night about his connections with David Graiver, the Argentinian banker who had invested the Montoneros' ransom money. As ambassador in the United States, Orfila had played host to Graiver during the latter's visits to the United States. Orfila's efforts to mediate between the Junta and the IACHR were noted in a June 1978 cable from Ambassador Castro (FOIA cable 04814).

25. From FOIA cable 04814 from Buenos Aires to Washington. The OAS guidelines for on-site visits were developed at the insistence of Tom Farer, who joined the IACHR in 1976 after serving as law professor at Rutgers University and adviser to the State Department. The IACHR was about to visit Panama at the invitation of Panamanian strongman Omar Torrijos. Torrijos was desperate to win approval of the Panama Canal Treaties by the U.S. Congress, and Farer calculated correctly that he would accept the conditions. This set a precedent for other missions.

26. "On basis fact that IACHR does not feel able accept conditional Argentina invitation we will inform EXIM Bank that, on foreign policy grounds, we recommend against financing for Argentina at this time" (FOIA cable 162533 from Washington to Buenos Aires).

27. Wrote Castro: "Some government officials believe that the IACHR has already gathered considerable derogatory material on Argentina and that a critical report will be written, no matter how forthcoming Argentina government may try to be" (FOIA cable 05032).

28. Castro met with General Reynaldo Bignone, the army Secretary General, and cabled: "In a dramatic fashion he [Bignone] lowered his voice and said: 'All of Argentina is hurt and confused by lack of understanding on the part of U.S.'" (FOIA cable 05645).

29. FOIA cable 6818.

30. The reply to Videla read: "I would be delighted to meet with you in Rome as you requested if this can be arranged September 4. This opportunity for us

to talk is both very welcome and timely and I look forward to it" (FOIA cable 222822 from Washington to the U.S. embassy in Rome, which passed the message on to Videla through the Argentinian embassy).

31. These arrangements were all relayed back to Washington by Castro in cables. Vaky did not, eventually, make the visit because Argentina did not abide by the timetable.

32. Castro met Viola on August 28 and found him at his most charming and elusive. Castro promised that military training places would be made available to Argentina in the United States as a gesture of good faith—and in expectation that the IACHR visit would soon be announced. "Viola was genuinely and deeply pleased. He thanked me for our efforts to try and understand their situation and problems. He then went immediately to the point of reducing human rights abuses. He said we are going to do it, we are committed to it, and he added he had recently had words with the troop commanders to this end. (I added that I hoped he didn't forget the police). . . . He asked for some patience . . . the security forces can't be transformed that fast."

If this suggested procrastination, worse was to come. Viola made no firm commitment to Newsom's request that the all-important "right of option" be restored: "He [Viola] said he had discussed the problems involved in getting this program moved with the President. They agreed that it ought to get off the ground and that the prohibition of visits by our consular officers to applicants made no sense. He said we are going to take care of this" (FOIA cable 07746). Viola did not, in the event, take care of it. The right of option was only partially restored by the Junta.

33. FOIA cable 08248 from Buenos Aires to Washington.

34. The New York Bar Association sent a mission to Argentina (April 1–7) to investigate the treatment of lawyers and the system of justice. Orville Schell, the mission chief, spoke at a House congressional hearing later in the year ("Human Rights and the Phenomenon of Disapearances," Hearings before the Subcommittee on International Organizations, September 20, 25; October 18 1979).

35. "Human Rights Group Opens Inquiry in Argentina." The judge who ordered the raid on the human rights groups, Martín Anzoateguí, was to play an important role in our story. (See below, Chapter 20, notes 35ff.) IACHR reviewed the harassment of the human rights groups and interviewed Judge Anzoátegui, who had ordered the seizure of documents. The IACHR's highly critical conclusions were printed in its report (OAS, *Report on the Situation of Human Rights in Argentina*, pp. 257–62).

36. It was clear that Thelma Jara de Cabezas's disappearance would be investigated when the IACHR visited Argentina, and the ESMA kidnappers tried to throw the visitors off the scent. In August, she was taken to a patissérie in Buenos Aires, where she met a reporter and photographer from a magazine and was forced to fabricate a story to the effect that she had fled to Uruguay to escape the violence. The farce was reenacted three times in Uruguay itself. Her story is described in *Nunca Más* (pp. 137–40). She survived to give testimony at the 1985 trial in Buenos Aires.

37. OAS, *Report on the Situation of Human Rights in Argentina*, p. 186. Villani described the changes made at the ESMA in his testimony at the 1985 trial.

38. Ibid., p. 6. Of the 5,580 complaints, 1,261 referred to cases already opened by the IACHR.

39. Ibid, pp. 50–52.

40. In, effect, if the Commission [IACHR] in violation of its mandate, were to agree to process a denunciation involving some alleged act of terrorism, in so doing it would implicitly place terrorist organizations on an equal footing with governments. Such organizations would be very pleased. But what government in the hemisphere would tolerate an implicit recognition of this kind?" (Ibid., p. 25).

41. The OAS representative in Buenos Aires was himself an Argentinian—which was most unusual. He helped to ensure that the Junta kept the OAS report from publication. Eventually it was published illegally by Emilio Mignone's CELS in 1982.

42. The confidential memo from Pastor to Videla carries an "Eyes Only" label, indicating the highest level of secrecy. This memo is in the author's possession.

43. From Memo D in the author's possession (p. 2). This document appears to be a speech from a senior Foreign Ministry official—possibly even Foreign Minister Pastor—to ambassadors. It was delivered in September 1980.

44. From a personal interview in Buenos Aires.

45. Pastor warned that the IACHR report could be used to intensify pressure against Argentina in the U.N. Commission.

46. Sixty-four disappearances were reported to Amnesty International in 1979.

47. Foreign Minister Pastor was to be preoccupied by the OAS report throughout much of 1980, and his memo reviews the various options, including the possibility of withdrawing from the OAS. In the event, the threat had its desired effect: the 1980 OAS Assembly did not pass a resolution criticizing Argentina. See below, Chapter 18, note 36.

48. Although the Junta suppressed the IACHR report inside Argentina, it was true to its promise not to penalize those who had given testimony to the IACHR team. In FOIA cable 8650 from the U.S. embassy in Buenos Aires (December 1979), Ambassador Castro said that the embassy had received no account of reprisals. Even ninety former prisoners who talked to the IACHR were unpunished.

Chapter 14. Martínez Prepares

1. Details of the December 18 1979 meeting from a memo in the author's possession.

2. The text of the Foreign Ministry note is published in Ragnar Hagelin's book *Mi Hija Dagmar,* p. 211. Details of Decree 310 from a document dated February 6 1980, in the author's possession.

3. Claus Ruser, deputy director of the Southern Cone section in the ARA, cabled Goodpaster from the State Department before the visit to say that the Junta wanted a full discussion about relations with the United States, including hu-

man rights (FOIA cable 019791, January 1980). The United States, for its part, wanted Argentina to join the grain embargo against the Soviet Union, or failing that, a commitment that Argentina would not exploit the embargo and fill the gap left by American farmers.

Neither side got what it wanted. The Junta agreed not to take commercial advantage of the embargo and immediately broke the promise (see below, note 8). Goodpaster merely promised "as a first step joint exercises, personnel exchanges, consultations on security matters." He also wrote that he had a "good discussion" with Videla about the forthcoming meeting of the U.N. Human Rights Commission in Geneva. Unfortunately, the contents of this discussion were not released to the author. (Details from FOIA cable 00313, sent by Goodpaster during a stopover in Rio de Janeiro.)

4. From Memo B in the author's possession, p. 49.

5. The Braiko visit is discussed in *El Mito de la Guerra Sucia* pp. 46–8. The authors downplay the relationship between the Junta and the Soviet Union during the dirty war and stress that the Argentinian Communist party was supportive of the Junta. In return, Communists were not targeted for disappearance.

6. The joint communiqué issued after Fokin's visit was recorded by Claus Ruser and transmitted back to Washington (FOIA cable 06287, August 1980). It stated that both nations "uphold the principles of respect for sovereignty of other countries. We oppose the creation of supranational organizations especially on human rights within the United Nations. The creation of these organizations would entail interference in the internal affairs of other states."

7. Memo D, in the author's possession, p. 1.

8. The figures on grain sales by Argentina to the USSR were produced at the April 1 1981 House hearings on Argentina ("Review of United States Policy on Military Assistance to Argentina," Hearings Before the Subcommittee on Human Rights and International Organizations and on Inter-American Affairs, pp. 6–9).

9. Memo D, in the author's possession, lists actions taken by the Junta not to provoke the United States. These included joining the boycott of the Moscow Olympic games. (See below, Chapter 18, note 41.)

10. "Dictatorships and Double Standards."

11. Jimmy Carter, *Keeping Faith: Memoirs of a President.* Carter's one chapter on human rights (pp. 141–51) lacks any political analysis, and the book contains no reference to Derian.

12. Derian announced her intention to resign in an interview with Ann Crittenden of the *New York Times,* "Human Rights and Mrs. Derian."

13. From an interview with the author. The Bureau of Human Rights and the regional bureau for Asia were in almost permanent conflict. John Salzberg joined Derian's office in 1979 after moving from Congressman Donald Fraser's staff and was assigned to East Asian affairs. He remembers telephoning one desk officer in the bureau for Asia and being interrupted by the man's superior. "Sorry, John, but we have orders not to talk to you." The orders came from Richard Holbrooke, Assistant Secretary of State for East Asia. There had been

bad blood between Salzberg and Holbrooke since the two had visited South Korea in 1978. When Holbrooke declined to refer to human rights at a press conference, he received a critical letter from Donald Fraser which he later blamed on Salzberg. Ray Bonner has a lively account of the feud in *Waltzing with a Dictator* (pp. 187–188). Patt Derian later told Salzberg that she had considered resigning over this incident. She took it to Christopher and then to Vance, but both refused to get involved. Derian reluctantly moved Salzberg to the African desk in the bureau and replaced him with someone less experienced and less controversial.

14. The one hundred seventy-six missing persons were named by the International Commission of Jurists in a report on February 11 1979.

15. For a detailed, impassioned account of Romero's work, and the way that Carter lost an opportunity to build a broad-based democratic coalition in El Salvador following the 1979 coup, see chapters 7 and 8 in Ray Bonner's *Weakness and Deceit: U.S. Policy in El Salvador.* pp. 145–67.

16. In an October 22 1979 memorandum to congressman Matthew McHugh, Brian Atwood from the State Department wrote that aid to El Salvador was justified under 502B for two reasons. First, the government was not guilty of "a consistent pattern of gross violations," as required by the law. "While the pattern of killings seems plain, gross and tragic," wrote Atwood, "the question of government responsibility is not as clear. There is a crucial distinction between a fledgling government that has publicly acknowledged its intention to control its security forces and one which deliberately engages in or tolerates abuses." Second, wrote Atwood, "[U.S.] national interest would be seriously prejudiced" if the left or right were to prevail in El Salvador. It was one of the most blatant uses of the loophole provided by 502B, and an illustration of how reluctant the United States was to pin the label of "gross violator" on governments which it considered allies.

See below Chapter 17, note 6 for more on Romero's death. Chapter 8 of Bonner's *Weakness and Deceit* deals with Romero's appeal to Carter.

17. The death of the four American churchwomen, and the long and dour struggle that faced their relatives in trying to obtain justice, has been the subject of countless articles and several books. The fullest account is to be found in a series of reports by the Lawyers Committee for International Human Rights in New York, which represented the families. In September 1981 the Lawyers Committee issued a detailed report complete with annexes (*A Report on the Investigation into the Killing of Four American Churchwomen in El Salvador*). For the aftermath of the murders and their importance to President Reagan's human rights policy, see below Chapter 19.

18. Shortly after the murders, the U.N. General Assembly was due to debate a resolution critical of El Salvador, and Secretary of State Edmund Muskie chaired a meeting to review how the U.S. should vote. According to one participant, who attended the meeting for the human rights bureau, John Bushnell claimed that the Salvadoran government had made important changes in the treasury police, one of the most notorious branches of the armed forces. This, he implied, justified the United States voting against the forth-

coming U.N. resolution criticizing El Salvador. The human rights bureau challenged Bushnell to come up with proof, which Bushnell failed to do, and Muskie directed the U.S. delegation at the General Assembly to abstain on the resolution.

A second meeting then took place on December 31 1980, at which Derian's office was excluded. More in despair than anger Derian penned a lengthy complaint to Muskie and laid out her reasons for opposing the resumption of military aid to El Salvador: it would relieve all pressure on the armed forces to solve the churchwomen's murder and stop further killing; it would render Napoleon Duarte "irrelevant" to the military, because his standing depended on being able to deliver U.S. military assistance. Derian's memo was to no avail. Three days before he stepped down, President Carter sent combat equipment worth five million dollars to El Salvador (Derian's memo in the author's possession).

19. On February 13 1980, the United States returned to the ILO after a two-year absence. Carter's decision to withdraw the U.S. from the ILO is still an issue of great controversy. For two very different analyses see Richard Melanson, "Human Rights and the American Withdrawal from the ILO" and Walter Galenson, *The International Labor Organization—Mirroring the U.N.'s Problems*. Melanson feels that Carter's decision to pull out in 1977 was a grave mistake. Galenson argues that it was not only justified, but that the ILO did not improve sufficiently to warrant return by the U.S. in 1980. For a detailed discussion of the damage caused by the U.S. withdrawal, see the report of the ILO Governing Body financial and administrative committee (November 15–18, 1977, reference GB.204/14/17).

20. For more on U.S. unwillingess to ratify human rights treaties and references see above Chapter 7, note 12. Derian's comments in favor of ratification can be found in "International Human Rights Treaties," Hearings Before the Senate Committee on Foreign Relations. November 14, 15, 16, 19 1979.

21. This April 8 1980 assessment of the disarray in the Nonaligned Movement was written after the 1980 session of the U.N. Human Rights Commission, which turned out disastrously for Argentina (memo in the author's possession).

Chapter 15. Shestack Breaks the Jinx

1. The International League for Human Rights began when a citizens group formed in France to protest the Dreyfus affair. This gave it French and Jewish connections that it has retained ever since. During a trip to Paris in 1927, the American civil rights campaigner Roger Nash Baldwin came into contact with the group. When the Second World War destroyed the group, Baldwin encouraged its reconstitution in the United States. It was incorporated in 1942 in New York as the International League for Human Rights.

See Laurie Wiseberg and Harry Scoble "The International League for Human Rights. The Strategy of a Human Rights NGO." The article gives valuable insights into the relationship between NGOs and the U.N.

2. Shestack had one serious disagreement with Theo van Boven over the distribution of written material. Shestack wanted to circulate a document on Sakharov, but van Boven refused to allow it on the grounds that Sakharov had not yet been the subject of a U.N. resolution. This seemed a technical point but it was van Boven's way of allowing NGO documents to circulate without violating the highly restrictive ECOSOC resolution 1919 of 1975, which had greatly curbed NGO participation (see Appendix 6). Shestack was furious, but van Boven argued there was no point in needlessly provoking the Soviets.

3. Shestack tried to break the frustrating U.N. impasse over South Africa. This issue traditionally came up early on the Commission agenda, and the United States had found itself forced to vote against resolutions condemning apartheid—usually because they called for economic sanctions. This opposition jarred with Carter's opposition to apartheid. Millard Arnold, a black lawyer on the delegation, hit on an idea. Why not call on the International Court of Justice to deliver an opinion about the legality of "banning," the insidious South African practice of putting "troublemakers" under house arrest? Shestack approved the idea and forwarded it to Washington, where it received a cautious welcome. He flew back to Washington for a hurried meeting with Maynes and Christopher. The issue then passed to Vance for final approval, but eventually Vance told Shestack to drop it because it could complicate the forthcoming elections in Rhodesia.

4. Al-Jabiri's role at the 1980 Commission is still a matter of speculation for many who attended. At first sight, he was challenging the Soviet Union by helping Shestack on Sakharov, but he may also have been helping the Soviet Union get out of a tight spot by postponing the debate. What is not clear is whether al-Jabiri was working alone or representing his government. For al-Jabiri's role on the disappearances see below.

    The International League for Human Rights published an open letter by Sakharov and gave details on his exile in 1983 ("Andrei Sakharov from Exile").

5. For Goodpaster's visit to Argentina and his discussions with Videla about the UN Human Rights Commission, see above Chapter 14, note 3.

6. Amnesty International, *Testimony on Secret Detention Camps in Argentina*. The report was based on the testimony of Oscar Alfredo González and Horacio Cid de la Paz, who was detained in no less than five secret camps. These did not include the ESMA. The importance of the Amnesty report lay in the fact that it disclosed details of the methodical system of coordination between the kidnapping patrols and the torture centers, and within the security forces. (See above, Chapter 3, notes 5ff.) González and Cid de la Paz would subsequently be blamed for collaboration by some relatives and even participating in torture of other prisoners, but no one has disputed the facts in their 1980 report.

7. According to cable 2299 (November 6 1979) from Martínez, the six communications came from: the International Federation of Women (163 cases listed); the International Federation of Human Rights (187 cases); Amnesty International (no cases mentioned); Argentina Lawyers in France (9 cases); World Christian Democratic Union (4,381 cases listed); Lawyers Committee for Human Rights (cases not listed). Martínez knew that "the Lawyers in France"

included his "bête noir" Rodolfo Matarollo, yet the only one of these six which he refused to answer—as a matter of principle—was Amnesty's. Martínez wrote that Amnesty was "politically motivated and violated the principle of confidentiality."

8. Al-Jabiri's group had recommended keeping Argentina under review for a year and it asked the government to explain the following: what had happened to the disappeared; what were the conditions of detention; what measures would be taken to ensure that law 22.068 declaring that the disappeared were legally dead would not be abused; what of the numerous indications that habeas corpus and amparo were not working; the persecution of lawyers; and what of the restrictions on the right of free expression and unions. (Summary record E/CN 4/R 56 Rev 1, February 20 1980.)

9. A copy of the French proposal in Martínez's files carried a terse message: "the project does not meet with Foreign Ministry approval" (from the author's files).

10. Sadi sent Martínez the names of nine disappeared persons on February 18 and followed it up with a letter two days later (in the author's possession). Sadi's letter added that Graciela Geuna (a young woman who had given testimony to Amnesty about detention camps) had expressed concern about her family. "I am sure her fears are unjustified but I thought of passing on to you her concern." Graciela Geuna's testimony was published by Amnesty in March 1980 (AMR 13/16/80). She was detained in the La Perla camp in Córdoba.

11. Figures about paper usage from "Waste Paper Recovery and Utilization of Recycled Paper. Case study: the Palais des Nations, Geneva" (note by the UN Secretariat, ENV/R.85, February 7 1978). The paper found that 271 million individual pages were printed at the Palace in 1977—a total weight of 997 tons.

12. "The 1980 U.N. Human Rights Human Commission and the Disappeared."

13. Martínez's April 8 1980 memorandum is in the author's possession.

14. "Review of the 36th Session of the United Nations Commission on Human Rights," Hearing before Subcommittee on Human Rights and International Organizations, April 29 1980.

15. Ibid.

16. Details of Shestack's meeting with ARA officials from an interview with the author.

17. See above Chapter 14, note 12. Normalization of relations between the United States and Argentina was preempted by the Junta's involvement in the brutal coup in Bolivia.

18. Shestack went on to serve on the U.S. delegations to the Madrid conference, ECOSOC, and the General Assembly. The United States was up for reelection to the U.N. Human Rights Commission at the ECOSOC meeting, and in spite of the unwritten rule that all five permanent members of the Security Council are guaranteed seats, Shestack found that he had to lobby furiously. Chile and Argentina both made it clear this was one tradition they would not be upholding. The United States won enough votes to guarantee reelection but it was far from resounding.

Later in the year, during the General Assembly, Shestack worked hard to coordinate a Western protest to U.N. Secretary General Kurt Waldheim on behalf of Sakharov. He also pressed for the U.N. Human Rights Division to be upgraded to a center in the U.N. bureaucracy.

Chapter 16. The Chairman Disappears

1. From a March 31 1980 cable in the author's possession.
2. From a memorandum in the author's possession, p. 6.
3. The West's first choice was Max van der Stoel, a former Dutch foreign minister. He declined, and the next choice of the Western group was Mark Colville. This would have marked a break with an unwritten rule that the five permanent members of the Security Council are not represented on U.N. human rights inquiries. Aware of the possibility of a Soviet veto, Jerry Shestack scribbled a note to Waleed Sadi, the Commission chairman, saying that he— Shestack—wanted to be on the working group. When the Soviets heard of this, they sent over a tall bony diplomat named Bykov to demand an explanation. This, said Bykov, is intolerable. Shestack let Bykov fume for a few minutes before offering to withdraw his own candidacy if the Soviets would accept Colville instead. They agreed.
4. *International Herald Tribune,* September 16 1980, article by the author.
5. Jerry Shestack was so concerned about al-Jabiri's fate that he made plans to visit Waleed Sadi in Jordan in the summer in the hope that Sadi could bring some pressure to bear on Iraq. Sadi was unable to keep the appointment. Al-Jabiri's life was probably saved by the campaign on his behalf. He is thought to be teaching in Iraq.
6. Between 1977 and 1979 officials from the GT 3/32 were sent abroad to Peru, Uruguay, Geneva, Venezuela, and Mexico to kill or kidnap Montoneros in exile.
7. The five Argentinians were Noemí Esther Gianotti de Molfino, Julia Inés Santos Acabal, Julio César Ramírez, Federico Frías Alberga, and Aldo Moran.
8. From a memorandum sent by the U.N. Working Group on Disappearances to Martínez on the case. Martínez cabled the note to Buenos Aires.
9. After CADHU's Spanish branch denounced involvement by the Junta, the Spanish police exhumed Molfino's body, but did not report anything that indicated foul play. CADHU's communiqué was sent to the working group on August 30, and a copy passed to Martínez. On September 18 1980 Martínez received the information in a cable from Argentina's embassy in Madrid.
10. From Ruser's August 23-September 5 human rights round-up (FOIA cable 07249).
11. Ruser reported in a September cable that "the probable involvement of Argentina security forces in the disappearance of three Argentine Montoñeros in Peru forced President Videla to cancel a trip to Lima that he wished to make to symbolically express his government's democratic intention" (FOIA cable 07745, September 1980).
12. Mignone was quoted in the *Washington Post,* September 13 1980.

Two laws on presumptive death were passed in September 1980. Law 22.062 (August 28 1979) entitled relatives to pensions and other rights if a person remained disappeared for a year. Law 22.068 (September 12 1979) stated that someone was to be presumed legally dead if he or she did not reappear within ninety days. For details, see the OAS *Report on the Situation of Human Rights in Argentina*, pp. 126–34.

These two laws were the first of several attempts by the military to bury the past and put the disappearances behind them. They caused an international outcry. "The government was somewhat surprised by the negative reaction," cabled Claus Ruser from Buenos Aires in September (FOIA cable 07442). During the first year, Ruser reported, there was only one case of a junior official declaring a "desaparecido" dead in the face of objections from relatives. He was reprimanded. In September 1980, the Attorney General preempted even this possibility by telling prosecutors that they could only invoke the law in the absence of relatives. The relatives greeted this as a victory, even though the law remained on the statute books.

Mario Amadeo, the author of the "presumptive death" laws, was much reproached by the human rights groups. During the 1980 session of the U.N. Sub-Commission, of which he was a member, he cabled Buenos Aires requesting information about the application of his own law and was told that 158 applications had been received in 1980 alone, which suggests that the law was more widely used than Ruser knew. According to one November 1979 cable from the U.S. embassy (FOIA 09276), Amadeo told human rights groups that he had presented the Junta with several other "recommendations all designed to improve the human rights situation in Argentina" which were ignored. Amadeo did not elaborate and he remained an equivocal figure for many human rights activists. (See above, Chapter 9, note 24.)

The Junta tried to justify the law on presumptive death in a letter to the U.N. (Reprinted in the first report of the U.N. Working Group on Disappearances, E/CN 4/1435 Annex XI.)

13. This information taken from the author's interviews with the Mothers in Buenos Aires.

14. Mario del Carril, a professor at Georgetown University, remembers escorting a group of Mothers around Washington. After one meeting at the National Security Council, the NSC official portentously said goodbye to Hebe de Bonafini with the words "vaya con dios" (God be with you). "God's already with us," replied de Bonafini quickly. "What we need is a few men on our side!" One of the Mothers was Angélica Mignone, Mónica's mother. Del Carril married Mónica's elder sister Isabel.

By 1979, the Mothers were effectively under U.S. government protection. In March 1978, Castro met with a group of Mothers for what his cable described as a "tour d'horizon" (FOIA cable 02379). The Mothers queried whether the sale of T-34 aircraft to Argentina was not covered by the U.S. arms embargo, but seemed most preoccupied by conflicting signals from the Junta about whether the disappeared were still alive. On August 28 Castro delivered a letter of support from President Carter's wife to the Mothers.

15. The story of the five "desaparecidos" who reappeared and then disappeared a second time was recounted in a long cable from Ambassador Shlaudeman (FOIA cable 09421). One of the five even visited home during the brief period of release, accompanied by one of his captors.

16. Shlaudeman's account of meeting the five parents from FOIA cable 09097.

17. Like the Mothers, the Grandmothers turned outside for help. The World Council of Churches in Geneva gave them sufficient funds to open a small, cramped office at the end of 1977.

18. From a Grandmothers report, reprinted as a supplement to Amnesty International's November 1981 newsletter. The Grandmothers began printing regular reports on their findings as early as 1978. These were transmitted and published by a wide variety of international NGOs.

19. The impetus for the creation of CELS came from Leonard Meeker, director of the Center for Law and Social Policy, a Washington-based public interest law firm. In 1978 (at the suggestion of Congressman Donald Fraser) Congress voted money for human rights defenders, and Meeker—a former U.S. ambassador to Rumania and State Department legal counsel—was invited to attend a meeting about how the money could be spent. Meeker submitted a proposal on July 27 1978, and USAID allocated $87,500 to be spent in Africa and Latin America. Meeker traveled to both regions. In Buenos Aires, Tex Harris introduced him to Emilio Mignone. Meeker met with a group of eight parents at the Mignones' apartment. "We thought some of the disappeared might still be alive in prison, so we got the idea of forming a legal group to initiate legal proceedings for their release." Meeker gave Mignone a copy of the by-laws of his own center in Washington, which the Argentinians adapted. On his return to the United States, Meeker recommended that most of the USAID money earmarked for Latin America—$40,000—should go to CELS. CELS secured USAID funding until President Reagan's election, when the money stopped. CELS has since survived on grants, chiefly from the Ford Foundation.

   Initially, Meeker transmitted the money through the Marine Midland Bank in New York. Then, for reasons which were never made clear to Meeker, the bank refused to continue the arrangement. Meeker then made the check out to Mignone, who picked it up during a trip to Washington. The rate of inflation was such that Mignone was able to make the USAID grant go a long way. Meeker remained a loyal friend of CELS and used his formidable State Department contacts to protest vigorously when CELS was raided in March 1981. (See below Chapter 20, note 36 ff.) Looking back, he feels that helping CELS get started was one of his major accomplishments.

20. Mignone was admired at the U.S. embassy in Buenos Aires. In March 1981, following Mignone's arrest and detention, Ambassador Shlaudeman sent the following appraisal:

   CELS offers the most effective legal help to the families of detained and disappeared persons. Through its personnel and especially through Mignone, it is extemely active in sustaining foreign concern about Argentina. Mignone, a Democrat and no terrorist, who travels widely undoubtedly has contact with people near the Montoneros when he is abroad. Finally, the sum of all of CELS' activities are aimed at one overriding proposition—making the military answer for the past. Others share this purpose but few are so effective at it (FOIA cable 01495).

For Mignone's arrest in 1981, see below, Chapter 20, notes 36ff.

21. The story of Angel's disappearance and his parents' campaign comes from interviews with Raul and Valentina at their home in Meyrin, Switzerland.

22. By 1979, Raul and Valentina had succeeded in obtaining 17,000 signatures throughout Switzerland. Raul spent 150 Swiss francs to print two thousand copies of a poem about his son. The pamphlet showed a boy with a sweet, dreamy expression, a pudding-bowl haircut, and big ears. The poem was aired on the BBC: "My son, how bitter are the days! what a disaster and a torment not to see you, to feel your presence near to me." Raul's wife, Valentina, with slanting eyes like an Indian, endured hundreds of newspaper interviews that posed the inevitable question: whether she thought her son was dead. She replied by producing five thick scrapbooks showing photos of her son, with a childish, misspelt legend on the cover: "Kidnaped by the armed forces of the tirany."

23. The first Latin American relatives group pre-dated the Mothers in Argentina. In October 1973, after the coup, the Chilean Catholic Church and others formed the "Ecumenical Committee for Peace." The committee was severely harassed, and in 1975 Pinochet forced Cardinal Enrique Silva to close it. Silva did so, but then formed the Vicariate of Solidarity within his Church to carry on the work. Pinochet was furious, but such was Silva's reputation that there was little he could do. Mothers of Chile's disappeared—thought to number around seven hundred—were allowed to set up an "agrupación" (group) within the Vicariate.

24. Patrick Rice's disappearance and reappearance furnished conclusive proof of the security forces' involvement. His testimony can be found in the IACHR report (OAS, *Report on the Human Rights Situation in Argentina,* pp. 209–14), and in the report of the November 1976 Amnesty mission to Argentina (pp. 30–32).

25. Figures from FEDEFAM bulletin, distributed at the 1983 Human Rights Commission.

Chapter 17. The Dialogue Starts, the Disease Spreads

1. The names of witnesses who appeared before the working group at its first session, and extracts from their testimony, can be found in the group's first report (E/CN.4/1435, January 26 1981).

2. This figure is taken from a special 1984 report by the Catholic Legal Aid Service "Socorro Juridico" to mark the fourth anniversary of the death of Archbishop Romero. The report put the estimates of deaths at 1,792 killings in 1979; 11,895 in 1980; and 16,276 in 1981.

3. On November 19 1981 García Villas' CDHES published a written appeal in local Salvadoran papers under the heading: "El Playón is an offense against

sensibility, an affront to Salvadorans and the entire human race." According to people who lived in the area, some four hundred corpses had been found on the lava bed over the previous two years.

4. This remarkable series of photos is printed in a report by Socorro Juridico (*La situación de los derechos humanos: Octobre 1979 – Julio 1981*.

5. Socorro Juridico started in 1975, when a group of law students from the Jesuit college of San José decided to offer free legal aid to the poor. Early in 1978 Archbishop Oscar Romero invited Socorro Juridico to work under the aegis of his office. Roberto Cuéllar gladly accepted. Shortly before, Romero had taken a group of mothers of disappeared persons under his wing, allowing them to use his name and meet in a small green outbuilding behind his administrative headquarters.

6. Such was El Salvador's passion for recording its own agony that the transcript of Romero's final service is interrupted with the words: "A shot rang out." Romero fell to the floor, blood pouring from his nose. He was bundled out of the chapel and into an ambulance by nuns, in a cameo that was eerily similar to the picture of the dead Christ on the wall of the cathedral. He died minutes later. (Details from *Sentir con la Iglesia*, Publicaciones Pastorales Catedrál, no. 61, March 24 1980, p. 22.)

7. A copy of the death squads' manifesto is in the author's possession. It called for the "physical extermination" of Communist cells, revolutionary groups, "common killers, robbers, assailants, rapists, homosexuals, prostitutes, drug addicts, military traitors, corrupt lawyers, poisonous professors, corrupt government officials, unscrupulous moneylenders, . . ."

8. Her testimony to the group is partially reprinted in the group's first report (E/CN4/1435, January 26 1981, Annex XIII). Colville's comments from an interview with the author.

9. The information in this chapter about José González and Nicaragua's independent human rights commission comes from interviews with the author.

U.S. marines occupied Nicaragua between 1912 and 1933. They withdrew after helping to create and train the national guard, under the command of Anastasio Somoza García. In 1936 Somoza forced the civilian president from office, seized power, and created a family dynasty that would last for forty-three years. By the time Jimmy Carter took power, Nicaragua was close to open civil war and the dictator Anastasio Somoza Debayle had a reputation throughout Latin America for corruption and brutality. On October 3 1978, the IACHR arrived in Nicaragua. Its report, published on November 17, was one of the most critical it ever produced (OAS, *Report on the Situation of Human Rights in Nicaragua*).

In June 1979 the Sandinistas launched a final offensive. On June 23 1979 the seventeenth consultation meeting of OAS foreign ministers decided—by seventeen votes to two with five abstentions—that Somoza's violations of human right had deprived him of political legitimacy. Those in favor included Argentina (which had been a strong supporter of Somoza) and the United States. Aware that the OAS debate was moving their way, the Sandinistas suspended their offensive. The United States made one final attempt to prevent a clean sweep by the Sandinistas by calling for the addition of two "moderates" to the five-member junta that had been set up by the Sandinistas to govern the country. (The junta was, in fact, a careful compromise of interests.) According to newspaper reports, one of the extra members was to be José Estéban González. The proposal was rejected out of hand. Early on July 18 1979 Somoza left for exile in Miami. After a chaotic two days of fighting the provisional government was installed in Managua on July 20 1979.

10. The World Council of Churches in Geneva promised $43,000 and sent a first installment of $15,000, with the balance to follow. González appeared in a WCC film that won a prize at a Leipzig film festival. When the U.N. Human Rights Commission called for a study on Nicaragua in March 1979, Theo van Boven's office drew on González's reports.

11. González denies newspaper reports that the United States and Venezuela wanted him as a sixth member of the Nicaraguan junta, but he does concede that Venezuelan President Héctor Campíns, a personal friend and Christian Democrat, strove to put together a government that was more centrist than that chosen by the Sandinistas.

12. It had been a brutal revolution in Nicaragua, nowhere more so than in Grenada, where a group of prisoners disappeared from the garrison of La Polvora shortly after the revolution. They included Francisco de Mayorga. On October 3 1979 José González accompanied Francisco's anxious wife Marlene to the area, where they found a depression in the ground and a human skull and some bones lying on the ground. They only needed to move three centimeters of soil to come upon the decomposing remains of a corpse, crawling with worms. Marlene recognized the trousers worn by her husband and broke down. But had González uncovered "forced and involuntary disappearances," or local scores settled after a brutal civil war? González had little doubt that it was the former, particularly as the victims were, like Francisco de Mayorga, lawyers and accountants, not Somoza's National Guardsmen. The Sandinistas held an inquiry, concluded that the La Polvora deaths had been caused by "fanatics," and arrested the commander. It is not known whether he was punished. For details see OAS, *Report on the Situation of Human Rights in the Republic of Nicaragua.*

13. International Commission of Jurists, *Human Rights in Nicaragua Yesterday and Today.* González's figures on disappearances are taken from his testimony to the U.N. Working Group on Disappearances (E/ CN.4/ 1435, January 26 1981, annex XV).

14. From the author's interview with Artucio.

15. The ICJ's main concern was with the tribunals that had been set up to try former National Guardsmen. Artucio and Fragoso warned that the charges were often vague, and that prisoners were being kept in detention for long periods without being charged as well as denied legal representation. Why did the ICJ not publish this second, more critical report on the Sandinista tribunals? Partly because MacDermot thought harsh criticism would backfire. The Sandinistas were already jittery and nervous. Three thousand five hundred former National Guardsmen had fled into Honduras. On April 10 1980 a group

of twenty had been captured in Nicaragua and confessed on television that further attacks were being prepared by "contras" (counterrevolutionaries). Another reason why the report was not published was that Artucio personally sympathized with the Sandinistas.

16. From the author's interview with Lord Colville.

17. For the group's comments and dialogue with the Sandinistas see its first report (E/CN 4/1435), pp. 58–61.

18. From an interview with the author.

19. Cited in Americas Watch, *Guatemala: the Group for Mutual Support,* pp. 2–4.

20. For the periodic waves of killing in Guatemala during the 1960s and 1970s see Roger Plant, *Guatemale: Unnatural Disaster* and Michael McClintock, *The American Connection Vol. 2.*

21. The best-known account of growing up an Indian in Guatemala is the biography of Rigoberta Menchu, an Indian leader whose father was killed when troops stormed the Spanish embassy in Guatemala City on January 31 1980 (*I Rigoberta Menchu*). See also *Indian Guatemala,* a sympathetic report by the Ecumenical Program for Interamerican Communication and Action.

22. Father Pellecer himself disappeared and reappeared in army hands after several months to denounce Guatemala's guerrillas. See below Chapter 23, note 17.

23. Figure from Amnesty International USA, *Disappearances: A Workbook,* p. 29.

Alberto Fuentes Mohr had had a distinguished career in government between 1966 and 1973, when he ran for election as vice-president but lost after widespread fraud. The presidential candidate was Efraín Ríos Montt, who seized power in 1982. Fuentes Mohr then went to work for the U.N. Conference on Trade and Development before returning to Guatemala in 1978. See below, Chapter 27, note 7, for the contemptuous way in which Fuentes Mohr's death was subsequently treated by the U.N. information department.

24. Resolution 32, adopted by the U.N. Human Rights Commission on March 11 1980, expressed satisfaction that the government had invited the IACHR to visit. It also expressed "profound concern" at reports of violations and asked the government to protect human rights.

25. For Julia Esquivel's testimony to the group see its first report (E/CN 4 1435, annex XIV).

26. Martínez's letter was sent to the working group on December 8 1980, and exerpted in the group report (E/CN.4/1435, annex IX).

27. The U.N. Human Rights Division sent four notes, containing forty-eight cases, to Martínez prior to, or immediately after, his appearance before the group on September 19. The first note from the working group (July 2 1980) contained the five names of the Argentinians who disappeared in Peru and was sent on to Buenos Aires by Martínez on July 4 (cable 559/80). The second note (July 15) contained eleven names and was dispatched on July 22 (cable 600/80). The third note (August 4) contained fourteen names and was sent on August 5 (cable 639/80) The fourth note (September 25) contained twenty-two names, and was sent to Buenos Aires on October 21 (cable 849/80).

The case on Dagmar Hagelin was submitted to Martínez on July 15 1980. It took the form of depositions by Dagmar's father, Ragnar, and by Norma

Susana Burgos, recently arrived in Sweden. During 1980 the group also submitted a sample five hundred cases to the Junta for an explanation.

28. For the case of Elena Holmberg, see above, Chapter 5. On the all-important question of whether Argentinian diplomats were aware of the disappearances see above, Chapter 8.

29. FOIA cable 08548, October 1980. Details of the Jauretche case were cabled to Martínez in Geneva from Buenos Aires.

30. The Inter-American Commission on Human Rights (IACHR) also appealed on behalf of Jauretche.

31. The persecution continued after Marianella García Villas left El Salvador. On January 28 1981 her house was blown up. On February 11, the police arrested a family that had rented a house belonging to her parents and queried them about the whereabouts of Marianella herself. (Details from CDHES bulletins.) On March 30 the Salvadoran armed forces issued a communiqué with a list of names under the heading "enemies of the people" that included Roberto Cuéllar and Marianella García Villas. From his exile in Mexico City Roberto Cuéllar compared the list with the names that had appeared on the death squad communiqué of May 11 1980 (see above, note 7). He found that many names were identical, and that some had since been killed. (From CDHES reports and author's interview with Cuéllar.)

Chapter 18. The Pressure Pays Off

1. Captain Jorge Vildoza, Petty Officer Victor Cardo, and Lieutenant Alberto Menotti were identified by Ana María Marti and filmed by an enterprising British television crew. Lord Avebury, the British peer who had accompanied the Amnesty team to Argentina in 1976, protested to the British Foreign Office, and the three slipped back to Argentina.

2. For Ana María Marti's story see above, Chapter 3. The report of the three women was distributed by CADHU.

3. Carlos Muñoz gave important testimony on July 30 1985 at the trial (*Diario del Juicio* 10). During his work at the ESMA, Muñoz was permitted access to large amounts of incriminating material and he even glimpsed thousands of names of prisoners on microfilm. A handful had the letter L against them, for "liberado" (freed). The rest had the letter T—"traslado" (transferred, or killed).

4. Miriam Lewin de García had tried to swallow cyanide when she was kidnapped in broad daylight. She gave testimony at the 1985 trial.

5. Burgos's testimony is reprinted in Ragnar Hagelin's account of his search for his daughter (*Mi Hija Dagmar*), pp. 194–204.

6. From the embassy's May 3–9 1980 human rights summary (FOIA cable 3909).

7. "Death Camp Man Goes Home." For Astiz's story after his return from South Africa, see below, Chapter 26.

8. Joelito Filártiga, the son of a well-known Paraguayan surgeon and human rights activist, died on March 29 1976 after being detained in a Paraguayan jail

and tortured by Norberto Peña-Irala, Inspector General of the police of Asunción. In 1979 Peña-Irala visited the United States and was rash enough to let his visa expire. The boy's father and sister, Joel and Dolly Filártiga, learned of this from human rights groups and brought a claim in court against Peña-Irala. The claim was dismissed in a district court, but this decision was reversed by federal judge Irving Kaufman in the Court of Appeals for the Second Circuit. In 1983 the Filártigas were awarded $375,000.

The Filártiga case is interesting and important. Judge Kaufman based his precedent-creating decision on the Alien Tort Statute, passed in 1789, which authorized U.S. federal courts to hear civil claims by aliens concerning violations of the "law of nations." Kaufman concluded that torture was a violation of this law. Although a subsequent ruling found against the Filártigas, it is still considered a landmark case in internationalizing the fight against torture and establishing a regime of universal jurisdiction. Peña-Irala has since returned to Paraguay and has not paid the damages.

For reading on the Filártiga case see: Claude, "Torture on Trial: The Case of Joelito Filártiga and the 'Clinic of Hope'," Drinan, "Cry of the Oppressed," pp. 54–57; Rodley, "The treatment of Prisoners under International Law," pp. 104–07.

Judge Kaufman wrote about his decision in "A Legal Remedy For International Torture?"

9. The fifteen countries were Argentina, Bolivia, Brazil, Chile, Cyprus, El Salvador, Ethiopia, Guatemala, Indonesia, Mexico, Nicaragua, Peru, the Philippines, South Africa, and Uruguay.

10. Thus, while neither Emilio Mignone's name nor that of his organization CELS mentioned, the name of his daughter Mónica does appear. The testimony of the six Argentinian groups that testified, including Mignone for CELS, are summarized and condensed into one annex. One young woman gave testimony to the group and displayed her wounds, and the group arranged for her to visit a Geneva physician, Dr. Bierens de Hann, who confirmed that the burns had probably been caused by a 220-volt "picana" (E/CN.4/1435, p.27). The doctor's name appears, but the victim's name does not. She is thought to be Graciela Geuna, who was detained at La Perla.

11. The report mentions the following detention centers: the ESMA; La Perla (3rd Army Corps); El Vesubio (3rd Infantry Regiment); El Jardín (Argentine and Uruguayan Intelligence forces); Club Atlético (Federal Police); Banco (Army); Olimpo (Army); Campo de Mayo (First Army Corps—the largest army base in Buenos Aires); Sheraton (Army Artillery unit); Quilmes (former police station); "Pozo" (another joint Uruguayan-Argentinian center); Police Station 40 (Provincial Police of Buenos Aires); Campito (La Plata, army); Unit 5 of the Buenos Pastor prison; Area 113 at Olmos (military and naval); the federal police coordination bureau. It is well to remember that this list appeared four years before the Argentinian commission on the disappeared (CONADEP) published its own list of military centers used in the dirty war.

12. "Review of United States Policy on Military Assistance to Argentina," Hear-

ings, House Subcommittee on Human Rights and International Organizations, April 1 1981, pp. 82–88.

13. In November 1980, Argentinian officials told Claus Ruser in Buenos Aires that
van Boven favored the working group holding public meetings. This, as Ruser
noted in a cable, was not true. There were, he noted, "differences" between
the United States and Argentina over the group's mandate (FOIA cable
08891).

14. Tom Farer and his IACHR colleagues arrived in Managua for the second time
on October 6 1980. They visited the La Polvora jail, where the alleged disappearances had occurred, and reviewed the dossier of José González on the
executions that had taken place there. González, they concluded, had been
correct—disappearances had occurred. But they also accepted that the government could not be held responsible: "While the Government of Nicaragua
clearly intended to respect the lives of all those defeated in the civil war, during
the weeks immediately subsequent to the revolutionary triumph, when the
Government was not in effective control, illegal executions took place which
violated the right to life and these acts have not been investigated and the
persons responsible have not been punished" (OAS, *Report on the Situation of
Human Rights in the Republic of Nicaragua*, p. 58).

15. E/CN.4/1435 add.1, February 16 1981.

16. After giving testimony to the group, González traveled to Spain where he
repeated his charge that hundreds had disappeared under the Sandinistas.
González was arrested when he returned to Nicaragua and was released from
jail only after an intervention by William Butler, president of the International
Commission of Jurists. The irony of González owing his freedom to the organization that he had criticized so harshly did not escape Niall MacDermot
and Alejandro Artucio. (For the circumstances of González's arrest and release
see OAS, *Report on the Situation*, pp. 144–46.)

17. In December, the U.N. group received a visit from Leonte Herdocia, who
headed a governmental human rights commission set up by the Sandinistas to
rival that of José González. Herdocia said it was pointless to inquire into disappearances that had happened during the revolution and regretted that it
would not be possible to arrange a visit for the U.N. group before the forthcoming meeting of the U.N. Human Rights Commission, in February 1981.
The Sandinistas, clearly, were piqued. The group's comments on Nicaragua
can be found in its report E/CN/4/1435, pp. 60–1. The Sandinista reply is
found in E/CN.4/1435/ Add.1, February 16 1981.

18. "Totalitarian" regimes like the Soviet Union, where the party has total control
over every aspect of life, do not need to employ the strategy of disappearances.
See, for instance, the report of the 1979 hearings on disappearances held by the
House Subcommittee on International Organizations. The report contains a
wealth of testimony on Argentina, but only three written submissions about
"totalitarian" disappearances: Nguyen Huu Hieu, who spent several months
in a Vietnamese re-education camp following the fall of Saigon in 1975 and
subsequently survived (pp. 488–91); Konstantin Pats, President of Estonia,
who was detained when the Soviet Union invaded Estonia in June 1940 and

subsequently died (p. 485); Raul Wallenberg, the Swedish diplomat who disappeared in Hungary in 1944 and is thought to have died in a Soviet jail (p. 432). None of these three cases fits the definition used by the U.N. Working Group on Disappearances: a "forced or involuntary" disappearance by one's own government.

19. For the neoconservative argument that "authoritarian" regimes permit limited freedom, see the statement that Michael Novak was preparing to deliver to the U.N. Human Rights Commission on February 28 1981 (Chapter 20, note 28, and Appendix 4).

20. Four communications alleging violations by East Germany of the right to leave were submitted by the International League for Human Rights in New York. These were reviewed by the preliminary group of subcommissioners—minus Vsefolod Sofinsky, whose visa was held up by Switzerland. The four subcommissioners accepted one, which was sufficient to ensure that East Germany went before the full Sub-Commission. By this time Sofinsky had arrived in Geneva, too late to get the blacklist modified. (For the treatment of East Germany by the 1981 Commission and the way in which the U.S. delegation jeopardized this, see below, Chapter 20, note 9.)

The communication against the United States from the Indian Law Resource Center in Washington argued that, by denying Hopi Indians the right to own the land on which they were living, the United States was violating articles 1, 9, 17, and 26 in the Universal Declaration (covering the rights to self-determination, ownership of property, and equal protection under the law). The United States replied with a 69-page counterargument which Beverly Carter, the U.S. subcommissioner, used to get the charge rejected. The ILRC subsequently obtained a copy of the government argument under the FOIA.

Japan found its way onto the 1503 blacklist in 1980 because of discrimination against the Korean minority in Japan.

21. The six governments under public indictment were South Africa, Chile, Israel, Guatemala, Equatorial Guinea, and El Salvador. The names of Chile and Guatemala also appeared on the 1503 blacklist and the report of the U.N. Working Group on Disappearances. The total number of governments under review by the U.N. for gross violations was twenty-six.

22. For an expression of Kirkpatrick's views about "selectivity" by the U.N., see below, Chapter 23, note 29.

The downside of "thematic" inquiries like those of the Working Group on Disappearances is that they weaken country studies and have a relatively small readership compared to country reports. But this was not apparent in 1980 and 1981, when the group was seen as an important complement to the country investigations and its reports were being avidly consumed by human rights groups in Latin America.

23. We should also urge the Argentines to cooperate with the UNHRC working group. This would include agreeing to an extension of its one-year term next February and acceptance of a visit to Argentina by the working group if it seeks its own invitation. The working group conceivably could provide a way out of Argentina's dilemma by offering a means of accounting for the disappeared that does not generally undermine

GOA interests. The working group is to report to the next Human Rights Commission session: we and the Argentines should be prepared to take its recommendations fully into account (ARA memorandum drafted by C. J. Whiteman on August 23 1980, in the author's files).

24. FOIA cable 00108 from Geneva, January 1981.
25. *New York Times,* March 5 1981.
26. FOIA cable 08850 from Buenos Aires, November 1980.
27. *Miami News,* October 20 1978.
28. From Argentinian Foreign Ministry Memo D in the author's possession, p. 6.
29. One Foreign Ministry analysis, written in July 1980, concluded that Argentina's only consistent friend had been neighboring Uruguay (Memo B in the author's possession).
30. From Memo D in the author's possession, p. 3.
31. From Memo B in the author's possession, p. 60.
32. "Argentine Rights Activist Wins Nobel Peace Prize," and "A Tireless Friend of the Dispossessed," *New York Times.*
33. The Nobel laureate's salary was referred to in a cable from Buenos Aires to Washington (FOIA cable 08283).
34. From memo D in the author's possession, p. 1. General Leopoldo Galtieri accused the Nobel committee of "interference" in Argentina's internal affairs, and a churlish communiqué by the Junta stated that Pérez Esquivel's activities "were effectively used to make the movement of various terrorist organizations easier." The Argentinian Church hurried to distance itself from Pérez Esquivel by pointing out that the Justice and Peace Commission had no formal ties to the Church.
35. When Harry Shlaudeman succeeded Raul Castro as U.S. ambassador in Buenos Aires on November 3 1980 he found the Junta obsessed by the upcoming OAS Assembly. "The paranoia level here strikes me as high," wrote Shlaudeman in one of his first cables back to Washington as ambassador. "A decision to tough it out would not be all that surprising" (FOIA cable 08712 from Buenos Aires to Washington).
36. Foreign Minister Carlos Pastor, the architect of the Junta's strategy, returned to Buenos Aires on November 28 and described the OAS decision as "one of the most resounding successes of Argentine diplomacy." It had, he continued, "written a definitive end to the human rights chapter." Argentina had carried the standard for Latin America and the United States had been isolated and snubbed (FOIA cable 09311 from the US Embassy in Buenos Aires).
37. FOIA cable 09311.
38. FOIA cable 09319.
39. *Buenos Aires Herald,* June 3 1980.
40. Kirkpatrick, "Dictatorships and Double Standards." See below, Chapter 19 for an analysis of the article and its impact.
41. From Memo D in the author's possession.
42. "The Nomination of Ernest W. Lefever," Hearings, Senate Foreign Relations Committee, May 1981, p. 78.

43. For the full text of Ruser's analysis of disappearances, see Appendix 3. For an analysis, see above, Chapter 2, note 34.
44. Ruser's account of Edith Bona's reappearance comes from a September cable from Buenos Aires entitled "Disappearance and Reappearance" (FOIA cable 07156).
45. From Memo B in the author's possession, p. 60.

Chapter 19. The Neoconservative Revolution

1. Philip Geyelin, "Human Rights Turnaround."
2. It was an article of faith to American neoconservatives that the Soviet Union was aggressive and expansionist, whether working through satellites like Nicaragua and Angola, or by direct invasion as in Afghanistan. For two statements of Kirkpatrick's views see "Les Combattants de la liberté" and "American Foreign Policy in a Cold Climate."

   A defense of the Reagan Administration's human rights policy can be found in Schifter's "Reagan's Human Rights Policy: Firm Foundation." Schifter was an architect of the policy during Reagan's two terms, as delegate-alternate and delegate on the U.N. Human Rights Commission, and as Assistant Secretary of State for Human Rights. He maintains that Alexander Haig's notorious January 28 1981 comment at a press conference that "terrorism would take the place of human rights" was unfairly seized upon by the press and that Haig quickly corrected this "fumble."

   Jerry Shestack criticizes the Reagan policy in the same issue of the *Harvard Human Rights Yearbook* ("An Unsteady Focus: The Vulnerabilities of the Reagan Administration's Human Rights Policy").
3. "South Africa: Strategy for Change."
4. For the background to the Nicaraguan revolution see above, Chapter 17, notes 9ff.

   On March 9 1981 the White House transmitted the first "Presidential Finding on Central America" to Congress, authorizing the CIA to spend $19.5 million to aid moderate opponents of the Sandinistas and interrupt the flow of arms from Nicaragua to other Central American nations. A series of National Security Council meetings in November 1981 recommended a ten-point plan for Central America that opened the way for a full-blooded covert CIA operation against Nicaragua. The meetings called for another 19.95 million dollars to train a team of five hundred Latin American commandos to complement one thousand Nicaraguan contras already being trained by the Argentinian Junta. The target was to be vital economic infrastructure in Nicaragua. The meetings drew up National Security Decision Directive 17, which President Reagan signed on November 23. In December 1981, Nicaraguan contras launched a series of attacks on Nicaragua's remote northeastern frontier, in an operation code-named "Red Christmas." (Chronology from Kornbluh, "Nicaragua: The Price of Intervention," pp. 14–25.)

5. For the OAS and Nicaragua see above, Chapter 18, note 14. It may be worth recalling that international human rights law in 1981 dealt with abuses by governments, not terrorists. It had nothing to say about "subversion," but plenty to say about torture and violations of the "right to life." It insisted that any government that has adopted the Universal Declaration—be it Argentina, El Salvador, the Soviet Union, or the United States—can be held to the same standards of behavior, irrespective of any evolution toward or away from democracy. It did not question the "legitimacy" of military governments, single-party systems, or governments that did not hold elections.

6. Haig, *Caveat,* p. 90. For the controversy surrounding Ernest Lefever's nomination see below, Chapter 21.

7. Details from Nossiter, "Questioning the Value of the United Nations."

8. Kirkpatrick explained why neoconservatives remained Democrats in a 1979 article, "Why We Do Not Become Republicans." Kirkpatrick finally switched parties and registered as a Republican in 1985.

  Jay Winik, Executive Director of the Coalition for a Democratic Majority (CDM), summed up the neoconservative philosphy—hawkish on foreign affairs, liberal on domestic—in "The Neoconservative Reconstruction," pp. 135–52.

9. Nossiter, "Questioning the Value of the United Nations."

10. Kirkpatrick, *Leader and Vanguard in Mass Society.*

11. COHA, the Council on Hemispheric Affairs, accused Georgetown University of aiding the Junta's public relations effort by hosting this seminar. Piñero Pacheco, a right-wing Argentinian entrepreneur, put up $25,000 toward the cost of the seminar. Two other Washington institutions refused to host it. (See above, Chapter 5, note 21.)

12. "Dictatorships and Double Standards."

13. "Authority in traditional autocracies is transmitted through personal relations: from the ruler to his [sic] close associates and from them to people to whom the associates are related by personal ties. . . . The fabric of authority unravels quickly when the power and status of the man at the top are undermined or eliminated" (ibid.).

14. "Generally speaking, traditional autocrats tolerate social inequities, brutality, and poverty, while revolutionary autocracies create them. . . . They claim jurisdiction over the whole life of the society and make demands for change that so violate internalized values and habits that inhabitants flee by the thousands" (ibid.).

15. "No idea holds greater sway in the mind of educated Americans than the belief that it is possible to democratize governments anytime, anywhere, under any circumstances" (ibid.).

16. Human rights groups were in no doubt that the regimes of the Shah and Somoza had practiced torture on a massive scale. Between April 18 and May 24 1978, the International Committee of the Red Cross visited 3,087 political detainees in eighteen prisons in Iran. Red Cross delegates interviewed eighty percent of the detainees and the doctors found that "almost all had scars on their legs and feet." The ICRC subsequently released the mission report after

the Ayatollah Khomeini's government released sections to show the Shah's regime in a poor light. Perhaps the most damning account of Somoza's brutality came in the report of the October 1978 mission to Nicaragua by the IACHR (OAS, *Report on the Situation of Human Rights in Nicaragua.* See above, Chapter 17, notes 17ff.)

17. Farer, "Reagan's Latin America." In addition to questioning Kirkpatrick's view of "authoritarian" regimes, reviewers suggested that she exaggerated the impact of U.S. actions during the civil wars in Nicaragua and Iran. In neither country, they suggested, could the United States have reversed the tide of opposition against the Shah or Somoza.

18. Council for Inter-American Security, *A New Inter-American Policy for the Eighties.*

19. "El Salvador has long been a country where violence is routine. According to [government] statistics homicide was in 1976 (one of the last normal years here) the third most common cause of death—after intestinal infections and gastric diseases" (from a January 15 1982 cable from the U.S. embassy in San Salvador, reprinted in the report "Human Rights in El Salvador," hearings, Subcommittee on Human Rights, House Foreign Affairs Committee, 1983). Human rights groups pointed out that the elevated murder rate in El Salvador was due to social injustice and an ineffective justice system which paid little heed to the needs of the poor. The sharp climb in killings in 1979 was clearly a product of political repression. Overall, however, describing violence as routine is unacceptable. It is an invitation, not only to indifference, but to more killing. Moreover, in terms of its terrifying impact on society and victims, violence in El Salvador is arguably no more "routine" than it is in Washington D.C.

20. "Questioning the Value of the United Nations."

21. *The Hobbes Problem,* pp. 127–37. This paper was delivered during the Institute's annual seminar on public policy. Kirkpatrick spoke at a panel on International Relations and Defense Policy. Other speakers included Lt. General Brent Scowcroft, William E. Colby, and Melvin Laird.

22. "U.S. Security and Latin America."

23. *Leader and Vanguard in Mass Society,* p. 77.

24. *The Hobbes Problem,* p. 130.

25. "The traditionalist death squads that pursue revolutionary activists and leaders in contemporary El Salvador call themselves Hernández Martínez Brigades, seeking thereby to place themselves in El Salvador's political tradition and communicate their purpose" (ibid., p. 133).

26. "The Catholic Left, whose interest in revolution on this earth has waxed as concern with salvation has waned and which acts through any organizational embodiment at hand" (ibid., p. 131).

27. "The present government has been inhibited in using the force at its disposal by our policy makers' powerful proclivity for believing that a government's using force is the equivalent of violating human rights" (ibid., p. 134).

28. "The principal function of terrorism is to disrupt the ordinary life of the society, disturb the normal expectations of ordinary people and destroy habit and order" (ibid., p. 134).

An important point made in the article is about violence. The article appears to distinguish between the traditional violence against people that has always been at the core of international human rights law—the violence of the machete that slits throats and gouges out eyes—and the violence of "subversion." The first is less sinister, if more spectacular, because it remains within the borders of traditional "authoritarian" society.

29. Kirkpatrick apparently recognized this. On the final page, one reads: "Hobbes argues that civil war and anarchy, being political problems, require political solutions. Autocracy is that solution he foresees. It is hardly an ideal one, surely not an acceptable one under our human rights program, but wholly in keeping with the priorities stated by that most eloquent of El Salvador's democratic leaders, Napoleon Duarte" (ibid., p. 136).

30. "U.S. Security and Latin America," p. 35.

31. Ibid., p. 38.

32. The four churchwomen, Dorothy Kazel, Jean Donovan, Ita Ford and Maura Clarke, were killed on the evening of December 2 1980 as they were driving from El Salvador's airport. Dorothy Kazel and Jean Donovan, members of the Maryknoll Society, were returning from an annual Maryknoll meeting in Nicaragua. For the impact of their death on President Carter's policy in El Salvador, see above, Chapter 14, notes 17 and 18.

33. "Ambassador Kirkpatrick, Reagan-Appointed Democrat, Speaks Her Mind on World, Domestic Politics." Kirkpatrick was not the only one to conclude that the four churchwomen were left-wing political activists. A March 3 1981 press release by the Council for Inter-American Security stated bluntly that one of the nuns was active in the Nicaraguan revolution. It also pointed out that Nicaraguan Foreign Minister Miguel D'Escoto was a Maryknoll member.

34. From an interview with Michael Posner, Executive Director of the Lawyers Committee for Human Rights.

35. On March 18 Alexander Haig told a hearing of the House Foreign Affairs Committee: "I would like to suggest to you that some of the investigations would lead one to believe that perhaps the vehicle that the nuns were riding in may have tried to run a roadblock or may have accidentally been perceived to have been doing so, and there may have been an exchange of fire ("Foreign Assistance Legislation for Fiscal Year 1982 (Part 1)," Hearings Before the House Committee on Foreign Affairs, March 13, 18, 19, and 23 1981, p. 163). Michael Donovan, brother of Jean Donovan, and William Ford, brother of Ita Ford, wrote to Haig on March 25 1981 to protest. See below, note 37 for Kirkpatrick's subsequent comments on the affair.

36. Unknown to the four American churchwomen, a Salvadoran National Guardsman at the airport thought their handbags were large enough to hold guns, and he notified his detachment commander, Sub-Sergeant Luís Antonio Colindres Alemán. Alemán ordered five guardsmen (Daniel Ramírez, Salvador Franco, Francisco Recinos, Carlos Palacios, and José Canjura) to change into civilian clothes and accompany him. When the four women arrived in their van at the checkpoint, they were stopped, searched, ordered back into the van,

and told to follow the guardsmen in the direction of Rosario de la Paz in their jeep. The jeep broke down. Franco was left to guard the jeep, and the other five drove off with the women. At an isolated spot, fifteen miles from the airport, Alemán ordered his men to shoot the women. (Chronology from *Justice Denied*, a March 1985 report by the Lawyers Committee for International Human Rights, the group which represented the families of the women.)

Carter suspended military aid to El Salvador immediately after the murders, and sent a three-person team to the country to investigate. The Salvadoran government also set up two investigations. The U.S. embassy, frustrated at the slowness of the investigations, started its own investigation and found evidence that identified the six guardsmen. It informed the Salvadoran government, which arrested the six on April 29 1981. CBS had already announced that the six guardsmen had been arrested in connection with the crime. The trial began on May 23 1984 and ended with the five perpetrators of the killings being found guilty. (Lawyers Committee, *Justice Denied*, pp. 69–77; Bonner, *Weakness and Deceit*, pp. 74–85.)

37. From the author's interview with Michael Novak, October 1983. Kirkpatrick was asked about her airport comments in a letter from Senators Percy and Pell. She wrote back explaining that the nuns were perceived as activists, just as were all the victims of violence in that country: "I think I have some sense of Mr. Donovan's anguish at the death of his sister and I am happy to take this opportunity to assure him and you that my words, spoken as a political analyst attempting to describe dispassionately a tragically violent scene, were in no sense intended as a smear." (Reprinted in Lawyers Committee, *Report on the Investigation*.)

38. "Chronology of Events Relating to the Death of Jean Donovan on December 2 1980," reprinted in Lawyers Committee, *Report on the Investigation*.

39. Kirkpatrick made the same point about Mike Hammer and Mark Pearlman, two Americans who were in El Salvador working with peasants on land reform for the American Institute for Free Labor Development (AIFLD) when they were gunned down at the Sheraton Hotel on January 3 1981, as they dined with a Salvadoran colleague, Rodolfo Viera. The killing provoked a wave of outrage in the United States. Kirkpatrick, who met with Viera and Hammer shortly before they died, said that their work in organizing peasant unions would not normally be viewed as political in a democratic society, but that in a highly polarized socety like El Salvador's it meant that they too were perceived as partisan. (For the AIFLD killings and the frustrating aftermath, see Lawyers Committee, *Justice Denied*, pp. 29–36.)

40. Donovan testified before the Senate Foreign Relations Committee. Lefever was asked about the comment at his own hearings before the committee on May 18 1981.

41. In contrast, the killing slowed in 1983 when the U.S. finally protested and threatened a suspension of arms. Vice-President Bush visited the country in December 1983 and delivered a list of senior army officers implicated in killings.

42. "U.S. Says Mrs. Kirkpatrick Met South African Army Intelligence Chief." On March 26, Congressman William Gray, vice-chairman of the black congressional caucus, called for Kirkpatrick's resignation. On May 12 1981, Gray questioned her about her meeting with the South Africans during hearings on the U.N. budget before the House Subcommittee on Foreign Operations (p. 540).

43. Like Patricia Derian, who had kept empty packing cartons in her office at the State Department, the neoconservatives liked to remind bureaucrats that they were outsiders—Democrats in a Republican administration and political scientists in a world of career foreign service officers. They had their own agenda which people could take or leave. As one commentator noted of Kirkpatrick in July 1982, "Far from pronouncing herself even a deputy vicar of policy, she has gone to great lengths in public speeches to describe herself as an intellectual academic who somehow woke up to find herself in the spotlight without knowing how she got there or being sure she likes it" (DeYong, "Worldly Ambitions and the Affairs of State").

44. For the collapse of the meeting on Namibia see below, Chapter 23, note 19.

45. From Haig's March 31 1981 address to the Trilateral Commission, the policy group comprised of opinionmakers from Japan, the United States, and Europe.

46. For Judge Kaufman's ruling on the Filártiga torture case, see above, Chapter 18, note 8. (Kristol, "The Common Sense of 'Human Rights'.")

47. In 1977 Howard Wiarda had written that individual rights did not have the same binding effect in a "Latin American context" that they had in the United States (*Human Rights and U.S. Human Rights Policies,* see above, Chapter 1, note 12). Ernest Lefever spoke out against the "universality" of human rights standards, in a *New York Times* article (January 24 1977).

48. The point about quiet diplomacy is that if you talk about it, it is no longer quiet. If we think that we can have more influence with the Argentina government by quietly speaking to them about particular cases that disturb us a lot, if we later announce, yes, we spoke to them and they did such and such then we are depriving them of any credit, we are claiming credit for ourselves, we are right back on sort of a public podium. We will have destroyed any possibility of the effectiveness of our policy" (hearings before the Subcommittee on Foreign Operations, May 12 1981, p. 548).

49. See below, Chapter 21, note 16 for Joyner's analysis and its relevance to the debate in Geneva.

Chapter 20. The Carrier Changes Course

1. Novak, "The Reagan approach to Human Rights Policy." Except where indicated, the material for this chapter comes from an interview with Michael Novak in October 1983.

2. From the interview with the author.

3. From *Rethinking Human Rights,* the collection of the statements that Michael Novak and Richard Schifter delivered to the Commission in 1981, p. 7.

4. Ibid., p. 9.
5. See, for example, Novak's "Arms and the Church." Michael Novak is a prolific and elegant writer. In 1981 he was working on a new book *The Spirit of Democratic Capitalism* in which he argued that no system in history had so released individual talent and energy, and garnered such rewards, as capitalism. Indeed, some of Novak's best statements to the Commission concerned the "right to development," including individual development, which he used to try to illustrate the superiority of capitalism over its competitors. But the attitude of the Reagan Administration toward the United Nations in these early days was so negative that there could be no question of trying to turn the Commission to advantage in this way. Furthermore, the concept of a "right to development" was anathema to American conservatives. When, later in 1981, Elliott Abrams argued that human rights could be useful to the Reagan Adminstration, he sugared the pill by insisting that "economic rights" did not exist. (See below, Chapter 22, note 6.)

    During his research, Novak concluded that a good part of Latin America's economic distress was due to its authoritarian culture and its antipathy to the work ethic and not, as Latin American bishops argued, to dependence on U.S. multinational corporations ("Why Latin America is Poor").
6. "Trusting the Yankees." "Michael Novak gave that body [the Commission] the most satisfying chastisement we've heard in five years for the anti-Israel calumnies it was spreading."
7. Novak and Schifter, *Rethinking Human Rights,* vol. 2, p. 16.
8. Kristol, "The Common Sense of 'Human Rights'."
9. Novak told the newspaper the *Courier* on March 3 1981: "For the first time in the history of the Commission and in the history of the European countries, we have been able to criticize East Germany on a question of marriage and emigration." On the afternoon of March 5, Valerian Zorin proposed a resolution deploring Novak's "political motivation" in this breach of confidentiality and proposing that East Germany be struck off the 1503 blacklist. The following day Novak apologized. Gabriel Martínez spotted an opportunity to use Novak's blunder to register his own concern at leaks in U.N. confidentiality and also squeeze some political mileage. He appealed to his Soviet friends to drop the reference to "politically motivated," which they did. The Commission passed a brief two-paragraph decision deploring Novak's leak. East Germany, however, remained on the 1503 blacklist. (Details from the U.N. summary records E/CN 4/ SR 1628 and 1629, March 9 and March 10 1981.)
10. "The Common Sense of 'Human Rights'."
11. For the background to the Sakharov resolution see above, Chapter 15, note 4ff.
12. The loss of the Sakharov resolution by Schifter and Novak was criticized by Professor David Weissbrodt on November 16 1981 at hearings by the House Subcommittee on Human Rights. Schifter responded in detail ("Review of the 37th session of the U.N. Human Rights Commission," Subcommittee on Human Rights and International Organizations).
13. From an interview with the author. Schifter tried to trace his parents when he

returned to Europe after the war, but without success. He did not disclose his loss publicly to journalists in Geneva until 1984.

14. In his memoirs, Secretary of State Alexander Haig confirms that the decision was made early on to oppose any further efforts to condemn Argentina in the U.N. Human Rights Commission:

> The U.S. decided to vote for Argentina in the U.N. Human Rights Commission. We knew that the Europeans would likely not vote with us and that there would be unfavorable press reaction, but Argentina had dramatically improved its record and, in our judgment, further improvement was more likely to be achieved by recognition of that fact than by reducing one of the most important nations in the hemisphere to the status of pariah (*Caveat*, p. 90).

Novak discussed his handling of Argentina at the 1981 Commission at length in hearings before the House Subcommittee on Human Rights, November 16 1981.

15. In addition to the problems facing any incoming administration that planned a radical change in policy, the Reagan Administration was also hampered by early rivalry between key members, particularly Jeane Kirkpatrick and Alexander Haig. During 1981, tension would also develop between Elliott Abrams and Kirkpatrick, two neoconservatives. See the profile of Kirkpatrick by Bernard Nossiter, "Questioning the Value of the United Nations."

16. From a January 29 1981 confidential background paper on disappearances prepared by R. D. Joyner in the human rights bureau. Acquired by the author under the FOIA.

17. "Nomination of Ernest W. Lefever," Hearings, Senate Committee on Foreign Relations, May 18, 1981, p. 80.

18. The author has not interviewed Ambassador Helman for this book. The information concerning Helman comes from cables acquired under the FOIA.

19. From FOIA cable 00100 from the U.S. mission in Geneva, January 1981. For more on Helman and the background to this cable, see Chapter 18, note 23.

20. Helman's cabled summary of the debate showed that the Soviet Union and the Nicaraguans were furious: "USSR said working group has been 'ineffective,' produced 'limited results' and allegedly accorded greater weight to NGO information than to government statements . . . [he] concluded by stating there was no reason to extend WG's mandate. Nicaragua said present government is not responsible for any disappearances that occurred before July 1979 revolution . . . he also questioned accuracy of some material included in WG report" (FOIA cable 01695, February 1981).

21. From FOIA cable 00950, January 1981.

22. From FOIA cable 041038.

23. On January 30 Martínez wrote to Luigi Cottafavi, head of the U.N. in Geneva, warning that terrorists might slip into the Commission and insisting on strict security checks. Ten days later came another intimidating note to Cottafavi from Martínez with brief biographical accounts of seven "terrorists," including Rodolfo Matarollo, and a reminder to Cottafavi that terrorists were capable of disguise.

24. Colville's reaction from FOIA cable 01542, February 1981. Helman's surprise from FOIA cable 01597, February 1981.
25. The author watched Martínez deliver this statement. Later, in 1985, I found his notes in a Foreign Ministry file in Buenos Aires. Helman noted Martínez's outburst in (FOIA) cable 01645, February 1981: "He [Martínez] accused U.N. secretariat of bias and improper procedures in servicing working group." For the case of Angel Nughes, see above, Chapter 16, note 22.
26. Colville discussed his change in attitude towards Martínez in a subsequent interview with the author. See below, Chapter 28 passim.
27. From an interview with the author.
28. The text of Novak's statement was cabled back to Washington by Helman in FOIA cable 01656, February 1981. For the text, see Appendix 4.
29. FOIA cable 01656. On March 4 1981 Anthony Lewis criticized Novak's statement in an editorial, "A Fearful Symmetry."
30. The article, "U.S. Helps Water Down Rights Unit," was written by the author.
31. "Review of the 37th Session of the U.N. Commission on Human Rights," Subcommittee on Human Rights, November 16, 1981, p. 16.
32. "We had the distinct impression that the Ambassador was not at all pleased about certain things that had happened in his country and thought they were far below the level of his civilization and its capacity" ("Nomination of Ernest Lefever," Senate Committee on Foreign Relations, p. 240).
33. Novak's statement to the Commission was cabled back to Washington in FOIA cable 02019, February 1981.
34. Novak, "The Reagan Approach to Human Rights Policy." Abrams's memo to Stoessel, his recommendation to Haig, and Haig's letter to Schifter and Novak were obtained by the author under the FOIA.
35. de Onis, "Argentina Arrests Key Rights Activists." The details of this incident were told to the author by Emilio Mignone in an interview.
36. Those arrested, in addition to Mignone and MacDonell, were José Westercamp, Boris Pasic, Carmen Lapaco, Marcelo Parrilli, Reynaldo Sabini, Lidia Sálazar, and Gabriela Iribarne. Iribarne was a house guest of Westercamp's and was released. CELS supporters in the United States rallied to their defense. Leonard Meeker, director of the Center for Legal and Social Studies in Washington, who had helped Mignone set up CELS, protested to Deputy Secretary of State Walter Stoessel. The Ford Foundation, which had given a substantial grant to CELS, telephoned the U.S. embassy in Buenos Aires to express concern that the Argentinian police might have seized documents embarrassing to the foundation.
37. "The Hunted in Argentina."
38. FOIA cable 052110, February 1981.
39. FOIA cable 01406, February 1981.
40. FOIA cable 054435, March 1981.
41. FOIA cable 01495. According to a June 5 1981 circular cable from the Argentinian Foreign Ministry, the case against Mignone was taken over by Federal

Judge Norberto Giletta from Judge Antoazegui. Giletta dropped the case and cleared the names of the six defendants.

42. FOIA cable 01503, March 1981.

43. U.N. letter to Martínez (reference G/SO 217/1 ARGEN) in the author's files.

44. March 3 1981 letter from Martínez to the U.N. working group (reference 43) in the author's files.

45. From a secret April 16 1981 cable (reference 355/81) from Martínez, in the author's possession.

46. Schumacher, "U.S. Military Courting Argentina Despite Ban on Aid by Congress."

47. Wrote Novak: "We take heart from a recent declaration by a human rights activist Emilio Mignone in Argentina: 'It's another style: maybe just now it's more effective for us.' Strong moderate elements in the government certainly agree. It will be to the glory of both Argentina and the U.S. if history bears us out" ("The Reagan Approach to Human Rights Policy").

48. Mignone wrote:

> I believe that an open policy on human rights matters as the one carried out by President Carter's administration is the most effective towards regimes such as the Argentine government. . . . However, and probably as a result of the previous actions of the Carter administration, the involvement of the Reagan government in the CELS case was effective and probably decisive. This involvement was also the consequence of the reaction of American public opinion to our arrests. . .

49. "Review of the 37th session of the U.N. Commission on Human Rights," Subcommittee on Human Rights, November 16 1981, p. 18.

50. After the author published an editorial in the *International Herald Tribune* critical of the U.S. performance at the Commission, Novak graciously answered the article point by point in a personal letter.

Chapter 21. Lefever's Calvary

1. Press release 3/17/81 from the Office of Senator Pell, cited by Orville Schell at the April 1 1981 congressional hearings on Argentina ("Review of United States Policy on Military Assistance to Argentina," Hearing, Subcommittee on Human Rights).

On March 18 1981 the *Washington Star* confirmed the story and reported that Viola planned to publish a list of between seven thousand and ten thousand names as a "gesture of goodwill" toward human rights groups.

2. *Clarín* (Buenos Aires), March 22 1981.

3. *Buenos Aires Herald,* March 22 1981.

4. See note 1.

5. From a Foreign Ministry letter in the author's files.

6. John Bushnell had been a fierce critic of Jerry Shestack and Patt Derian, as well as one of the Junta's foremost defenders, while serving in the key position of senior deputy Assistant Secretary of State for Inter-American Affairs. He was rewarded by being appointed acting Assistant Secretary of State in early

1981, until the post was filled by Thomas Enders, whose credentials as a hard-line anti-Communist were even more impressive. During his stint, Bushnell did manage to register his skepticism at Carter's human rights policy during several congressional hearings, and express understanding and sympathy for the Junta and also Pinochet in Chile. (See, for instance, "U.S. Sanctions Against Chile," Hearing Before the Subcommittees on International Economic Policy and Trade, and on Inter-American Affairs, March 10 1981, pp. 37–53.) Bushnell was posted to the embassy in Argentina after the Malvinas/Falklands war. He appeared to undergo a change of heart about the Junta after attending the trial in 1985. (See below, Chapter 30, note 8.)

The proposal on Argentina referred to by Ambassador Aja Espil, by Congressman Gerry Studds, was rejected by a vote of twenty to fifteen. It called on President Reagan to certify that the Junta had fulfilled the recommendations of the 1979 IACHR mission on the issue of the disappeared.

7. *Prisoner Without a Name, Cell Without a Number.*
8. Cable 355/81 (April 16 1981) in the author's files. See above, Chapter 14, note 22.
9. The material for this section comes largely from interviews and the reports of the hearings held by the Senate Foreign Relations Committee on Ernest Lefever's nomination. The 577-page report is essential reading for anyone interested in U.S. human rights policy and the contrast between Patricia Derian's philosophy and that of the neoconservatives. ("Nomination of Ernest Lefever," Hearings Before the Committee on Foreign Relations," May 18, 19; June 4, 5 1981; Referred to hereafter as "Lefever Hearings.")

In May 1989 the author interviewed Ernest Lefever by telephone. I found him still bitter at what he termed his "crucifixion" in 1981 and still convinced that he was the victim of a left-wing conspiracy. "I was Borked before Bork," he said, in reference to the rejection of Judge Robert Bork for the Supreme Court. Jeane Kirkpatrick held exactly the same views as he did, said Lefever, but the left "had not caught its breath" by the time of her nomination hearings in January 1981. By the time of Lefever's hearing, they were out for blood.

Lefever said that he had seen himself portrayed in a cartoon with a skull and crossbones. He remains deeply bitter about the committee chairman, Senator Charles Percy, whom he describes as "supercilious and self-righteous," and he is still convinced that Patt Derian was "sympathetic to the revolutionary left." For Lefever's views on the universality of human rights see above, Chapter 19, note 47.

Lefever told the author that he made a mistake in describing torture as being in the "Iberian tradition." It was, he says "a dumb statement." Apart from anything else, the Germans and Russians have proved to be equally proficient as the Iberians. He still believes that the annual State Department reports ("Country Practices") are "arrogant and inappropriate."

10. The World Council of Churches and the (U.S.) National Council of Churches stood for the kind of church activism that Lefever and other neoconservatives detested. Both organizations opposed the sale of infant formula in developing countries and supported the call for a "new international economic order." In August 1978 the WCC announced a grant of $85,000 to the Patriotic Front

guerrillas who were fighting the Smith regime in Rhodesia. Lefever attacked the WCC for funding terrorists in a 1979 book, *Amsterdam to Nairobi: The World Council of Churches and the Third World.*

11. "Human Rights and U.S. Foreign Policy," Hearings Before the Subcommittee on International Organizations July 12 1979, p. 218.

12. Lefever Hearings, p. 75. This scandal, when it came to light in South Africa, was labeled "Muldergate."

13. The boycott of Nestle was aimed at enforcing a code to prohibit the promotion of infant formula. The code was adopted by the Geneva-based World Health Organization in May 1981. For the code, and U.S. opposition, see below, Chapter 23, note 20. Lefever told the Senate committee that Nestle paid his center $25,000. It also emerged in the hearings that he had commissioned Herman Nickel, editor of *Fortune* magazine, to write an article. The article, entitled "The Corporation Haters," was published and widely distributed. Nickel later became U.S. ambassador to South Africa under the Reagan Administration. (Lefever Hearings, pp. 364–71 and 450–57. For a chronology of the baby foods affair see p. 325.)

In a May 1989 telephone interview with the author, Lefever said that Nestle was one of several corporations which supported his center. "We would have reprinted the *Fortune* article whether or not Nestle had paid a donation. We reprint lots of things. We believe in robust debate."

14. Lefever Hearings, pp. 166, 328.

15. Ibid., p. 108.

16. Ibid., p. 357. The quote is taken from a written memorandum, entered by Lefever for the record.

17. Falcoff, "The Timerman Case." "New Timerman Book Stirs Dispute on Author," by Colin Campbell, *New York Times* Service.

18. Lefever Hearings, p. 78.

19. Evans and Novak, "The Weapon Against Lefever." Argentina's ambassador in Washington, Aja Espil, cabled the text of the article back to Buenos Aires (cable 1298, in the author's files).

20. Stanislawski, "Lefeverish Activity."

21. A reference to Buckley's article is made in Hadar, "Sparks Fly Over 'Quiet Diplomacy'."

22. Kristol, "The Timerman Affair." Timerman was arrested on April 15 1977 as part of a large military investigation into Graiver's alleged connections with the Montoneros. Graiver died in a plane crash in August 1976. One analysis from the U.S. embassy in Buenos Aires suggests that Kristol's analysis was wrong—and that the Graiver investigation, and Timerman's arrest, had more to do with the internal power struggle in the military than anything else. "Enough has been said in the public record to suggest that those behind the probe may be wild men searching for evidence to support their preconceived notions." The cable (FOIA cable 02820, April 1977) also noted that the operation was conducted with customary brutality, several journalists having been murdered.

23. "The Strange Behavior of Mr. Timerman."

24. President Reagan was so angry at the vote that he refused to accept Percy's recommendation for an Illinois federal judge.
25. Cable no 1777/1778 (June 13 1981), retransmitted from Buenos Aires to Gabriel Martínez in Geneva.
26. "The leadership of the Argentina Jewish community as well as most of its members, differs profoundly with Timerman both over the situation of Jews in Argentina and how best to secure the community's interests" (FOIA cable 08548, October 1980). What particularly irked Argentinian Jews, wrote Ruser, was Timerman's refusal to be termed "an exiled Argentinian." This "feeds the mills of anti-Semites here." Ruser went on to note that following an attack on "fascism" and "anti-Semitism" in Argentina by the exiled Timerman, a Jewish cemetery in Buenos Aires was desecrated.
27. FOIA cable 08636, October 1980.
28. Lewis, "The Timerman Affair."
29. Campbell, "Weisenthal Denies Slighting Timerman"; Evans and Novak, "The Weapon Against Timerman"; McGrory, "Timerman Shatters the Silence."
30. Cable 369, transmitted by the Argentinian Foreign Ministry to Geneva on June 30 1981.
31. "Argentina Responds to Timerman Affair," The article was cabled to Argentinian embassies (no. 1446 in the author's files).
32. "Timerman Incredulous That Tapes Stir Doubts."
33. Falcoff, "The Timerman Case."
34. Section 725 of the December 1981 International Security and Development Act. For an analysis of the act and its application for Chile and El Salvador as well as Argentina see Moeller, "Human Rights and United States Security Assistance."

Chapter 22. Abrams Recoups

1. Some of the material for this chapter comes from the author's interview with Elliott Abrams in 1983.
2. McClaughry's memo in the author's possession. McClaughry suggested that the "fundamental right to own private property" should be vigorously promoted and backed up by redirecting American trade with the Soviet Union away from state-controlled corporations to the "Soviet counterparts" of American firms with the aim of "subtly undermining the centralized statist economy of the USSR."
3. Dowie, "Abrams: Learning to Live with Torture."
4. The memo was entered in the record of the House Subcommittee on Human Rights hearing on the 37th Session of the U.N. Commission on Human Rights (November 16 1981) and is in the author's possession. For the background see Schifter, "Reagan's Human Rights Policy: Firm Foundations."
5. "The Soviets are a special case for they are the major threat to liberty in the world. Human rights must be central to our assault against them if we are to rally Americans and foreigners to . . . fight Soviet aggression" (ibid.).

6. "We propose that Country reports be turned to our policy goals. Our reports should a) be objective; b) weigh not only the concerned government's conduct but also its human rights record and orientation of opposition within the country; c) look not only at individual cases of human rights violations but also at long term structural questions, so as to give perspective to discussions of Communist versus non-Communist dictatorships; and d) avoid describing human needs (jobs, housing) as "rights" which both confuses the issue of liberty with that of wealth and implies that government has an equally central role in both" (ibid., p. 6).

7. For the controversy over economic and social rights see above, Chapter 7, notes 16 and 17.

8. The Inter-Agency Group on Human Rights and Foreign Assistance, headed by Deputy Secretary of State Warren Christopher, brought together representatives from all interested state bureaus plus representatives of the Departments of Treasury, Defense, Agriculture, Commerce, and Labor, the National Security Council, and USAID. See above, Chapter 13, note 4.

9. Letelier and Moffitt (a researcher at the Institute for Policy Studies in Washington) were killed by a car bomb in Washington on September 21 1976. A U.S. grand jury indicted the head of Chile's secret police (DINA) and two other DINA officials for the crime. Section 726 of the International Security and Development Act banned U.S. aid to Chile until the killers were brought to justice. (For an account of the killing see Dinges and Landau, *Assassination on Embassy Row*.)

10. Americas Watch and ACLU, *Report on Human Rights in El Salvador*. A copy of Shaffer's February 4 1982 memo to Abrams is in the author's files.

11. During 1981, one Salvadoran was granted political asylum in the United States out of 6,199 who officially applied. On June 22 1981 and September 23 1981 the UNHCR appealed to the United States not to return any Salvadorans to El Salvador on humanitarian grounds. On September 1 1981 the Reagan Administration told the UNHCR that twelve thousand to eighteen thousand Salvadorans were deported back from the United States every year, and that claims that they were persecuted were motivated by "political rather than humanitarian concerns." (Details from UNHCR memoranda in the author's possession.)

12. The 1981 report—the first issued by the Reagan Administration—was effectively completed by the time Abrams arrived at the Human Rights Bureau. It was in the 1982 report that he worked his definitional sleight of hand.

13. Maechling, "Human Rights Dehumanized." Abrams's letter was printed in *Foreign Policy 53*.

14. The October 27 1981 memo stated: "In forums such as the U.N. we must address the Soviets' abuses of freedom and liberty."

15. FOIA cable 02403 from USUN New York. The author submitted a FOIA request on Kirkpatrick's visit to Buenos Aires. In spite of the considerable press coverage it received, the State Department was only able to find this one document pertaining to the visit.

16. *New York Times,* June 27 1981.

17. The Mothers' activities were recorded in cable 379 from the Argentinian consulate in New York, retransmitted by the Foreign Ministry to Geneva (cable 1444, in the author's files).

18. Schumacher, "Latins Get Taste of Kirkpatrick Style."

19. From an October 1983 interview with the author.

20. Ibid.

21. Details from an Americas Watch memo, dated May 21 1982. (See below, note 25.)
    Jaime Castillo Velasco had been Justice Minister in the Christian Democratic administration of Eduardo Frei in the 1960s and had already been exiled once by Pinochet. After he returned, Castillo set up the Chilean Human Rights Commission, and on December 10 1978 Theo van Boven, the Director of the U.N. Human Rights Division, was invited to the ceremony to receive its founding statutes. Castillo was mentioned by many inside and outside Chile as a possible president if Chile ever escaped from Pinochet's military rule.

22. Kirkpatrick's comments and the expulsion of Jaime Castillo were sharply criticized by the *Washington Post* in an editorial ("'Quiet Diplomacy' in Action," August 23 1981).

23. Riding, "Costa Rica Up in Arms over Mrs. Kirkpatrick."

24. See, for instance, "Mrs. Kirkpatrick, Loudly," *New York Times,* August 22 1981. During a May 1989 interview with the author, Ernest Lefever underlined the similarity between his views and Kirkpatrick's at the start of 1981. He suggested that the reason why Kirkpatrick was not subjected to the same barrage of criticism was that her nomination hearings took place in January. His took place in May, by which time the critics were prepared.

25. Neier's May 21 1982 memo is in the author's files.

Chapter 23. The Knives Sharpen

1. The author is grateful to Theo van Boven for access to his personal files for material for this chapter.

2. Beltramino's statement from van Boven's personal files.

3. Statement by Santos Nestor Martinez from van Boven's personal files.

4. FOIA cable 01678, USUN New York to Washington and Geneva.

5. From an interview with the author.

6. Colville's letter (reference G/SO 217/ 1 ARGEN) from Argentinian Foreign Ministry files in the author's possession.

7. See above, Chapter 8, note 10.

8. Because of geographical quotas, it can take several months to hire full-time U.N. staff officials. Given that the working group was being extended by only one year at a time, van Boven's only alternative was to hire temporary staff.

9. Trucco's memorandum to Buffum from van Boven's personal file. Antonio Fortín Cabezas had been recommended to van Boven by Edmundo Vargas Careno, the Chilean Executive Secretary of the Inter-American Commission on Human Rights (IACHR). For Fortín's background and association with Emilio Mignone, see above, Chapter 16.

10. For more on the Reagan Administration's efforts to impose zero growth on the U.N., see below, notes 19ff.

11. Voting figures from U.N. press release GA/AB/2088 (December 1 1981).

12. "Review of the 37th Session of the U.N. Commission on Human Rights," Subcommittee on Human Rights, November 16 1981, p. 16.

13. From the group's second report (E/CN 4/1492, December 31 1981), p. 40, par. 77.

14. From a November "grimgram" ("Violence Week in Review") cable from the U.S. embassy in San Salvador (cable 08898, November 1981).

15. This report so alarmed the Americans that they discreetly approached Tom McCarthy, van Boven's assistant, for more information. In cabling this back to Washington, Ambassador Swaebe asked that McCarthy's name be protected (cable 12387). The U.N. group was unable to confirm the meat-packing charge, and it did not appear in the second report.

16. Ambassador Arriolla himself would subsequently confirm that van Boven was correct, and that the Guatemalans were stalling when he resigned in disgust against the abuses of the Lucas García regime. General Efraín Ríos Montt chose Ariolla as Foreign Minister when he seized power in 1982, whereupon Arriolla continued his campaign to delay any U.N. investigation. Three more U.N. candidates would be proposed in 1982 and 1983 before the Guatamalans finally accepted Lord Colville of Culross. For the background to disappearances in Guatemala and the U.N. response, see above, Chapter 17, notes 18–25. For Colville's efforts on behalf of the Guatemalan disappeared, see below, Chapter 28.

17. Apart from his drugged appearance on September 30 1981, the chief argument for Pellecer's having been brainwashed rested on two facts. First, a companion of Pellecer was killed during the kidnapping. Second, a well-known Indian leader, Emeterio Toj, was also kidnapped. Toj was subsequently freed by guerrillas. He later described how he had been brainwashed and forced to denounce the guerrillas.

The author put in a FOIA request on the Pellecer affair and received thirty-one documents. The early cables from the U.S. embassy Guatemala City share the jubilation of the government of Guatemala at having scored a major propaganda coup. But when no action was taken against the groups that Pellecer had implicated (including the Jesuits), doubts evidently began to set in. A month later, the U.S. embassy cabled: "In spite of all the publicity given to Pellecer, his case remains an enigma to many. He has surfaced only twice in carefully controlled circumstances, partly for his own security" (FOIA cable 096877). By December 1981 Pellecer had still not been allowed out of army custody and the U.S. State Department was beginning to respond to worried inquiries on Pellecer's behalf with the words: "We appreciate and share your concern for Father Pellecer." Following the 1982 coup in Guatemala, Pellecer slipped out of the news. Mark Colville visited him in 1984 while on a U.N. mission after Pellecer had left the Jesuits and married. Colville himself told the author that he was convinced that Pellecer had worked with the guerrillas. See below, Chapter 28, note 12.

18. According to the cabled account of the meeting,

> Cohen team assessed its meeting with Director van Boven, principal U.N. secretariat official in human rights field, as a standoff. Van Boven, with a background in Dutch Democratic Socialist circles, already possessed considerable background and knowledge of internal El Salvador politics, and some prejudices which he does not attempt to hide. We doubt that he was fully convinced by the case he heard (FOIA cable 01797, February 1981, from the U.S. mission in Geneva).

19. Before his retirement from the U.N., U.N. Under Secretary General Brian Urquhart told the author he assumed that South Africa felt under less pressure to withdraw from Namibia after President Reagan's election on November 4 1980. The new administration was on record as favoring "constructive engagement" with South Africa and was more concerned by Cuba's presence in Angola than South Africa's occupation of Namibia. On April 15 and 16 1981, Assistant Secretary of State-designate Chester Crocker told South Africa's Foreign Minister Botha in Pretoria that the U.S. would understand if South Africa linked the withdrawal of Cuban trops to South Africa's withdrawal from Namibia. (A memo of the conversation in the author's possession.) The South Africans were only too happy to agree, and the linkage remained one of the major obstacles to a Namibian settlement during the 1980s. It was completely artificial: South Africa's presence was illegal, whereas the Cubans were invited in by the Angolan government.

20. Negotiations on a Law of the Sea treaty began in 1973. By 1980—after important imput by Republicans Henry Kissinger and Elliot Richardson—a package had been agreed on that gave the United States more than most: free passage for its fleets, sovereignty over a large coastal zone, and guaranteed access for Western mining consortia to the minerals on half the deep sea bed. Angered at the prospect of any regulation of deepsea mining whatsoever, Reagan dismissed the U.S. negotiating team. One hundred and fifty nations then waited a full year while the U.S. reviewed the treaty and finally demanded changes that could not be accommodated without undoing the treaty. As a final slap the United States blandly announced that the parts of the treaty which met with U.S. approval were already customary international law. The Reagan Administration voted against the treaty.

   Baby foods. WHO drew up a code to ban the advertising of infant formula as part of its "primary health care" program aimed at preventing disease in the Third World. (Breast milk immunizes infants, whereas infant formula can kill them if mixed with foul water.) The Reagan Administration understood the health risks. In an April 9 1981 memorandum, John Bryant from DHHS analyzed reports from Brazil, Papua New Guinea, and Canada, which showed that "very high rates of infant malnutrition were associated with a combination of factors including advertising" (memo in the author's possession).

   The United Nations budget. The Reagan years were marked by a long U.S. campaign to cut the U.N. budget and reduce the U.S. contribution. In the author's view this was both unreasonable and destructive. The budget for the entire U.N. system (the U.N. and specialized agencies) grew from $402 million in 1971 to $1,313 million in 1980. Part was paid in the form of assessed

contributions; the rest was voluntary. The United States paid twenty-five percent of the assessed budget ($149.7 million in 1980). The Reagan Administra-
tion proposed cuts of $32 million in voluntary contributions to such stalwart
organizations as UNICEF, OAS, UNDP (U.N. Development Program), and
the U.N. Environment Program, but Congress promptly reinstated and even
increased some of the funds. The decision to delay assessed U.S. payments to
the U.N. and fifteen major agencies allowed the United States to save $600
million over four years without formally breaking its treaty obligations.
(Figures, together with analysis, from the testimony of Marion Creekmore,
acting Assistant Secretary of State for International Organizations, before the
Subcommittee of the Committee on Appropriations April 7 1981; and the testimony of Elliot Abrams, Assistant Secretary of State for International Organizations, before the Subcommittee on Foreign Operations, May 12 1981.)

21. Nossiter, "Questioning the Value of the United Nations."
22. From Garza, "Jeane Kirkpatrick—the Iron-Woman Image and Other Myths."
23. Seymour Maxwell Finger, himself a former senior diplomat at the U.S. mis-
    sion to the United Nations, analyzed these appointments in "The Reagan-
    Kirkpatrick Policies at the United Nations."
24. Details from an interview with Dr Pilón.
25. Heritage Foundation, "The United States and the United Nations: A Balance
    Sheet."
26. The U.N. budget for 1984/1985 grew by only 0.7 percent over the previous
    biennium—indicating a far greater sense of fiscal responsibility than that
    shown by the U.S. government. In spite of this, the U.S. Congress allocated
    only $100 million to international organizations instead of the $206 million
    the United States was treaty-bound to pay. To make matters worse, the money
    arrived ten months later, two days after the U.N. ran out of money. A last-
    minute compromise reached between the administration and Congress over
    the ballooning U.S. budget arbitrarily reduced U.S. funds to agencies like
    FAO and WHO—without any regard to whether they had met U.S. concerns
    about U.N. spending.
27. President Reagan finally put an end to the ordeal on September 13 1988, when
    he announced he would certify that the U.N. had reformed itself, and would
    recommend full funding, but it has proved impossible for the U.N. to escape
    the thicket of congressional curbs and restrictions, and the legacy of hostility
    left by Reagan. As of this writing, the U.S. still owes the U.N. system many
    millions of dollars of unpaid dues.
28. "Human Rights and Wrongs in the United Nations," speech by Kirkpatrick
    to the Third Committee reprinted in American Enterprise Institute, *The Rea-
    gan Phenomenon*, p. 46–53.
29. The U.N. had not "ignored" the case of Sakharov. Indeed, Sakharov might
    still have been on the agenda if Kirkpatrick's team in Geneva had acted less
    naively earlier in the year. East Germany was still under indictment for a "con-
    sistent pattern of gross violations"—again, no thanks to the United States.
    The U.N. Working Group on Disappearances had drawn attention to the
    dirtier aspects of the Nicaraguan revolution. While the U.N.'s inaction over

Pol Pot was lamentable, the Reagan Administration recognized the Khmer Rouge's claim to a U.N. seat, and encouraged UNICEF to deliver food to Khmer Rouge guerrillas at the Thai-Kampuchean border.

Kirkpatrick's skepticism about the U.N. was based largely on her view that it was comprised of regional "blocs" which repeatedly joined forces to criticize U.S. allies (especially Israel) and vote through budget increases which the U.S. was expected to pay for. Blocs also exacerbated conflicts by forcing smaller nations to take a position on issues like the Middle East conflict. The United States itself was not a member of a regional bloc because of its global role as a superpower. (For a detailed statement of Kirkpatrick's views see "The United Nations as a Political System.")

This analysis clearly did not apply to the U.N. Human Rights Commission in 1981. The previous year, Jerry Shestack had welded the Western bloc into a formidable unit in this body, and demonstrated that the Commission's bloc system could be supremely useful to the United States when it came to issues on which the Nonaligned group was divided. The Commission's "blocs" did carry dangers, but they were not the kind identified by Jeane Kirkpatrick. They were best illustrated by the Swedish torture convention that was presented to the Commission in 1978. Under the unwritten rule (noted above in Chapter 7), permament members of the Security Council were guaranteed seats on the U.N. Commission. The U.S., France, and Britain thus received three of the West's eleven seats. But Sweden, which was far more committed to human rights, shared one seat with Finland and Denmark. Sweden surrendered the Scandinavian seat to Denmark in 1980—at precisely the time that the convention was falling foul of an Argentinian and Soviet filibuster. The Swedes found themselves fretting from the sidelines as an observer as Gabriel Martínez picked away at their draft.

30. On February 25 1982, the Lawyers Committee for International Human Rights sent a letter of protest to Ambassador Kirkpatrick about the Chile and Guatemala votes.

31. The proceedings of the Managua seminar were printed in U.N. document ST/ HR/ SER.A/11.

32. During the sixteen ballots, Salim reached the minimum nine votes required on four occasions.

33. FOIA cable 12325, from the U.S. embassy in Peru (October 1981). After his election as U.N. Secretary General, Pérez de Cuéllar said that as Director General of the Foreign Ministry in 1968 he had had no choice but to swear in the military regime. An Associated Press story with this information was widely printed (*Bangkok Post*, December 14 1981).

34. FOIA cable 04637. In spite of his long stint as Peruvian ambassador in New York, little was known about Pérez de Cuéllar at the State Department. As late as December, to judge from the cable, doubts still persisted at the U.S. mission in New York.

35. The candidates in the final ballot, in addition to Pérez de Cuéllar, Ortíz de Rosas and Sadruddin Aga Khan, were Carlos Lulio Arosemena Monroy, former president of Ecuador; Santiago Quijano-Cabellero of Colombia; Shridath

Ramphal of Guyana (Secretary-General of the Commonwealth Secretariat in London); and Rafael Salas of the Philippines.

36. U.N. Press Release SG/SM/451 (January 12 1982).

Chapter 24. The Dictators Triumph

1. Seven miners were reported killed in disturbances at the Wujek mine, and another died on the way to the hospital. Fifty were seriously injured.

   The best U.N. account of the events in Poland following the December 1981 declaration of martial law is to be found in the report of a commission of inquiry established by the International Labor Organization (ILO). The report was published by the ILO in 1984, causing Poland to suspend its membership in the ILO (*Official Bulletin of the International Labour Office*, special supplement, vol. LXVII, Series B).

2. The Polish government was also scrupulous about keeping the U.N. Secretary General informed about its emergency measures, as required by the International Covenant on Civil and Political Rights, which Poland has ratified.

3. Michael Novak's press briefing was recorded by the author.

4. The Guatemalan ambassador in Geneva was Ana María Lucas de Rivera. Early in the Commission session, the World Council of Churches submitted an eyewitness account of a massacre of Indians by helicopter gunships in a ravine in Guatemala. The testimony came from a nun, Sister Petronila. Van Boven had it circulated as an official U.N. document (E/CN 4/ 1501/ Add 1, February 18 1982).

5. The role of the Presidential Agency in the killing was first disclosed by the Amnesty International Report "Guatemala: a Government Program of Political Murder." For more details see McClintock, *The American Connection*, pp. 169–78.

6. The author has seen a copy of Olivares's memo, but was not allowed to make a photocopy. For the background, and the author's efforts to confirm the U.S. role in van Boven's dismissal, see Appendix 1.

7. U.N. Press Release HR/1140 (February 1 1982).

8. For the text of William Buffum's memorandum, see Appendix 1.

9. This account of the telephone conversations comes from the author's interview with van Boven.

10. The author was informed by one Brazilian diplomat in Geneva that the Foreign Ministry in Brasilia had a long cable on file from the Brazilian mission in New York about this promise.

11. This cable was sent to Geneva at 2:00 P.M. Mexican time on February 1 by Mario Luís Palacios at Argentina's Embassy in Mexico. Palacios retransmitted the following message to Martínez from Héctor Gross Espiell:

    Ecuador's Under Secretary of Foreign Affairs called yesterday to Martínez Cobo on the business of reaching a decision among the Latin American group over the Director of the Human Rights Division. Martínez Cobo is not interested. My personal opinion is that before taking a position, it might be useful to sound out Pérez de Cuéllar to see what possibilities exist. You can reach me by telex for whatever reason at the embassies of Argentina or Uruguay here in Mexico. I will be in Geneva the last week of February, and we can deal with the problem them. At any event, many thanks from me. I embrace you. Héctor Gross Espiell. (This cable, reference ELCA 4, is in the author's files.)

Gross Espiell knew how to hedge his bets. He had managed to coexist with the repressive Urugayan regime while conducting U.N. investigations into human rights in Bolivia.

12. For the text of Buffum's February 17 statement, see Appendix 1.

13. The author broke the story of van Boven's dismissal in the *London Guardian* on the morning of February 8 1982, before van Boven spoke. Van Boven's statement, referring to "major policy differences with the leadership of the Organization," was printed in U.N. press release HR/1156 (February 10 1982).

14. From FOIA cable 01748.

15. FOIA cable 01760.

16. From a FOIA memorandum (February 11 1982), in the author's files.

17. In cable 347, sent February 17 1982. Copy in the author's files.

18. From the group report (EC/N.4/1492, December 31 1981) pp. 11–32.

19. EC/N.4/1492, annex V.

20. Freund, *Argentina Special Action* newsletter.

21. Mignone's press conference was reported in *La Nación* on January 6 1982. The story of di Bernardo's reappearance was reported in an agency (Noticias Argentinas) report. A copy of the charge against Mignone (case a-34) is in the author's files.

22. "This man has already submitted information to the working group, which is meant to work in private, so what is he doing here? What is more, he was arrested in Argentina earlier this year on the serious charge of violating state security. He has even called for sanctions against his own government!" In fact, the case against Mignone in Argentina was now closed, but Martínez didn't mind: he could use Mignone's arrest as evidence that he was "politically motivated." Nor could he be contradicted, because under Commission rules ICJ did not have the right to reply.

    This account is from the notes of the author, who was present when Martínez spoke. Martínez himself cabled back an account of his address from Geneva to Buenos Aires (cable 470 February 1982 in the author's files).

23. In an interview with the author, Novak said about Martínez: "Maybe he had some purpose. . . . But I couldn't find it. . . . It seemed to me exhibitionism . . . or venting emotion . . . mad pointless play to humiliate Mignone and embarrass . . . him. I don't remember thinking of anything useful. . . . It was like seeing something mad going on and thinking of stepping into the middle: what are you going to do?"

24. Statement by Mignone in the author's files.

25. Martínez later told the Senegalese delegate, Abdoulaye Dieye, who was the first to speak out on behalf of the ICJ, that he had been responsible for the worst day of Martínez's life. (Information from Niall MacDermot.)

26. From the summary record of the March 18 1982 session of the Commission (E/CN 4/ 1982/ SR 61.) This session was held specifically to review an article by the author in the *International Herald Tribune* (March 8 1982), giving details of the confidential vote on East Germany. The five-member committee had recommended keeping East Germany on the blacklist for another year.

Cuba proposed to take no action, but was defeated by nineteen votes to ten with fourteen abstentions. A second vote, to accept the recommendation, was accepted by twenty votes to twelve, with eleven abstentions. As a result, East Germany remained under review.

According to the records, Martínez claimed that van Boven was responsible for this leak to the author, which was not true. During the closed session he also blamed van Boven for a long series of embarrassing leaks since 1977:

> The Argentinian delegation is profoundly troubled by the publication in the international press, year after year, of information reserved for the use of the U.N. secretariat, or information which is false and malevolent on such and such a topic—just like this current situation. It is troubling to note that these stories always appear in the same sources (the *Guardian*, the *Washington Post*, the *Tribune de Génève*, the *Journal de Génève*, *Le Monde*, the *International Herald Tribune*) and that they are always written by the same journalists accredited to the United Nations: Iain Guest, Isabelle Vichniac, André Naef (E/CN.4/ 1982/ SR 61 para. 5).

Chapter 25. The Angel's Wings are Clipped

1. See below, note 9ff. for sources used on the Falklands war.
2. Verbitsky, *La Ultima Batalla de la Tercera Guerra Mundial,* pp. 133–35 and Burns, *The Land that Lost its Heroes* pp. 29ff. give dramatic accounts of the collapse of the Argentinian economy under military rule.
3. Galtieri had been commander of the Second Army Corps during the dirty war, and several detainees reported having seen him visit secret detention centers. Adriana Arce, who was held at a factory outside Rosario city, told the CONADEP commission that during one visit, Galtieri told her that he held her life in his hands (*Nunca Mas,* p. 199).
4. *Latin America Weekly Report,* November 13 1981. For an account of the embassy lunch see the *Sunday Times* Insight Team, *The Falklands War,* p. 60.
5. Mallea Gil's paper was obtained by the *Washington Post* (Diehl, "Argentina Suggests Desire for Normal Relations with U.S."). The plan was also revealed in *Clarín* (Buenos Aires, June 27 1982). Argentina's military regimes had shown little enthusiasm for membership of the Nonaligned Movement since 1976. According to a Foreign Ministry memo in the author's possession, it had brought Argentina few practical benefits, done nothing to ease the diplomatic pressure on Argentina over human rights, and required Argentina to take positions that were patently at odds with its policy. These included criticism of South Africa and Israel (one of Argentina's main arms suppliers, in spite of the military's anti-Semitism) and support for the PLO.
6. Verbitsky, *La Ultima Batalla,* p. 107. Verbitsky gives a detailed account of Argentina's two-pronged strategy in Central America for helping the United States by putting pressure on the Sandinistas and giving military support to right-wing regimes, chiefly in El Salvador (pp. 80–109). For three U.S. accounts, see Kornbluh, *Nicaragua: The Price of Intervention,* pp. 22ff.; Sklar, *Washington's War on Nicaragua,* pp. 84–89; Gutman, *Banana Diplomacy,* pp. 49–55.

7. Verbitsky, *La Ultima Batalla,* p. 100.

8. Ibid., p. 108. Verbitsky writes that senior Argentinian navy officers received incessant signals from their U.S. counterparts that the United States would welcome a South Atlantic naval alliance against the Soviet Union. Between August and October 1981, naval exercises named "Ocean Venture" took place in the Atlantic involving 120,000 men from fourteen nations, further underlining the U.S. determination to protect sealanes from any Soviet threat.

9. For the historical background to the war and the conflicting claims of Britain and Argentina, see *Sunday Times* Insight Team, *The Falklands War,* pp. 32–43. The Argentinian position was that the islands were previously occupied by Spain and so passed to Argentina when Argentina won independence from the Spanish. According to the British, Britons landed on the islands first in 1690. Although Britain left the islands uninhabited for long periods, Britain never relinquished the claim.

10. Jenkins and Avignolo, "Britain's Pearl Harbour."

11. For the background to Massera's plan, and the involvement of the ESMA detainees see above, Chapter 5, note 27.

12. Jenkins and Avignolo, "Britain's Pearl Harbour." Human rights groups accused Lombardo of having caused the death of a young crippled woman, Rosa Ana Frigerio.

13. Ibid.

14. For the early chronology and the U.S. determination to remain neutral, see below, note 21.

15. *Sunday Times* Insight Team, *The Falklands War,* pp. 68–69.

16. Ambassador Gabriel Martínez was informed of the Ana María Martínez disappearance in a cable from Buenos Aires on February 18 1982 (reference no. 338, in the author's files). This cable gives no clues as to the identity of the killers.

17. "Galtieri . . . saw them [the Malvinas] as a short-cut to popularity. The military, after five years in power, was almost completely discredited; the economy was in serious disarray; the beginnings of public unrest could be discerned; there was even dissent in the armed forces. The Junta badly needed a success" (*The Falklands War,* p. 30).

18. Rouco's January 24 column cited in *The Falklands War,* p. 28; the March 3 *La Prensa* column in *La Ultima Batalla,* p. 108.

19. Lewis, "A Not-So-Comic Opera."

20. The author put in a FOIA request for material on the controversial dinner and was told that only one document was found. This was the transcript of an April 11 1982 interview given by Kirkpatrick on "Face the Nation." Denying that Argentina had been guilty of "armed aggression," she said: "Now, look, one has to be clear about this I think. Armed aggression would take place in a clearcut way against territory on which there was clear-cut ownership . . . and we have said we have no position on who owns these islands." Britain's allies in Europe maintained from the start that this did not justify an Argentinian invasion. A U.S. legal scholar was quoted in an article as saying that under the U.N. Charter "peace is the primary concern. In this

view, peace is more important than justice" ("Basis for U.S. Action Cited," *New York Times,* May 2 1982).

21. The United States was so keen to remain neutral before the fighting actually began that it even avoided passing messages between the two sides. On February 27, after talks between Argentina and Britain ended inconclusively in New York, the British delegation asked the U.S. to urge restraint on Argentina. The reaction of U.S. ambassador in Buenos Aires Harry Shlaudeman was that this might imply taking sides. Shlaudeman cabled: "Regarding Luce's inquiry . . . the cost to us here of being perceived as leaning towards the British in this dispute which arouses Argentine passions, could be high and the Argentines would find ways of indicating their displeasure, such as in their actions on Puerto Rico" (FOIA cable 01112).

U.S. Assistant Secretary of State Thomas Enders visited Buenos Aires early in March. Britain repeated its request and asked Enders to ask Argentina to cool down. Whether Enders did so is disputed. Britain concluded that he did not (*The Falklands War,* pp. 26–27). Certainly Enders had other items on his agenda. He wanted Argentinian support for a U.N. investigation into Poland, continuing help in Central America, and even troops for the Sinai peacekeeping mission ("Central America Dominates Enders' Meetings," *Buenos Aires Herald,* March 9 1982).

After Davidoff's landing on South Georgia, the role of the United States became a matter of acute importance. On March 29 at 4:00 P.M., Deputy Secretary of State Walter Stoessel met with Argentina's ambassador to the U.S. Esteban Takacs. One hour later, he met with Sir Nicholas Henderson, the British ambassador. According to a briefing memorandum prepared for Stoessel by Assistant Secretary of State Enders, Britain's Foreign Secretary Lord Carrington had asked the United States to take Davidoff's men off the South Georgias in a U.S. ship. Enders's memorandum to Stoessel strongly suggests that this would not be acceptable to Argentina. It recommends that the U.S. urge both sides to "cool passions," but not much more, and expresses doubts as to whether the United States would achieve much by taking a more active role and offering its good offices. (Part of the memorandum was released to the author under a FOIA request.) At this late stage the Reagan Administration was still absolutely determined not to take sides.

22. *The Falklands War,* pp. 123–24.

23. "The number of reported violations of all kinds fell dramatically compared to previous years." For the section on Argentina see *Country Reports on Human Rights Practices for 1981,* U.S. State Department, February 1982, pp. 328–35. For the October 27 1981 "Eyes Only" memorandum from Assistant Secretary of State Kennedy to Alexander Haig, see above, Chapter 22, note 4ff.

24. *Clarín,* February 8 1982.

25. "Unions Rally to the Flag in Argentina," *Washington Post,* April 7 1982; "Military Seeking Popular Support of Argentines," *Washington Post,* April 13 1982.

26. "Argentina Says a Cease-Fire is in Effect in the Falklands," *New York Times,* June 15 1982.

27. According to Alexander Haig, Kirkpatrick warned President Reagan that supporting Britain against Argentina would buy the United States a hundred years of animosity in Latin America (*Caveat,* p. 269). Haig himself saw the British victory as welcome and long-overdue proof of Western mettle. (For Haig's account of his doomed shuttle diplomacy, and his much-publicized difference with Kirkpatrick during the war, see *Caveat,* pp. 260–301 and "Kirkpatrick Feud With Haig is Noted," *New York Times,* May 31 1982.)

28. Kirkpatrick, *Leader and Vanguard in Mass Society,* pp. 187ff. In answer to a questionnaire for the book, sixty-two percent answered that Argentina should be more independent from the United States.

29. "U.S. Support for Britain Imperilling Latin Policy," *New York Times,* May 16 1982.

30. See above, Chapter 18, note 6.

31. Martínez cabled back details of the discussions in a series of cables to Buenos Aires. Cable 126 (February 26 1982) states that Australia, together with Argentina, India, Brazil, and the Soviet Union "have difficulties" over the principle of universal jurisdiction. Britain had dropped its objections the previous year. (From the author's files.)

32. Meyer, "Liability of Prisoners of War for Offences Committed Prior to Capture: the Astiz Affair." Meyer was the legal officer at the British Red Cross Society at the time. The International Commission of Jurists took a more conventional view and stated that a civil suit by relatives of Astiz's victims would not have succeeded in Britain because torture was not yet considered an international crime, in spite of the Filártiga decision (ICJ, "The Case of Captain Astiz."). Nigel Rodley states the arguments for and against without taking a firm position either way (*The Treatment of Prisoners Under International Law,* pp. 102–04).

(For the Filártiga case, see above, Chapter 18, note 8.)

Chapter 26. The Unplugging

1. Schumacher, "Argentina's Jubilant Rebirth of Politics." Raúl Alfonsín headed one of the two factions of the Radical party known as the "Movement of Renovation and Change." He was not quite the country lawyer that he was sometimes made out to be, although he was only just emerging as a mainstream political figure. His father had come from Spain and opened a store in the small town of Cuascomús, near Buenos Aires. Raúl then studied at the national military school before switching to law. He had entered the National Congress in 1963, but lost his seat three years later when President Arturo Illia, from the Radical party, was ousted in a military coup and Congress dissolved. He took advantage of a split in the Radical party to take control of the progressive wing. By 1983 he was the party's most dominant politician as well as its choice for president.

2. Two draftees, Luis Pablo Steinberg and Luis García, disappeared while they

were at the army college in 1976, when Bignone was the college director. Bignone would be indicted by a judge for their deaths ten days after turning over power to Alfonsín on December 10 1983. He was subsequently charged with destroying evidence on the dirty war while president.

3. Goodsell, "Argentina's Army Brass Stay on Top of the Heap."
4. Schumacher, "With the Military and Economy Weakened, Unions Flex Their Muscles."
5. Diehl, "Argentina's Army Rulers Seek to Block Human Rights Inquiry."
6. For Elena Holmberg's murder, and the presumed involvement of the ESMA GT 3/32, see above, Chapter 5, note 34ff. In 1982, Amnesty International put out a briefing paper on the Holmberg and Dupont cases (AMR/13/28/82).

Gregorio Dupont learned the identity of his brother's killers in 1986 after another tortuous story of murder and intrigue. In 1981, Swiss police arrested two Argentinian police officers, Luís Martínez and Rubén Bufano in Geneva, when they tried to pick up the ransom money for a Uruguayan financier, Carlos Koldobsky. Bufano and Martínez were subsequently extradited back to Argentina. Koldobsky's lawyer also represented the family of Marcelo Dupont, and during the investigation, he learned from one of Martínez's associates, known as Stilke, that Stilke had taken part in the Dupont operation working with the 601 Battalion (army intelligence unit). The lawyer subsequently tried to get Stilke prosecuted, but found that he was too late: Stilke was covered by the 1987 "due obedience" law.

If the aim in killing Marcelo Dupont was indeed was to discredit Massera, then the army succeeded. In June 1983 a judge put Massera into preventive detention for having organized the murder in 1977 of Fernando Branca, a former business associate and the husband of his mistress. Massera was to remain behind bars until the trial of the commanders in 1985, when he was sentenced to life imprisonment. Gregorio Dupont rejoined Argentina's diplomatic service and was posted to Geneva, Gabriel Martínez's old haunt, as deputy chief of mission, where he now works with Julio Strassera.

7. This account is taken from a March 9 1983 update of the Center for Legal and Social Studies (CELS), reproduced by Americas Watch. The graves in Grand Bourg and the case of Miguel Angel Sosa were also the subjects of an Amnesty International briefing paper of October 26 1982 (AMR 13/51/82).

Anonymous graves were found in twelve cemeteries. The total number of bodies was put at around fifteen hundred, but only a handful could be identified. The discovery of the graves caused a major confrontation between judges and human rights groups. Most of the files on the NNs remained closed on the orders of judges, and on January 19 1983 Mignone issued a statement warning that judges as well as soldiers could expect to face charges once civilian rule was restored. When an appeals court ruled on February 10 that the father of one NN (Norberto Gómez) was not even entitled to act as a plaintiff in the case involving his son's murder, Mignone applied to have the court declared incompetent to handle the case.

8. "400 Bodies Found," *Buenos Aires Herald,* October 23 1982.
9. From the author's interview with Mrs. Epelbaum.

10. These statistics from the March 1983 CELS report, p. 12: "Foreign Governments Demand Information on Disappeared."

11. For a chronology of incidents and threats against human rights groups see the March 1983 CELS report, p. 23.

12. Schumacher, "Argentine Rally Erupts in Violence."

13. *Country Reports on Human Rights Practices for 1982,* U.S. State Department, p. 386.

14. "Politicians Criticize Junta Terms for Accord," *Buenos Aires Herald,* November 13 1982.

15. Americas Watch, *The State Department Misinforms: A Study of Accounting for the Disappeared.*

16. From Hoge, "British Advance Halted, Argentines Say."

17. Pirmín Azorena disappeared on April 30 1977, Billy Lee Hunt on April 8 1977, and Toni Agatina Motta in 1980. The embassy files drawn up in 1977 made it clear that the Argentinian military were involved. On April 16 1977, the U.S. consul had even received a note from the Mendoza police saying that a warrant for Hunt's arrest had been issued by the Eighth Mounted Brigade.

18. "Americans Listed Among the Missing in Argentine 'War'," *Washington Post,* May 20 1983.

19. FOIA cable 03467. This cable refers to the destruction of the files, as does FOIA cable 06602.

20. Lawyers Committee et al., *Critique—Review of the Department of State's Country Reports on Human Rights Practices for 1982.*

21. The document's full title was *Final Document of the Military Junta on the Struggle Against Subversion and Terrorism.* It was approved by an institutional act, and fiercely condemned by human rights groups inside and outside Argentina. This was the second attempt by the Junta to ensure that the military was not prosecuted for its actions in the dirty war. (The first, in March 1982, had taken the form of an informal statement of intent by Interior Minister Alfredo St. Jean.)

22. "Vatican Assails Argentine Junta over Its Report on War on Leftists," *New York Times,* May 4 1983.

23. Lewis, "Gently With Gangsters."

24. "Incidente con Madres de Plaza de Mayo tras una reunión en la CGT."

25. International Commission of Jurists, "Argentina's Draft Amnesty Law for Torturers and Assassins."

26. President-elect Alfonsín and his advisers were less than thrilled by this gesture, which they interpreted as an indication that the United States was eager for Argentina's military to maintain a prominent role under democracy, when Alfonsín's actual goal was the exact opposite. All in all, the Reagan Administration showed itself singularly insensitive to the problems facing Argentina's fragile democracy. In November 1983, Lieutenant General Robert Schweitzer, chairman of the Inter-American Defense Board, visited Argentina to talk to senior military officials without telling Alfonsín. Several of those he met would be summarily retired by Alfonsín. (See "The Military Obstacle to Latin Democracy," *Foreign Policy* 73, Winter 1988–89.)

Chapter 27. Betrayal in Geneva

1. The information on these relatives and their groups comes from personal interviews with the author.

2. The group's third report, fifty pages long, was made available on January 21 1983 (U.N. Document E/CN.4/1983/14). During 1982 the group received reports on 2,340 disappearances. 1,733 were submitted to eleven governments, together with a request for information, 400 as a matter of urgency. The eleven governments, the total number of disappearances submitted by the U.N. group between 1980 and 1983, and the answers received from the governments were: Argentina—1,377 cases, 0 replies; Bolivia—32 cases, 7 replies; Cyprus; El Salvador—1,232 (870 in 1982), 72 replies; Guatemala—1,050 cases, 4 replies; Honduras—66 cases, 2 replies; Indonesia—23 cases, 0 replies; Mexico—73 cases, 1 reply; Nicaragua—81 cases, 3 replies; Philippines—201 cases, 51 replies; Uruguay—33 cases, 2 replies.

3. See above, Chapter 18, note 9 for the group's first report. As a rough rule of thumb, it was estimated in 1981 that each printed page of a U.N. document cost fifty dollars.

4. Details from an interview between Herndl and the author. Herndl's career prior to 1982 was distinguished: 1977–1982, chief of the legal department in the Austrian Foreign Ministry; 1975–1977, director of Kurt Waldheim's executive office; 1973–1975, director of the U.N. Security Council staff; 1969—1973, official in the Security Council secretariat. According to one friend, Herndl's two years with Waldheim were deeply unhappy. Waldheim reportedly treated him abominably.

5. In a January 12 1984 internal memorandum to his staff entitled "Challenges of 1984," Herndl wrote: "The [U.N.] organization is faced with all the complexities of the modern world and must nevertheless seek to make a positive contribution in co-operation with the Governments of member states which make up the Organization." (Herndl's memo in the author's possession.)

6. This article was written by the author for the *London Guardian*. The errant press release was the background release for the overall 1983 session of the Commission and, as such, was widely read (U.N. document HR/1302/ January 24 1983).

7. The report was entitled "The Assassination of Alberto Fuentes-Mohr—The Violation of Human Rights in Guatemala." For the background on Fuentes Mohr and the way his assassination forced Guatemala onto the U.N.'s human rights agenda, see above, Chapter 17, note 23.

8. Novak's praise for Argentinian "cooperation" came in an impromptu press conference, the text of which was cabled back to Buenos Aires on March 13 1982 by Martínez: "Novak recalled that in the past other countries—Argentina, Bolivia, El Salvador—had refused to cooperate with international investigations of human rights violations in their countries. After reconsideration, they 'have appeared before the Commission in a cooperative spirit,' he said."

9. The six infants were Mónica Silvia Alarcón; Elena Noemí Francisetti and her step-brother Humberto Ernesto Francisetti/Colauti; Andres Moscato/La

Bunda; Juan Pablo Moyano; Carla Graciela Rutilo. The cases were sent back to Buenos Aires on July 12. Martínez received a reply on September 9 1983. (From the author's files.)

10. Copy of Colville's letter in the author's files. Martínez's flattering September 15 1983 statement to the group was cabled back to Buenos Aires. (Cable 2873, in the author's files.)
11. Foreign Ministry note from the author's files.
12. Martínez's nine-page letter to the working group, dated December 2 1982, in the author's files.
13. María de Mariani's press conference was reported in the Argentinian paper Clarin on February 28 1983.
14. The U.N. group's third report (E/CN.4/1983/14) contains no reference to Martínez's duplicity.
15. Martínez's January 19 letter to Herndl in the author's files.

Chapter 28. The Politicized United Nations

1. For an account of the measures taken by West Germany's democratic government after the Second World War see the paper by John Herz for the Aspen Institute Conference on State Crimes. Herz worked in the Office of Strategic Services in Germany after the war. He points out that West Germany was faced by several essential tasks if it wanted to make a fresh start: first, to establish a correct image of Hitler's regime; second, expunge the Prussian militaristic mentality that turned Germany into such an aggressive and warlike state; third, punish those responsible for war crimes; fourth, purge those who had sympathized with the Nazis. Goals one and two have been achieved, suggests Herz; goals three and four have not. One hundred eighty-five senior Nazis were prosecuted at Nuremberg, with thirteen receiving the death penalty, and eight life imprisonment. Thereafter, however, the Allies lost their stomach for prosecutions. Between 1962 and 1985 some six thousand guilty verdicts were passed down by German courts, of which one hundred sixty were life sentences. The Law for Liberation from National Socialism and Militarism of March 1946 called for a program of de-Nazification, but so many Germans had been Nazis that this quickly ran out of steam.
2. For the cruelty of the Macías regime see Cronje, *Equatorial Guinea: The Forgotten Dictatorship*. Macías Nguema was overthrown in a coup on August 3 1979; he was tried and condemned to death with six others. Alejandro Artucio, from the International Commission of Jurists, attended the trial and concluded that it was fairly conducted (ICJ, *The Trial Against Macias in Equatorial Guinea: History of a Dictatorship*.) Fernando Volio Jiménez visited Equatorial Guinea in November 1980. The U.N. lived up to its side of the bargain and started to coordinate development assistance, but President Nguema, who succeeded his uncle Macias, did not, and democracy is still a long way from being restored in Equatorial Guinea.
3. Marianella García Villas was killed by Salvadoran government troops early on

March 14 while she was investigating charges that the government had used chemical weapons against civilians in guerrilla-held areas. The circumstances of her death were controversial: some human rights groups maintained that she had been raped and tortured, but this was denied by the government, which pointed out that traveling in a guerrilla zone carried risks. For her September 1980 appearance before the U.N. Working Group on Disappearances, see above, Chapter 17.

4. The report states that Nicaragua was told of eighty-one disappearances, and that the Sandinistas had clarified only three. In fact, the Sandinistas had given other information, which is referred to vaguely as "replies from the government relating to other cases referred to in the text" (E/CN.4/1983/14, pp. 30–31).

5. These figures were provided to the author by a member of the Sub-Commission who requested anonymity.

6. The material for this section comes from the author's interviews with Lord Colville and Colville's own reports. Colville's first report was issued on November 4 1983 for the U.N. General Assembly (A38/485, November 4 1983). Following the August 8 1983 coup which overthrew Ríos Montt, he visited the country again between November 24 and November 29 1983 and produced a second, more detailed report for the 1984 session of the U.N. Human Rights Commission (E/CN.4/1984/30).

7. Readers can find Colville's explanation in E/CN.4/1984/30, pp. 9–13: "I do not propose to comment on events prior to President Ríos Montt's accession. Thereafter, however, there continue to be allegations of massacres by the army" (par. 4.11). This is the extent of his criticism of Rios Montt's brutal rule. Colville accepts that a massacre took place at Chichupak, in the province of Baja Verapaz, but does not allot responsibility. He then devotes two pages to vigorously disputing other allegations of massacres. This was to be his approach over the next two years.

8. The dispute between Colville and the NGOs spilled out into the press. (See, for instance, "Peer in 'Whitewash' Row over Guatemala Report," *London Sunday Times,* February 12, 1984.)

    During the years that Colville was the U.N. rapporteur in Guatemala, the Americas Watch group mounted several investigations to Guatemala and vigorously challenged all attempts to downplay violations committed under Ríos Montt and Mejía Víctores. This involved the Watch in a furious argument with the U.S. State Department in late 1982 (Americas Watch, *Human Rights in Guatemala: No Neutrals Allowed*). The Americas Watch also engaged in a running dispute with Colville as soon as it became clear that he too would try to disprove reports of massacres. The Watch criticized Colville in *Comments on Lord Colville's Report* and in *Four Failures: A Report on the U.N. Special Rapporteurs on Human Rights in Chile, Guatemala, Iran, and Poland.* For another highly critical account see *Guatemala: The Group for Mutual Support,* Ch. 7.

9. Wrote Colville about the Santiago Ixcán massacre: "The only possible conclusion at present must be that this event is entirely fictitious" (E/CN.4/1985/19,

Feb 8 1985, par. 41). Colville similarly examined, and dismissed, six other alleged massacres.

The initial report on Santiago Ixcán can be found on page 4 of Enfoprensa's *Información de Guatemala* (no 2/6, March 9–15 1984).

10. Colville's visit to the village was hurried, translation was difficult (no one on his team spoke the Quiché dialect), and Colville was accompanied by two Guatemalan military officers in civilian clothes. These were not the best conditions for a forthright discussion.

In addition, Colville's summary of the alleged massacre left out some important information. The original report from Enfoprensa had contained the following paragraph: "In 1978 Santiago Ixcán had approximately 1000 families, distributed into ten hamlets nearby, but many were killed in repeated attacks by the army and many others sought refuge on Mexican territory." According to Colville's report, the village numbered approximately 410 persons when he visited in August 1984. What had happened to the rest? When the author put this question to a representative of the exiled Guatemalan Human Rights Commission, who was attending the U.N. Commission meeting in Geneva, he was told that the massacre had happened in one of the outlying hamlets. This is not inconceivable given that Enfoprensa had reported one hundred villagers reported killed. Colville told the author that during his helicopter sweep over Santiago Ixcán he saw one nearby village which appeared completely deserted. His army guide said that all the people were out to work, but even Colville found this hard to believe. The point is that while the reports of the massacre may have been exaggerated, there was still sufficient doubt for Colville to be more nuanced. Most important, his detective work was vitiated by the fact that he never applied his zeal to a similar examination of abuses by the army.

11. A/38/485, November 4 1983, par. 138.

12. Colville allowed a team from Thames Television (U.K.), of which he is a director, to accompany him to Guatemala, but refused to give Rex Bloomstein, the producer, a copy of this conversation with the commander until it was too late to be useful.

Colville encountered plenty of evidence in Guatemala to confirm his own political instincts. He met Luís Pellecer, the former Jesuit priest whose disappearance and reappearance had caused such an uproar in 1981. Pellecer, now married, told him that he had indeed sympathized with the guerrillas. On August 16 1984, during a visit to refugees in Mexico, Colville also heard from a former guerrilla who claimed to have been recruited by Jolanda Aguilar Urizar, the young woman whose repeated rape at the hands of the police had been denounced by Julia Esquivel back in September 1980 before the U.N. Working Group on Disappearances. This kind of information confirmed his suspicions that Esquivel was connected to the guerrillas. (In fact, she strove to remain totally independent from them.) Once again, however, Colville undermined his position by adopting the opposite approach—total skepticism—when dealing with charges against the armed forces.

13. Julia Esquivel, it will be recalled, gave evidence to the U.N. working group in September 1980. For the background to Guatemala's disappearances see above, Chapter 17, notes 19ff. For the work of the GAM in the difficult years of 1984–1986 and an excellent comparison between the mothers of the disappeared in Guatemala, El Salvador and Argentina, see Schirmer, "Those Who Die for Life Cannot Be Called Dead." Americas Watch, *Guatemala: The Group for Mutual Support* is essential reading.

14. E/CN.4/1983/14, January 21 1983, par. 63.

15. A/38/485, November 4 1983, p. 35. Colville notes having submitted the list of disappeared from San Carlos in his February 1984 report, written after Ríos Montt had fallen (E/.CN.4/1984/30, February 8 1984, par. 6.2.2).

16. E/CN.4/1984/30, February 8 1984, par. 6.2.4.

17. Americas Watch, *Guatemala: The Group for Mutual Support,* passim.

18. Colville refers to this in paragraph 67 of his February 1985 report (E/CN.4/1985/19 February 8 1985). See pp. 13–17 for disappearances.

19. FOIA Cable 01198, February 1985, from the U.S. embassy in Guatemala City.

20. Colville's decision to reinterpret his mandate from the Commission and suspend his review of the disappearances is harshly criticized in Americas Watch, *Four Failures,* p. 17.

21. In 1987, on a U.S.-supported initiative, the U.N. Human Rights Commission decided to remove the consideration of Guatemala from the category of "consistent pattern of gross violations," and place it under the neutral category of "advisory services." This implied that the violations had ceased, even though no less that three U.N. investigations (on torture, disappearances, and summary executions) showed this was not the case.

    See "Guatemala: the U.N. at Odds with Itself" in Human Rights Internet, *On the Brink of a Mid-Life Crisis,* pp. 84, 85.

    For an example of U.S. enthusiasm for Colville see *Country Reports on Human Rights Practices for 1984,* U.S. State Department, p. 552. The report notes that the United States supported the extension of Colville's mandate although it opposed the resolution on Guatemala at the U.N. Commission—even though the number of kidnapping and disappearances rose in 1984 over the previous year. See Americas Watch, *Four Failures* (p. 33) for the charge that the Reagan Administration used Colville's report to justify returning asylum-seekers to Guatemala.

22. The author learned this from Mr. Zoller.

23. Kinzer, "In Guatemala, a Rights Group Battles Fear, Murder, and the Government."

24. According to one cable from the U.S. embassy in Guatemala City, Colville told a press conference that he was "very sad" about the relatives' reaction and that the GAM was angry that he had not clarified cases "of special interest to its members" (FOIA Cable 09108, September 1985).

25. For a reference to the U.N. reports on violations in Guatemala in 1986 and 1987 see above, note 21.

26. Together with Rice, the FEDEFAM directors were Loyola Guzmán from Bo-

livia, Rosario Ibarra de Piedra from Mexico, Cecilia Rodrigues from Chile, Elizabeth Martínez from El Salvador, and Zenaida Velásquez from Honduras.

27. For the connection between Sakharov's Moscow Human Rights Committee and the International League for Human Rights, and for Shestack's efforts on Sakharov's behalf at the 1980 Human Rights Commission, see above, Chapter 15, note 4.

28. Ermacora's report on Afghanistan can be found in U.N. document E/CN.4/1985/21, February 19 1985.

29. This trend actually began in 1982, when Pérez de Cuéllar was asked by the Commission to find a rapporteur to examine human rights in Poland. Pérez de Cuéllar had served as Peru's ambassador in Poland and he effectively killed the inquiry in exchange for a Polish promise to release a young U.N. official from jail. I am not saying here that Pérez de Cuéllar has similarly influenced all other reports since. But I am saying that having the U.N. investigating Iran and Iraq for torture has not helped U.N. peace efforts in the Persian Gulf, and that this has combined with the rapporteurs' own desire to play a "healing" (i.e., political) role to ease pressure on governments. One can see the result in the extraordinary February 1988 decision by the U.N. Human Rights Commission to drop Iraq from the 1503 blacklist soon after the disclosure that Iraq had used poison gas against Kurdish villages.

   The elimination of Herndl's post—previously occupied by Theo van Boven—removed the crucial buffer that protected the U.N. human rights secretariat from political pressures. It is worth recalling that Herndl was dismissed as a result of the U.N. financial crisis brought on by the United States in 1986.

   The author's verdict on Herndl is disputed by Nigel Rodley, who headed Amnesty International's legal office during the period covered by this book. Rodley points out that Kurt Herndl was a strong advocate of the U.N. convention against torture and helped steer the convention through its final stages.

30. Once again, Rodley takes issue with this severe conclusion. He argues that by 1988, three thematic U.N. investigations (torture, summary executions, and disappearances) existed, and that all three were effective. It might interest readers to know that Michael Posner, executive director of the Lawyers Committee for Human Rights and a leading U.S. lobbyist, disagrees. Posner feels that thematic inquiries weaken the United Nations by diverting attention from single-country probes.

   I agree with Rodley, although with qualifications. As of writing, the thematic inquiries are certainly the most effective arm of the U.N.'s human rights machinery. In addition, the disappearances group did enjoy something of a revival after Toine van Dongen from Holland and Diego García Sayan from Peru were nominated to it. Since that time, it has conducted on-site investigations to Peru, Colombia, Guatemala, and Bolivia, and held meetings in Latin America. FEDEFAM has become a respected source of information, and the group's reports acknowledge the importance of the NGOs. In addition, in 1988, the Soviet Union permitted the group to be extended for two years at a time. In short, the group can celebrate its tenth anniversary, in March 1990, with some satisfaction.

Overall, however, the story of the U.N.'s human rights machinery since the cut-off date for this story has been one of repeated failure to expose serious government abuse, either in the confidential 1503 procedure or in public debate. Iraq, Guatemala, Haiti, and Colombia are among the governments which have been treated with kid gloves for political reasons. The U.N. has quite simply lost the stomach for confronting governments. The United States has contributed to this failure by obsessively using the Commission to try and win condemnation of Cuba, while vigorously continuing to defend other governments which are practicing worse abuses.

Ironically, the U.N. Working Group on Disappearances has kept up the pressure on democratic Argentina. Refusing to turn the page on the dirty war, the group has continued to harry Alfonsín's government to take a tougher position in confronting the military. Julio Strassera, prosecutor at the 1985 trial who is now posted to Geneva, has tried without success to change the group's position, which is in striking contrast to the sympathy it showed to the dictators in 1982 and 1983.

References to the group's recent reports: E/CN.4/1984/21 (December 9 1983); E/CN.4/1985/15 (January 23 1985); E/CN.4/1987/15 (December 24 1986); E/CN.4/1988/19 (December 31 1987); E/CN.4/1989/18 (January 18 1989). In 1988 the group investigated 3,500 cases in twenty-four countries.

31. The government of Raul Alfonsín lifted its objections to the draft torture convention in February 1984, opening the way to its adoption by the General Assembly on December 10.

32. Instead of purging diplomats who had worked closely with the Junta, President Alfonsín left it to the Foreign Ministry to institute its own housecleaning. No career diplomats were dismissed, although Juan Arlia, who headed the Foreign Ministry human rights coordinating office, was placed on the retirement list. Ana Carmen del Richter, who had worked so zealously with Gabriel Martínez, was posted to the Argentinian consulate in the Chilean city of Antofagasta.

33. "Vienna Roundtable on World Monetary, Financial, and Human Resources," U.N. press release DEV/350, September 4 1984.

Chapter 29. Alfonsín's Compromise

1. For the text of Ruser's cable, see Appendix 3. Jaime Malamud-Goti's paper was delivered at the November 1988 Aspen Institute seminar on State Crimes.

   A June 1984 Amnesty International internal briefing document (AMR/13/03/84, p. 16) lists the eleven decrees relating to human rights passed by Argentina's congress between December 10 1983 and April 11 1984. Additional material for this section also comes from Americas Watch, *Truth and Partial Justice in Argentina* and Mignone et al., "Dictatorship on Trial."

2. "Dictatorship on Trial." The February 14 1984 revision to the military code (law 23.049) is still a matter of great controversy. Some argue that it expanded

military jurisdiction and weakened the Nuremberg principle that war criminals can plead "due obedience" to orders, others, that it did the exact reverse.

Military jurisdiction. The argument that the 1984 law extended military jurisdiction over civilians comes first from the fact that the military would now prosecute military personnel for offenses committed against civilians—something that had not previously been the case. In addition, the reform applied to civilians such as police officials, coastguards, border guards, etc., who had taken part in the dirty war. They would now be judged for their role in the dirty war by military courts on charges such as torture, robbery, and kidnapping of civilians which would previously have been heard before civilian judges prior to the coup.

The counterargument, which was put to the author in an interview with Julio César Strassera, the prosecutor at the 1985 trial, was that the reform only covered past crimes committed during the dirty war and that in the future the military would find its jurisdiction reduced and strictly limited to breaches of discipline by military personnel. In addition, any charges arising from the dirty war that were not taken up by the military within six months could go to the civilian federal appeals court.

Due obedience. There is general agreement that the 1984 reforms allowed junior officials to plead "due obedience." It must be stressed, however, that principle 4 of the Nuremberg principles referred only to "international crimes" and that it was not intended to dilute the cardinal rule of obedience to superior officers, which is considered essential to the discipline of any army. (See above, Chapter 7, note 11.) The first draft of the 1984 law was very broad: it stated that anyone acting under orders during the dirty war should be presumed innocent. During the debate, however, the clause "except when they committed atrocious acts" was added. This wording opened the way for the prosecution of hundreds of lower-ranking officers, and this possibility was not weakened by the 1985 trial, as some had feared (see below, notes 21ff). But it did lead to near-mutiny by the armed forces. As a result, the June 1987 law dropped even the exception (see below, note 22).

3. For the sequence of events, see Mignone et al., "Dictatorship on Trial," pp. 138–39.
4. During 1984, sixteen senior officers were identified as having contributed to the Falklands disaster. In August 1985, the prosecutor of the armed forces Supreme Council recommended that ten be prosecuted and six acquitted. This, as the U.S. embassy observed in a cable to Washington was a welcome sign by Alfonsín's government that the military was willing to try its own (FOIA cable 06630, August 1985). Galtieri was sentenced to twelve years detention for the Falklands disaster. The military was totally unwilling to try itself for the dirty war. All were pardoned by President Menem in 1989.
5. Chavez, "Grisly Deeds Leave Argentine Army Unabashed."
6. The harshest criticism of CONADEP came, predictably, from the Mothers. Issue 1 of *Madres,* December 1984, attacked CONADEP and accused its chairman, Ernesto Sabato, of collaborating with Videla. There is not space here to write the history of CONADEP, dramatic though it was. But it is important

to note that its members included several people (like Bishop Jaime de Nevares) who had been stalwart supporters of the Mothers during the dictatorship. Many members of the human rights community, like Graciela Fernández
Meijide, not only supported CONADEP but actually went to work for it.
(Fernández Meijide had lost a son in the disappearances and served as Secretary of the Permanent Assembly on Human Rights.) The CONADEP secretariat was divided up into five separate departments. She was appointed to
head the department that collected testimony.

7. The author interviewed Dr. Eduardo Rabossi, a member of CONADEP, in
Buenos Aires. Dr. Rabossi gave testimony at the trial. For more about the
organization of CONADEP and its staff see *Nunca Más,* pp. 443–71 and
"Como Trabajo la CONADEP" (How CONADEP Worked) in *El Periodista*
(Buenos Aires, September 22 1984).

8. *Nunca Más,* p. 16.

9. See above, Chapter 10, passim.

10. *Nunca Más,* p. 79.

11. The total lack of military cooperation, combined with the fact that CONADEP
could not subpoena witnesses, meant that CONADEP was forced to accept
testimony from several questionable witnesses. Orestes Vaellos, Nestor Sen-
dón, Sergio González, and Julio Emmed were all former police officials who
had been charged with common crimes. Emmed testified that Christian von
Wernich, the military chaplain for the Buenos Aires provincial police force,
gave his blessing to the murder of three young people. After giving his testimony, Emmed said he had been visited by CONADEP officials in jail and
offered $20,000 if he would testify.

12. CONADEP never came out and stated that the "desaparecidos" were dead,
but *Nunca Más* strongly implies it. The Mothers expressed their anger at what
they called this "philosophy of death" in issue 2 of *Madres*. Yet the *Nunca Más*
annex, which contains the names of the disappeared registered by CONADEP,
uses the age that the victims would have been at the time of the denunciation,
not when they were detained. This, clearly, is a gesture to the relatives. For
more, see below, "The Aftermath."

13. "All civilized nations, including our own, have written into their constitutions
guarantees that can never be suspended, even in the most dire emergencies:
the right to life, the right to personal integrity, the right to due legal process"
(*Nunca Más,* p. 8).

14. ". . . [how the trial] will impact on the already charged political athmosphere
as the Alfonsín government struggles to confront its mounting problems"
(FOIA cable 03083, April 1095).

15. Overall, as the U.S. embassy noted, Alfonsín did not want to put the armed
forces on trial, even though the tactic of disappearances had been expressly
aimed at spreading responsibility as widely as possible throughout the ranks.
This was why other military hard-liners, members of the fourth junta, and the
more notorious torturers like Astiz, were not in the dock alongside the nine
former commanders.

16. Although the nine were being tried in a civilian court, they were being charged under the military code, which requires oral proceedings.

17. *Somos,* an Argentinian weekly, September 27 1985. Strassera's background under dictatorship was eagerly devoured by the press, which asked why Strassera had not followed up the petitions for habeas corpus that had arrived on his desk. The newspapers dredged up one damaging comment. In one March 19 1979 legal opinion Strassera wrote: "The constitutional nature of the institutional acts [of the Junta] have been recognized by the Supreme Court," implying that the coup had been legal. Now, here in court, he would be arguing it was unconstitutional.

    Strassera himself freely admits that he kept his head down during the military regime and that he had no idea of the extent of the killing. After he took on the task of prosecuting the former commanders, he was utterly appalled by what he found. Several people say that he became slightly obsessed. "Something snapped in him," says Juan Gasparini, an ESMA survivor. Strassera was so harshly critical of the armed forces, and conducted such an effective trial, that he received death threats. He was posted to the Argentinian mission in Geneva as a roving ambassador, in charge of human rights.

18. See above, "Prologue."

19. FOIA cable 09348, October 1985.

20. Galtieri was not exempted by the 1984 or 1987 due obedience laws because he had served as head of a security zone, but Menem's 1989 pardon squashed the case against him.

21. FOIA cable 10298, December 1985.

    See above, note 2, and Chapter 7, note 10, for the way the Nuremberg trials had sought a balance between the soldier's need to obey orders—obviously critical for maintaining discipline and ensuring an efficient military—and his duty to a higher law when it comes to crimes against humanity.

22. The period covered by this book ends with the 1985 trial, but the trial was followed by a series of jarring military mutinies that unsettled democracy and provoked new concessions from Alfonsín, thus serving as a somber postscript. These disturbing events whittled down the number of officers awaiting trial, until Alfonsín's successor as president, Carlos Menem, issued a pardon on October 6 1989. A brief chronology follows:

    December 1983. Alfonsín allows the military to initiate prosecutions for human rights abuses. If these are not taken up within six months, prosecutions pass to civilian judges. Alfonsín also revises the military code so as to put most of the responsibility on senior commanders, thus opening the way to the plea of due obedience. (See above, note 2.)

    December 1985. The trial verdict against the nine former commanders does not, as feared, absolve lower ranks from responsibility. Five of the nine are convicted. Of the four acquitted, three are subsequently tried in different courts for different crimes.

    December 1986. Several officers refuse to respond to summonses and are supported by the military hierarchy. The government responds by passing the "punto final" (full stop), which requires a 60-day deadline for new prosecutions. Human rights groups hurry to meet the deadline. Some 400 individuals still face prosecution.

April 1987. 1200 middle-ranking officers in Córdoba and Buenos Aires rise in protest when an officer is called to trial in Córdoba, and demand a total amnesty. Alfonsín intervenes in person. This is followed by the June 1987 "Due Obedience" law which effectively grants an amnesty for everyone below the rank of brigadier general. This reduces the number of those awaiting trial to between twenty-five and thirty.

January 1988. Lieutenant Colonel Aldo Rico stages a brief revolt in the town of Monte Casseros.

December 3 1988. Colonel Mohamed Ali Seneildin leads a group that seizes the Villa Martelli barracks. Four persons die.

January 1989. Forty civilians from "Movimiento Todos por la Patria" (All for the Fatherland), a group that has operated legally since 1986, attack the army barracks at La Tablada in Buenos Aires province, alleging that a military coup is imminent. Twenty-eight are killed and eighteen arrested. The dead include Jorge Baños, a human rights lawyer, giving rise again to charges that the human rights groups have been infiltrated by the left.

1989. During 1989, prison conditions for the handful of those still in jail are less than onerous. Emilio Massera, architect of the ESMA murders, slips out to spend a day with his family, while Leopoldo Galtieri even keeps his official car.

October 6 1989. Newly elected President Carlos Menem signs four decrees pardoning one hundred sixty-four officers involved in the uprisings, thirty-nine officers and sixty-four civilians indicted for their actions in the dirty war. Those freed also include Galtieri, Anaya, and Lami Dozo, jailed for the Malvinas/Falklands fiasco. Excluded from pardon are Firmenich, Videla, Massera, and Ramón Camps. This leaves Carlos Suárez Mason as the sole officer still facing possible prosecution for human rights abuses.

For purposes of this book, the crucial event in this sequence is probably the June 1987 law on due obedience. As Juan Méndez points out in *Truth and Partial Justice in Argentina,* the concept of "due obedience" contained in the June 5 1987 law was broader than the 1984 revision to the military code, which had at least made an exception for "atrocious and aberrant acts." (See above, note 2.) The June 1987 law exempted only three offenses—rape, theft, and falsification of civil status (the crime by which the disappeared infants were given false identities and given to other families). Human rights groups argued that the June 1987 due obedience law violated both Argentina's constitution, which guarantees equality before the law, and the new U.N. torture convention, which upholds the Nuremberg principle that no one can plead orders as an excuse for practicing torture.

23. Inevitably, the verdict left the relatives angry and deflated. For the Mothers' reaction see Schirmer, "Those Who Die for Life Cannot Be Called Dead."

24. FOIA cable 10298, December 1985.

Chapter 30. The Denuncia

1. The material for this section is taken from the author's interviews with Theo van Boven and van Boven's testimony at the trial on April 23 1985 (printed in *Diario del Juicio*).
2. Van Boven's reference to fascism was the only part of his testimony that made the international press ("Argentina Junta Compared to Nazis," *International Herald Tribune*, April 25 1985).
3. By coincidence, Jeane Kirkpatrick was also present in Geneva the same day as van Boven, participating at a round table on refugees. The two did not meet.
4. Carlos Cabeza in *Diario del Juicio* 4, p. 2.
5. FOIA cable 04734, June 1985.
6. FOIA cable 04734 gave a full account of Derian's testimony, which was also reprinted verbatim in *Diario del Juicio* 9, July 23 1985.
7. FOIA cable 04734. See above, Chapter 12.
8. See above, Chapter 26, note 13.
9. From FOIA cable 04303.
10. From a U.S. embassy memo obtained by the author under the FOIA. As well as trying to discourage Tom Farer, the IACHR refused to allow Edmundo Vargas, its Chilean-born Executive Director, to testify.
11. Mignone managed to get in a sharp jab at Videla: "Other officers who were in the same course at college recall his inability to assume responsibility and remember that his tendency to cynicism and deceit characterized his whole military career." *Diario del Juicio* made Mignone its witness of the week in July 1985.
12. The author watched part of the trial with Matarollo from the press benches. This was satisfying for me, too, since my first article from Geneva in 1977 had been about Martínez and Matarollo.
13. *Diario del Juicio* 15 provides some interesting statistics about the trial: 500 separate files from the Supreme Council of the Armed Forces (each file containing 200 pages); 4,000 diplomatic notes; 709 individual cases; 833 witnesses, including 64 military personnel, 13 priests, 15 journalists, and 12 foreigners; 1.3 million photocopied pages; 80 testimonies from witnesses like Ana María Martí, recorded at embassies abroad; 30 people employed on the trial; 78 separate sessions, of which the longest was 13 hours, 25 minutes; longest single testimony—the 5 hours and 40 minutes spent by Victor Basterra recalling how he had forged documents and taken photos while detained at the ESMA; 672 journalists accredited to cover the trial, 158 of them foreigners.
14. From Martínez's testimony on May 16 1985, reprinted in *Diario del Juicio*.
15. *El Periodista*, December 15 1985.
16. "With Astiz's Liberation, Impunity Becomes Law" (*Madres*, March 5 1985).
17. For Astiz and his story see Americas Watch, *Truth and Partial Justice in Argentina*, pp. 41–46.
18. Hagelin, *Mi Hija Dagmar*, pp. 155ff.

Notes to Aftermath.

1. The bodies of the Lanouscou family had been been exhumed in the San Isidro cemetery. The exhumation had found the clothes of a fifth family member, five-month-old Matilde, but no bones. Snow confirmed the finding: Matilde had not been killed with the rest of her family, and could thus be assumed to be alive.

    Clyde Snow's involvement in Argentina began in 1982, when a group of Grandmothers visited the headquarters of the American Association for the Advancement of Science and met Eric Stover, director of the AAAS Committee on Scientific Freedom and Responsibility. In June 1984 Stover organized a visit to Argentina of five American forensic experts to advise on identifying the unknown dead. They included Snow and Mary-Claire King, a geneticist from California. During the visit, Snow was asked by a judge whether a skeleton could be identified as having been Héctor Hidalgo Sola, the ambassador to Venezuela who disappeared (see above, Chapter 5, note 31). Snow compared the bones with Sola's medical records and concluded that the dead man was not Sola. (For Stover's account of the discovery see "The Disappeared of Argentina: Not Without Trace.")

    The use of science in the cause of human rights was still in its infancy and the first thing that Snow had to impress on his Argentinian hosts was to use extreme care in uncovering the bodies. By carelessly handling the skeletons, cemetery workers could lose vital clues like teeth and bullets. Snow started by uncovering the feet of the body, which showed the way it was lying. He then carefully removed all the earth from around it, checking to see that there were no other traces of bones.

2. Paula Eva Logares was twenty-three months old when she was kidnapped by a band of armed men with her parents in Montevideo at 3:30 in the afternoon of May 18 1978. Her parents then disappeared. Paula was adopted by Rubén Luis Lavallén, a police detective at the San Justo detention center. Lavallén had ingeniously concealed his adopted daughter's real identity. He maintained that she was born on October 29 1977 at a family residence, without medical assistance, and that her birth had been registered belatedly on May 18 1978 (the date of her abduction in Uruguay). Jorge Héctor Vidal, the police obstetrician, had forged the new birth certificate, and another police officer had allowed Lavallén to use his private address. The forgery meant that Paula was registered as being almost two years younger than she was, which placed her two years behind her contemporaries in school.

    In 1980, the Grandmothers received a tip-off about Paula's true identity. Lavallén had now retired and was in charge of security at the Mercedes Benz factory in Buenos Aires. He moved, and dropped out of sight. Three more years passed before the Grandmothers received another anonymous phone call at the end of July 1983. Elsa Pavón de Aguilar, the child's grandmother, went to stake out a house, found the local school, and watched Paula at play. She was convinced that she was watching her granddaughter. She then learned that

Lavallén was making plans to leave the country, so she applied for a court order to stop Lavallén. The judge ordered a genetic test on both Pavón and Paula.

This test was conducted by the geneticist Mary-Claire King. Tests of this kind are commonly used in paternity suits, by matching blood groups, red cell enzymes, and plasma protein, but they had never before been used to legally prove a relationship between grandparent and grandchild. The test proved 99 percent positive, but Judge Edgardo Fegoli was still not convinced. He received an urgent visit from a group of child psychologists who had volunteered their services to the Grandmothers. They argued that Paula would have to find out about her true parents some day, and that the longer the delay the greater the trauma. The judge summoned Lavallén, who replied that he and his wife had provided a loving home for Paula. Breaking up yet another family would only create more grief all round. Eventually Paula was returned to her grandparents. (On October 14 1986 the PBS series "Nova" broadcast an excellent film about the work of Clyde Snow and Mary-Claire King in Argentina. Transcript available from WGBH, Boston.)

3. "Exigimos Respeto," (We demand respect), *Tiempo Argentina*, March 11 1985.

The exhumation of Liliana Pereyra was one of ten performed by Clyde Snow during this, his second visit to Argentina. Snow returned at the invitation of Eduardo Rabossi, formerly member of CONADEP and now Sub-Secretary of Human Rights at the Ministry of Interior. Rabossi's department was charged with identifying the unknown dead, and Snow gave a series of training sessions for Argentinians in addition to performing the exhumations.

Twenty-one-year-old Liliana Carmen Pereyra Assarri, a bank employee, was abducted in Mar del Plata on October 5 1977, when she was five months pregnant. Several months later, her mother was told that she had been killed in a shootout on July 15 1978, and buried in the Parque cemetery in Mar del Plata. Liliana's mother waited until 1983 before looking through the cemetery records until she found an entry that appeared to correspond to a young woman of her daughter's age. Meanwhile, Ana María Martí and the two other former detainees at the ESMA school had been released and testified to having seen Liliana in the ESMA. Shortly after Liliana gave birth, naval personnel from the Mar del Plata base came and took her away.

When Liliana Pereyra's mother heard that Snow was once again in Argentina, she asked for his help. When he finally examined the skeleton in the Parque cemetery, Snow concluded that a slight misshapenness in the pelvic bone indicated that the young woman gave birth shortly before she died. In addition, Snow found no smaller bones inside the pelvic region to indicate a fetus. The upper left canine tooth was missing, and the back of the skull shattered by a shot. He was even able to identify the make of the gun—an Ithaca shotgun—from the pellets. Liliana's mother confirmed that her daughter had been to the dentist shortly before her abduction. She also produced a chest X-ray of Liliana's which would seem to correspond to the skeleton.

Eric Stover and Clyde Snow both testified at the trial of the nine commanders on April 24 1985. A group known as the Argentine Forensic Anthropology Team (EAAF) has continued Snow's work, but as of late 1988 roughly only twenty of the hundred bodies exhumed had been identified.

4. In late 1986, María Adela de Antokoletz led a break-away movement of Mothers who were angered by de Bonafini's authoritarian style and open attacks on Alfonsín.

Bibliography

The material for this book comes from four main primary sources: submissions by the author under the U.S. Freedom of Information Act; Argentinian government documents and cables collected by the author in Argentina; United Nations documents; interviews conducted by the author. Published material is also used.

PRIMARY SOURCES

Freedom Of Information Act (FOIA)

Between 1983 and 1988 I submitted twenty-seven requests for information under the Freedom of Information Act. The material released is referred to throughout in the text as FOIA, followed by the origin, number and date of the cable.

Argentinian government cables

In September 1985 I traveled to Buenos Aires to cover the trial of the nine former military commanders and was given unconditional access to the enormous amount of material collected by the prosecution. This included files from the Argentinian mission in Geneva. No restrictions were imposed on my use of the material. Most of these documents are dated and authored, and are referred to as such in the text and notes.

While in Buenos Aires I also made copies of several longer Foreign Ministry memoranda. These are neither dated nor authored, but the approximate date is clear from their contents, and their authenticity has been confirmed by Argentinians. The first memo, eighteen pages in length, was written in early 1977, and is referred to in the text as Memo A. Memo B is a sixty-page document entitled "Human Rights: The external situation of the Argentinian government between 1976 and 1980." Memo C, written in mid-1977, is thirty-eight pages in length and is entitled "Human Rights." Memo D, eight pages long, is the text of an address that was delivered by a senior Foreign Ministry official to colleagues shortly before the November 4 presidential elections in the United States. It is written on headed Foreign Ministry paper and is stamped "secret."

United Nations documents

The reader will find references to U.N. documents, including those under the confidential 1503 procedure. It will be clear from the text that I consider the confidentiality of the 1503 procedure to have been widely abused by governments. It is also important to note that journalists are under no moral or legal obligation to respect the confidentiality of this procedure—particularly as governments cynically leak 1503 material as and when it serves their purpose. Nonetheless, I have generally limited my use of 1503 material to what was provided by Argentinian authorities in Buenos Aires. In 1983 the government of Argentina asked the U.N. to make public all the 1503 material pertaining to Argentina. Uruguay followed suit. This material has not been made widely available because of budgetary constraints at the U.N.

Interviews conducted by the author

These will be referred to where appropriate. It is not possible to list the names of all those who have generously helped me in the preparation of this book and have provided me with guidance and information during my work as a journalist, but I am duly grateful.

PUBLISHED MATERIAL

The following bibliography is arranged in eight sections, covering: (1) Argentina, Latin America, and disappearances; (2) Uruguay; (3) El Salvador; (4) Guatemala; (5) Nicaragua; (6) the United Nations, the OAS, and the international human rights movement; (7) United States human rights policy; (8) U.S. government and congressional material.

Argentina, Latin America, and Disappearances

"Americans Listed Among the Missing in Argentine 'War'." Washington Post, May 20 1983.
Americas Watch. *Chile Since the Coup.* New York, August 25 1983.
———. *The State Department Misinforms: A Study of Accounting for the Disappeared in Argentina.* New York, October 1983.
Amnesty International. *Report of the Mission to Argentina, November 6–15 1976.* Amnesty Publications, London, 1977.
———. *Testimony on Secret Detention Camps in Argentina.* Amnesty Publications, London, 1980.
———. *The State of Siege and Political Imprisonment in Argentina.* Amnesty International External Paper, AMR 13/18/82, 1982.

Amnesty International USA. *Disappearances: A Workbook.* An Amnesty International USA Publication, April 1981.

Andersen, Martin Edwin. "Argentina's Dirty Secrets." *The Nation,* March 13 1989.

———. "Kissinger and the 'Dirty War'." *The Nation,* October 31 1987.

———. "The Military Obstacle to Latin Democracy." *Foreign Policy* 73, Winter 1988–89.

Anderson, Jack. "The Art of Making Bad Look Good." *New York Daily News,* May 30 1978.

"Argentina Junta Compared to Nazis." *International Herald Tribune,* April 25 1985.

"Argentina Responds to Timerman Affair." *New York Times,* July 3 1981.

"Argentina Says a Cease-Fire is in Effect in the Falklands." *New York Times,* June 15 1952.

"Argentine Rights Activist Wins Nobel Peace Prize." *New York Times,* October 14 1980.

Aspen Institute for Humanistic Studies. *State Crimes: Punishment or Pardon.* Proceedings, Conference on State Crimes, Rye Woods, N.Y., November 4–6 1988.

Association of the Bar of the City of New York. *Report of the Mission of Lawyers to Argentina,* April 1–7 1979.

Berman, Maureen, and Roger Clark. "State Terrorism: Disappearances." *Rutgers Law Journal,* vol. 13, 1983.

Bonasso, Miguel. *Recuerdos de la Muerte (Recollections of Death).* Bruguera, Buenos Aires, 1984.

Bousquet, Jean-Pierre. *Las Locas de la Plaza de Mayo (The Crazy Women of the Plaza de Mayo).* Fundación para la democracia, Buenos Aires, 1983.

Burns, Jimmy. *The Land That Lost its Heroes.* Bloomsbury, London, 1987.

———. "The Church in Argentina" and "A Church that Failed." *The Tablet,* April 1985.

Campbell, Colin. "New Timerman Book Stirs Dispute on Author." *New York Times Service,* 1981.

———. "Weisenthal Denies Slighting Timerman." *New York Times,* June 14 1981.

Chavez, Lydia. "Grisly Deeds Leave Argentine Army Unabashed." *New York Times,* December 26 1984.

Claude, Richard Pierre. "The Case of Joelito Filartiga and the 'Clinic of Hope'." *Human Rights Quarterly,* vol. 5, 1983, pp. 275–95. Reprinted with changes in Stover and Nightingale, eds., *The Breaking of Bodies and Minds,* pp. 79–100; and in Claude and Weston, eds., *Human Rights in the World Community: Issues and Answers,* pp. 272–81.

Claude, Richard Pierre and Burns H. Weston, eds. *Human Rights in the World Community: Issues and Answers.* University of Pennsylvania Press, Philadelphia, 1989.

CONADEP (The Argentine National Commission on the Disappeared). *Nunca Más (Never Again).* Buenos Aires University Press, 1985. Volume 1 of *Nunca Más* is the report of the commission, Volume 2 the CONADEP list of disappeared. *Nunca Más* is also available in English. Farrar, Straus, Giroux, New York, 1986. References in the text are to the Spanish version.

"Death Camp Man Goes Home." *South African Sunday Tribune,* June 12 1981.

De Onis, Juan. "Argentina Arrests Key Rights Activists." *New York Times,* February 28 1981.

El Diario del Juicio (The Journal of the Trial). Editorial Perfil, Buenos Aires. The newspaper which covered the trial of the former commanders between March 1985 and January 1986, reported verbatim on important testimony, and printed transcripts of the prosecution, defense, and verdict.

Diehl, Jackson. "Argentina Suggests Desire for Normal Relations with U.S." *Washington Post,* July 7 1982.

———. "Argentina's Army Rulers Seek to Block Human Rights Inquiry." *Washington Post,* August 10 1982.

Dinges, John and Saul Landau. *Assassination on Embassy Row.* McGraw-Hill, New York, 1980.

Duhalde, Eduardo. *El Estado Terrorista Argentina (The Terrorist State of Argentina).* El Caballito, Buenos Aires, 1983.

Evans, Ronald and Robert Novak. "The Weapon Against Timerman." *Washington Post,* June 17, 1981.

Falcoff, Mark. "The Timerman Case." *Commentary,* July 1981.

Foster, Douglas. "After the Terror." *Mother Jones,* February/March 1985.

"400 Bodies Found." *Buenos Aires Herald,* October 23 1982.

Fragoso, Heleno. *The Situation of Defense Lawyers in Argentina.* Report prepared for the International Commission of Jurists, Geneva, March 1975.

Freund, Marketa L. "The Law and Human Rights in Argentina." *Worldview,* May 1979.

———. *Argentina Special Action.* Amnesty International Newsletter, November 21 1982.

Frontalini, Daniel and María Cristina Caiati. *El Mito de la Guerra Sucia (The Myth of the Dirty War).* CELS Publication, Buenos Aires, 1984.

Garro, Alejandro. "The Role of the Argentine Judiciary in Controlling Governmental Action Under a State of Siege." *Human Rights Law Journal,* vol. 4, no. 3, 1983.

Gasparini, Juan. *La Pista Suiza (The Swiss Trail).* Legasa, Buenos Aires, 1986.

———. *Montoñeros: Final de Cuentas (Montoñeros: The Final Reckoning).* Puntosur, Buenos Aires, 1988.

Gibson, Janice and Mika Haritos-Fatouros. "The Education of a Torturer." *Psychology Today,* November 1986.

Goodsell, James. "Argentina's Army Brass Stay on Top of the Heap." *Christian Science Monitor,* August 11 1982.

Government of Argentina. *Evolución de la Delinquencia Terrorista en la Argentina (Evolution of Terrorism in Argentina).* Buenos Aires, 1979.

Graham-Yooll, Andrew. *Portrait of an Exile.* Junction Books, London, 1985.

Hadar, Leon. "Sparks Fly over 'Quiet Diplomacy'." *Jerusalem Post,* June 20 1981.

Hagelin, Ragnar. *Mi Hija Dagmar (My Daughter Dagmar).* Sudamericana, Buenos Aires, 1984.

Herz, John. Paper presented at the Aspen Institute for Humanistic Studies Conference on State Crimes, Rye Woods, N.Y., November 6 1988.

Hilton, Isabel. "Death Squad Secrets Revealed." *London Sunday Times,* May 8 1983.

Hoge, Warren. "British Advance Halted, Argentines Say." *New York Times,* June 11 1982.

———. "The Case of Captain Astiz." *ICJ Review,* June 1982.

"Human Rights Group Opens Inquiry in Argentina." *New York Times,* September 7 1978.

"The Hunted in Argentina." *New York Times,* March 5 1981.

"Iglesia y Dictadura." *El Periodista,* Buenos Aires, September 22–28 1984.

"Incidente con Madres de Plaza de Mayo tras una reunión en la CGT." *Políticá,* Buenos Aires, September 9 1983.

International Commission on International Humanitarian Issues. *Disappearances.* Zed Books, London, 1986.

International Commission of Jurists. "Argentina's Draft Amnesty Law for Torturers and Assassins." Press release, June 16 1983.

Jenkins, Simon and María Laura Avignolo. "Britain's Pearl Harbour." *London Sunday Times,* March 22 and March 29 1987.

Kirkpatrick, Jeane. *Leader and Vanguard in Mass Society: A Study of Perónist Argentina.* MIT Press, Cambridge, Mass., 1971.

Kristol, Irving. "The Timerman Affair." *Wall Street Journal,* May 29 1981.

"Latin America's Terrorist International." *London Economist Foreign Report,* March 23 1977.

Lawyers Committee for International Human Rights. *Violations of Human Rights in Argentina.* New York, 1980.

Lawyers Committee for International Human Rights, Americas Watch, Helsinki Watch. *Critique: Review of the Department of State's Country Reports on Human Rights Practices for 1982.* New York, February 1983.

Lernoux, Penny. *Cry of the People.* Doubleday, Garden City, N.Y., 1980.

Lewis, Anthony. "A Fearful Symmetry." *New York Times,* March 4 1981.

———. "The Timerman Affair." *New York Times,* June 14 1981.

———. "A Not-So-Comic Opera." *New York Times,* April 8 1982.

———. "Gently With Gangsters." *New York Times,* May 23 1983.

Madres. (*Mothers*) The monthly journal of the Mothers of the Plaza de Mayo. Sociedád Impresora Americana, Buenos Aires, 1985–.

Maechling, Charles. "The Argentina Pariah." *Foreign Policy,* vol. 45, Winter 1981–82.

Martí, Ana María. Testimony delivered at the French National Assembly on October 12 1979.

McGrory, Mary. "Timerman Shatters the Silence." *Washington Star,* June 14 1981.

Méndez, Juan. *Truth and Partial Justice in Argentina.* Americas Watch, New York, 1988.

Meyer, Michael. "Liability of Prisoners of War for Offences Committed Prior to Capture: The Astiz Affair." *International and Comparative Law Quarterly,* vol. 32, October 1983.

Miguens, José Enrique. *Honor Militar, Conciencia Moral y Violencia Terrorista (Military Honor, Moral Conscience and Terrorist Violence).* Sudamericana Planeta, Buenos Aires, 1986.

Mignone, Emilio. *Witness to the Truth.* Orbis Books, New York, 1988. First published in Argentina as *Iglesia y Dictadura* (*Church and Dictatorship*). Ediciones del Pensamiento Nacional, Buenos Aires, 1986.

Mignone, Emilio, Cynthia Estlund, and Samuel Issacharoff. "Dictatorship on Trial: Prosecution of Human Rights Violations in Argentina." *Yale Journal of International Law*, vol. 10, no. 1, fall 1984.

"Military Seeking Popular Support of Argentines." *Washington Post,* April 13 1982.

Mine, Douglas Grant. "Argentina Accused of Gulag Operation." Associated Press, May 1 1983.

Munck, Ronaldo. *Argentina—from Anarchism to Perónism*. Zed Press, London, 1987.

Naipaul, V.S. *The Return of Eva Perón*. Vintage Books, New York, 1981.

Nosiglia, Julio. *Botín de Guerra* (*War Booty*). Abuelas de la Plaza de Mayo, Buenos Aires, 1985.

Omang, Joanne. "Latin American Left, Right Say U.S. Militarized Continent." *Washington Post,* April 11 1977.

Organization of American States. *Report on the Situation of Human Rights in Argentina*. OAS, Washington, D.C., April 11 1980.

Peri, Camille. "Getting to Know the Lord of Life and Death." *Mother Jones,* September 1987.

"Politicians Criticize Junta Terms for Accord." *Buenos Aires Herald,* November 13 1982.

Rock, David. *Argentina, 1516–1987: From Spanish Colonization to the Falklands War and Alfonsín*. I.B. Tauris, London, 1986.

Schirmer, Jennifer. "Those Who Die for Life Cannot Be Called Dead: Women and Human Rights Protest in Latin America." *Harvard Law School Human Rights Yearbook,* vol. 1, 1988, pp. 54–61.

Schoultz, Lars. *Human Rights and United States Policy Toward Latin America*. Princeton University Press, Princeton, N.J., 1981.

Schumacher, Edward. "U.S. Military Courting Argentina Despite Ban on Aid by Congress." *New York Times,* April 8 1981.

———. "Argentina's Rebirth of Politics." *New York Times,* July 21 1982.

———. "With the Military and Economy Weakened, Unions Flex Their Muscles." *New York Times,* August 15 1982.

———. "Argentina Rally Erupts in Violence." *New York Times,* December 16 1982.

Shestack, Jerome. "The Case of the Disappeared." *International League for Human Rights,* vol. 8, winter 1980.

———. "On Private and State Terror—Some Preliminary Observations." *Rutgers Law Journal,* Spring 1982.

Simpson, John and Jana Bennet. *The Disappeared*. Penguin Books, New York, 1985.

Stover, Eric. "The Disappeared of Argentina: Not Without Trace." *New Scientist,* November 15 1984.

Stover, Eric and Elena O. Nightingale, eds. *The Breaking of Bodies and Minds: Torture, Psychiatric Abuse, and the Health Professions*. W. H. Freeman, New York, 1985.

Sunday Times Insight Team. *The Falklands War*. Sphere Books, London, 1983.

Timerman, Jacobo. *Prisoner Without a Name, Cell Without a Number*. Penguin Books, New York, 1982.

"Timerman Incredulous That Tapes Stir Doubts." *New York Times*, July 5 1981.

"A Tireless Friend of the Dispossessed." *New York Times*, October 14 1980.

"Unions Rally to the Flag in Argentina." *Washington Post*, April 7 1982.

"Vatican Assails Argentine Junta over Its Report on War on Leftists." *New York Times*, May 4 1983.

Verbitksy, Horacio. *La Ultima Batalla de la Tercera Guerra Mundial (The Final Battle of the Third World War)*. Legasa, Buenos Aires, 1985.

Zalaquett, José. "Confronting Human Rights Violations Committed by Former Governments: Principles Applicable and Political Constraints." Paper presented at Aspen Institute for Humanistic Studies Conference on State Crimes, Rye Woods, N.Y., November 4–6, 1988.

Uruguay

Amnesty International. Uruguay under Torture, 1975–1977 Amnesty International Publications, London, 1978.

———. *Report on Human Rights Violations in Uruguay*. Amnesty International Publications, 1983.

A Collective of Uruguayan exiles living in Switzerland. Uruguay 1982, Uruguay 1983, and Uruguay 1984.

Labrousse, Alain. *The Tupomaros*. Penguin Books, New York, 1973.

Lawyers Committee for International Human Rights. *Uruguay: The End of a Nightmare? A Report on Human Rights Based on a Mission of Inquiry*. New York, 1986.

El Salvador

Americas Watch and American Civil Liberties Union. *Report on Human Rights in El Salvador*. Vintage Books, New York, March 1982.

———. *At Odds with Knowledge*. New York, June 1982.

Association of the Bar of the City of New York. *Justice in El Salvador. Report of a Mission of Inquiry*. New York, January 31 1983.

Bonner, Ray. *Weakness and Deceit: U.S. Policy and El Salvador*. Times Books, New York, 1984.

Moeller, James. "Human Rights and United States Security Assistance: El Salvador and the Case for Country-Specific Legislation." Commentary in the *Harvard International Law Journal*, vol. 24, 1983.

Nash, Richard. "Certifying Human Rights: Military Assistance to El Salvador and the International Security and Development Cooperation Act of 1981." *Columbia Human Rights Law Review*, vol. 14, 1982–1983.

Horton, Scott and Randy Sellier. "The Utility of Presidential Certifications of

Compliance with United States Human Rights Policy: The Case of El Salvador." Commentary in the *Wisconsin Law Review,*

Lawyers Committee for International Human Rights. *A Report on the Investigation into the Killing of Four American Churchwomen in El Salvador.* New York, September 1981.

———. *Justice in El Salvador: A Case Study.* New York, 1982. (Updated in 1983 and 1984.)

———. *Justice Denied: A Report on 12 Unresolved Cases.* New York, March 1985.

Guatemala

Americas Watch. *Human Rights in Guatemala: No Neutrals Allowed.* New York, 1982.

———. *Comments on Lord Colville's Report,* New York, November 29 1983.

———. *Guatemala: The Group for Mutual Support 1984–1985.* New York, 1985.

Amnesty International. *Human Rights in Guatemala: Report of a Mission.* Amnesty International Publications, December 5 1979. An accompanying Amnesty memorandum, sent to the government of Guatemala, was also distributed. (Amnesty publications AMR 34/45/79.)

———. *Guatemala: A Government Program of Political Murder.* Amnesty International Publications, London, 1981.

Ecumenical Program for Interamerican Communication and Action (EPICA). *Indian Guatemala.* Washington D.C., 1984.

Enfoprensa. *Información de Guatemala* 2/6 March 9–15 1984.

McClintock, Michael. *The American Connection,* vol. 2. *State Terror and Popular Resistance in Guatemala.* Zed Press, London, 1985.

Kinzer, Stephen. "In Guatemala, a Rights Group Battles Fear, Murder, and the Government." *New York Times,* April 19 1985.

Menchu, Rigoberta. *I Rigoberta Menchu.* Verson Editions, London, 1984.

"Peer in 'Whitewash' Row over Guatemala Report." *Sunday Times,* London, February 12 1984.

Plant, Roger. *Guatemala: Unnatural Disaster.* The Latin America Bureau, London, 1978.

Simón, Jean-Marie. *Guatemala: Eternal Spring, Eternal Tyranny.* W.W. Norton, New York, 1987.

War on Want. *Bitter and Cruel. Report of the Mission of a British Parliamentary Human Rights Group.* London, 1985.

Nicaragua

Amnesty International. *Report on the Amnesty International Missions to the Republic of Nicaragua: August 1979, January 1980 and August 1980.* Amnesty International Publications, London 1982.

Artucio, Alejandro and Heleno Fragoso. *Human Rights in Nicaragua: Yesterday and Today*. International Commission of Jurists, Geneva, July 1980.

Gutman, Roy. *Banana Diplomacy: The Making of American Policy in Nicaragua 1981–1987*. Simon and Schuster, 1988.

Kornbluh, Peter. *Nicaragua: The Price of Intervention*. Institute for Policy Studies, Washington, D.C., 1987.

Organization of American States. *Report on the Situation of Human Rights in Nicaragua*. Washington, D.C., June 1979.

———. *Report on the Situation of Human Rights in the Republic of Nicaragua*. Washington, D.C., June 1981.

Sklar, Holly. *Washington's War on Nicaragua*. South End Press, London, 1988.

The United Nations, the OAS, and the international human rights movement

Individual U.N. documents, including reports by the Working Group on Disappearances, are cited in the text and notes, with document reference numbers.

Agee, Philip. *Inside the Company: CIA Diary*. Stonehill, New York, 1975.

Alston, Philip. "The Universal Declaration at 35: Western and Passé or Alive and Universal."*ICJ Review*, December 1983.

Americas Watch. *Four Failures: A Report on the U.N. Special Rapporteurs on Human Rights in Chile, Guatemala, Iran, and Poland*. New York, January 1986.

Amnesty International. *Report on Torture*. Duckworth, London, 1973, revised in 1975.

———. *Report and Recommendations of an Amnesty International Mission to the Government of the State of Israel, June 3–7 1979*. Amnesty International Publications, London, 1980.

———. *Torture in the Eighties*. Amnesty International Publications, London, 1984.

———. *When the State Kills: The Death Penalty Versus Human Rights*. Amnesty International Publications, London, 1989.

Borchgrave, Arnaud de and Robert Moss. *The Spike*. Crown Publishers, London, 1980.

Buergenthal, Thomas. "Inter-American System for the Protection of Human Rights." In Meron, ed., *Human Rights in International Law*.

Brookings Institution. *The United Nations and Human Rights*. Washington, D.C., 1956.

Cronje, Susan. *Equatorial Guinea: The Forgotten Dictatorship*. Anti-Slavery Society, London, 1976.

Derian, Patricia. "Human Rights and American Foreign Policy." Reprinted in *Universal Human Rights*, vol. 1, no. 1.

Desmond, Cosmas. *Persecution East and West: Human Rights, Political Prisoners, and Amnesty*. Penguin, London, 1983.

Dinstein, Yoram, "The Right to Life, Physical Integrity, and Liberty." In Henkin, ed., *The International Bill of Rights*.

———. *Chile Briefing*. Amnesty International briefing paper AMR 22/13/88.

Drinan, Robert. *Cry of the Oppressed: The History and Hope of the Human Rights Revolution*. Harper and Row, New York, 1987.

Dunant, Henri. *A Memory of Solferino*. The American National Red Cross, 1959.

Durand, André. *From Sarajevo to Hiroshima*. André Dunant Institute, Geneva, 1978.

Galenson, Walter. *The International Labor Organization: Mirroring the U.N.'s Problems*. Heritage Foundation, Washington, D.C., 1982.

Gerson, Allan. *Israel, the West Bank and International Law*. Frank Cass, 1978.

Goodrich, Leland and Edvard Hambro. *Charter of the United Nations*. World Peace Foundation, Boston, 1949.

Guest, Iain, "U.S. Helps Water Down Rights Unit." *International Herald Tribune*, February 27 1981.

Hannum, Hurst, ed. *Guide to International Human Rights Practice*. University of Pennsylvania Press, Philadelphia, 1984, updated 1986.

Henkin, Louis. *The Rights of Man Today*. Westview Press, Boulder, Col.

——— ed. *The International Bill of Rights: The Covenant on Civil and Political Rights*. Columbia University Press, New York, 1981.

Higgins, Rosalyn. "The European Convention on Human Rights." In Meron, ed., *Human Rights in International Law*,

Human Rights Internet. *On the Brink of a Mid-Life Crisis. Report of the 1988 Session of the U.N. Commission on Human Rights, February 1–March 12 1988*. Boston, 1988.

Humphrey, John. *The Great Adventure: Human Rights and the United Nations*. Transnational, Dobb's Ferry, N.Y., 1983.

International Commission of Jurists. *States of Emergency: Their Impact on Human Rights*. ICJ, Geneva, 1983.

———. *The Trial against Macias in Equatorial Guinea*. ICJ, Geneva, November 1979.

———. *Final Report of the Mission to Chile, April 1974, To Study the Legal System and Protection of Human Rights*. Geneva, 1974.

International League of Human Rights. *Andrei Sakharov from Exile*. New York, October 1983.

Joyce, James Avery. *Broken Star*. Christopher Davies, Swansea, UK, 1978.

Kaufman, Irving. "A Legal Remedy for International Torture?" *New York Times Magazine*, November 9 1980.

Kay, David A. *The United Nations Political System*. Wiley, New York, 1967.

Kuper, Leo. *Genocide*. Penguin Books, New York, 1981.

Leigh, David. *The Wilson Plot*. Heinemann, New York, 1989.

Lefever, Ernest. *Amsterdam to Nairobi. The World Council of Churches and the Third World*. Ethics and Public Policy Center, Washington, D.C., June 1979.

———. "Limits of the Human Rights Standard." *New York Times*, January 24 1977.

Lifkovsky, Sidney. "The U.N. Reviews Its NGO Policy." *Reports on the Foreign Scene*, no. 10. American Jewish Committee, New York, January 1970.

Lillich, Richard and Frank Newman. *International Human Rights: Problems of Law and Policy*. Little, Brown, Boston, 1979.

Melanson, Richard. "Human Rights and the American Withdrawal from the ILO." *Universal Human Rights*, vol. 1, no. 1.

Meron, Theodor, ed. *Human Rights in International Law: Legal and Policy Issues.* Clarendon Press, Oxford, 1984.

Nossiter, Bernard. "U.N. Rights Body Has Poor History of Biased Reports." *Washington Post,* November 23 1977.

Organization of American States. *Basic Documents Pertaining to Human Rights in the Inter-American System.* OAS, Washington, D.C., March 1 1988.

Power, Jonathan. *Against Oblivion.* Fontana Books, London, 1981.

Ramcharam, Bertie. "The Good Offices of the United Nations Secretary-General in the Field of Human Rights." *American Journal of International Law,* vol. 76, no. 1, January 1982.

——— ed. *The Right to Life in International Law.* Martinus Nijhoff, Amsterdam, 1985.

Rodley, Nigel. *The Treatment of Prisoners Under International Law.* Clarendon Press, Oxford, 1987.

Russell, Ruth. *A History of the United Nations Charter.* Brookings Institution, Washington, D.C., 1958.

Shihata, Ibrahim. *The World Bank and Human Rights: An Analysis of the Legal Issues and the Record of Achievement.* Unpublished 1989 memorandum by the World Bank's legal counsel.

Tolley, Howard, Jr. *The U.N. Commission on Human Rights.* Westview, Boulder, Col., 1987.

United Nations. *Is Universality in Jeopardy?* Report of a 1985 U.N. symposium. United Nations Department of Information, New York, 1987.

———. *Human Rights: A Compilation of International Instruments.* United Nations Publications, New York, 1988.

———. *Selected Decisions Under the Optional Protocol.* United Nations Publications, New York, 1985.

———. *United Nations Action in the Field of Human Rights.* United Nations Publications, New York, 1988.

Urquhart, Brian. *A Life in Peace and War.* Harper and Row, New York, 1987.

Valtikos, Nicholas. *International Labour Law.* Kluwer, Amsterdam, 1979.

Van Boven, Theo. *People Matter: Views on International Human Rights Policy.* Meulenhoff, Amsterdam, 1982.

Vasak, Karel, ed. *The International Dimensions of Human Rights,* vols. 1 and 2. Revised and edited for the English edition by Philip Alston. Greenwood Press, New York, in conjunction with UNESCO.

Vishinsky, Andrei. "Human Rights and Human Freedom—A Russian View." *New York Times Magazine,* March 24 1946.

Walters, F. P. *The League of Nations.* Oxford University Press, London, 1952.

Weissbrodt, David. "Fact-Finding by NGOs." *Virginia Journal of International Law,* vol. 22, no. 1.

———. "The Contribution of International Nongoverment Organizations to the Protection of Human Rights." In Meron, ed., *Human Rights in International Law.*

Will, George. "A Right to Health." *Newsweek,* August 7 1988.

Wiseberg, Laurie and Harry Scoble. "The International League for Human Rights. The Strategy of a Human Rights NGO." *Georgia Journal of International and Comparative Law*, vol. 7, 1977.

Zuijdwijk, Ton. *Petitioning the United Nations—a Study in Human Rights*. St. Martin's Press, New York, 1982.

United States Human Rights Policy.

Albert, Paul. "The Undermining of the Legal Standards for Human Rights Violations in United States Foreign Policy: The Case of 'Improvement' in Guatemala." *Columbia Human Rights Law Review*, vol. 14, 1982–1983.

"Ambassador Kirkpatrick, Reagan-Appointed Democrat, Speaks Her Mind on World, Domestic Politics." *Tampa Tribune*, December 25 1980.

Amnesty International USA. *Ratification Now*. Washington, D.C., 1989.

"Basis for U.S. Action Cited." *New York Times*, May 2 1982.

Bonner, Raymond. *Waltzing with a Dictator: The Marcoses and the Making of American Policy*. Times Books, New York, 1987.

Brown, Cynthia, ed. *With Friends Like These: The Americas Watch Report on Human Rights and U.S. Policy in Latin America*. Pantheon Books, New York, 1985.

Buckley, William. "The Strange Behavior of Mr. Timerman." Universal Press Syndicate, May 30–31 1981.

Carter, Jimmy. *Keeping Faith: Memoirs of a President*. Bantam Books, Toronto, New York, 1982.

Cohen, Roberta. "Human Rights Diplomacy: The Carter Administration and the Southern Cone." *Human Rights Quarterly*, 1982.

Cohen, Stephen. "Conditioning U.S Security Assistance on Human Rights Practices." *American Journal of International Law*, vol. 76, 1982.

Corry, John. "Jeane Kirkpatrick—Call Her Madam and Color Her Tough." *Life Magazine*, April 1981.

Council for Inter-American Security. *A New Inter-American Policy for the Eighties*. Washington, D.C., 1980.

Crittendon, Ann. "Human Rights and Mrs. Derian." *New York Times*, May 31 1980.

Crocker, Chester. "South Africa: Strategy for Change." *Foreign Affairs*, Winter 1980–1981.

Crosland, Susan. "Surviving Under Diplomatic Fire." *Sunday Times*, London April 14 1984.

Del Guidice, Marguerite. "Abrams Stresses Ideological Battle." *Boston Globe*, November 20 1981.

DeYong, Karen. "Worldly Ambitions and the Affairs of State." Review of *Dictatorships and Double Standards* by Jeane Kirkpatrick. *Washington Post Book World*, July 18 1982.

Dowie, Mark. "Abrams: Learning to Live with Torture." *Mother Jones*, December 1985.

Draper, Theodore. "The Ambassador's Theories." Review of *Dictatorships and Double Standards* by Jeane Kirkpatrick. *New York Times Book Review*, July 25 1982.

Evans, Roland and Robert Novak. "Human-Rights Zeal that Costs U.S. Jobs." *Washington Post,* September 18 1978.

———. "The Weapon Against Lefever." *Washington Post,* June 17 1981.

Farer, Tom. "Reagan's Latin America." *New York Review of Books,* March 19 1981.

Finger, Seymour Maxwell. "The Reagan-Kirkpatrick Policies at the United Nations." *Foreign Affairs,* Winter 1983/84.

Garza, Melita. "Jeane Kirkpatrick: The Iron-Woman Image and Other Myths." *The Independent,* October 29 1981.

Geyelin, Philip. "Human Rights Turnaround." *Washington Post,* December 12 1980.

Haig, Alexander. *Caveat: Realism, Reagan and Foreign Policy.* Macmillan, New York, 1984.

Harrison, Lawrence. "We Don't Cause Latin America's Troubles—Latin Culture Does." *Washington Post,* June 29 1986.

Heaps, David. *Human Rights and U.S. Foreign Policy: the First Decade.* A report for the American Association for the International Commission of Jurists, December 10 1983.

Heritage Foundation. *The United States and the United Nations: A Balance Sheet.* Heritage Backgrounder, January 21 1982.

Institute for Policy Studies. *The Southern Connection: Recommendations for a New Approach to Inter-American Relations.* Washington, D.C., February 1977.

International Human Rights Law Group. *U.S. Legislation Relating Human Rights to U.S. Foreign Policy.* Washington, D.C., third edition, 1982.

Kirkpatrick, Jeane. "Dictatorships and Double Standards." *Commentary,* November 1979.

———. *Dictatorships and Double Standards: Rationalism and Reason in Politics.* Simon and Schuster, New York, 1982.

———. *The Reagan Phenomenon—and Other Speeches on Foreign Policy.* American Enterprise Institute, 1983.

———. "The United Nations as a Political System: A Practicing Political Scientist's Insights into U.N. Politics." *American Foreign Policy Newsletter,* vol. 5, no. 5, October 1983.

———. "American Foreign Policy in a Cold Climate." *Encounter Magazine,* November 1983.

———. *The Hobbes Problem: Order, Authority and Legitimacy in Central America.* American Enterprise Institute Public Policy Paper, Washington, D.C., December 9–11 1890.

———. "U.S. Security and Latin America." *Commentary,* January 1981.

———. "Why We Do Not Become Republicans." *Commonsense,* 1979.

———. "Les Combattants de la liberté." *Géopolitique,* Paris, Spring 1986.

"Kirkpatrick Feud with Haig is Noted." *New York Times,* May 31 1982.

Kissinger, Henry. Arthur P. Salomon Lecture, 1977. Reprinted, *Washington Post,* September 25 1977.

Kristol, Irving. "The Common Sense of 'Human Rights'." *Wall Street Journal,* April 8 1981.

Lawyers Committee for Human Rights. *The 1988 Project.* New York, December, 1988.

Lethwaite, Gilbert. "U.S. Human Rights Policy Debated." *Baltimore Sun*, February 9 1983.

Loescher, Gil. "U.S. Human Rights Policy and International Financial Institutions." *The World Today*, December 1977.

———. "Carter's Human Rights Policy and the 96th Congress." *The World Today*, April 1979.

Luard, Evan. "Human Rights and Foreign Policy." *International Affairs*, Autumn 1980.

Maechling, Charles. "Human Rights Dehumanized." *Foreign Policy*, vol. 52, Fall 1983.

"The Military Obstacle to Latin Democracy." *Foreign Policy*, vol. 73, summer 1988–1989.

"Mrs. Kirkpatrick, Loudly." *New York Times*, August 22 1981.

Newsom, David, ed. *The Diplomacy of Human Rights*. University Press of America, Washington, D.C., 1986.

Nossiter, Bernard. "Questioning the Value of the United Nations." *New York Times Magazine*, April 11, 1982.

Novak, Michael. "The Reagan Approach to Human Rights Policy." *Wall Street Journal*, April 28 1981.

———. "Arms and the Church." *Commentary*, March 1982.

———. *The Spirit of Democratic Capitalism*. Simon and Schuster, New York, 1982.

———. "Why Latin America is Poor." *Atlantic Monthly*, March 1982.

Novak, Michael and Richard Schifter. *Rethinking Human Rights*, vols. 1 and 2. Speeches at the 37th and 38th session of the U.N. Human Rights Commission. Reprinted by the Foundation for Democratic Education, 1981 and 1982.

"'Quiet Diplomacy' in Action." Editorial, *Washington Post*, August 23 1981.

Riding, Alan. "Costa Rica Up in Arms over Mrs. Kirkpatrick." *New York Times*, August 19 1981.

Schifter, Richard. "Reagan's Human Rights Policy: Firm Foundation." *Harvard Human Rights Yearbook*. vol. 2, Spring 1989.

Schumacher, Edward. "Latins Get Taste of Kirkpatrick Style." *New York Times*, August 5 1981.

Schwarz, Mary. "Jeane Kirkpatrick, Our Macho U.N. Ambassador." *National Review*, January 21 1983.

Shestack, Jerome. "An Unsteady Focus: The Vulnerability of the Reagan Administration's Human Rights Policy." *Harvard Human Rights Yearbook*, vol. 2, spring 1989.

Stanislawksi, Howard. "Lefeverish Activity." *New Republic*, May 30 1981.

"Symposium: Human Rights and U.S. Foreign Policy." *Universal Human Rights*, vol. 1, no. 1, January 1979.

Tremblay, Anne. "Jeane Kirkpatrick—Woman in the News." *Working Woman Magazine*, May 1983.

"Trusting the Yankees." *Wall Street Journal*, March 2 1981.

Unger, Brooke. "Hard Choices." *The Independent*, November 25 1981.

The United Nations Association of the USA. *United States Foreign Policy and Human Rights*. December 10 1979.

"U.S. Blocks Rights Data on Nations Getting Arms." *New York Times,* November 19 1975.

"U.S. Says Mrs. Kirkpatrick Met South African Army Intelligence Chief." *New York Times,* March 24 1984.

"U.S. Support for Britain Imperilling Latin Policy." *New York Times,* May 16 1982.

Walzer, Michael. "Totalitarianism versus Authoritarianism." *New Republic,* July 4 and July 11, 1981.

Weintraub, Bernard. "Reagan's Human Rights Chief: No Liberal Mole." *New York Times,* October 19 1982.

Weissbrodt, David. "Human Rights Legislation and U.S. Foreign Policy." *Georgia Journal of International and Comparative Law,* supplement to vol. 7, summer 1977.

Wiarda, Howard J., ed. *Human Rights and U.S. Human Rights Policy.* American Enterprise Institute, Washington, D.C., 1982.

Winik, Jay. "The Neoconservative Reconstruction." *Foreign Policy,* vol. 73, winter 1988.

U.S. Government and Congressional material

Entries are arranged chronologically.

Country Reports on Human Rights Practices. The annual reports issued by the U.S. State Department, in pursuance of Section 502B and 116(d) of the Foreign Assistance Act.

International Protection of Human Rights. The Work of International Organizations and the Role of U.S. Foreign Policy. Hearings before the Subcommittee on International Organizations and Movements. House Committee on Foreign Affairs. 93rd Congress, First Session. August 1; December 7 1973.

Human Rights in the World Community: A Call for U.S. Leadership. Report of the Subcommittee on International Organizations and Movements. House Committee on Foreign Affairs. March 27 1974.

Chile: The Status of Human Rights and Its Relationship to U.S. Economic Assistance Programs. Hearings before the Subcommittee on International Organizations. House Committee on International Relations. 94th Congress, Second Session. April 25; May 5 1976.

Human Rights in Argentina. Hearings before the Subcommittee on International Organizations. House Committee on International Relations. 94th Congress, Second Session. September 28, 29, 1976.

The Status of Human Rights in Selected Countries and the U.S. Response. Report prepared for the Subcommittee on International Organizations. House Committee on International Relations. July 25 1977.

Human Rights Conditions in Selected Countries and the U.S. Response. Report prepared for the Subcommittee on International Organizations. House Committee on International Relations. July 25 1978.

U.S. Participation in International Organizations and Programs. Report of staff mission, House Committee on Foreign Affairs, October 6–November 11 1978.

Review of the 35th session of the United Nations Commission on Human Rights. Hearing before the Subcommittee on International Organizations. House Committee on Foreign Affairs. 96th Congress, First Session. April 9 1979.

Human Rights and U.S. Foreign Policy. Hearings before the Subcommittee on International Organizations. House Committee on Foreign Affairs. 96th Congress, First Session. May 2, 10; June 21; July 12; August 2 1979.

Human Rights and the Phenomenon of Disappearances. Hearings before the Subcommittee on International Organizations. House Committee on Foreign Affairs. 96th Congress, First Session. September 20, 25; October 18 1979.

International Human Rights Treaties. Hearings before the Senate Committee on Foreign Relations. 96th Congress, First Session. November 14, 15, 16, 19 1979.

Review of the 36th Session of the United Nations Commission on Human Rights. Hearing before the Subcommittee on International Organizations. House Committee on Foreign Affairs. 96th Congress, Second Session. April 29 1980.

U.S. Economic Sanctions against Chile. Hearing before the Subcommittees on International Economic Policy and Trade and on Inter-American Affairs. House Committee on Foreign Affairs. 97th Congress, First Session. March 10 1981.

Review of United States Policy on Military Assistance to Argentina. Hearing before the Subcommittee on Human Rights and International Organizations and on Inter-American Affairs. House Committee on Foreign Affairs. 97th Congress, First Session. April 1 1981.

Foreign Assistance Legislation for Fiscal Year 1982. Part 1. Hearings before the House Committee on Foreign Affairs. 97th Congress, First Session. March 13, 18, 19, 23 1981.

Hearings before the Subcommittee of the Senate Committee on Appropriations. 97th Congress, First Session. April 7 1981.

Hearings before the Subcommittee on Foreign Operations. House Committee on Appropriations. 97th Congress, First Session. May 12, 1981.

Nomination of Ernest W. Lefever. Hearings before the Senate Committee on Foreign Relations. 97th Congress, First Session. May 18, 19; June 4, 5 1981.

Review of the 37th Session and Upcoming 38th Session of the U.N. Commission on Human Rights. Hearing before the Subcommittee on Human Rights and international organizations. House Committee on Foreign Affairs. 97th Congress, First Session. November 16 1981.

The Genocide Convention. Hearings before the Senate Committee on Foreign Relations. 97th Congress, First Session. December 3 1981.

Implementation of Congressionally Mandated Human Rights Provisions, vols. 1 and 2. Hearings before the Subcommittee on Human Rights and International Organizations. House Committee on Foreign Affairs. 97th Congress, first session. July 14, 30; September 17; November 5, 17; December 10, 1981. February 23; March 9, 17 1982.

U.S. Participation in the United Nations. Hearings and Markup before the House

Committee on Foreign Affairs. 97th Congress, Second Session. April 22, 27; May 4, 1982.

Review of State Department Country Reports on Human Rights Practices for 1981. Hearing before the Subcommittee on Human Rights and International Organizations. House Committee on Foreign Relations. 97th Congress, Second Session. April 28 1982.

Latin America and the United States after the Falklands/Malvinas Crisis. Hearings before the Subcommittee on Inter-American Affairs. House Committee on Foreign Affairs. 97th Congress, Second Session. July 20; August 5 1982.

Review of the 38th Session and Upcoming 39th Session of the U.N. Commission on Human Rights. Hearing before the Subcommittee on Human Rights and International Organizations. House Committee on Foreign Affairs. December 10 1982.

Human Rights in El Salvador. Hearings before the Subcommittee on Human Rights and International Organizations, and on Western Hemisphere Affairs. House Committee on Foreign Affairs. 98th Congress, First Session. July 26, 1983.

The U.S. Role in the United Nations. Hearings before the Subcommittee on Human Rights and International Organizations. House Committee on Foreign Affairs. 98th Congress, First Session. September 27; October 3 1983.

Testimony by Alejandro Artucio. Hearings before the Subcommittee on Human Rights. House Committee on Foreign Affairs. 98th Congress, Second Session. May 15 1984.

Soviet presence in the U.N. Secretariat. Report of the Senate Select Committee on Intelligence, U.S. Senate. May 1985.

Review of the U.N. Commission on Human Rights. Hearing before the Subcommittee on Human Rights and International Organizations. House. Committee on Foreign Affairs. 99th Congress, Second Session. June 25 1986.

Index